NORTHERN GREECE

DANA FACAROS
UPDATED BY AMBER CHARMEI

www.bradtguides.com

Bradt Guides Ltd, UK
The Globe Pequot Press Inc, USA

Bradt GUIDES
TRAVEL TAKEN SERIOUSLY

NORTHERN GREECE
DON'T MISS...

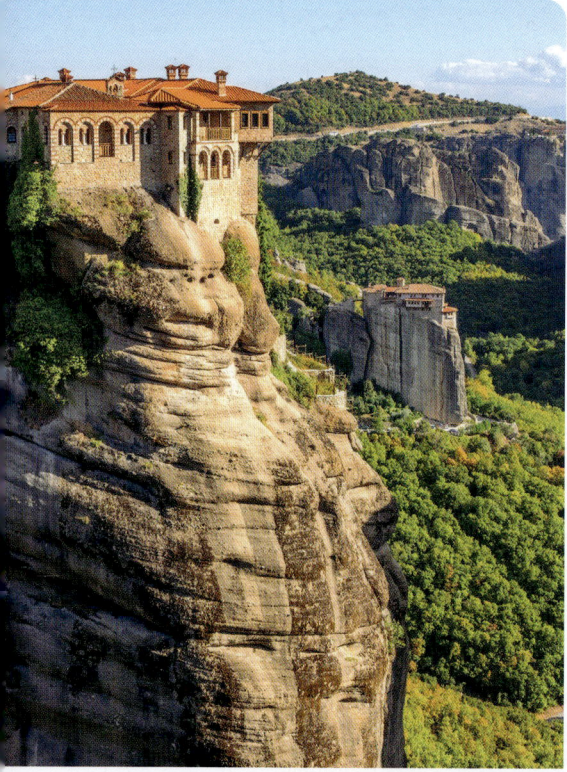

METEORA
The otherworldly streak in Greek monasticism reached its peak (literally) in Meteora; besides visiting the monasteries, hike on trails through the towering pinnacles. Pictured: Varláam Monastery **PAGE 316**
(GME/S)

THESSALONÍKI
With its UNESCO World Heritage-listed Roman and Byzantine sites and enormous student population, Thessaloníki deftly combines old and new **PAGE 59**
(Sa/S)

BEACHES
Northern Greece has beaches to suit every taste, from immaculate sands with chic bars to intimate coves accessible only by sea. Pictured: Karýdi Beach, Sithonía, Chalkidikí PAGE 114
(Mi/S)

PELION VILLAGES
The Pelion is famous for its traditional villages, each centred around a sociable *plateia* under the shade of a plane tree – Makrinítsa's is one of the finest PAGE 347
(NN/S)

PINDUS NATIONAL PARK
The majority of Greece's spectacular national parks are in the north, including the Pindus National Park with the world's deepest canyon: the Víkos Gorge PAGES 253 & 278
(VB/S)

NORTHERN GREECE
IN COLOUR

above left (LP/S) — A traditional 18th-century *archontikó* (mansion) typical of the Pelion PAGE 343

above right (EV/S) — Although tourism is now a mainstay on the islands, fishing still has its place. Pictured: fishing boat on Thássos PAGE 193

below (Mo/S) — On the shores of Lake Pamvótida, Ioánnina with its storied citadel is a serene delight PAGE 260

Vibrant Xánthi is nicknamed the 'City of a Thousand Colours' PAGE 206 — above left (GT/S)

Traditional Carnival costumes in Náoussa PAGE 146 — above right (ST/S)

Pastries in Komotiní, one of Thrace's 'sweet' cities PAGE 212 — middle right (DL/S)

A statue of Aristotle at Ancient Stageira, his birthplace, in Chalkidikí PAGE 115 — below left (PK/S)

Named after the Turkish word for 'plane tree', Tsinári is among the most enchanting areas of Thessaloníki's Áno Póli district PAGE 88 — below right (T/S)

JOIN
THE TRAVEL CLUB

THE MEMBERSHIP CLUB FOR SERIOUS TRAVELLERS
FROM BRADT GUIDES

Be inspired
Free books and exclusive insider travel tips and inspiration

Save money
Special offers and discounts from our favourite travel brands

Plan the trip of a lifetime
Access our exclusive concierge service and have a bespoke itinerary created for you by a Bradt author

Join here:
bradtguides.com/travelclub

Membership levels to suit all budgets

Bradt GUIDES

TRAVEL TAKEN SERIOUSLY

AUTHOR

Dana Facaros wrote her first travel guide to the Greek islands in 1977, then married her college sweetheart, Michael Pauls, and dragged him into the fray. They have been at it ever since, writing guides and apps and contributing to a number of UK publications, including the *Sunday Times, Sunday Times Travel Magazine, Daily Telegraph, Wanderlust* and *Holiday Which?*. Over the past decades they have lived in Greece, Spain, Italy, Ireland and southwest France, where they are currently based.

UPDATER

Amber Charmei was a 15-year-old with a backpack and tattered copies of The Colossus of Maroussi and Greece and Yugoslavia on $5 a Day when she first touched down in Athens from downtown NYC in 1981, catching ferries around the Dodecanese and sleeping on stacks of kilims as she travelled around with her artist parents. After studies in Art and Architectural History, she traded Manhattan for Thessaloniki, lured by its deeper backstory and sweeter melons, and contributes features on art, gastronomy and cultural experiences to *Greece Is* and other publications as well as working on guidebooks whenever the opportunity arises.

AUTHOR'S STORY

Dana Facaros has been in love with Greece since she was 14 years old and spent a summer on her father's native island, Ikaria. She studied ancient Greek, mythology and the Classics during a brief stint at university, and she has been visiting and writing about the country since 1977, when she wrote her first guidebook – to the Greek islands. Dana later co-authored the Cadogan guide to all Greece with Linda Theodorou, published in 2003. While researching that book she concentrated on northern Greece. Since then, she has become a Greek citizen and writes frequently about Greece for the *Sunday Times* and *Sunday Times Travel Magazine*. While writing *this* guide to northern Greece, she was inspired to create the Greek Food Decoder app, which she often wished she had had in the tavernas off the beaten track.

Second edition published November 2025
First published 2020
Bradt Travel Guides Ltd
31a High Street, Chesham, Buckinghamshire, HP5 1BW, England
www.bradtguides.com
Print edition published in the USA by The Globe Pequot Press Inc,
PO Box 480, Guilford, Connecticut 06437-0480

Text copyright © Dana Facaros, 2025
Maps copyright © Bradt Travel Guides Ltd, 2025; includes map data © OpenStreetMap contributors
Photographs copyright © Individual photographers, 2025 (see below)
Project Manager: Elspeth Beidas
Cover research: Pepi Bluck, Perfect Picture

The author and publisher have made every effort to ensure the accuracy of the information in this book at the time of going to press. However, they cannot accept any responsibility for any loss, injury or inconvenience resulting from the use of information contained in this guide. All rights reserved. No part of this publication may be reproduced, stored in a retrieval system, or transmitted in any form or by any means, electronic, mechanical, photocopying, recording or otherwise without the prior consent of the publisher.

ISBN: 9781804692820

British Library Cataloguing in Publication Data
A catalogue record for this book is available from the British Library

Photographs AWL Images: Karol Kozlowski (KK/AWL); Shutterstock.com: Abdullah Durman (AD/S), Andrei Nekrassov (AN/S), Apostolis Giontzis (AG/S), Arnaoutis Christos (AC/S), Constantinos Iliopoulos (CI/S), David Havel (DH/S), Desislava Lyungova (DL/S), dinosmichail (DM/S), Eric Valenne geostory (EV/S), Georgios Tsichlis (GT/S), Gestiafoto (G/S), GoodMan_Ekim (GME/S), Havoc (H/S), Heracles Kritikos (HK/S), Jesus Giraldo Gutierrez (JGG/S), Klagyi (K/S), Lefteris Papaulakis (LP/S), Mistervlad (Mi/S), monticello (Mo/S), Nataliya Nazarova (NN/S), Panos Karas (PK/S), rawf8 (R/S), risteski goce (RG/S), sam_thanasis (ST/S), sandsun (Sa/S), stoyanh (Sto/S), Sven Hansche (SH/S), tilialucida (T/S), Tony_Papageorge (TP/S), trabantos (T/S), Valery Bocman (VB/S), Ververidis Vasilis (VV/S), Victor Marinov (VM/S), vlas2000 (V/S)
Front cover Roussánou Monastery, Meteora (KK/AWL)
Back cover, clockwise from top Kalamítsi, Sithonía Peninsula (T/S); *kouloúri* bread (R/S); colourful street in Xánthi (GT/S)
Title page, clockwise from top left Mount Falakró (AC/S); *archontikó* in Áfyssos (AG/S); Dalmatian pelican, Préspa National Park (VM/S); mosaic in Ancient Dion (AN/S)

Maps David McCutcheon FBCart.S. FRGS

Typeset by Ian Spick, Bradt Guides
Production managed by Gutenberg Press Ltd; printed in Malta
Digital conversion by www.dataworks.co.in

Paper used for this product comes from sustainably managed forests, and recycled and controlled sources.

Acknowledgements

DANA FACAROS A big fat Greek ευχαριστώ πάρα πολύ to everyone who contributed to this book, beginning with Linda Theodorou, who wrote much of the Epirus and Thessaly chapters in an earlier incarnation of the guide. I also thank Chronis Pechlivanidis of Onos TV for all his many contributions to Thrace, Vasilis Georgiades for his expertise on Thrace and Eastern Macedonia, Angela Giannakídou of the Ethnologicial Museum in Alexandroúpolis, Sotiris Malassiotis for his tips on hiking, Michael Pauls for his research, Chris Malumphy for crossing the Atlantic to help out at home so I could return to northern Greece, cousin Filia Xilas-Pattakou for answering all my picky little questions, and to Andy Bostock for his kind permission to mine the *Practical Information* chapter and Athens section of his Bradt Guide to the Peloponnese. Also I would like to express my deeply felt gratitude to the team at Bradt, especially my dauntless, eagle-eyed editor, Susannah Lord, and Rachel Fielding, who just knew that northern Greece deserved its own guidebook.

AMBER CHARMEI Warmest thanks to Angela Giannakídou, founder and president of the Ethnological Museum of Thrace, and Museum Co-ordinator Valentina Sokrátous for the introduction to a fascinating region, to Apóstolos Karagiannópoulos and Ioánnis Foúntas of The Kontós House – Museum of Theóphilos for their kindness and insights, and to Polyxéni Karéna of the Museum of the City of Vólos. Thank you also to Andréas Giórgos Láppas and Father Nectários of the monastery Ágia Eleóussa on the island in Lake Pamvotida by Ioánnina, and Sister Paraklíti of the Monastery of Ágios Stéfanos at Meteóra for their hospitality. And a heartfelt thanks to the team at Bradt – Creative Director Anna Moores for bringing me onboard, Commissioning Editor Claire Strange, my editor Elspeth Beidas for her patience and dedication to detail – and to Dana Facaros for entrusting me with this book. Through her excellent work, and the adventures I experienced updating it, my appreciation of northern Greece has grown deeper still.

Contents

	Introduction	**vii**
PART ONE	**GENERAL INFORMATION**	**1**
Chapter 1	**Background Information** Geography 3, Climate 3, Natural history and conservation 3, History 6, Government and politics 18, Economy 18, People 19, Language 19, Religion and beliefs 20, Education 21, Culture 21	**3**
Chapter 2	**Practical Information** When to visit 29, Highlights 29, Suggested itineraries 30, Tourist information and tour operators 31, Red tape 32, Getting there and away 33, Health 35, Safety 38, Women travellers 38, Travelling with a disability 39, LGBTQIA+ travellers 39, Travelling with children 39, What to take 39, Money and budgeting 40, Getting around 41, Accommodation 43, Eating and drinking 45, Public holidays and festivals 49, Shopping 53, Sports and activities 53, Museums and archaeological sites 54, Opening times 55, Media and communications 55, Cultural etiquette 56, Travelling positively 56	**29**
PART TWO	**THE GUIDE**	**57**
Chapter 3	**Thessaloníki (Θεσσαλονίκη)** History 59, Getting there and away 63, Getting around 66, Tourist information and tour operators 67, Orientation 70, Where to stay 70, Where to eat and drink 72, Entertainment and nightlife 75, Shopping 77, Sports and activities 78, Other practicalities 78, What to see and do 79	**59**
Chapter 4	**Chalkidikí (Χαλκιδική)** History 102, Getting there and away 103, Tourist information and tour operators 103, Sports and activities 103, Central Chalkidikí 106, Kassándra Peninsula 108, Sithonía Peninsula 111, Chalkidikí's east coast 114, Akté Peninsula 116, Mount Athos (Ágion Óros) 119	**102**

Chapter 5	**Central Macedonia (Κεντρική Μακεδονία)** Tourist information 129, Mount Olympus National Park 129, Véria 137, Vergína 142, Náoussa 145, Ancient Pella 150, Édessa 152, Gouménissa and Mount Páiko 157, Kilkís 159, Lake Kerkíni National Park 161, Sérres 162, South of Sérres 167	129
Chapter 6	**Eastern Macedonia (Ανατολική Μακεδονία)** History 173, Kavála 176, Ancient Philippi 183, Mount Pangaíon 186, Dráma 188, The Néstos River and Gorge 191, Thássos 193	173
Chapter 7	**Thrace (Θράκη)** Xánthi 206, Komotiní 212, Alexandroúpolis 217, The Évros 220, Samothráki 225	202
Chapter 8	**Western Macedonia (Δυτική Μακεδονία)** History 232, Kastoriá 236, East of Kastoriá 243, Flórina 246, Préspa National Park 248, Kozáni 250, Pindus National Park 253	232
Chapter 9	**Epirus (Ήπειρος)** History 256, Ioánnina 260, The Zagorochória 271, Kónitsa and around 279, Métsovo 280, Dodona 283, The Tzoumérka 285, The Ambracian Gulf 288, Párga 296, Sývota 300, Igoumenítsa 301	256
Chapter 10	**Thessaly (Θεσσαλία)** History 303, Lárissa 305, Around Lárissa 309, Tríkala 313, Meteora 316, West of Tríkala: Pýli, Eláti and Pertoúli 324, Kardítsa 326, Lake Plastíra 327, Loutrá Smókova 330	303
Chapter 11	**Magnesía (Μαγνησία) and the Pelion Peninsula** Vólos 331, The Pelion 342	331
Chapter 12	**The Sporádes (Σποράδες) Islands** History 353, Skiáthos 354, Skópelos 361, Alónissos 367	353
Chapter 13	**Athens (Αθήνα)** History and mythology 375, Getting there and away 375, Getting around 376, Tourist information and city tours 376, Where to stay 377, Where to eat and drink 377, Other practicalities 377, What to see and do 378	375
Appendix 1	Language	381
Appendix 2	Glossary	386
Appendix 3	Further Information	389
Index		392
Index of Advertisers		400

LIST OF MAPS

Alexandroúpolis	218	Náoussa, Around	147
Alónissos	368	Nikopolis, Ancient	294
Amphipolis, Ancient	169	Párga, Sývota and around	296
Athens, Central	374	Philippi, Ancient	184
Central Macedonia: east of the Axiós River	158	Samothráki	226
		Sérres	163
Central Macedonia: west of the Axiós River	128	Skiáthos	355
		Skópelos	362
Chalkidikí	104	Sporádes Islands, The	352
Dion, Ancient	134	Thássos	194
Eastern Macedonia	174	Thassos, Ancient	197
Édessa	152	Thessaloníki and around	58
Epirus	258	Thessaloníki: city centre	64
Ioánnina	262	Thessaloníki: Ladádika and Plateía Aristotélous	68
Kastoriá	237		
Kavála	177	Thessaly	304
Kavála: town centre	179	Thrace (Thráki)	204
Komotiní	213	Tríkala	314
Lake Plastíra	328	Tzoumérka, The	285
Lárissa	306	Véria	139
Magnesía and the Pelion Peninsula	332	Vólos	335
		Western Macedonia	234
Meteora	317	Xánthi	207
Mount Athos	120	Zagorochória, The	273

HOW TO USE THIS GUIDE

PRICE CODES Throughout this guide we have used price codes to indicate the cost of those places to stay and eat listed in the guide. For a key to these price codes, see page 44 for accommodation and page 46 for restaurants.

MAPS
Keys and symbols Maps include alphabetical keys covering the locations of those places to stay, eat or drink that are featured in the book. Note that regional maps may not show all hotels and restaurants in the area: some establishments may be located in towns shown on the map.

Grids and grid references Several maps use gridlines to allow easy location of sites. Map grid references are listed in square brackets after the name of the place or site of interest in the text, with page number followed by grid number, eg: [68 E3].

Introduction

Northern Greece is in many ways a world apart. Those who already know Athens and southern Greece could look at it as the Hellenic version of Scotland; very familiar yet different, a land of astonishing natural beauty – spectacular mountains, rivers, lakes and gorgeous coastlines – its history filled with highlanders from dozens of clans, who even dressed in kilts, when they joined up with Alexander the Great. Lively student-filled Thessaloníki could be the Edinburgh of the south, only with more sun.

This being Greece, there are renowned beach resorts, including Chalkidikí, Thássos and Párga, and attractions you've probably already heard of: Mount Olympus, home of the gods; the extraordinary monk-topped pillars of Meteora; the gold-filled Royal Tombs in Vergína; the Víkos Gorge – deepest for its width in the world; the idyllic landscapes of the Pelion and the Sporades islands (as seen in *Mamma Mia!*); and Ancient Philippi, where Octavian and Mark Antony defeated Brutus, and St Paul founded the first church in Europe. Thessaloníki, St Paul's second stop, was the second city of the Byzantine Empire for a thousand years, and boasts World Heritage-listed churches filled with mosaics. Lovely lakefront Ioánnina was the capital of Lord Byron's colourful despot, Ali Pasha. But never far are places well off the mass tourism radar, especially in the mountains where goat bells and nightingales are the loudest sounds, where waterfalls splash near 200-year-old stone bridges that span the stream below.

Northern Greece defies stereotypes, offering unexpected delights in spades. There are lofty ski resorts, forests filled with wild mushrooms and bears, natural mud baths, a steaming hot river and petrified forests, firewalkers, some of Europe's last silk-makers and a carnival dedicated to penises. The heart of the ancient kingdom of Macedon that gave the world Alexander the Great, northern Greece would later find itself on the front lines of the death throes of the Ottoman Empire. Its recent history was convulsed with war and upheavals and mass movements of people, leaving it a unique mix of ethnicities and religions that in many ways add to its fascination – not to mention its exotic pastries.

Northern Greece was the home of the Olympian gods, of centaurs, Achilles, and Jason and the Argonauts, but it was also the land of the uncanny and haunting, of Dionysos, god of wine and ecstasy, mystical musician-prophet Orpheus, and the mysteries of the Great Gods of the Underworld on Samothráki. It's where you'll find Dodona, the 4,000-year-old oracle of whispering leaves, and the Necromanteion, where Odysseus and many others journeyed to converse with the dead. They're all part of a thick hummus created over thousands of years of myth, poetry and history, which makes Greece's north so fascinating to explore.

FEEDBACK REQUEST

At Bradt Guides we're aware that guidebooks start to go out of date on the day they're published – and that you, our readers, are out there in the field doing research of your own. You'll find out before us when a fine new family-run hotel opens or a favourite restaurant changes hands and goes downhill. So why not tell us about your experiences? Contact us on 📞01753 893444 or e info@bradtguides.com. We will forward emails to the author who may post updates on the Bradt website at w bradtguides.com/updates. Alternatively, you can add a review of the book to Amazon, or share your adventures with us on Facebook, 𝕏 or Instagram (@BradtGuides).

Part One

GENERAL INFORMATION

NORTHERN GREECE AT A GLANCE

Location Balkan peninsula, between the Aegean and Ionian seas, south of Albania, North Macedonia and Bulgaria, and west of Türkiye
Size 98,818km^2
GDP per capita €25,300
Population 3,947,390 (2021 census)
Life expectancy 81.2 years
Climate Mediterranean and Continental
Regional Capitals Thessaloníki, Ioánnina, Lárissa
Other main towns Vólos, Kastoriá, Kavála, Tríkala, Véria, Komotiní, Alexandroúpolis
Main airport Thessaloníki
Language Modern Greek
Religion Greek Orthodox, with a Muslim minority
Currency Euro (€)
Exchange rate €1 = US$1.15, €1 = £0.85 (September 2025)
International telephone code +30
Time GMT +2 (+3 in summer)
Electrical voltage 230V/50Hz, two-pin plugs
Public holidays 1 January, 6 January, 25 March, 1 May, 15 August, 28 October, 25 December, 26 December (see also page 49)

1

Background Information

GEOGRAPHY

Northern Greece is a mostly mountainous region, with 26 peaks over 2,000m, located at the south end of the Balkan peninsula. In this guide it consists of five administrative regions: Central Macedonia, Eastern Macedonia and Thrace, Western Macedonia, Epirus and Thessaly. Albania, North Macedonia, Bulgaria and Türkiye are to the north and east; to the west is the Ionian Sea, and the Aegean to the south and east. The Pindus mountain range cuts across the west, reaching 2,637m at Mount Smólikas; to the north, the deeply wooded Rhodope range defines the frontier with Bulgaria. Olympus (2,917m), the highest mountain in Greece, divides the regions of Central Macedonia and Thessaly. Five islands are close to its shores: Thássos, Samothráki, and the Sporádes (Skiáthos, Skópelos and Alónissos).

Thessaloníki, Greece's second city and port, stands at the head of the Thermaic Gulf, at the top of the great three-pronged peninsula of Chalkidikí and near the delta of three major rivers, the Axiós, the Loudías, and the Aliákmonas, the longest river (298km) to flow entirely through Greece. Other major rivers include the Évros in the far east, which defines the border with Türkiye; the Strymónas, which runs from Bulgaria into the Aegean at Amphipolis; the Néstos that flows from Bulgaria into a large delta east of Kavála; and the Pineiós that traverses Thessaly from the Pindus and Meteora before crossing the Vale of Tempe and flowing into the Aegean. In Epirus, the Voïdomátis flows through the Víkos Gorge, before joining the Aoös and flowing into Albania.

CLIMATE

Northern Greece has a Mediterranean climate near the coasts and a continental climate at higher altitudes, especially on Olympus and in the Rhodope and Pindus mountains, where heavy snow is common in winter. Occasionally, in winter, Macedonia is buffeted by the mighty Vardaris wind that descends down the Vardar valley from North Macedonia, then meets the high mountains of Greece, where it picks up steam and swoops down to Thessaloníki. Although there are occasional thunder showers, spring is lovely everywhere, especially in the months of May and June. Summers can be very hot, especially on the plain of Thessaly where 40°C is not uncommon, but the Aegean coasts and islands are cooled by the *meltémi* wind from the north, which can occasionally wreak havoc with ferry schedules. The rainiest season is in autumn, especially after mid-October, but it's also when the mountain woodlands burst into colour.

NATURAL HISTORY AND CONSERVATION

With forests covering a quarter of its territory, along with its seacoasts, lakes, rivers, wetlands and mountains, northern Greece can claim one of the most diverse

1 | BACKGROUND INFORMATION

biospheres in the world. Wolves and bears roam its mountains, and the birds are spectacular (of Europe's estimated 475 species, 436 thrive here or regularly visit). Artificial Lake Kerkíni, a legend among birders, stands out as a rare example where human intervention has actually improved the wetlands; now Lake Kárla just north of Pelion, which was short-sightedly drained in the 1960s, has been re-flooded as a haven for wildlife. Eagles and vultures float over the mountains and cliffs; the Dadiá Forest, near the Évros Delta, is a haven for rare birds of prey. The unique half-salt-half-freshwater Lake Vistonída in Thrace was first studied by the father of biology, Aristotle.

Closer to the ground, Greece's extraordinary range of flora boasts some 6,000 native species – Mount Olympus is one of UNESCO's World Biosphere Reserves. Grevená and the east slopes of the Pindus, where mammoths once roamed, is renowned for its incredible array of wild mushrooms. The Pelion is a botanical wonderland, known since antiquity as the 'healing mountain'.

Greece was a Johnny-come-lately to conservation – until recently many Greeks saw their country only as something to exploit: if the law forbade building on forested land, the obvious solution was to burn the forest. In the past three decades the situation has improved dramatically. Now only Spain has more EU Blue Flag beaches – and Chalkidikí, by the way, is the national champ. Northern Greece boasts 157 protected European Natura 2000 sites and 12 national parks (including one European Geopark, Víkos-Aoös National Park in Epirus, supported by UNESCO). However, this protected status was no defence against the devastating wildfires that Greece experienced in 2023. Over 20 people died in the fires at Evros (most of them asylum seekers) and over 50% of Dadia National Park burned down. Natural regeneration of the forest has been progressing, according to the WWF, and raptors have returned to nest – hopeful news after a traumatic event.

The Dadia forest is among numerous forest and wildlife reserves in northern Greece, including virgin areas in East Macedonia where access is strictly limited. The country has made great strides in saving its wetlands, 11 of which are considered of international importance by Ramsar (w ramsar.org). Another bright spot is the designation of the crystalline seas around Alónissos as a National Marine Park, with untouched islets and a diversity of marine life, including the most endangered species in Europe, the monk seal (page 371). For a complete list of all the protected sites, see w biodiversity-greece.gr.

BIRDLIFE *with James Lowen*
With extensive areas of natural landscapes ranging from upland forests to coastal wetlands – much of which remains little adulterated by human activity – northern Greece has developed a strong reputation for exciting birdwatching, including for seeing species that can be hard to find elsewhere in Europe. Greece overall boasts almost 200 internationally recognised 'Important Bird Areas', and roughly 250 bird species breed (more than Italy, which is twice the size) – the large majority in the north. Throw in several score species that winter, or stop off on spring and autumn migration, and you have plenty of feather at which to aim your binoculars, whatever the time of year.

The region's large number of waterbodies explains an impressive diversity of wildfowl. Three species of swan occur, with mute resident but the yellow-billed pair of whooper and Bewick's both winter visitors to the northeast. Greater white-fronted goose is a localised but reasonably common winterer, the odd flock being joined by a sizeable gathering of the globally threatened lesser white-fronted goose. Common winter ducks include Eurasian teal, Eurasian wigeon and mallard. Two internationally rare diving ducks, ferruginous duck and common pochard, are most readily seen on passage and in winter, respectively. Another scarce relative, white-headed duck, is rare but regular in winter, with Lake Vistonída a stronghold. On migration, look for the dapper garganey. Although unrelated, grebes resemble ducks: little and great crested are locally common residents; in winter, black-necked gathers in coastal waters.

Wetlands harbour an impressive variety of attractive, long-legged waterbirds. Northern Greece holds a third of Europe's Dalmatian pelicans, making it a birder's must-see (notably at Lake Kerkíni); great white pelican also occurs but is scarcer. Little bitterns weave through waterside vegetation; glossy ibis is a common sight on migration. Black-crowned night-herons and squacco herons forage near the water's edge, whereas little and great egrets favour deeper water. White storks often nest atop buildings, and hordes of greater flamingo lope through saline lagoons. Large wetlands are also favoured by the scarecrow-like pygmy cormorant, a speciality of southeast Europe – albeit one outnumbered by the heftier great cormorant.

Waders (shorebirds) are often seen on saltpans, saltmarshes and other coastal habitats. With its preposterously long pink legs, black-winged stilt is the most eye-catching – though pied avocet (a winter visitor) runs it close. Kentish plovers scurry beside saline lagoons, northern lapwing and Eurasian curlew are common in winter, and wood sandpiper and greenshank are among the commonest passage waders. Of gulls, yellow-legged and black-headed are the most abundant, but Mediterranean – the most striking and slender-billed – the most desirable. Common tern breeds widely, but the so-called 'marsh terns' (black, white-winged and whiskered) primarily migrate through in spring, their buoyant flight including dips to pluck insects off the water surface.

The raptors most likely to be spotted are the aptly named common buzzard and common kestrel, followed by short-toed eagle and Eurasian sparrowhawk, with red kite increasingly seen in winter. Marsh harrier hunts low over wetlands, but mountains form the realm of griffon vulture – and those in the northeast are also the treasured location of Greece's sole Egyptian and cinereous vultures. Greater spotted, white-tailed and eastern imperial eagles hulk around major wetlands in winter, and red-footed falcon pursues insects on spring migration. Four types of owl – Eurasian scops, tawny, little and long-eared – are relatively common and widespread, with Eurasian eagle-owl a fan of sparsely populated rocky places.

A quartet of colourful Mediterranean birds are crowd-pleasers. Look for golden oriole (yellow and black, or green) around poplars, Eurasian hoopoe (peach, black and white) trotting along the ground, and European roller (pink and blue) and European bee-eater (a rainbow) on wires. In the skies above, admire a trio of swifts – Alpine, common and pallid – plus various swallows and martins.

Of half-a-dozen species of woodpecker, the mightiest is black woodpecker, which favours mixed montane woods, particularly with firs. These also provide the realm of the rare white-backed woodpecker, while commoner sylvan species include the perky crested tit, timid coal tit, trunk-hugging short-toed treecreeper and a trio of sprites: the diminutive goldcrest, sparkling firecrest and silvery eastern Bonelli's warbler.

Continuing the montane theme, northern Greece harbours several localised rock-loving birds whose habitat or altitudinal affinities are inscribed in their name, whit Alpine chough, Alpine accentor and rock bunting. Further 'rock stars' such as common and blue rock thrushes, crag martin and western rock nuthatch reside readily at lower altitudes, occupying cliffs and outcrops: the nuthatch breeds in crevices, securing its nest-hole from predators by sealing it with mud.

1 | BACKGROUND INFORMATION

Such low-lying rocky areas often sit amid phrygana – bushy scrub on poor soils. This habitat boasts its own particular birdlife, with European stonechats and eastern black-eared wheatear demanding attention by using prominent lookouts, while Sardinian and eastern subalpine warblers skulk in the thickets below. In terrain with taller vegetation, other warblers might attract attention through song: Eurasian blackcap and common whitethroat will be familiar to people hailing from western Europe, but eastern olivaceous and eastern orphean warblers – as their name implies – will not. Keep an ear out too for common nightingale and for sombre tit, the latter keenly sought by birders.

Finally, in open areas of lowlands, from cultivation to coastal margins, gardens to olive groves, a wide range of species can be enjoyed. Red-backed and woodchat shrikes hunt bees and beetles from elevated perches. Spotted flycatchers sally from secluded perches. Zitting cisticola yo-yos high in the sky while giving its simple, repetitive song. White wagtail and meadow pipit scamper along the ground, supplemented by yellow wagtails in summer. Crested lark runs along roadsides, with Eurasian skylark (winter) and greater short-toed lark (summer) providing additional interest. Flocks of thrushes, mainly fieldfare and redwing, roam widely in winter. European serin gives its jingling song from tall trees, while more familiar seed-eaters include common linnet and European greenfinch. Of the closely related buntings, corn is the most common, cirl is smartly attired, Cretzschmar's and ortolan are resplendent in pastel hues, and black-headed is an unequivocal stunner. In northern Greece there is much feathered beauty to admire.

HISTORY

History looms large in the Greek psyche, sometimes astonishing in its achievements, sometimes like a nagging live-in mother-in-law. In Greece today, much of the historical narrative is speculative, regionally fragmented, or twisted and glossed over to fit into a political agenda. This is not unique to Greece, but the Greeks have been doing it longer than most – since the 8th century BC.

EARLY DAYS: PREHISTORIC NORTHERN GREECE Traces of Palaeolithic inhabitants have been found throughout Greece, but the north first becomes interesting in Neolithic times, when the revolution in agriculture and domestication of sheep and goats from Asia Minor arrived in southern Macedonia and Thessaly. The oldest known Neolithic farming settlements in Europe have been unearthed at Néa Nikomedía near Véria (7th millennium BC) and Sésklo near Vólos (6500BC); both had simple houses around a palace-like structure, and the latter imported obsidian from the Cycladic island of Mílos and made elegant pottery, the delightful little clay figurines of people and animals that are one of the glories of the Vólos Archaeology Museum. A contemporary of Néa Nikomedía and Sésklo, Dikili Tash (Orthópetra) near Philippi yielded the oldest goldwork in the Balkans. Dispilió on Kastoriá's lake yielded the mysterious wooden tablet that at least one scholar believes is the earliest writing. In 2007 another very early civilisation was found in the Western Macedonian lake region at Amýntaio, including a house with a wooden floor carbon dated to 7,300 years ago. Finds at Aianí (page 252), inhabited from Neolithic times but in close contact with the later Mycenaeans, suggest it may well have been the embryo of the ancient kingdom of Macedon.

At the beginning of the Bronze Age (c3200–1050BC), a slow and somewhat shadowy incursion of foreigners (Proto-Greek-speaking Indo-Europeans) introduced bronze metal-working techniques and the swing plough. These innovations stabilised agriculture, allowing permanent settlements with lands radiating out several miles. These led to craft specialisation and the use of symbols such as seals or pot marks denoting a specific place, saying 'here we are and this is ours'. The oldest oracle in Greece was founded around the same time at Dodona in Epirus.

The elegant, sea-trading Minoan culture of Crete that reached as far as Skópelos and Samothráki in northern Greece, began to decline after 1500BC – the time of the cataclysmic explosion of Santoríni – and it wasn't long before the horse-taming, chariot-riding Indo-European Mycenaeans filled the power vacuum, with their sky god and a social hierarchy that valued warriors. Indo-European Thracian tribes set up shop in northeast Greece (and Bulgaria and European Türkiye) in 1300BC.

Mycenae gave its name to the era, dominating fellow city-states in some kind of loose federation. Massive fortified palaces went up in the Peloponnese, in Athens and central Greece. The north was largely beyond the boundaries of their world, though there may have been a Mycenaean state at Iolkos (modern Vólos), mentioned in mythology as the place from which Jason and the Argonauts set sail. For reasons not entirely clear, the wealthy and powerful Mycenaean cities crashed dramatically about the time of the fall of Troy (c1180BC), which was followed soon after by the destruction of the citadels of the conquerors made famous by Homer. It was the beginning of the 'Greek Dark Age', as a much-reduced population in tribal bands struggled on in isolated pockets. The Mycenaean word for 'chief' or 'baron', *basileus*, survived to become the Classical Greek 'king', suggesting that at least some of the tribes were remnants of the Mycenaeans.

1180–500BC: FROM THE DARK AGE TO THE ARCHAIC This period may have been a Dark Age, but a lot was happening while the lights were out. When the curtain rises on the Archaic Age in the 8th century BC, what do we find? Sea trade booming again, and diverse groups of Greeks speaking different dialects: Ionian in Attica, on most of the Cyclades and the Anatolian coast; Aeolian in the west in Thessaly; and Dorian in the Peloponnese, some of the islands, and Macedonia (remembered in the myth of three sons of Hercules, whose descendant founded the dynasty of kings at Aigai; page 142). All wrote in an alphabetic script learned from the Phoenicians and began to mint coins. The Panhellenic Oracle at Delphi was established as religious arbiter and political legitimiser, and the founding of the Olympic Games (in 776BC) marked the beginning of the Greek calendar. And there was a renaissance in the arts, too; heroic story cycles developed, including Jason and the Argonauts and the Homeric epics involving the 'second generation' of heroes.

Nurturing all of these developments is that quintessentially Greek institution, the *polis* or city-state. A 'citadel' in Homer (8th century BC), the word *polis* by Archaic times had evolved to denote a city-state not unlike the medieval *comuni* of Italy. Because of the country's geography, with its natural internal boundaries of mountains or sea, there were hundreds of city-states, many of them quite small; Athens, which encompassed all of modern Attica, was exceptionally large. Autarchy, or self-sufficiency, was a city-state ideal, leading to endless wars in the fight for resources. Hoplite formations made up of citizens replaced the Homeric military elite (although these lingered in ancient Macedon and Thessaly, which boasted the best horses and cavalry in Greece).

Also a *polis* could clone itself. Population growth in the 8th century BC dictated that some citizens had to leave; they founded colonies around the Black Sea, Libya, in the western Mediterranean and notably among the Thracians along antiquity's gold coast, including Thássos, Abdera and the many ancient cities of Chalkidikí.

1 | BACKGROUND INFORMATION

City-states fought and competed, but the need for the hoplites to return to their own farms precluded long-term conquests. Sparta was the exception, having enslaved its neighbours as helots to do all the farm work. Their political system, based on the repression of a large majority, led to the creation of a military machine coupled with permanent political paranoia. Panhellenic shrines and games aside, the analogy that fits Hellenic culture is that of a maladjusted family whose members got together at holidays, but who had nothing good to say about the family the rest of the year.

500–338BC: THE CLASSICAL MOMENT Meanwhile, the Greek city-states in Ionia (Asia Minor) had been gobbled up, first by Croesus of Lydia, who in turn was gobbled up by the Persians, at the time the greatest empire in the world. In 499BC the Ionian Greeks revolted and, remembering old ties, Athens sent troops to help; they burned the Persian capital at Sardis and went home. The furious Persians vowed revenge. In the long struggle that followed, the Greek city-states would band together (at least sometimes) to repel the common enemy: a decade after Athens and Plataea famously repulsed an expeditionary force at Marathon in 490BC, Persian king Xerxes arrived with the biggest army and navy Europe had ever seen – traces still remain of the canal Xerxes dug at Néa Róda in Chalkidikí – and things looked especially grim. Some 300 Spartans fought to the death in a delaying action at Thermopylae. Later, the Athenian fleet won a resounding victory at Salamis, and the Spartans led the Greek armies in trouncing the Persians at Plataea in 479BC.

Although Sparta had played a leading role in the war, most city-states, still fearing the Persians (who were ever ready to keep the pot boiling by aiding one Greek faction against another), turned for protection to Athens and its fleet by forming the Delian League, which soon became a de facto Athenian empire. Under Pericles, Athens became a radical democracy and built the Parthenon while laying down the basics of Western civilisation in art, poetry, drama and philosophy. Power and money made the city the centre of the Greek world, but they would also be its downfall.

Fifty years of tension between Sparta and Athens finally boiled over in the Peloponnesian War in 431BC. In this cataclysmic pan-Greek conflict, the north had a role to play too, as both sides coveted its wealth of gold and silver. A revolt against Athens in Potidaea helped touch off the war, and the Spartan conquest of Amphipolis and its mines in 424BC deprived Athens of a considerable part of its finances. Athens' final defeat in 404BC ended the city's pretensions as boss over the Greeks, and it inaugurated a period of constant warfare and instability.

As the city-states beaverishly undermined one another (the cities of Chalkidikí are a prime example), a new actor on the stage looked down from the north and saw only ripe pickings. The Macedonians and their royal family had been considered rather inferior Greeks by the Athenians, but their king, Philip II, who came to the throne in 359BC, was a keen student of great Theban general Epaminondas, who had defeated the Spartans, and, thanks to his gold mines, he was by far the wealthiest ruler in Greece. He was determined not only to prove the southern Greeks wrong, but to do something even the Athenians in their most reckless moment had never envisaged: eliminate the Persian threat, once and for all.

As a prelude, Philip snatched up the Greek colonies in the north and annexed Thrace and Thessaly. Old enemies Thebes and Athens joined forces against him, only to be crushed at Chairóneia (338BC), the death knell of the old city-state. Two years later Philip was assassinated; his son Alexander shocked Greece into

HISTORY

submission by destroying rebellious Thebes. He left a viceroy in Macedon and led his father's planned expedition to Persia and never returned, too busy conquering the world to pay attention to Greece.

338BC–AD330: HELLENISTIC AND ROMAN GREECE Alexander's death in 323BC left a political mess as his generals fought endlessly over his conquests, but his legacy would be the great cultural and economic revival in the eastern Mediterranean, known as the Hellenistic Age. Suddenly the Greek world had quintupled in size, while it enjoyed boom times in a great cross-cultural current. Athens still had its reputation, but the focus of cultural life slowly shifted to Rhodes, Alexandria and Pergamon. New cities appeared in the north. Macedonian King Cassander founded Thessaloníki in 315BC, while Demetrios Poliorketes (the 'Besieger'), son of another of Alexander's generals, built a new town near Vólos called Demetrias, and made it his base for fighting Cassander and the other would-be heirs of Alexander. Demetrios 'freed' Athens (from Cassander) and restored democracy in 307BC, on his way to becoming King of Macedon in 294BC. Greek cities would often be given their 'freedom' in the Hellenistic and Roman eras, and many did enjoy considerable autonomy, as long as they remembered who was boss.

Throughout the 3rd century BC, the generals' descendants kept Greece convulsed in endless warfare and instability. The struggles exhausted the country, and made it easy for Rome and its legions to move in. Open conflict with Macedon began in 215BC, during the Second Punic War, when the Romans intercepted a Macedonian ambassador with the draft of a treaty between his country and Carthage. After a series of wars, the Romans defeated the Macedonian phalanx decisively in 197BC at Cynoscephalae.

ST PAUL IN NORTHERN GREECE

St Paul personally brought Christianity to Greece in AD49, after a dream he had of a tall Macedonian man asking him to come. Accompanied by Luke (the Evangelist, and author of the Acts of the Apostles), Silas and Timothy, he landed briefly in Samothráki and then Neapolis (modern Kavála), on his way to Philippi (the first of four visits), where he made his first converts in Europe. Paul caused a commotion when he cast an evil spirit out of a servant girl; the girl and her demon had been supporting the family by telling fortunes, and they dragged Paul and Silas off to the Roman magistrates, who flogged and imprisoned them. A midnight earthquake miraculously knocked down their prison door, but Paul and Silas refused to escape, demanding that the magistrates come and explain why they had so mistreated two Roman citizens. The prison guard was so impressed with their steadfastness that he converted, along with his family, and the magistrates let them go on their way.

After that Paul and Silas hurried to Thessaloníki, where Paul talked in the synagogue for three Saturdays and made enough converts to found a church, before he was run out of town by hostile Jews and escaped to Véria (Berea). Here he received a friendlier reception, but his enemies in Thessaloníki got wind of it and came after him – Paul's friends helped him to escape. Timothy and Silas remained in Véria, while a local named Sopatros (or Sosipatros) accompanied Paul for years. Paul's time in Macedonia is recounted in the New Testament's Acts, and he himself wrote the Epistle to the Philippians and the Epistles to the Thessalonians.

1 | BACKGROUND INFORMATION

After several uprisings, Rome took direct control of all Greece in 146BC. One of its first acts was to build the Via Egnatía across northern Greece from modern Igoumenítsa to Byzantium, opening the way to conquests in the east. The country later witnessed two key moments in Roman history: Octavian and Antony's defeat of Brutus and the conspirators who assassinated Caesar at Philippi (42BC); and Octavian's victory over Antony and Cleopatra's fleet at Actium (31BC).

Rome hauled off as much art as it could and divided Greece into provinces. The Romans professed to having been 'conquered' by Greek culture, a pretty compliment, and used Athens as a finishing school for their élite. But if the Romans considered themselves as part of the Hellenic family and went to great lengths to link themselves to the heroes of Homer, the Greeks could never really have seen them as anything more than 'Big Brothers'. Still, like every other era in history, people made the best of it; Roman rule did bring peace, and it offered a better life than the barbarians, who began knocking at the door in AD252, when the Goths invaded Macedonia.

By this time, Thessaloníki on the Via Egnatía had supplanted Athens as the most important city in Greece. As pressure from the invaders increased, the Roman empire divided itself like an amoeba into two parts; Thessaloníki briefly served as eastern capital until AD330, when emperor Constantine moved to Byzantium and changed its name to his own, Constantinopolis. Historians call the resulting eastern half the Byzantine Empire, but the Greeks of the time still referred to themselves as 'Romans'.

AD330–1204: THE BYZANTINE EMPIRE Under the Byzantines, Greece lost much of its importance, except for the north where Thessaloníki continued to prosper. Christianity spread early and pervasively. Edicts by Emperor Theodosius ordered that ancient temples be razed to make way for Christian churches, usually built from the same stones. Although many cities in Greece kept their chins up, the general picture is one of terrible decline. Barbarian invasions continued periodically, and catastrophic earthquakes in AD521 and 551, coupled with devastating outbreaks of plague in AD541–43, left vast swathes of Greece underpopulated. The 7th-9th centuries AD were grim, marked by the violent controversy of Iconoclasm over the use of images in the Church. New peoples, mostly Slavs, arrived to fill the empty spaces in Greece as the bureaucrats in Constantinople moved populations like chess pieces in order to keep up their tax base. Enough Greeks remained to absorb the invaders, and within a few generations most of the newcomers would be linguistically and culturally assimilated.

The light begins to flicker on again after future emperor Nikephóros Phokás liberated Crete from the Saracens (AD961) and Basil II defeated the Bulgars who had threatened the north. New churches and monasteries were built, especially on Mount Athos. Much of Greece, however, was deteriorating into a handful of large fiefs owned by absentee landowners (often the monasteries themselves); Constantinople's crushing taxes and clumsy statist economy meant a continuing impoverishment of the hinterlands. By 1204, the Byzantine Empire was such a decadent and misgoverned entity that few were unhappy to see it taken over by the 'Franks' (the Greek word at the time for any Westerner) in the Fourth Crusade, an incursion masterminded by the merchants of Venice, who had a bone to pick over trading concessions in the east.

1205–1821: FRANKS, BYZANTINES AGAIN AND TURKS Although the flimsy Latin Empire in Constantinople soon reverted to the Greeks, there was little resistance to the invading Ottomans, who initially took Thessaloníki in 1387. The Byzantines reclaimed the city a few years later, before losing control to the Republic of Venice, which was unable to hold out against the determined Ottomans – the Ottomans finally came to stay for good in 1430 (and would remain for close to five centuries). They also snapped up much of the rest of Greece in the 15th century. They were welcome in some quarters simply because it was Ottoman policy to leave the Orthodox Church alone. The Porte (Sultan) left local communities some freedoms except where taxes were concerned, combined with vicious reprisals whenever their authority was challenged. Under the Turkokratía, life for the peasants actually improved thanks to the end of the fighting and high taxes that had so plagued the region in the past, although the *devşirme* system (the every-five-years Ottoman patrols, which took the strongest Christian boys to convert to Islam and serve the Ottoman empire in a variety of capacities, with the possibility of reaching the highest ranks) was deeply resented.

Thessaloníki remained the most important city in Greece, especially after 1492, when Sultan Bayezid II welcomed the Jews expelled from Spain by Ferdinand and Isabella ('You venture to call Ferdinand a wise ruler,' the Sultan scoffed. 'He who has impoverished his own country and enriched mine.'). The city's population also included Bulgars, Turks (Atatürk was born there) and a score of other nationalities, making it one of the great cosmopolitan trading centres of the Mediterranean.

Significantly for the future, parts of Greece, such as Souli in Epirus, never truly submitted to the Turks, and the pashas were constantly reduced to some form of power-sharing with local Greek leaders whom they could, of course, never quite trust. In spite of setbacks and disappointing efforts to oust the Turks by Morosini (Venice) in 1684 and Orlov (Russia) in 1770, Greek freedom fighters in klephtic bands fought and were defeated again and again, then headed for the hills and bided their time. Their numbers increased dramatically in the 1700s, and an entire culture grew up around these free mountain spirits that would prove hard to give up when independence came.

1821–1922: INDEPENDENCE AND THE GREAT IDEA The revolutionary fires that swept through Europe at the end of the 18th century found plenty of kindling among Greeks. Poet Rígas Feraíos of Thessaly, fired up by the French Revolution, provided the inspiration, and, after he was killed on the Sultan's orders, a group of diaspora Greeks living in Odessa formed the Filikí Etareía ('Friendly Society'). This secret society would do much to co-ordinate activities between well-wishers abroad and Greeks in Greece.

The War of Independence began in the Peloponnese in 1821, and continued for more than six years through a parade of atrocities and political infighting. In the end, the Great Powers, namely Britain, Russia and France, came to assist the Greek cause, and the decisive Battle of Navarino (20 October 1827) gave the new Greek state the Peloponnese and the mainland up to a line between the cities of Árta and Vólos. They also came up with a king for Greece: Otto, son of Ludwig I of Bavaria, who immediately offended local sensibilities by giving Bavarians all the official posts, including the building of the new capital over the bedraggled village that was Athens.

The fledgling Greek state was born with a mission: the Megáli Idéa, or 'Great Idea', of liberating and uniting all the Greeks into a kind of Byzantium Revisited. Otto's arrogance and inadequacies led to his eventual dethronement in 1862, but the Great Powers found a replacement in George, son of the King of Denmark (who, as a young naval cadet, learned of his new job in a newspaper wrapped around his sardine sandwich). In 1864, the National Assembly made Greece a constitutional monarchy, a system that began to work practically under Prime Minister Trikoúpis in 1875. During the long reign of well-liked George I (grandfather of Philip, the late Duke of Edinburgh), Greece began to develop, with shipping as its economic base.

Meanwhile, the north remained under Ottoman rule, and Thessaloníki flourished: a rapidly modernising commercial city with trams and electric lights long before many places in Greece had them, and an energetic population that was nearly half Jewish. Modernism, however, brought new kinds of troubles. Greek Nationalists and anarchists threw bombs and raised riots, while radical circles among the Ottomans in the city gave birth to the Young Turk movement. Their revolt in the city in 1908 brought them to power, beginning the bloodshed and misery their policies would spread over the Ottoman lands for the next 12 years.

In 1910, Eleftherios Venizélos became prime minister of Greece for the first of many terms. He deftly used the two Balkan Wars of 1912–13 to annex his native Crete, the North Aegean islands, Thessaloníki, Macedonia and southern Epirus. But for Greece every up had a down: King George I, ready to celebrate the golden jubilee of his reign, was assassinated in Thessaloníki on 18 March 1913.

When World War I broke out, his son Constantine I (married to Kaiser Wilhelm's sister) supported the Germans while remaining officially neutral, while Venizélos set up a separate government in support of the Allies in Thessaloníki to stand against the Turks, Bulgarians and Austrians. When Serbia was on the brink of falling to the Central Powers, the Allies decided to create a new 'Macedonian Front'. French and British divisions landed in Thessaloníki, and after the fall of Serbia they were joined by Italian, Serbian and Russian troops and Greek volunteers. The Greek 'National Schism' went Venizélos's way when the Allies recognised the prime minister as the government and blockaded the southern areas of Greece that supported Constantine before bluntly ordering the king and his eldest son, George, to abdicate and leave his second son, Alexander, as interim king; Venizélos then sent Greek troops to the Macedonian front.

Though Greece had chosen the winning side, for Thessaloníki the war was a disaster. Beside the disruptions in trade, the great fire of 1917 destroyed much of the old city, leaving a quarter of its population homeless and most of the rest unemployed.

During the Paris Peace Conference, Greece was rewarded with Eastern and Western Thrace, up to the Bosporus, but Venizélos wanted more. Türkiye was prostrate, and Britain, France and America agreed to a Greek occupation as a preliminary to a local plebiscite on the future of the Greek lands of Anatolia. Tragically, the Greek landings were accompanied by atrocities against the Turks, who began to rally around national hero Mustafa Kemal (later Atatürk). Venizélos was defeated in elections and went to France, while the royalists brought back King Constantine in 1920 on promises of a 'small but honourable Greece'.

But Smyrna (now Izmir) was too tempting a prize. Constantine's incompetent, foolhardy government ordered the army to march on Ankara, thinking to destroy Kemal's armies. Instead it was the Greeks who were routed, in September 1922, abandoning Smyrna to the Turkish Army as the city was consumed in flames. It was the death of the Megáli Idéa. Constantine abdicated; Colonel Nikólas Plastíras took over, and in the bitterness that followed he executed five ministers and a general as scapegoats. Turkish–Greek relations had reached such a nadir that their leaders agreed that a population exchange was the only solution in the 1923 Treaty of Lausanne.

While usually referred to as the Asia Minor Catastrophe internationally, the Greeks often just call it the 'Catastrophe'. The country, with a then population of 4.8 million, was faced with the difficulties of finding housing and work for 1.3 million refugees, 160,000 of whom ended up in Thessaloníki. Some 380,000 Muslims were sent to Türkiye, although a dispensation was given to Western Thrace, where a large Muslim minority remains to this day, with the tacit understanding that Greeks could remain in Istanbul.

There were enough refugees to change the politics of Greece, and most of them supported Venizélos. The monarchy was abolished in 1924, and after a bad interlude of military dictatorship under General Pángalos, Venizélos was elected prime minister again in 1928. Trade unions and the Greek communist party, the KKE, gained strength. Venizélos made peace with Greece's neighbours (he visited Türkiye in 1930 and even nominated Atatürk for the Nobel Peace Prize).

WORLD WAR II AND THE GREEK CIVIL WAR What Venizélos couldn't heal was the increased polarisation of Greek political life, especially as the Great Depression led to violent labour unrest. Venizélos himself barely survived an assassination attempt; martial law was declared, coups were attempted, and in 1935, after a faked plebiscite, George II returned to Greece, with General Ioánnis Metaxás as his prime minister.

Metaxás assumed dictatorial control under the 'Regime of the Fourth of August'. He exiled the opposition, instituted rigorous censorship, banned the use of the Slav language in the northwest, and crushed the trade unions and all leftist activities. Although he imitated the Fascists in some ways, Metaxás had sufficient foresight to prepare the Greek army in advance against occupation, and on 28 October 1940, as the story goes, he responded with a laconic '*Óchi!*' (No!) to Mussolini's ultimatum that his troops massed on the Albanian border be allowed to occupy strategic points in Greece.

The Greeks heroically pushed the invading Italians back into Albania, in the first victories over the Axis in the war, but refused British offers of assistance at first in the futile hope of preventing Germany from joining the conflict. When Hitler's help for Italy came in April 1941, it was crushing, and in spite of a fierce resistance, by mid-month the severely outnumbered British, New Zealanders and Australians, along with the Greek government, were fleeing south to North Africa. After the Battle of Crete in May, all Greece was in the hands of the Nazis, who divided the country into occupation zones: German in Athens, Thessaloníki and Central Macedonia; Bulgarian in Eastern Macedonia and Thrace (the region it long claimed); and Italian for much of the rest.

A huge number of civilians died in Greece; an estimated 500,000 starved to death in the Great Famine of the first winter. Communism had been gaining ground all through the 1930s; now, the miseries of the occupation politicised Greeks who in the past had hoped only to be left alone. The EAM and its army, the Greek People's Liberation Army (ELAS), led the resistance and destroyed all other groups. They had vast popular support – Márko Vafiádis's Macedonian division of ELAS liberated Thessaloníki and is credited with saving the lives of thousands of Jews – but their politics were hardly palatable to Churchill, who made the famous 'percentages agreement' with Stalin, later agreed in Yalta, to keep Greece within the Allied sphere of influence.

Stalin, however, failed to tell Greek communists about his deal, and the Greek Civil War – the first campaign of the Cold War – broke out three short months after liberation. It began with a fight for the control of Athens – the 'December

1 | BACKGROUND INFORMATION

Events' (Dekemvrianá) – with British troops fighting members of ELAS, their former resistance allies. The Communists abstained from the elections of March 1946, leading to the victory of right-wing royalists, followed by a referendum that voted in favour of the return of the monarchy in the person of Constantine I's son Paul. Long-drawn-out guerrilla campaigns and atrocities followed in the mountains of northern Greece and the Peloponnese. Stalin kept his pledge not to meddle in the conflict, though the Communists were able to mount their raids into the country from bases in Albania and Yugoslavia. As Britain's containment policy was taken over by the USA under the Truman Doctrine, American money and advisors poured into Greece. The Civil War dragged on until 1949, when Marshal Tito withdrew his support; leftists who were not shot or imprisoned went into exile (page 233).

1950–1974: INTERESTING TIMES Greeks call the next two decades the 'Years of Stone'. Recovery was slow, even if orchestrated by America, and the Greek diaspora that began in the early 1900s accelerated so fast that entire villages became ghost towns. In 1952, Greece and Türkiye became full members of NATO, an uncomfortable arrangement from the start because of the unresolved issue of Cyprus.

In 1955, US-backed Konstantínos Karamanlís of Macedonia became prime minister, inaugurating eight years of relative stability and prosperity as agriculture, industry and tourism grew, although the opposition criticised his pro-Western policies. He even managed to reach a compromise over Cyprus with Türkiye and Great Britain, when the island became independent in 1960.

The royal family, especially the forceful German-born Queen Frederíka, was unpopular; there were strikes and powerful anti-American feelings. Karamanlís quarrelled with King Paul, resigned and lost the next elections in 1963 to centre-left warhorse George Papandréou, who gave a portfolio to his son Andréas, an economics professor at Harvard (and once Adlai Stevenson's campaign manager in Minnesota), whose mildly inflationary policies horrified the right. At the same time, King Paul died and was succeeded by his son, the conservative, 23-year-old Constantine II.

The combination did not bode well; a quarrel with the king over reforming the military led to Papandréou's resignation in 1965. Constantine called for elections; before they could take place, a coup by an obscure group of army officers on 21 April 1967 caught both right and left by surprise. The 'Colonels', most of whom were of peasant stock and resentful of Athenian politicians, established a dictatorship and imprisoned George and Andréas Papandréou. Colonel George Papadópoulos made himself prime minister. Constantine attempted a ridiculous counter-coup and then fled to Rome.

Under the Colonels, human rights were suppressed, absurd censorship undermined cultural life, and secret police imprisoned and tortured dissidents – or their children. Yet Greece's strategic position in the volatile eastern Mediterranean and in NATO were reason enough for the USA to prop up the regime. The internal situation went from bad to worse, and on 17 November 1973 students of the Polytechnic School in Athens went on strike. Tanks were brought in and many were killed. Popular feeling rose to such a pitch that Papadópoulos was sacked, only to be replaced by his arrester, the brutal head of the military police, Dimítrios Ioannídes.

In an insane bid for popularity, Ioannídes tried to launch a coup in Cyprus, to assassinate the island's leader, Bishop Makários, and replace him with a president who would declare the union of Cyprus with Greece. It was a fiasco. Makários fled, and in July 1974 the Turkish army invaded Cyprus, occupying 40% of the island.

The Greek military rebelled, the dictatorship resigned and Karamanlís hurriedly returned from his exile to form a new government, release the political prisoners and order a ceasefire in Cyprus.

1974 TO THE PRESENT Karamanlís and his conservative New Democracy (ND) party easily won the November 1974 elections. The monarchy did less well in a subsequent plebiscite, and Greece became a republic. That same year Karamanlís realised his fondest dream when the country was anchored to the European Economic Community, becoming a full member of the EU in 1981. Karamanlís brought stability but neglected the economic and social reforms Greece needed. These, along with a desire for national integrity in the face of American meddling, were to be the ticket to populist Andréas Papandréou's victories beginning in 1981. His party, PASOK (the Panhellenic Socialist Movement), promised much, beginning with withdrawal from NATO and the EU, and the removal of US airbases.

A national reconciliation with the exiled resistance fighters was at the top of the agenda; women were given more rights, and even excess accents were kicked out of the written language as a heady liberalisation swept the land. PASOK easily triumphed again in the 1985 elections, in spite of Papandréou's failure to deliver Greece from the snares of NATO or the EU, or keep any of his promises on the economic front. Inflation soared, and Greece had to be bailed out by a huge EU loan accompanied by an unpopular belt-tightening programme – an early-warning alarm bell that no-one heeded.

Scandals brought Papandréou down in 1989, when Néa Demokratía leader Konstantínos Mitsotákis, a former resistance fighter, took a slim majority in the elections, promising to grapple with Greece's economic problems. His austerity measures soon proved even more unpopular than Papandréou's scandals, and in October 1993 Papandréou was re-elected. He kept Greece in his thrall as Yugoslavia disintegrated, pushing Balkan nationalist buttons over what would become known for decades as the Former Yugoslav Republic of Macedonia and siding (verbally, mostly) with the Serbs, as Orthodox brethren were oppressed by the so-called Muslim hordes. As Papandréou played the gadfly, the once-reviled 'capitalist club', the EU, poured massive funds into Greece, resulting in new roads, schools, sewers and agricultural subsidies.

In late 1995 as Papandréou's health declined, technocrat Kósta Simítis toughed it out to get PASOK's nod. The economy improved, and with the aid of Papandréou's son George as foreign minister, Greece positioned itself as a regional leader and prime investor in the Balkans. Even Greek–Turkish relations improved, after each country rushed to the other's aid after the earthquakes in 1999. And what seemed to be the icing on the cake for many ordinary Greeks who yearned for peace and stability, the country joined the Eurozone that same year – only minus any much-needed structural economic reforms.

ND leader Kóstas Karamanlís, nephew of the former prime minister, was elected in 2004 and at first everything went swimmingly: against the odds, in 2004 Greece won the UEFA European Championship for the first time, then held the 2004 Olympics – pulling off a successful games at the last minute, although with huge cost overruns. Further feathers in the national cap included winning the Eurovision Song Contest and the European basketball championships, both in 2005.

Behind the scenes, however, all was not well; even back in 2004, the European Commission suspected that the Greek government had cooked the books and hid the country's soaring debts to meet the fiscal requirements to join the euro. The economic crisis that began in 2008 hit the Eurozone in 2009, as PASOK's George

1 | BACKGROUND INFORMATION

A GREEK MYTHOLOGY WHO'S WHO

Like all good polytheists, the Greeks filled their pantheon with a kaleidoscopic array of divinities. They may be more anthropomorphic than Egyptian or Indian gods but, having evolved over 1,000 years, are nonetheless full of fathomless contradictions, subtleties and, above all, regional nuance. The Greeks had no 'Bible', no written book of dogma or ritual. The only recognised higher authority was the Delphic oracle, and it was famous for its ambiguities. The Olympians, the immortal dozen, became a recognised hierarchy by the Archaic period, mostly thanks to Homer and Hesiod, but even they were never cut and dried.

In reality, Greeks everywhere felt quite free to create their own peculiar perspective on their gods, and to hang on to any indigenous local ones they fancied. Naturally imaginative and idiosyncratic, they turned their stories of the gods into an art form as much as a religion. If one aspect of Zeus didn't appeal or fit the bill, he could be morphed by adding an epithet: Zeus of Oaths, Zeus the Saviour, Zeus of the Flies, ad infinitum. Different areas could claim the same divinity as their own home-grown god. If none suited, a god could be borrowed: even in ancient times, equating a minor local god or a foreign god with an Olympian was something of a parlour game. Of course, the gods were often conscripted to do duty on the political level. Politicians have always had a nice appreciation of their usefulness, especially in time of war.

And, like elderly aunts, the Greeks could never bear to throw anything out. Once a taboo, god or ritual became part of their religious furniture, it stuck around in one form or another, resulting in early chthonic deities rubbing shoulders with later, more rationalised versions of themselves. Local nymphs, naiads, river gods and dryads ran about; a whole host of early giants, heroes, half-animal deities such as centaurs, satyrs and snake men were constantly on the loose in the 'dream time' of the Greek collective religion. But we all have to start somewhere; the following is a short rundown of the big guns.

The one-time weather god turned big shot on Olympus was **Zeus** (or Dias, or Jupiter to the Romans). A version of the Indo-European sky god, he was lord of the thunderbolt, with a libido to match. Zeus was wed to his sister **Hera**, the goddess of marriage, who had the handy knack of renewing her virginity annually in a river

Papandréou, son of Andréas, was elected – just in time to deal with the massive sovereign debt crisis. The bailout agreements between Greece and the 'troika' (the European Commission, European Central Bank and IMF) would last nearly a decade and eventually total more than a quarter of a trillion euros, in exchange for swingeing austerity cuts that set off violent protests as salaries and pensions were slashed, age of retirement and taxes were raised, banks closed, spending was cut to the bone, and unemployment soared, especially among the young; unable to find work, some 500,000 Greeks emigrated abroad.

Growth slowly, erratically, began again in 2013 – at the same time as Greece found itself on the frontlines of the European refugee crisis, as migrants escaping political turmoil, mainly from the Middle East and Afghanistan, began crossing over to the Greek islands from Türkiye, nearly all hoping to make their way to Germany. The tension led to the rise of ultra-nationalist extreme right party Golden Dawn, who won seats in parliament in 2014, the same year that radical left-wing coalition SYRIZA won the majority under Aléxis Tsípras, with the promise of renegotiating the deal with the troika, which ended up a shambles.

(it didn't improve their relationship). Although she began in Mycenaean times or earlier as a goddess of fertility, Hera's special role in myth was as the wronged, jealous wife. Zeus had two brothers: **Poseidon**, who ruled the sea, managed the rivers and caused earthquakes; and **Hades**, god of the shadowy underworld and realm of the dead, who kept a low profile except when he went hunting for a wife and kidnapped Persephone, Demeter's daughter. **Demeter**, goddess of corn and growing things, did not need to throw her weight around – when she was unhappy, nothing grew. **Aphrodite**, the goddess of love, is nearly as old as the earliest gods, and had a weird beginning. Born from the foam produced by the severed genitals of Uranos when his son Kronos castrated him, she was a force to be reckoned with.

The second generation of Olympians were the offspring of Zeus. **Athena**, the urbane virgin goddess of wisdom, handicrafts and ceramics, was born right out of the forehead of Zeus, his own ideal female; she was always associated with Athens in particular. **Ares**, a Thracian interloper, was the god of war. Oddly enough, given Greek history, he was not popular, and often resembles a whining bully. **Hermes** was a one-man courier service, a go-between who watched over travellers and merchants and took everybody on their final journey to Hades. **Hephaestos**, son of Hera and lame husband of Aphrodite, was ridiculed for his less-than-perfect body, but revered for his fire and forge, which produced the weapons and baubles of the gods.

Apollo, patron of the Ionians, the god of light, music, reason, poetry and prophecy, was the nonplus ultra of a rationalised Greek god, but even he could lose his cool on occasion. His twin, **Artemis**, the tomboy, was the virgin moon goddess of the hunt. The temperamental, cross-dressing **Dionysos**, god of wine, orgies and theatre, came from Thrace but was popular everywhere. And we forgot **Hestia** (Vesta), the virgin goddess of the hearth and Zeus's sister, and **Helios**, the sun god – which makes 15 (so much for the magic number 12). Among the supporting cast, two in particular stand out: **Pan**, the woodland god who gave his name to posterity in the word 'panic', and **Heracles**, a god-hero in a class by himself, and a big favourite with the Dorians.

Relations with Recep Erdoğan's Türkiye have been rocky: issues over the border flare up, either by the Turkish air force flying into Greek airspace in the Aegean, a situation worsened after the 2016 attempted coup in Türkiye, when several Turkish military personnel sought political asylum in Greece. Greece refused to send them back, and in response the controversial 'one in, one out' controls the EU negotiated with Türkiye to control migrant crossings have been put on the shelf. In 2018, some 30,000 migrants crossed into Greece, nearly half of whom crossed over the Évros River. An increasing number have been Turks, seeking asylum in Greece.

In 2018, Greece had a record tourism year, which helped the national coffers, although the country as a whole managed just over 2% growth, and in 2019 the IMF announced that Greece was growing and one of the best performers in the Eurozone. Still, the economy had lost nearly a quarter of its pre-2009 value. Unemployment (up to 40% among 15–24-year-olds) is terrible. Greece is one of the poorest countries in Europe, and it will be decades before the country pays back its debt pile of 180% of GDP. In the meantime, the government has embarked on a number of schemes to earn extra cash: selling off assets, running a controversial 'golden passport' scheme, etc.

One bright spot has been the settling of the long-running diplomatic feud over the name of the Former Yugoslav Republic of Macedonia when votes squeaked through both parliaments in Athens and Skopje, in the face of nationalist protest on both sides of the border to accept 'North Macedonia' as its official name.

When SYRIZA garnered only 23.7% of the vote in the EU elections in May 2019, Tsípras called a snap general election on 7 July, when the ND under Kyriákos Mitsotákis, son of the former prime minister, won an outright majority of seats in parliament (158 compared with 86 for SYRIZA). Harvard- and Stanford-educated banker and first post-bailout prime minister Mitsotákis promised to lower taxes, complete an array of stalled projects and put an end to corruption, red tape and tax dodging.

The COVID-19 pandemic brought every other concern to a halt, but Greece fared better health-wise than some nations, thanks to the leadership (and strong measures) of physician Sotíris Tsiódras, who was appointed to co-ordinate management of the response to the pandemic. Post-pandemic Greece has seen a surge of tourism – 36 million visitors in 2023, and over 41 million in 2024, many of them concentrated in tourism hotspots. Residents continue to reckon with the impact of the increase in tourism on day-to-day life, the environment, the country's infrastructure, and the rising cost of living. Greece returned to the polls in May 2023, but no majority was reached. In a second election in June of that same year, Kyriákos Mitsotákis and ND reached 158 seats, but as of early 2025 they face some challenges – the anniversary of a controversial 2023 railway tragedy, tourism development threatening natural wonders, and a sharp rise in housing prices are among the factors giving rise to a simmering discontent.

GOVERNMENT AND POLITICS

In 2011, northern Greece's five regions (page 3) were further devolved into regional units around major cities. Politically they veer towards the centre-right, although Thessaloníki has historically stood out for its liberal, all-inclusive policies. The Central Macedonia region also encompasses the autonomous self-governing Monastic State of Mount Athos, with its spiritual affairs cared for by the Patriarch in Istanbul and its state affairs managed by the Greek Foreign Ministry.

In northern Greece, with its complicated and often tragic history, minority issues and sensitivities are rarely far below the surface. Although the 2019 agreement of both sides to call the Former Yugoslav Republic of Macedonia 'North Macedonia' was hailed internationally, nationalist resentment lingers on the ground (in the Greek parliament the bill passed with only a majority of seven). Another issue has been the rights of the Muslim community in Thrace, which were defined in the Treaty of Lausanne in 1923, which compelled Muslims to take their domestic disputes to a mufti under Sharia law – a rule that finally changed in 2018 with the ruling of the European Court of Human Rights.

ECONOMY

Central Macedonia – which includes Thessaloníki, with Greece's second most important port, its third-busiest airport, one of the country's biggest universities, and a vibrant service-based economy (not to mention a huge chunk of the north's tourism revenues) – is recovering the fastest in northern Greece from the economic crisis. Otherwise, agriculture is a mainstay throughout Macedonia, which has the country's richest and best irrigated farmland. Tobacco, the cash crop for more than a century, is still widely grown, but cereals and fruits are now more important, along with high-value crops such as wine, peppers and saffron. Corn, cotton and cattle are produced on the great plain of Thessaly, although in the Pindus Mountains and in Epirus, where much of the soil is too poor for crops, animal husbandry (sheep and goats) are important. EU projects such as the funding of the Egnatía Ódos highway across northern Greece has helped open up isolated pockets in Epirus and Western Macedonia, two of the poorest and most isolated regions, and there are plans on the table to build a modern railway along the route.

PEOPLE

The majority of people in northern Greece are ethnic Greeks, including a large number of descendants of the refugees forced to relocate in 1923 from western Türkiye, the Pontus (the south coast of the Black Sea) and Cappadocia; many others, still alive, arrived after the Istanbul pogrom of 1955. Often, towns and villages with a 'Néa' (new) in front of their name recall a beloved old home, while cultural organisations keep alive traditional festivals, of costumes, music, cuisine and patron saints, such as the Panagía Soumelá of the Pontic Greeks (page 251). There are the once-nomadic Sarakatsáni shepherds who roamed across the Pindus and Rhodope mountains (page 165); anthropologists and linguists believe they may well be the descendants of the ancient Dorian Greeks who took to the mountains and stayed aloof from history for centuries, preserving a dialect, costumes and near-Homeric patriarchy along the way.

Although the Greek government, for complicated historic reasons, refuses to recognise any minority outside the Muslim community in Western Thrace (page 202), it's easy to see why the French word for a mixed salad is a '*macédoine*'. Northern Greece is home to some 200,000 Aromanians (or Vlachs), the once semi-nomadic descendants of the ancient Dacians who have lived in and around the Pindus Mountains at least since the Middle Ages. In the northwest, there are thousands of Slavic-speaking Macedonians (or 'Slavophone' or 'bilingual' Greeks as Athens prefers; page 233). There are Albanian Arvanites who have lived in Greece for centuries. In the east, along with Turkish-speaking Muslims are Muslim Pomaks and Muslim Roma, and much smaller communities of Armenians. Jews, both Greek and Sephardic descendants of exiles from Iberia, once lived throughout the north until the Holocaust; today the majority, estimated at 1,200, live in Thessaloníki. A massive wave of Albanians who arrived in the 1990s after the fall of Communism are today the largest expatriate community, while the most recent newcomers are refugees, mainly from Afghanistan, Iraq, Syria and recently Türkiye, many of whom end up in the region's several refugee camps, and most of whom hope to relocate to other EU countries in the north.

LANGUAGE

Greek holds a special place as the oldest spoken language in Europe, going back at least 4,000 years. From the ancient language, Modern Greek, or *romaíka*, developed into two forms: the purist, or *katharévousa*, and the popular, or Demotic, *demotikí*, the language of the people. These days few purist words are spoken, but you will see the old *katharévousa* on shop signs and official forms. Even though the bakery is called the *foúrnos*, the sign over the door will read ARTOPOLEION, 'bread-seller',

1 | BACKGROUND INFORMATION

while the general store will be the PANTOPOLEION, 'seller of all'. You'll still see the pure form on wine labels as well. At the end of the 18th century, writers felt the common language wasn't good enough; archaic forms were brought back and foreign ones replaced. Upon independence, this somewhat stilted, artificial construction became the official language of books, documents and even newspapers.

The more vigorous and natural Demotic soon began to creep back; in 1901 Athens was shaken by riots and the government fell when the New Testament appeared in *demotikí*; in 1903 several students were killed in a fight with the police during a *demotikí* performance of Aeschylus. When the fury subsided, it looked as if the Demotic would win out until the Papadópoulos government (1967–74) made it part of its puritan 'moral cleansing' of Greece to revive the purist *katharévousa*. The debate was settled in 1978 when Demotic was made the official tongue.

Modern Greek is spoken by all, but not surprisingly quite a few minority languages are current as well: many Vlachs speak Aromanian, an eastern Romance language related to Romanian, while Albanian Arvanites have kept alive an old Albanian dialect, Arvanitika. Muslims in Thrace speak Turkish, as well as Greek, while the Pomaks speak a dialect of Bulgarian and the Roma speak southern Vlax Romani. Ladino, the medieval Spanish dialect of Thessaloníki's Jews – once the city's dominant language – has all but vanished.

English is mandatory in school and most Greeks travel so far and wide that even in the most remote places there's usually someone who speaks English. However, while Greek, usually spoken with great velocity, isn't a particularly easy language to pick up by ear, it is very helpful to know at least the alphabet – so that you can find your way around – and a few basic words and phrases (page 381).

RELIGION AND BELIEFS

The majority of people (including the Aromanians, the Arvanites, the Slavophones) belong to the Eastern Orthodox church, but northern Greece is also home to the country's Muslim minority, who live in Eastern Macedonia and Thrace, and a small handful of Jews, mostly in Thessaloníki.

Orthodoxy is so fundamental to Greek identity that for centuries deciding who was Greek or not depended on speaking Greek and being baptised into the church. One reason for this deep national feeling is that, unlike everything else (see from page 10), the Orthodox church has scarcely changed since the 4th century AD. As Constantinople took over as the capital of the Roman Empire and Greek – the language of the New Testament – took over from Latin, the Greeks believe their church to be the only true successor to the church founded by St Peter in Rome. Therefore, a true Greek was for centuries called a Romiós or Roman, and the Greek language was called Romaíka.

The Orthodox church is considered perfect and eternal; if it weren't, believers could never expect to be saved on Judgement Day. This sense of timelessness has spared Greeks the changes that have rocked the West, from the Reformation to the Second Vatican Council to controversies over abortion, birth control and so on. Anyone (as long as they're male) interested in Orthodoxy in its purist form should visit Mount Athos, where even the clocks and calendar are Byzantine.

This determination never to change anything explains the violence of Iconoclasm, when in the early 8th century, Emperor Leo III, shamed by what his Muslim neighbours called 'idolatry', deemed the images of divine beings to be sacrilegious. The Iconoclasm opened up a first major rift with the West, and it worsened in AD800 when the Patriarch of Rome (aka the Pope) crowned Charlemagne as Emperor, usurping the position of the Byzantine Emperor in Constantinople. Further divisions arose over the celibacy of the clergy (nearly all Orthodox priests marry before they're ordained) and the use of the phrase *filioque*, 'and the son', in the Holy Creed. This phrase was enough to cause the final schism in 1054 when the papal legate, Cardinal Humbert, excommunicated the Patriarch of Constantinople and the Patriarch excommunicated the Pope.

The Ottoman Sultans not only tolerated the Orthodox church, but astutely imparted considerable powers to the Patriarch in return for his guarantee of Greek good behaviour. The church helped to preserve Greek tradition, language and identity through the centuries of Turkish rule, but on the other hand, it left Greece a deeply conservative country in some ways. Despite church bigwigs doing all they could to prevent Greece from building its first crematorium, one opened in Évia in 2019. Orthodoxy demands that bodies be buried, even if bodies have to be exhumed after a few years and re-interred in ossuaries because of a lack of space.

EDUCATION

Greeks know the value of a good education, and many parents have gone into debt to make sure their children take all the courses they need at the night schools, the *frontistíria*, that complement the mandatory state education to make sure they pass the highly competitive university exams. One of the many tragedies of the recent economic crisis and massive unemployment rates has been the brain drain of the young and well educated – an estimated half a million have departed looking for work, in a national population of fewer than 11 million.

CULTURE

ART AND ARCHITECTURE
Archaic, Classical and Hellenistic (8th–5th centuries BC) Like many peoples, the ancient Greeks were inveterate storytellers, but with a twist: their focus was not so much on what happened but on how and why it happened. Fired by a 'divine discontent' and lust for fame, architects, sculptors, painters and potters constantly innovated as they strove for an ideal that became the 'classic' standard.

There was a lot happening in northern Greece during this period, but 99% of it has been lost in earthquakes, wars, and re-using old stones. Many of the archaeological sites here are of partly excavated long-gone cities (including Stageira, birthplace of Aristotle, and Abdera, birthplace of Democritus). All have certain things in common: an acropolis, often walled, with the city's oldest shrines, and below, an agora, usually translated as 'marketplace', although it was much more: both the heart of civic life and a sacred temenos, marked by boundary stones, forbidden to the criminal and the unclean. In the agora you'd find the council chamber (bouleuterion), the presidential committee chamber (prytaneion), fountain house, and shrines, temples, altars and statues dedicated to civic gods or heroes. Along the sides, colonnaded stoas housed shops and banks, offering shelter from the elements, where Greeks could indulge in their favourite pastime – talking. Elsewhere within the city walls there would often be baths, fountain houses and latrines, and a quarter devoted to athletics and the body beautiful, with a gymnasium ('place where one goes naked') attached to various schools for young men.

Urban planning became a science in the mid 5th century BC with the geometrician Hippodamos of Miletus, who laid out neat grids of streets to encourage *isonomia*, or social equality: Olynthos in Chalkidikí is the best-preserved example in Greece. In the early 4th century BC, Athens rebuilt its theatre in stone, and soon every city had one, scooped into the convenient side of the acropolis hill: there are well-preserved ones in Dodona, Philippi, Thássos and Lárissa. In Aigai (Vergína), the sacred city of the kings of Macedon, Philip II set a new bar in grandeur with one of the largest, and most lavishly innovative palaces in antiquity, which would become an inspiration for later Roman emperors and their architects – his palace in Pella was nearly as large.

Vitruvius wrote that the Greeks discovered perspective in the 5th century BC, and the story goes that one painter, Zeuxis, even deceived the birds, which tried to pluck grapes from his picture. The best Classical and Hellenistic-era paintings to survive are in a handful of Macedonian tombs in Vergína and Lefkadía – works that display techniques that would only be rediscovered in the Renaissance – and the painted funeral steles of Demetrias, in Vólos's Athanasákio Archaeological Museum. Floor mosaics, first seen in the 5th century BC at Olynthos, developed into masterly imitations of paintings in Ancient Pella and Ancient Dion, and in the newly discovered, enormous Kásta tomb in Amphipolis.

Alexander was the first to use images of himself as propaganda. His favourite sculptor, Lysippos, used less perfect but more lifelike proportions (with a notably smaller head) and statues meant to be seen in the round. By the time Alexander died (323BC), the problems of pose, anatomy, proportions and drapery had been resolved. Now artists could only exaggerate; a Baroque sensationalism and complexity, all windswept drapery, violence and passion, became prominent in works such as the *Winged Victory* (now in the Louvre in Paris) from the Sanctuary of the Great Gods in Samothráki, which was lavishly rebuilt by Alexander's successors and stands out as one of the most interesting Hellenistic-era sites in the region. Thanks to the custom of burying the dead with gold, there are superlatively worked wreaths, jewellery and more in Vergína and the Archaeology Museum in Thessaloníki, which also has the astonishing 4th-century BC bronze Dervéni Krater (page 94), obviously the work of Benvenuto Cellini in a former incarnation.

Roman The *pax romana* ended the rivalries between the Greeks but also pretty much dried up their inspiration, although a stream of workmanlike sculptors, architects and other talents found a ready employment in the Roman Empire, cranking out copies of earlier masterpieces. Nikopolis (Actium) is essentially Roman, as is Philippi and the visible remains of Thessaloníki, starring Galerius' wonderful Rotunda and arch, and the walls built by Theodosius, and the (copies of) the 2nd-century BC figures of *Las Incantadas* now in front of the Archaeology Museum in Thessaloníki. The 2nd-century AD *Tumulus of Mikrí Doxipára* in Thrace with its chariot and horse burial, is the only one in Greece. And in 2018, the largest Roman villa in Greece was discovered in Amýntaio, filled with art and lavishly covered with beautiful floor mosaics – though this is not yet open to the public.

Byzantine The founding of Constantinople in AD330 coincided with the official recognition of Christianity. The earliest churches were modelled on the three-aisle Roman basilica: see Thessaloníki's 5th-century AD Panagía Acheiropoiétos (page 88), one of the oldest churches still in use. Mosaics decorated the walls with glittering tiny tesserae; Thessaloníki again has some of the earliest surviving works, perhaps none as charming as the church of Ósios David, where the pagan delight in the material world still lingers; other beautiful examples are in that city's Museum of Byzantine Culture. In the 6th century AD, under Justinian, architects striving for a more Christian architecture placed what would become the classic dome over a cruciform supported by squinches or pendentives, although it took several tries to get it right (as with Basilica B, at Philippi).

CULTURE

Most early churches in Greece fell victim to the earthquakes and barbarian invasions that troubled the next few centuries. By the time the Greeks were ready to build again, the Greek cross plan had been mastered; the 8th-century Ag Sofía in Thessaloníki is an early example, and one of the few surviving churches built during the Iconoclasm (AD726–843), when figurative art was equated with idolatry and icons tossed on to the pyre.

The Middle Byzantine or Macedonian Age (named after the Macedonian emperors, AD844–1025) that followed the defeat of the Iconoclasts brought a cultural revival and a vast building programme of churches and monasteries. Painted or mosaic decoration was often in the 'hierarchical' formula that symbolically reproduced the universe; it was especially popular in *katholikóns* (monastery churches). Christ Pantocrator ('all-governing') reigns in the dome of heaven, surrounded by angels, while just below the Virgin and John the Baptist intercede for humanity. The Virgin and Child occupy the central apse, while surrounding vaults and upper registers show the Dodekaorton, the 'Twelve Feasts' of the church, while in the lower, terrestrial zone are saints, prophets and martyrs (whose gory deaths were a favourite subject in the narthex).

Byzantine art under the Comnene emperors (12th–14th centuries) marked a renewed interest in antique models: the stiff, hieratic figures are given more naturalistic proportions in graceful, rhythmic compositions. Occasionally the emperors sent imperial mosaicists to decorate their foundations – leaving exquisite examples in Thessaloníki. Other beautiful examples from the period are the Moní Molyvdosképastou near Kónitsa, Panagía Kosmosotíra in Féres, Mavriotissa in Kastoriá, and the Moní Kipínas, built into a sheer cliff in 1212, one of several remarkable monasteries in the Tzoumérka.

THE ART OF ICONS

After the Iconoclasm, the Second Council of Nicaea gathered to set the rules for images in the church, seeking an idiom that would portray spiritual truths. Orthodoxy teaches that Christ is the perfect God and the perfect man, and it was essential to avoid representing only his human side in art, so it was decided that icons should have only two dimensions to emphasise their spiritual aspect. Early Byzantine costumes, as described in early church texts, would be the dress code. Light should come from within the holy figures, not from an outside source. Human proportions could be distorted, employ unnatural colours (faces often have greenish highlights) and avoid any sense of time, so several events with the same personages are depicted on the same plane.

'The artistic perfection of an icon,' as Timothy Ware wrote in *The Orthodox Church* (1963), 'was not only a reflection of the celestial glory – it was a concrete example of matter restored to its original harmony and beauty serving as a vehicle of the spirit.' The result is that even in the depiction of the bloodiest martyrdoms there is a certain trance-like detachment; often an icon's most striking feature are the intense, staring eyes.

Icons never play on the heartstrings or ask the viewer to relive the agony of the Passion or coo over a baby Jesus; the Virgin (the Panagía, or 'all-holy'), cocooned in black, has none of the beauty and charm of a Renaissance Madonna. Unlike the ancient Greeks, who gave their divine figures the famous calm Classical gaze, a reflection of earthly mathematical perfection, the saints of Orthodoxy have eyes that mirror the soul.

1 | BACKGROUND INFORMATION

The Late Byzantine period began in 1261, with the recovery of Constantinople by the Paleologos emperors. The humanist and naturalistic influences of the next century combined to produce, apparently independently, the Byzantine equivalent of the trecento art of Siena, Italy, with a greater attention to colour, perspective, landscape, and architecture. Thessaloníki's Ag Apostóli and Ag Nikólaos Orphanós are two fine examples; others are in monasteries on Mount Athos and in Meteora's Great Meteoron.

1460–1912: Ottoman The Ottomans left northern Greece a wide array of mosques (those in Thrace are still in use), hammams and public buildings. Standouts include the unique pyramid-roofed Bayezid mosque in Didymóteicho (1420), which recently, like Notre Dame in Paris, caught fire as it was being restored. Tríkala's Osman Shah Mosque is the only one in Greece built by Istanbul's great builder Sinan. Thessaloníki and Ioánnina have fine examples from the period, but the most enchanting single structure is Kavála's Imaret, now a luxury hotel, paid for by Muhammad Ali of Egypt. One of the joys of northern Greece are its graceful arching stone bridges, most of them built by the expert masons from the remote Mastorochória, 'Master-builder villages', in Epirus who travelled far and wide.

The Greeks themselves are best represented by their defiant monasteries, often built in inaccessible places – on cliffs, in ravines and most spectacularly on the pinnacles of Meteora. Epirus, Véria and Kastoriá had thriving local schools of Byzantine art and architecture in the 16th and 17th centuries. Although most people lived simply, the better to avoid the attention of the taxman, merchants in the 18th and 19th centuries left impressive mansions in Kastoriá and Siátista, in the Zagorochória and on the Pelion. Silversmiths in Epirus were renowned across the Ottoman Empire for their intricate work (the superb Silversmithing Museum in Ioánnina celebrates the craft; page 267). It was also a thriving period for textiles, costumes, jewellery and ceramics. Local folklore museums are always worth a look; there are remarkable ones in Alexandroúpolis, Ioánnina, Thessaloníki and Kozáni.

ANTIPAROCHÍ   *Amber Charmei*

It used to be common to lament the surge of building that took place in the cities and larger towns of Greece in the middle of the 20th century. But a closer look reveals that the urgent demand for housing in Greece's urban centres was met with a fair degree of style, a Mediterranean sense of independence, and an innovative approach to financing. With much of the nation's land already divided into small lots and privately owned, Greece's modern apartment buildings were constructed largely through individual initiatives. A builder would approach a homeowner and propose an equal exchange – called *antiparochí* – in which the original homeowner would trade the small house and its land for some apartments in the building to be erected in its place. Other apartments would be sold in advance in order to pay for the materials and building costs. Generally receiving more than one apartment in the arrangement, the original homeowner even had a dowry to provide for his or her children, with the added advantage of having them close by. As to style and decór, Greece's booming cinema industry provided a blueprint for this new way of life; Finos Films' tremendous output often featured urban Greeks in stylish modern apartments, with all the latest mod-cons.

CULTURE

GREEK MODERN ART: FROM THE GENERATION OF THE '30S TO THE AVANT-GARDE
Amber Charmei

The Asia Minor Catastrophe (page 13) was a shock to the collective Greek psyche. In its wake, an urgent quest for 'Greekness' emerged, finding a host of expressions throughout the arts over the following decades. The naïf artist Theóphilos Hatzimichaíl (often referred to by his first name) was championed by the influential Paris publisher Tériade (Stratís Eleftheriádis, originally of Lésvos). Theóphilos' purity of approach and faithfulness to the folk idiom inspired many artists of this younger generation. More profoundly influential still was Fótis Kóntoglou. A Greek of Asia Minor and a master iconographer, he considered Byzantine art to be the authentic, unadulterated expression of Greek identity. Major artists of the generation apprenticed with Kóntoglou, including the modern figurative painter Yánnis Tsaróuchis and the surrealist Níkos Engonópoulos (who was also a fine poet). Even as they came later to embrace abstraction, the works of Yiánnis Móralis were informed by the same quest, as were the ethereal works of Giórgos Gounarópoulos and Spýros Vasilíou. Greece also has a fine history of modern printmaking, with artists such as Tássos (Alevízos), Vasílis Sperántzas, Yánnis Kefallinós, Váso Katráki and Giórgos Sikeliótis. As the 20th century progressed, Greeks artists both at home and in the Greek diaspora were pioneers of various avant-garde movements such as Arte Povera, Pop Art, Abstract Expressionism, and Kinetic Art, among them Theódoros Stámos, Chrýssa (Vardéa-Mavromicháli, best known internationally by her mononym), Jánnis Kounéllis, Aléxis Akrithákis, Tákis (Panayiótis Vassilákis), Ópy Zoúni and Yánnis Gaítis.

Modern times In the last years of the Ottoman Empire and into the early 20th century, public buildings of urban northern Greece were often constructed in a Neoclassical style, while the industrial elite favoured eclecticism (page 97) for their own grand mansions. In rural areas traditional and often strikingly beautiful vernacular styles prevailed, especially in mountain villages and on the islands. The need to provide housing for a million refugees in 1922–23 and the brutality of the Occupation and Civil War have all taken a toll since, followed by a rash of modern apartment blocks and hotels that mushroomed up in the 1960s as people moved into the cities and tourists began to flock to the coasts.

In the 1970s, the Greek tourism board embarked on an ambitious programme to preserve the country's rapidly depopulating but beautiful old villages. In some 600 'traditional settlements', they offered to restore buildings for free and make use of them for ten years, usually as guesthouses or restaurants, then return the buildings, no strings attached, to their owners. Now laws in many areas insist that new building conform to local styles: among the most beautiful villages in the north are the Zagorochória and the Pelion's mountain villages, but also Parthenónas (page 112), Palaiós Panteleímon (page 133), Áno Poróia (page 162), the two villages on Skópelos (pages 366 and 367), Theológos (page 200), Nymphaío (page 244), Syrráko and Kalarrýtes (page 287), and Ampelákia (page 311).

You'll find a sprinkling of modern art. The often-enigmatic Italian-Greek artist Giorgio de Chirico (1888–1978) was born and spent his youth in Vólos, and constantly referenced his native land in his work (although Vólos didn't get to keep any of his paintings, you can ride on a historic section of the old narrow-gauge

1 | BACKGROUND INFORMATION

railroad designed by his father, engineer Evaristo de Chirico; page 338). In Vólos you can discover the charm of Greece's top naïf painter, Theóphilos Hatzimichaíl (1866–1934; page 341).

To delve into the modern and contemporary Greek art scene, visit Lárissa's G I Katsígras Museum, and Thessaloníki's MOMus Museum of Contemporary Art and the Telloglio Foundation of Art; other collections are in the Avéroff Museum in Métsovo and Museum of Contemporary Art in Ellinikó.

MUSIC Greece has an extremely rich musical culture, with influences going back to ancient Greece (in the Dion archaeology museum you can actually see one of their instruments, the hydraulis – the world's first organ) along with Byzantine church music. Balkan and Anatolian influences are also strong; music, at least, knows no borders.

Each region has its own folk songs, which are still very popular at village weddings and local celebrations (*panegýri*), played on bagpipes (*tsamboúna*), clarinet (*klaríno*), hand drum (*toubeléki*), *violí* (violin), *kítara* (guitar), *laoúto* (a large mandolin, used for backing, traditionally picked with an eagle's quill) and the double-stringed hammer dulcimer (*sandoúri*). Besides the notes available in the West, Greek music also draws on a whole range of quarter tones and time signatures that come straight from ancient Greece (especially in Epirus, Macedonia and Thrace, where 7/8 and 11/16 is common), all of which would have made Beethoven jump out of the window.

Modern northern Greek music owes much to the influences brought over by the Asia Minor Greeks in 1923, who piled their longing and homesickness into *rebétiko*, the soulful Greek urban blues, while introducing the bouzouki, the long-necked metallic string instrument so closely associated with popular Greek music. Thessaloníki was an important centre, with performers such as Sofía Vémbo (1910–78), whose feisty spirit and patriotic songs during World War II inspired the troops and earned her the affectionate name 'Songstress of Victory'; Thessalonian bouzouki virtuoso Manólis Chiótis (1920–70); and bouzouki-player/songwriter Vassílis Tsitsánis (1915–84) from Tríkala, who composed two of the most famous wartime songs, 'Ómorfi Thessaloníki' (Beautiful Thessaloníki) and 'Synafiasméni Kyriakí' (Cloudy Sunday), which summed up the bitterness of the Occupation. Other renowned musicians from Thessaloníki include songwriter Dionýsis Savvópoulos (b1944), often called the Bob Dylan of Greece; singer Marinella (b1938), the 'Great Lady of Song'; and *baglamás* (a petite, long-necked bouzouki) player Níkos Papázoglou (1948–2011).

In more recent decades Thessaloníki has perhaps been better known as a cradle of Greek underground and experimental rock and metal, with such bands as Xýlina Spathiá, Trýpes, Firewind, the electro-pop Mikro, and pop band Onirama. Then there's Koza Mostra, who make use of traditional music and perform in kilts (most memorably in the 2013 Eurovision Song Contest, with their anti-austerity anthem 'Alcohol Is Free'). The city was also the birthplace, in 1978, of classical pianist and composer George-Emanuel Lazarídis, founder of the Music Village International Festival on Mount Pelion (w music-village.gr) at Ag Lavréntios.

Two of the most renowned contemporary Greek composers came from the north, though they didn't stay there long: Xánthi-born Mános Hadjidákis (1925–94), who with Míkis Theodorákis pioneered *énthechno*, or art song cycles (as well as composing orchestral music and the Oscar-winning song from the film *Never on Sunday*); and electronic music maestro Vangelis, who wrote the film scores for *Chariots of Fire* and *Blade Runner*, born in Vólos in 1943.

CULTURE

LITERATURE Northern Greece gets important mentions in the *Iliad* and the *Odyssey*, early poets Anacreon (Abdera) and Archilochos (Thássos) came with the Greek colonists to Thrace, Thucydides wrote *The Peloponnesian War* while in exile here, and Euripides wrote *The Bacchae* in Macedon. Surviving native talent from northern Greece was mostly philosophical, giving the world Aristotle of Stageira, Democritus and Protagoras of Abdera, and one of the very few known female philosophers of antiquity, Hipparchia of Maroneia. In Thessaloníki's Archaeology Museum you can see Europe's oldest surviving manuscript, the Dervéni papyrus from 340BC – the time of Philip II of Macedon – which managed to not get completely burned up in a funeral pyre. St Paul, of course, wrote several Epistles in *Koine* Greek to his northern Greek congregations, now in the New Testament. In the 9th century AD SS Cyril and Methodius of Thessaloníki, the Apostles of the Slavs and co-patron saints of Europe, invented a whole new alphabet: Cyrillic.

Throughout the turbulent centuries that followed, the church helped to preserve not only Greek culture, but also literature: the monastic libraries of Mount Athos and Meteora are treasure troves. Beginning in the 1500s, Thessaloníki's Jews wrote and printed a vast array of books in Ladino, many of which are preserved in the city's Jewish Museum.

Magnesía was an important centre of the Greek Enlightenment: revolutionary poet Rígas Feraíos of Velestinís (1757–98) was one of the first to write in *demotikí*, the people's language, rather than the formal, scholarly *katharévousa*; all Greeks learn his battle hymn 'Thoúrios' ('It's finer to live one hour as a free man than 40 years as a slave and prisoner.'). Alexándros Papadiamántis of Skiáthos (1851–1911; page 359), the 'Dostoyevsky of Greece', was a key figure in the development of Greek prose.

Finding translations of anything else from northern Greece is next to impossible, but there are some excellent books in English on the region. Travellers of eras past shared their impressions of northern Greece as it was in the Ottoman Empire in works including *Seyahatnâme*, Evliya Çelebi's fanciful 17th-century travelogue; *Travels in Northern Greece*, by the topographer and diplomat William Martin Leake (originally published in 1835); and sections of Herman Melville's *Journal of a Visit to Europe and the Levant, 1856–1857*. Four of the best modern works for a general read are Patrick Leigh Fermor's *Roumeli*; Nicholas Gage's *Eleni*; Mark Mazower's extremely informative *Salonica, City of Ghosts* and Kapka Kassabova's *Border* (for details, see page 390).

CINEMA Thessaloníki is the centre of the Greek film world, with its numerous festivals (page 82) and the country's only film museum. In fact, Greek (and Balkan) cinema got its start in northern Greece in 1905 with *The Weavers*, filmed by brothers Yanáki and Miltiádis Manákis in Avdélla (page 255), who would later document many of the great events of the early 20th century both in Greece and in North Macedonia. On an international level little happened afterwards until award-winning director Théo Angelópoulos (1935–2012) came to Flórina to make *Ulyssses' Gaze*, in 1995 – in which Harvey Keitel stars as a Greek film-maker in search of lost reels of film by the Manáki brothers. Angelópoulos, known for his slow, evocative, often ambiguous style, also set other films in Thessaloníki, including *Eternity and a Day* (1998) and *Trilogy: The Weeping Meadow* (2004).

Quite a few people know (and have come to) northern Greece thanks to a pair of hit films: *For Your Eyes Only* (1981), the James Bond vehicle partly filmed in Meteora (which was scarcely on tourism's radar before), and *Mamma Mia!* (2008), filmed on Skópelos, Skiáthos and the Pelion. More recently, the political thriller

1 | BACKGROUND INFORMATION

Beckett (2021) put Epirus on the cinephile map before taking viewers to the streets of Athens. Thessaloníki and the surrounding region has also risen in popularity as a filming location for international productions, including *Tin Soldier* (2023), *The Bricklayer* (2023) and *Dirty Angels* (2024).

Significant films have been set in the region without actually being shot there, including Costa-Gavras's superb *Z* (1969), filmed in Paris and Algeria during the dark days of the military dictatorship. The region's history and myths are the basis for dozens of dire Hollywood films, including at least two about Alexander the Great, although your author confesses to a certain fondness for the stop-motion action classic *Jason and the Argonauts* (1963).

2

Practical Information

With Andrew Bostock

WHEN TO VISIT

Any time is a good time to see some part of northern Greece. Winter offers a lively city scene in Thessaloníki, a chance to play in the snow in the many ski resorts, or see archaeological sites in lonely splendour. The carnival season that precedes Lent is both a great time to let Dionysian abandon take hold and to witness wild and mysterious folk traditions rooted in a pre-Christian past. Spring is a time for wildflowers, pleasant temperatures and for participating in Greek Easter, the biggest holiday on the calendar. May and June are generally calm and warm (beach hotels stay open from Easter or May into September or October) and great for hiking or touring by car. July and August are the most popular months for sun lovers and people with children – the busiest, hottest and priciest time. The coasts are cooled by winds, but inland it can be stifling. The weather generally stays fine into mid-October, with the bonus of brilliant colour in the mountain forests. The wet season begins at the end of October when it can rain 'tables and chairs', as the Greeks say.

HIGHLIGHTS

CHALKIDIKÍ (Page 102) The huge three-pronged peninsula is lined with stunning Blue Flag beaches and the most glamorous high-end resorts in northern Greece. The easternmost peninsula, the 1,000-year-old monastic republic of **Mount Athos**, couldn't be more different and fascinating to visit – as long as you're a man.

ÉDESSA (Page 152) The little city that puts paid to any idea that Greece is an arid country: channels of water stream through the centre of Édessa before plummeting over a cliff in a mighty waterfall.

IOÁNNINA (Page 260) The capital and silver-working centre of Epirus is one of the most atmospheric cities in Greece, with its beautiful lake, island, castle and other sites associated with the notorious Ali Pasha, immortalised by Byron.

KAVÁLA (Page 176) This attractive port has an evocative historic centre and sandy beaches, and lies only a short hop from **Ancient Philippi**, where St Paul introduced Christianity to Europe, and the island of **Thássos**, a pine-wooded, beach-fringed jewel and ancient powerhouse.

METEORA (Page 316) The medieval monasteries atop their towering pinnacles are one of the most striking sights Europe can offer and, since their star turn with James Bond, attract visitors and pilgrims by the coachload. Not to be missed, but go in the off season to avoid the queues.

2 | PRACTICAL INFORMATION

MOUNT OLYMPUS (Page 129) The highest mountain on the Balkan Peninsula and home of the gods is spectacular from all angles, either from the summit or from the ancient city of **Dion**. Even if you don't make the ascent, there are ravishing walks on all sides.

PELION PENINSULA (Page 342) 'Bucolic' seems to have been invented for this rugged peninsula dangling from Mount Pelion. Where centaurs once roamed, its stunning villages, rushing streams, traditional mansions converted into guesthouses, beaches, heritage railway and breathtaking natural beauty are a year-round attraction.

PRÉSPA LAKES (Page 248) Tucked way up on the borders of North Macedonia and Albania, these two ancient lakes ringed by towering mountains have a unique, otherworldly atmosphere.

SAMOTHRÁKI (Page 225) Thrace's lush, wooded mountain in the sea – site of the Sanctuary of the Great Gods of the Underworld – is full of lingering mystery.

THE SPORÁDES ISLANDS (Page 353) The three emerald islands off the coast of Magnesia are among the most beautiful in Greece: beachy fun-in-the-sun Skiáthos; serenely idyllic Skópelos; and Alónissos, with Greece's oldest national marine park and now also an underwater archaeological museum.

THESSALONÍKI (Page 59) Once the second city of the Byzantine Empire, modern Greece's second city is buzzing with life and youth, with great restaurants and clubs alongside World Heritage mosaic-filled Byzantine churches and a fantastic archaeology museum.

VERGÍNA (Page 142) Otherwise known as Aigai, the capital of ancient Macedon, this is where Philip II built his extraordinary palace, and where his son Alexander the Great buried him in a royal tumulus, filled with glittering gold works and unique frescoes from the 4th century BC.

THE VÍKOS GORGE AND ZAGOROCHÓRIA (Pages 278 and 271) The world's deepest canyon offers some of the most spectacular trekking in Greece. Just as spectacular are the surrounding Zagorochória: traditional mountain villages of stone, linked by cobbled mule paths and spectacular stone arched bridges.

SUGGESTED ITINERARIES

Below are suggestions on how best to organise a driving tour of the highlights.

A WEEKEND Thessaloníki is a year-round destination – in fact it's livelier out of season with its numerous festivals (page 82) and a large student population ensuring its famously sociable street life. Visit the city's World Heritage-listed Byzantine churches, the Galerius Palace complex and Rotonda, its fabulous archaeology and Byzantine museums and take in the vibrant restaurant and bar scene in and around the Ladádika district.

EIGHT DAYS IN ANCIENT MACEDON Spend the first two days in Thessaloníki, as described above.

Day 3	Head south to Ancient Dion in the morning and to Litóchoro on Mount Olympus in the afternoon for a brief stroll up the beautiful Enipéas Gorge.
Day 4	Take the scenic route via Trílofos to Vergína for a morning in Ancient Aigai; then to Aristotle's school, the tombs of Lefkádia, and Náoussa.
Day 5	Visit Alexander's birthplace, Ancient Pella, then take the fast Egnatía Ódos east to Philippi, overnighting in Kavála.
Day 6	Take in Amphipolis and Aristotle's birthplace, Stageira; then late in the afternoon, Ouranoúpolis.
Day 7	Enjoy a cruise around Mount Athos, and relax on the beach.
Day 8	Visit Olynthos and more of Chalkidikí, depending on your flight arrangements.

TWO WEEKS Follow the eight-day itinerary opposite for the first three days.

Days 4–5	From Litóchoro, drive through the Vale of Tempe to Vólos and the Pelion.
Day 6	Cross the plain of Thessaly in 2 hours to Kalambáka for Meteora.
Day 7	Have lunch in Métsovo, then travel on to Ioánnina.
Days 8–9	Explore the Zagorochória and Víkos Gorge.
Day 10	Visit Kónitsa with its beautiful bridge and Samarína, before winding up to Kastoriá.
Day 11	Spend the morning in Kastoriá, and the afternoon at the Préspa Lakes; overnight there or in Flórina.
Day 12	Take in Édessa and the hot springs of Loutrá Pózar.
Day 13	Head to Véria for the Byzantine churches and nearby Vergína for the royal tombs and new Polycentric Museum of Aígai.
Day 14	Make time for a visit to Ancient Pella before returning to Thessaloníki.

THREE WEEKS Follow the two-week itinerary above for days 1–14, then from Pella take the highway around Thessaloníki for Lake Kerkíni, and overnight in Sérres.

Day 15	Go hiking or kayaking in the Néstos Gorge; then overnight in Xánthi.
Day 16	Spend time in Xánthi and Ancient Abdera, then cross the Néstos Delta for Alexandroúpolis.
Day 17	Explore the Évros Delta, Féres and Souflí, or alternatively – if ferry schedules permit – make an overnight/day trip to Samothráki.
Day 18	Visit Ancient Philippi and Kavála.
Day 19	Amphipolis, Stageira and Ouranoúpolis.
Day 20	Take a morning cruise around Mount Athos, or see more of Chalkidikí or Thessaloníki.

TOURIST INFORMATION AND TOUR OPERATORS

With the economic crisis, many local tourist offices have closed, but to make up for it, quite a few local and regional governments, as well as private individuals, have maintained useful websites in English; some are even up to date. The **National Tourist Office**'s website (w visitgreece.gr) offers an excellent overview.

UK
Andante Travels ☏01722 786745; w andantetravels.co.uk. 10-day expert-led archaeology & art-based tours of Epirus & Macedonia; 9-day Albania & Macedonia tour along the Via Egnatía.

2 | PRACTICAL INFORMATION

Exodus Travels ✆ 020 3553 5013; w exodus.co.uk. Walking tour in the Zagóri & Meteora.
Explore ✆ 01252 391103; w explore.co.uk. 15-day tours of Ancient Macedonia.
Martin Randall Travel ✆ 020 8742 3355; w martinrandall.com. Cultural tours in northern Greece.
Naturetrek ✆ 01962 733051; w naturetrek.co.uk. Birdwatching tours on Lake Kerkíni.
Peter Sommer Travels ✆ 01600 888220; w petersommer.com. Superb cultural tours on the archaeology, food & wine of Macedonia.
Ramblers Walking Holidays ✆ 01707 817262; w ramblersholidays.co.uk. Self-guided treks of Mt Olympus, the Pelion, Vikos Gorge & more, & walking tours in the hills of Chalkidikí.
Responsible Travel ✆ 01273 823700; w responsibletravel.com. Botanical painting, yoga or pilates in the Pelion, self-driving, walking & trekking holidays in northern Greece, etc.
Sunvil ✆ 020 8568 4499; w sunvil.co.uk. International operator offering tailor-made trips, beach holidays in Chalkidikí, & packages to the Pelion & the Sporades.
TravelLocal w travellocal.com. A UK-based website where you can book direct with selected local travel companies, allowing you to communicate with a ground operator without having to go through a 3rd-party travel operator or agent. Your booking with the local company has full financial protection, but note that travel to the destination is not included. Member of ABTA, ASTA.

GREECE

Greek Adventure ✆ 24620 87999; w greekadventure.com. Offers a wide variety of local guided excursions, including river trekking to Olympus in the Orlias gorge, rafting in the Aliákmonas, hiking in Meteora, & Olympus treks.
Keytours ✆ 21092 33166; w keytours.gr. Runs a variety of tours across Greece including tours of Thessaloníki, & excursions to Meteora, Mount Athos & Ancient Pella.
Natural Greece ✆ 21303 46261; w natural-greece.gr. Birdwatching tours, wildlife conservation, bears of the North Pindus, & more.
Olympos Trek ✆ 24109 21244; w olympostrek.gr. Based in Lárissa, with a vast range of activities, including some for families, in eastern Thessaly & beyond.
Trails Beyond ✆ 21179 00603; w trailsbeyond.gr. Small group & bespoke tours, including kayaking on Lake Plastíra, horseriding, & the Víkos Gorge.
Trekking Hellas ✆ 21033 10323; w trekkinghellas.gr. Offers excursions with English-speaking guides throughout northern Greece, mountain walks, rafting & much more.
True Adventure m 69729 34764; w trueadventure.gr. Vólos-based company offering day- & week-long adventures, ski touring, kayaking & trekking in lesser-known parts of northern Greece.
Walking Holidays m 69485 08120; w walkingholidays.gr. Vólos-based operator, offering small-group guided treks in the Pelion, Meteora, Zagóri, Pindus & Olympus.

RED TAPE

Citizens of EU member states and holders of passports from some 50 nations do not need a **visa** for stays of up to 90 days in a period of 180 days. These include Australia, Canada, Israel, Japan, Malaysia, Mexico, New Zealand, Singapore, South Korea, Switzerland, the UK and the USA. Check before travelling at w mfa.gr/en/services/visas-for-foreigners-traveling-to-greece/countries-requiring-or-not-requiring-a-visa. All EU members can stay in Greece for up to three months, and longer under certain conditions; see w migration.gov.gr/en/polites-ee-meli-oikogeneias for more details. If you want to stay longer, it is best to contact a Greek embassy (see opposite) before your trip.

Note that, from the last quarter of 2026, citizens of visa-exempt countries, including the UK, USA, Canada and Australia, will be required to pay a fee and obtain an ETIAS travel authorisation (w travel-europe.europa.eu/etias_en) in order to enter Greece. A new Entry-Exit System (EES; w travel-europe.europa.eu/ees_en) is also set to be introduced on 12 October 2025, to replace the requirement for stamping passports.

This will be rolled out gradually at border crossings over the following six months, with full implementation across the EU by 10 April 2026. Check before you travel.

Be aware that your passport may not be checked if arriving from another EU country, but you need to have it stamped to avoid problems leaving the country.

EMBASSIES For many countries the closest consulates are in Thessaloníki, while all embassies are in Athens. Check w embassypages.com/greece for a constantly updated list, including Greek consulates and embassies abroad.

GETTING THERE AND AWAY

BY AIR International airports handy for northern Greece include Athens, Thessaloníki, Vólos, Skiáthos, Kavála, Ioánnina and Préveza.

Flights to Athens Direct year-round flights to Athens International Airport (Elefthérios Venizélos; \ 21035 30000; w aia.gr) leave from London and, less frequently, Manchester (3½–4hrs). EasyJet (w easyjet.com) is often cheapest. Other airlines that currently serve these routes are British Airways (w britishairways.com), Aegean (w en.aegeanair.com) and Olympic Air (w olympicair.com) – compare dates and prices with w skyscanner.net.

Athens is also accessible by air from most of the rest of the world (again, check w skyscanner.net).

Getting to and from Athens airport For details on getting to central Athens, see page 375.

By car Athens airport is 30km southeast of the city and has the usual range of car hire companies. From the airport, getting to northern Greece is simple: follow the toll road towards Athens, and turn off right on to the National Road (E75) towards Vólos (3½hrs), Thessaloníki (5hrs) or Ioánnina (4½hrs).

By train The suburban (Proastiakós) trains run once an hour between 06.00 and 22.00 from the airport to Lárissis station in Athens. For suburban and mainline train information, and to purchase tickets online, visit w hellenictrain.gr/en/ticket-purchase; better still, download the app – it's easier to use. Alternatively, call \ 14511 for information, although be aware that there is a charge of about €1/min from a mobile or €0.65 from a landline, and they may be slow. The Intercity train to Thessaloníki takes 5 hours, with fares from €43 one way.

By bus The X93 bus (\ 11185; w oasa.gr/en/visit-athens; €6; buy tickets from the kiosk) from just outside the airport building runs to KTEL Stathmós Kifissoú, the Athens bus terminal, in about 1 hour. Buses are frequent and run through the night (although late at night you're better off waiting at the airport rather than in the bus terminal).

There are frequent buses from Athens to all the main cities in northern Greece, all run under the auspices of KTEL, the national bus company, but locally managed by each municipal region. The main ticket hall has different ticket desks organised by destination. Once you have your ticket, be sure to ask for the number of the bay from which your bus will depart.

By taxi Airport taxis to the city centre cost, at the time of writing, a flat rate of €40 from 05.00 until midnight, and €55 from midnight until 05.00.

2 | PRACTICAL INFORMATION

Flights to Thessaloníki Direct flights from the UK and Ireland to Thessaloníki tend to run only in the summer and shoulder season, but leave from most major regional airports. The website w skyscanner.net will bring up your options, or see EasyJet (w easyjet.com), British Airways (w britishairways.com), Aegean (w en.aegeanair.com), Jet2 (w jet2.com), Olympic (w olympicair.com), Ryanair (w ryanair.com) and Tui (w tui.co.uk).

Flights to smaller airports There are summer flights from various UK airports to Kavála, Préveza, Skiáthos and less often to Vólos with EasyJet, Olympic and Tui.

BY TRAIN From the UK, take the **Eurostar** (w eurostar.com) across the Channel and connect with a fast train; if you're lucky, a journey from London St Pancras to Ancona or Venice can take as little as 14 hours but average at 21 hours, changing in Paris (Gare du Nord to Gare de Lyon). See w seat61.com for options – although it's almost impossible to find a train cheaper than a flight, especially after adding on the ferry crossings to Greece (see below). Or you can go overland via Paris (change to the Gare de l'Est) to Sofia, calling at Munich and then continue from Sofia to Thessaloníki by bus.

BY CAR OR MOTORCYCLE If you live in the UK and are planning to be in Greece for any length of time, it may make sense to bring your car or motorcycle. Before leaving, consult w aade.gr/en/greeks-abroad-non-residents (select 'private passenger vehicles' then 'temporary importation of private vehicles') for complete details, including the length of time you may keep the car in Greece; once there, hold on to your ferry tickets for proof of date of entry. Although this is rarely checked, if you are caught out (for instance if you have an accident or are caught speeding) your car will be immediately impounded and the fine to release it can be more than the car is worth.

Do note: UK drivers with photocard driving licences can use them in Greece, but those with paper licences will need an International Driving Permit (see w gov.uk/foreign-travel-advice/greece/safety-and-security).

The quickest route is by way of Calais, through France and Switzerland, then on to Italy, where you catch a ferry (see below), though this entails quite heavy road tolls in France and Italy (Calais to Ancona €39), and also the Swiss road tax (CHF40). If you sail from Venice – a magical place to sail out of or into as the ferry seems to go through the old city – then the drive can be done in 13 hours. The sea crossing takes just over a day, meaning you could do the whole trip over a long two days (sleeping on the ferry to Igoumenítsa).

If you stop overnight on the way to or from Italy at a campsite or budget hotel, and travel deck class on the ferry, it will cost around €500 per couple one way. If you are going to be in Greece for a month or more this can compare favourably with the cost of a flight and car hire (and you can carry a lot more stuff). If your visit is going to be an extended one, to avoid difficulties when you leave, you can also ask to have your car stamped in your passport on arrival. If you leave Greece without your car, you must have it withdrawn from circulation by a customs authority.

BY SEA Ferries to Greece from Italy nearly always run overnight. The main port for northern Greece is Igoumenítsa, which can be reached from Venice (25–29hrs; from €440 return with a car), Ancona (16hrs; from €430 return), Bari (10hrs; from €230 return) and Brindisi (7½–10hrs; from €216 return). Do book in advance (which you can do via w ferryhopper.com, w directferries.co.uk, w ferries.gr or w aferry.

HEALTH

TRAVELLING OVER THE BORDERS

Northern Greece has borders with four countries, which you might be tempted to visit. Note that some countries require a passport to be valid for at least three or even six months beyond your planned stay.

ALBANIA EU, UK, Australian and US citizens can enter without a visa for up to 90 days, as can holders of multiple-entry Schengen visas or multiple-entry UK or US visas. For detailed up-to-date information, and to obtain a visa if necessary, see w e-visa.al/apply.

BULGARIA EU nationals need only a valid passport or national ID card for entry. Non-EU nationals must present a return ticket and show sufficient funds for their stay (€100/day). For more information, see w mfa.bg/en/services-travel/consular-services/travel-bulgaria/visa-bulgaria.

REPUBLIC OF NORTH MACEDONIA At the time of writing, all EU, Schengen, UK, Canadian and US citizens can enter without a visa; for details and length of stays see w mfa.gov.mk/en/page/432/visa-requirements-for-entering-the-republic-of-north-macedonia.

TÜRKIYE At the time of writing, many visa requirements have been lifted. To see if you need a visa, visit w evisa.gov.tr, where you can also get a visa in advance if needed. You'll need a passport with at least six months' validity. If you do not need a visa, make sure to still get an entry stamp on arrival, and a departure stamp when you leave, so as to avoid possible fines or difficulties in the future.

---

co.uk). There are various forms of accommodation on board: the cheapest, 'deck' class, does not mean you are confined outside. You are allowed in the communal areas, and in the low season will often find a spot to stretch out and sleep. In high season you may have to sleep out on the deck, although there are usually plenty of sheltered areas (a sleeping mat or pop-up tent is an advantage, though some ferry companies discourage them, especially while the boat may still be boarding).

HEALTH *with Dr Daniel Campion*

The health issues you will face here are not much different to those of most other European countries. There are no vaccinations needed for entry, although it's always wise to be up to date with tetanus, which comes combined with diphtheria and polio immunisations. EU, EEA and UK citizens are entitled to a certain level of free medical care (apply for an EHIC or GHIC card before travelling), although comprehensive health insurance is always advisable. Also be aware that 'free' health care in Greece doesn't cover all you might expect: there are charges, generally small, for prescriptions, tests and, increasingly, check-ups. If you should need a stay in hospital, and if you don't have a Greek family to supply food and comfort, do note that nursing care tends to be minimal.

Prescription medicines are widely available, but do bring along enough for your trip, together with your prescription. Pharmacists are well trained and able to prescribe an extensive amount of medication, although in some touristy areas, they might hesitate, fearful of being sued, and refer you to a doctor. In most towns and cities there is a rotation schedule so that there is a pharmacy on duty after hours and on weekends. Visit w vrisko.gr/en/pharmacy-duties and enter your location to find the closest.

Most areas are served by a health centre, which is generally staffed around the clock and open for drop-in enquiries in the morning from 08.00. It's first come, first served. Expect to pay all medical expenses up front (unless you have an EHIC or GHIC card); papers will be supplied for you to be reimbursed by your insurance provider. If you think you have been ripped off, hang on to receipts.

If you do not have a medical emergency, and don't want to bother with bureaucracy or spend time in a waiting room at a health centre or hospital, you can find an appointment with a general practitioner or any type of specialist, including dentists, at w doctoranytime.gr/en. Select your location and the type of doctor you're looking for and a list of options will appear, including contact information and available appointments, as well as a price list (you may need to create a free account and log in to see the price list, or just call the office). It depends upon the specialisation and the service, but visits very often cost between €30 and €50.

TRAVEL CLINICS AND HEALTH INFORMATION A list of current travel clinic websites worldwide is available on w istm.org. For other journey preparation information, consult w travelhealthpro.org.uk (UK) or w wwwnc.cdc.gov/travel (USA). All advice found online should be used in conjunction with expert advice received prior to or during travel.

MEDICAL PROBLEMS
Sun and heat This is a very serious matter; there were several fatalities due to exposure to heat and sun in the summer of 2024, usually cases of hikers and walkers getting lost, dehydrated and disoriented. Don't underestimate the Greek sun. Even ignoring the possibility of skin cancer, **sunburn** can spoil any holiday and in serious cases can put you out of action for days. Wear a high-SPF suncream and hat in the sun. Heatstroke is also a risk, so stay hydrated – always carry a bottle of water. Tap water is safe to drink, but if you have a delicate stomach, you may want to stick to bottled water.

BITES AND STINGS Between May and October, **mosquitoes** can be a major irritant, especially around the wetlands. Some people react badly to mosquito bites, but they are usually harmless. There are, however, some more serious mosquito-borne diseases that are becoming more prevalent. These include malaria and dengue fever, although at the time of writing they have been limited to southern Greece. In 2018 there was an unprecedented number of cases of West Nile virus. Although severe symptoms were rare, there were more cases of encephalitis, meningitis, and acute paralysis than would usually be expected. Wild birds act as the reservoirs for the virus and the mosquitoes pick up the virus from feeding on their blood. The virus can infect humans and horses. The *Culex* mosquitoes that carry the virus are more prevalent from dusk till dawn. The West Nile virus season tends to run from mid-June to November.

Mosquitoes are most prevalent at dusk and can be effectively combated by sleeping under permethrin-impregnated bed nets or window screens, and plug-in repellents or battery-operated repellents (the liquid ones work best and can be easily bought in supermarkets). If you are camping, you have to go with the smelly option; cheap, burnable coils work reasonably well, and a good spray-on repellent is worthwhile (look for a high DEET content: 50–55% is optimum). At the first sign of dusk, you can also thwart the little vampires by covering up in long-sleeved shirts and trousers. The *Aedes* mosquitoes that carry dengue fever are more prevalent during daylight hours so bite avoidance is paramount 24 hours a day.

Snakes are much maligned by Greeks, but rarely do anyone harm and tend to flee at any sign of human presence; in rural areas be cautious of holes and crevices in stone walls or wood piles. Some snakes may be venomous, such as the horned viper (the horn is more of a little bump on its head, and it often has a zigzag pattern running down its back). If they feel cornered, they will make a hissing sound like radio static before attacking. Their bite is painful, but not lethal, and there is antivenom available. If you do get bitten, try to limit movement of the affected limb, and seek immediate medical attention.

Scorpions and large brown **centipedes** with pincers are also known to give painful stings or bites. Seek treatment at the nearest medical centre or pharmacy. In the water look out for **sea urchins**, especially on shallow rocks. If a spine becomes embedded, you'll need to remove it, and if you try to force them out, the spines may break and embed themselves even deeper. Soak the affected area in hot water no hotter than 45°C. Carefully remove any superficially embedded spines with tweezers in the direction they went in. Do not attempt to remove spines embedded deeply in the skin; let medical professionals handle those. **Jellyfish** (especially the oval transparent ones, the *tsoúchtres*) stings are painful and will eventually just go away; hydrocortisone cream and antihistamines can ameliorate the discomfort. Less common but more dangerous, the *drákena*, or **weever fish**, with a poisonous spine, hides in the sand waiting for its lunch. If you step or sit on one (rare, but it happens), you'll feel a mix of excruciating pain and numbness; it's possible the spine may be embedded, in which case you will need to seek medical attention. Whether that's the case or not, you may want to seek medical advice for any swelling – a pharmacist is a good source of information in this or any similar situation, and can recommend if you also need to see a doctor.

Ticks Ticks are unfortunately a menace, especially if you mean to spend a lot of time in the mountains between April and November, posing a risk of Lyme disease and tick-borne encephalitis (TBE). The latter is potentially fatal, so it is important to do everything to avoid tick bites. Cases of TBE have been reported around the

TICK REMOVAL

Ticks should ideally be removed intact, and as soon as possible, to reduce the chance of infection. You can use special tick tweezers, which can be bought in good travel shops; or failing this, with your fingernails, grasp the tick as close to your body as possible, and pull it away steadily and firmly at right angles to your skin without jerking or twisting. Applying irritants (eg: Olbas oil) or lit cigarettes is to be discouraged as a means of removal since they can cause the ticks to regurgitate and therefore increase the risk of disease. Once the tick is removed, if possible douse the wound with alcohol (any spirit will do), soap and water, or iodine. If you are travelling with small children, remember to check their heads, and particularly behind the ears, for ticks. Spreading redness around the bite and/or fever and/or aching joints after a tick bite imply that you have an infection that requires antibiotic treatment. In this case seek medical advice.

city of Thessaloníki. There is a TBE vaccine that comprises two doses given at least two weeks apart, but preferably longer, with a third dose given 5–12 months later if there is continued risk. To reduce the risk of tick bites, avoid walking in tall grass, tuck trousers in socks, wear a repellent containing 20–30% DEET or 20% Picaridin, and wear light-coloured clothes (the lighter the better to spot any ticks); always inspect yourself after an excursion. Pay particular attention to the hairline, behind the ears, the groin and the armpits, where ticks love to hide.

Plants Various plants have sap or oil that can cause irritation when they come into contact with the skin. And berries can be poisonous – if you're not absolutely sure what it is, don't taste it.

Rabies Bats in Greece may carry a rabies-like virus which can be passed to humans. If you have any encounter with a bat and may therefore have been in contact with bat saliva, then seek medical help promptly. Prompt rabies vaccination after exposure will prevent the disease from developing.

TOILETS You might encounter the occasional 'Turkish' toilet in Greece, which consists of two foot-stands and a hole in the ground, but they are increasingly rare. What hasn't changed is the inability of the Greek sewer system to cope with toilet paper, or anything else more substantial. These all go into the bin provided next to the toilet, unless you want the embarrassment of causing a flood.

SAFETY

When travelling in Greece take the same precautions you would at home. Do, however, take extra care on public transport, especially around Athens, where gangs of pickpockets have been reported. Any crime should be reported to the tourist police (❧ 1571), who will have an English speaker on their staff. They can also be useful in disputes with hotel owners and taxi drivers. If you get into trouble, contact Advocate Abroad (w advocateabroad.com/greece/lawyers), which has a network of English-speaking lawyers.

Forest fires are, unfortunately, a normal part of the Greek summer; always dispose of cigarettes and broken glass carefully in the countryside. Minor earthquakes are not uncommon; larger ones are much less common and modern Greek buildings are built to withstand them. If you do find yourself in a big one, then go outside into an open area if you can do so quickly and safely; if not, get under the sturdiest piece of furniture available.

Hikers and mountaineers should always exercise caution – lives are lost each year in Greece due to exposure (in any season), overheating and dehydration, or sudden snows. Always venture out in pairs or in a group rather than solo, and inform others – such as the staff at the mountain shelters – of your route and your expected time of return. Apart from exposure to cold and snow, or dehydration if you get lost, the biggest danger you'll face in the mountains is zealous **sheepdogs**, trained to ward off bears and wolves. Avoid livestock pens and herds of animals.

WOMEN TRAVELLERS

Women travellers, especially on their own, might find some male attention unwelcome. Situational awareness is key. In areas where one sees few women, it's especially wise to exercise caution.

WHAT TO TAKE

TRAVELLING WITH A DISABILITY

Although hotels, resorts, major museums, churches and restaurants increasingly have facilities for wheelchair users, getting around northern Greece can prove a challenge for those with limited mobility. Access on public transport – trains, buses, small planes and ferries – is limited, and the steepness of the natural terrain means many villages have steps for streets or cobblestoned pavements. That said, six of the country's most popular destinations, including Thessaloníki and Chalkidikí, have been the focus of improvements covered by the **National Accessibility Authority** (w accessible-eu-centre.ec.europa.eu/national-accessibility-authority-greece_en). **Get Your Guide** (w getyourguide.com) offers listings for wheelchair-accessible tours to various sights in northern Greece.

To arrange assistance on Greek trains, ring in advance (21301 21121; 08.30–20.30 daily) or fill in the form at w hellenictrain.gr/en/form/forma-metaforas-amea. For more information about the accessibility of specific stations, you can visit w hellenictrain.gr/en/transport-persons-special-needs-reduced-mobility.

A number of beaches offer solar-powered SEATRACs to aid wheelchair users; **Tobea** (w tobea.gr; tobealtd), the company that makes them in Greece, has a map of their locations on their website.

The UK's **gov.uk** website (w gov.uk/government/publications/disabled-travellers) provides general advice and practical information for travellers with disabilities preparing for overseas travel. A comprehensive list of rights of travellers with disabilities can be found at the EU site w europa.eu/youreurope/citizens/travel/transport-disability/reduced-mobility/index_en.htm. More useful information is available at w disabledtravelers.com.

LGBTQIA+ TRAVELLERS

Greece legalised same-sex marriage in February 2024 – the first Christian Orthodox country to do so. Thessaloníki and Athens are increasingly openly LBGTQIA+ friendly, with smaller cities catching up slowly – public displays of affection could possibly still bring you some unwelcome attention in more rural or conservative areas.

TRAVELLING WITH CHILDREN

Greeks love children, and children usually love Greece. Depending on their age, they travel for free or receive discounts on ships and buses. However, don't count on pharmacies stocking your brand of infant formula – it's safest to bring your own supply. Take extra precautions against the strong sun.

Greek children usually have an afternoon nap (as do their parents) during the hottest part of the day, so it's quite normal for them to eat late and stay out after midnight in summer. Although Greek superstitions are dying out, one involving children still holds strong: if you compliment a child's beauty or intelligence, follow it with a ritual dry spit sound 'phtew, phtew, phtew' in the direction of the admired one. The 'spitting' wards off evil spirits. If you neglect this, don't be surprised if the mother does the 'phtew-ing' for you, and adds the sign of the cross and a small prayer to the Virgin to boot.

WHAT TO TAKE

CLOTHING AND FOOTWEAR Loose, cool clothes and a sun hat are the rule in summer; lightweight clothing is more comfortable and safer than bare skin under the sun. However, even in August, evenings can be chilly, and a pair of long trousers may come in handy for walks among prickly things or to protect against mosquitoes. Pack some sturdy, comfortable shoes if you mean to do any walking – though trainers are usually good enough. Plastic swimming shoes are handy for rocky beaches and as a barrier to spiny sea urchins – you can easily buy them near any beach if you don't want to carry them around with you.

Note that modest dress is required in churches and monasteries. For both sexes this means shirts with sleeves and no shorts, and for women, at monasteries especially, skirts or dresses that cover the knee rather than trousers. A sarong makes a handy cover-up. Monasteries often have skirts and sarongs available to wear over your clothing.

ELECTRICITY The electric current is 220 volts, 50Hz; plugs are continental two-pin or three-pin for big items such as washing machines. UK travellers will need an adaptor; North Americans will need a transformer in addition to an adaptor. It's a good idea to buy an adaptor in the airport, or before you travel, as they can be hard to find in Greece.

OTHER ITEMS Bring along enough prescription drugs for your trip, along with the prescription itself, and suncream, which may be cheaper at home. Soap, washing powder, a clothes line, a Swiss army knife for picnics and a towel are essential budget traveller's gear. Torches come in handy for moonless nights, caves and examining frescoes in churches. Binoculars are also useful for examining frescoes and mosaics in high church domes, and they're essential for birding – the many protected wetlands make northern Greece a paradise for local and migrating birds.

Remember that Greeks are inveterate night people: bring earplugs if you're not.

MONEY AND BUDGETING

MONEY Greece uses the euro (pronounced *evró*; euro cents in Greek are *leptá*) and Greeks often use cash for transactions. Major hotels, petrol stations, luxury shops and resort restaurants take credit cards (look for the little signs), and guesthouses, shops, tavernas and even kiosks also increasingly have card machines. Check with your card issuer, whether a debit card or a credit card, before leaving in order to see if there is a surcharge for transactions while in Greece. If you plan to spend time in a remote area, bring cash.

The word for bank is *trápeza*, derived from the word *trapézi*, or table, used back in the days of moneychangers; general hours are weekdays from 08.30 to 14.00. Most small towns and villages of a thousand or so people will have at least one bank, or an ATM. These tend to accept Visa and Mastercard most readily, but in summer resort areas with few machines they can run out of cash. Always try to choose ATMs by banks rather than in airports or tourist areas, which usually have worse exchange

TYPICAL PRICES

0.5 litre of beer	€3.50	postcard	€0.50
bottle of water (0.5 litre)	€0.50	street snack (*koulouri*)	€0.70
chocolate bar	€1.20	T-shirt	€12
loaf of bread	€0.90	32 GB memory card	€11
petrol (per litre)	€1.85		

rates; and if asked to view your transaction in your own currency, always refuse in order to avoid sneaky bad exchange rates. Your bank at home will probably charge as well, either a set rate or a percentage of what you withdraw. All transactions with foreign credit cards now carry an extra €2–3 'direct access fee' in Greece to help fill the banks' empty coffers, so it's best to take out a good sum every few days.

BUDGETING Greece is no longer a cheap country in which to travel: petrol prices have soared, and cheap hotels now cost about the same as in the rest of Europe (at least in summer), although eating out remains pretty affordable in the tavernas. For a couple staying in a reasonable hotel, eating one meal out a day at a taverna, having a few drinks and using a hire car daily, costs will come to around €80–100 per person.

GETTING AROUND

BY AIR There are domestic flights from Athens to Thessaloníki, Alexandroúpolis, Ioánnina, Kastoriá, Kavála, Kozáni, Préveza (summer only) and Skiáthos and other Greek airports. Olympic (w olympicair.com) and Aegean (w aegeanair.com) are the main carriers, but also see Sky Express (w skyexpress.gr).

BY TRAIN Trains are the cheapest way to get around northern Greece, although routes are increasingly limited. (Many places that used to have train service now have a train to the nearest destination where a train still runs, then a bus operated by the train company to continue, which has no discernible advantage over the bus.) Moreover, following a railway disaster in 2023, the train has fallen out of favour with many Greeks.

During the austerity crisis Greece sold off its floundering railway (OSE) to Italy's Ferrovie dello Stato. Information on routes and schedules is available at w hellenictrain.gr/en, where you can also purchase e-tickets up to 10 minutes before departure. The free app 'HT New Platform' is much easier to use and enables the ticket to be available on your phone. There's also a call line 14511, with a charge of €0.65/min from a landline and €0.98 from a mobile phone, if you don't have digital access.

A fast train links Athens to Thessaloníki via Lárissa (page 66), now a 5-hour journey, with four departures daily. Rail buffs won't want to miss the very-narrow-gauge Little Pelion Train, which now runs a heritage route (page 350).

BY BUS Greek public bus services (KTEL) are run by the provinces, with different ticket booths in Thessaloníki's central Macedonia bus station, which can be confusing; destinations are grouped by region, each with its own ticket counter. Each regional KTEL also has its own website, some more useful than others. Tickets can often be purchased online, but note that a paper ticket still must be picked up at the ticket counter, at least 15 minutes before departure. Once aboard, however, buses are fast and efficient, at least on main routes, and the buses themselves are modern, comfortable and air conditioned (although the toilet is seldom open). On intercity routes, you buy a ticket in advance and seating is assigned; in July and August and during the holidays, reserve early to get a seat, especially on buses to and from Athens as well as on popular tourist routes, such as from Thessaloníki to Kalambáka (Meteora) and to destinations in Chalkidikí.

In Thessaloníki, note that there are two separate KTEL stations. Buses to Chalkidikí leave only from the KTEL Chalkidikí, a separate dedicated depot east

PRACTICAL INFORMATION

> **AMMON EXPRESS**
>
> If you're based in Thessaloníki, Ammon Express (23105 00225; w ammonexpress.gr) with its online bookings and four pick-up spots in the city offers an easy way to reach northern Greece's star attractions without a car, providing transport by coach, as well as express tickets, with an English-speaking assistant on board.
>
> Destinations include Pella and Vergína; Meteora, Édessa and the Pozar Spa; Dion and Mount Olympus; Lake Kerkíni; Chalkidikí; Mount Athos with a cruise; Véria and Náoussa with wine tastings, with many trips starting at around €50.

of the city (in the direction of the airport; a taxi from the centre costs around €10). Departures for all other destinations are from the KTEL Macedonia, west of the city (past the train station; a taxi from the centre costs around €9). Both depots can be reached by local bus service. Buses for Athens and some other destinations may also leave from the train station before stopping at the KTEL Macedonia on their way out of town.

On rural routes, buy tickets from a conductor or the driver on the bus. If there are only a couple of buses a day, they tend to be first thing and in the early afternoon, designed for local students and shoppers.

BY CAR OR MOTORBIKE Unless you want to confine yourself to the major towns or a beach, the easiest way to get around is by hiring a car. In peak season you can get a small car for around €30 a day. Navigating is generally easy with most apps, but every now and then you may need to get creative with the spelling of your destination on account of the variety of possible transliterations from Greek. Also, depending on the app, there may be no distinction as to whether a road is paved or a dirt road – relevant in some remote areas. The unexpected can happen in Greece, so do get the most comprehensive insurance cover you can. A photo licence from any EU country is valid, as is one from the UK (though check if your car-hire company has additional requirements); other nationals should have an International Driving Permit. Allow enough time to obtain one from your local automobile association before leaving.

Traffic regulations and signalling comply with standard practice on the European Continent (ie: driving on the right). As a rule, local speed limits are 50km/h in built-up areas, 70km/h on rural roads and 100km/h or 120km/h on motorways, but there are plenty of (often inexplicable) exceptions. Speed cameras are beginning to appear, but police traps with radar guns are more common. If people driving towards you flash their headlights, they are warning that you are about to pass one of these.

There are tolls at intervals along the national highway E75 (adding up to €31.25 for 502km) and along the Egnatía Ódos, although these are negligible. Unleaded 95 is the basic fuel, and currently hovers around €1.85 per litre, but the price changes often. In the majority of petrol stations there are pump attendants. Some might close on Sundays or during the night.

Although driving in and around Athens and Thessaloníki isn't much fun, the rest of Greece is fairly easy and pleasant. There are few cars on most roads, but always be prepared for surprises: low visibility in the mountains, flocks of goats and sheep just around the bend, abruptly ending asphalt and world-class pot-holes. Roads passing through villages are often single lane, and dotted with sleeping dogs. Toot your horn at blind corners and listen out for those coming the other way. Greek drivers tend to believe the rules of the road don't apply to them, so are liable to tailgate even on mountain roads (pull over when it's safe and let them get on with it), or use the hard shoulder as a personal fast lane. Occasionally, you might have to drive on dirt roads, often to reach an archaeological site. Even on good ones, drive slowly, to avoid throwing up stones and pebbles. If you are in a hire car, you are often not covered for damage to its underside, or for driving off-road (even if you have hired a 4x4).

In case of an accident, remain calm and wait for the police to arrive; they are normally efficient, polite and fair. For roadside assistance, get coverage from the rental car company, or before leaving home look into European or international coverage from your regular roadside assistance provider.

In resort areas you can hire scooters, motorbikes or even quad bikes. For any but the smallest of these you should have a specific licence, and if you are not experienced, you should probably steer clear.

BY TAXI Taxis are cheaper than in most other European countries and can be a useful alternative to public transport. In towns they run on the meter (on tariff 1, changing to tariff 2 if they drive out of town). In rural areas there are often set prices for various journeys, but it's always best to agree on the charge before starting. A rough estimate of cost would be €1 per kilometre, with a minimum fare of €4.

BY BIKE Despite (or perhaps because of) its mountains, many people enjoy cycling in northern Greece, but it's best to avoid July and August because of the heat. Many of the resorts hire out street and mountain bikes, and bike rental shops are easy to find in most cities and larger towns. Bringing your own bike on your flight is often possible as well; check with the airline.

MAPS Greek maps get better all the time, although no map company could keep up with the rate of change, especially on hiking maps. Anavasi (w anavasi.gr) produces excellent, regularly updated 1:125,000 touring maps of Epirus and Thessaly, and a 1:250,000 GPS-compatible map of all Greek regions of Macedonia. They also do 1:50,000 and 1:25,000 paper and geo-referenced maps that are particularly useful to hikers and cover much of northern Greece; their useful app – Anavasi mapp – has hiking maps for the mountains and islands of Greece and works offline. Geopsis (w geopsis.com) specialises in eastern Macedonia and Thrace, with excellent additional information. Terrain Maps (w terrainmaps.gr) produces a series of useful regional 1:200,000 maps and a specialist one of Mount Athos.

Maps are also sold at many bookshops in major Greek cities but can be hard to find elsewhere. Stanfords (w stanfords.co.uk), with shops in London, Bristol and Manchester, stocks most of the maps listed and can also process special orders; it also has an excellent online store.

ACCOMMODATION

Northern Greece has a vast range of accommodation, from five-star glamorous resorts to traditional inns and campsites.

HOTELS Nearly all Greek hotels have websites, where you can – at least in the case of larger hotels – book rooms online (in some cases you can save money by doing this directly, but for smaller hotels you'll have to contact them by phone or email or rely on w booking.com or similar). Off season (ie: mid-September to

2 | PRACTICAL INFORMATION

ACCOMMODATION PRICE CODES

Prices are based on the cost of a double room per night in high season.

€€€€€	Luxury	€300+
€€€€	Very expensive	€150–300
€€€	Expensive	€100–150
€€	Moderate	€60–100
€	Budget	up to €60

mid-July) you can generally get a discount, sometimes as much as 40%. Bear this in mind when looking at price categories. Charges include a government tax, a community bed tax, a stamp tax, and a recently added Climate Crisis Resilience Tax. There may also be an optional 10% surcharge for stays of only one or two days, and an air-conditioning surcharge in cheaper hotels, as well as a surcharge for an extra bed. If your hotelier fails to abide by the posted prices, or if you have any other reason to believe all is not on the level, take your complaint to the tourist police (↘ 1571). In July and August, hotels may require a minimum three-day (or longer) stay.

GUESTHOUSES AND STUDIOS Guesthouses, often with basic studios (sink, table and chairs, a couple of gas rings, fridge, utensils and dishes), are generally family-run affairs and cheaper than hotels. Many are purpose-built blocks, but in some places (notably in the Zagorochória and Pelion) you'll find charming bed-and-breakfast conversions of traditional mansions. Depending on facilities and location, a double room or studio will run between €40 and €60 for two people sharing in high season. Until June and after August, prices are always negotiable. Owners will often drop the price per day the longer you stay.

APARTMENTS AND VILLAS Although apartments and villas used to be concentrated in resorts, you can now find them nearly everywhere in northern Greece. In addition to the usual booking sites, also try:

Five Star Greece w fivestargreece.com. Luxury, upmarket villas on the Pelion, Skiáthos, Skópelos, Alónissos & Diáporos.
Le Collectioniste w lecollectionist.com/en. Villas on the Ionian coast & Skiáthos.

Novasol w novasol.co.uk. Villa holidays in Epirus & Chalkidikí.
Sunvil ↘ +44 (0)20 8568 4499; w sunvil.co.uk. Well-run company with self-catering properties in Chalkidikí, Epirus, Kavála, Thássos, Skópelos, etc.

CAMPING Greece in summer is perfect for sleeping out of doors. Unauthorised camping is illegal (the law was enacted to displace Roma camps), though each village enforces the ban as it sees fit; it's especially well enforced at seaside locations. It often depends on the proximity of organised campsites – these are liberally scattered along the coasts, but you can also find them near attractions such as Meteora. They are sometimes geared towards campervans and charge on a sliding scale. For two people with a small tent and a normal car, prices start at €17 a night. The most minimalist campsites have toilets (but not always toilet paper) and showers (but not always hot water). In general, the standard is pretty good, with small shops and a bar, sometimes a taverna and a pool. There's a complete list at w greececamping.gr.

In remote areas in the mountains no-one cares if you wild camp (often it's the only option), but if you do, make sure you leave no sign of your presence. If the police are in some places lackadaisical about enforcing the camping regulations, they come down hard on anyone lighting a fire in a forest, and with good reason – Greece has seen some devasting wildfires in recent years. The penalties can range from a big fine to even some jail time.

EATING AND DRINKING

> Life's fundamental principle is the satisfaction of the needs
> and wants of the stomach.
>
> Epicurus, 3rd century BC

Epicurus may have lent his name to gourmets, but in reality his philosophy advocated maximising simple pleasures: rather than continually seeking novelty, Epicurus suggests making bread and olives taste sublime by fasting for a couple of days. In that way Greeks have long been epicureans: centuries of occupation and poverty taught them to relish food more than cuisine. But what has changed in the 21st century is that cuisine has inescapably arrived.

BREAKFAST, LUNCH AND DINNER In resort areas, hotels and restaurants offer familiar breakfasts, lunches and dinners at familiar western European hours. One recent incentive among hotels is to win the coveted 'Greek breakfast' label, meaning they feature homemade flaky pies, breads, cakes, yogurt and honey. Greeks themselves get by with something light, supplemented mid-morning with a cheese pie or other snack.

You can eat lunch at noon, but if you want to do as the Greeks do in summer, get your sightseeing business done by 14.00, then indulge in a long lunch with wine, followed by a nap to avoid the afternoon heat. Get up at 18.00 for a swim and an ice cream, followed by the *vólta*, the evening stroll and a drink. Greeks rarely eat before 21.00, in summer especially, and meals can go on into the small hours. Children are welcome (they too nap in the afternoon).

An average taverna meal – if you don't order a major fish – usually costs around €20–30 per person with carafes of house wine. Bread will come whether or not you've ordered it, with a small service charge added. Prices at sophisticated, blatantly touristy, places with views can be much higher. In many resorts, waiters are paid a cut of the profits (which is why some obnoxiously tout for custom); tipping is technically discretionary but increasingly common – rounding up generously or adding 5–10% will be warmly appreciated. A law designed to catch tax evaders requires that you take a receipt (*apóthixi*) 150m from the door; the police make periodic checks.

CLASSIC GREEK DISHES Greek cooking methods tend to be simple, with strong Turkish and Italian influences. One criticism levelled at Greek food is that it's served tepid. Once you get used to it, you realise that many dishes are actually tastier once they're left to cool in their own juices, especially in the summer.

Many dishes need no introduction (but always taste better in Greece) – taramasalata (*tamará*), moussaka, *gýros*, stuffed vine leaves (*dolmadákia*), Greek salads with feta, Greek yogurt and baklava have achieved the universality of lasagne and chicken tikka. A classic meal begins with little plates (*mezédes*) shared around the table: olives, tzatziki (cucumbers and yogurt), prawns, *tirosaláta* (feta cheese dip),

RESTAURANT PRICE CODES

Prices are based on the cost of an average meal per person not including drinks.

€€€€€	Top end	€60+
€€€€	Very expensive	€40–60
€€€	Expensive	€30–40
€€	Moderate	€20–30
€	Inexpensive	up to €20

tirokapterí (a pungent cheese dip), salted fish, roasted peppers, cheese or spinach pies (*spanakópita*), a salad, or *saganáki* (fried cheese sprinkled with lemon).

Main courses could be a gorgeously fresh omelette, or an oven dish or stew (called 'ready dishes' as they're already prepared) such as lamb *kleftikó* (slow cooked with wine and vegetables), *stifádo* (spiced beef stew with baby onions), *kokinistó* (beef cooked with tomatoes and a hint of cinnamon), lamb or veal *youvétsi* (baked with tomatoes and tear-drop pasta), or *kréas stin stámna* (lamb or beef baked in a clay dish). Meats grilled to order come under the heading *tis óras* ('the on times'): pork chops (*brizóles*), lamb cutlets sold by the kilo (*paidákia*), kebabs (*souvláki*), minced steak (*biftéki*), meatballs (*keftédes* or *sousoukákia*), sausage (*lukániko*) or chicken (*koutópoulo*).

Seafood is fresh and delicious, but sometimes expensive, although you can usually find cheapies like whitebait (*marídes*), sardines (*sardéle*), cuttlefish (*soupiá*) and squid rings (*kalamári*). Baked or fried *bakaliáros* (fresh Mediterranean cod) is always a treat and shouldn't break the bank. Some places serve fish soups – *psarósoupa* (with potatoes and carrots) or *kakaviá* (Greek bouillabaisse), which are meals in themselves with hunks of fresh bread and a bottle of wine. Prawns (*garídes*) are lightly fried or baked with garlic, tomatoes and feta (*garídes saganáki*), a popular dish from the 1960s, as is spaghetti with spiny lobster (*astakomakaronáda*). Often each type of fish has its own price, priced by weight; you may be asked to pick out the one you want and the owner puts it on the scale in front of you.

Greeks make lovely sweets, puddings, cakes and ice creams, but tend to eat them in the late afternoon after their siesta, although desserts are now common in restaurants as well.

VEGETARIAN AND VEGAN DISHES Because of historic poverty, the use of olive oil over butter and the demands of Orthodox fasts (which forbid animal and dairy products), Greece has many traditional vegetarian (*chortofágos*) dishes. During Lent, restaurants go out of their way to prepare vegan dishes – when the artichokes (*anginares*), stewed with potatoes and fresh dill, are not to be missed. Any time of the year you'll find pulses, in starters such as *gigántes* (giant butter beans in tomato sauce) or *revíthia* (chickpeas, baked or in soups or fritters), bean soups (*fasoláda*) and occasionally lentils (*fakés*). Other vegan standbys are *ládera* (fresh vegetables cooked in olive oil), a host of salads, *patzária* (beetroot drizzled with olive oil and vinegar), *yemistá* (peppers or tomatoes stuffed with rice), *bríam* (potato and aubergine or courgette, baked with olive oil), *imams* (aubergine stuffed with tomato and onion), various *keftédes* (fritters from carrot to courgette to tomatoes), *dolmádes* (rice and dill-filled vine leaves), and, everywhere, endless supplies of chips, usually fried in olive oil. Although *skordaliá*, the classic garlic dip, is traditionally made simply with puréed potatoes or bread and olive oil, some places now do it with soft cheese.

SPECIALITIES OF NORTHERN GREECE Dining out is one of the joys of northern Greece, with its recipes brought over with refugees in 1923 from Asia Minor and the Black Sea; Thessaloníki has long been one of the food capitals of Greece, although it's probably best known for its *bougátsa*, flaky pies introduced after 1923. The handmade pastry is left to prove until doubled in size, then tossed in the air three to seven times until it becomes thin, filled with creamy custard or soft cheese (but you can also find spinach or minced meat), then baked and sold in *bougatsaría*. Every town in the north has at least one.

You'll find old Ottoman-era dishes such as *hunkár begendí* (stewed lamb with aubergine purée), Thracian *kavourmás* (lean beef or pork cooked slowly in broth and fat, with spices, then preserved in a jar or formed into a log, sliced and eaten as a *mezé* or with potatoes), Izmir-style meatballs in a spicy tomato sauce (*soutzoukákia*) and *pastoúrma* (Anatolian-style pastrami, made from beef, lamb or camel; Sary in Dráma is famous for it). You may even see *mantza*, a traditional Pomok dish of veal combined with vegetables or pasta. The sweets of the north, many brought over by Anatolian pastry chefs – including Xánthi's *karióka*, Véria's *revaní*, Komotiní's *soutzouk loukoum* and *kazán dibí*, Kalambáka's *halvah sapouné*, and Sérres's *akanés* – are renowned.

Epirus is a land of cheeses and pies (egg pie, pastry pie, milk pie), feta cheese and *anthótyro* (fresh whey cheese made from sheep or goat's milk) pie, pies filled with lamb and *trahanás* (a dried pebbly mixture of grain and yogurt or fermented milk, an ancient way of preserving milk, often made into soups). Métsovo's smoked cheese is often used to make *bougiourdí* (cheese baked with tomatoes and peppers); also look out for *batzossaganáki* (fried local cheese). But wherever you go you'll find surprises: Pelion's chestnuts, little apples, and wild herbs; buffalo milk cheeses and meats from Lake Kerkíni; red saffron from Krókos; honey from Chalkidikí; cherries from Édessa; giant peaches (*yiármades*) from Véria; beans from Préspa; red and green peppers from Flórina; wild mushrooms from everywhere in the mountains; and even truffles (*troúfes*) around Meteora and Grevená. Every *gýros* counter has a shaker of *boúkovo*, 'the chilli flakes of the Balkans', similar to hot paprika, which is sprinkled on soups, stews, beans, roast or grilled meats.

RESTAURANTS, TAVERNAS, ETC Because dining is an integral part of social life, Greeks eat out as often as they can. *Estiatória* (restaurants) are generally formal affairs; while tavernas are more like family-run bistros and can range from beach shacks to barn-like affairs with live music in the evening. At the seaside you'll find fish tavernas, *psarotavérnes*, specialising in all kinds of seafood from sea urchins and octopus stew to red mullet, swordfish, bream and sardines. Note that fresh line-caught wild fish in a taverna are priced by the kilo and they can run up the bill quite a bit; many Greeks find the expense very worthwhile. Most fish tavernas carry one or two meat dishes for fish-haters who may be dragged along. If you're a red-blooded meat-eater, then head for a *psistariá*, specialising in charcoal-grilled chicken, lamb, pork, beef or *kokorétsi* (lamb's offal, braided around a skewer).

Every village has at least one pizzeria and a *gyrádiko* (*gýros* stand) or *souvlatzídiko* (*souvláki* stand) for cheap meaty fills. At any neighbourhood *mageirío* you'll find a steam table laden with home-style specialities, vegetarian and vegan dishes among them. Everything is also available to take away. Bakeries sell an array of sweet and savoury hot pies; for something sweet, just look at the lovely displays in any *zacharoplasteío* or pastry shop.

CAFÉS AND BARS Every village larger than a dozen houses will have a *kafeneíon*: a coffee house, but more importantly a social institution where men (and increasingly women) gather to discuss the latest news, read the papers, nap or play cards and incidentally drink coffee. The bill of fare can be quite basic: Greek coffee (*café ellinikó*) – also known with less political correctness as Turkish coffee – is prepared in a little copper pot (*brikí*) in 40 different ways although *glykó* (sweet), *métrio* (medium) and *skéto* (no sugar) are the standard orders. It is always served with a cold glass of water. Other coffees, unless there's a proper Italian espresso machine, won't make the earth move: '*nes*' (ie: Nescafé) has become a Greek word, and comes either hot or whipped and iced as a frappé, which was invented in Thessaloníki; many Greeks now prefer iced espressos or cappuccinos. When you order any kind of coffee in Greece, they'll ask how you want it – sweet, medium or no sugar; let the server know if you prefer sugar on the side (Greek coffee is the exception – you order it as you wish to drink it). Tea, soft drinks, brandy, beer and ouzo round out the old-style *kafeneíon* fare.

That grand old Greek institution, the *ouzerí*, is still around, although these days many have morphed into the Greek version of tapas bars – the *mezedopoleío*, with a wide assortment of little plates easily made into a full meal. The national aperitif, ouzo (first commercially distilled in Týrnavos, in Thessaly in the 19th century), is clear and anise-flavoured, and served in tall glasses, which habitués dilute and cloud with water and sometimes ice. Modern Greek *rakí* is similar to grappa, and usually not anise-flavoured; try it in *rakómelo* (mulled with cinnamon, cloves and honey as a winter warmer). In much of northern Greece the tipple of choice is *tsípouro*, pomace brandy (similar to *rakí* but distilled in a different way, invented by the monks on Mount Athos in the 14th century); it is usually anise-flavoured but not always. *Mezedopoleíos* that specialise in it are called *tsipouradíka*; Vólos is famous for them. And although they specialise in *tsípouro*, they also serve wine and beer. Many cities now have wine bars, too – great places to discover the wonderful wines of northern Greece (see opposite).

Every flyspeck town tends to have at least one music bar, playing the latest hits (foreign and/or Greek). They come to life at cocktail hour and again at midnight; closing times vary but dawn isn't unusual in the summer. In general, they're not cheap and are sometimes outrageously dear; it can be disconcerting to realise that you paid the same price for your gin fizz as you paid for your entire meal earlier in the taverna next door. However, remember that the measures are triples by British standards. If in doubt, stick to beer – Amstel or Heineken, or the national brands Mythos and Fix. But do try the local brands: Vergina (page 215), brewed in Komotiní, is a popular choice. There's also an active craft beer movement; look out for beers from Sknipa and Nymphi from Thessaloníki, Marmita from Kavála, Lola (Pineios) from Lárissa, Epirus Brewery and Vólos Brewery, among many others.

WINE

Bronze is the mirror of the form; wine of the heart.
Aeschylus

Greece has 300 different indigenous vines, and there could well be something to the myths that wine was invented here; the famous wine in the Odyssey that Odysseus used to intoxicate the Cyclops came from Marónia in Thrace (page 216). Despite Greece's head start in winemaking some 4,500 years ago, the average Greek wine in recent decades was precisely that – average, a victim of the pan-European phylloxera epidemic and the 20th-century wars that ravaged and depopulated the country.

Since the 1980s, however, foreign expertise, better-educated winemakers and modern techniques have put wines on the map, and one of the joys of travelling

PDO WINE REGIONS OF NORTHERN GREECE

AMÝNTAIO Similar to Náoussa, but from higher altitudes on the Western Macedonia shores of Lake Vegorítida, this yields dry reds and rosés and sparkling dry and demi-sec.

ANCHÍALOS A new PDO region, along the west coast of the Pagasitic Gulf, Rhodítis and Savvatianó produce a soft and fruity white.

GOUMÉNISSA Greece's smallest PDO region, a soft dry red, grown on the lower slopes of Mount Paíko, but using Negóska as well as Xinómavro.

NÁOUSSA Macedonia's best-known tannic red, cultivated from Xinómavro on the slopes of Mount Vérmio, where winters are cold and summers are hot.

PLAGIÉS MELÍTONA The region around Porto Carras on the Sithonía Peninsula of Chalkidikí, one of the largest privately owned wine estates in Europe and home of Château Carras and Límnio, a drought-resistant grape from the island of Límnos and perhaps the oldest varietal in the world – it was even mentioned by Homer.

RAPSÁNI Dry red wines blended from three grapes indigenous to Xinómavro 'tamed' with Krasáto and Stavrotó varietals, grown on the lower slopes of Mount Olympus.

ZÍTSA Epirus's high-altitude (600m plus) fresh white wine, made from indigenous Debína grapes, Zítsa comes dry, medium dry or lightly sparkling. While in the region, seek out the even higher-altitude wine Katógi of Métsovo, a Cabernet Sauvignon grown at 1,150m – the highest vineyard in Greece.

in northern Greece for wine lovers is discovering the small vineyards unknown outside the region, preserving local varietals in a multitude of microclimates.

The showcase red grape of the north is dark, complex, tannin-rich Xinómavro (page 148), used in some of the most prominent Greek appellations, both PDO (Protected Designation of Origin) and PGI (Protected Geographical Indication). These are shown in the box above.

For more details, check out the Wines of Greece (w winesofgreece.org), and the Wine Roads of Northern Greece (w winemakersofnorthgreece.gr) with its eight different wine routes and a complete list of wineries open for tours, along with restaurants and hotel recommendations.

PUBLIC HOLIDAYS AND FESTIVALS

Most businesses and shops close down for the afternoon before and the morning after a religious holiday. If a national holiday falls on a Sunday, the following Monday is often observed. The Orthodox Easter (and Lent) is variable and generally falls a week or two after Easter is celebrated in the Western church.

In Greece, Easter is even more important than Christmas, the time when far-flung relatives return to see their families back home, with feasts and fireworks.

2 | PRACTICAL INFORMATION

After Easter and 1 May, spring (*ánixi* – the opening) has officially arrived, and the tourist season begins.

PUBLIC HOLIDAYS

1 January	**New Year's Day** (Protochroniá; also Ag Vassílis, aka Basil, the Greek Father Christmas) Many head to the casino to try their luck – supposedly a clue for the rest of the year.
6 January	**Epiphany** (Ta Fóta/Theofánia) When the priest blesses the sea by hurling a cross in the water, which swimmers battle to retrieve for good luck.
February–March (variable)	**'Clean Monday'** (Katharí Theftéra; precedes Shrove Tuesday and follows Carnival) Everyone flies kites and eats seafood.
25 March	**Annunciation/Greek Independence Day** (Evangelismós) Parades of schoolchildren in traditional costumes, led by the top student in each class.
April, usually	**Good Friday** (Megáli Paraskeví), **Easter Sunday** (Páscha) and **Greek Easter Monday** (Theftéra tou Páscha).
1 May	**Labour Day** (Protomayá) Everyone heads to the countryside to pick wildflowers.
Seventh Monday after Greek Easter	**Pentecost** (Pentikostí)
15 August	**Assumption of the Virgin** (Koímisis tis Theotókou)
28 October	**'Ochí' Day** In celebration of Metaxás's 'no' to Mussolini in 1940.
25 December	**Christmas** (Christoúyena)
26 December	**Gathering of the Virgin** (Sináxi Theotókou)

FESTIVALS Every village has its *panegýri*, or patron saint's day, some celebrated with a special church service, others with events culminating in a feast and music and dancing till dawn. It's also worth remembering that the main partying often happens the night before a saint's day. There are also many cultural festivals throughout the year – music, dance, film and more. Check the related websites for the most up-to-date information.

January

Kalí Vrýsi	One of several villages in Eastern Macedonia that celebrate the **Baboúgera**, with prancing 'goat men' (page 189); 6 January.
Kastoriá	**Ragoutsária**: Dionysian masks and frolics over three days, with dancing and music; 6–8 January.
Kleisoúra	The **Argoutsária**, or winter Dionysia, with masks, music, and dancing in the street; on New Year's Day. Also in Kozáni.
Xilaganí	**Festival of Babo**; 8 January. Also in other villages (page 211).

February

Týrnavos	**Bouráni**: 'Clean Monday' here is celebrated with a whacky, rowdy penis festival (page 310).

PUBLIC HOLIDAYS AND FESTIVALS

Xánthi	The biggest **Carnival** in northern Greece: a three-week-long festival leading up to the 40 days of fasting before Greek Easter, culminating on Clean Monday. There are other major celebrations in Náoussa (page 146), Vólos and Skópelos (page 364).

March
Thessaloníki	**Thessaloníki Documentary Festival** (w filmfestival.gr/en/documentary-festival); over 250 international documentaries, plus workshops, talks and related events over ten days in early March. Fantastic.

April
Thessaloníki	**Dance Festival** (w tdf.gr): one of the biggest jazz, salsa, street, Latin, etc dance competitions in the Balkans.

May
Karditsa	**International Choral Festival** (International-Festival-Of-Karditsa)
Kavála	**Cosmopolis International Festival** (w visitkavala.gr/en/sightseeing/festival-cosmopolis): music, dance and film; starts in May and runs through to December. See also page 181.
Lagadás	**Firewalkers** (page 100): celebrating the feast of SS Constantine and Helen; 21 May.
Préveza	**Jazz Festival** (w prevezajazzfestival.com); founded in 2003, this is Greece's second-largest international Jazz festival. Late May/early June.
Wineries	**Open Cellar Day**: tours, tastings and special events at wineries all over Greece. Usually the second or third weekend.

June
Keramotí	**Mussels and Sardines Festival**, with a fishing contest, live music and dancing; first weekend.

July
Kastaniés	**Ardas Festival** (w ardasfestival.gr): Balkan music festival for the young along the banks of the Árdas River near the borders of Türkiye and Bulgaria; over four to five days in mid-July.
Vlásti	**Earth Festival** (EarthFestivalVlasti): an alternative music festival, in the mountains above Kozáni; early July.
Vovoúsa	**Vovoúsa Festival** (w vovousafestival.gr): exhibitions, films, workshops and performances dedicated to the mountains; late July to early August.

July/August
Nestório	**River Party** (w riverparty.net): plenty of concerts, which attract thousands of Greek and foreign campers; late July or early August.

2 | PRACTICAL INFORMATION

Olympus	**Olympus Festival** (w festivalolympou.gr): since 1972 the biggest festival in northern Greece, featuring music, dance and theatre by Greek and international performers in venues large and small all around the big mountains; throughout July and August.
Pelion	**International Pelion Festival** (w pelionfestival.com): master classes for strings, piano and voice, and intimate chamber music concerts in the evenings; usually last two weeks of July.
Philippi	**Philippi Festival** (w visitkavala.gr/en/sightseeing/festival-filippon): ancient drama and music in Philippi, Thássos and Kavála; July to August.
Sani Resort	**Sani Festival** (w sani-resort.com/festivals/sani-festival): music festival featuring jazz, classical and world music; early July to mid-August.

August

Géfira (near Thessaloníki)	**International Festival of Folk Dances and Music** (f CulturalClubGefiraThessaloniki); late August to early September.
Néa Karváli	**Sun and Stone International Festival** (w www2.cioff.org/events-festival.cfm/en/259/Greece); traditional folk dances; usually late August.
Samothráki	**Pulsar Festival** (w pulsarfestivalgreece.com): rock, electronic, New Age music, etc; second week.

September

Dráma	**International Short Film Festival** (w dramafilmfestival.gr); mid-September.
Ioánnina	**Photometria** (w photometria.gr): photography festival, with seminars, competitions and exhibitions; September through part of October and other events throughout the year.
Kalambáka (Meteora)	**Mushroom Festival** (w meteoramuseum.gr/mushroom-festival); September.
Lekáni	**Potato Festival**, plus traditional Pontian music and dancing; first Sunday of the month.
Thessaloníki	**Street Mode** (w streetmode.gr): a massive festival of street arts; early September. Also: **Thessaloníki International Fair** (w tif.helexpo.gr) – the biggest in the Balkans, mid-month; and **Reworks** (w reworks.gr) – a massive contemporary music festival, usually late September. See also page 82.
Xánthi	A very lively **Old Town Festival**, with art, food and drink and partying in the streets; early September.

October

Gríva (by Gouménissa)	**Chestnut Festival**: roast chestnuts, wine, cheese and more, plus traditional dancing, by the slopes of Mount Paíko; last weekend.
Lárissa	**Open Nights Festival** (f Open.Nights.Off.Art) An interdisciplinary art festival on a different theme each year; usually around the middle of the month.

SPORTS AND ACTIVITIES

Néa Perámos	**Tsípouro Festival**: drinking, nibbling seafood *mezédes* and dancing by the sea; last weekend.
Platamónas	**Livestock Festival**: an outdoor feast featuring 600kg of goat stew, along with a bazaar of local goodies; first Sunday of the month.
Thessaloníki	**Dimítria** (**w** dimitria.thessaloniki.gr): big-name events celebrating the city's patron saint; first three weeks. The website should go live a few months before the festival. Also the **Thessaloníki Animation Festival** (**w** tafestival.gr); late October.

November

Thessaloníki	**Thessaloníki International Film Festival** (page 82); over ten days in early November.
Wineries	**European Wine Tourism Day** Tours, tastings and special events. Generally the second Sunday.

December

Tríkala	**Christmas festivities** that attract a million visitors a year, with a Christmas theme park, light displays and 'Mill of Elves' for children; mid-month–6 January.

SHOPPING

Supermarkets (Greeks love Lidl) now sell almost everything you could want, especially the large ones at the edge of bigger towns, but independent butchers and greengrocers still thrive. In rural areas, vans go from village to village selling everything from vegetables, through fresh fish and live chickens, to plastic chairs. Mountain honey and herbs, often sold on the roadside, are superb, as are wines, olives and oil, but these need to be packed with care (and be aware of restrictions on liquids in hand luggage if you are flying). Jewellery is not cheap, but can be excellent quality; Epirus has long been famous for silver.

SPORTS AND ACTIVITIES

Northern Greece, with its beaches, mountains, lakes, rivers, gorges and waterfalls, was made for active holidays. Several Greek firms (page 32) organise a wide variety of half-day to week-long experiences in the great outdoors. A great resource is **Xtreme Greece** (**w** xtremegreece.gr), with a listing of local firms offering extreme and not-so-extreme sports, as well as a heads up on all the rallies, races and other events around the country.

BIRDWATCHING With its lakes, forests and deltas, and position on major fly paths, northern Greece is prime birdwatching territory: Lake Kerkíni, the Évros Delta and Dadiá Forest are legendary, but there are many other wetlands and Natura 2000 sites. See **w** birdwing.eu/sites-of-northern-greece.

CANOEING, KAYAKING AND WHITE-WATER RAFTING Northern Greece has some of the best paddling spots in the Balkans, notably the Aoös Voïdomátis, Árachthos, Kalarítikos and Aspropótamos rivers in Epirus and the Néstos in Eastern Macedonia and Thrace.

2 | PRACTICAL INFORMATION

HIKING Towering mountains, spectacular gorges and exceptional flora and fauna make northern Greece wonderful walking territory. Long-distance hiking, however, is strictly for the adventurous: paths can be unexpectedly blocked, or dangerously eroded or washed out, streams may be impassable and the way-marking is poor; be prepared for long diversions.

In the 1980s two European long-distance trails were extended to Greece. The **E4** starts in westernmost Portugal and crosses into Greece from Bulgaria at Promachónas north of Sérres, passing through Flórina, Meteora and Mount Olympus in the north before crossing into Central Greece and ending up on Cyprus. Welsh walker John Pone describes it wonderfully in his blog, w johnpone4greece.blogspot.com. The **E6** begins in Finland and crosses Greece from Igoumenítsa to Alexandroúpolis. The **Pindus Trail** (f) team is progressing with their work to open 600km+ (370+ miles) through the Pindus Mountains, partly along the E6. The section from Vovoúsa to Dístrato and on to Samarína has been cleared and signposted.

But there are shorter lovely hikes everywhere – in the Pindus Mountains, the Vália Cálda, Zagóri, Víkos–Aoös and Tzoumérka in Epirus, around Olympus and the Pelion Peninsula, in the Rhodope Mountains and Néstos Gorge. Hiking map company **Anavasi** lists all the mountain refuges with a map and their contact details (w anavasi.gr/refuges/index-en.php).

SKIING Greece may not be ready to challenge Switzerland, but it's a lot cheaper, and you'll find decent slopes around Métsovo in Epirus; Mount Pelion; Falakró in Eastern Macedonia; 3-5 Pigádia, Elatochóri, Kaimaktsalán, Séli and Sérres in Central Macedonia; and Vígla Pisodéri/Vérno (Flórina) and Vasilítsa in Western Macedonia.

SPAS Some of the most popular spas are the thermal baths of Loutrá Pozar near Édessa, Loutrá Ag Pareskeví in Chalkidikí, the mud baths near Philippi at Krinídes and the hot springs at Ágkristro north of Sérres.

WATERSPORTS Greece was made for watersports, and by law all the beaches, no matter how private they might look, are public. Almost all meet European guidelines for water cleanliness, although a few could stand to have less litter on the sand. Beaches often have umbrellas and sunbed concessions and snack bars, and if there's a breeze you'll probably find a wind- or kitesurfing board to rent. Bigger resorts offer paragliding, jet skis and waterskiing. Some of Greece's best beaches are on the second leg of Chalkidikí, including Vourvouroú, Karýdi and Karvourótrypes. Pelion, too, is famous for its beaches, with Mylopótamo and Damouchári among the many standouts. Syvotá and Párga on the Ionian coast are also justifiably popular.

Scuba-diving, once strictly banned to keep divers from snatching antiquities and to protect Greece's much-harassed marine life, is permitted between dawn and sunset in specially defined areas; local diving excursions will take you there.

MUSEUMS AND ARCHAEOLOGICAL SITES

Because of financial pressures, the opening times of Greek sites have become more erratic. As a general rule, even the smallest museum and site (if it is fenced) should be open 08.30–15.00 Wednesday to Monday throughout the year, though it's always a good idea to ring ahead and check before setting out. Larger, better-known sites will extend these hours in the summer.

Concessions on entry fees are available to the under 16s, over 65s (EU citizens), and EU students among others, who often get in free. Owing to hard times, there has been a sharp increase in many entry fees, some as much as doubling, but to encourage off-season travel, government-run sites offer a 50% discount on entrance fees from November to March. Admission is free to all on Melina Mercouri Memorial Day (6 March), International Monuments Day (18 April), International Museums Day (18 May) and European Heritage Weekend (the last Saturday and Sunday of September), as well as 28 October and the first Sunday of every month from November to March.

OPENING TIMES

Most shops and supermarkets are open 08.00–21.00 Monday to Friday and to 20.00 on Saturday, but some smaller shops still close in the afternoons for siesta, and may not reopen on Monday and Wednesday evenings. Outside of tourist areas, where shops tend to stay open daily in summer until midnight, everything closes down on a Sunday. Banks are open 08.00–14.00 Monday to Friday. Post office hours are 07.30–14.00 Monday to Friday, although in regional capitals main post offices are open 07.30–20.30 Monday to Friday and 07.30–14.30 on Saturdays. Pharmacies keep similar hours to shops, and in cities will display the details of the nearest after-hours pharmacy.

MEDIA AND COMMUNICATIONS

INTERNET Nearly all hotels and cafés now provide a free Wi-Fi connection, and this has spread to some surprisingly rural locations. Speeds are often comparable to what you might expect in the UK or USA.

LOCAL NEWS The local, daily edition of the *International New York Times* contains a translation of parts of *Kathimerini*, one of the better Greek newspapers; check online at w ekathimerini.com. Other good sources in English are the daily updates on Greek Reporter (w greekreporter.com); Navtemporiki (w naftemporiki.gr/English), and the Athens-Macedonian News Agency (w amna.gr/en). Online magazine *Greece Is* (w greece-is.com) is packed full of interesting up-to-date articles about the country's culture, gastronomy and nightlife.

POST The postal service in Greece is efficient. Most larger villages have a post office and they will hold poste restante mail sent to you care of them for a month. Postboxes (*grammatokivótio*) and signs for post offices (*tachidromío*) are bright yellow and easy to find. Post offices are open from Monday to Friday 07.30–14.00, although in large towns they may be open until 20.00, and on Saturday mornings as well. Stamps (*grammatósima*) can also be bought at kiosks and in some tourist shops, although they may charge a small commission. Postcards cost the same as letters and are given the same priority (they take about three days to the UK).

TELEPHONE With the rise of the mobile phone, public telephones operated by cards are often out of order, although you might still find a metered phone by a kiosk. Most foreign mobile phones will pick up a Greek network, but non-EU residents might want to check with their provider about roaming charges – they can easily add up. The alternative for longer stays is to buy a local Greek SIM card from one of the three main providers – Vodafone, Cosmote or Nova – or get an e-SIM before arrival. All Greek phone numbers have 10 digits now: those starting with a '2' are landlines; those starting with a '6' are mobile numbers.

2 | PRACTICAL INFORMATION

CULTURAL ETIQUETTE

Greeks traditionally treat strangers as guests, and you will get on with them best if you act like one. Cultural mores are generally little different from the rest of Europe, but there are a few pointers to keep in mind. Walking around wearing very little, except on or very near the beach, is frowned upon. Similarly, topless sunbathing for women, while generally accepted, might raise the odd eyebrow if done on the village beach in front of everyone having lunch – exercise discretion. Nudism is forbidden by law, but tolerated in numerous designated or out-of-the-way areas.

Tipping on American scales is not customary, but tips for good service are always welcome in cafés, bars and restaurants; with taxi drivers, just round up the bill by a little. Visitors to churches and monasteries are expected to dress respectfully, although many people ignore this. At the least you should cover knees and shoulders (men and women both; see also page 322). Raising your hand, palm out, as if to signal 'stop' is a serious sign of disrespect (annoyed drivers do it quite a bit; saying 'Naaa' adds to the insult).

TRAVELLING POSITIVELY

Despite hard times, Greece has little need of overt public charity. If you want to help the country, there is one excellent way you can do so: visit, especially outside of July and August (when the country groans under the mass of tourism – in 2024 it had over 40 million visitors), travel around, spend money in locally owned businesses, learn about the culture and people, and fall in love with the place. If you want to volunteer to help the refugees in northern Greece, see w carecenter.gr; many organisations do not last after the funds have dried up, but this one, affiliated with the Evangelical Churches of Greece, seems to have some staying power.

Greek tap water is perfectly safe to drink, and inexpensive plastic bottles of spring water are widely available (and responsible for untold pollution, taking up half the available room in landfill sites). Buy one and refill.

Part Two

THE GUIDE

3 | THESSALONÍKI (ΘΕΣΣΑΛΟΝΙΚΗ)

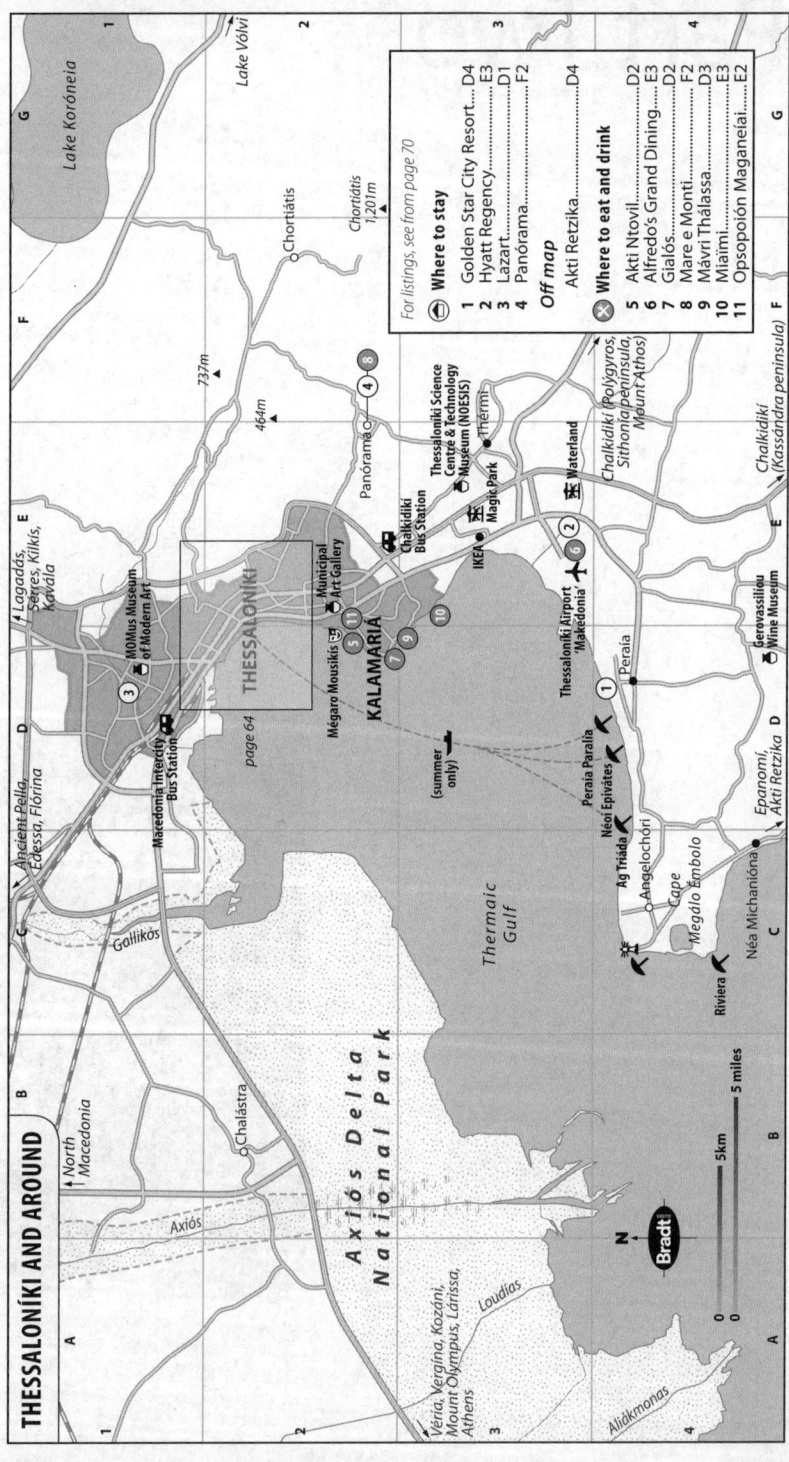

3

Thessaloníki (Θεσσαλονίκη)

Sheltered at the top of the Thermaic Gulf, Thessaloníki (or Salonica), with a population of over 1 million in the metropolitan area, is the second city of Greece. But you'll rarely hear Greeks indulge in the banter that often characterises the relations of first and second cities, like Barcelona and Madrid, or Rome and Milan; in fact, many Athenians readily admit that Thessaloníki is a much nicer place to live, where life unwinds at a less hectic pace (its motto is χαλαρά – *chalará* – or 'taking it easy'). Many of the 150,000 university students who come here to study never leave, adding to its vibrant cultural life, its great bar and restaurant and festival scene, and sizzling nightlife.

Thessaloníki boomed in the Middle Ages while Athens snoozed, and its most compelling monuments are Byzantine: 22 churches still stand, several of which – the Rotonda, Ósios David, Ag Dimítrios, the Panagía Acheiropoiétos, Ag Apostóli and Ag Sofía – are UNESCO World Heritage sites. The upper city, the main Muslim district in Ottoman times, is cocooned in towering late Roman walls, while the lower city stands on tiers like a choir singing to the sea. Thessaloníki has always been cosmopolitan: it's one of only a few European cities to boast an urban population for an uninterrupted 2,500 years, one that has known great joy and great darkness, too.

HISTORY

Thessaloníki is one of the few Greek cities to know its birthday – 315BC, when King Cassander founded a new city named after his wife (page 60). To populate his foundation, Cassander used carrots and sticks to relocate the inhabitants of 26 older towns in the area, the largest of which, Therme, gave its name to the Thermaïkós Kólpos, the Thermaic Gulf.

Thessaloníki only really blossomed after the Romans conquered Macedon in 146BC, and blazed the Via Egnatía – the extension of the Via Appia and first Roman road outside of Italy, from Albania to Byzantium – and developed Thessaloníki into a commercial and military port. Cicero was exiled here in 58BC, and in AD42, after the Battle of Philippi, the city was declared a free city by the victors, Antony and Octavian. St Paul (page 9) came in AD50, and later addressed two epistles to the church he founded. In the late 3rd century AD, as the vortex of the empire moved away from Rome, Emperor Galerius made Thessaloníki his capital.

Although the city was disappointed when Constantine rejected it in favour of the puny town of Byzantium for his 'new Rome', Constantinople, he did finance a new artificial port as compensation. Theodosius I (AD379–95) often made Thessaloníki his base and built its mighty walls; in AD380, when he thought he was dying, he converted to Christianity and issued the Edict of Thessaloníki, supressing paganism and banning the Olympics.

3 | THESSALONÍKI (ΘΕΣΣΑΛΟΝΙΚΗ)

> ### ALEXANDER THE GREAT'S MERMAID SISTER
>
> The daughter of Philip II, and half-sister to Alexander, was born on the same day in 353BC that the king won a battle in Thessaly that led to his domination of that region (hence her name, Thessalonike – 'Victory in Thessaly'). Raised by Alexander's mother, Olympias, Thessalonike was in Pydna (page 136) when Cassander murdered Olympias, but he spared Philip's daughter to marry into the ruling family and solidify his claims to the throne of Macedon. While she was a child, Alexander was said to have washed her hair with the water of immortality. History says one of her three sons murdered her, but legend says she became a mermaid, who stopped passing ships to ask: 'Is Alexander the king still alive?' Greek sailors knew they had to reply that 'Yes, he lives, and reigns, and conquers the world' or she would sink the ship and drown all hands on board.

By Justinian's time, Thessaloníki was the *symvassilévousa* (co-reigning city) of the Byzantine Empire, much visited for its trade fair and the relics of its patron saint, Dimítrios. It remained a Greek outpost even after the Avars and Slavs occupied the rest of Macedonia; in the 9th century AD it became the cultural centre for the entire Balkan region after two Thessalonian brothers, Methodius and Cyril, converted the Slavs to Christianity and created an alphabet for their language. Its prosperity attracted unwelcome visitors, too: among them the Saracens, who captured and sold off 22,000 inhabitants as slaves in AD904. After the Fourth Crusade in 1204, the city briefly became the capital of the Latin kingdom of Thessaloníki before returning to the Greeks.

THE ORIGINAL NAVEL-GAZERS In the late 13th century, Thessaloníki was the fulcrum of the Orthodox Hesychasm ('Quietness') movement, which advocated the contemplation of God through 'total' prayer that concentrated body, mind and soul. The regard of the body as a healthy, godly thing was revolutionary at the time; a suggestion by St Nikephoros the Hesychast that young monks should fix their eyes on their navels, to 'attach the prayer to their breathing', led to the accusation that the Hesychasts were '*omphalopsychoí*', having their souls in their navels. The nobility supported the Hesychasts, while a popular party, the Zealots, found it distinctly non-Greek. Under Thessaloníki's Hesychast archbishop and later saint Gregory Palamás (1296–1359) the pot boiled over; anathema followed anathema, and in 1342 the Zealots hurled the nobles over the walls. Yet the Hesychast period coincided with a splendid age of painting and church building.

THE OTTOMAN CONQUEST Thessaloníki first fell to the Ottomans in 1387. Ruler Manuel Paleológos had wanted to resist, but the inhabitants forced him out of town so they could surrender. And as usual, when a city surrendered, the Ottomans treated it lightly. A small garrison was installed in the castle, and one church was made into a mosque; the worst imposition was the 'tax of sons', the *devshirme*, when families would be compelled to give up sons to become Muslims, who would be trained for the civil service or as janissaries.

In 1402, however, the Ottoman army suffered a devastating defeat by Mongol khan Tamerlane; the Sultan Bayazid was captured and died in captivity, setting off a battle for the Sultanate. Manuel Paleológos took advantage of the disarray to marry his daughter to one of the pretenders to the throne in exchange for the return of Byzantine rule to Thessaloníki. But in 1421, the young, talented and ambitious

Murad II became Sultan, and one of his first concerns was to recapture the city, so he sent an army to besiege it.

The Byzantines in Constantinople were too weak to help; the Venetians were invited in but could do little. Three-quarters of the population fled, and when Murad, who was married to a Greek and sympathetic towards the Greeks, offered promises of good treatment in exchange for surrendering, most of the inhabitants who remained were willing. But the archbishop held out. Murad showed up in person in March 1430 to deliver the coup de grâce, but not before offering them one last chance to surrender. When the archbishop still refused – in spite of the desperate pleas from his flock – Murad offered his soldiers everything in the city: all of its people and all of its riches. As they breeched the walls, the Venetians and some lucky Greeks escaped on the galleys; the rest were killed or enslaved.

OTTOMAN RULE Although it remained a strategic port, military base and janissary command post, much of Ottoman Selanik (as it was known) resembled a ghost town until the Sephardim were welcomed into the city after 1492 (page 62). Once again business thrived; every week caravans set off for Skopje, Sofia and Vienna. Even by Balkan standards, the city was such an ethnic mix that even poor peddlers spoke half a dozen languages; more than half the population was Jewish, a third Greek, and the rest a mix of Turks, Serbs, Bulgars, Armenians, Albanians and Vlachs.

It worked well enough until the 1800s: after attempts to join in the Greek War of Independence in 1821 were crushed, many Greek Thessalonians moved south to the new Kingdom of Greece, leaving only 4,000 in the city. The Ottomans, feeling history was slipping through their fingers, began the Tanzimat, or 'reorganisation': founding schools, reforming commerce and trade and establishing the Bank of Salonica with assistance from financiers in France and Austria. In 1869, the walls of the lower city were demolished to allow the city to grow. A new modern port for steamships replaced the dilapidated old docks, new rail links to Skopje (1871) and Constantinople (1896) were built, and full legal equality was granted to Ottoman citizens regardless of their religion. The Young Turks rallied here for reforms – for a constitutional monarchy and multi-party democracy in the Ottoman Empire – before the overthrowing of the absolutist Sultan 'Abdul the Damned' in 1908.

TRAGIC 20TH CENTURY During the two Balkan Wars that followed (1912–13), Thessaloníki was the glittering prize claimed by both Greece and Bulgaria. It turned into a race: 'Thessaloníki at all costs!' declared Prime Minister Eleftherios Venizélos. The Greek army arrived first by just a few hours, and held the city after fierce street fighting; three days later, King George rode through Thessaloníki in triumph. When he returned in March 1913, he was assassinated (page 92). Ethnic tensions simmered – only to be exacerbated by the outbreak of World War I, which led to the arrival in 1915 of a large Allied Expeditionary Force of 400,000 troops from the Commonwealth, France, Italy, Russia and Serbia. Their presence brought a boom to the local economy after the austerity of the Balkan Wars: a dozen newspapers in seven languages were printed, and theatre, cinemas and cafés overflowed.

Then on 18 August 1917, a spark from a homemade stove in a refugee's hovel ignited a straw bed, leading to a fire that spread quickly through the narrow medieval streets, fanned by the wind – there was no fire service, and the Allies had requisitioned much of the available water. It destroyed a square kilometre of the lower city, leaving 70,000 homeless, including most of the city's Jews. Venizélos ordered the city not to be rebuilt quickly, but commissioned French urban planner

3 | THESSALONÍKI (ΘΕΣΣΑΛΟΝΙΚΗ)

MOTHER OF ISRAEL

By the 4th century BC, there were Jewish communities in all the commercial cities of the eastern Mediterranean, including the Thessaloníki visited by St Paul. By the 12th century, as traveller Benjamin of Tudela reported, the Jews in the city had become so assimilated that they spoke Greek as their first language and called themselves Romiots, 'citizens of Rome' (the Byzantine Empire). The emperors tolerated them as God's chosen people and the Ottomans, when they took over, treated them as they treated the Christians, as a *millet*, or nation, with religious and, to a large extent, legal autonomy.

The Ottoman attitude was in stark contrast to the persecutions in the West. In 1492, when Spain expelled the Sephardim, Sultan Bayezit II welcomed them. Some 20,000 settled in Thessaloníki, and they were soon joined by thousands of other Jews fleeing persecution in central Europe, Naples and Sicily. The wealthy, well-educated and well-connected Sephardim outnumbered the local Romiots, and their liturgy and language, Ladino (derived from medieval Spanish), became the local language of commerce. Their 36 synagogues, with names such as Aragon and Toledo, did much to keep medieval Spanish culture alive. Brothers Judah and Samuel Benveniste, grandsons of the Court Rabbi of Castile, brought their vast collection of books to Thessaloníki and became great civic benefactors, establishing libraries and public parks. Samuel Usque gave Salonica its nickname the 'Mother of Israel' in his 16th-century epic poem *Consolation for the Tribulation of Israel*.

Because the Jews were associated in Greek minds with their Ottoman protectors, many were massacred in southern Greece during the War of Independence. Survivors fled north to Thessaloníki, swelling the Jewish population to its peak at c90,000. Troubles came again after the city became part of Greece, and Athens

Ernest Hébrard to lay out a modern city of boulevards and broad squares. With the exchange of populations in 1923, 160,000 ethnic Greeks from Asia Minor more than doubled the population, and earned Thessaloníki a new nickname – Phtochtómana, 'Mother of the Poor'. The influx of refugees gave the city an ethnic Greek majority for the first time in centuries.

The rebuilding had hardly begun when World War II broke out. The Italians bombed the city in 1940, killing 232, before it became the first city in Greece to fall to the Germans, on 8 April 1941. The Nazis quickly got to work, forcing the Jews into a ghetto by the railway station before deporting most to Auschwitz and Bergen-Belsen. Few returned; Thessaloniki lost 95% of its Jewish population during the war.

After the war and Civil War, Thessaloníki slowly found its feet again to take its place as the second most important commercial port in Greece. An earthquake in 1978 caused severe damage, especially to the Byzantine churches, but most were restored in time for Thessaloníki's year as Cultural Capital of Europe (1997). In 2011, the city elected independent leftist, ecologist and anti-nationalist Yiánnis Boutáris, a scion of the famous wine family (page 148), as mayor, who has promoted the city's Jewish and Muslim multi-cultural past, LGBTQIA+ rights and the legalisation of marijuana, and welcomed Jewish and Turkish tourists, infuriating hardliners; in May 2018 he was even beaten up by far-right protesters. But emphasising the city's rich multi-cultural past has paid dividends in visitor numbers to the city. In 2019, independent candidate Konstantínos Zérvas, Boutáris's vice mayor, defeated the Néa Demokratía candidate and served as mayor of Thessaloníki for the next four years. Stélios Angeloúdis, an independent sought to drag the idiosyncratic old city into contemporary Greek life. Greek was imposed as the official language, and many traditional religious laws had to be adapted to the laws of the new state.

It was the beginning of the end for the Mother of Israel. After the great fire of 1917, many Sabbetaians (page 98) moved their businesses to Istanbul; in 1923, when the influx of Greek refugees from Asia Minor made the Jews a minority, many left Thessaloníki for Athens, Palestine or France, including mathematician Raphaël Salem and Daniel Carasso (founder of Danone), and the ancestors of Nobel-prize-winning author Patrick Modiano, Diane von Fürstenberg, Nicolas Sarkozy and the Dassaults of the aerospace conglomerate.

In hindsight, they were the lucky ones. Throughout the 1930s, the German consulate had been taking notes on the 56,000 Jews who remained in the city, and the Occupation began with the plundering of their most precious books, manuscripts and ritual items. Families were evicted from their homes to make way for Nazis. There were systematic desecrations of the Jewish cemetery. All Jewish men were mobilised for civilian labour under appalling conditions. The chief rabbi raised a huge sum to pay for their release, but in February 1943 Eichmann's right-hand man, Dieter Wisliceny, arrived to implement the 'Final Solution' and sent 48,974 to Auschwitz.

Only 1,950 ever returned after the war. But in this impoverished, refugee-filled city, with its extreme housing shortage, the Jews had few friends; when survivors tried to reclaim properties that had been expropriated during and after the war, very few ever succeeded, and most left for good, for Palestine or America. Today, about 1,000 Jews remain in Thessaloníki, who support two synagogues, an elementary school, retirement home, and the Jewish Museum (page 83).

candidate with the unofficial support of PASOK, won the next election and took office in 2024.

GETTING THERE AND AWAY

BY AIR Thessaloníki's Makedonia airport [58 E3] (23109 85177; w skg-airport.gr; ⊕ 24hrs daily), 15km southeast of town, is linked by direct seasonal flights with a dozen cities in the UK along with several flights a day from Athens.

Getting from/to the airport Every 30 minutes, **bus** 01X or night bus 01N links the airport to the railway station and the Macedonia Intercity Bus Station by way of the Via Egnatía through the city centre, with a journey time of around 40 minutes under ideal traffic conditions (fare €1.80; for schedules, see w oasth.gr). Buy tickets from the machines on board (the machines take only coins and do not give change), or from the ticket kiosk by the bus stop.

Taxis take about half an hour. There's a flat fee for the city centre of €25 (€35 between midnight and 05.00). There's a taxi stand outside the arrivals area, or book in advance with Welcome Pickups (21117 68284; w welcomepickups.com).

Car hire A number of well-known car-rental firms have desks at the airport.

Aegean 23105 00801; w aegeancar.gr

Avis 23108 88100 (port), 23104 75888 (Peraia, past the airport); w avis.gr

3 | THESSALONÍKI (ΘΕΣΣΑΛΟΝΙΚΗ)

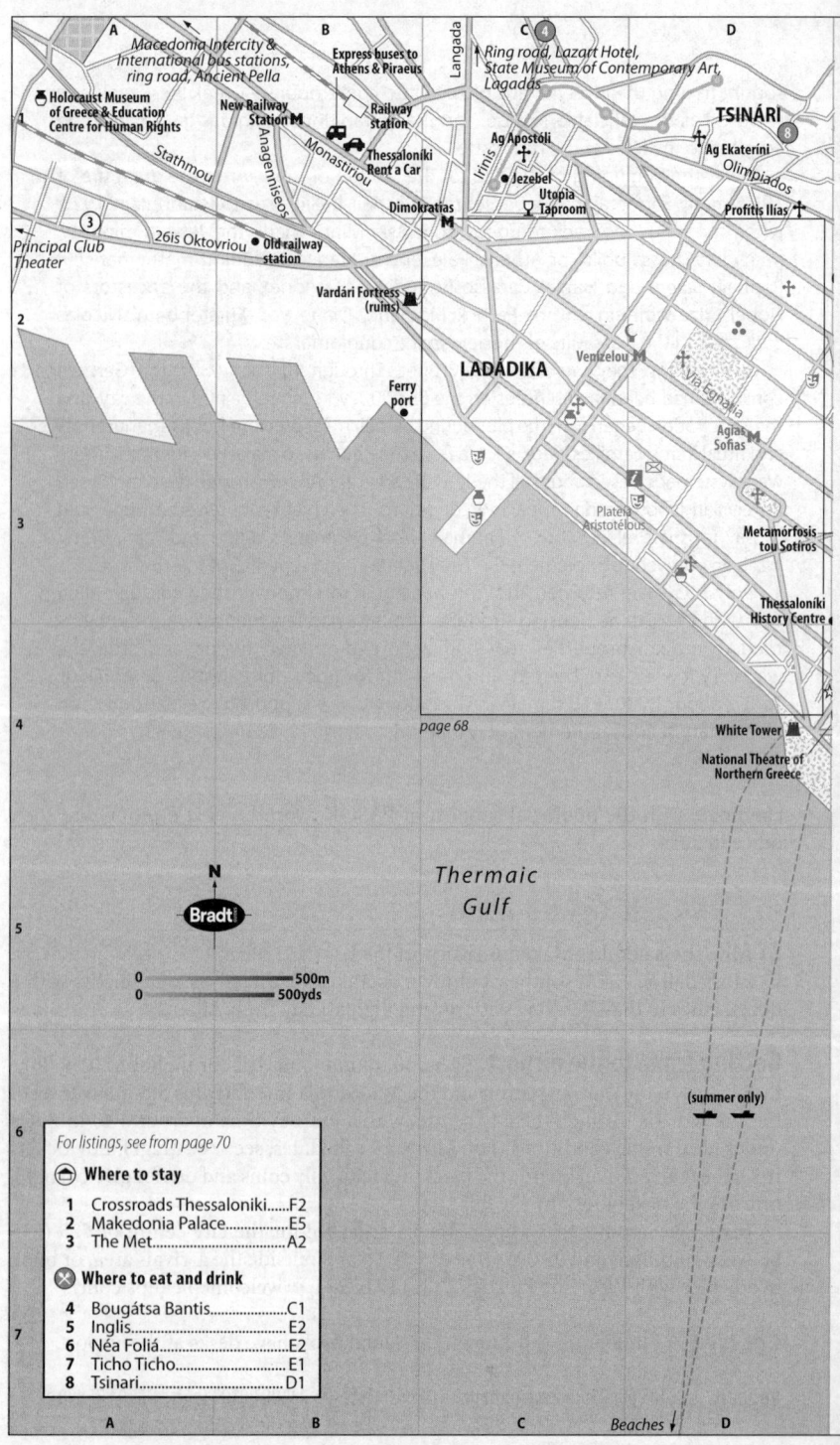

For listings, see from page 70

Where to stay
1. Crossroads Thessaloniki......F2
2. Makedonia Palace..............E5
3. The Met..................................A2

Where to eat and drink
4. Bougátsa Bantis..................C1
5. Inglis......................................E2
6. Néa Foliá...............................E2
7. Ticho Ticho..........................E1
8. Tsinari...................................D1

GETTING THERE AND AWAY

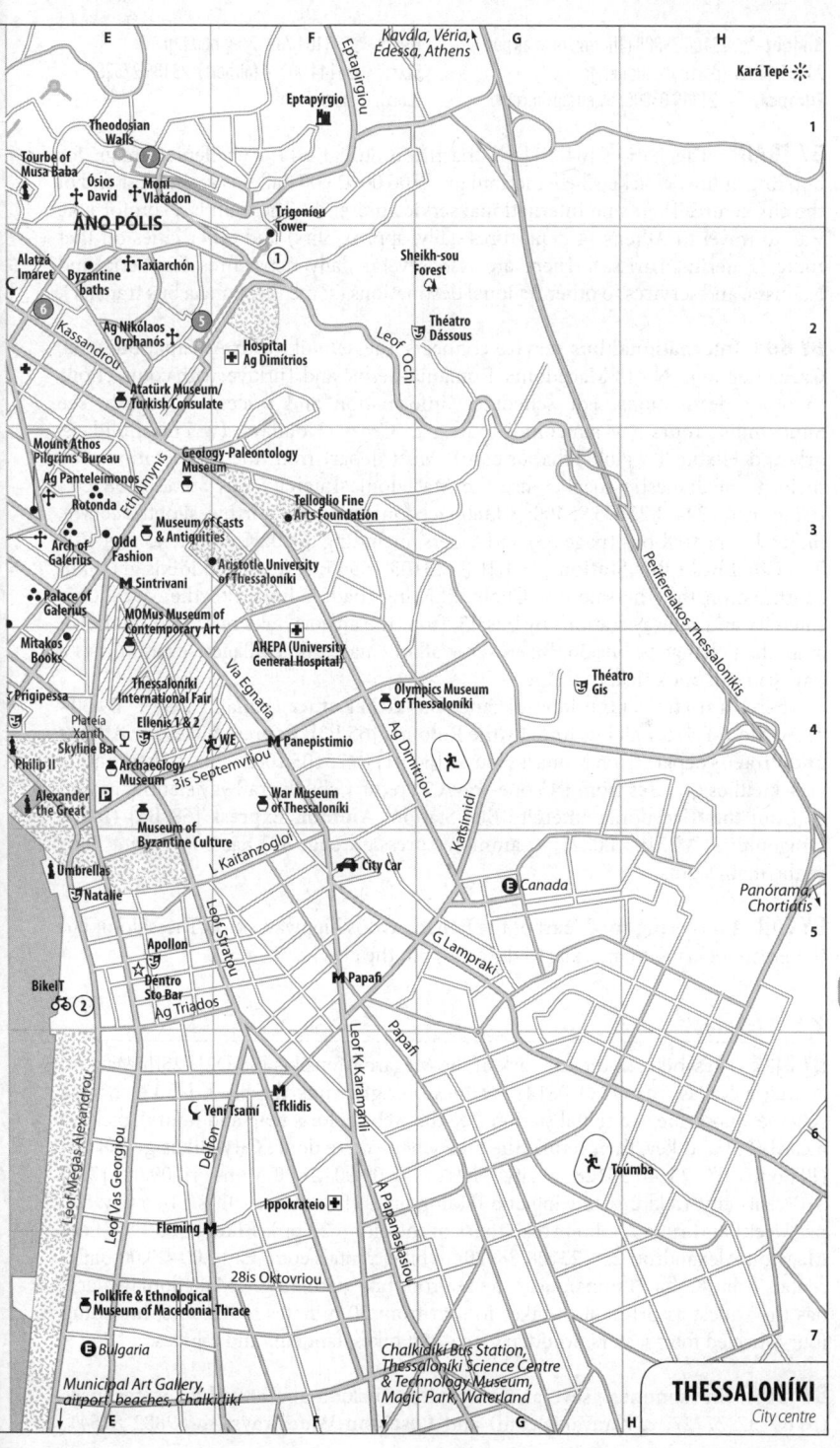

3 | THESSALONÍKI (ΘΕΣΣΑΛΟΝΙΚΗ)

Budget ⎹ 23104 75888 (Thermi, near airport), 23105 40827 (port); **w** budget.gr
Europcar ⎹ 21119 03000; **w** europcar.com
Hertz ⎹ 23104 73952; **w** hertz.gr
Sixt ⎹ 23144 00224 (airport), 23105 27528 (port); **w** sixt.global

BY TRAIN The station [64 B1] (Monastiríou St; ⎹ 14511; **w** hellenictrain.gr, for booking online: **w** tickets.hellenictrain.gr; ⏲ 06.00–23.00 daily) is at the west end of the city centre. There's no international service presently. The train is a comfortable way to travel to Athens (4 departures daily, approx 5hrs) and other cities on that route (Katerini, Larissa). There are also several daily departures for Véria and Naoussa, and services to other regional destinations (some involving a bus transfer).

BY BUS International bus service connects Thessaloniki with Albania, Bulgaria, Czech Republic, North Macedonia, Romania, Serbia and Türkiye, with connections to other destinations. For schedules, information and prices in English, see Simeonidis Tours (**w** simeonidistours.gr), Crazy Holidays (**w** crazyholidays.gr), and Flixbus (**w** global.flixbus.com). Most depart from the train station. The majority of domestic coaches use the Macedonia Intercity Bus Station [58 D1] (Giannitsón 244; ⎹ 23105 95400; **w** ktelmacedonia.gr), 5km northwest of the centre, linked by the 01X bus (page 63) and others, including the 02K, 12, 31, 45 and 45Y. The **Chalkidikí Bus Station** [58 E2] (⎹ 23103 16555; **w** ktel-chalkidikis.gr), 9km southeast on the Thessaloníki–Chalkidikí ring road, is linked to the Macedonia Intercity and railway stations by bus 45; from the airport, take bus 79 to the IKEA stop, then change to bus 36. Buses serve all of Chalkidikí's villages several times a day; you can book tickets online.

There's a useful central long-distance bus **ticket office** (Egnatía 119; ⏲ 09.30–17.30 Mon–Fri) for all bus lines by the Rotonda [65 E3]. **Express buses for Athens and Piraeus** depart from Monastiríou 67 [64 B1] (⎹ 23105 10835; buy tickets online at **w** ktelthes.gr; fares from €45 one-way/€72 return), by the railway station, as well as from the Macedonia Intercity Bus Station. **Ammon Express** [68 B4] (Íonos Dragoúmi 3; ⎹ 23105 00225; **w** ammonexpress.gr; page 42) has convenient links to the main sights.

BY CAR A busy **ring road**, part of the Egnatía Ódos highway, skirts Thessaloníki to the north, offering many exits to descend into the city.

GETTING AROUND

BY BIKE **Thessbike**, in the car park of the Mégaro Mousikís [58 D2] (25th Martíou & María Kállas; **m** 69780 08141; **w** thessbike.gr), runs the city's I-Bike sharing scheme. Subscribe at a rental station (see the website for a map and hours), pick up a card (€3) and key, then return the bike when you're done. **City-Bikes.gr** [68 F4] (Plátonos 1; ⎹ 23140 35128; **w** city-bikes.gr; ⏲ 09.00–21.00 Mon–Fri, 09.00–17.00 Sat) rents city, trekking, touring and folding bikes (from €8 for 4hrs/€14 a day/€60 per week) and runs 2½-hour bike tours of the city (€25 pp). **BikeIT** [65 E5] (Leof Megálou Alexándrou 2; ⎹ 23108 88920; **w** bikeitrentals.com; ⏲ 10.00–23.00 daily; rentals from €3 for 30mins), near the seafront bike path, in the Makedonia Palace, has the widest assortment of bikes to rent from 30 minutes to 4 hours, including four-wheeled four-seaters, wooden Coco-Mat bikes, tandems and e-bikes.

BY BOAT In summer, several companies, including **Karavákia waterbuses** (**m** 69737 77727; **w** karavakia.com) and **Poseidon Waterways** (**m** 69882 81541,

69882 85873; w poseidonwaterways.com), run boats departing from the port and the White Tower [64 D4] for the beaches and tavernas of Néoi Epivátes, Peraía and Ag Triáda, with fares costing €10 one-way, €16 return.

BY BUS The city has a good bus system (11085, 23109 81100; w oasth.gr). Single-ride fares are €0.90, two trips within 70 minutes are €1.10, three trips within 90 minutes are €1.30, and four trips within 2 hours are €1.80 (over 65s & under 18s pay half). Tickets can be purchased at ticket kiosks, some regular kiosks (*períptera*) and some convenience stores, or in the machines on the buses themselves, though they take only coins and give no change. Main stops have electronic signs, indicating wait times. While most sights are within walking distance in the centre, buses that may come in handy are numbers 10 or 11 from the train station, which cross town on the Egnatía; bus 22 from Plateía Aristotélous to the Áno Pólis; and buses 5 and 6 from Plateía Eleftherías, which follow the seafront to Néa Kríni, passing near the Archaeology Museum and the museums on Vasilissis Ólgas Street. The **Culture Bus** (bus 50; €2/€1) makes a circuit past the city's most important sights, starting at the White Tower and heading up to the Áno Pólis.

BY CAR The one-way system and local tendency to double-park everywhere can test your patience. If you do decide to drive, the biggest central car parks are in Plateía Eleftherías [68 C4], by the railway station [64 B1], and behind the Archaeology Museum [65 E4].

Car hire The following car hire companies have offices in the city centre (see page 63 for car rental at the airport).

City Car [65 F5] Doiránis 38; 23102 02029; w citycars.gr

Thessaloníki Rent a Car [64 B1] Monastiríou 28; 23105 27888; w thessalonikirentacar.gr. Will deliver to the airport or any hotel.

BY METRO First proposed by planner Ernest Hébrard in the early 1920s, the first metro line in traffic-clogged Thessaloníki at last opened at the end of November 2024. Extensions will gradually be added to reach the airport. Work began in 2006, but interesting archaeological discoveries – including a Byzantine-era market and a Roman cemetery – caused lengthy delays. The excavations at the Ágia Sofía stop along Egnatía are particularly interesting (page 87).

BY TAXI Since the COVID-19 pandemic, sharing a taxi is much less common – feel free to refuse if the driver proposes to pick someone else up along the way (which also confuses the calculation of the fare). If you can't find a taxi at a taxi stand or flag one down in the street, try **Radio Taxi Makedonia** (23105 55111, 23105 50500) or **Radio Taxi Mercedes** (23105 25777). Alternatively, book taxis online at **Taxithess** (m 69721 54399; w taxithess.gr), which has a price calculator and is good for reaching hotels outside the centre. You can also book a taxi via the Uber app. However you get a taxi, make sure the meter is on. All taxis by law must have a price list posted in plain sight, explaining surcharges for late-night rides, for the airport, for luggage, etc.

TOURIST INFORMATION AND TOUR OPERATORS

The **tourist information office** [69 D5] (23102 29070; w thessaloniki.travel; 09.00–15.00 Mon–Fri) is located centrally, on Plateía Aristotélous.

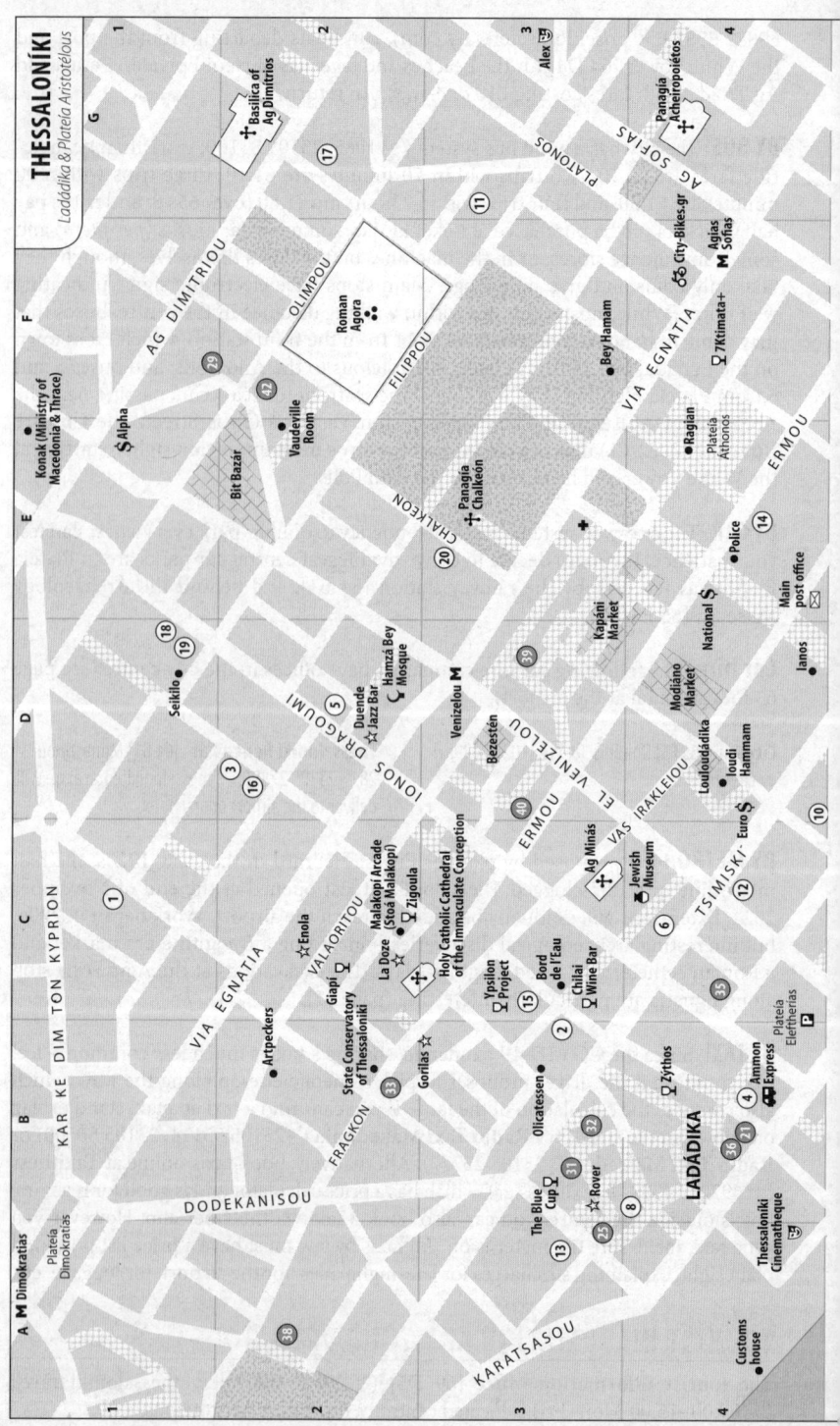

TOURIST INFORMATION AND TOUR OPERATORS

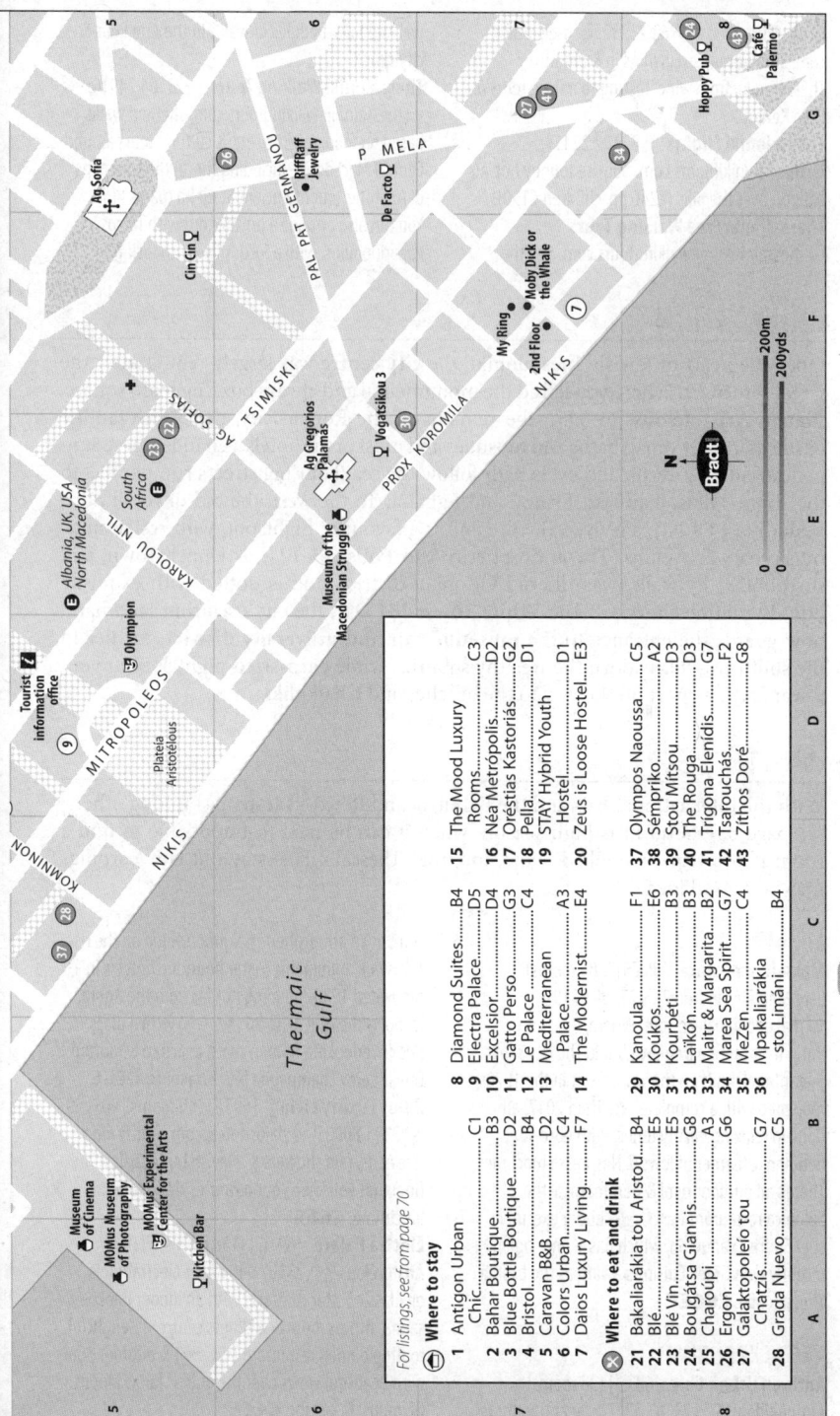

Grek.Addict m 69763 23232; w grekaddict.com. Small group excursions in & around Thessaloníki, from wine-tasting to nature tours on Lake Kerkíni.
Thessaloníki Flights 23102 22413; w thessalonikiflights.com. Sunrise tour by hot-air balloon over the hills (€240 pp, children €150).
Thessaloníki Free Walking Tours w thessalonikifreewalkingtours.com. See the website for schedules of walks in the Áno Pólis & city centre.
Thessaloníki Walking Tours 23104 24916; w thessalonikiwalkingtours.com. Themed walks based on food, *rebétiko*, etc, & cultural tours around Central Macedonia, including the 'In the Footsteps of Aristotle' tour of Ancient Stageira (page 115). You can also arrange a private tour with Tassos Papadopoulos, with a focus of your choosing.

ORIENTATION

Once the heart of Jewish Thessaloníki, the **city centre** was largely rebuilt after the Great Fire in 1917: here you'll find the monumental and always buzzing main square, **Plateía Aristotélous** [69 D3], the remains of the Roman city, the big Byzantine basilicas, the Ottoman baths and mosques and most of the hotels. A handsome 4.5km pedestrian boardwalk and cycle path follow the sea. Four big streets run parallel to the shore: Nikis, Tsimiski, Ermoú and Egnatía. To the west, the old olive oil port, **Ladádika** [68 B4], survived the fire and is a favourite nightspot, with restaurants, music bars and clubs. The atmospheric **Áno Pólis** [65 E1], or Upper Town, still surrounded by walls, was the old Ottoman district, and is dotted with exquisite little Byzantine churches. The **White Tower** [64 D4], the city's seafront landmark, now guards the entrance to the **museum, fair and university district**; further to the southeast villas adorn the wealthy suburbs, while barn-sized nightclubs are out towards the airport on the way to the beaches and Chalkidikí.

WHERE TO STAY

With the International Fair and the Dimítria and Reworks festivals (among others; see page 82), autumn is high season, when it can be next to impossible to find a room if you haven't booked. Note, too, that Thessalonians stay out late: earplugs may be a good idea.

LUXURY
Makedonia Palace [65 E5] (284 rooms) Leof Meg Aléxandrou 2; 23108 97197; w makedoniapalace.com. Where VIPs from Putin to Catherine Deneuve bunk. The city's first 5-star hotel, built on the waterfront in the 1970s, reopened with a complete facelift in 2017, all done in relaxing earthy tones, with Coco-Mat bedding & feather pillows & Nespresso machines. There's an outdoor pool & hammam, & the Salonica restaurant (€€€€€) under executive chef Sotíris Evangélou, which has – once again – recently won Greek Cuisine's award as the best in Thessaloníki. €€€€€

VERY EXPENSIVE
Antigon Urban Chic [68 C1] (38 rooms) Antigonidón 15; 23105 23573; w antigonhotel.com. In an atmospheric neighbourhood on the rise, this sleek, minimalist 5-star boutique hotel is in a renovated 1930s building not far from the Agora. It sports the cool A-Bistro (€€€€) with a glass floor overlooking Roman ruins, a jacuzzi & rooftop Duval-Leroy champagne bar. B/fast inc. €€€€
Daios Luxury Living [69 F7] (49 rooms) Níkis 59; 23111 80005; w daioshotels.com. Comfy king-size beds, rain showers & a lavish buffet b/fast (inc) that will keep your batteries charged until lunchtime. €€€€
Electra Palace [69 D5] (138 rooms) Plateía Aristotélous 9; 23102 94040; w electrahotels.gr. Classic 5-star comforts with an indoor pool, sauna, fitness room & wellness centre, a delightful rooftop garden restaurant (€€€€) & outdoor pool with beautiful views over the gulf as far as Mount Olympus. B/fast inc. €€€€

WHERE TO STAY

Excelsior [68 D4] (34 rooms) Kominón 10; ☎23100 21020; w excelsiorhotel.gr. Hotel from 1924, recently completely overhauled & featuring bright chic rooms with French balconies & all the mod cons, including Nespresso machines & customised minibars, award-winning fine Greek dining with a French twist (€€€) & b/fast buffet (inc) served on the roof garden. €€€€

Hyatt Regency [58 E3] (152 rooms) Km13 on the Thessaloníki–airport road; ☎23104 01234; w thessaloniki.regency.hyatt.com. By the airport, plush 5-star hotel rooms with marble baths, with a lovely outdoor pool the size of a small lake, fitness centre & Ambrosia restaurant (€€€€€) serving superb Greek & Mediterranean dishes under chef Apostólos Altánis. €€€€

Lazart [58 D1] (74 rooms) Kolokotróni 16, Stavroúpoli; ☎23160 15000; w lazarthotel.com. Colourful 5-star choice near the State Museum of Contemporary Art & the outdoor concert venue Moni Lazariston, 10mins north of centre, with a range of spacious rooms, including family suites. There's an outdoor pool, gym, spa with a full range of treatments, free parking & a charging station for electric cars. B/fast inc. €€€€

The Met [64 A2] (212 rooms) 26is Oktovríou 48; ☎23100 17000; w themethotel.gr. Near the new port, this flash design hotel sprinkled with contemporary art boasts a 22m rooftop pool with mighty views, spa & rejuvenation centre, & a bar with a gold-plated wall. Minimalist rooms in white, black & charcoal come with Coco-Mat beds & pillows, complimentary T1 smartphones & even amenities for your pooch. Designer restaurant Chan (evenings only; €€€€) has a modern Greek & Asian menu. Free shuttle bus to Plateía Aristotélous & free parking if you book via their website. €€€€–€€€

EXPENSIVE

Bristol [68 B4] (16 rooms) Cnr Katoúni & Oplopioú 2; ☎23105 06500; w bristol.gr. Located in the former Ottoman post office in Ladádika, this is a romantic little hotel with plush cotton sheets on queen-size beds & handwoven carpets on sturdy wooden floors. Rooms are equipped with Nespresso machines, tea kettles & minibars. €€€

Mediterranean Palace [68 A3] (118 rooms) Salamínos 3; ☎23112 40200; w mediterranean-palace.gr. This luxurious hotel with classic décor is located across from the ferry terminal & right next to lively Ladadika. It's a particularly family-friendly choice, with a children's library, board games, family rooms, cots & children's menus. €€€

The Modernist [68 E4] (40 rooms) Ermoú 32; ☎23160 09990; w themodernist.gr. In a 1920s building near the Modiáno Market, the city's sleekest minimalist Danish-inspired design hotel opened in 2018. Its high-ceilinged rooms are sized from small to extra large (there's a family room too) & come with comfy beds with cotton linens, Marshall speakers, Nespresso machines & custom furniture; there's a roof garden for b/fast & cocktails. €€€

Bahar Boutique Hotel [68 B3] (16 rooms) Edéssis 10, in Áno Ladádika; ☎23105 53433; w baharboutiquehotel.com. 'Bahar' means 'spring' in Turkish, & this family-run hotel in an 80-year-old shop in the hip Valaorítou district, 500m from Plateía Aristotélous, has vintage design details plus 3-layer Coco-Mat beds. €€€–€€

Golden Star City Resort [58 D4] (44 rooms) P Kountouriótou 73, Peraía; ☎23920 22755; w goldenstarhotel.com. Take bus 78 to the IKEA stop, then change to the 72 for the Peraía Paralía to sleep opposite a sandy beach in a Coco-Mat bed, with excellent 4-star amenities (including mini fridges with freezers), plus free umbrellas, sunbeds, & parking 40m away. They also have bikes to rent for adults & kids, & a restaurant (€€€) on the beach. Greek b/fast inc. €€€–€€

The Mood Luxury Rooms [68 C3] (18 rooms) Katoúni 31; ☎23105 55088; w themoodthessaloniki.gr. Classy rooms & 3 suites done up in black, white & greys in a historic building in Ladádika, with minibars, espresso machines & a wine bar. B/fast €10. €€€–€€

MODERATE

Akti Retzika [58 D4] (18 studios/apartments, 6 bungalows, 3 furnished tents) Epanomí; ☎23920 44786; w retzikas.gr. Lovely beachside studios & apartments with balconies & kitchenettes, as well as bungalows & furnished tents for a glamping experience. €€

Blue Bottle Boutique Hotel [68 D2] (20 rooms) Episkopou Amvrosiou 16; ☎23105 20090; w bluebottlehotel.gr. Stylish contemporary rooms in a fresh palette, on a quiet street close to the lively nightlife scene around Valaorítou St. Organic b/fast (inc with some bookings). €€

Caravan B&B [68 D2] (13 rooms) Cnr Rebélou & Vabaká; ☎23130 62780; w thecaravan.gr. Fun, informal hotel opened in 2016, run by a young team in a listed Neoclassical building of 1929 near the Hamza Bei Mosque. Bright high-ceilinged rooms, good for families (there are plenty of toys) & café bar. Parking €14; Greek b/fast €9. €€

Colors Urban Hotel [68 C4] (26 rooms) Tsimiskí 13; \23102 72829; w colorshotel.gr. True to its name, this hotel has bright colours, king-size beds with a pillow menu, sat TVs & a spa with 16 massage treatments, & a garden bar, where the buffet b/fast (extra charge) is served. Child & pet friendly. €€

Diamond Suites [68 B4] (7 rooms) Dóxis 8; \23103 85846; w diamondsuites.gr. Colourful design rooms with really big windows & king-size beds in Ladádika, with an espresso wine bar & b/fast served in your room (€10). Parking in walking distance (€10). €€

Gatto Perso [68 G3] (17 rooms) Mitsaíon 10; \23102 21445; w gattoperso.gr. In a 1926 building near the Roman Agora, the 'Lost Cat' was restored with 1930s vintage charm & kitchenettes; options vary from studios to 1-bedroom apartments. Parking can be arranged in walking distance. €€

Le Palace Hotel [68 C4] (53 rooms) Tsimiskí 12; \23102 57400; w lepalace.gr. Palace might be a bit of an overstatement, but this family-friendly hotel of character from the 1930s has Coco-Mat beds & 6 pillow choices. They have agreements with private car parks 500m away. Tasty Greek b/fast inc. €€

Panórama [58 F2] (50 rooms) Analípseos 26, Panórama, 11km east of Thessaloníki; \23103 44871; w hotelpanorama.gr. Comfortable, stylish rooms & restaurant terrace on top of Panórama (€€€) with a fabulous view over the entire city & sunset (bus 58 from Plateía Dikastiríon). Greek b/fast inc. €€

BUDGET

Crossroads Thessaloníki [65 F2] (3 rooms – 12 beds total) Athanasiou Diakou 1; \23102 03700; m 69703 82250; w crossroadsthess.gr. Eco-friendly, convivial bunk rooms with shared baths near the Byzantine walls & a balcony with a panoramic view. B/fast €6.50. €

Néa Metrópolis [68 D2] (35 rooms) Sygróu 22; \23105 30363; w neametropolis.gr. Just off the Egnatía, a reliable choice in an older building; basic en-suite rooms, with AC & fridge. Continental b/fast €5. €

Oréstias Kastoriás [68 G2] (37 rooms) Agnóstou Stratiótou 14; \23102 76517; w okhotel.gr. Pleasant, functional & (relatively) quiet choice with AC off Olympiádos St, by the Roman Agora. €

Pella [68 D1] (79 rooms) Íonos Dragoúmi 65; \23105 24221; w pella-hotel.gr. In the heart of the city, pleasant hotel from the 1960s, now spruced up with Coco-Mat beds, AC & Wi-Fi; parking nearby for €14/day. Under 10s stay for free. €

STAY Hybrid Youth Hostel [68 D1] (70 rooms) Íonos Dragoúmi 61; \23112 44600; w thestay.gr. Run by a team of music lovers & travellers, this hostel with a street mural on the outside is 2 blocks west of the Roman Agora; inside there's a mix of en-suite sgl, dbl & trpl rooms, dorms (with up to 8 beds, lockers & female-only shared bathrooms on each floor) & even 3-bedroom apartments; plus a rooftop terrace & sunbeds, cheap garage parking. Buffet b/fast & meals available. €

Zeus is Loose Hostel [68 D1] (90 beds total – 15 dbl rooms, 15 dorm rooms) Klisoúras 13 at Chalkéon St; \23111 18713; w zeusisloose.com. Floor-to-ceiling windows overlooking the large central park above Aristotle Sq & a sociable rooftop bar with great views make this an appealing budget choice in the centre of town. There's a mix of en-suite dbl rooms (with dbl beds, twin beds or bunk beds) & dorms (mixed or female-only), with 4–6 beds each with lockers, curtains & individual lights. There's a bathroom in each room plus a bathroom on each floor. €

WHERE TO EAT AND DRINK

Thessaloníki is the gastronomic capital of Greece. If you need just a snack, pick up a *kouloúri* (a crunchy, sesame-covered bread ring that has been popular since the Byzantine era) from a street vendor. Or try one of Thessaloníki's many *mezedopoleíos* (page 75), where lighter dishes or Greek-style tapas are served alongside local wines, ouzo, *tsípouro*, etc until late. The city claims to have more cafés and bars per person than any other in Greece, and it's hard to argue. In 1957 during the International Fair it even saw the invention of that Greek summer essential, the *frappé*, when an employee of Nestlé, Dimítri Vakondíos, couldn't find any hot water for his usual instant coffee break, so put his coffee in the chocolate milk shaker the company had on exhibit, and hey presto!

Many restaurants close in August, so always ring ahead then.

RESTAURANTS
Top end
Alfredo's Grand Dining [58 E3] Regency Casino, 12km on the Thessaloníki–airport road; ☏ 23104 91234; w thessaloniki.regencycasinos.gr; ⊕ 21.00–02.00 Wed–Sun. Perfect spot for celebrating a big win at the roulette tables or any other special occasion. Executive chef Apóstolos Altánis has won every award going for running the best restaurant in town, famous for such dishes as salmon Waldorf & seafood ravioli with a lobster & beurre blanc sauce, with a wine list to match. €€€€€

Olympos Naoussa [68 C5] Leoforos Nikis 5; ☏ 23102 75715; w olymposnaoussa.gr; ⊕ 13.00–23.00 daily. Olympos Naoussa was Thessaloniki's most celebrated restaurant for generations. After a 3-decade hiatus, it's back, with award-winning chef Dimitris Tasioulas' creative & classic cuisine, sometimes including *hünkâr beğendi* – tender beef in a tomato sauce served over a smoky aubergine purée – the restaurant's historic signature dish. €€€€€

Very expensive
Akti Ntovil [58 D2] Themistoclí Sofoúli 86, Kalamariá; ☏ 23104 07000; w aktintovil.gr; ⊕ noon–midnight daily. Waves nearly lap the tables at this superb new favourite in the chic Kalamariá district. A large menu of elegant fresh seafood dishes & beautiful views of the city. (The restaurant's name is the Latin transliteration of the Greek transliteration of Deauville beach, which is adjacent.) €€€€

Grada Nuevo [69 C5] Kalapothaki 14; ☏ 23102 71074; ⊕ 13.00–23.00 daily. Fine dining for lovers of pristine seafood – an oyster bar, 2 caviars, fish tartares & carpaccios, & inventive, skillfully cooked dishes. €€€€

Marea Sea Spirit [69 G7] Margariti Lori 13; ☏ 23102 57696; w mareaseaspirit.gr; ⊕ noon–midnight daily. A superb menu of elegant, classic fresh seafood dishes plus marinated & smoked fish preparations, a variety of oysters,

& a good selection of Greek & international wines. €€€€

Mávri Thálassa [58 D3] Nik Plastíra 3, Kalamariá; ☏ 23109 32542; w mavri-thalassa.gr; ⊕ noon–23.00 daily. The city's top seafood palace, with 112 seafood dishes to choose from (their fish in lemon sauce is famous) & a list of more than 200 wines. €€€€

Miaïmi [58 E3] Thétidos 18, Kalamariá; ☏ 23104 47996; w maiamirestaurant.gr; ⊕ noon–midnight daily. Opened in 1945 & still going strong, with tables under a huge awning next to the sea; wonderful fresh fish & excellent wines. €€€€

Expensive
Charoúpi [68 A3] Dóxis 4; ☏ 23105 26262; m 69885 26262; ⊕ 13.00–01.00 daily. On the edge of Ladádika, a contemporary restaurant featuring superb Cretan cuisine made with ingredients such as *stamnágathi* (spiny chicory) brought up especially from the big island along with the finest Cretan wines. €€€

Mare e Monti [58 F2] Venizélou 13, Panórama; ☏ 23103 43344; w mare-e-monti.gr; ⊕ 19.30–01.00 Tue–Sat, 13.00–18.00 Sun. The city's best Italian restaurant left the seaside for the hills, but the locals still drive up for its superb range of antipasti & pasta dishes, & pizzas cooked in a proper pizza oven. €€€

Opsopoión Maganeíai [58 E2] Komotinís 6; ☏ 23108 89699; w maganie.gr; ⊕ 14.00–01.30 Tue–Sat. Near the Mégaro Mousikís, small restaurant famous for perfect Mediterranean cuisine, including lovely homemade gnocchi in parmesan cream & superbly tender beef, in a laid-back jazzy atmosphere. Book a couple of days in advance. €€€

Sémpriko [68 A2] Frágkon 2; ☏ 23105 57513; ⊕ noon–23.00 daily. Near the courthouse & Byzantine walls, the 'Co-operative' has been a top address ever since it opened in 2012, renowned for its exceptional food (it's also a gourmet grocery

store). Try their famous melt-in-your-mouth *chilópites* pasta with *kavoúrma* (pork confits), mushroom risotto & *spalobrizóla* (rib steak) & a wide selection of Greek cheeses. Booking essential. €€€
Zíthos Doré [69 G8] Tsirogiánni 7; ☏ 23102 79010; w zithos.gr; ⊕ 10.00–02.00 daily. Same owners as Zíthos (page 76) & similar retro style occupying the former premises of the famous café Doré overlooking the White Tower. Excellent dishes with an Anatolian touch; good veggie choices. €€€

Moderate

Gialós [58 D2] Kalamariá Marina; ☏ 23104 42121; ⊕ 12.30–midnight daily. A lovely setting in the marina & a classic seafood taverna menu – steamed mussels, grilled sardines, fried red mullet – make this a popular choice with locals. €€€–€€
Bakaliarákia tou Aristou [68 B4] Katouni 3; ☏ 23105 42906; w mpakaliarakia-aristou.gr; ⊕ 10.00–18.30 daily. Crisp, batter-fried salt cod, a mound of fried potatoes, garlicky *skordaliá* & a fried hot pepper, served on a sheet of paper & enjoyed preferably with a bottle of chilled retsina, is a Thessaloníki classic. €€
Blé Vin [69 E5] Georgíou Stavroú 14 at Ag Sofías; ☏ 23102 31201; ⊕ 17.00–midnight daily. At the intersection of 2 lively pedestrian streets in the heart of downtown, Blé Vin is a wine-forward delight, with intelligent, creative plates featuring locally sourced artisanal products & a great list of Greek & international wines, available in pours of both 60ml & 125ml. €€
Ergon [69 G6] Pávlou Melá 42; ☏ 23102 88008; w ergonfoods.com; ⊕ 09.00–01.00 daily. Massive shop of Greek delicacies, plus a restaurant serving them up for b/fast, brunch, lunch & dinner. €€
Inglis [65 E2] Irodótou 32; ☏ 23103 11367; ⊕ noon–23.30 daily. This informal vine-draped taverna in the Áno Pólis first opened its doors in 1914. Now run by an enthusiastic team, it serves great local specialities – melt-in-the-mouth pork shank & *hunkár begendí* (braised lamb with smoked puréed aubergine). €€
Maitr & Margarita [68 B2] Vérias 2, off Frágkon; ☏ 23140 07586; ⊕ 14.00–01.00 daily. Fun bistro in a former commercial building with unusual dishes, including pasta with Cretan smoked pork (*apáki*),

an extra special version of the classic Greek salad & unusual cheeses from around Greece. Arrive when it opens to avoid the queue. €€
Mpakaliarákia sto Limáni [68 B4] Fasianoú 2; ☏ 23105 12600; f mpakaliarakiastolimani; ⊕ 10.00–18.30 daily, but best before 15.00 or 16.00. The exact same classic menu as its neighbour Bakaliarákia tou Aristou (see left). Sit at whichever one has a table. €€
Néa Foliá [65 E2] Aristoménous 4; ☏ 23109 60383; f Η Νέα Φωλιά; ⊕ 14.00–midnight daily, closed summer. Just off Ag Sofías, a charming little restaurant that's been going strong since 1967, serving lip-smacking hearty, homestyle yet inventive specialities based on the best of the season. Excellent wines by the carafe. €€
The Rouga [68 D3] Karípi 28; ☏ 23102 41727; f rouga1999; ⊕ 13.00–01.00 daily. Filled with antiques, old photos & old-fashioned charm; famous for seafood & the best moussaka in town. Book (especially) for Sat night. €€

Inexpensive

Kánoula [68 F1] Raktiván 8; ☏ 23102 22185; w kanoula.gr; ⊕ 13.00–midnight daily. Behind the Ministry of Eastern Macedonia & Thráki, tiny old-fashioned taverna with exceptionally good food at kind prices: don't miss the stuffed mushrooms. Organic wines by the carafe. €
Kourbéti [68 B3] Cnr Vaíou 2 & Lykoúrgo; ☏ 23105 20631; f Το Κουρμπέτι; ⊕ 11.00–04.00 Sun–Fri, 11.00–06.00 Sat. Small, lively, Ladádika taverna that draws a fun crowd, with tasty home-cooked dishes (very tender chicken & pork) & often live *rebétiko*. €
Laïkón [68 B3] Polytechníou 24; ☏ 23105 23433; ⊕ noon–04.00 daily. Old-fashioned, beloved *souvláki* joint in Ladádika, a night-owl favourite. €
MeZen [68 C4] Rogkóti 3; ☏ 23102 32749; w mezen.gr; ⊕ noon–23.30 daily. A little bit of Vólos: a *tsipourádiko* with a huge choice of spirits to go with your nibbles. Order from the menu or the traditional way, in which each glass of *tsípouro* comes with a generously sized, generally fish-forward meze for a progressive meal full of tasty surprises. €
Stou Mítsou [68 D3] Vláli 11, Kapáni market; ☏ 23155 15504; ⊕ 10.00–midnight Mon–Sat. Tiny, charming *kafeneíon* serving meze of seasonal ingredients sourced from the market & their own bread from a wood oven. €

Ticho Ticho [65 E1] Stergíou Polidórou 1; 23102 45351; 09.00–01.00 daily. Delightful *mezedopoleíon* with a large terrace in the Áno Póli, with views of the city walls & great meze. €

Tsarouchás [68 F2] Olýmpou 78; 23102 71621; 24/7. One of Thessaloníki's last traditional *patsatzidíko* taverns, specialising in *patsás*, tripe & veal trotter soup – the classic stomach-coating hangover cure (they do other dishes too). Busiest in the wee hours. €

Tsinari [64 D1] A Papadopoúlou 72; 23102 84028; 13.00–midnight daily. A delightful & extremely photogenic old school *mezedepoleíon* from 1885 in the heart of the Áno Pólis. €

PASTRY SHOPS

Blé [69 E5] Ag Sofías 19; 23102 31200; w bletastegallery.com; 08.00–midnight daily. High-design bakery made of volcanic stone, with a remarkable 12m wood oven – the tallest in the world. Lovely breads, cakes, chocolates, all-natural ice creams, French & Italian sweets, & coffees.

Bougátsa Bantis [64 C1] Panagías Fanoroménis 33; 23105 10355; 06.30–15.00 Mon–Sat, 06.30–13.00 Sun. Destination-worthy *bougátsa*, with a variety of top-quality fresh fillings in delicate hand-stretched phyllo by 2nd-generation *bougátsa* master Philippos Bantis.

Bougátsa Gíannis [69 G8] Mitropóleos 106; 23102 57375; bougatsa_giannis;

20.00–15.00 daily. For late-night munchies: the city's favourite all-night *bougátsa* shop. 'Créma' with a heap of Merenda (Greek Nutella) & minced meat with a heap of Greek yogurt are among the favourites.

Galaktopoleío tou Chatzís [69 G7] Pavlou Melá 16 at Tsimiskí; 23102 84620; 08.00–23.45 Sun–Thu, 08.00–00.45 Fri & Sat. The latest generation of the Chatzís family has a shining new shop & treasured old recipes. Chatzís has been an institution since 1908, specialising in *Politiká glyká* ('Constantinople-style' sweets). They maintain a herd of buffalo for their rich kaymak (thick cream), & they're also the last place in the city that makes *bóza*, a soft drink made from fermented millet that was all the rage in centuries past.

Koúkos [69 E6] Vogatsikoú 10; 23102 42403; 07.00–22.00 Mon–Sat, 08.00–21.00 Sun. A classic since 1953, serving great coffee, pastries & superb savoury pies.

Trígona Elenídis [69 G7] Goúnari 13 near Tsimiskí; 23102 57510; w elenidis.com; 09.00–20.00 Wed–Mon, from 10.00 Sun. In 1944, Agapitos Valogiórgis invented what has become *the* pastry of the city, the *trígona Panóramatos*, a flaky triangular pastry filled with fragrant custard with a hint of syrup. This place, founded in 1960, is famous for them; there's also a branch on Iktínou 1 in the centre & at Kominión 69 in Panórama.

ENTERTAINMENT AND NIGHTLIFE

Thessaloníki is proud to be a town that never sleeps, thanks in part to Greece's largest student population. Nightlife hubs include Ladádika and Valaorítou, the medieval district inhabited by Venetian and Genoese merchants, and more recently by tailors and seamstresses, the student-filled Plateía Navarínou by the Rotonda and the two central pedestrian streets, Iktínou and Zéfxidos.

This city loves films, and many cinemas play English-language films with subtitles; open-air cinemas are good fun in the summer – films are screened in their original language with Greek subtitles.

For details of Thessaloníki's annual festivals, see page 82.

BARS, CAFÉS, OUZERÍS AND MEZEDOPOLEÍOS

7Ktimata+ [68 F4] Kastritsíou 5, near Plateía Áthonos; 23102 87750; 7ktimata; 13.00–01.00 Mon–Sat. A deliciously cosy place to try 42 of Macedonia's finest wines from 7 small but excellent estates (*ktímata* in Greek), with platters of cheese & cured meats, accompanied by mellow jazz.

The Blue Cup [68 B3] Salamínos 8; 23109 00666; w thebluecup.gr; 08.30–03.00 Mon–Thu, 08.30–05.00 Fri–Sat, 10.00–03.00 Sun. In Ladádika, serving the best coffee in town, as well as fancy herbal teas, sandwiches & excellent cocktails through the night.

Café Palermo [64 D4] Filikís Etaireías 3; 23102 79958; 10.00–02.00 daily. Charming Art Deco-

style hideaway, filled with antiques & soft jazz, & serving proper Italian espressos.
Chilai Wine Bar [68 C3] Ag Miná 4; ☎ 23130 54550; f; ⏰ 08.00–02.00 Mon–Sat, 08.00–midnight Sun. Beautiful designer wine bar in Ladádika.
Cin Cin [69 F5] Iktínou 22; ☎ 23102 23350; f; ⏰ 10.00–02.30 daily. Cool décor with a touch of camp & a big terrace, for superb cocktails, delicious snacks & French-style desserts.
De Facto [69 G6] P Melá 19; ☎ 23102 63674; ⏰ 08.30–03.00 Mon–Sat, 08.30–midnight Sun. A classic café-bar with vintage décor.
Giapí [68 C2] Katholikón 1; ☎ 23105 39603; f giapibar; ⏰ 20.00–02.00 Tue–Sat. A favourite for its good DJs playing anything from experimental electronica to 60s garage & occasional live sets. A perfect stop while checking out the Valaorítou district.
Hoppy Pub [69 G8] Nikifórou Foká 6, inland from the White Tower; ☎ 23102 69203; f; ⏰ 17.30–01.30 Tue–Sat. A very friendly must for beer lovers, featuring an enormous selection of craft beers.
Kitchen Bar [69 A5] Pier A; ☎ 23105 02241; f; ⏰ 09.00–02.00 Wed–Sun, 09.00–midnight Mon–Tue. Popular hangout with fantastic views & seating on the water's edge in a former industrial building. Good b/fast & cocktails, including many original ones, nibbles & desserts.
Skyline Bar [65 E4] Egnatía 154, on top of the OTE tower; ☎ 23102 65460; w skyline. bar; ⏰ 10.00–01.00 Sun–Thu, 10.00–02.00 Fri & Sat. The easy way to see the city, this recently renovated bar 76m up on top of the telecommunications tower makes a complete rotation every hour from 19.00 to midnight.
Utopia Taproom [64 C1] Gladtonos 11; f Utopia-Taproom-est-2023; ⏰ 17.00–01.00 Sun–Thu, 17.00–02.00 Fri & Sat. Greek craft beers plus negronis on tap, on a square in one of the most interesting neighbourhoods of the moment.
Vogatsikou 3 [69 E6] Vogatsikoú 3 (just off Níkis); ☎ 23102 22899; f; ⏰ 09.00–03.00 daily. Elegant bar with great staff, & great drinks from a huge selection of bottles. One of the best.
Ypsilon Project [68 C3] Edéssis 5; ☎ 23105 30480; f; ⏰ 09.00–02.00 Mon–Fri, 09.00–03.00 Sat–Sun. Hip bar & art space combo.
Zíthos [68 B4] Katoúni 5; ☎ 23105 40284; w zithos.gr; ⏰ 10.00–02.00 daily. The oldest restaurant in Ladádika, with lovely high ceilings, a great selection wines & craft beers & delicious meze.

CLUBS AND MUSIC BARS
Déntro Sto Bar [65 E5] Leof Vas Georgíou 25; ☎ 23108 11885; ⌨ dentrostobar; ⏰ 08.00–05.00 Mon–Sat, 08.00–midnight Sun. Near the Makedonia Palace hotel, with a pretty garden terrace & retro bar within.
Duende Jazz Bar [68 D2] Dimarchou Vamvaka 5-3 at Elefthérios Venizélos 45; m 69426 15002; f; ⏰ 1 or 2 shows per week, check Facebook for programme. Near Plateía Aristotélous, elegant bar with cool live jazz & blues.
Gorilas [68 B3] Verías 3; ☎ 23130 86274; f Γορίλας; ⏰ 09.00–03.00 Tue–Thu, Sun, 09.00–04.00 Fri–Sat. Great cocktails & great music; one of the liveliest bars in the city.
La Doze [68 C2] Vilará 1; ☎ 23105 32986; ⏰ 19.00–05.00 daily. Dark arty bar famous for its long list of delicious margaritas; different DJs every night. Gallery upstairs.
Prigipessa [64 D4] Filikís Etairías 5, near the White Tower; ☎ 23102 73542; w prigipessa.gr; ⏰ check website for programme & hours. Best place to hear live *rebétiko*.
Principal Club Theater [64 A1] Mylos complex, Andréou Georgíou 56 ; ☎ 23104 28088; w principalclub.com. Live venue at the west end (bus 31, stop Ichthyoskala), where Morrissey, Thievery Corporation & Motorhead have played; featuring every kind of music from electronica to rockabilly.
Rover [68 B3] Salamínos 6, Ladádika; ☎ 23105 44304; ⏰ 10.15–04.00 Sun–Fri, 10.15–06.00 Sat. Hopping bar with live bands from around the world & tasty cocktails at €9 a piece.

CINEMAS
Thessaloníki Cinematheque [68 A4] Pier A; ☎ 23105 08598; w filmfestival.gr. Shows films in original language, at the museum (page 84), at the 2 screens in Olympion [69 D5] (Plateía Aristotélous 10) & at the 2 cinemas in Warehouse 1 (see website for schedules).

Open-air cinemas
Alex [68 G3] Olýmpou 106; ☎ 23102 69403; f CINE ALEX
Apollon [65 E5] Sarantapórou 4; ☎ 23108 28642; f Apollon Open Air Cinema

SHOPPING

Ellenis 1 & 2 [65 E4] Leof Stratoú, by the Archaeological Museum; ☎23102 92304; ⓕ cinellinis

Natalie [65 E5] Meg Alexándrou 3; ☎23108 29457; ⓕ Natali Cinema

CONCERT, DANCE AND THEATRE VENUES

Mégaro Mousikís [58 D2] 25 Martíou & Megálou Alexándrou; ☎23108 95800; w tch. gr. Inaugurated in 2000, by the sea, this is Thessaloníki's main performance venue, divided into 2 buildings: M1, a 9-storey hall with a 1,400-seat auditorium; & M2, with smaller venues designed by Arata Isozaki, where films are shown on the rooftop in summer.

National Theatre of Northern Greece [65 E4] Ethnikís Amýnis 2; ☎23152 00000; w ntng.gr. The biggest cultural organisation in Greece, presenting drama, dance & opera in several indoor & outdoor theatres in the city & in even the smallest villages across the region.

Théatro Dássous (Forest Theatre) [65 F2] Seich Sou Forest; ☎23152 00200; w ntng.gr. Another outdoor theatre of the National Theatre of Northern Greece, with a capacity of over 3,800, located in a beautiful forest setting above the city, easily reached by public transportation.

Théatro Gis (Theatre of the Earth) [65 F4] Triandría; ☎23152 00200; w ntgn.gr. One of the outdoor performance spaces of the National Theatre of Northern Greece, with a capacity of over 4,300. Located above the city.

LGBTQIA+ THESSALONÍKI Thessaloníki is one of the most welcoming & tolerant cities in Greece, hosting its own Pride parade since 2011 & the host city of EuroPride in 2024. Most bars are gay-friendly, especially:

Enola [68 C2] Valaorítou 19; m 69365 63656; ⏱ 23.30–05.00 daily. Thessaloníki's most popular gay bar, with cocktails & dancing.

Zigkouala [69 C2] Siggroú 9 (Malakopí Arcade); m 69823 67904; ⓕ zigkoualathebar; ⏱ 19.00–03.00 Tue–Thu, 19.00–05.00 Fri & Sat. Friendly, cosy spot in the heart of the Valaorítou district with great music & cocktails. Pet-friendly.

SHOPPING

Designer clothing and boutiques are clustered on Mitropóleos, Tsimiskí, Venizélou, Ag Sofías, Ermoú, and Egnatía streets. The Valaorítou area is the place to look for up-and-coming designers and unusual shops, especially along Verías Street. For food, start at the **markets**: Modiáno [68 D3], Kapáni [68 D4], and Plateía Áthonos [68 E4] with its little markets selling delicacies to take home, as well as wicker and woodwork.

BOOKS

Ianos [68 D4] Platéia Aristotélous 7; ☎23102 77004; w ianos.gr; ⏱ 09.00–21.00 Mon–Fri, 09.00–20.00 Sat. The city's biggest bookshop, with books in English & a huge selection of maps & music.

Mitakos Books [65 E4] Eth Amýnis 28; ☎23123 15707; ⏱ 09.00–17.00 Mon & Wed, 09.00–15.00 & 17.00–20.00 Tue, Thu & Fri, 10.00–15.00 Sat. Books for students of English, but lots of others too.

DESIGN, ACCESSORIES, ARTS AND CRAFTS

2nd Floor [69 F7] Proxénou Koromilá 50; ☎23102 66931; w 2ndfloor.gr. Cool architecture & design products in Thessaloníki's most exclusive shopping district.

Artpeckers [68 B2] Valaorítou 12; ☎23104 39276; w artpeckers.com; ⏱ 10.00–18.00 Mon & Wed, 10.00–19.00 Tue, Thu & Fri, 10.00–15.00 Sat. Award-winning homeware, bags & accessories, inspired by Greek mythology. Made in local workshops from Greek materials.

Seikilo [68 D1] Filíppou 5; ☎23160 19635; w seikilo.com; ⏱ book in advance for tours, which take place at 11.00 & 16.00 Mon–Fri & 11.00 Sat. Superb introduction to the world of ancient Greek music from a family that specialises in handcrafted reproductions of ancient Greek musical instruments & board games. They also offer workshops & seminars.

3 | THESSALONÍKI (ΘΕΣΣΑΛΟΝΙΚΗ)

FOOD
Moby Dick or the Whale [69 G7] Morgentaou 5; 23102 53781; w mobydick.wine; ⏰ 10.00–14.00 & 17.00–21.00 Mon–Sat. A serene shop specialising in natural, biodynamic & low-intervention wines, including selections from many Greek producers.

Olicatessen [68 B3] Viktor Hugo 4; 23130 30286; w olicatessen.gr. Superb delicatessen in the centre of Ladádika, specialising in artisan olive oils & other products from across Greece, as well as housewares & natural cosmetics. They also offer seminars & tastings, of olive oil, cheese & wine, vegan produce, soap-making & more.

Ragian [68 E4] Balanoú 13 (Plateía Áthonos); 23150 03907; w ragian.gr. Branch of the Pontic cheese, yogurt & delicacy-maker of Váthi (page 160).

CLOTHING AND JEWELLERY
Bord de l'Eau [68 C3] Edessis 5; 23105 20911; w bdl.gr. Inside the bar of the same name, the studio of 3rd-generation jeweller Yánnis Gounarídis, who creates contemporary designs with wood, metals & turquoise.

Jezebel [64 C1] Paparrigopoúlou 21 A (near the church of the 12 Apostles); 23105 43557; w elenk.gr; ⏰ 10.30–15.00 Mon–Sat & 17.30–20.30 Tue, Thu & Fri. Very chic, intelligent, minimalist clothing. Designer Eleni Kíki makes each piece herself by hand. Affordably priced, travel-friendly pieces.

My Ring [69 F7] Chrysostómou Smýrnis 9; 23130 15805; w myringdesign.gr. Playful, colourful pieces in plexiglass, created by a graphic designer.

RiffRaff Jewelry [69 G6] Pavlou Melá 29; 23102 41238. A charming shop featuring the works of several independent designers. Lovely charms, & innovative window displays.

VINTAGE
Oldd Fashion [65 E3] Meleníkou 5; m 69752 09572; f. Expertly curated vintage street fashion, especially strong in '70s through '90s looks. Very friendly shopping experience.

Vaudeville Room [68 E2] Gkarmbolá 3; 23140 19045; ⏰ 11.00–17.00 Tue–Fri, 11.00–16.00 Sat. Beautiful pieces with a focus on the '30s through the '60s.

SPORTS AND ACTIVITIES

Recently opened in the HELEXPO Fair Grounds is the **WE** [65 F4] (cnr Leofóros 3 Septemvríou & Lampráki Grigoríou; 23102 84700; w weskg.gr; ⏰ 09.00–23.00 daily) recreational centre. It has a roller-skating rink, climbing wall and circus equipment.

OTHER PRACTICALITIES

BANKS
Alpha Bank [68 E1] Ag Dimitríou 66; 23102 86646

Eurobank [68 D4] Tsimiskí 27; 23103 74200

National Bank [68 E4] Plateía Aristotélous 6; 23102 50216

HOSPITALS
AHEPA (University General Hospital) [65 F4] Kyriadíki 1; 23133 03110; w ahepahosp.gr

Hospital Ag Dimítrios [65 F2] Eléni Zográphou 2; 23133 22100; w oagiosdimitrios.gr

Ippokrateio [65 F6] Konstantinoupóleos 49; 23133 12000; w ippokratio.gr. With specialist maternity/paediatric units.

PHARMACIES
Thessaloníki has many pharmacies, & there will always be some on duty, at any time of the day or night, including holidays & w/ends. To find a pharmacy on duty, look for an illuminated green cross, which indicates the pharmacy is open. Otherwise, check the list posted in the window of any pharmacy (even if closed), or consult w xo.gr/pharmacies-on-duty/thessaloniki.

Deligiorgis [69 F5] Ag Sofías 23; 23102 60163; ⏰ 08.30–21.00 Mon–Fri, 09.00–17.00 Sat

Pharmacy128 [65 E2] Ag Dimitríou 128; 23111 17000; ⏰ 08.00–21.00 Mon–Fri, 08.00–20.00 Sat

Tsakíroglou [68 E3] Egnatía 72; 23102 36468; ⏰ 08.00–21.00 Mon–Fri, 08.00–17.00 Sat

WHAT TO SEE AND DO

POLICE
Police station [68 E4] Aristotélous 18; \23102 53341

POST OFFICE
Main post office [68 E4] Vasiléos Irakleíou 38; \23102 77434; ⊕ 07.30–14.45 Mon–Fri

WHAT TO SEE AND DO
CITY CENTRE
Plateía Aristotélous [69 D5] Stretching back seven streets from the waterfront to the base of the Áno Pólis, Thessaloníki's main square is where the city parties and protests. It was laid out by Ernest Hébrard in 1918, after the Great Fire, as part of his plan to give the previously higgledy-piggledy Ottoman city a Parisian-style axis as a focal point, starting with a large horseshoe on the seafront, embraced by grand façades (although Greece's economy precluded anything as grand as the Frenchman had planned), while many of the other buildings, erected only in the 1950s, are lined with porticoes sheltering cafés and restaurants. A statue of its namesake, the great philosopher Aristotle from Macedonia, lounges in front of the National Bank at number 6.

Roman Agora [68 F2] (Plateía Dikastiríon; \ 23133 10400; ⊕ summer 08.00–20.00 Wed–Mon, 13.30–20.00 Tue, winter 08.30–15.30 daily; combined ticket for the Roman Agora & the Palace of Galerius €8, concessions €4) In the 1960s, while digging foundations for its law courts at the top of Plateía Aristotélous, the workers stumbled across the Roman Agora (or forum), the administrative centre of the ancient city. Built between the 1st and 3rd centuries AD, it was planned as a unified ensemble around a 146m-long square paved in marble, framed on three sides by one- and two-storey Corinthian porticoes. One of the most lavish buildings (along Agnóstou Stratiótou) has been identified as either the library or a temple to the imperial cult, and there's a 3rd-century AD Odeion, or concert hall, where performances are still held. The impressive cryptoporticus (underground passage) once held shops. The **Museum of the Roman Agora** is beneath the Agora and has an interesting exhibition about the history of the site and the early history of the city.

Panagía Chalkeón [68 E3] (Cnr Egnatía & Chalkeón 2; \ 23102 72910; ⊕ 07.15–09.15 daily, plus evening services beginning at 17.30 in winter & 18.30 or 19.00 in spring, summer & autumn; free) Set in a garden of cypress trees and roses that is hidden beneath street level in the western corner of the park below the Roman Agora, is the picturesque 'Our Lady of the Coppersmiths'. An inscription above the entrance tells us it was built in this 'once profane place' in 1028 by one Christóphoros from Lombardy, who was also buried there. This is historically the district of the coppersmiths, and still is today; in the Ottoman era, the church temporarily became the mosque of the coppersmiths. The brick church is constructed in a cross-in-square plan and has an elaborately textured exterior of arches and set-backs; a tall, narrow dome rises out of the centre and a pair of smaller ones mark the narthex. The frescoes – which are currently being restored and may mostly be hidden by scaffolding – are dark, but are of special interest because they date from the early 11th century: The Last Judgement in the narthex is especially good.

Bey Hamam [68 F3] (Cnr Egnatía & Mit Gennadíou; \ 23102 26931; ⊕ open only for special exhibitions) The first Ottoman bathhouse in the city was built in 1444 by Sultan Murad II. It had sections for men and women, the former more

THE ENCHANTED ONES

Just south of the Agora was a Hellenistic bathhouse and a 2nd-century AD portico, supported by four pillars sculpted with figures of the gods in high relief. As the centuries passed, the portico was built into the courtyard of a Jewish merchant's house. Standing 13m high, it loomed over the surrounding rooftops and was a beloved landmark. The Sephardim called the beautiful figures Las Incantadas, 'the Enchanted Ones', and they told the legend that the portico was once part of a stoa in a royal palace in Thrace. The Queen fell in love with Alexander the Great, and at night he would visit her by creeping through the stoa. Her husband found out and had magic spells cast on the stoa, but Aristotle found out and warned Alexander to stay away that night. When the Queen became impatient to see her lover, she led several of her courtiers into the stoa, and all immediately turned to stone. The king followed, curious to see if the spell had worked, only to be turned into stone himself.

Before the White Tower, the Enchanted Ones were the symbol of Thessaloníki, but they would meet a French Lord Elgin in the person of a palaeographer named Emmanuel Miller. Miller had come to Greece in 1864 to search for Byzantine manuscripts to present to Napoleon III, only to be thwarted by the monks of Mount Athos and Meteora. Rather than return home empty-handed, Miller asked French diplomats to ask the Sultan for permission to take the Incantadas to France, and not believing it would ever happen then went to Thássos and started excavating the ancient city for trophies, believing 'you should not leave anything, otherwise the English will grab it'.

But to Miller's surprise, the French diplomats succeeded. As the operation to break up the portico and move Las Incantadas began, furious crowds of Christians, Jews and Turks tried to stop them – but to no avail. Today they are in the Louvre, and although Thessaloníki failed to get them back, the Louvre sent consolation copies to the city in 2015 (page 92).

opulent, with a special apartment for the Bey under a stalactite ceiling. The Greeks, who used it until 1968, called it Loútra Parádeisos, 'Paradise Baths'. Today the baths are used for temporary exhibitions.

Basilica of Ag Dimítrios [68 G2] (Ag Dimitríou 97; ☏ 23102 70008; ⊕ 06.00– 22.00 daily; free) Overlooking the Agora, this basilica dedicated to Thessaloníki's patron saint is one of the largest churches in Greece. Yet Dimítrios, Great Martyr of Orthodoxy and second only to George as a military saint, as well as patron saint of children and horses, is a rather elusive character. In Thessaloníki they say he was a Roman soldier, born in AD280 who converted to Christianity and instructed children in the faith, although the action that led to his martyrdom in AD304 was his blessing of his friend Nestor, who defeated Galerius' favourite gladiator at wrestling. The emperor, a sore loser, imprisoned Dimítrios in the Roman baths, where he was run through with a spear. A myrrh-scented oil oozed from his wounds; hence his epithet, Myrovlítis, 'the streamer of myrrh'.

The Christians built a chapel over his grave as soon as it was permitted, in AD313. In the 5th century, when the Prefect Leontius was cured of paralysis by the sacred oil, he founded a large five-aisled, wooden-roofed basilica, which was rebuilt in the 7th century exactly as it was after an earthquake and fire. It was converted into a mosque in 1491, and when it became a church again in 1907 and its whitewash cleared away, its 43m nave was found to have splendid mosaics – just before most of them were destroyed forever in the 1917 fire.

The basilica was rebuilt between 1918 and 1948 as it was, preserving as much as possible; the result resembles its contemporaries in Ravenna. The **baptismal font**, the size of a paddling pool, in the square in front of the basilica, originally stood in the atrium. As you enter the nave from the narthex, you'll see on the left an engraved 15th-century Easter calendar and the Venetian Renaissance wall **tomb of Loukas Spantounis** (1481), not something you see every day in Greece (Spantounis was a prominent merchant in the city); on the right, there's a curious wall painting of a man being chased by a unicorn.

Originally the walls were clad in marble, but as time went on the faithful replaced it with votive **mosaics**. Two survive on the west wall: a beautiful fragment of *Dimítrios with an Angel* blowing a trumpet on a rainbow-coloured background, and on the right a garden scene showing a *Dedication of Two Children* to the saint. Most of the columns are survivors from the 5th-century basilica, and their capitals offer a rare ensemble of early Christian sculpture: animals, geometric figures or lacy Theodosian acanthus.

The other mosaics (5th–9th centuries) are on the piers around the sanctuary. On the right, a young, wide-eyed *Dimítrios with Two Founders of the Church* stands before the city walls; *Dimítrios and a Deacon* (who was told by the saint in a dream that the church would be rebuilt after a fire), and an excellent *St Sergius*, dressed as a Roman military officer, hands raised in prayer. On the left there's a sombre Virgin and St Theodore, and the charming *Dimítrios with Two Children*. All the saints wear mantles with a different coloured fabric sewn on the left, a convention showing their status. To the right, a baby basilica attached to the church, the **Chapel of Ag Euphémius**, has expressive paintings of Christ's miracles (1303).

Crypt (08.30–15.00 Mon, Wed & Thu, 09.00–13.30 & 19.00–22.00 Fri, 07.30–14.30 Sat–Sun; free) The basilica's labyrinthine crypt, long forgotten, was revealed by the fire in 1917. Now used to display sculptural fragments, it incorporates a stretch of Roman road and baths where Dimítrios was martyred. Here too is the apsidal martyrium of AD313 and the fountain into which the miraculous myrrh seeped from the wall of the saint's tomb, which pilgrims collected in lead flasks. A phial of earth soaked in blood (presumably Dimítrios') was discovered under the altar; similar phials were valued gifts for emperors. The Friday evening service held in the crypt is a special experience.

Alatzá Imaret [65 E2] (Kassándrou 91–93; 23102 78587; for exhibitions) Built in 1484 by the Grand Vizer Ishak Pasha, this mosque and house of charity has remnants of its original paintings inside – worth a look if it's open. Its name comes from its minaret – destroyed in 1912 – that was completely covered with colourful diamond-shaped stones (*alatza*). The nearby bathhouse, the **Yeni Hammam**, is now a club.

Konak (Ministry of Macedonia and Thrace) [68 E1] (Cnr Ag Dimitríou & Filímonos) Built over the old merchants' caravanserai and designed as the Ottoman governor's palace by Italian architect Vitaliano Poselli in the 1890s, this remains one of Thessaloníki's grandest buildings.

Just south of the Konak, more Roman ruins are being excavated, while Venizélou Street – originally named after the Ottoman governor Sabrí Pashá, who modernised

FESTIVALS AND EVENTS IN THESSALONÍKI

Thessaloníki is a famously sociable town with a full cultural calendar. After the locals return from the beaches, the season gets a soft opening at **Beer Fest** (SoulfoodThessaloniki) – four days of many selections of beer, street food and live music in September. Things then start up strong mid-September with the **International Fair** (w thessalonikifair.gr). A Thessaloníki institution for decades, the fair is one of the largest in southeastern Europe, welcoming over 1,500 exhibitors and honouring a different county each year. These can be festive, if hectic, days to be in town: not only are hotel rooms scarce, but the Prime Minister comes to give an annual address during the fair, frequently occasioning protests and other traffic disruptions. Following the International Fair is **Reworks** (w reworks.gr), a pioneering festival of electronic and experimental music, art and events over several days in late September. Later in September and throughout October is the **Dimítria** (w e-dimitria.gr); since 1965, this annual celebration of theatre, dance and music has taken place at various venues throughout the city. The Dimitria also now includes the **Thessaloníki International Short Film Festival** (tisffest). The **Thessaloníki Animation Festival** (w tafestival.gr) usually takes place in late October. Then, at the end of the month or early November, the city fills with activity for the **Thessaloníki International Film Festival** (TIFF; w filmfestival.gr): ten days of screenings in multiple locations plus masterclasses and events. Greek and international productions from emerging as well as established directors compete for the Golden Alexander. Screenings are in English or with English subtitles. November is also a fine

the district, creating this cosmopolitan thoroughfare to connect the Konak to the port – descends to the sea, into the city's old commercial district, still buzzing with colourful markets.

Bit Bazár [68 E2] (Between Venizélou, Olýmpou & Filíppou sts) The old flea market, originally shops opened by the refugees of Asia Minor, is a charmingly atmospheric 'secret' courtyard, with a mix of antique and vintage shops and inexpensive student bars.

Hamzá Bey Mosque [68 D2] (Cnr Venizélou & Egnatía) Built in 1468 by the wealthy Evrenos family and named after the military commander, and featuring an enclosed courtyard, this is among the finest and largest Ottoman mosques outside Türkiye. Although listed in 1928, it suffered decades of neglect (it spent years as the Alcazar cinema), but in 2006 archaeologists began the long, slow process of restoring it to its former glory.

Bezestén [68 D3] (Venizélou 40) Just to the south of the Hamzá Bey Mosque and on the other side of Egnatia is the 15th-century Ottoman Bezestén – an indoor fabric market, still in use. This was where the most precious textiles, perfumes and jewellery were sold (and could be guarded); in its heyday it had 100 stalls and, according to 17th-century traveller Evliya Çelebi, 'visitors literally lose their senses from the scent of musk, amber and the other perfumes'. A façade of the 1960s and an Art Nouveau apartment building surround the Bezestén, making for a fine snapshot of the complex urban space. A warren of alleys across Venizélou lead into the **Kapáni Market** [68 D3] (Vláli St; ⊕ 05.00–around 15.00 Mon–Sat), on this site

WHAT TO SEE AND DO

month for oenophiles, kicking off on the 1st with **International Xinomavro Day** (w winemakersofnorthgreece.gr), a celebration of the region's indigenous grape with tastings and events at local wineries, wine bars and restaurants. The second Sunday in November marks the **Day of European Wine Tourism** (w winesofgreece.org), with special events at regional wineries (several are very close to the city). After the winter holidays – usually in February – the city puts on a fine **Apokries**, the Greek carnival that precedes Lent. The equivalent of the Latin world's Shrove Tuesday is **Tsiknopempti** – this 'meat-smoke' Thursday finds grills set up not just at restaurants but on private balconies and in front of petrol stations, shoe repairs, etc, from noon through an increasingly loud and festive night. **Kathara Deftera** – 'Clean Monday' – festively ushers in the Lenten season preceding Easter with kite flying and picnicking on taramasalata (fish roe spread), *laganas* (a flat bread made especially for the holiday), olives and seafoods. Ten days in March bring another highlight for cinephiles, with the **Thessaloníki International Documentary Festival** (TIDF; w filmfestival.gr/el/documentary-festival), held, like the TIFF, at the grand Olympion Cinema and the screening rooms in the port. **Pride** (w thessalonikipride.com) fills the city with positive energy in June. Thessaloníki also has a fantastic **International Biennale of Contemporary Art** (w thessalonikibiennale.gr), which includes a festival of performance art. There is also a **Photo Biennale** (w photobiennale-greece.gr) with exhibitions at spaces all across the city. Both take place in odd-numbered years.

since the 15th century and rebuilt after the Great Fire of 1917, where you can find everything from capers to underpants.

Modiáno Market [68 D4] (Ermoú 37; ✆ 21110 88972; ⊕ shops: 08.00–20.00 Mon–Sat, some also Sun; restaurants 11.00–02.00 daily) This colourful indoor market once specialising in meat and fish was begun in 1922 and named after its architect, Elí Modiáno, scion of a prominent Jewish family (page 96). It has recently been stylishly renovated and now has a broad selection of speciality food shops – a pleasant stop for a coffee or a browse. Behind it, on Kominón, is the flower market, the **Louloudádika,** next to the charming 16th-century **Ioudi (or Bazar) Hammam** (Jewish baths) which look to be in great nick but are never open.

Jewish Museum [68 C4] (Ag Mínas 13; ✆ 23102 50406; w jmth.gr; ⊕ 09.00–14.00 Mon–Fri, also 17.00–20.00 Wed, 10.00–14.00 Sun; €8, students €3) Founded in 2001 in an arcade that survived the Great Fire, this museum tells the story of the city's Jewish community over the past 2,000 years. There are paintings (including one of the original arrangements of Las Incantadas; page 80), photographs and historical documents, tombstones from the vast Jewish Cemetery that once occupied the site of the university and relics of long-lost synagogues and business. A new memorial section is dedicated to the victims of the Holocaust.

Ag Minás [68 C3] (I Dragoúmi 10; ✆ 23102 72700; ⊕ 08.30–13.00 & 18.00–20.00; free) Founded in the 5th century AD and nicknamed the 'Ark' for the animals sculpted on its cornice (which now live in the Museum of Byzantine Culture; page 94), Ag Minás was the protector of the market. After it burned down, it was rebuilt in 1852. Two teardrop-shaped windows adorn the façade; inside there's a touch of central European Rococo.

Holy Catholic Cathedral of the Immaculate Conception [68 C3] (Frángon 19; ✆ 23105 39550; w ccthess.gr) This fin-de-siècle work by Vitaliano Poselli, uniting elements of Baroque and Neoclassicism, has served the Catholic community of Thessaloníki since the late 19th century. The leafy street it sits on – Frangon – is named for the Franks, the Frangi. This was the heart of the Frangomachala – 'Frangi' were the Latin Christians of the Ottoman empire, a term that grew to encompass the prosperous international community generally, here and in other Ottoman cities.

State Conservatory of Thessaloníki [68 B2] (Frángon 15) This Baroque and Neoclassical mansion with its mansard roof was originally built for the notorious businessman and money-lender Jackie Abbot (his fortune began with a monopoly on leeches). The mansion in turn changed hands and became the Ottoman Bank, shortly after which it was blown up by the anarchist group the 'Boatmen of Thessaloníki' and subsequently reconstructed. The only trace of the 1903 episode remaining is the damage to the statue of a woman behind the decorative iron fence.

Malakopí Arcade (Stoá Malakopí) [68 C2] (Villará & Syggroú sts) Built originally as the Banque de Salonique on the grounds of the old Allatini mansion, also by Vitaliano Poselli (page 97), this ornate neo-Baroque arcade serves as the heart of the busy Valaorítou district. Its clock stopped at the very moment of the 1978 earthquake and has not been reset since.

Plateía Eleftherías [68 C4] (At the south end of Venizélou) 'Freedom Square' marked the end of the Byzantine walls, and when they were demolished in 1869 it became the main sea entrance to the city, surrounded by banks, hotels and restaurants, most of which were destroyed in the Great Fire. On 'Black Saturday' (8 July 1942), the Nazis ordered, seemingly out of the blue, that all Jewish men between the ages of 18 and 45 report there for forced labour, where they were surrounded by German soldiers with automatic weapons, who publicly humiliated them as they queued up in the hot sun. The **Holocaust Monument** (1997) in the shape of bodies consumed in a flaming Menorah was sculpted by the Glid brothers.

MOMus Museum of Photography [69 A5] (Warehouse A, Navárchou Vótsi 3; ✆ 23105 66716; w thmphoto.gr; ⏰ 11.00–19.00 Tue–Wed & Fri–Sun, 11.00–20.00 Thu; €4, concession €3, or €6 for a combined ticket with the MOMus Experimental Center for the Arts) The warehouses along Pier A at the end of Plateía Eleftherías have found new uses: one is the only state-run museum in Greece dedicated to photography, with a fascinating archive of Greek photographs through the ages, featuring changing exhibitions by themes or by photographer.

Museum of Cinema [69 A5] (Warehouse A; ✆ 23103 78570; w filmfestival.gr/museum; ⏰ 09.00–15.00 Mon–Tue, 09.00–19.00 Wed–Fri; €3, concessions €2) Adjacent to the Museum of Photography, the Museum of Cinema covers the history of Greek cinema with an engaging, English-language-friendly exhibit with equipment, old hand-painted posters, photos, etc.

MOMus Experimental Center for the Arts [69 A5] (Warehouse B1; \ 23105 93270; w momus.gr/en/museum/experimental-center-arts; ⊕ 10.00–18.00 Tue, Wed & Fri–Sun, 10.00–22.00 Thu; €4, concessions €3, or €6 for a combined ticket with the MOMus Museum of Photography) This is the most avant-garde of the MOMus spaces, with changing exhibitions and events representing the most interesting currents in contemporary artistic expression across a variety of media.

Ladádika The huge customs house [68 A4] (1910) just down the waterfront is another work by Elí Modiáno; behind it was the artificial port created in AD323, by the Emperor Constantine, as Thessaloníki's consolation prize for not being chosen as his new capital. Back then the sea reached inland as far as Frágon Street. It silted up over the centuries, and a new quarter, the Ladádika ('Olive Oil Market'), grew up on little lava-paved lanes, now all fixed up, brightly painted and converted into bars, clubs and restaurants. Katoúni is one of the prettiest streets with its colourful façades and old street lights.

Vardári Fortress [64 B2] (North end of Frágon St) Remains of the 16th-century fortress built by Suleiman the Magnificent stand over layers of walls that once protected Constantine's port. Just north, busy **Plateía Dimokratías** was the location of the fabled Golden Gate, Thessaloníki's front door until the 19th century, now gone without a trace and replaced by a statue of Prince Constantine, liberator of the city in 1912 if later a problem-causing king during World War I.

Old railway station [64 B2] (Palaioú Stathmoú) The district northwest of Ladádika, where lumber was once shipped out, is known as Xyládika, with the 'new' railway station (new since the 1960s) and bus station. From the old station, beginning in March 1943, all Jewish citizens of Thessaloníki were squeezed into freight wagons and shipped to Auschwitz-Birkenau. Now the site is destined to host the striking octagonal **Holocaust Museum of Greece and Education Centre for Human Rights** [64 A1] (w holocausteducenter.gr), whose construction is slated to begin soon. Funded by Germany and the Stávros Niárchos Foundation, and designed by Germany's Heide & Von Beckerath and Israel's Efrat-Kowalsky Architects, it will tell the history of Thessaloníki's Jewish communities.

THE OLD IMPERIAL CITY AND AROUND
Palace of Galerius [65 E3] (Plateía Navarínou; \ 23102 04868; ⊕summer: 08.00–20.00 Wed–Mon, winter: usually 08.30–15.30 Wed–Mon; combined ticket with Roman Agora €8, concessions €4) When Galerius made Thessaloníki his capital in AD300, he built a massive complex to match his imperial dignity, covering 18ha – now all far below the modern street level. Visible sections include the courtyard and rooms in the southeast corner; the adjacent octagon, with lavish marbles, was probably the throne room.

Arch of Galerius [65 E3] (Cnr D Goúnari & Egnatía) From the palace, a covered portico once extended to the sacred precinct of the Rotonda by way of the *decumanus maximus* – Thessaloníki's main street since its foundation (now the Egnatía). The crossing point of the *decumanus* and the portico was marked by the Arch of Galerius (or Kamara, as the locals call it). Only a quarter of the original domed double gateway survives, with reliefs all busy in the Late Imperial style celebrating Galerius' triumphs against the Sassanid Persians (here portrayed as little men in pointy hats) in AD298. Although the faces have been carefully hacked off, you can pick out the emperor fighting on horseback, addressing his troops, riding his chariot and reigning and sacrificing with his father-in-law Diocletian, who fancied that he was the incarnation of Jupiter and Galerius was his Hercules. The two were rabid persecutors of Christians – Galerius alone martyred some 3,000, to please Diocletian – but on his deathbed Galerius felt which way the wind was blowing and signed an edict of tolerance.

Rotonda [65 E3] (Plateía Ag Georgíou; ✆ 23102 04868; ☉ summer: 08.00–20.00 Wed–Mon, winter: 08.30–15.30 Wed–Mon; €6, concessions €3; bring binoculars) If the Arch of Galerius looked to late Roman triumphal arches as its model, this remarkable round building, constructed at the same time, echoes the Pantheon. Yet no-one is sure what it was meant to be – Galerius' mausoleum (although his body was never brought here), or possibly a temple to the Cabeiri (page 227). The walls of brick and rubble masonry, 6m thick, enclosed a space 24m in diameter, originally covered with coloured marble and relieved by barrel-vaulted niches for statues. The tremendous dome, 30m high, was made of brick, and like the Pantheon there was once a central hole to let in light and air – and rain; the floor was equipped with drains.

In the 4th century AD, the Rotonda was converted into the church of the Asómatoi (the 'body-less ones', aka the Archangels). A now-destroyed ambulatory was built around it; mosaics were lavished on its walls; and the east bay was widened to make a sanctuary – which undermined the integrity of the circular structure. In a 10th-century earthquake, the dome collapsed and had to be repaired, and two buttresses were built to shore up the sanctuary. In 1591, it was converted into a mosque, and has the only minaret in Thessaloníki that survived a nationalist rampage after the assassination of King George I in 1913 – even though he was shot by a Greek (page 92).

In its prime, the church glittered with some of the oldest Christian mosaics in the eastern Mediterranean, made up of c34 million tesserae, which survive only in fragments. But what fragments – still fresh and glowing from the cusp of a new world age, Hellenistic in style but full of wonder and promise. In the centre was the figure of Christ Pantocrator (now lost), in a lush heavenly garden in a rainbow supported by four angels, whose heads, wings and hands survive. The next band contained the Apostles, although they too have been lost, except for their feet. Below them, eight saints martyred under Diocletian, their arms spread in the *orans* or prayer gesture, stand before delightful stage façades studded with gems and hung with pearls, where peacocks frolic.

Ag Panteleímonos [65 E3] (Cnr Egnatía & Iansonídou; ✆ 23102 220020; ☉ rarely) Down from the Rotonda's entrance is medieval Ag Panteleímonos, a nubby quilt of brick and tile, and one of several churches in the city whose original name and date are disputed: by the architecture it is late 13th century, a good example of the complex tetrastyle cross-in-square plan. It was transformed into a mosque in 1548, and a few of its damaged wall paintings survive.

Metamórfosis tou Sotíros [65 E3] (Egnatía 140; ✆ 23102 23009; ☉ rarely) This little church (c1350), with its jauntily tilted octagonal dome surrounded by restaurant tables, may have been a monastic funerary chapel. The earthquake of 1978 revealed its secrets: its rare plan, a *tetraconch* (four-sided shell) inscribed in a square, and forgotten wall paintings.

WHAT TO SEE AND DO

> **THESSALONÍKI'S BIGGEST ARCHAEOLOGICAL SITE**
>
> When excavating the corner of Venizélou and Egnatía streets for a metro station, workers uncovered an extraordinary stretch of 6th-century AD Thessaloníki, including 77m of the *decumanus maximus*, paved with marble, along with remains of wealthy residences and public buildings. All in all, some 300,000 items were unearthed during the construction of the metro. The greatest prize was found near Ag Sofía: a headless but beautiful statue of Aphrodite, along with colourful mosaic floors from the 4th century AD.

Thessaloníki History Centre [65 E3] (Plateía Ippodrómou; ☏ 23102 49803; w thessaloniki.gr; ⊕ 08.00–14.00 Mon–Fri; free) This city-run research centre has a library and changing exhibitions, often with fascinating photographs. It overlooks the square marking the site of the hippodrome, with a line of palms echoing the monument-lined *spina* that once divided the racetrack.

Chariot racing was the rage in Thessaloníki, and in AD390 the city's favourite charioteer tried to seduce a slave boy belonging to Emperor Theodosius' commander, the stern Goth Botheric. Scandalised, Botheric imprisoned the charioteer; outraged, the Thessalonians murdered Botheric; furious, Theodosius (then in Milan) ordered his army to murder the Thessalonians. Although the emperor eventually cooled down and sent a messenger to cancel the order, it was too late: his commanders had already invited the population to the hippodrome to watch their favourites race, then locked the gates, and in a 3-hour killing spree, the army massacred more than 7,000 men, women and children. Afterwards, when Theodosius tried to attend Mass in Milan, the bishop (and later saint) Ambrose barred the way and wouldn't let him in for eight months, until he made penance – a first for an emperor, setting an important precedent for the Church. Theodosius also decreed a new law, mandating a 30-day pause between a death sentence and an execution.

Ag Sofía [69 G5] (Plateía Ag Sofías; ☏ 23102 70253; ⊕ 07.00–21.00 daily; free) Thessaloníki's Byzantine cathedral, dedicated to Holy Wisdom, was built in the 8th century over a 5th-century church built in turn over a Roman bath. Originally it was once much grander, with a large atrium (now marked by a palm garden) and an elaborate Turkish portal from its days as a mosque, both of which were victims of an Italian air raid in 1941.

The interior with its huge dome on pendentives is reminiscent of the Ag Sofía in Istanbul. It is filled with a mosaic of the *Ascension*, dated to shortly after the end of the Iconoclasm, which illustrates what was lost in the Rotonda's dome: Jesus the Pantocrator 'Ruler of All' on a rainbow, supported by two angels, although the artist's attempt to adapt the figure of Christ to the curved surface gives him a curiously stumpy look. All around him, standing in a stylised rocky landscape, are the apostles, gazing up in astonishment and consternation while the Virgin stands serene between a pair of angels; the quotation here is from Acts I ('Men of Galilee, why do you stand gazing up into heaven?'). The golden mosaic of the Virgin and Child in the apse, also from the 9th century, replaced the original simple cross (you can still see its 'ghost'); the mosaics in the barrel vault, with monograms of Constantine VI and Empress Irene, are rare survivors from the Iconoclasm. Some of the columns have charming Theodosian capitals. The subterranean chapel just to the right of Ag Sofía, labelled the 'catacombs' of

3 | THESSALONÍKI (ΘΕΣΣΑΛΟΝΙΚΗ)

Ag Ioánnes Pródomos (St John the Baptist), was really the 5th-century baptistry, built over a Roman nymphaeum.

Panagía Acheiropoiétos [68 G4] (Ag Sofías 56; ☏ 23102 72820; ⏱ 10.00–noon & evening hours which change by season daily; free) This basilica was built in AD431, shortly after the Council of Ephesus recognised Mary as the Mother of God, making it one of the oldest churches dedicated to Mary still in use. Its name, 'The All Holy Virgin Made without Hands', was derived from an icon of the Virgin reputedly painted by angels. Converted into a mosque by Murad II to celebrate his conquest of the city – look on the west side of the church for the marble column inscribed in Ottoman Turkish 'Sultan Murad Conquered Thessaloníki in 833' (1430) – it was restored after serving as an emergency shelter for refugees in 1923. The interior is impressive in its simplicity, its three aisles divided by monolithic colonnades, crowned with superb 5th-century AD 'Theodosian' capitals (named after Theodosius II). These are decorated with ancient Corinthian-style acanthus leaves perforated to resemble lace, which either stand upright or blow in a violent wind, sometimes every which way. Charming late 5th-century AD gold-ground mosaics of fruit, flowers, fountains, birds and geometric designs similar to those in the Rotonda decorate the soffits of the arches. Of the frescoes, all that remains are portraits of 18 martyrs along the right arcade. In the left aisle, look for the floor mosaics, once part of the Roman bath.

Ag Gregórios Palamás [69 E6] (Cnr Ag Sofías & Mitropoléos; ⏱ 07.00–20.00 daily; free) The city's current Orthodox cathedral, Ag Gregórios Palamás (dedicated to the Hesychast leader who was re-buried here; page 60), was rebuilt after a fire in 1890. The church was designed by the famed Neoclassicist Ernst Ziller, and after a hiatus in construction it was completed by the architect Xenophon Paionidis.

Museum of the Macedonian Struggle [69 E6] (Proxénou Koromilá 23; ☏ 23102 29778; w imma.edu.gr; ⏱ 09.00–14.00 Mon–Fri, until 20.00 Wed, 10.00–14.00 Sat; €4, concessions €2; English translation available) Dedicated to the 20th-century wars that led to the current boundaries between states, this museum has photos, relics and documents, and an audiovisual history. Appropriately enough, it is housed in a handsome Neoclassical mansion designed by Ernst Ziller (architect of many of Athens' finest buildings, as well as the adjacent cathedral Ag Gregórios Palamás) that served as the Greek consulate before the Balkan Wars, where the Procouncil Koromilá was instrumental in assuring that Thessaloníki became Greek instead of Bulgarian (there was fierce hand-to-hand fighting between the armies nearby, the Greeks having the distinct advantage of a machine gun posted on top of Ag Sofía's old minaret).

ÁNO PÓLIS In the shadow of the mighty ramparts begun by Emperor Theodosius, the Áno Pólis, or Upper City, is the former Ottoman district that survived the Great Fire. How letters ever get delivered here, where narrow streets turn into stairs with names invisible to the naked eye, is a credit to Thessaloníki's postal workers. Occasional signs point towards the Byzantine churches that are its glory (although their opening hours tend to change without notice; ask at the tourist office or call ahead if there's something you really want to see). The best way to visit is to catch a bus to the Acropolis (literally 'the top of the city') and stroll down. Bus 23, which leaves from Plateía Eleftherías and ascends Venizélou, drops you at the stop Platanos, by the Moní Vlatádon (see opposite) – an excellent starting point.

WHAT TO SEE AND DO

Eptapýrgio [65 F1] (Northeast cnr of the Acropolis; ☏ 23109 68843; ⊕ 08.00–16.00 daily, towers open until 14.00 Wed–Mon; free) The 'Fort of Seven Towers' (actually it has ten) is still often known by its Turkish name, Yedí Koulé. Built in the 14th century, and added to by the Venetians in 1420 as a last line of defence, it housed the city's governor until 1890, when it was converted into a prison, which would feature in numerous *rebétiko* songs. It closed in 1989, and a small part is open to visits. The splendid main gate, with a Turkish inscription of 1431, was cobbled together with numerous ancient bits and pieces, including pretty Byzantine reliefs of peacocks.

Theodosian Walls [65 E1] Some 4km of the brick and rubble masonry walls that once encompassed the entire city survived the demolition of 1869. Built by Theodosius (AD380s–395), in part over Cassander's Hellenistic walls, they are 4.6m thick and stand up to 10.5m, interspersed with rectangular towers; brick arches were built to reinforce the walls in case they were sapped, but add a decorative note; here and there you can see bits of Roman temples. Inscriptions in red brick testify to repairs over the past 1,400 years. Eptapyrgíou Street has the best-preserved stretch, but also the bloodiest: in 1345, in the Hesychast revolt, the Zealots tossed aristocrats off the top on to stakes below. The stout round tower in the south wall, the 15th-century **Trigoníou Tower** [65 F2] (the Zincirli Kule, 'Chain Tower', to the Ottomans), was the focus of the Turkish assault in 1430. It still fires cannons – at midnight on New Year's Eve.

Moní Vlatádon [65 E1] (Eptapyrgíou 64; ☏ 23102 46357; ⊕ 07.30–11.00 & 17.30–20.00 daily; free) Thessaloníki's only active Byzantine monastery was founded in the mid 14th century by the Hesychasts Dorothéos and Márkos Vlátis, pupils of St Gregory Palamás. The church was rebuilt over an 11th-century predecessor, and, unusually, the dome is supported directly on the walls. The frescoes, uncovered in 1981, date from c1370. The right chapel marks a spot where in AD51 St Paul preached, although his message wasn't well received by the local Jews, who ran him out of town. Outside, the monastery's peacocks enjoy a superb sunset view over the city; on a clear day you can see Mount Olympus, about 80km away as the crow flies.

Ósios David [65 E1] (Cnr Bouboulínas & D Poliorkití – hard to find, but persist; ☏ 23133 10400; ⊕ 09.00–15.00 Mon–Sat, 07.00–noon Sun; free) Once part of the Latómou, the monastery 'of the Quarry', this winsome Byzantine church dedicated to Ósios ('Blessed') David from the outside looks like someone's home: a tiled porch faces a little courtyard full of potted plants. Its story is typically obscure: allegedly it was built by the secretly baptised Theodora, daughter of Galerius, who dedicated it to St David the Tree-Dweller, who spent his whole life in Thessaloníki up an almond tree. Then the nave was amputated for conversion into a mosque.

If mosaics could sing, Ósios David's 5th-century AD *Epiphany* in its concave niche would warble like a nightingale. Hidden under calves' skins (likely during one of the Byzantine Iconoclastic periods) and rediscovered in 1920, this is only one of three known mosaics from the period. The iconography is striking: it shows a young, beardless but serious-minded Christ, surrounded by the light of glory (*doxa*). Under his feet the rivers of Eden – Physon, Geon, Tigris and Euphrates – flow into the Jordan, personified as a man with fish swimming along his body. Symbols of the Evangelists surround the *doxa*: an endearing ox and lion earnestly clutch their books. Next to the lion, Ezekiel (whose vision this is) is bent over in fear and ecstasy, representing the emotional response to God; on the right, the prophet Habakkuk, in the typical position of an ancient philosopher, smiles in deep thought, representing the rational.

Also take a close look at the 12th-century murals discovered in 1976: although overshadowed by the mosaic, the *Nativity*, the *Bathing of the Christ Child* and *Baptism* are among the finest surviving works from the era.

Ag Nikólaos Orphanós [65 E2] (Irodótou 1; ✆ 23102 70591; ☉ usually 10.00–13.00 Mon & Thu; free) Built in the early 14th century by Serbian king Milutin, who married a daughter of the emperor and frequently visited Thessaloníki, this little church was amputated at some point and the brickwork is simple by standards of the day, but the vivid frescoes (1310–20) are the best preserved in the city, and show a naturalism, concern for colour and feeling typical of the Paleologian era. In the *Marriage of Cana*, the Virgin, usually a sorrowful character in Byzantine art, whispers to her son, just as any mother would, that their hosts have run out of wine and need a timely miracle to fill the carafes.

Atatürk Museum [65 E2] (Apostoloú Pavloú 17; ✆ 23102 48452; ☉ 10.00–17.00 Tue–Sun; free; bring your passport in case you're asked) The founder of modern Türkiye was destiny's child; born here on the edge of the Áno Pólis in 1881, his father hung his sword over his cradle to dedicate him to a military career and his maths teacher later gave him his name Kemal, 'the perfect one'. After attending a military academy in Istanbul, Kemal was appointed in 1907 to a unit in Thessaloníki, at the time a hotbed of the Young Turk movement. He joined the march on Istanbul to depose reactionary Sultan Abdul Hamid, but never returned; after the First Balkan War, his family was forced to leave Thessaloníki. In 1935, the city donated the house to the Turkish government (which also has its consulate here); the museum has personal items, school reports and some original furnishings. In the garden, don't miss the pomegranate tree planted by Kemal's father.

Taxiarchón [65 E2] (Theotokopoúlou 40, just off Akropóleos; ✆ 23102 09546; ☉ usually) Behind its rebuilt façade, this 14th-century church is a handsome little stone and patterned brick structure that lost most of its frescoes when it served as a mosque.

Byzantine baths [65 E2] (Cnr Theotokopoúlou & Kríspou; ✆ 23109 68860; ☉ 10.00–13.00 Wed & Fri; free) Restored in 2015, these are the best-preserved Byzantine baths in Greece, built in the late 1200s with tepid, hot and cold rooms, and in constant use until the last bather towelled off in 1940.

Tourbe of Musa Baba [65 E1] (Plateía Terpsithéas) Sufi dervishes were once a powerful force in the city, and this 16th-century hexagonal tomb of their beloved mystic was a favourite shrine for Christians as well, who identified Musa Baba with St George. Just north of here is the **Tsinári** district (named after an ancient plane tree – *çinar* in Turkish), one of the most picturesque corners of the Áno Pólis, with a clutch of old-fashioned *ouzerís* and tavernas along the tiny lanes.

Profítis Ilías [64 D1] (Olympiádos 20; ✆ 23102 73790; ☉ 09.00–noon & sometimes 18.00–19.30) Built in the 14th century in a panoramic setting on a mound overlooking the city, this church dedicated to the Prophet Elija is the only Athonite (tetrastyle cross-in-square plan with side choirs) church in the city, a style invented by St Athanásios at the Great Lávra; its masonry (white ashlar alternating with courses of brick) is rare in Macedonia, but common in churches in Constantinople. Only a few of the rich murals of 1360 survive – the *Massacre of the Innocents* in the narthex is strikingly realistic in its cruelty.

Ag Ekateríni [64 D1] (Cnr Ioús & Sachtoúri; ✆ 23102 25580; ⊕ 08.00–noon daily & evening hours changing with the seasons) Built in a complex tetrastyle cross-in-square, the church of St Catherine has five domes and a closed ambulatory, its decorative brickwork accented with ceramics, giving it a nubby texture. Only fragments of its beautiful frescoes of 1315 survived its conversion into the Yakup Pasha Mosque in 1500.

Ag Apostóli [64 C1] (Olýmpou 1; ✆ 23105 37915; ⊕ 07.30–noon daily & evening hours changing with the seasons) A bit off on its own, this beautiful church is a vision amid dull apartment blocks from the 1970s. Founded c1312 by Patriarch Nephon I and similar in style to Ag Ekateríni, the Holy Apostles was part of one of the richest foundations in the city. The domes are pierced with numerous openings, admitting beams of light to illuminate the elegant mosaics inspired by the Chora monastery in Istanbul, although they were never completed. Yet they represent the summit of, and one of the last examples of, Paleologian mosaic art – more naturalistic and earthy in detail, yet endowed with the Hellenistic grace that marked the curtain call of Byzantium. In the dome, as usual, the *Pantocrator* holds pride of place, surrounded by prophets and Evangelists, while the *Twelve Holy Feasts* decorate the vaults and west wall – scenes of the *Nativity* (with a nurse testing Jesus's first bath), *Resurrection*, *Transfiguration* and *Entry into Jerusalem*. When the patriarchal largesse dried up (Nephon was deposed in 1314), the remaining walls were painted: the *Tree of Jesse* in the ambulatory, the *Hand of God* holding the souls of the righteous, the *Birth of John the Baptist*, *Herod's Feast* and *Salome* performing an unusual feat – dancing while balancing the Baptist's head on a tray on her own head.

Stroll around the surrounding streets while you are here, as many interesting art and design studios have recently started to open in the vicinity.

MOMus Museum of Modern Art [58 D1] (Kolokotróni 21, take bus 34 from Plateía Aristotélous & get off at Moní Lazaristón; ✆ 23105 89143; w momus.gr/en/museum/museum-modern-art; ⊕ 10.00–18.00 Tue, Wed & Fri–Sun, noon–20.00 Thu; €6, concessions €3) Founded in 1997, when Thessaloníki was European Capital of Culture, this museum in the former Moní Lazaristón houses a surprise: the Costákis collection of Russian avant-garde art, considered among the most important collections outside Russia itself.

THE MUSEUM DISTRICT Thessaloníki's biggest museums, its university and fair are clustered just south of the city centre. Beginning at the esplanade in front of the White Tower, the 3.5km waterfront promenade was completed in 2013 around the city's new landmark: the cascading *Umbrellas* (1997) [65 E5] by sculptor George Zongolópoulos (1903–2004), reflecting the colours of the sky and sea and beautifully illuminated at night.

White Tower (Lefkós Pýrgos) [64 D4] (✆ 23102 67832; w lpth.gr; ⊕ Apr–Oct 08.00–20.00 Wed–Mon, 13.00–20.00 Tue, Nov–Mar usually 08.30–15.30 daily; Apr–Oct €6, concessions €3; Nov–Mar €3) Thessaloníki's landmark tower with its massive 360° views began as part of the seafront walls of Theodosius, but at the end of the 15th century it was rebuilt as a stout 32m cylinder, probably by the Venetians. Under the janissaries, the Sultan's praetorian guard who were a law unto themselves, it earned the name Bloody Tower for the frequent executions within its walls. When Sultan Mahmoud II purged the janissaries in 1825, the tower was whitewashed (the story goes that a prisoner offered to do the work himself in exchange for freedom) and has been the White Tower ever since. It has served numerous purposes over the decades: as part of the city's air defences and a communications tower for the Allies in World War I, as a meteorological station for the university and, today, as an exhibition space, over six floors, on Thessaloníki's history.

A **statue of Philip II** [65 E4] scrutinises the tower with his one bad eye from across Leofóros Mégas Aléxandros, while towards the waterfront a large equestrian **statue of Alexander the Great** (1973) [65 E4], the son who inherited his ambitions, has become a favourite photo spot.

Archaeology Museum [65 E4] (Manólis Andrónikos 6; 23133 10201; w amth. gr; ⊕ 09.00–16.00 daily, high season to 17.00; Apr–Oct €8, concessions €4, Nov–Mar €4, EU citizens up to 25 free, all children up to 5 free) Thessaloníki's archaeology museum is one of the best in Greece, highlighting the extraordinary wealth and craftsmanship of Ancient Macedonia. Before you go inside, though, have a look at the replicas of 2nd-century BC **Las Incantadas** (page 80) gifted from the Louvre (where the original still resides), decorated with figures of a Maenad, Dionysus, Ariadne, Leda, Ganymede, one of the Dioscuri, Victory and Aura, a personification of the breeze.

THREE FAMOUS ASSASSINATIONS

With its convoluted 20th-century history it's not surprising that Thessaloníki has had its share of intrigue, including three mysterious assassinations with international repercussions. The first occurred shortly after the city became part of Greece on 5 March 1913, when the well-loved 67-year-old King George I was taking a stroll by the White Tower only to be shot in the back at close range by a certain Alexándros Schinás, who may have been an alcoholic vagrant, an anarchist, or a man delirious from tuberculosis. After questioning and probably torture at the hands of the gendarmes, Schinás fell or was pushed out of the police station window to his death. The assassination set off a nationalist anti-Turkish, anti-Bulgarian frenzy in the city. But were there others behind the killing with geopolitical motives? George's son Constantine was married to the Kaiser's sister, and it wouldn't be long before the outbreak of World War I…

The second occurred on 7 May 1948, during the height of the Greek Civil War. George Polk, a well-known American journalist for CBS radio, had arrived in Thessaloníki en route to the northwest mountains, where he intended to interview Márkos Vafeiádis, then leading the communist guerrillas. Polk had been covering the war and was critical of both sides, and notably of the Truman administration's unqualified support of the corrupt right-wing government in Athens. Only Polk disappeared the day after he arrived in Thessaloníki and was found a week later, his hands and feet bound, and a bullet in his skull, in the Thermaic Gulf. The Americans pressured Greece for an arrest and conviction, and Grigóris Staktópoulos, a local journalist who had had a brief association with the Greek Communist party, was tortured by the Security Police into a rambling confession of being an accomplice, and spent 11 years in prison. Everyone who

Inside, the exhibits are arranged thematically. The lower level is dedicated to **Prehistoric Macedonia**, with finds from a 23m mound (or tell) from c3200BC in Toúmba, the neighbourhood just south of the centre – mounds that later inhabitants considered magical places. On the ground floor, the section **Towards the Birth of Cities** (1100–700BC) has finds from the colonies from southern Greece set up in the north, which influenced the then-coalescing kingdom of Macedonia. Next, **Macedonia from the 7th century BC to Late Antiquity** has intriguing everyday items, including some fine vases and sculptures – the torso of a kouros in a clingy robe, a Classical-era funeral stele from Néa Kallikráteia of a girl holding a dove, and later sculptures, imbued with a homely charm as proportions start to waver from the golden mean.

The section on **Thessaloníki** has a superb 4th-century BC marble door of a Macedonian tomb (page 144) with all its bronze fittings: wheels once allowed it to open effortlessly. Another tomb, robbed just before it was excavated in 1984, still yielded beautiful marble couches charmingly painted with griffons, a bull, gods and a red-shoed Silenus. There's the lovely 5th-century BC Aphrodite of Thessaloníki, displays on Galerius' ambitious building programme and finds from his palace, including a painterly mosaic of Ariadne and Dionysos from the 3rd century AD. The Roman statues include an Augustus as a hero, an early example of the 'propaganda' statues erected across the empire (later, the Romans would save money by sending out bodies in togas with replaceable heads). There's also part of the Ionic temple of Aphrodite discovered in 2000 in Plateía Antigonidón. It has an unusual history: it was built in Ancient Ainea (near the modern beach resort of Epanomí), a once prosperous

has followed the case since is convinced that Staktópoulos was framed by officials who, pressured by the USA, very much wanted to close the case and end the bad publicity. But who killed Polk? Over the decades, suspicion has lingered on the Communists, right-wing politicians, the security forces, or even rogue American, British or Soviet agents. Appeals to the Greek Supreme Court over the decades by Staktópoulos and then by his widow went unheard. Scores of books and articles have been written about the case, and it's remembered annually in the USA with the prestigious George Polk Awards in Journalism.

The third assassination, of prominent left-wing deputy and peace activist Grigóris Lambrákis, is the best known, thanks to Z, Vassílis Vassilíkos's novel made into a film by Costas Gávras in 1969. Lambrákis had marched with the Campaign for Nuclear Disarmament in 1963 in the UK, and at Bertrand Russell's suggestion, had tried to organise a similar peace march from Marathon to Athens – which was banned by the Greek government. So Lambrákis, who had parliamentary immunity, walked the 26 miles on his own, holding his banner with the word ΕΛΛΑΣ and the peace symbol. His popularity and ideal of freeing Greece of foreign entanglements alarmed the right, and on 22 May 1963, after delivering a powerful keynote speech at a peace demonstration in Thessaloníki, two extremists in a three-wheeled vehicle struck him with a club, while the police stood by and watched. Lambrákis died in hospital five days later; half a million people attended his funeral in Athens. Thessaloníki prosecutor Chrístos Sartzetákis later uncovered the links between the assassins and an organisation of right-wing thugs linked to the police and allegedly NATO's secret anti-communist 'stay behind army' that operated in Europe until the end of the Cold War.

city reputedly founded by and named after Aeneas, Aphrodite's son, then hurriedly disassembled and relocated to Thessaloníki after the Battle of Actium, because the city supported loser Antony and needed to butter up victor Octavian (soon to be Augustus), whose great uncle Julius Caesar claimed descent from Aphrodite.

The last section is dedicated to the **Gold of Macedonia**, the metal that funded Philip II's meteoric rise to power. There are dazzling displays of gold from 121 6th-century BC tombs in Síndos, in the suburbs of Thessaloníki. Men were buried with their weapons, women with their jewellery, and both with miniature items useful in the afterlife – furniture and mule carts, one pulled by terracotta mules. Some tombs contained gold masks or lozenges that covered the mouths of the dead. You need a magnifying glass to pick out the granulation and filigree on the necklaces.

A cemetery in Dervéni, on the road to Kavála, yielded a glittering hoard from the second half of the 4th century BC, including one of the great masterpieces of Hellenistic art: the bronze **Dervéni Krater** (c320BC), the only intact relief metal vase to survive antiquity, made with such a high quantity of tin in the alloy that it looks gold-plated. According to its inscription, its owner was a nobleman of Lárissa, probably a hostage of Philip II; its creator was a Greek Cellini, who some critics have tentatively identified as Lysippus. The theme is a Dionysian revel. Hammered out in the most exquisite repoussé, ecstatic bacchants whirl in fluttering garments across the main body of the vase, watched by a man wearing one boot, identified as Thracian king Lykourgos, who was punished by Dionysos with madness for his impiety. Ariadne and Dionysos are shown seated, Ariadne pulling back her veil as her husband stretches a sensuous leg over her thigh. The other elements are of cast bronze – the extraordinary four figures weary from the dance around the neck: Dionysos and a maenad, and a satyr and maenad who are the very definition of erotic languor. Even the handles are unique, anticipating rococo soup tureens, decorated with bearded heads framed in screw-tailed snakes.

The next exhibit, the **Derveni Papyrus** (340BC), has been recognised by UNESCO as 'Europe's oldest book'. It was bizarrely preserved by being burned in a funeral pyre (usually papyrus can't survive in the damp Greek soil). The 266 fragments, laboriously recovered and translated into modern Greek and English, hold a copy of a late 5th-century BC hexameter poem ascribed to Orpheus that starts 'Close the doors, you uninitiated'. Written in an allegory full of secret meanings, it appears (to the uninitiated) full of fuzzy philosophical ramblings about the essence of Zeus.

Museum of Byzantine Culture

[65 E4] (Leof Stratoú 2; ✆ 23133 06422; w mbp.gr; ⊕ Apr–Oct 08.00–20.00 Wed–Mon, 13.00–20.00 Tue, Nov–Mar 08.30–15.30 daily; Apr–Oct €8, concessions €4, Nov–Mar €4 or free 1st Sun of month, EU citizens up to 25 free, all children up to 5 free) Where the archaeological collection ends, this museum, directly behind, picks up the story. Early Christian art shows the continuity of pagan styles, even in the tombs, although instead of 'Farewell' the epitaphs read 'Sleeping' or 'At Rest'. The earliest art here emphasises hope – the young, beardless Good Shepherd amid sweet visions of a heaven filled with birds, fruit and wine: crucifixions wouldn't become popular until the 6th century AD. And judging by the mosaic floor and paintings from a 5th-century AD dining room, life on earth, at least for some, was good, too. There are bittersweet photos of the mosaics in the Basilica of Ag Dimítrios, lost in the fire of 1917, and a fresco showing Susannah and the Elders, unique in Greece. After the puritanical Iconoclasm, there was an explosion of art to fill the new monasteries founded by the Macedonian emperors (AD867–1056). There's also a video installation on the Byzantine castles along the Via Egnatía, gorgeous icons, and a chic café/restaurant.

WHAT TO SEE AND DO

Thessaloníki International Fair [65 E4] (TIF HELEXPO, Egnatía 154; ⍲ 23102 91598; w helexpo.gr/en) Founded in the early Middle Ages and revived in 1926, Thessaloníki's September fair is the biggest in the Balkans, but the space also hosts numerous events throughout the year. The big landmark nearby, on **Plateía Xanth** [65 E4] (ΧΑΝΘ, Greek for YMCA), is a Flash Gordon-style OTE telecommunications tower from 1966, now home to the revolving Skyline Bar (page 76).

MOMus Museum of Contemporary Art [65 E4] (Within the TIF HELEXPO grounds; ⍲ 23102 40002; w momus.gr/en; ⊕ 10.00–18.00 Tue, Wed & Fri–Sun, noon–20.00 Thu; €6, concessions €3) International art dealer Alexander Ιólas was instrumental in founding this museum after the earthquake of 1978, donating close to 507 works by artists such as Andy Warhol (who was first discovered by Ιólas in New York in the late 1940s) and Niki de Sainte-Phalle, as well as internationally known Greek artists, forming the initial core of the collection. The museum also manages the Xydis and Apergis collections, plus the contemporary works of the Foundation of the Macedonian Museum of Contemporary Art and of the State Museum of Contemporary Art and the collection of sculptures of the Foundation Alex Mylona Museum of Contemporary Art. The museum has a full programme of dynamic exhibitions and is also the main sponsor of the Thessaloníki Biennale of Contemporary Art, held in odd-numbered years.

War Museum of Thessaloníki [65 F4] (Gr Lambráki 4; ⍲ 23102 49803; w warmuseum.gr/en; ⊕ Apr–Sep 09.00–19.00 daily, Oct–Mar 09.00–17.00 daily; €4, concessions €2) The all-too-frequent conflicts that took place in Greece in the 19th and 20th centuries are the subject here, with collections of uniforms, posters, weapons, medals, awards and photographs. There's also a large exhibit on singer Sofía Vémbo, the 'Singer of Victory' whose songs boosted Greek morale during World War II.

Aristotle University of Thessaloníki (AUTH) [65 F3] (⍲ 23109 96000; w auth. gr) Founded in 1925, in the newly liberated territories of northern Greece, the university's main building is in a mansion that had been converted into a military hospital on Éthnikis Amýnis Street. The university has several museums, many awaiting renovation – including the fascinating Criminology Museum.

Geology-Paleontology Museum [65 E3] (Ground floor in the right wing of the old Faculty of Sciences, cnr Éth Amýnis & Ag Dimitríou; ⍲ 23109 98540; w auth. gr/en/museums-archives-en/geology-en; ⊕ 09.00–noon Thu, but best to call first; free) Come here to ogle minerals from the mines of Chalkidikí, marbles, fossils of invertebrates and vertebrates, casts of primitive primates and *hominidae*, including the 9.5 million-year-old head bone of the great ape *Ouranopithecus macedoniensis* and the controversial Petrálona skull (page 107).

Museum of Casts and Antiquities [65 E3] (Basement of the New Philosophy building, cnr Éth Amýnis & Egnatía; ⍲ 23109 97301, 23109 97279; w auth.gr/en/museums-archives-en/ekmageia-en; ⊕ 09.00–14.00 Tue, Wed & Fri for hall A, Mon & Thu for Hall B, call to confirm) This collection of 900 casts of Greek and Roman sculpture, along with archaeological finds (coins, terracotta figurines, lamps), is divided into two halls, open on alternate days. The **Chrístos Tsoúntas Hall** has casts of prehistoric works, copies of famous bronzes, and the Parthenon frieze; the **Konstantínos Romaíos Hall** has pediments from the Temple of Zeus at Olympia, Classical and Hellenistic sculpture, reliefs from the Arch of Galerius, and more.

Olympics Museum of Thessaloníki [65 F4] (Cnr 3 Septemvríou & Ag Dimitríou; ☏ 23109 68531; w olympicmuseum-thessaloniki.org; ⊕ 09.00–19.00 Mon–Fri, 10.00–16.00 Sat, 10.00–14.00 Sun; €5, 15 & under free) Aside from the one in Ancient Olympia, this is Greece's only Olympics museum. Under the auspices of the IOC, it contains multimedia displays on the history of the ancient and modern games, with overviews of each Olympiad since 1896, as well as the Paralympics. There's lots of memorabilia – items belonging to modern Olympics founder Pierre de Coubertin, equipment from each sport, artefacts from all the games, including the ones not held during the World Wars, and changing exhibitions.

Telloglio Fine Arts Foundation [65 F3] (Ag Dimitríou 159A; ☏ 23102 47111; w teloglion.gr; ⊕ consult website for current exhibitions & hours) Founded in 1972 by Alíki and Néstor Télloglou and housed in a new building at the north end of the campus, the Telloglio holds thematic exhibitions of modern art, both Greek and international.

SOUTHEASTERN SUBURBS Thessaloníki's residential districts extend southeast of the centre. In the 19th century this was the quarter of the wealthy and cosmopolitan of all faiths, and just before the Balkan Wars beautiful mansions were built, especially along Vasilissis Ólgas Street. Several are still standing, most of them now housing cultural institutions.

Folklife and Ethnological Museum of Macedonia-Thrace [65 E7] (Vas Ólgas 68; ☏ 23108 30591; w lemmth.gr; ⊕ 09.00–15.30 Fri–Tue, 09.00–21.30 Wed; €2) This neo-Gothic meets Art Nouveau villa was built in 1911 by Eli Modiáno for his father, Jacob Modiano. Upon the liberation of Thessaloníki in the first Balkan war, it was acquired by the state with the intent of being given to the Greek royal family for their use. However, during World War I the National Schism divided Greece, with the royalists wishing to remain neutral while the followers of Eleftherios Venizelos favoured joining the war on the side of the Allies. The Provisional Government of National Defence was based in Thessaloníki, with the former Villa Modiano its headquarters. The villa now serves as an excellent child-friendly museum, with two permanent collections – on traditional watermills (and how they work) and an excellent collection of traditional costumes – as well as temporary exhibitions from the museum's extensive collections. Follow up with a drink in the garden café.

Yení Tsamí [65 E6] (Archaiologikoú Mouseíou 30) Rarely open, but worth seeing from the outside if you're exploring the neighbourhood, this 'New Mosque' was built in 1902 by Italian architect Vitaliano Poselli for the Sabbetaians. It's as unique as the community that built it (page 98): a domed neo-Renaissance mosque with touches of the Alhambra and Art Nouveau, dotted with discreet Stars of David and an inscription in Arabic reminding worshippers to 'pray toward Mecca, never toward Jerusalem'. In the immediate aftermath of the population exchange in 1922 it housed refugees from Izmir, and in 1925 it housed the archaeology museum, which is how the street got its name. Today it's sometimes used for special exhibitions. For Eid al-Fitr in 2024, for the first time in over a century, the Yení Tsamí also opened for prayer.

A VERY FINE FIN DE SIÈCLE *Amber Charmei*

The mansions of Thessaloníki's Belle Epoque serve as an exuberant expression of the city's cosmopolitan, multi-cultural spirit and European orientation. While the elite of Athens favoured a more restrained Neoclassicism – a style that suited the identity of the capital of the new Greek State – Thessaloníki's Beau Monde embraced unrestrained eclecticism, uniting a variety of architectural styles and elements. The district was once filled with such mansions, along what is today Vasilíssis Olgas and in the surrounding seaside district; happily, a few remain. The **Villa Allatini** at Vasilíssis Olgas 198, designed by Vitaliano Poselli for the family of bankers and industrialists (page 84), who also owned the Allatini mills at the waterfront close to the mansion, is the grandest of them all, set inside its own tremendous park. The balls held here, with as many as 700 guests, were legendary. In 1909, the villa was augmented by a Turkish bath in order to serve as the genteel prison of the deposed Ottoman Sultan Abdul Hamid (this whole district was once called the Hamidiye in his honour). He remained there until the city changed hands and became part of Modern Greece in 1912.

Returning toward the centre and passing the **Casa Bianca** (the Municipal Art Gallery; see below), a work of 1911–13 by Piérro Arrigóni, we come to the **Villa Mordoch**, at Vasilíssis Olgas 162, by Xenophon Paionídis. Notable for its onion dome, the villa was originally built for Ottoman military commander Seifullah Pasha. Further down the street are two mansions designed by Piérro Arrigóni for the Kapandjí family – successful Ma'min (page 98) industrialists. The villa **Mehmet Kapandjí** with its grand tower at number 108 has a neo-Gothic gravity and a fine double staircase; you can have a peek inside, as after a particularly storied history this is now a branch of the Cultural Foundation of the National Bank of Greece and is frequently open for exhibitions. The colourful **Villa Ahmet Kapandjí** at Vasilíssis Olgas 105 is among the neighbourhood's most elaborate constructions, with Art Nouveau flourishes, polychrome masonry, Moorish details and charming lacy eaves. Other fine examples of Thessaloníki's eclecticism include Eli Modiano's **Villa Modiano** with its mansard roof (now the Folklife and Ethnological Museum of Macedonia-Thrace; see opposite) and the **Yení Tzamí** (see opposite), Poselli's masterpiece for the Ma'min community.

Municipal Art Gallery [58 E2] (Vas Ólgas 182 ; 23133 18538; ⏰ 09.00–15.00 Tue–Sat; subject to change, call for updated hours; free) The city's extensive art collection, from Byzantine icons to contemporary Greek painting, etchings and sculpture, is housed in the splendid Casa Bianca, an Art Nouveau mansion designed for the industrialist Fernandez-Diaz, and named for his wife Blanche, by Piero Arrigóni. It hosts major exhibitions in conjunction with other galleries in Greece and abroad.

AROUND THESSALONÍKI
Sheikh-sou Forest (or Kedrinós Lófos, or Chília Déndra) [65 G2] Above the university, Thessaloníki's biggest city park is a favourite place for walks. Head to a spot called **Kará Tepé** [65 H1] for beautiful views over the city and the gulf.

3 | THESSALONÍKI (ΘΕΣΣΑΛΟΝΙΚΗ)

> ### SACRED SINNING: THE SABBETAIANS
>
> When the Sephardim emigrated from Iberia, they brought along not only their customs and language, but also their cabbalist schools, which made them especially receptive to the millennial messianic speculation that flared up in the 17th century among Christians and Jews alike. Interpreters of mystic texts concluded that the years 1638 and 1666 would be years of wonders and redemption and maybe the end of the world.
>
> In 1638, a keen student of the texts, the charismatic Sabbetai Zevi from Smyrna, proclaimed himself the Messiah and attracted followers, especially in Thessaloníki. Ottoman rulers didn't care about their subjects' private beliefs as long as they maintained decorum, but in 1666, as Zevi became famous and rumours swirled of improper behaviour, Sultan Mehmed IV ordered his arrest. Zevi was given the choice of either becoming a Muslim or death – and, to the surprise of most observers, he chose to convert, explaining it as the ultimate sacrifice of the Messiah. Some 300 Jewish families in Thessaloníki followed him in his 'sacred sin' and called themselves the Ma'min, the 'Faithful'; Ottomans, who doubted their sincerity, called them Dönmeh ('Turn-coats'), while other Jews considered them apostates. The Ma'min were an influential community: pioneers in enlightened education, successful international industrialists, cosmopolitan intellectuals, architectural patrons and local politicians, including the last mayor of the Ottoman era. In the neighbourhood by the water extending east from the White Tower are the two splendid Kapandji mansions, as well as the Yení Tsamí (page 96).

Panórama (Πανόραμα) [58 E2] (11km east on the slopes of Mount Chortiátis; take bus 58 from Plateía Dikastiríon) This busy and leafy suburb, with hotels and restaurants, commands a fine view of the Thermaikós. Just east of the suburb is the Platanákia (w platanakia-natura.gr), a popular family-friendly destination for a short hike alongside the stream or a coffee in the shade.

Chortiátis (Χορτιάτης) [58 F2] Site of a horrific Nazi reprisal, this now peaceful village and mountain (1,201m), another 18km southwest (bus 57, then 61 from centre), lures in city dwellers for mountain walks and biking, and its neat tavernas specialising in game, lamb and *kokorétsi* (lamb innards braided on skewers – they taste better than they sound).

Thessaloníki Science Centre and Technology Museum (NOESIS) [58 E3] (6km on the Thessaloníki–Thérmi road – take a taxi; \ 23104 83000; w noesis.edu. gr; ⊕ summer 09.30–16.30 Tue & Thu–Fri, 11.00–19.00 Wed & Sat–Sun; for winter hours consult website or call; may close 1 week in Aug; admission €12, concessions €8, inc audio-guide in English) This is full of science fun for all ages, and one of the best places to while away a rainy day – it even has a good restaurant with views over the gulf. The Science Centre boasts a state-of-the-art digital **Planetarium**, the **Cosmotheatre** presenting giant 3D films (both for ages over five) and the chance to ride a **Motion Simulator** that combines 3D stereoscopic shows with motion (for ages over seven and over 120cm). The **Technology Museum** has exhibits on ancient Greek engineering reproduced in life-size wooden models, plus a classic car collection and a hands-on interactive techno-park full of clever gadgetry.

Family tickets are available. Go at the weekend to avoid school groups.

WHAT TO SEE AND DO

Theme parks If the kids need payback for all those churches you've made them see, there are two options nearby: **Magic Park** [58 E3] (km12 on the airport road; ☏23104 76770; w magicpark.gr; ⊕ w/ends & school hols) is an old-fashioned funfair park. A little further out is **Waterland** [58 E3] (Néo Rýsio, off the Chalkidikí road; ☏ 23920 72025; w waterland.gr; ⊕ Jun–mid-Sep 10.00–18.00, mid-Jul–mid-Aug 10.00–20.00), a massive waterpark with a small zoo. Special shuttle buses depart from several stops in the city – call the number above and press '9' for English to listen to the schedule.

Beaches If Chalkidikí isn't on the cards, there are Blue Flag beaches closer to the city. **Peraía Paralía** [58 D4] (bus 78 to the IKEA stop, then change to 72, or go by boat – page 66), with its 7.5km narrow stretch of sand, is a big favourite, lined with bars and sunbeds. Its western extension **Néoi Epivátes** [58 D4] is the favourite of the young, with its 900m Baxe Beach lined with plane trees, tavernas and bars that stay open late on summer nights. There are two other Blue Flag beaches further west at **Ag Triáda** [58 D4].

Next along the coast is **Angelochóri** [58 C4] (bus 76 from the station) with its landmark lighthouse on Cape Megálo Émbolo, a favourite spot for watching sunsets. Its beach is one of the best for kitesurfing, while beyond is a Natura 2000 lagoon. There's a beautiful sandy beach called **Riviera** [58 C4] just south before the fishing port of **Néa Michanióna** [58 C4] (bus 71 from the station), and several further south at **Epanomí** [58 D4] (bus 70 from the station, or 69A or 69K from IKEA).

Gerovassilíou Wine Museum [58 D4] (Epanomí; ☏23920 44567; w gerovassiliou. gr; ⊕ 10.00–16.00 Mon, Thu & Fri, 13.00–19.00 Wed, 11.00–17.00 Sat–Sun; tour of cellar, vineyards & museum €5, students €2.50, under 18s free; tastings from €15) Owner Vangélis Gerovassilíou has been a key figure in the promotion of indigenous Greek varietals, saving one – white Malagousiá – from extinction. The museum has a display on the history of wine and historic items, including one of the world's largest collections of corkscrews (2,600 and counting). Throughout the winery and vineyards are many first-rate works of art and major sculptures by Greek and international artists.

Lagadás (Λαγκαδάς) [58 E1] (16km northeast of Thessaloníki; bus 83M leaves several times a day – call ☏23105 31678 or see w ktelthes.gr/slide/no-83-lagkadas-thessaloniki for times; ☏ 23940 22221; ⊕ 08.00–23.00 daily) This town has the closest spa and thermal springs to the city, the **Loutrá Lagadá**, with two domed Byzantine tubs; the Justinian opened in AD900 and the Mygdonia in 1400. Both are still in use, alternating days between the genders in the daytime (⊕ 08.00–18.00) and available by advance booking for private use in the evenings (⊕ 18.00–23.00); there are also modern tubs, jacuzzis and personal tubs.

Axiós Delta National Park [58 B3] (8km southwest of Thessaloníki; ☏ 23107 94811; w axiosdelta.gr; entry at the birdwatching tower, or by the visitor centre; free) The great delta and rice fields formed by the Axiós (Vardar), Gallikós, Loudías and other rivers is a major wetlands area, where wild horses and water buffalo roam. By its southernmost section, where Greece's longest river, the Aliákmonas, meets the sea at **Néa Agathoúpoli** (50km from Thessaloníki), there's a **birdwatching tower** (⊕ 10.00–14.00 Mon–Sat; free) with telescopes, where 215 species have been spotted – with luck you might see a pair of white-tailed sea eagles, along with

3 | THESSALONÍKI (ΘΕΣΣΑΛΟΝΙΚΗ)

WALKING ON FIRE

Lagadás is famous for its fire-walkers, the Anasternárides ('groaners'), who on the evening of 21 May dance barefoot over burning coals to the drum and *lýra*, holding aloft icons of SS Constantine and Helen. The story goes that c1250, in the Thracian town of Kósti, as the church of Ag Konstantínos went up in a blaze, its icons could be heard groaning, and some of the villagers rescued them without coming to any harm. Since then, both the icons and the ability to walk on fire in a trance have been passed down in their families. The families moved to Macedonia in 1914 when Kósti became part of Bulgaria; besides Lagadás, other Anasternárides live in Marvoléki (Drama), Ag Eléni (south of Sérres) and Melíki (by Véria), where the ceremony also takes place, and usually includes the sacrifice of a garlanded calf and sheep, to be eaten after the fire-walk. The Dionysian echoes of all this hardly meets the approval of the Orthodox church, which in the past has excommunicated the fire-walkers and done all it could to suppress the rite. These days, however, the Anasternárides have taken on the trappings of a folklore troupe: special buses come up from Thessaloníki (get there by late afternoon for a good view), and the fire-walking takes place over three evenings (19–21 or 20–22 May; the Feast Day of Konstantínos and Eléni itself is 21 May) to accommodate the crowds. If you can't make it in person, they usually show it on Greek television.

thousands of ducks, pochards, Dalmatian pelicans, purple herons and shelducks. In summer, though, especially at sunset, beware the mosquitoes.

The visitors' centre (✆ 23107 94811; ⊕ 10.00–15.00 Mon–Sat) is in Chalástra [58 B2], 25km from the city.

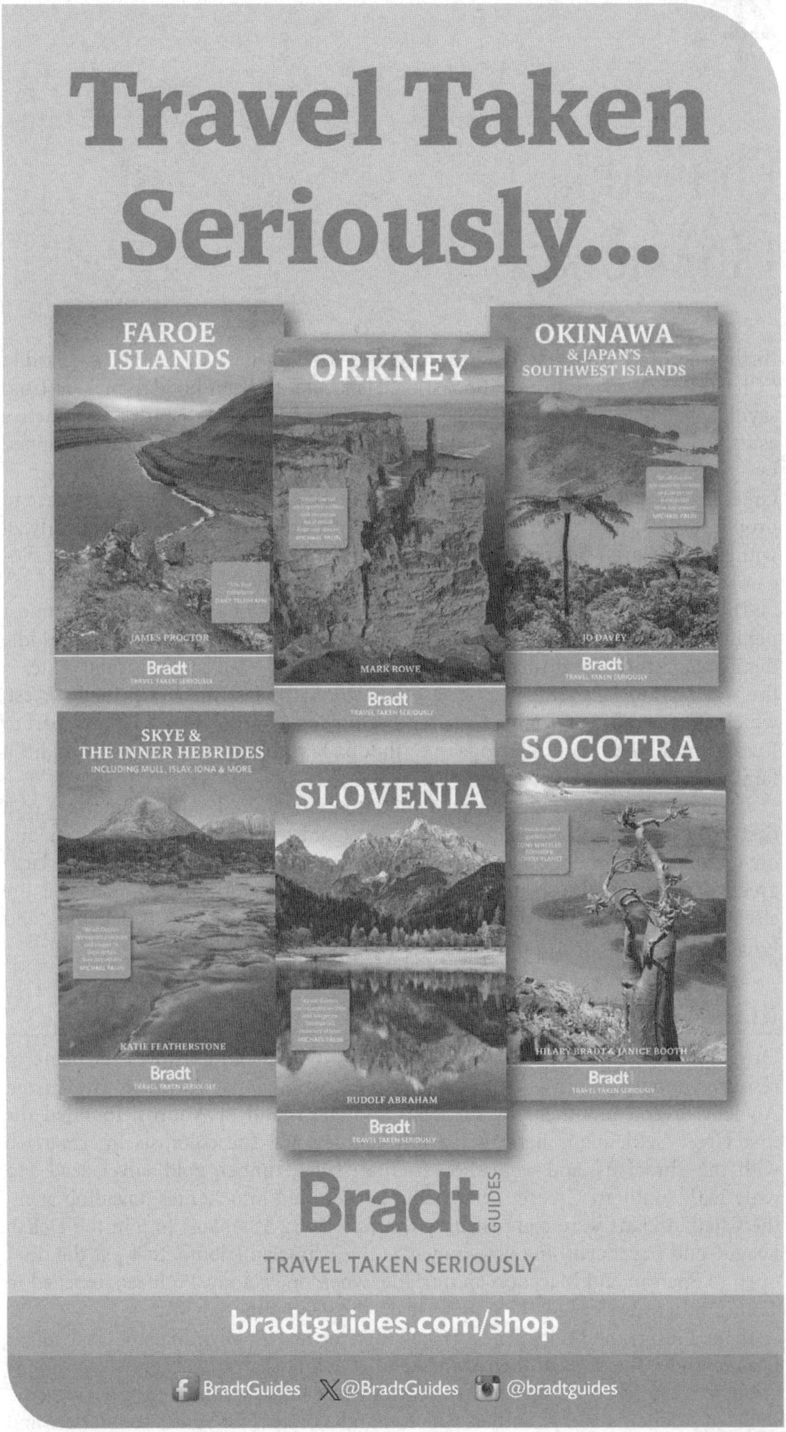
Travel Taken Seriously...
FAROE ISLANDS
JAMES PROCTOR
Bradt
TRAVEL TAKEN SERIOUSLY
ORKNEY
MARK ROWE
Bradt
TRAVEL TAKEN SERIOUSLY
OKINAWA & JAPAN'S SOUTHWEST ISLANDS
JO DAVEY
Bradt
TRAVEL TAKEN SERIOUSLY
SKYE & THE INNER HEBRIDES
INCLUDING MULL, ISLAY, IONA & MORE
KATIE FEATHERSTONE
Bradt
TRAVEL TAKEN SERIOUSLY
SLOVENIA
RUDOLF ABRAHAM
Bradt
TRAVEL TAKEN SERIOUSLY
SOCOTRA
HILARY BRADT & JANICE BOOTH
Bradt
TRAVEL TAKEN SERIOUSLY
Bradt GUIDES
TRAVEL TAKEN SERIOUSLY
bradtguides.com/shop
BradtGuides
@BradtGuides
@bradtguides

3

4

Chalkidikí
(Χαλκιδική)

Birthplace of Aristotle and northern Greece's favourite playground, Chalkidikí ('Chalcidice' in many history books, or 'Halkidikí' to keep holiday-makers from saying 'chalk') resembles a giant bear paw, with a history and spirit as distinctive as its geography. Along the three dangling claws, pines back sandy beaches lapped by a turquoise sea, planted with more Blue Flags per square metre than any part of Greece – 93 at the current count. This is your best chance in northern Greece to drop a serious chunk of change at a luxury hotel or gourmet restaurant (nearly all within the resorts) but there are also more affordable hotels, apartments, studios galore – often booked by package holiday firms – campsites and humble tavernas.

The closer to Thessaloníki and its airport, the busier the shore. The westernmost peninsula, Kassándra, is the summer resort for half of Thessaloníki. The middle peninsula, Sithonía, still has wild patches; while the eastern peninsula, Akté, is the way station to another world: Mount Athos, the last theocracy in the West, which after decades of decline is currently enjoying a boom, thanks in large part to Russian and other eastern European Orthodox faithful, many of whom combine a family beach holiday with a visit.

If Chalkidikí's 'claws' get most of the attention, the inland is something of a best-kept secret, with farmland, mountains, gold mines, dense pine woods and olive groves that produce a whopping percentage of Greece's table olives (the large green ones are the most famous), and literally tonnes of honey, much of it the elsewhere somewhat rare pine honey. That of wild thyme flowers is delicious, and for something unique, try the chestnut.

HISTORY

Originally home to the Thracian Paeonian tribe, Chalkidikí owes its name to resource-hungry colonists from Chalkís, Évia, who, along with their rivals from Ancient Eretria (another city on Évia) and the island of Ándros, founded the first Greek settlements here in the 8th century BC. The colonists intermarried with the Thracians, and were soon trading slaves, timber, gold, silver, lead and wine with southern Greece. After being conscripted into Xerxes' invading army, the Chalkidikians were compelled by the victorious Athenians to join the Delian League and pay a crushing tax, known as the 'Thracian tribute', that left the door open to Spartan and Macedonian intrigue; when one colony, Potidaea, rebelled in 432BC, Athens besieged it, helping to spark the Peloponnesian War.

In the 390sBC, the 32 city-states of Chalkidikí formed the Olynthian (or Chalcidian) League under the aegis of their own capital, Olynthos, a rare, progressive example of ancient Greek co-operation that excited the jealousy of the neighbouring city-states of Apollonia and Acanthus, which found a pretext for Sparta to interfere and conquer. Weakened and subsequently caught in the meshes of Philip II, who coveted the gold and silver mines on Chalkidikí's east coast, the cities turned to Athens for help, and in 348BC Philip responded by destroying every last one.

Depopulated, Chalkidikí slipped out of history until the 9th century AD, when the first monks arrived on Athos. Over the centuries, Byzantine emperors granted much of the rest of Chalkidikí's land to the monasteries as dependencies (*metóchia*) to support the holy men. Settlements of labourers grew up around the fortified towers that protected the coasts from pirates, and even under the Ottomans life carried on pretty much the same until the locals, notably on the Kassándra Peninsula, joined the Greek War of Independence and were massacred in 1821. In 1923, the *metóchia* were confiscated to provide land for the Asia Minor refugees, who built some 30 new towns, most of them named after their old homes with a 'new' (Néa) in front.

GETTING THERE AND AWAY

For Thessaloníki's Chalkidikí Bus Station, see page 66. The region is blessed with a good bus service and website (w ktel-chalkidikis.gr), where you can check schedules and book e-tickets (note that you still may need to exchange the e-ticket for a paper one at the ticket counter before departure). Main stations, where you may have to change, are at Polýgyros (\ 23710 22309; 70mins from Thessaloníki; €6.90) and Néa Moudaniá (\ 23730 21228; 60mins; €6.90).

TOURIST INFORMATION AND TOUR OPERATORS

There are several useful websites covering the region, including the general, up-to-date website w visit-halkidiki.gr.

BOAT TRIPS In addition to the cruises listed here, you can also hire a boat (see below; €80/day) to visit the little island of Diáporos.

Athos Cruises \ 23770 71071; m 69861 07451; w athos-cruises.gr. 3hr morning cruises around Mount Athos from Ouranoúpoli (€25 pp, ages 6–12 €12.50, under 6s free). Afternoon cruises are available 15 May–15 Oct, as well as cruises to Ammoulianí. Book online.
Ormos Travel Órmos Panagiás; \ 23750 31522; w ormostravel.com. Runs 2 Mount Athos cruises (€35 pp, ages 6–12 €17.50, under 6s free), one to view 8 monasteries with a stop for lunch, & another to view 4 monasteries plus a stop at a lagoon for a swim & light lunch on board. They depart Órmos Panagiás at 09.15 & return at 17.00 or 17.30. You can also skip the monasteries altogether on a beach & lagoon cruise. Book cruises a day in advance by phone or email.

SPORTS AND ACTIVITIES

There are some 20 **walking** trails in Chalkidikí, from easy to challenging – for online maps see w komoot.com/guide/17659/hiking-in-chalkidiki. There are also cycling routes at w komoot.com/guide/17662/cycling-in-halkidiki, and mountain biking routes at w komoot.com/guide/17660/mtb-trails-in-halkidiki.

BOAT AND KAYAK HIRE
Diaporos Boat Rentals Vourvouroú; m 69863 12501; w diaporos-boats.gr. Explore the Sithonía coast & islands on your own; from €80 for 4.
On Waves Vourvouroú; m 69739 79529; w onwaves.gr. Boat rental for independent explorations plus private excursions

4 | CHALKIDIKÍ (ΧΑΛΚΙΔΙΚΗ)

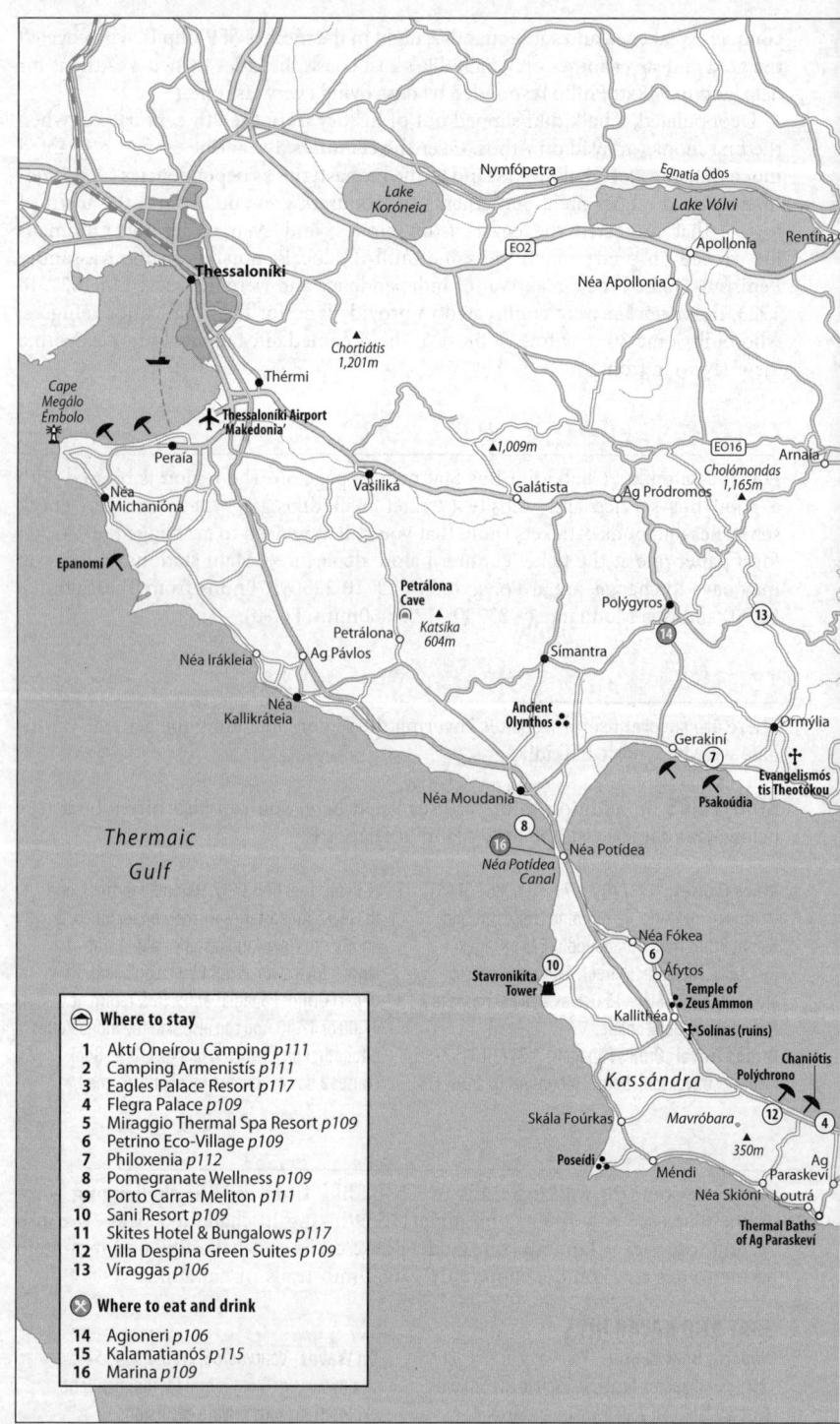

SPORTS AND ACTIVITIES

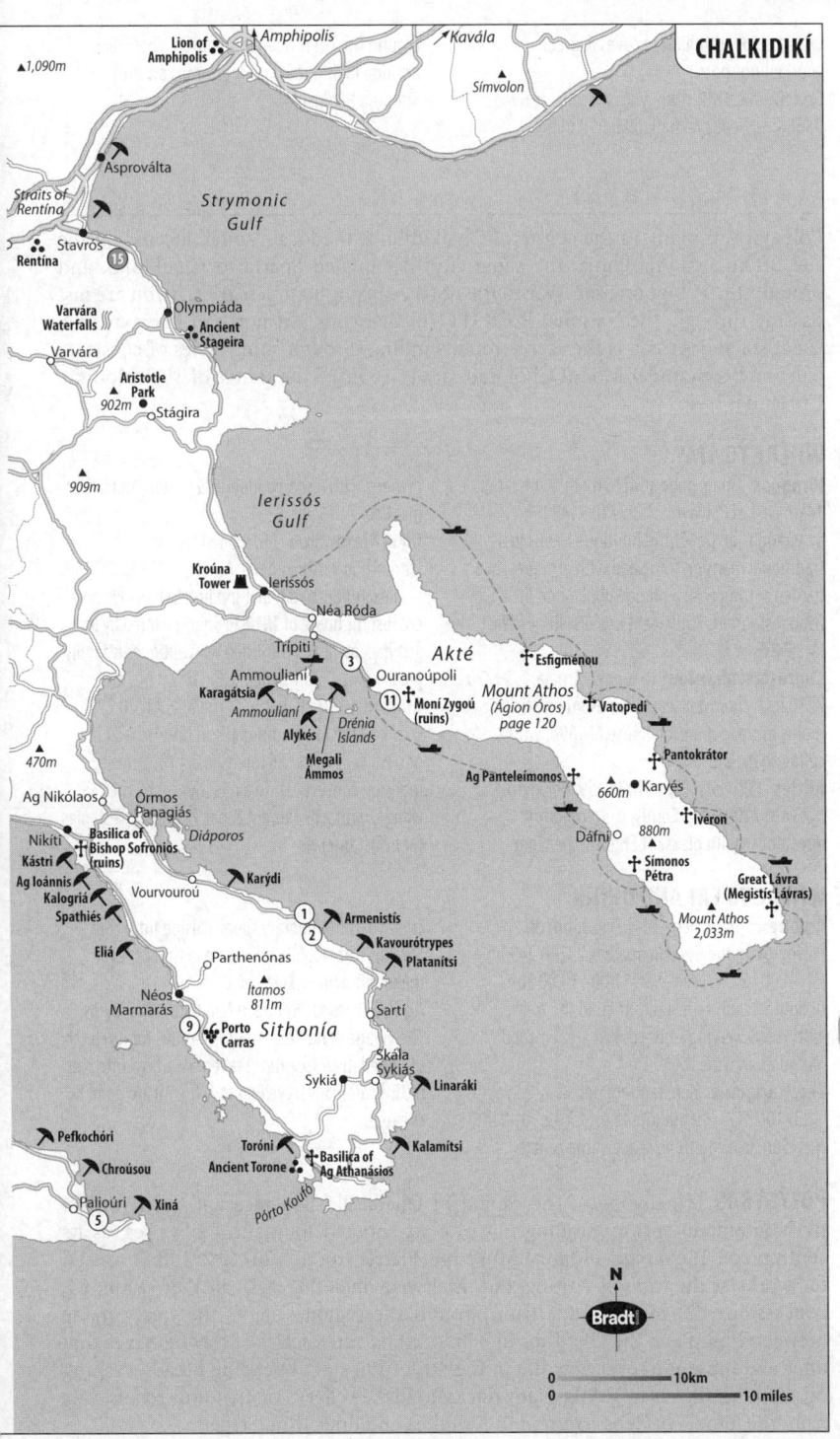

with a skipper to hidden coves & great snorkelling spots. **Sea Kayak Halkidiki** Vourvouroú; m 69452 35686; w seakayakhalkidiki.gr. Paddle around the islets near Vourvouroú. They also arrange hiking tours up Mt Ítamos on the Sithonía Peninsula.

CENTRAL CHALKIDIKÍ

Polýgyros, roughly in the centre of Chalkidikí, is the local capital, located on the site of Ancient Apollonia, the same city that invited Sparta to Chalkidikí, and brought the Peloponnesian War to the north, causing so much grief. If you are just passing through, the National Road (EO16) that runs just north of Polýgyros via Galátista and Arnaía is the scenic route winding through sunny vales of chestnut, oak and beech under Mount Cholómondas (1,165m) – the source of Thessaloníki's Christmas trees.

 WHERE TO STAY

Víraggas [map, page 104] (6 rooms) Vrástama, 14km east of Polýgyros; 23710 71429; w viraggas.gr. Delightful boutique rooms in a traditional mansion furnished with antiques, in a garden setting with a plunge pool, good little Slow Food restaurant, & adjacent *rakí* distillery. B/fast inc. €€€–€€

Chorostasi Mansion (6 rooms) Arnaía; 23720 22102; w chorostasi.com. Handsome rustic chic rooms in stone mansion house of 1896, with a coffee shop. €€

Klities (5 rooms) Politechníou 59, Polýgyros; 23710 21001; . Comfy, contemporary guesthouse with pleasant English-speaking owners, with a shared lounge & continental b/fast inc. €€

Oikia Alexándrou (10 rooms) Plateía Patriárchou Vartholoméou, Arnaía; 23720 23210; w alexandrou-traditional-inn.hotelschalkidiki.net/en. Historic house of 1812, lovingly restored by its architect owners & furnished with antiques & family possessions. Comfy bedding. Big b/fast inc. €€

Oikia Mitsiou (6 rooms) Arnaía; 23720 22744; w oikia-mitsiou-traditional-inn.hotelschalkidiki.net/en. Very colourful rooms in a 19th-century mansion converted into a guesthouse by the village, with a restaurant & bar. Excellent fresh pies for b/fast (inc). €

✖ WHERE TO EAT AND DRINK

Agioneri [map, page 104] 2km south of Polýgyros on the Gerakiní road; 23710 24500; 14.00–22.00 Wed–Sat, 11.00–19.00 Sun. Delightful country restaurant amid the trees, with views, serving slow-cooked meats; good Macedonian wine list. €€€

The Marigoula Konstantinoupoléos 7, Polýgyros; 23710 23171; w marigoula.gr; 12.30–01.00 Tue–Sun. In a charming space in the centre, creative, contemporary Greek cuisine from chef Sofoklís Yiagtzóglou, who (rare in Greece) even makes his own pickles. €€€

Ag Pródromos Between Galátista & Polýgyros. The village of Ag Pródromos is famous for its clutch of grilled meat (*psistariá*) tavernas, a favourite stop of Thessalonians travelling to & fro. All are good & cheap. €

POLÝGYROS (Πολύγυροσ) The capital of Chalkidikí is a pleasant town, with a fresh mountain spring gurgling out of a six-spouted fountain, Éxi Vríses, as its centrepiece. The **Archaeological Museum** (Plateía Iróon; 23710 22148; closed for works at the time of writing, but otherwise open 08.30–15.30 Wed–Mon; €4, concessions €2) houses finds from around the region. There's the treaty made between Philip and the Olynthos in 356BC, coins and a series of clay figurines that offer a glimpse into everyday life in the 4th century BC: kneading bread, washing up, bathing (but also riding giant ducks), plus jewellery, vases, tomb reliefs, bits from the temple of Zeus Ammon in Kallithéa and finds from Stageira.

GALÁTISTA (Γαλάτιστα; 21km northwest of Polýgyros) The village of Galátista, famous for its honey, is dominated by a massive late Byzantine tower, near a pair of working watermills.

PETRÁLONA CAVE (Σπήλαιο Πετραλώνων; 39km west of Polýgyros; ☏ 23730 73365; w petralonacave.gr; ⊕ guided tours summer 08.00–20.00 daily, winter 09.00–15.00 Tue–Sun; €8, concessions €4) In 1959, villagers searching for water on the edge of Mount Katsíka (604m) discovered this beautiful stalactite cave, tinted red from bauxite deposits. It was filled with a remarkable range of fossils – prehistoric rhinos, lions, bears and sabre-toothed tigers, and, embedded in a stalactite, a 25–35-year-old humanoid cranium. This has been a source of huge controversy. Áris Poulianós, who led the excavation team, claims it represented a new species of hominin, *Archanthropus europaeus petraloniensis*, and dated it to around 700,000BC, 'the first man out of Africa' along with traces of fire. Since then other studies have dated the skull to 200,000–170,000BC and identified the skull as *Homo erectus*, or *Homo heidelbergensis*, the species that may have been the common ancestor of Neanderthals and modern humans. But as other very early hominins have been discovered in Europe, notably Tautaval Man in southwest France, the controversy rages on.

ANCIENT OLYNTHOS (Όλυνθος; 21km southwest of Polýgyros; ☏ 23710 22060; w odysseus.culture.gr; ⊕ 08.00–15.00 Wed–Mon; €4, concessions €2) Pre-Hellenic for 'wild fig', Olynthos was briefly the most important city in Chalkidikí. Spread over two flat hills, the higher one was settled by Bottiaians, a Thracian tribe from Imathia, in the 7th century BC, after King Perdiccas I of Macedon conquered their homeland. In 480BC, Xerxes drafted the Bottiaians and their ships to his cause, but when they rebelled the next year, the Persians destroyed the city.

In 432BC, as coastal populations broke away from Athens (and from the onerous 'Thracian' tribute Athens charged to belong to its Delian League) the Chalkidikians built a new Olynthos on the north hill, laid out to accommodate 30,000 inhabitants, as the headquarters of the Olynthian (or Chalcidian) League. Philip II courted the league after it was fatally weakened by its Spartan overlords in the Peloponnesian War, but the relationship went sour in 349BC, and he besieged it. Back in Athens, the great orator Demosthenes gave his three famous Olynthiac speeches that rallied the Athenians to its defence, but the wily Philip caused a diversion by attacking Évia while obliterating Olynthos before the Athenians arrived, leaving behind his calling card for archaeologists: arrowheads inscribed 'Philippos'.

Because it had only lasted 84 years, Olynthos is the best-preserved example of a purely Classical city in Greece, laid out in a Hippodameian grid in blocks of ten houses, in two rows of five, with a channel between to take rainwater from the roofs. Walls on rubble foundations were built with sound anti-seismic flexibility, their baked bricks strengthened with timber ties. Uniformity ended indoors, however, where householders arranged rooms as they pleased around stone-paved courtyards, each with their own cistern, family altar and *pastas* (portico), leading into the residential area. *Androns* (men's banqueting rooms) were decorated with the oldest floor mosaics ever found, including one of *Bellerophon on Pegasus Attacking the Chimera*. One house still has its bathtub. Of the Archaic-era city on the south hill, recent excavations have revealed two avenues, the agora and the prytaneion.

ORMÝLIA (Ορμύλια) Southeast of Polýgyros, Ormýlia hosts one of the best-known convents in Greece, the **Evangelismós tis Theotókou** (w ormyliamonastery.com), a dependency of Símonos Pétras on Mount Athos, founded in the 1970s. Many of its 120 nuns are doctors working in the Ormýlia Foundation (w ormyliafoundation.gr), which specialises in free screening for breast and cervical cancer. They also run a farm, producing olive oil and fruit liqueurs, and the Ormýlia Art Diagnosis Centre (w artdiagnosis.gr), using the latest technology for the preservation and promotion of art and culture in archaeological sites, Byzantine churches and more. The nuns are also famous for their singing on Sunday mornings.

ARNAÍA (Αρναία) This village east of Polýgyros is a favourite weekend retreat of the Thessalonians, a beautifully restored Brigadoon of stone and wooden houses, cobbled lanes and fountains, surrounded by orchards and vineyards. A popular first stop is the main square, where you can refresh yourself in the spring of cold water that flows from beneath the plane tree. Arnaía was famous for its colourful handmade carpets and wall hangings, and has a **Weaving Museum** (m 69429 49250; ⊕ 10.00–18.00 Fri–Wed, closed holidays) close to the central square (behind the National Bank) in a building that belonged to weaver Charikleía Dimitrakoúdi (d2003), with exhibits dedicated to the art of weaving, including displays on wool dyeing and looms, and a traditionally decorated room. Directly across from the Weaving Museum is the **Historical and Folklore Museum** (⊕ 10.00–18.00 Fri–Wed) housed in a historic mansion and displaying beautiful utilitarian items from the good old days. Both museums share a single admission price of €2; large groups should ring ahead (Municipality of Arnaía: \23723 50130). Another worthwhile stop, just 400m from the square on Aristotélous Street, is the church of St Stephen (Ágios Stéfanos) with its timber roof and floor of glass. Built in 1812, it burned down along with the rest of the village in the revolution of 1821. It was rebuilt shortly afterwards, but then nearly completely destroyed by fire once again, in 2005. That is when three earlier structures were revealed, including an early Christian basilica (from about AD400) and a Byzantine temple of the 10th–11th centuries. Tombs found in the excavation are visible through the glass floors.

KASSÁNDRA PENINSULA

Kassándra (Κασσανδρα; Ancient Pallini) is technically an island, cut off at its neck by a 1,250m canal at **Néa Potídea** (Νέα Ποτίδαια). Ancient Potidaea was Chalkidikí's only Corinthian colony, founded c600BC – the settlers obviously felt at home on an isthmus – and it maintained a close relationship with its mother city, which encouraged it to revolt against Athens in 432BC. A two-year siege ensued (Socrates, one of the Athenian hoplites, was famous even then – for going barefoot on ice) before Athens prevailed and replaced its population with Athenians. Philip II in turn snatched it and gave it to Olynthos to curry favour, then razed it. Cassander re-founded the town as Kassandría, which gave its name to the entire peninsula. He dug the canal (re-dug in the 1930s by an American company) and made the city Macedon's ship-building centre. You can see ruins of the great walls built out of ancient buildings under Byzantine emperor Justinian; they were last repaired by the Venetians in 1426 in a vain attempt to turn back the Turks. Fertile Kassándra was Chalkidikí's most prosperous peninsula until 1821 and the Greek War of Independence, which Kassandrans enthusiastically joined, only to realise that they were hardly prepared to fight. They back-pedalled, but the Pasha of Thessaloníki would have none of it and slaughtered them and demolished their villages, and for decades afterwards the peninsula was given over to shepherds. Today, with its 40km of beaches, it is all filled up again. With its slightly quicker access from Thessaloniki, Kassándra is largely considered the liveliest of the peninsulas, with a greater concentration of beach bars and nightlife options.

WHERE TO STAY
Beach hotels and resorts are open from April to October unless otherwise stated, and many offer shuttles from Thessaloníki's airport. Nearly all will have minimum stays.

Ikos Oceania (290 rooms) Néa Moudaniá; ☎ 23730 95100; w ikosresorts.com. Recently renovated, this chic resort is one of the most popular in the region, with its 4 à la carte restaurants (€€€€€–€€€), beach, pools, spa, sports & all the other bells & whistles; all inclusive. €€€€€

Pomegranate Wellness Hotel [map, page 104] (172 rooms) Néa Moudaniá; ☎ 23730 43070; w pomegranatespahotel.com. One of the newest 5 stars, located just north of the Néa Potídea canal, with a 1st-class spa & excellent restaurant, Hermes (€€€€€), serving arty creative cuisine with a Greek touch. €€€€€

Sani Resort [map, page 104] (694 rooms & suites, 252 bungalows) Sáni; ☎ 0800 949 6809; w sani-resort.com. One of the most famous resorts in Greece, an immaculately landscaped, award-winning complex encompassing 5 hotels (each catering to different types of guest), 7 sandy beaches, infinity pools, 4 spas, a bird sanctuary, a marina with yacht charters & every sport (including Chelsea FC coaching for 4–16-year-olds), 26 boutiques, 15 bars & 19 restaurants in every price range. They are also known for the annual music & performing arts Sani Festival (w sani-resort.com/festivals/sani-festival), strong on jazz, each Jul/Aug. €€€€€

Miraggio Thermal Spa Resort [map, page 104] (300 rooms) Kanigtro, Palioúri; ☎ 23744 40000; w miraggio.gr. This award-winning all-suites resort opened in 2016 on 16.6ha of coast near the end of Kassándra, complete with a 3,000m² thermal spa & thalassotherapy pool, beaches, marina for super-yachts, high-tech concert hall, amusements, & gourmet restaurants (€€€€€) under chef Zacharías Koprídis. Many suites have private pools. B/fast inc. €€€€€–€€€€

Flegra Palace [map, page 104] (82 rooms) Palioúri–Áthitou road; ☎ 23740 61702; w flegrahotels.com. A 9min walk from Chaniótis Beach, with contemporary rooms in Mediterranean colours in a palmy garden surrounding a large pool overhung by a glass-bottom terrace, all beautifully lit in the evening. Good restaurants (€€€€) & cocktail bar; delicious Greek b/fast buffet inc. €€€€–€€

Petrino Eco-Village [map, page 104] (34 rooms) 700m from the sea, north of Áfytos; ☎ 23740 91635; w petrino-hotel.gr. Rooms & suites in stone houses, some sleeping 4, with traditional furnishings, deep colours & plenty of wood & stone in a pretty setting with a pool; it also has a beach 800m away. The excellent restaurant (€€€) serves tasty dishes (with lots of game in season) prepared in an outdoor wood oven. €€€

Blue Bay (69 rooms) 200m from the sea in Áfytos; ☎ 23740 91645; w bluebayhotel.com.gr; ⊕ May–Oct. Warm & welcoming hotel in a lofty position on the edge of town, where all rooms have lovely views over the gulf. Pool, restaurants, & steps down to the beach. €€€–€€

Villa Despina Green Suites [map, page 104] (4 rooms) Polýchrono; m 69424 02111; w villadespinasuites.com. Set in a flower-filled garden, energy-efficient, well-equipped 2-bedroom suites which have been awarded the EU Ecolabel; a 200m walk from the beach. €€€–€€

WHERE TO EAT AND DRINK
Many of the best restaurants are in the resorts.

Marina [map, page 104] Néa Potídea, by the canal; ☎ 23730 41570; w marina-fish.gr; ⊕ year-round, from noon or 13.00 through dinner service daily. This popular destination restaurant from Thessaloníki is widely regarded as one of the best fish & seafood restaurants in Chalkidikí – a favourite of chefs dining out. Beautiful modern room, gorgeous presentation. Make sure to book. €€€

Sousouráda & Sgourós Skatzóchiros Áfytos; ☎ 23740 91594; Sousourada Restaurant; ⊕ May–mid-Oct 18.00–midnight daily. One of the best restaurants in Chalkidikí, with a lovely terrace, serving creative Greek cuisine made with top ingredients. Great Greek wine list, especially the reds. €€€

Théa Thálassa Áfytos; \ 23740 91044; w theathalassa-afitos.gr; ⊕ noon–midnight daily. The 'Sea View' offers just that, along with wonderful seafood, including a mouthwatering risotto. €€€

Giannikos 1962 In the main square of Palioúri; \ 23740 92214; giannikostaverna; ⊕ 12.30–23.30 daily. Towards the very tip of the peninsula, everything a Greek taverna should be, & outdoor tables for people-watching. €€

Imeros Cocktail Bar Áfytos; m 69743 18194; ⊕ 10.00–02.00 daily. Delicious cocktails & coffees in a shady courtyard, served with a smile, sometimes with live music.

WHAT TO SEE AND DO South of the bridge that connects the peninsula to the rest of Chalkidikí, Kassándra's tourism vocation begins in earnest. The road passes through flat lands to reach **Sáni** on the Thermaic Gulf, named after an ancient colony of Ándros and now a luxurious 400ha eco-friendly estate surrounded by pine woods (page 109). Like Porto Carras (page 113) it was begun in the 1960s on mosquito-plagued marshland and pine forest purchased from the monks on Mount Athos, in this case by public contractor Anastásios Andreádis (whose family still own it) and civil engineer Leonídas Zisiádis. The 16th-century **Stavronikíta Tower** on the coastal bluff overlooking the resort is typical of the ones built by the Athonite monasteries; the nearby hill hosts the summer Sáni Festival, featuring classical and jazz musicians, often playing works especially commissioned for the festival.

A similar tower guards **Néa Fókea**, where the road crosses over to the east coast of the peninsula. Here **Áfytos** (Άφυτος) or Áthyos is Kassándra's prettiest village, its traditional stone houses and cobbled lanes hugging the slope down to the beach, which has some of the warmest waters in the Med. **Kallithéa** (Καλλιθέα), next south, has a good white sandy and often crowded beach adorned with the foundations of a 4th-century BC Doric **Temple of Zeus Ammon** (⊕ summer 08.00–15.00 Wed–Fri; free). This was the most important sanctuary in Greece dedicated to the ram-horned Greco-Egyptian king of the gods – whom Alexander the Great believed (or pretended to believe) was his real father, according to the oracle in the Libyan oasis of Siwa, which also predicted he would conquer the world. Unlike most ancient temples, which faced east, this had north–south orientation. South of Kallithéa at a spot called **Solínas**, there are the pretty mosaic floors from a 5th-century AD basilica, showing a pair of deer in paradise.

Above the next beach resort, **Polýchrono** (Πολύχρονο), you can take a 3km walk to **Mavróbara** ('Turtle Lake'), abode of two species of endangered turtle. **Chaniótis** (Χανιώτης) boasts some of the liveliest beach bars on the peninsula. Surrounded by the pines that gave it its name, **Pefkochóri** (Πευκοχώρι) has long narrow coarse-sand-and-fine-gravel beach, lined with chic restaurants and bars. **Chroúsou** (Χρούσου) has a great semi-circle of white sand and plenty of beach bars; if it's all too crowded, try the tiny curl of beach towards the end of the peninsula at **Xiná** (Ξυνά).

Just west, the modern, sulphur-rich **Thermal Baths of Ag Paraskeví** (\ 23740 71358; prices and hours at w halkidikispa.com) are dramatically perched on the cliffs at **Loutrá**. Continuing up the southwest coast, the fishing village of **Néa Skióni** (Νέα Σκιώνη) replaces Ancient Skioni. Set high on the bluff, it was besieged by Athens in 423BC to punish it for having welcomed Spartan general Brasidas during the Peloponnesian War; it resisted heroically for two years, and when it fell the Athenians slaughtered every male.

The cape up the coast was colonised very early on, by 1000BC by the Eritreans of Évia who called it Mende (**Méndi**; Μένδη) after the abundant mint that grew there. Mende controlled the trade route from the south to Thrace, mined gold and produced wine that was exported as far as Italy (a 5th-century BC shipwreck found off Alónissos was loaded with 3,000 amphorae of the stuff). It was a big player in Athens' Delian League, until it revolted to join Brasidas, who went on to win a famous victory against Athens at Amphipolis (page 168). It avoided Skióni's fate, and managed to stay independent until 315BC when Cassander forced the population to settle his new town of Kassandría. Its suburb **Poseídi** (Ποσείδι), mentioned by Thucydides, has the remains of a sanctuary of its namesake Poseidon.

SITHONÍA PENINSULA

The Sithonía (Σιθωνία) peninsula offers 100 mostly white sandy beaches and most in the way of postcard visions of Chalkidikí – deeply wooded ravines ending in delectable coves, with fragrant pines running down to the white sand, lapped by a turquoise sea. While there are a couple of lively campgrounds and some popular beach bars, this is generally thought to be the quieter leg of Chalkidikí, with a few pleasingly remote stretches of coastline.

WHERE TO STAY

Danai Beach Resort (55 rooms) Nikíti; 23750 20400; w danairesort.com. Surrounded by lush gardens, these elegant bungalows have every luxury & plenty of marble; some suites have private pools. Excellent b/fast buffet featuring organic ingredients; there are watersports, tennis, spa, & pool; they even offer dog walking. Among the excellent restaurants is the Squirrel Gourmet (€€€€€) on a terrace facing the sea – one of the best in all Greece, featuring superb French Mediterranean cuisine & vegan dishes. €€€€€
Ekies All Senses (64 rooms) Vourvouroú; 23750 91000; w ekies.gr. The area's 'eco-luxury' resort, located 300m from the exotic white sands of Karýdi Beach; features dbls & a range of suites with minimalist design, Coco-Mat beds & pillow menu, spa & pool. It also boasts exceptional restaurants, including Bubo (€€€€), in an idyllic setting, & the Treehouse (€€€€) restaurant with 6 tables, high up in a pine tree overlooking the sea. €€€€€
Porto Carras Meliton [map, page 104] (376 rooms) Porto Carras; 23750 77000; w portocarras.com. The height of 1970s resort design, with a huge range of facilities (page 113). Also here are the Porto Carras Sithonía Beach (346 rooms) with a casino & the Marina Village & Yacht Club, with apartments sleeping up to 4. €€€€€
Ikos Olivia (291 rooms) Gerakíni; 23730 95100; w ikosresorts.com. All-inclusive sister resort of Ikos Oceania (page 109) with all the goodies, including a selection of à la carte restaurants & suites with private pools. €€€€€–€€€€

Anthemus Sea Beach Hotel & Spa (200 rooms) Eliá Beach, Nikíti; 23750 72001; w anthemussea.gr. On a private cove, a 5-star complex with 3 lagoon pools, spa, gourmet restaurant (€€€€) & a great roof garden bar, with live piano music. €€€€
Aktí Oneírou Camping [map, page 104] Sárti, 12km south of Vourvouroú; 23757 70910; w aktioneirou.gr. Isolated in the pines, on a golden sandy beach with views of Mount Athos, the 'Dream Coast' enjoys a lovely setting, with a wide range of accommodation, from bungalows to mobile homes, as well as pitches for tents & caravans, & a smart beach bar & restaurant. €€€–€€
Camping Armenistís [map, page 104] Sárti; 23750 91487; w armenistis.gr. From hosting campers who are self-equipped to renting bungalows, caravans & glamping tents, this sociable beachside campground is a favourite. A beach bar/café, children's activities, & watersports provide plenty of activity by day, & a full calendar of concerts, festivals, DJs, outdoor film screenings & so on keep things going later on. €€€–€
Chorostási (4 rooms) Parthenónas; 23750 72890; m 69747 10028; w horostasi.gr; ⊕ all year. Stélios & Tánia Mallinís are the nicest hosts; their studio apartments each sleep 4 & have a balcony with a sea view & fireplace. €€
Oreiades (6 rooms) Parthenónas; 23750 72461; ⊕ all year. Very hospitable, cosy rooms with verandas (1 sleeping 4), lovely views, fireplaces & a café. Greek b/fast inc. €€

4 | CHALKIDIKÍ (ΧΑΛΚΙΔΙΚΗ)

Parthenon (18 rooms) Parthenónas; m 69443 82384; w parthenonas-chalkidiki.com; ⊕ all year. Rooms in several houses, furnished with antiques & kitchenettes; rates include a delicious homemade b/fast on the terrace. €€

Philoxenia [map, page 104] (155 rooms) Psakoúdia; ☏ 23710 51960; w philoxenianet.gr. At the top of the peninsula, 4-star ecological family-oriented complex in walking distance of the village & beach. €€

Thalassokipos (13 rooms) Vourvouroú; ☏ 23750 31945; m 69776 64945; w thalassokipos.com. Bright, recently renovated studios & suites sleeping 4 with balconies & lovely sea views, & the Moonlight Lounge Bar for jazz & modern Greek music. €€

Galini (22 rooms) Sárti; ☏ 23750 94352; w galini-chalkidiki.com. Your classic Greek rooms & studios with balconies by the beach. B/fast €5. €€–€

Villa Karavitsi (21 rooms) Néos Marmarás; m 69723 11098; w karavitsi.gr. Modern stone buildings & standard rooms (including 2-room studios, sleeping 5) in a large garden setting by a pebble beach, with sunbeds & beach bar, serving great homemade b/fasts. €

✖ WHERE TO EAT AND DRINK

Arsanas Nikíti; ☏ 23750 23235; ⊕ 13.00–23.00 daily. On the beach, delicious seafood salad & pasta, & a creative chef, Michális: put yourself in his hands & see what he comes up with. €€€

Blue Maris On the beach road just south of Néos Marmarás; ☏ 23750 71290; w blue-maris.gr/restaurant; ⊕ Jun–early Sep 12.00–23.00 daily. Another classic, in business since 1964; dishes have touches of Old Smyrna's cuisine. €€

Gorgona Vourvouroú; ☏ 23750 91461; ⊕ noon–23.30 daily. Formerly the Pullman, a favourite since 1965, for seafood on the beach. €€

Mouragio Gerakiní; ☏ 23710 54060; w gerakini-mouragio.gr; ⊕ Apr–Oct all day, Nov–Mar noon–15.00 Sun–Thu, all day Fri–Sat. Wonderful traditional taverna, with tables under a massive pergola, serving tasty *mezédes* including crispy pies, creamy mushrooms, *bouyourdí* (baked feta, tomato & hot pepper dip), seafood & meat mains. Great choice of wines, too. €€

Okyalos Néos Marmarás; ☏ 23750 72244; w okyalos.gr; ⊕ Apr–Oct 12.30–01.00 daily. Excellent family-run seafood spot overlooking the port, with a big choice. €€

Café Bar Anoi Parthenónas; m 69458 76262; ⊕ May–Sep 19.00–midnight Mon–Fri, 10.30–14.00 & 19.00–midnight Sat & Sun. Lovely views, especially at sunset, & frequent live music in the summer.

WHAT TO SEE AND DO The holiday fun begins in earnest at **Nikíti** (Νικήτη), with a modern seafront and a lively beach scene and a handsome 700-year-old village, Palaiá Nikíti, tucked behind, with stunning views from its lofty church of Ag Nikítis. Nikíti's predecessor, Ag Geórgios, 2km south, has the ruins of the early 5th-century AD **Basilica of Bishop Sofronios** with good mosaics and bits of fresco. Chalkidikí is the **honey** capital of Greece, with 6,500 beekeepers managing hives that produce 2,000 tonnes of honey a year, a third of the national production; Nikíti, base of the Síthon Honey co-operative (w honeysithon.gr), likes to remind you that Democritus, the father of nuclear theory, who lived to be 107, said: 'You need to wet your insides with honey and your outsides with oil.'

South of Nikíti, the coast is scalloped with magnificent beaches – **Ag Ioánnis** and **Kástri**, with turquoise waters and lots of people; lush, sandy-bottomed **Kalogriá**, one of the most photographed; shallow **Spathiés** and pebbly 2km **Eliá Beach**, protected by trees – all the way to **Néos Marmarás** (Νέος Μαρμαράς). True to its name, this village was founded by refugees from Marmaras, Türkiye, and is now a big jumbly resort, the largest on Sithonía's west coast, with a few fishing boats bobbing in the port.

In the hills above Néos Marmarás, immersed in olive, quince and pomegranate groves, **Parthenónas** (Παρθενώνας), 'the Town of Virgins', is a remnant of quieter, pre-beach holiday times. Some 700 people lived here before it was abandoned in the

1960s. But visitors found it charming, and eventually people moved back, restoring the houses along the cobbled streets. The little inns offer a peaceful alternative to the busy coast, and in the middle of July it hosts a mini outdoor film festival.

From Parthenónas you can drive up to Sithonía's lofty backbone, **Mount Ítamos** (or Dragoudélis, 811m), up to the 800m plateau, with a pretty little country church and rare European yews (*ítamos*) that gave their name to the mountain; one mighty example, just northeast of the summit, is more than 2,000 years old. There are also magnificent examples of the European black pine, and views of the great pyramid of Mount Athos. You'll need a 4x4 to explore the unmarked forest roads.

You can make a complete circuit of the peninsula by way of the huge beach at **Toróni** (Τορώνη). At its end lie the foundations and mosaic floor of the 5th-century

PORTO CARRAS: VIP CHALKIDIKÍ

It's hard to imagine, but in the 1960s Chalkidikí was little known outside of Macedonia. The change began in 1963, when ship-owner Yiánnis Carrás of Chíos (1907–89) was on a cruise with Greek VIPs (including film star Melína Mercoúri, future Culture Minister) to celebrate the millennium of Mount Athos, when bad weather forced them to shelter on empty marshland south of Néos Marmarás. Carrás saw something in the mosquito-ridden swamp that no-one else had seen before, and perhaps inspired by the Aga Khan's recent purchase of the Costa Smeralda in Sardinia, bought 1,763ha, stretching from Mount Melíton to the shore, much of it formerly monastic property. This included 9km of coast dotted with 25 sandy coves, and what would become the biggest marina in northern Greece.

Land was drained for an 18-hole golf course and an experimental farm with 45,000 olive trees and vineyards. Most Greek wine at the time was plonk; Carrás was the first to reach out to experts, especially the great oenologist Émile Peynaud from Bordeaux, who researched and planted Greek and French varietals appropriate to the geography and climate. Now the PDO region of Plagiés Melítona, this is the largest privately owned organic wine estate in Greece, known for its white Malagousiá grapes and red Límnio, mentioned by Hesiod in the 7th century BC and considered the oldest surviving varietal.

In 1973, Carrás had architect Kóstas Kapsambélis build the 2,000m² Villa Galini as a private residence to host his friends. The design was inspired by the monasteries of Mount Athos, and decorated by mosaic tiles by Yves St Laurent. Here he received his guests, including Rudolf Nureyev, pianist Gina Bachauer (her piano is still there), François Mitterrand and Salvador Dalí, who lived in suite 303 and designed one of the bathrooms. Although the resort itself was commissioned from Walter Gropius, work didn't begin until after his death. The first hotel, the Village Inn, opened in 1976, followed in 1979 by the Porto Carras Melíton, a cross between an Inca temple and cruise liner, and the Sithonía, with a casino, open-air cinema, equestrian centre, nine tennis courts, a diving centre, spa (the biggest in southern Europe), three helipads and two ports for hydroplanes. In 2003 it hosted an EU summit along with the heads of NATO.

Since 2000, the resort has planted 324ha of new organic vineyards and built the new Varelàki wine bar, a new winery and tasting room (\ 23750 77437; w domaineportocarras.com). Vineyard tours can also be arranged.

AD **Basilica of Ag Athanásios** and a little promontory, sprinkled with the walls of **Ancient Torone**, a Bronze Age settlement and then a Greek colony that became briefly Chalkidikí's most important city, and then like so many, a battleground in the Peloponnesian War. South of Toróni, maquis covers the rugged shores and cliffs that girdle **Pórto Koufó** (Thucydides' Kofos Limin, 'Deaf Port', because it's so big that if you stand in the bay you can't hear the sea). Once a pirate base, it's the most sheltered anchorage in the region, a pretty lake of a bay with a small fishing village and beach.

The wild south of Sithonía is dotted with corrugated metal goat sheds, but the shores are punctuated with spectacular beaches. **Kalamítsi** (Καλαμίτσι) is a peaceful haven, with an excellent beach and fish tavernas. There's a magic moment as you approach **Skála Sykiás** (Σκάλα Συκιάς) when the whole Akté Peninsula comes into view, the tremendous cone of Mount Athos piercing the sky, often through a necklace of cloud. Skála Sikiás has a set of beautiful little beaches (signposted **Linaráki**), and there are others to the north, by **Sárti** (Σάρτη), that are even finer: **Platanítsi** and stunning **Kavourótrypes**, 'Crab Holes' (or 'Orange') beach, where the shallow water is crystal clear and the pockets of white sand are decorated with pale granite, whipped by the elements into petrified froth (although in recent years it has become a victim of its own beauty, and fills up by 11.00 with nowhere to park); and, 8km further north, **Armenistís**, where the sea comes in every shade of blue and green.

There's another idyllic, picture-perfect beach, **Karýdi**, with pine trees and a great bar just south of the resort with the fun-to-pronounce name, **Vourvouroú** (Βουρβουρού), looking across to pine-clad **Diáporos** (Διάπορος), the largest of nine islets. Pirates used to hide in its sheltered bay, where the water stays warm enough for swimming until late September, and there's fine snorkelling around its coral reefs. Just north is **Órmos Panagiás** (Όρμος Παναγίας), a laid-back fishing village with excursion boats around Mount Athos (page 103).

CHALKIDIKÍ'S EAST COAST

This rugged, wooded coast, is gold and silver country, where mining began c600BC and later funded Alexander's campaign in Asia. In ancient times this region was dominated by Stageira, birthplace of Aristotle. Under the Sultans, the dozen local 'Iron Villages' or Mantemóchoia were obliged to send their silver to the Sultan, but in exchange the miners were granted a certain amount of autonomy – as long as the Sultan got his share of the silver. In 1821, however, when the villagers joined the Greek revolt, they were forced to support 10,000 soldiers sent to guard the mines. In 1893, the mines were run under a French-Ottoman company, and the last vestiges of communal ownership ended. In recent years, Canadian firm Eldorado has leased the mines, notably at Olympiáda, and believes they could become Europe's most productive gold mines.

GETTING THERE AND AWAY KTEL Thessaloníki buses (w ktelmacedonia.gr) run to Stavrós and Olympiáda (for Ancient Stageira) six times a day (1hr 45mins; €4.50) on the Asproválta route.

WHERE TO STAY

Liotopi (16 rooms) Olympiáda; ︎23760 51257; w hotel-liotopi.gr; ⊕ May–Oct. Owner Louloúdia runs a charming hotel near the beach, with bright pastel-tinted rooms. Excellent & varied homemade b/fast, with

plenty of fresh fruits; free cooking lessons once a week. **€€€–€€**

Electra (30 rooms) 28is Oktovríou, Stavrós; ︎23970 65135; w electrahotel.gr; ⊕ all year. Modern, family-run hotel, a short walk from the

centre & 5mins from the beach. Bright airy rooms, all with balcony; restaurant & excellent buffet b/fast inc. €€
Hotel Akroyiáli (17 rooms) Olympiáda; 23760 51257; w hotel-germany.gr; ☉ all year. Greek in spite of its former name as the Hotel Germany, with tidy rooms right on the beach, half with sea views, all with fridges, plus an excellent taverna by the beach, the Akrogiali (☉ May–Oct; €€).

Guests have free use of the hotel's mountain bikes; Dimitri, the 3rd-generation owner & brother of Louloúdia of Liotopi, is a mine of local information. €€
Athos (14 rooms) Kon Palaiológou 10, Stavrós; 23970 61353; w athoshotel.net; Hotel Athos; ☉ Jun–Sep. Vintage 1973, with simple but pleasant rooms with balconies facing the plane grove & beach. €

✕ WHERE TO EAT AND DRINK

Kalamatianós [map, page 104] 2km on the Olympiáda road, Stavrós; 23970 61073; w kalamatianos.restaurant; ☉ May–Sep 13.00–23.00 daily. Excellent spot in a garden by the sea, featuring perfectly grilled or golden fried seafood, stuffed squid with cheese & sun-dried tomatoes or shrimp & tomato rice in a parmesan basket. Lovely local produce & wonderful salads, & an excellent wine list. €€€
Lefteris Stavrós main street; 23970 65594; ☉ 17.00–23.00 daily. Popular, family run & serving generous portions of all the Greek favourites with panache. €

STAVRÓS (Σταυρός; at the east end of the straits of Rentína; page 167) This unpretentious resort has a little amusement park and a large beach backed by the **Plataniá**, a rare park of century-old plane trees right by the sea. Some measure 8m in circumference and resemble dancers frozen in a fandango. Another tree in Stavrós, the huge Plátanos of Apollonía, is an official 'Monument of Nature'.

OLYMPIÁDA (Ολυμπιάδα) This low-key beach resort and mussel fishery was the port of Ancient Stageira, and named after Alexander's mother when she was exiled here by Cassander, who famously loathed anything to do with Alexander. Here she tried to protect Alexander's widow, Roxana, and her grandson Alexander IV, before Cassander had her sent to Pydna – and her death, in 316BC. He then imprisoned Roxana and her son in Amphipolis, before having them killed as well.

ANCIENT STAGEIRA Colonists from Ándros founded this city in 650BC, lured by the forests and gold. Aristotle was born here in 384BC, son of Nicomachos, court physician to Amyntas III (father of Philip II) and Phaistis, a wealthy woman from Chalkís in Évia. Orphaned at 13, Aristotle may have spent time in the Macedonian royal court; by age 17 he was attending Plato's Academy in Athens, where he stayed for 20 years until Plato's death c348BC, when he was said to have been miffed at not being made head of the Academy. Any thoughts of returning home to Stageira were moot because, as a member of the Olynthian League (page 107), it had been destroyed by Philip II in 349BC.

Aristotle spent the next few years in Asia Minor and on Lésvos inventing biology with Theóphrastus (of Eresos, like the poet Sappho), before Philip managed to lure him back to Macedon – with the promise of rebuilding Stageira – to instruct his son Alexander (page 149). In 335BC, Aristotle returned to Athens and founded the Lyceum, where he wrote most of the texts that made him one of the founding fathers of philosophy, as well as inventing logic, physics, optics, geology, epistemology, politics, taxonomy, metaphysics, ethics and literary criticism.

After Alexander's death, accusations of impiety led Aristotle to move to his mother's estate in Chálkis ('I will not allow the Athenians to sin twice against philosophy,' he stated, referring to Socrates). He died there and in 322BC his bones were brought to Stageira, where the locals built him an impressive monument and inaugurated a festival, the Aristoteleia, in his honour. Yet when Strabo visited 300 years later, Stageira was abandoned. There was briefly a Byzantine town here, before it was completely forgotten.

Aesthetics weren't the reason because the **archaeological site** (\ 23710 22060, 23102 85163; ⊕ 08.30–15.30 Wed–Mon; free), on a pair of hills over a little peninsula, couldn't be more fetching, with views across to Thássos on the horizon. Excavations since 1990 have revealed the **acropolis** set in beautifully triangular walls, roads, a large house (Aristotle's, perhaps), a large altar, the massive ashlar foundations of a Classical-era stoa, the agora, a temple on the north hill (where the original colony was founded), and two 6th-century BC temples (including a circular *thesmophoríon* of Demeter). In 2016, archaeologist Kóstas Sismanídis announced that he had discovered, after 20 years of research, what he was sure (though he admits no-one will ever know for certain) was **Aristotle's tomb** hidden under a Byzantine-era tower: a vaulted, hastily erected Hellenistic building near the agora, with a marble floor and coins from 322BC, and traces of an altar outside.

The 19km **Aristotle Trail** links Ancient Stageira to modern Stágira, passing through the Natura 2000 'Aristotle's Forest' near the idyllic **Varvára Waterfalls**, a delightful place for a soak on a hot afternoon. If you're not hiking, you can get there on the road from Olympiáda to **Varvára** (Βαρβάρα), following the dirt track to a car park and the signs for ΚΑΤΑΡΑΧΤΗΣ.

Modern **Stágira** (Στάγιρα) was named before the discovery of the ancient city 8km northeast; in Ottoman times, it was called Siderokafsía (blast furnace) and for a while it hosted the Sultan's mint. Above the village, in the remains of a Byzantine fort, a large marble **statue of Aristotle** (1956; labelled, simply, 'the Stageirite') broods over the views of the Ierissós Gulf. This is the centrepiece of **Aristotle Park** (\ 23760 41327; ⊕ 08.00–21.00 daily; €2), featuring outdoor interactive science exhibits based on the scientist's writing on physics, including a pentaphone, telescope and solar clock. From here the often-empty coastal road to the Akté Peninsula winds through miles of pines.

AKTÉ PENINSULA

Akté (Ακτή), Chalkidikí's magnificent easternmost peninsula, 56km long and mantled in virgin forests and wildflowers, ends in the autonomous Monastic State of the Holy Mountain, or Mount Athos (page 119).

GETTING THERE AND AROUND
By road There are six KTEL **buses** a day from Thessaloníki to Ierissós (1hr 20mins; €11.90) and Ouranoúpoli (1hr 40mins; €13.90). On Mount Athos, buses link Dáfni to Karyés, and to the other monasteries.

Ouranoúpoli has a 24-hour paying **car park** (\ 23770 71212) near the port.

By sea The little port of **Trípiti** has ferries several times a day year-round to Ammoulianí island (€2.20 pp, cars €10.10).

To Mount Athos Boats are the only way to get to the Holy Mountain, and it's wise to book a place two weeks in advance. Sailings are from Ouranoúpoli for west-coast monasteries or Ierissós for the east-coast monasteries, although the latter can be cancelled in bad weather – ring the relevant boat company to check.

The **Microathos Shipping Company** (m 69951 05105; w microathos.gr) runs ferry and high-speed connections from Ouranoúpoli to several monasteries and

AKTÉ PENINSULA

Dáfni, the port of Karyés (port info: 23770 23682). **Agioreitikes Grammes** also runs boats from Ouranoúpoli (23770 71149; w agioreitikes-grammes.com), a speedboat from Ierissós (23770 21041) and eight-seater taxi-boats. A small boat from Dáfni links up with the ferry from Ouranoúpoli and carries on up to the east-coast monasteries.

TOURIST INFORMATION The town of Ierissós has a very helpful website (w dimosaristoteli.gr) that covers the entire peninsula.

Pilgrims' Bureau Office Main street, Ouranoúpoli; 23770 71422; 06.00–13.00 daily

WHERE TO STAY

Eagles Palace Resort [map, page 104] (147 rooms) 4km north of Ouranoúpoli; 23774 40050; w eaglesresort.gr. Where the Aga Khan stayed & Maria Callas spent her last holiday: built in 1973 in the style of Mount Athos, with beautiful gardens, luxurious, minimalist rooms & suites, & 17 bungalows with private pools, on an immaculate white sand beach. All kinds of watersports, plus tennis court, a spa, indoor & outdoor pools, 8 restaurants & bars, & facilities for families, too. Free shuttle from Thessaloníki airport for stays of 5+ nights. €€€€€

Ayia Marina Suites (11 rooms) Ouranoúpoli; 23770 71271; w ayiamarinasuites.com. In easy walking distance of the centre & beach, luxurious contemporary suites with balconies facing the garden or sea. €€€€

GKEEA (16 rooms) Vas Georgioú, Ierissós; 23770 22533; w hotelgkeea.gr. Contemporary, comfortable boutique hotel near the beach, with kettles & fridges. €€€–€€

Helianthus Guesthouse (9 rooms) Main square, Ammouliání (a little island – take the boat from Tripití); 23770 51155; w helianthus.gr. Attractive dbls & trpls in earth colours, with goose down pillows & king-size Coco-Mat beds. B/fast inc. €€€–€€

Skites Hotel & Bungalows [map, page 104] (25 rooms) Ouranoúpoli; 23770 71140; w skites.

gr; May–Oct. Secluded in gardens near the monastic border, ecologically built whitewashed bungalows with chestnut ceilings, furnished with antiques & wrought-iron beds with mosquito nets. A path leads through the garden to the pebbly beach with a wooden pier, where everyone goes to watch the sunset; there's a bar & good restaurant (€€). B/fast inc. €€

Sunrise Hotel (46 rooms) Right on the sea, 300m from the port of Ammouliání (take the boat from Tripití); 23770 51173; w ammouliani-sunrise.gr. Airy, modern rooms, most overlooking the sea, with balconies & small garden. Buffet b/fast inc. €€

Macedonia (18 rooms) Ouranoúpoli; 23770 71085; w hotel-makedonia.gr; all year. Sweet & simple 2-star, right in the centre, 50m from the beach. B/fast €5. €€–€

Pension Irini (13 rooms) Ouranoúpoli; 23770 71443; w pansionirini.gr. Lovely Irini runs these spotless studios with true Greek hospitality; excellent b/fast inc. €€–€

Xenios Zeus (20 rooms) Ouranoúpoli; 23770 71274; w ouranoupoli.com/zeus; all year. Simple, welcoming, family-run favourite for pilgrims to Athos (they will store your bags); Herbert Marcuse & the director Théodoros Angelópoulos are among the many famous guests who have stayed. €€–€

WHERE TO EAT AND DRINK

Kritikos Ouranoúpoli; 23770 71222; w okritikos.com; 11.30–00.30 daily. Set just in from the shore, long-time favourite for spaghetti with lobster – or just about any other fish you fancy. Big portions, & 60 Greek wines to choose from. €€

Taverna Tzanis Ammouliání; 23770 51322; 09.00–01.00 daily. Founded by refugees as a *kafeneíon* in 1924, Tzanis is now the island's best-known restaurant, famous for its prawn & mussel dishes, plus lovely views on the waterfront, overlooking the beach & Mt Athos. Book in summer. €€

4 | CHALKIDIKÍ (ΧΑΛΚΙΔΙΚΗ)

WHAT TO SEE AND DO The story goes that in 655BC colonising expeditions from Chalkís and Ándros arrived at the neck of the peninsula at the same time, and both sent scouts racing ahead to stake their claim. When the scout from Ándros saw that he would never catch his Chalkís rival, he hurled his javelin ahead, and in arbitration Ándros was declared to have won the site 'by the point of their spear'. They named the colony Akanthos, after the abundant acanthus, the plant with curling leaves that features on the capitals of Corinthian columns. Akanthos grew rapidly, thanks to nearby mines, minting coins by 530BC. Today known as **Ierissós** (Ιερισσός), it has a large beach and boat-building yards, with bits of Ancient Akanthos signposted off the main road: amid the chicken coops, look for a Classical temple and altar under a metal roof and, further up, the walls of the citadel. The landmark 15th-century **Kroúna Tower** (visible only from the outside), just northwest of the centre, was once part of the Hilandaríou monastery.

The *tirokomío* (cheese factory) in Ierissós holds the record for producing the world's largest goat cheese, the 'caprine rock' that weighed 939kg. Just as unexpectedly, a statue of Don Quixote made of scrap metal stands in front of the **Cultural Centre of Ierissós**, which houses the only 3D cinema (Vas Konstantínou 6; 23770 21130; w axtada.gr) in northern Greece, showing three regularly scheduled films during the day: *Journey to Mount Athos* (a virtual visit to the monks' world), *Angels Are the Light for Monks*, and the underwater *Sea World*; check the website for schedules. Real fish swim in the tanks of the town's seawater-fed **Aquarium** (⊕ always; free) along the waterfront promenade.

In 492BC, 500 Persian ships of Mardonios' invasion fleet were wrecked in a storm off the Athonite Peninsula. A decade later, Xerxes, planning his massive invasion of Greece and determined to avoid the same fate, sent an army of slaves to spend three years digging a ditch wide enough for two triremes to sail abreast. Although Herodotus wrote that the Great King wanted 'to leave something to be remembered by', the 2.9km canal between **Néa Róda** (Νέα Ρόδα) and **Trípiti** (Τρυπητή) has silted up so completely that the modern road now follows its traces; the curious little hills alongside were the excavated earth and rubble. In the past few years, a more tangible Hellenistic temple and Archaic house have been excavated at Néa Róda, associated, respectively, with Alexarchos and the ancient city of Sani (page 110).

Trípiti is the port for Chalkidikí's only inhabited island, **Ammoulianí** (Αμμουλιανή), once a dependency of Vatopédi Monastery and inhabited by a few monks, shepherds and farmers. In 1925, it was given to Greek refugees from the islands in the Sea of Marmara, who fished, farmed, and have converted Ammoulianí, girdled with 30 beautiful beaches, into a tourist hotspot. The main organised beach is **Alykés**, on a shallow turquoise sea south of the village, with lovely sunsets (there's a shuttle from the port); **Megali Ámmos** is the furthest south, safe for tots with fine white sand and an excellent taverna on the cliff; and sheltered, less-crowded **Karagátsia** is 2km from the village on the west coast, with a beach bar. The other thing to do is hire a boat to visit the eight uninhabited **Drénia Islands** – though the main beach, on a calm, shallow lagoon, with its parasols and seafood tavern, can get too crowded in season.

Sandy coves line the coast south to **Ouranoúpoli** (Ουρανούπολη), the 'City of Heaven' and the end of the road for women, children and permit-less men, unless they take a sightseeing cruise (page 103). Surprisingly, its name pre-dates any monasteries, or even Christianity: Ouranoupolis was founded in 315BC near an older city, Sani (one of many destroyed by Philip II), by proto-hippie guru Alexarchos, brother of King Cassander, who fancied he was the sun. He founded a utopian commune, imposing his own alphabet and a dialect 'incomprehensible even to the god of Delphi'. No-one knows how long it lasted, although some of its coins were discovered.

Modern Ouranoúpoli is a sprawling beach resort, where you'll hear as much Russian as Greek, and where shops sell walking poles, rucksacks, icons, fancy priest kits and a surprising amount of jewellery, presumably to amuse wives and girlfriends left behind.

The picturesque **Prosphóriou Tower** (23770 71585; ⊕ Apr–Oct 08.30–15.30 Wed–Mon, Nov–Mar closed; €3, concessions €2), the tallest monastic watchtower on Chalkidikí, watches over the village fishing fleet. The first version of the tower dates from 1018 but had to be rebuilt after damage from earthquakes and fires; its wooden interior and roof are 20th century. It originally sheltered the warehouses and boat of the *metóchi* of Vatopédi Monastery, but after 1924 was inhabited by refugees from the island of Marmara. The tower was the later home of Joyce and Sydney Loch, workers for a Quaker refugee organisation, who came here for a holiday in the 1920s and never left, helping, among other things, to promote the local carpet weavers. Now restored, the tower houses a chapel and a museum of antiquities, including 6th-century BC helmets and jewellery, to go with its views.

A 1km archaeological walk from the tower leads to the border of Mount Athos and the ruins of **Moní Zygoú** (⊕ 08.30–15.30 Wed–Mon; €3, concessions €2), a large Athos-style monastery, founded in the 10th century, but abandoned by 1199.

MOUNT ATHOS (ÁGION ÓROS)

One of the Aegean's greatest landmarks, the pale crystalline cloud-garlanded limestone cone of Mount Athos (2,033m) punctuates the end of the Akté Peninsula. The Greeks call it the Ágion Óros (Άγιον Όρος), the 'Holy Mountain', and there is no place like it; a thousand years of isolation and devotion have permeated the land to create a unique mystical otherworldliness. In myth, Athos, one of the giants who challenged Zeus and co for world domination, hurtled a mighty rock at Olympus. But Poseidon deflected it with his trident and the rock landed here, some say on top of Athos himself – all 2,033m of it, a landmark for miles around.

The monasteries of Athos resemble castles, and within their walls they have safeguarded the soul of Orthodoxy, shielding it from a millennium of Western influences and ecumenicalism. Together, they form the world's greatest museum of Byzantine art, but a living museum: the monks sing Byzantine hymns, paint icons and prepare incense as they've done for centuries, keeping safe exquisite reliquaries, icons and some 12,000 illuminated manuscripts, nearly half of those surviving in Greece. Days are marked by the Julian calendar (putting Athos 13 days behind the rest of the world), the hours by Byzantine time, which starts the clock for each new day at sunset.

Since 1988, Mount Athos has been a UNESCO World Heritage Site, and it's also a unique Natura 2000 site: even the flora and fauna are Byzantine, and incredibly rich and diverse, thanks to a ban on grazing animals for the past 1,000 years. Jackals still roam the wilder reaches.

HISTORY Athos could have had a very different fate, had architect Deinokrates had his way. One day he appeared in Alexander the Great's court in Asia, naked except for a lion-skin and club. Intrigued by his Heracles get-up, Alexander heard his proposal: to sculpt Mount Athos into his likeness, with a fortified city in one hand and a lake in the other, which would spill over as a waterfall into the sea. History doesn't record how long Alexander mulled over the idea (he rejected it because there wasn't enough surrounding farmland to support the city), but he was

4 | CHALKIDIKÍ (ΧΑΛΚΙΔΙΚΗ)

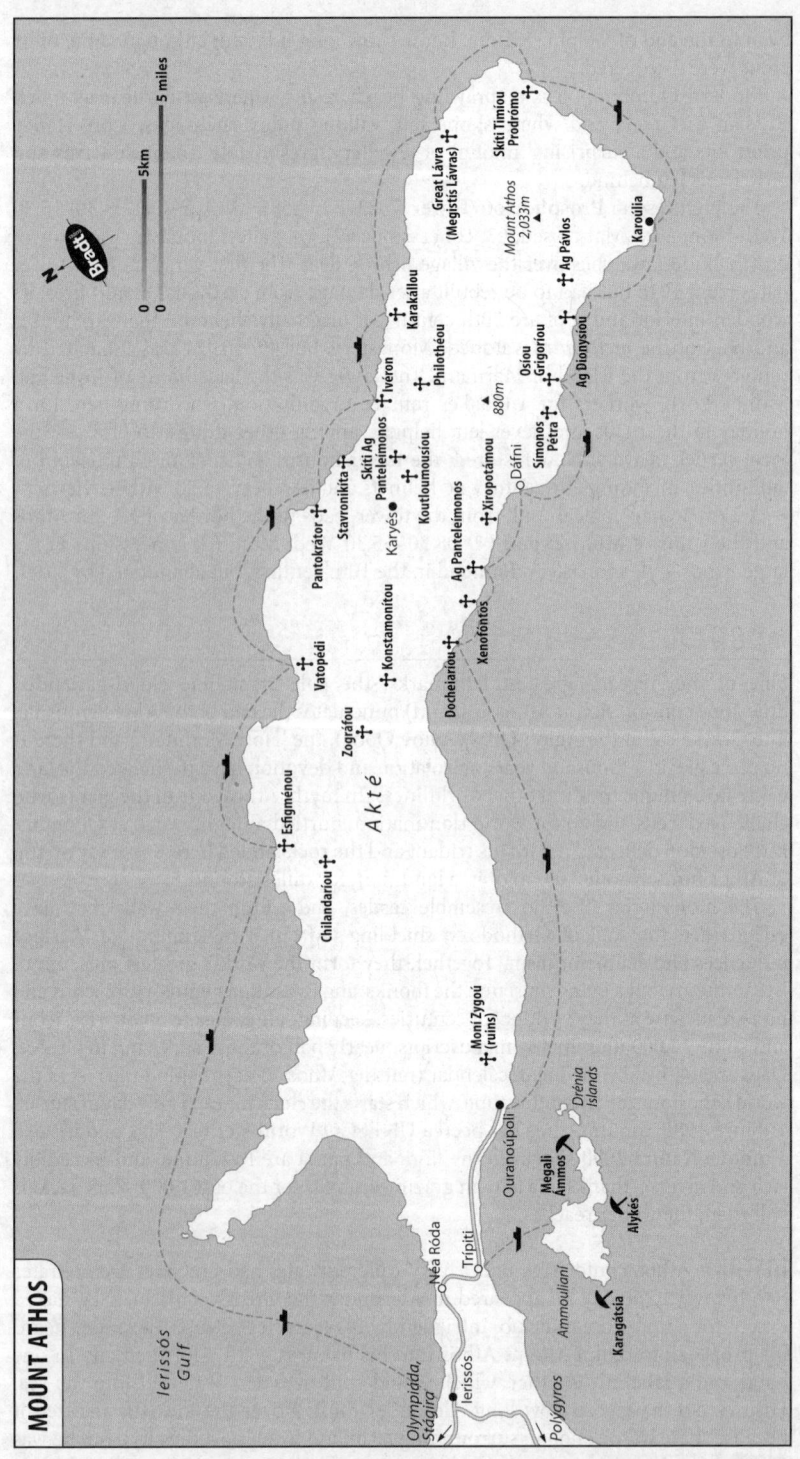

impressed enough to hire Deinokrates and later to commission him to lay out his grandest foundation, Alexandria in Egypt.

Legend has it that in later centuries the Virgin Mary was sailing to Cyprus to visit Lazarus when her ship was blown in a storm to the Bay of Ivéron. Enchanted by its beauty, she prayed that it might be hers, and heard a voice from heaven: 'Let this place be your inheritance and your garden, a paradise and a haven of salvation.' The first hermit, St Peter the Anchorite, arrived in the late 8th century AD; his small cave survives near the Great Lávra. As the influx of spiritual athletes grew, fleeing the Iconoclasts, Emperor Basil I proclaimed the peninsula their exclusive domain in AD885.

In AD963, the first monastery, the Great Lávra ('community of hermitages') was founded by St Athanásios with funds from a guilt-wracked Nikephóros Phokás, who had promised Athanásios that he would become a hermit if he succeeded in taking Crete from the Saracens, but instead fought for the imperial throne. A faction of ascetic hermits, led by Pávlos Xeropotomíou, accused Athanásios of introducing luxury to Athos. But Athanásios had friends in high places, and in AD971 his rules were inscribed in the Próto Typikó, or charter that governs Athos. In 1045 the peninsula was named the 'Holy Mountain' and declared off limits to all except for Orthodox Christian monks and adult males. Other holy men, many financed by princes, went on to establish monasteries, *skete* (dependencies) and hermitages (180 in its heyday, or so they say) including Moldavian, Albanian, Bulgarian, Russian, Romanian, Serbian, Georgian, Wallachian and Amalfitani houses, with 40,000 monks.

Their wealth attracted pirates – hence the high walls. More trouble began in 1204 with the Latin occupation, but the restoration in 1261 of Michael VIII Paleológos in Constantinople brought no respite: attempting to bully Athos into accepting the union of the Eastern and Western churches, his men tortured and burned 26 monks alive. Although his son Andronicus II was an anti-Unionist, his Catalan mercenaries, when dismissed for bad behaviour, occupied the Kassándra Peninsula and spent the next two years plundering and burning monasteries, leaving only 25 standing.

In 1453 Athos submitted at once to the Ottomans, and in return the Sultans let the peninsula maintain its independence, although heavy taxes took a toll. There was a revival in the 18th century, when the Mount took a leading role in the Greek enlightenment, with the founding of the Athonite Academy near Vatopédi; in 1821, many monks joined the Greek War of Independence. In 1926, after the monasteries were compelled to give up most of their dependencies to the Asia Minor refugees, a new charter made Athos an autonomous part of the Greek state, subject only in its external relations to the Ministry of Foreign Affairs.

By the 1970s the monasteries on Athos were dilapidated, with few new monks taking their vows, but in recent decades there have been big changes: an influx of young monks has increased the population to around 2,000 on the Holy Mountain; and at least half of the 40,000 annual visitors are Russian – Vladimir Putin has been twice. In 2003, the European Parliament passed legislation to lift the ban on women, as a 'violation of sexual equality and EU legislation governing discrimination', but it was rejected by the Greek government. In 2008 mobile phones and the internet arrived, at least in some monasteries.

The recent (and controversial) building of roads on the Holy Mount has disturbed some of its medieval peace, but the income from a discreet increase in logging and tourism has enabled the monasteries – wonderfully rambling complexes that have evolved (or devolved) over time – to make much-needed repairs and renovations. And, although they are cut off, the monasteries have felt the rumblings of political discord ever since the decision in 2018 by the Ecumenical Patriarch Bartholomew I

4 | CHALKIDIKÍ (ΧΑΛΚΙΔΙΚΗ)

VISITING MOUNT ATHOS

Mount Athos is the Garden of the Virgin, and she will brook no rivals: since 1063, it has been *ávaton* or off limits to all females coming within 500m, with the exception of wild animals (the monks do turn a blind eye to cats, though, or else the place would be overrun by mice). Boys are allowed, usually with their fathers, in spite of the 'no smooth-faced person' rule enacted to keep out women disguised as men – it has happened, at least once, in 1953, when a Greek woman succeeded. The Greek government then passed a law punishing any future transgressors with a year in prison, although when a Ukrainian people-smuggler dropped four Moldavian women off on Athos's coast in 2008 and the police detained them, they were forgiven by the monks.

GETTING THERE AND AWAY For details, see page 116.

PERMITS To visit, men need a permit from the **Mount Athos Pilgrims' Bureau** in Thessaloníki [65 E3] (Egnatía 109; 23102 52578; e athosreservation@gmail.com; 09.00–16.00 Mon–Fri & 09.00–14.00 Sat; English spoken). Each day 100 permits (*diamonitíria*) are reserved for Orthodox visitors and ten for non-Orthodox. You can book up to six months in advance. By March most of the summer spaces are filled; out of season, you may get in on short notice, especially if your dates are flexible. There are several helpful websites with up-to-date information, including **Friends of Athos** (w athosfriends.org) and **Visit Mount Athos** (w visitmountathos.eu).

The *diamonitírio* grants four days on Athos, but you can apply for a two-day extension at the Holy Community in Karyés. Before embarking at Ouranoúpoli or Ierissós (see page 117 for details; arrive at least an hour early) you will need to show your permit, and pay the fee of €35 (€25 for Orthodox, €18 for students). Non-Greek Orthodox should bring their baptismal certificates or other proof from their church.

STAYING AT THE MONASTERIES All visitors are expected to stay at the monasteries and you'll need to ring ahead to reserve a bed (but not on Sundays or holidays, when no-one will answer the phone). Gates close at sunset. On arrival, the gatekeeper

of Constantinople to grant the Ukrainian church the right to have its own head. Patriarch Kirill of the Russian church, which regards Ukraine as its domain, furiously responded by splitting the Russian church away from Constantinople and forbidding his followers from taking communion in any church where Bartholomew is blessed.

MOUNT ATHOS TODAY The peninsula is divided into 20 territories, each controlled by a 'ruling monastery'. Each has a deputy on the Holy Council that governs Athos in conjunction with an annually elected executive board of four. The 20 monasteries follow a rigid hierarchy of precedence, from the Great Lávra, Vatopédi and Ivíron down to the newest, Konstamonítou. Although several were originally idiorrhythmic (each monk 'going his own way', working and providing his own food), as of 1992 all monasteries are coenobitic, where the monks live and eat communally. Most have several dependencies. These include *skete* or daughter houses, ruled by a prior; *kelliá*, like farmhouses with a chapel and usually three or four monks; even smaller will check your *diamonitírio* and direct you to the guest master (*archontáris*), who will offer you *tsípouro* (pomace brandy), *loukoúmi* (aka Turkish delight), cold water and coffee, give you the timetable of services and meals, then escort you to the dormitory (equipped with toilets and basins; some now have hot showers). Hospitality is free, although an offering 'for the church' might be accepted. Many monks speak some English.

After resting, at around 16.00, monks and visitors attend Vespers in the monastery church (*katholikón*). After Vespers, bells summon residents to the refectory (*trápeza*) opposite the katholikón; the Abbot (*Igoúmenos*) enters first, followed by the monks and the visitors (note that some monasteries have special customs about church attendance and meals for the non-Orthodox). Meals, which consist of olives, vegetables, rice, pasta, beans, fruit, cheese and good Athos wine, are eaten in silence, while a monk reads aloud from the Bible. Meat is never eaten, and fish is served only on feast days. On fast days (Monday, Wednesday, Friday, Lent and before major feasts) monks abstain from wine, oil, and dairy products.

After supper, visitors then return to the katholikón for Compline (the evening liturgy), after which relics are displayed for the veneration of Orthodox pilgrims. Afterwards there is free time, when you can chat with the monks. All retire with the sun at around 21.00 or 22.00, then wake up at around 03.00 or 04.00 to attend Matins, Hours and the Divine Liturgy, immediately followed by breakfast (similar to dinner) at 07.00. The monks then go about their work, and visitors are expected to continue their pilgrimage (you can stay at a monastery for more than one night, but only by special request).

OTHER PRACTICALITIES Because of the amount of walking, take as little as possible, but do pack a good map, water bottle, stout shoes, hat, insect repellent, snacks, a torch and matches (many monasteries have no electricity). Dress is casual, but shorts are out. The monks don't swim; if you do, do it out of their sight. Photography is allowed, but not videos, and you will need the Abbot's permission to take pictures of the monks or any interiors. **Karyés**, the 'capital', has basic shops, a post office, doctor, restaurants, a simple hotel and police station, but no bank or money-changing facilities.

kalýves and *kathiímata*; and smallest of all *hesychastéria*, huts or caves in the cliffs, mostly in the 'Desert of Athos' at the south end of the peninsula, where hermits live in isolation and prayer, living off what passers-by drop in their baskets.

Today many young, savvy monks and novices live on Athos – so don't expect to find only doddering eccentrics, as travellers encountered a few decades ago. The Bulgarian, Russian, Romanian and Serbian houses are undergoing such a renewal that there is fresh concern over maintaining the Mount's 'Greekness'.

Since permits are checked before you embark, it's no longer necessary to go to Karyés, the seat of the Holy Community (and only capital in the world without a women's WC), unless you want a two-day extension. The oldest building on Athos is here, the 10th-century church of the **Protáton**, with lovely 14th-century frescoes by Manuel Pansélinos.

THE MONASTERIES In four or six days on Athos it's impossible to see everything. While all the monasteries have relics and icons, works of art and rich libraries (to examine them, you'll need a letter of introduction, preferably from an Orthodox bishop), you may want to concentrate on the famous ones, such as the Great Lávra, Vatopédi, Ivíron and Símonos Pétra. The following are thumbnail sketches of the monasteries – for more information, there are several good books (page 389).

Along the west coast from Ouranoúpoli

Zográfou (Μονή Ζωγράφου; ⎰ 23770 23247; e zografergo@gmail.com) The first (hidden from the sea) is the Bulgarian monastery, founded in the 10th century and famous for its miraculous icons. Its name, 'the painter', comes from an icon of St George that mysteriously appeared here.

Konstamonítou (Μόνη Κωνσταμονίτο; ⎰ 23770 23228) Half hidden in a wooded ravine, Konstamonítou comes last in Athos's hierarchy; its katholikón dates from 1871.

Docheiaríou (Μονή Δοχειαρίου; ⎰ 23770 23245) Founded by a companion of St Athanásios who was in charge of stores (*doleiarios*), its buildings, mostly 16th-century, were a gift from the prince of Wallachia. The katholikón, with excellent frescoes of 1568 by Cretan master Tzortzis, houses the famous icon Panagía Gorgoepikoös, 'she who grants requests quickly'.

Xenofóntos (Μονή Ξενοφώντος; ⎰ 23770 23249; w imxenophontos.eu) This monastery was founded in the AD900s by the Blessed Xenofóntos but was largely rebuilt after a fire in 1817; it has an enormous katholikón (1809–1919), containing two 13th-century mosaic icons, and also an older katholikón, frescoed in 1544 by the Cretan School.

Ag Panteleímonos (Μονή Αγίου Παντελεήμονος; ⎰ 23770 23252; e rpm. palomnik@gmail.com) Green onion domes, symbolising heaven, mark the Russian monastery, or the 'Roussikon'. Founded in the 10th century on the mountainside, the present monastery was built closer to the sea by the Russians in 1765. It resembles a small city and once held 1,500 monks in a failed attempt to take over Athos by sheer force of numbers; today it has room for 500 guests.

Xiropotámou (Μονή Ξηροποτάμου; ⎰ 23770 23251) Xiropotámou is an attractive monastery overlooking the bay above Dáfni. Founded according to varying traditions in the 6th or 10th century AD, its current buildings and katholikón date from the 18th century; it holds the largest piece of the True Cross in the world and the precious, tiny 6th-century steatite 'Paten of Pulchería'.

Koutloumousíou (Μονή Κουτλουμουσίου; ⎰ 23770 23226; w koutloumous. com) Up by Karyés and in existence since the 10th century, the monastery is thought to have been founded by Emperor Alexios I Komnenos. Its katholikón of 1540 was fully frescoed in the style of the Cretan school, much of it repainted in the 19th century. There are also several other chapels, a bell tower and a fountain of Tinian marble. The monastery's **Skíti Ag Panteleímonos** (Σκήτη Αγίου Παντελεήμονος) is nicknamed 'the American monastery' because of its many Western monks.

Símonos Pétra (Μονή Σίμωνος Πέτρα; ⎰ 23770 23254; e hospitality@ simonopetra.gr; w simonopetrafoundation.org) South of Dáfni rises this extraordinary, most photogenic monastery on Athos, its seven storeys hanging high on a sheer cliff, 214m over the sea. Named for its 13th-century founder, the hermit Simon, it has suffered more than most from fires, having been razed in 1891; many of its dependencies burned down in 1990. Its prize relic is the hand of Mary Magdalene.

Osíou Grigoríou (Μονή Οσίου Γρηγορίου; 23770 23218; e filoxenia@imog.gr) A lower rock supports this monastery founded in the 14th century by the Blessed Gregory of Sinai and rebuilt after a fire in 1761; its katholikón has 18th-century frescoes by the Kastoriá school and celebrated icons of the Virgin and St Nikólaos.

Ag Dionysíou (Μονή Διονυσίου; 23770 23687) A steep and narrow rock holds this monastery, founded in the 14th century by St Dionysos of Korseos and fairly untouched since the 18th century. The katholikón has excellent frescoes by Cretan painter Tzórtzis, and a beautiful gilded iconostasis; the treasury and library are especially rich, thanks to its royal benefactors, the emperors of Trebizond.

Ag Pávlos (Μονή Αγίου Παύλου; 23770 23741; e moni@agiou-pavlou.gr) In a ravine at the foot of Mount Athos, Ag Pávlos was founded by the ascetic monk Pávlos of Xiropótamo (9th or 10th century). Its greatest relics are nothing less than the Gifts of the Magi – you've always wondered what happened to them! The katholikón dates from 1844, although the chapel of Ag Geórgios has some of the finest frescoes on Athos, painted in 1555.

Down the east coast from Ierissós
Chilandaríou (Μονή Χιλανδαρίου; 23770 23797; e pilgrims@hilandar.org) Hidden from the coast in wooded hills, Chilandaríou's founders, Prince Stefan Nemanja and his son St Sávvas, gave up thrones to become monks, and the monastery was given in perpetuity to the Serbs by Emperor Aléxis III in 1198; even Tito sent the monks a tractor. The katholikón has frescoes of 1320 (repainted) and a fine mosaic floor; it possesses relics of several saints, cameos and important icons, including the Panagia Tricherousa (the Virgin of three hands). In 2004 a fire destroyed much of the monastery, but the icons and library were saved.

Esfigménou (Μονή Εσφιγμένου; e info@esphigmenou.gr) In rough weather waves lap the walls of Esfigménou ('tied with a very tight cord'), a late 10th-century monastery. Those sometimes rough seas could be seen as a metaphor; the fundamentalist monks here have been in conflict with Patriarchate of Constantinople on several issues, including meeting with representatives of the Catholic church. They have also been in conflict with the authorities, which has at times escalated into violence. Much can be read of the disputes over the last two decades from various news sources. The monks' own view of events can be found at w esphigmenou.com.

Vatopédi (Μονή Βατοπεδίου; 23778 88088; e filoxenia@vatopedi.gr; w vatopedi.gr) Home to 120 monks, this great rambling country estate of a monastery was founded cAD980 by three monks from Edirne, although the derivation of its name, 'bramble field', is unknown. Its 10th-century katholikón has excellent frescoes of the Macedonian school (although repainted) and its treasury houses major relics: the Virgin's girdle (aka her belt), the rod that held the sponge soaked in vinegar given to Christ, plus a superb diptych, portable icons and 2,000 illuminated manuscripts. It's also the only monastery with an Emmy, donated in 2012 by American actor/musician Jonathan Jackson, to celebrate his conversion to Orthodoxy in that year.

THE LAND DEAL THAT ROCKED GREECE

In the early 1990s the Vatopédi Monastery was in dire straits – almost derelict, overrun by rats, the frescoes black from candle smoke – when a new Abbot, Ephraim, with a group of young Cypriot monks took over and began the restoration work, picking up funds from the EU, VIPs and politicians in Greece and elsewhere. Prince Charles visited for three summers in a row in the early 2000s. During the clean-up the abbot discovered, in the old library, a deed to Lake Vistonída (page 211) bestowed by the emperor in Constantinople from 1080, covered in golden seals. Nearly all the properties once owned by the monasteries had been expropriated by the Greek government in the 1920s, but not the lake, which is home to the Agios Nikólaos Monastery, a dependency of the Vatopédi Monastery. The lake had previously been designated a nature reserve, but in 1998 the designation somehow lapsed, and the monastery took over the lake.

Abbot Ephraim and his financial whizz, Father Arsénios, tried then to sell the lake to the Ministry of Finance in 2004, but the government didn't have any money. So they suggested they swap the lake (which collected no rents) for government land, and in 2008 were given 73 different properties owned by the Ministry of Agriculture, including the abandoned gymnastics centre for the 2004 Olympics. They convinced the government to re-zone properties for commercial use, with the idea of selling them off to investors, to raise money to restore Vatopédi. The monastery made at least €100 million on what Abbot Ephraim and Father Arsénios called the 'holy exchange'.

When the affair and the involvement of the politicians hit the headlines in August 2008, the public presumed the monks' business dealings had to have come from fraud. It triggered the resignation of two ministers, the deal was cancelled, and it helped trigger the fall of the New Democracy government of Kósta Karamanlís, leaving the next government under Socialist George Papandréou to discover that Greece had a €30 billion hole in its finances, setting off the crisis and bailout. The new Minister of Finance filed a lawsuit against the monastery, demanding the return of government property, and the case went on for years; Abbot Ephraim spent three months in prison in 2011, but in 2017, when the case finally went to court, both monks and ministers were acquitted.

Pantokrátor (Μονή Παντοκράτορος; 23770 23880; e filoxenia@pantokrator.gr) Sitting on a headland, Pantokrátor was founded by two Byzantine nobles in the 14th century but suffered fires in 1773 and 1948; it has a famous icon of the Virgin known as the 'Elder'.

Stavronikíta (Μονή Σταυρονικήτα; 23770 23255) The smallest monastery resembles a little castle and enjoys great views over the big mountain. Its foundation in the 10th century is lost in legend; its katholikón has frescoes by the great Theophanes (c1520), although its most famous icon is that of St Nicholas of the Oyster, named for the creature stuck to it (the mark is still visible) when the monks pulled it from the sea.

Iviron (Μονή Ιβήρων; 23770 23643; e ivironfiloxenia@gmail.com) Like Stavronikíta, Iviron is linked to Karyés by road. It was founded in the AD900s by

Duke John Tornikios of Iberia (not Spain, but the medieval kingdom of Georgia), hence the monastery's name. When its famous jewelled icon of Panagía Portaïtissa painted by St Luke cured the daughter of Tsar Alexis in the 17th century, the monks were given the monastery of St Nicholas in the middle of Moscow. Its katholikón (11th–16th century) has a fine mosaic floor; the treasury houses the robe of Emperor John Tzimiskés (the successor to Nikephóros Phokás) and the library has three 10th-century chrysobulls and 2,000 codices.

Philothéou (Μονή Φιλοθέο; 23770 23256; e philotheou.filoxenia@gmail.com) Another late 10th-century foundation, on a plateau that once had an Asklepeion, this shelters one of Orthodoxy's most famous icons, the Glykophiloúsa, or 'Sweet-Kissing One'.

Karakállou (Μονή Καρακάλλου; 23770 23225) High above the sea, this monastery resembles a picturesque 16th-century fort, has a mighty defence tower and katholikón with frescoes from the 1700s.

Great Lávra (or Megistís Lávras) (Μονή Μεγίστης Λαύρας; 23770 23761; e iera.moni.megistis.layras@gmail.com) Last, on the wild slopes where its founder battled with demons, is the most venerable and imposing monastery, home to 420 monks. The refectory and katholikón, built by St Athanásios and the model for every subsequent monastery church, have superb frescoes by Theophanes (1535); its treasury and library are the richest on Athos and house the magnificent imperial robe and crown of Nikephóros Phokás. It has the most important dependencies as well, including the **Skíti Timíou Pródromou** (Σκήτη Τιμίου Προδρόμου) inhabited by Romanian monks, and the hermitages in the sheer cliffs of **Karoúlia**.

From the Great Lávra you can make the ascent of Mount Athos; Robert Byron, who wrote a fascinating traveller's tale of his visit to Holy Mountain (page 390), claimed he could see the plains of Troy from the summit.

5 | CENTRAL MACEDONIA (ΚΕΝΤΡΙΚΗ ΜΑΚΕΔΟΝΙΑ)

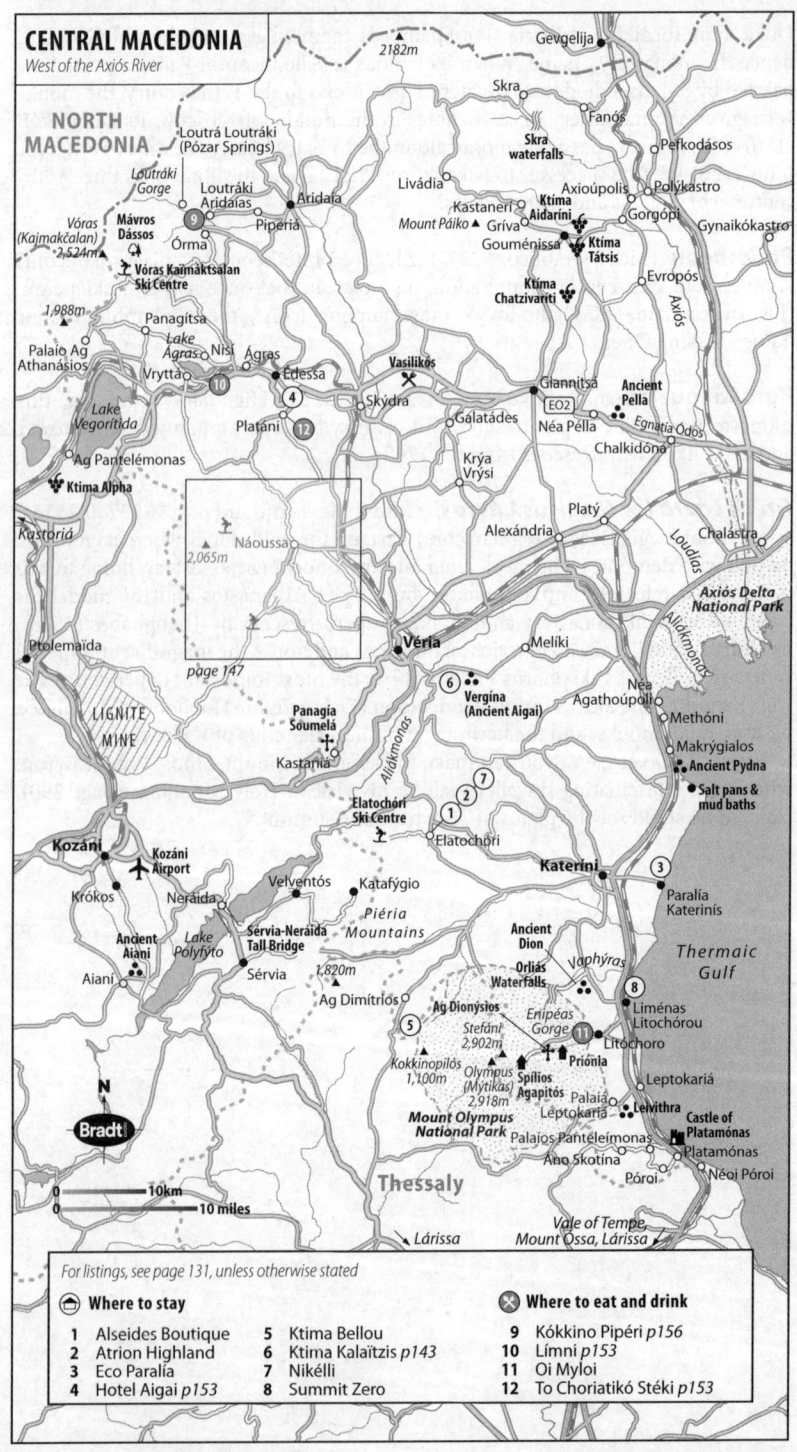

For listings, see page 131, unless otherwise stated

Where to stay
1. Alseides Boutique
2. Atrion Highland
3. Eco Paralía
4. Hotel Aigai *p153*
5. Ktima Bellou
6. Ktima Kalaïtzis *p143*
7. Nikélli
8. Summit Zero

Where to eat and drink
9. Kókkino Pipéri *p156*
10. Límni *p153*
11. Oi Myloi
12. To Choriatikó Stéki *p153*

5

Central Macedonia (Κεντρική Μακεδονία)

The most populous Greek region after Attica, Central Macedonia encompasses Thessaloníki and Chalkidikí (which get their own chapters), but also Mount Olympus, the home of the gods and the heart of the ancient kingdom of Macedon, where Alexander the Great was born and raised and where he spectacularly buried his father Philip II in Ancient Aigai (Vergína). It encompasses the fabled wine-growing region of Imathia, the old biblical and Byzantine town of Véria, or Berea, where St Paul preached, Édessa the city of waterfalls, Lefkádia with some of the best surviving painted Macedonian tombs, and Amphipolis, where the largest Macedonian tomb discovered so far has recently been excavated. And to the north in the Rhodope Mountains are the undiscovered cities of Sérres and Kilkís, bird-filled lakes and wetlands (notably Lake Kerkíni), and fertile valleys and plains where tobacco, cotton and cattle thrive – in fact, a beefy diet helped to make Alexander's army into tough hombres.

TOURIST INFORMATION

Central Macedonia's tourist information website (w visit-centralmacedonia.gr/en) is packed full of useful information and suggestions.

MOUNT OLYMPUS NATIONAL PARK

Olympus (Όλυμπος) originally meant 'mountain', and scattered around the Mediterranean some 20 other mountains bear the same name. But this, the highest peak on the Balkan peninsula at 2,918m, its summits wreathed in cloud, its precipices echoing with thunder, was always *the* Olympus, the abode of Zeus and his argumentative clan. In Homer, the palaces of the gods lay in the mountain's 'mysterious folds'. At the tallest of its 52 peaks, in ancient times known as the Pantheon (now more prosaically called Mýtikas, 'nose'), where the sun always shone and the air was too thin for mortals to breathe, the deities would gather to hear Zeus arbitrate on his Throne, the sheer armchair (and greatest climbing challenge on the mountain) today better known as Stefáni (2,902m).

Olympus was one of the last famous European mountains to be climbed (in 1913) – not because of Zeus's thunderbolts, but because of the *armatoloí* (irregular militia) and kidnapping *klephts* who haunted it until Macedonia became part of Greece in 1912. In 1938, high Olympus and its deeply wooded eastern slopes were designated Greece's first national park; in 1981, UNESCO included it in the list of

World Biosphere Reserves. It's famous for its birds – some 156 species have been counted here, and some 1,700 Mediterranean and central European plants have been found (25% of all the flora in Greece, including the rare Bosnian pine), and of the rare little plants above the treeline 23 species are unique to Olympus. The lions that attacked the camels in Xerxes' army are gone, but Zeus's golden eagles still float overhead, and wolves, jackals, wild cats and deer roam in the woodlands. Litóchoro (Λιτόχωρο) on the east slopes, the classic gateway to Olympus, is in a superb setting, just 5km up from the coast.

GETTING THERE AND AROUND

By train Litóchoro (w hellenictrain.gr/en) has eight trains a day from Thessaloníki (55mins), while Kateríni to the north on the Athens–Thessaloníki line has 11. Note that Litóchoro train station is beside the sea, 6km east of the town, and at a lower elevation.

By bus Buses (\ 23105 95428; w ktelpierias.gr) run nearly every hour from Thessaloníki to Kateríni bus station (Vérias 9; 45mins; €6.90), with connections to Litóchoro (10 a day; 25mins; €2.50), Elatochóri (3–5 a day; 45mins; €3.10), and the beach resorts. Frequent local buses go to Díon (40mins; €1.60) from outside Kateríni's bus station, 1km walk away, on Vardáka Partheníou Street.

By taxi There's a taxi rank in Litóchoro at the roundabout by the church of Ag Nikólaou, just past the municipal park (\ 23523 05050). Also try Íranto Theológos (m 69872 58949) or Sákis Prokóvas (m 69371 76667), the mountain marathon taxi driver. A taxi to Prióinia will cost around €30.

TOURIST INFORMATION The **Olympus National Park Information Centre** (Litóchoro; \ 23520 83000; w olympusfd.gr; ⊕ 09.00–16.00 daily, May–Oct until 18.00 daily) is packed with information on the flora and fauna and on the mountain itself. The website (search 'Mountain Routes') has details in English on the 12 main trails in the national park from easy to dangerous, including routes less travelled but spectacular from western points such as Kokkinopilós (1,100m), and details of its eight refuges (always ring to book a bed) and emergency shelters.

 WHERE TO STAY
Litochóro
Olympus Mediterranean (23 rooms) Dionýsou 5; \ 23520 81831; w mediterraneanhotels.gr/olympus. Part Neoclassical, part rustic chic 4-star hotel with a sauna & indoor pool, some rooms with a jacuzzi & fireplace. B/fast inc. €€€

Bayiri (6 rooms) Politechníou 3, off Plateía Nauftikón; m 69723 38348; w bayiri.gr. Rooms in a beautifully restored old stone building, full of traditional charm. Very helpful owners; great homemade b/fast inc. €€

Olympus Hotel Villa Drossos (14 rooms) Archelloú 20; \ 23520 84561; w villa-drosos.com. Bright & pleasant, with a garden & pool & tidy if smallish rooms. Parking; b/fast inc. €€

Villa Pantheon (12 rooms) Ag Dimitríou; \ 23520 83931; w villapantheon.gr. On the road leading to the gorge, big rooms & wonderful views, 8 with fireplaces; b/fast inc. Possibly closed for part of winter. €€

Archontikó Aphrodite (22 rooms) Plateía Eleftherías; \ 23520 81415; w arhontiko-aphrodite.gr. Run by the charming Aphrodite herself, friendly atmosphere, & useful mosquito nets over the beds. Possibly closed for part of winter. €€–€

Enipeas (22 rooms) Enipéas 2; \ 23520 84328; w enipeysrooms.gr. Older hotel, with lovely views, balconies & easy parking. B/fast inc. €

Around Olympus

Ktima Bellou [map, page 128] (12 rooms) Ag Dimítrios; ☎ 23517 70021; **w** ktimabellou.gr. West of Olympus, a stunning hotel with breathtaking views, built in the traditional style but according to best environmental practices, with some rooms in stone cottages, equipped with energy fireplaces, Coco-Mat beds, handmade furniture & traditional art. There's a pool, & an organic farm supplying the restaurant (€€). Wonderful b/fast inc. Closed w/days for some of the winter (w/ends open). €€€

Dimatis (13 rooms) Ag Dimítrios; ☎ 23510 84202; **w** dimatis.eu. A village *kafeníon* & inn from the 1920s, recently converted into an attractive hotel with suites, family rooms & attic rooms, with fireplace. Excellent restaurant (€€) featuring organic veg, game & the family's own Amýntaio wine. Minimum stay 3 nights at w/ends. B/fast inc. €€€–€€

Nikélli [map, page 128] (19 rooms) Elatochóri; ☎ 23510 82218; hotel_nikelli_elatochori. Boutique hotel with big rooms, all with balconies to take in the splendid views, & an excellent restaurant (€€) serving dishes made with produce from the hotel's garden. 2 nights' min stay; b/fast inc. €€€–€€

Alseides Boutique Hotel [map, page 128] (10 rooms) Elatochóri; ☎ 23510 82812; **w** alseides.gr. Elegant antique-filled boutique hotel, with views down to the sea & sitting room with a fireplace; sauna, hammam & gym. B/fast inc. €€

Atrion Highland Hotel [map, page 128] (16 rooms) Elatochóri; m 69722 41024; **w** atrionhotel.gr. Beautiful cosy rooms furnished with family heirlooms. Wonderful host; excellent b/fast inc. €€

Feggarópetra Magic Mountain Inn (6 rooms) Palaíos Panteleímonas; ☎ 23520 22725; fegaropetrainn. Charming owners Joanna & Marios have made this a magical place, with fun folk art & comfy beds in an old mansion. There are gorgeous views over Olympus & the coast, plus a large terrace with a pergola, bar & hammock. Parking 3mins away. Delicious b/fast inc. €€

Kýmata (50 rooms) Frouríou 37, Platamónas; ☎ 23520 41240; **w** hotelkymata.gr. Right on a stony beach tucked under the fortress, this bright luminous white hotel is well signposted; being far away from the road noise, the loudest sound is the waves (*kýmata*). B/fast inc. €€

Eco Paralía [map, page 128] (13 rooms) Marína Merkoúri 10, Paralía Katerinís; m 69457 51057; EcoHotelParalia; ⊕ Jun–Aug or Sep. Built to the best environmental standards; rooms have Coco-Mat beds, kettles & satellite channels. There's also a wellness centre, roof garden, canoes to borrow & free bikes; b/fast inc. €€–€

Summit Zero [map, page 128] (4 rooms) On the beach at Grítsa (Liménas Litochórou); ☎ 23520 61406; **w** summitzero.gr; ⊕ year round, winter by request. Hostel with bunk beds in rooms sleeping 4–6, with shared bathrooms & a bar (the owner's family make their own wine & *tsípouro*), plus links to a full range of activities. Bring your own towels. €15 pp/night. €

✕ WHERE TO EAT AND DRINK

Gastrodromio en Olympo Ag Nikólaou 36, Litochóro; ☎ 23520 21300; **w** gastrodromio.gr; ⊕ Easter–Oct 13.00–23.00 daily, winter may be closed some days. Award-winning restaurant founded in 2003 by chef Andréas Gávris, creating lovely dishes with prime ingredients from around the country; exquisite steaks but also vegan dishes, plus 30 Greek cheeses, & 500 wines, mostly from indigenous grapes. Book. €€€

Mezé Mezé Ag Nikólaou 40, Litochóro; ☎ 23520 82271; ⊕ 12.30–22.30 daily. Big variety, big portions, & friendly staff. Get there early in summer to bag an outdoor table. €€

Oi Myloi [map, page 128] At the Enipéas Gorge entrance, at the western edge of Litóchoro; ☎ 23520 83111; OiMyloi.Litochoro; ⊕ summer 11.00–23.00 Tue–Sun, winter Sat–Sun only. Lovely old spot by an old watermill, with a leafy terrace, grilled lamb, pasta with prawns, etc. €€

Olympos Gitema Ag Nikólaou 50, Litochóro; ☎ 23520 21525; Olympus-Γήτεμα; ⊕ 12.30–23.30 daily. A bright contemporary interior, meat-forward traditional dishes, lovely platings, & warm service. €€

SPORTS AND ACTIVITIES The trekking season runs from May to mid-October, but to climb to the top of Mount Olympus, you'll need to wait until late May or

5 | CENTRAL MACEDONIA (ΚΕΝΤΡΙΚΗ ΜΑΚΕΔΟΝΙΑ)

June, after the snows have melted. Even then winds and storms are not uncommon; check the weather report in Litóchoro before setting out. One of the top mountain guides in Greece, **Marinídis Bábis** (m 69743 35299; w guideolymp.com) is based in Litóchoro. Outdoor specialists **Greek Adventure**, **Trekking Hellas** and **Olympos Trek** (all page 32) offer a huge range of activities, including guided climbs to the summit, in the mountains of Pieíra around the Vale of Tempe and Óssa just south in Thessaly. Local **Olympus Paths** (m 69860 53465; w olympuspaths.com) also specialises in guided walks and treks.

Elatochóri Ski Centre [map, page 128] 8km from Elatochóri; ℅ 23510 72200; w xionodromika. gr/en/ski-centers/elatochori-ski-center; ⊕ Dec– Mar. North of Olympus, with 10 slopes ranging from 1,974m to 1,410m, & 5 lifts, plus snowboard & sledge slopes.

WHAT TO SEE AND DO Somewhat unexpectedly for a mountain village, Litóchoro has a proud past in the merchant navy, thanks to the many Greek refugees who arrived after the fall of Constantinople in 1453. Former sailors run the **Maritime Museum of Litóchoro** (Ag Nikólaou 5; ℅ 23520 81402; w nmlitohorou.gr; ⊕ Jul–Aug 20.00–22.30 daily, also 10.00–noon Sun; other times ring ahead; €2, under 12s free) evoking the past with paintings and models of ships, maps, mines, navigational equipment and more.

From Litóchoro, the classic ascent of Olympus starts up the E4 into the stunning sheer-sided **Enipéas Gorge**, with seven beautiful wooden bridges over the river, passing the **cave hermitage Ag Dionýsios** and the **Monastery of Ag Dionýsios** (⊕ Apr–Sep) founded c1500 by St Dionýsios of Mount Athos. It's 9km as the crow flies (the path is 15.5km) and it takes about 5 hours to reach **Priónia** (1,100m), 18km by road from Litóchoro, with the source of the Enipéas and a café/restaurant (m 69324 84868; ⊕ 08.00–18.00 daily, in winter open w/ends only; €). Alternatively you can take the bus or taxi up and walk down – although there are also a lot of 'ups' on the way down).

From Priónia it's 3 hours' walk (4.5km) through the forest, with many rare Bosnian pines, to the **Spílios Agapitós (Zolotas) refuge** (2,040m; ℅ 23520 81800; ⊕ mid-May–Oct; €), with beds for 110 and a restaurant. This is the base for the 3km, 3-hour ascent of **Mýtikas** (2,918m), rated medium-difficult, although the very last leg is a precipitous, slippery scramble on the rocks, where you might run into a people jam on the narrow trail.

AROUND MOUNT OLYMPUS The region north of Olympus, Piéria, was according to Hesiod the birthplace of the Nine Muses, daughters of Zeus and Mnemosyne (Memory). Inland from **Leptokariá** (Λεπτοκαρυά) – the biggest resort on the coast – and south of Palaiá Leptokariá was **Leivithra** (Leibethra), inhabited from Mycenaean times to the 1st century BC and once a favourite home of the muses; one version of the myth has it that Orpheus was born here, the son of Kalliope, the muse of Epic Poetry and the Thracian king of Oiagros. It was here that the women buried the limbs of Orpheus, after tearing him to bits (page 203). The **archaeological site** (℅ 23520 33884; w leivithra.culture.gov.gr/en/park-of-leivithra; ⊕ 08.00–15.00 Mon–Fri by appointment; free) is scattered over three areas; the acropolis at Kástri is set amid the trees and doubles as a festival venue, near a new educational park. Sections of an ancient mule path laboriously built over the mountains from Leivithra to Thessaly were uncovered during the digs.

Many mountain villages like **Palaiá Leptokariá** were all but abandoned in the rush to the coast in the 1950s and 60s, but in recent years, descendants of the

> ### TEA OF THE GODS
>
> The Greek mountains are full of healing herbs, but Mount Olympus tea, or *Sideritis scardica*, has always been one of the most valuable. The scientific name derives from *sideros*, Greek for 'iron', referring to its ancient role in healing wounds inflicted by iron weapons. Endemic to the Balkan peninsula, it has been over-harvested in both Greece and Bulgaria because of the renewed interest in its virtues as an antioxidant and anti-inflammatory. One of the few places where it grows abundantly, however, is over 1,000m up the slopes of Olympus, where commercial cultivation is underway.

property owners have returned to convert old houses into holiday homes or inns and tavernas, especially at lovely **Palaíos Panteleímonas** (Παλαιός Παντελεήμωνας), where tavernas serve *tsípouro* made from arbutus (fruit from the strawberry trees that surround it). There's a beautiful path from here to **Póroi** (Πόροι) and **Áno Skotína** (Άνω Σκοτίνα), the latter with a 17th-century church, Ag Athanásios.

The unspoiled west flanks of Olympus and lush mountains of Piéria have attracted some upmarket mountain lodges, notably **Elatochóri** (Ελατοώρι) near the ski slopes and **Ag Dimítrios** (Αγ Δημήτριος).

Olympus Riviera Piería's shore consists of 16 sand and pebble beaches one after another, most backed by pine woods – a package holiday paradise rimmed with hotels, apartments and campsites with signs in a bewildering array of languages and alphabets. The one minus this Riviera shares with the Italian one is the proximity of the railway to the shore and the night trains that use it. The southernmost beaches, **Néoi Póroi** and **Platamónas** (Πλαταμώνας), enjoy theatrical views of the **Castle of Platamónas** (car park off the National road; ⊕ summer 09.00–15.00 Tue & Wed, 09.00–20.00 Thu–Mon, winter 08.30–15.00 Wed–Mon; €3) on the lofty headland. Built on the site of Ancient Heraclea, a Macedonian frontier town guarding the entrance into the Thermaic Gulf and **Vale of Tempe** (page 310), the castle was built by the Lombard Crusaders under Orlando Piche in 1204, but was taken after a terrible siege in 1218 by Theodore Angelus, Despot of Epirus. Within the well-preserved walls are bits of ruins of churches, an ironworks, and the 'black plane tree' where the Turks hanged rebels during the fighting in 1912.

Orliás Waterfalls (Off the road from Litóchoro to Díon, near the sign for the Petrostroúgga refuge) The Helicón (or Orliás) River tumbles down the gorge in a series of falls and pools that make it one of the prettiest places around for a swim; it's clear but cold. The path to the biggest waterfall takes about an hour from the sign by the road; in summer get there early to avoid a scrum, and bring your swimsuit and swim shoes.

Ancient Dion Another name for Zeus was Dias, and this ancient city north of Mount Olympus supposedly stood where Deukalion (the Noah of Greek myth) erected the first altar to the father of the gods after the flood. As the Macedonian kings claimed Zeus as an ancestor, Dion became important in the late 5th century BC under King Archelaos, who founded the Olympian Games in honour of Zeus and his daughters, the Nine Muses.

It was during these games that Philip II was given a superb but skittery stallion, which no-one could mount until the eight-year-old Alexander piped up and asked to

5 | CENTRAL MACEDONIA (ΚΕΝΤΡΙΚΗ ΜΑΚΕΔΟΝΙΑ)

try, then rode into the sun because he had noticed the horse was startled by his own shadow. 'Oh my son, look thee out for a kingdom equal to and worthy of thyself, for Macedon is too little to hold thee,' his proud father exclaimed. Alexander named the stallion Bucephalus, and later rode him to India. Dion was also the place where the Macedonians sacrificed to Zeus before leaving for battle, as Alexander did in splendid style before going to Persia, presiding in a tent that held a hundred dining couches.

Although Cassander surrounded the city with walls that stood up to 10m tall in places, the Hellenistic city was devastated by the Aetolians in 219BC, but soon rebuilt. It thrived under the Romans into early Christian times, becoming a bishopric in the 4th century AD, until earthquakes and barbarian invasions led to Dion's abandonment.

Archaeological Park of Ancient Dion (\ 23510 53484; w odysseus.culture.gr; ⊕ Jun–Oct 08.00–20.00 daily, Nov–May 08.30–15.30 Thu–Mon; €8, concessions €4, inc museum) 'Park' is no exaggeration: on the Vaphýras River, it covers 150ha, including the scattered ruins of Ancient Dion, woods, meadows and lush swampy

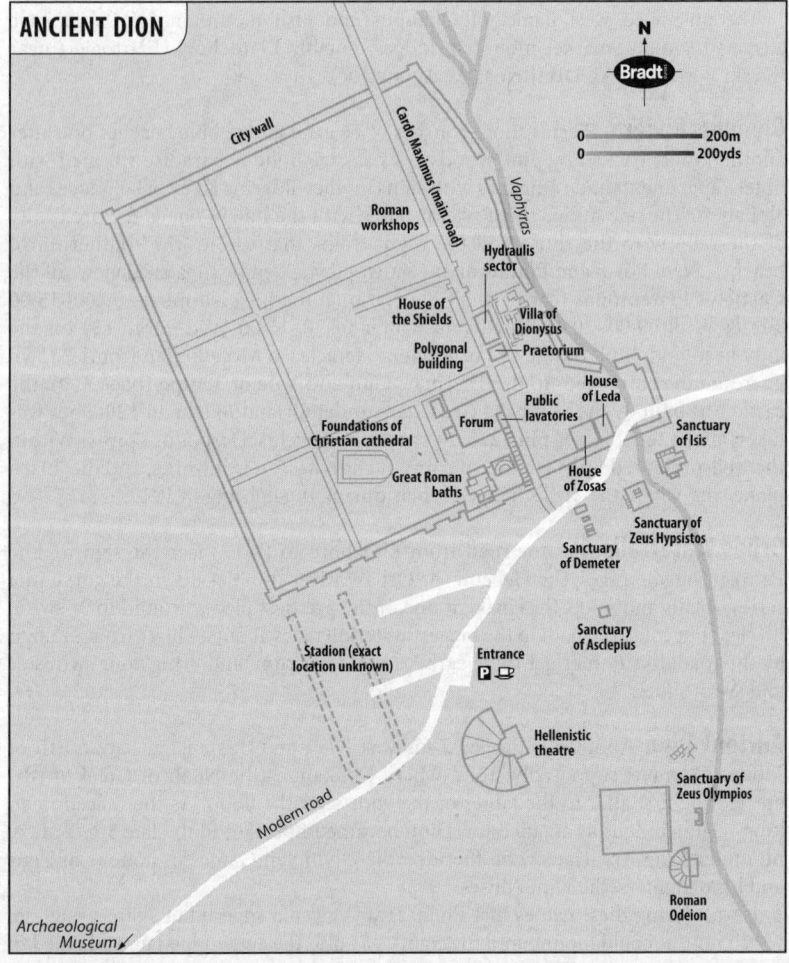

ponds; birds twitter, frogs croak and pretty blue dragonflies dart over the ruins. This river was famous in mythology: its headwaters were on Olympus, where it was known as the Helicón, but when the maenads who murdered Orpheus (page 203) tried to wash the blood from their hands, it ducked underground, rather than be polluted, then re-emerged at Dion under a new name, Vaphýras.

The sites are well signposted. A left turn from the entrance leads to the ruins of the city; except for a protruding bit by the river – possibly a jetty – it was an almost-perfect square grid. The main street, the **Cardo Maximus**, is wide and was nicely paved by the Romans. Walk up the little path on the left to the luxurious **bath complex**, the most important of the ten found in the city, with walkways to take you over the impressively intact mosaic floors and hypocaust system. Statues of Asklepios and his children found at the north end (now in the museum) suggest that at least part of the complex was used for therapeutic purposes. The **Roman forum** stood near here.

Follow the signs to the large **Christian cathedral** that was never finished. Returning to the Cardo, the **Hydraulis sector** (named after the instrument discovered there; page 136) is the site of the vast **Villa of Dionysos** (cAD200), which had a row of shops facing the street, baths, a shrine to the wine god, four peristyle courts with pools and a banquet hall. Here archaeologists uncovered the superb mosaic copied from a Hellenistic painting of the Dionysos in a chariot borne by amphibious panthers (now in its own building; page 136).

Heading back down the main street are **Roman workshops** and the **House of the Shields** decorated with reliefs from the 4th century BC, which may once have been the base of a victory monument disassembled and moved here. Further up, opposite the **Praetorium** or guesthouse, don't miss the well-preserved **public lavatories** where citizens could socialise while relieving themselves. The large **Polygonal building** was square on the outside, with a 12-sided courtyard within. A mosaic of wrestlers is preserved inside, suggesting it had something to do with sports, but no-one is sure. Just within the southeast walls, the **House of Leda** and **House of Zosas** contain copies of their original states – now in the archaeology museum.

The cluster of four sanctuaries just outside the city walls are often soggy if not completely inundated; there's a **Sanctuary of Asclepius**, a **Sanctuary of Zeus Hypsistos** ('the most high') with a mosaic of a white bull and double axes, and a **Sanctuary of Demeter** (originally designed in the shape of a Mycenaean megaron and from the 6th century BC, pre-dating the rest of Dion). A bridge crosses the Vaphýras – which was navigable in antiquity – to the often-flooded, evocative Hellenistic **Sanctuary of Isis**, a pretty complex decorated with copies of the statues found in situ. The Macedonian rulers followed Alexander in adopting his syncretising ways, and replaced Artemis with the gentler Egyptian Isis as the goddess of childbirth; the flooding symbolised the goddess's native Nile, and it's certainly true that the sanctuary is more often than not completely submerged, along with its side temples dedicated to Isis, the goddess of fortune, and to Aphrodite Hypolimpidia ('under Olympus').

A path through the lush woodlands leads to the once-roofed **Roman Odeion**, used for concerts or lectures. Nearby, there are the few blocks remaining of the massive 22m altar of the **Sanctuary of Zeus Olympios** and the rows of stones where oxen would be chained in preparation for their sacrifice in a hecatomb – a hundred at a time. Originally this was a grove, filled with gilded statues of the kings of Macedon and 25 famous bronze equestrian statues by Lysippus of Alexander's Companions who fell at the young king's first great victory over the Persians at Granicus. The Aetolians wrecked them all.

Under Philip II, the surrounding fields were used to drill the Macedonian phalanx, which with its full body shields and the long spears he had invented (*sarissa*; page 155) was said to resemble a charging porcupine. This wall of pikes acted as an 'anvil' to hold the centre, while the heavy cavalry (mostly recruited from horsey Thessaly) would swing around and 'hammer' the enemy. Philip learned the tactics as a hostage of Epaminóndas in Thebes, and Alexander would use them over and over, with a hundred variations. The field is closed off by a **Hellenistic theatre**, with modern seating for the Olympus Festival. It has a rare surviving feature, a 'ladder of Charon' – a corridor under the orchestra that allowed actors to emerge up the steps from the 'Underworld'. The Stadion was probably near here.

Archaeological Museum (500m from Archaeological Park, in modern Díon town; 23510 53206; Jun–Oct 08.00–20.00 Wed–Mon, 11.00–19.00 Tue, Nov–May 08.30–15.30 Wed–Mon; combined ticket with Archaeological Park) The museum houses Hellenistic and Roman finds: statues of the four philosophers from the Villa of Dionysos, others from the sanctuaries and baths, and funerary steles, including an expressive one of a mother and child by a 5th-century BC sculptor.

Upstairs, there's a real rarity: the 1st-century BC hydraulis, the oldest example yet found of the world's first keyboard instrument, discovered in the Dionysos Villa. Invented in the 3rd century BC by Ktesibius of Alexandria, an engineer who specialised in air- and water-powered mechanisms, it was a hit in ancient Rome (Nero claimed to perfect it). It was later forgotten in the West until AD757, when the Byzantine emperor sent one as a gift to Rome, where it developed into the modern church organ. Dion's hydraulis was reproduced by the European Cultural Centre at Delphi – it sounds like a melancholy train whistle heard underwater, the rhythms emphasised by the clack of the keys and creaking water pump (there's a film of a concert on the ground floor). Another musical find in Dion was a woman's funeral stele that yielded the first image of a *nabla*, a six-string instrument with a sound box on the bottom and two tuning strings on the sides, often played at ancient banquets, and known in the Temple of Solomon.

Archaeological Store (Opposite the museum; same hours as museum; included in park ticket) Threatened with water damage, the superb mosaic of Dionysos in his chariot from the Villa of Dionysos was detached and relocated here in its very own building in 2017, after starring in a special Dion exhibition in the Onassis Foundation in New York City; a film explains how it all happened. The surrounding cases hold the latest finds from the site.

TOWARDS THESSALONÍKI Kateríni, the capital of Piería, has a glorious view of Mount Olympus, and seriously busy traffic that makes you just want to get out as soon as possible. **Makrýgialos** (Μακρύγιαλος) to the north is famous for the delta's mussels (some 90% of the entire Greek haul) and holds a festival celebrating the molluscs during the last ten days of July.

Just south are the remains of **Ancient Pydna** (08.00–14.00 daily; ; free – if he's not busy, Thanásis the enthusiastic guardian will give you a free guided tour), Macedon's most important port before the foundation of Thessaloníki and where Alexander's meddlesome mother Olympias was stabbed to death in 317BC by an assassin employed by Cassander during the fight between the Successors. In 168BC, Pydna also witnessed the final battle of the Macedonian Wars, pitting 38,000 Romans under Lucius Amelius Paulus against 43,000 Macedonians under King Perseus. The Romans, having learned a trick or two from Hannibal, had laboriously brought their secret weapon – 22 elephants – around Mount Olympus. In spite of the common belief that Pydna once and for all proved the superiority of the legion over the phalanx, many military historians in fact blame Perseus' failure to follow Alexander's tried and true methods of bringing in the cavalry 'hammer' for Macedon's wretched defeat (20,000 killed and 11,000 imprisoned, compared with 1,100 Roman dead). Perseus fled to Samothráki, but he was captured, forced to take part in Amelius' triumph in Rome, and died. In Byzantine times Pydna was called Kítros, and the site has what remains of the cathedral and **castle** after it was attacked by Frankish and Catalan mercenaries. You can also have a look at the second-most important **salt pans** (*alykí*) in Greece – and their popular **mud baths** (⊕ always).

Methóni, with its Blue Flag beach, was an Athenian colony, the last one to survive in northern Greece until Philip II besieged it in 354BC; he lost an eye in the battle, and when Methóni surrendered he sent the Athenians home and gave their land to his men. Just to the north (2.5km) is some excellent birding at the Nea Agathoúpoli birdwatching tower by the wetlands (❧ 23107 94811; ⊕ 10.00–14.00 Mon–Sat), part of the **Axiós Delta National Park** (page 99). Information and binoculars are provided, and there are also paths through the wetlands for a closer look. Having some insect repellent on hand is a good idea.

The rest isn't too exciting unless you're a farmer: Central Macedonia's rich, fertile, well-watered plains provide many of the good things in Thessaloníki's markets.

VÉRIA

Straddling the Tripótamos, a tributary of the Aliákmonas River, Véria (Βέροια; population c75,000) is the lively capital of Homer's 'lovely Imathia', the rich plain densely planted with strawberries, vineyards, peach and apple orchards and a gorgeous frilly sight in spring before the blue backdrop of Mount Vérmio (2,065m). It was the cradle of the Hellenistic kings of Macedon, descended from Alexander's general Antigonus I Monophthalmus ('the one-eyed'). Pompey and his army wintered here before meeting Caesar at Pharsalus (Fársala; page 312).

Known as Berea in the Bible, Veria had an important Jewish community; Acts VII tells how St Paul and Silas came here and noted that the local Jews 'were more noble than those in Thessaloníki…they searched the scriptures daily'. Under the Byzantines, it became the most important city in the region after Thessaloníki, and was filled with members of both faiths, especially after the local Romiot Jews were joined by the Sephardim. Some 300 watermills powered the city's textile works that made its wealth, and along with Kastoriá, the city became a leading

> **KING MIDAS**
>
> In myth, Imathia was the gardens of King Midas, 'where roses grow wild – wonderful blooms, with sixty petals each, and sweeter smelling than any others in the world'. One day his gardeners found Dionysos' tutor, Silenus, under the roses, sleeping off too much wine. When Midas safely delivered Silenus back to Dionysos, the god granted him his wish: that all he touched turned to gold, which of course backfired when he nearly died of thirst and starvation before Dionysos told him to go east and wash his hands in the Pactolus River. Midas stayed in Anatolia to become the heir to the childless Phrygian King Gordius (who tied the famous Gordian knot cut by Alexander), leaving Macedonia to be occupied by the Dorian heirs of the hero Makedon.

centre of Byzantine art in the latter half of the 15th century, counting some 72 churches, many of which were provincial versions of churches of Constantinople; today some 48 have survived, earning the city the nickname 'Little Jerusalem'.

Véria also has a new feather in its cap: in 2010, its Central Public Library (w libver.gr) won a million-dollar prize from the Bill & Melinda Gates Foundation, while two large wind farms are under construction in the Vérmio mountains.

GETTING THERE AND AROUND

By train The station [139 C1] (\ 23310 24444; w hellenictrain.gr/en) is 3km north of town (linked by bus to the centre). From Athens or Thessaloníki, change at Platý (Πλατύ) for Véria (three services a day); three trains also run direct from Thessaloníki and take 1 hour (from €5).

By bus Véria's bus station [139 B3] (\ 23310 22988; w ktelnimathias.gr) is at Trempesína 8, just off Venizélou. There are buses roughly every 45 minutes from Thessaloníki (\ 23310 22342; €7.40) and frequent links to Vergína (20mins), Náoussa and Édessa.

By taxi There are ranks at the bus station [139 B3] and by the Bema of St Paul [139 A5]. Or call \ 23310 62555.

By car There's an easy-to-find 24/7 parking garage on Mitropóleos Street, next to the town hall (Dimarchío) [139 B4]. Otherwise be prepared for a long walk.

TOURIST INFORMATION Discover Veria (\ 23313 50608; w en.discoververia.gr) has a wealth of visitor information on what to see and do in the town and surrounding areas.

ORIENTATION It's easy to get lost in Véria. Busy main Mitropóleos Street was a branch of the Via Egnatía; the deeply grooved paving stones, discovered in 1997 in front of the Dimarchío await their next chariot. It descends from **Plateía Orologíou** (or Raktiván) [139 A5], the site of the ancient acropolis, and links up with the other main street, Venizélou, at a Y-shaped angle with Eliá Street, which leads to the garden belvedere **Párko Eliá** [139 C4], with its restaurant, café and 180° views across the Imathian plain. Along the Tripótamos River the Jewish **Barboúta** (Μπαρμπούτα) [139 A4] quarter preserves a 19th-century synagogue and 18th- and 19th-century mansions; others are just north in the **Panagías Dexiás** (Παναγίας Δεξιάς) [139 A4] quarter. Many of Véria's Byzantine churches (several of which were once camouflaged as houses, hidden from pesky Turkish officials) are tucked behind Mitropóleos Street in the old Christian **Kyriótissa** (Κυριώτισσα) [139 B4] quarter, where old houses have been converted into restaurants and bars.

WHERE TO STAY

Olganos VL Boutique Hotel [139 A4] (7 rooms) 10th Merarchías 7; \ 23310 72226; w olganos.com. Handsome design hotel in a century-old building in Barboúta, full of interesting textures: stone & brick walls, wooden floors, beamed ceilings with a mix of antique & contemporary details. Sat TV & kettle in the rooms. Good b/fast €7. €€€–€€

Aiges Melathron [139 D5] (54 rooms) 1km from the centre on the Náoussa road; \ 23310 77777; w aigesmelathron.gr. Modern 4-star hotel, the only one with a pool & children's pool. Easy, free parking; good buffet b/fast inc. €€

Kókkino Spíti [139 A4] (12 rooms) Olgánou 10, near the Old Synagogue; \ 23310 74440; w kokkinospiti.gr. Boutique rooms

VÉRIA

in a handsome 19th-century mansion, with parquet floors & old wooden beams & antiques, overlooking the wooded banks of the Tripótamos River in the old Jewish quarter of Barboúta. Lovely b/fast €7. €€

Makedonía [139 B4] (39 rooms) Kontogeorgáki 50; 23310 66902; w makedoniahotel.gr. Central, smart hotel, recently renovated, on the edge of the old town, with a roof garden. B/fast inc. €€

Veritas Boutique Art Hotel [139 B3] (6 rooms) Aristotélous 8; 23310 68100; w hotelveritas.gr. Colourful, hip rooms, each dedicated to a famous contemporary Greek, in a Neoclassical building in the centre, located over a popular bistro. B/fast inc. €€

Villa Eliá [139 C4] (27 rooms) Eliás 10; 23310 26800; w hotel-villaelia.gr. Convenient & central hotel with big rooms near the park & belvedere; if you let the owners know, they can arrange parking. €€–€

✖ WHERE TO EAT AND DRINK

12 Gráda [139 A4] Cnr Sofoú 11 & Dimosthénous; 23311 00112; w 12grada.gr; ⏱ 13.00–23.00 Tue–Sun. In a traditional building overlooking the Tripótamos River, the '12 Steps' is a wonderful wine

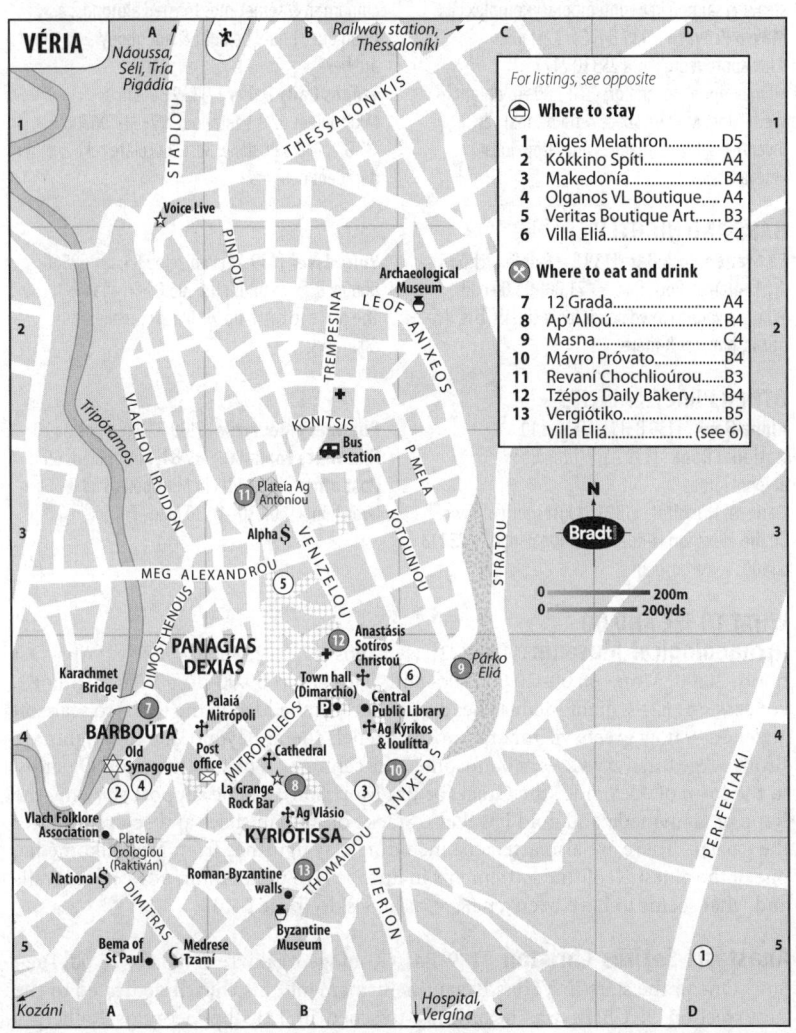

5 | CENTRAL MACEDONIA (ΚΕΝΤΡΙΚΗ ΜΑΚΕΔΟΝΙΑ)

bar run by sommelier & chef brothers, offering 80 wines & a constantly changing menu of delicacies, with an Anatolian touch to match your chosen glass or bottle. €€€
Vergiótiko [139 B5] Oumaídou 2; 23310 74133; f; ⏰ until 01.00 daily. Beef is the speciality at this rustic taverna, built into the rock. Some of the beef is from the owner's family's cattle, aged in house. This is some of Greece's finest meat: succulent steaks cooked to order, stewed beef cheeks, & a number of other hearty classics & Náoussa wines. €€€
Masna [139 C4] Eliás Park; 23310 64000; w elia-veria.gr/masna; ⏰ noon–midnight daily. Great views & fresh pasta from Italy, grilled rib-eye steaks & salmon in a contemporary complex. €€
Mávro Próvato [139 B4] Cnr Kastanias 41 & Kontogeorgaki; 23310 21211; w mavroprovatoveria.gr; ⏰ 13.00–midnight Wed–Mon. Modern space & traditional yet inventive salads & mains. Wines from local vineyards. €€

Ap' Alloú [139 B4] Patriárchos Iokeím 5; 23310 20199; f Απ' Αλλού; ⏰ 14.00–midnight daily. Charming spot in an old house near Ag Vlásio, offering a mix of classic Greek & Mediterranean dishes, with good vegetarian choices. €
Revaní Chochlioúrou (Χοχλιούρου) [139 B3] Plateía Ag Antoníou; 23310 22737; ⏰ 08.30–21.00 daily. Since 1886, this little shop has made the best version of Véria's famous *revaní*, a cousin of the Middle Eastern *basbousa* or *samali* – a sweet, moist cake made with fine semolina flavoured with lemon zest, drizzled with an orange citrusy syrup, & sprinkled with cinnamon & sometimes toasted almonds; a good one should be light & not gooey – as they are here.
Tzépos Daily Bakery [139 B4] Cnr Mitropoleos 67 & Venizélou; 23313 06706; ⏰ 07.00–23.00 daily. Best chocolate cake & other decadent delights.

BARS AND NIGHTLIFE
La Grange Rock Bar [139 B3] Patr Ierarchón 14; f Lagrange-Rock-Bar; ⏰ 21.00–05.00 daily. Where a young crowd heads for cocktails, DJs, live music, billiards & more.

Voice Live [139 A1] Venizélou 85; m 69860 80004; f; ⏰ midnight–06.00 Fri–Sat. The place to catch up with new Greek bands & singers.

OTHER PRACTICALITIES
Alpha Bank [139 B3] Malakoúsi 10
National Bank [139 A5] Mitropóleos at Ippokrátous
General Hospital [139 C5] Just south of town on the Alexandrias-Kozanis national road; 23313 51100; w verhospi.gr

Pharmacy Mourtzíla [139 B2] Trempesína 20
Pharmacy Foukala [139 B4] Mitropóleos 65
Post office [139 A4] Cnr Mitropóleos 33 & Ierarchón; ⏰ 07.30–14.30 Mon–Fri

WHAT TO SEE AND DO
Archaeological Museum [139 C2] (Aníxeos 47; 23310 24972; ⏰ Apr–Oct noon–20.00 Mon, 08.00–20.00 Tue–Sun, Nov–Mar 09.00–17.00 Tue–Sun; €3, concessions €2) A giant Medusa head – formerly embedded in the walls, to scare off attackers – now greets visitors rather than repels them. Beyond, the highlights are Bronze Age funerary vases, a handsome 2nd-century AD bust of river god Olganos, in the form of Alexander the Great (or Jim Morrison), a table support showing the Rape of Ganymede and gold jewellery. Stacks of Roman steles and sculpture litter the garden. There are also artefacts, including clay figurines from Néa Nikomédia, one of the oldest Neolithic settlements in Europe (7th millennium BC) – it had walls and what seems to have been a palace, as at Sésklo (page 340).

Anastásis Sotíros Christoú [139 B4] (Kontogeorgáki 1; ⏰ 08.30–15.00 Tue–Sun) One of the stars in Véria's Byzantine firmament, this church dedicated to the Resurrection of Christ was beautifully frescoed in 1315 by Geórgios Kalliérges of Thessaloníki, an elegant painter of saints and angels. It's the only work he ever signed, although someone else painted the scene under the porch, of a river and men hugging each other, wearing flying-saucer halos.

Ag Kýrikos and Ioulítta [139 B4] (Kontogeorgáki; ⊕ 08.30–15.00 Tue–Sun) Built in the 14th century and surrounded by some of the oldest houses in the city, there is a rich collection of frescoes inside, mostly from the 16th century.

Palaiá Mitrópoli [139 A4] (Vas Konsantínou 32, off Kentrikís; ☎ 23310 29737; ⊕ 09.00–17.00 Wed–Mon; free) Built in the 11th century over a 5th-century AD church, the Old Cathedral echoes the great Basilica of Ag Dimítrios in Thessaloníki in its design, and re-uses some of the capitals and columns of its predecessor. Converted into a mosque under the Ottomans, it reopened in 2016 after a long restoration, which revived the rich colours of its important 12th–14th-century frescoes that once completely covered the interior. The **new Cathedral** [139 B4], a block away on Mitropóleos Street, was probably begun in the 1400s, after the old one was converted into a mosque; it too has some of its original frescoes.

Old Synagogue [139 A4] (Olgánou; m 69838 80329; ⊕ noon–15.00 daily, contact Mrs Evi Meska for visits at other times; €3, under 18s free) Just down by the river in the colourful Barboúta quarter, Véria's surviving synagogue, rebuilt in stone in 1850, may well replace an earlier version known by St Paul in AD50 – which would make the site one of the oldest in Europe. The bishop of Véria saved the building from the Nazis, but he couldn't save the congregation from the death camps. The pedestrian stone bridge [139 A4] over the river is named after its Turkish architect, Karachmet.

Byzantine Museum [139 B5] (Thomaídou 26; ☎ 23310 76100; ⊕ Apr–Oct noon–20.00 Tue, 08.00–20.00 Wed–Mon, Nov–Mar 09.00–17.00 Wed–Mon; summer €4, concessions €2, winter €2 for everyone) Housed in a large flour mill of 1911 – its restoration won a Europa Nostra prize – this museum is filled with art going back to the 5th century AD, including pretty mosaic floors, murals and an exceptional icon collection with three masterworks, an *Ag Dimítrios*, a *Christ Pantocrator* and a *Virgin Hodegétria* ('she who points the way') gesturing towards an infant Jesus, attributed to Geórgios Kalliérges. While there, walk down the nearby steps to see the **Roman-Byzantine walls** [139 B5] along Thomaídou Street, supporting rickety old houses and balconies.

Ag Vlásio [139 B4] (Gr Xenópoulou 3) Built in 1320, this little church has frescoes on the life of St Blaise and icons, some attributed to Kalliérges.

Bema of St Paul [139 A5] (Mavromicháli, just above Plateía Orologíou; ⊕ always; free) This is what the coach tours come to see: the humble tribune steps where St Paul preached, which were given a royal mosaic treatment in 1961.

Medrese Tzamí [139 A5] (Apostólou Paúlou) Behind the bema this well-preserved mosque of 1850 was built out of the stones of the church of St Paul, and is named after the adjacent theological school, which burned down in 1922.

Vlach Folklore Association [139 A4] (Cnr Veróis & Evraíon Martiron; ☎ 23310 64315; w vlahoi.gr) Although Vlachs have been documented in Véria since Byzantine times, they moved into the area en masse from the Pindus during the late 18th–19th-century troubles, keeping their flocks in the surrounding mountains. The association has a choir, dance groups and a Museum of Aromanian Music with recordings.

VERGÍNA

Some 12km east of Véria, past the Aliákmonas River dam, the road rises into the gentle foothills of Mount Piería to a village created by 1922 Greek refugees from the Pontus and Caucuses. But people have lived here since the cows came home, or at least since the 11th century BC, the date of the oldest of the area's 500 tumuli. One of these mounds had some old stones that the locals called the 'little palace' of a certain queen Vergína (Βεργίνα) who gave her name to the village. Decades earlier, in the 1860s, the French had begun excavations and found a Macedonian tomb, but war and troubles prevented further investigations until 1937, when it became a project of the archaeology department of the University of Thessaloníki. War stopped work again until 1959. Archaeologist Manólis Andrónikos, who had begun research as a student at Vergína, returned to lead the dig.

British classicist N G L Hammond, who knew Macedonia so well that he was recruited as an SOE officer in the region during World War II, had theorised that Vergína (not Édessa, as many believed) occupied the site of Ancient Aigai, the first capital of the kings of Macedon. Convinced that Hammond was right, Andrónikos set to work on the Great Tumulus, 110m in diameter (once believed to be the largest in Greece, although it is dwarfed by the Kásta tomb at Amphipolis, which is so large that people just presumed it was a hill). Excavations showed that the clay and gravel of the tumulus had fragments of damaged funerary steles from 300–250BC – which slotted in with the historical fact that Gaulish mercenaries of King Pyrrhus, left to guard Aigai in 274BC, had plundered its cemetery. And in 1977–78 Andrónikos found, under all the rubble, what he had sought: the royal tombs. What he hadn't expected was to find one unplundered, with the fabulous treasure and ashes of Philip II – confirmed by the forensic reconstruction of the skull showing the horrific eye wound he suffered at the battle of Methóni.

HISTORY Greek historians wrote that Karanos (or some say Perdiccas), the son of the king of Argos – a descendant of Hercules – was the forefather of Macedonia's Argead ('Argive') dynasty. The myth has it that in the late 9th century BC before the first Olympiad (776BC), when his brother became king of Argos, Karanos wanted a kingdom of his own and was told by the Oracle at Delphi to head north and follow a herd of goats, which he duly did and named his foundation Aigai ('many goats'). For a country on the fringes of the Hellenic world, this essential Greek ancestry, duly confirmed in 500BC by the Hellanodikai (official Olympic judges), was important, as non-Greeks couldn't compete in the games. Even after the Macedonian court moved to Pella, Aigai retained its importance, especially as a royal burial ground: a prophesy warned that if a king were buried anywhere else, the Argead dynasty would end, which was proved correct when Alexander the Great was buried in Egypt.

In 336BC, at the height of his power, Philip II rebuilt the royal palace at Aigai in a grand style never before seen in Europe, then invited his nobles and representatives of the Greek city-states to attend the wedding of his daughter Cleopatra to her maternal uncle Alexander of Epirus. It was a magnificent show of bling, designed to impress the Greeks, and after the wedding Philip invited everyone to a ceremony at Aigai's theatre, which he planned as a send-off to his conquest of Persia. Signs for the latter were auspicious: there had been double poisonings in the Persian royal family, the Greeks in Asia Minor were ripe to revolt and the Delphic oracle had told him: 'Wreathed is the bull; the end is near, the sacrificer is at hand.' Philip, of course, interpreted the 'bull' as the king of Persia.

Only one row of seats survives in the theatre today, but try to imagine the bowl filled with perfumed dignitaries. First, in solemn procession, come splendid statues of the Olympian gods, followed by a surprise: a statue of Philip himself, enthroned as a 13th god (a conceit later adopted by the Roman emperors). Then his 20-year-old son Alexander III and new son-in-law, Alexander, enter the theatre, just ahead of Philip, who is about to enter, alone. Instead – a horrible shout, as Philip's bodyguard Pausanias stabs him to death. In the confusion Pausanias almost gets away to waiting horses before he is killed.

Conspiracy theories began immediately, many pointing to Alexander's mother, Philip's estranged wife Olympias, although the only contemporary account to survive, by Aristotle, says a tawdry sexual humiliation was the motive. After the murder, Alexander the Lyncestian stood beside Alexander in the theatre to nominate him as successor, and the assembled Macedonians raised their shields and beat them with their spears, to signify their accord.

WHERE TO STAY AND EAT

Ktima Kalaïtzis [map, page 128] (11 rooms) Metóchi Prodrómou, 5km west of Vergína; 23310 92092; w ktima-kalaitzi.com. Charming guesthouse on a hill, surrounded by vines, with lovely views. Splurge on a stay in the beautiful wood-panelled Grand Suite (€€€). Good restaurant (€€€) with a limited menu. B/fast €7. €€

Pension Vergina (12 rooms) Aristotélous 55; 23310 92510; . Simple but friendly rooms of 1970s vintage in an overgrown house, in walking distance of the Royal Tombs. €

Stou Charátsi Anageníseos 1; 23310 92593; noon–22.30 Wed–Mon. The place to dine après tombs, with a shady terrace & simple Greek eats. €

WHAT TO SEE AND DO

Polycentric Museum of Aigai (23310 92580; w aigai.gr; summer 08.00–20.00 Wed–Mon, noon–20.00 Tue, gradually earlier closings Sep–Oct, winter 09.00–17.00 Wed–Mon; combined ticket for museum, Royal Tombs and Palace €20, concessions €10) At the end of 2022, under the direction of archaeologist Angelikí Kottarídi, the much-anticipated new Central Museum Building of Aigai opened, providing a conceptual gateway to the sites and related findings, and more broadly to the life of the Hellenistic world. The museum experience unfolds through innovative displays of the findings, arranged in thematic compositions of artistic merit, and digital displays (the planned 'Alexander the Great, from Aigai to Oikoumeni') as well as works by contemporary artist Chrístos Bokóros.

Royal Tombs of Aigai (23310 92347; w aigai.gr; see Polycentric Museum of Aigai, above, for hours and prices) In 1998, the Great Tumulus was arranged as a spectacular museum. Here, the bright light of day is left behind for the atmospheric penumbra of the tomb, where golden treasures glow magically, just out of reach (thanks to fibre-optic lighting in almost invisible cases).

Manólis Andronikos discovered four tombs in the mound. One was next to a *heröon*, built for the worship of the 'hero' Philip, but destroyed when the tumulus was built. The second, the **Persephone Tomb**, takes its name from the finest ancient wall painting to come down to us, a frieze of the Rape of Persephone attributed

5 | CENTRAL MACEDONIA (ΚΕΝΤΡΙΚΗ ΜΑΚΕΔΟΝΙΑ)

TOMBS INSPIRED BY PLATO

At the end of the Classical age, it seems that the Macedonian élite turned to Plato's *Laws* when it came to tomb design for the elite:

> Their tomb shall be constructed underground, in the form of an oblong vault of porous stone, as long lasting as possible, and fitted with couches of stone set side by side; in this when they have laid him who is gone to rest, they shall make a mound in a circle round it and plant thereon a grove of trees, save only at one extremity, so that at that point the tomb may for all time admit enlargement.

And so the Macedonians built their subterranean tombs, with simple or elaborate temple façades, closed by a marble door on metal hinges. Most had two vaulted chambers: an antechamber in the front, sometimes with a marble throne, and a tomb chamber in the back, with marble banquet couches for the deceased (although bodies were usually cremated on pyres just outside the tombs and placed in urns) and tables for offerings. Philip II himself may have set the fashion, in the tomb he built for his mother, Eurydice, in Aigai.

But where he and later Macedonians varied from Plato is in the offerings and decoration they lavished on the furnishings and walls of the tombs. The paintings are especially striking; in vibrant reds, blues, pinks, greens, violets and blacks, garlands, hunting and battle scenes, architectural features, the myth of Persephone and portraits – the best surviving examples we have of Classical and Hellenistic Greek painting.

to Nikomachos, a painter famous for his speedy work, who captured motion with quick brushstrokes, subtle colours and an unerring line – Hades, sceptre in one hand and the despairing Persephone in the other, leaps into his chariot, drapery flapping, while the maiden's companion crouches in fear and Hermes assists Hades; Demeter on her 'Mirthless Rock' and the three Fates are much fainter. This tomb, plundered in antiquity, may well have belonged to King Antigonus II Gonatas (d239BC, grandson of the first Antigonus, Alexander's one-eyed general who went on to rule most of Asia).

The Persephone Tomb did, however, distract robbers from the **Tomb of Philip II**, its façade decorated with a faded but excellent frieze of Alexander hunting lions. 'In the funeral which Alexander arranged for his father, in accordance with tradition, the magnificence of the ceremony surpassed all expectation,' wrote Diodorus Siculus. A gold chest emblazoned with the star of Vergína held the king's remains and a superb gold wreath with 313 oak leaves and 68 acorns; there's an exquisitely worked gold and ivory shield and other armour, silver and bronze vessels and a magnificent chryselephantine burial couch; among the delicate surviving ivories are portraits of Philip, Olympias and Alexander. The tomb's antechamber yielded a smaller gold chest containing burned bones, remnants of gold and purple cloth, a gold wreath of myrtle and a splendid diadem; these belonged to one of Philip's wives, probably a Thracian, who committed suttee and so was specially honoured. Others were cremated on top of Philip's tomb to placate his ghost: the crucified corpse of the assassin Pausanias, his sons and presumed co-conspirators, and even the getaway horses. Homer's heroes would have approved, but a 4th-century BC Athenian would have found it all a bit de trop.

Next to it, the **Prince's Tomb** is believed, by virtue of the age of its occupant and wealth of its fittings, to have belonged to Alexander IV – the 13-year-old son of Alexander the Great, who was assassinated with his mother, Roxane, in 323BC on the orders of Cassander. A decorative red, blue and white frieze in the antechamber shows a chariot race. The burial was in a silver hydra with a gold wreath around its shoulder; a gold-plated collar and ivory miniatures, including a remarkable Dionysos and Ariadne following Pan, were among the offerings. At the end, a film (in English) puts it all in perspective.

Palace (⊕ see Polycentric Museum of Aigai, page 143, for hours and prices)
The City of Aigai extended to the north, along with the sparse remains of the fatal **theatre** and a pair of **sanctuaries**, one to Cybele and one to Eucleia, the goddess of good repute – perhaps her most important sanctuary in Greece – built by Philip II during his grand project to transform Aigai (until then a collection of villages) into a cultural capital, the Athens of the north.

The centrepiece of this was Philip's greatest work, the **Palace**, residence and administrative centre, the Versailles of its day and the largest building of Classical times – 107m long, 12,500m², three times the size of the Parthenon – built on a commanding height so that it would dominate the landscape for miles around. The architect is believed to have been Pytheos, one of the chief designers of the Mausoleum of Halicarnassus, one of the Seven Wonders of the World, and this palace was equally revolutionary, becoming the prototype for future palaces around the Hellenistic and Roman world. Built of 26,000 cubic metres of limestone quarried from Mount Vérmio, carried along the Aliákmonas on a pontoon then carted another 20km here, the palace was covered with precious marble inlays and mosaics, bronze sculpted doors, frescoes – one of the greatest painters of antiquity, Zeuxis was here – and luxury roof tiles and decorations. The exterior was covered with a shiny fine marble stucco that mirrored the sun.

The palace was entered on the east side through a monumental two-storey Propylon, a triple gateway. A southern gallery was a throne room, while a much larger northern gallery was used for lectures. Beyond is a large peristyle courtyard, with 16 columns on each side – the first in history, able to fit in 8,000 people, and which may have been a secret garden; the banquet hall, where some 450 guests could lounge on their dining couches still has a superb floral pebble mosaic. In the 2nd century AD the Romans destroyed it, and its beautifully cut stone went into building Véria. Where earlier kings in Aigai may have lived no-one knows – so far. Only 1/800th of the site, a series of settlements covering 800,000ha² between the modern Vergína and Palatítsia, has been excavated.

Along the road back to Vergína you can have a look at the exterior of two tombs. The **Rhomaios Tomb** (signposted 'Macedonian tomb'), named after its discoverer, has a pretty Ionic façade and inside an impressive marble throne, over 2m high and carved with sphinxes. The **Tomb of Eurydice**, built by Philip II for his mother, is the oldest Macedonian tomb found so far (c340BC). It too contained a marble throne, painted with the Rape of Persephone, set before a delightful trompe l'oeil façade in coloured plaster with four Ionic columns.

NÁOUSSA

Founded as the Roman colony of Nova Augusta, Náoussa (Νάουσα) enjoys a beguiling setting on the slopes of Mount Vérmio, overlooking orchards and vines. Synonymous with some of Greece's finest wines, its full name is 'Heroic Náoussa':

during the Greek War of Independence, the local women, rather than be enslaved by the Ottomans, threw themselves and their children off the bridge into the Arápitsa River – a site marked by a bronze statue of a grimly determined-looking woman and child. Its unique **Carnival** features locals dressed up as scimitar-bearing Genítsari (janissaries) and Boúles (boys who would be dressed up as girls trying to avoid the *devsirme* – the Ottoman 'tax of children' when officers selected the most likely boys to train as janissaries). They lead the masked 'soldiers' in traditional costumes, hopping and shaking their jingling breast plates to the beat of an archaic-sounding drum, the *daoúli*, and wailing quarter tones of the *zournas*, or fife; it's easy to imagine Alexander the Great's army doing something similar.

Náoussa has a few streets of old houses and a pretty municipal park, but its setting and climate are the main attractions, headlined by the celebrated **Grove of Ag Nikólaos**, 3km southwest on the Arápitsa River, an oasis of waterfalls and springs bubbling up under ancient plane trees, filled with happy ducks. Roads hairpin up deeply forested Mount Vérmio, where in autumn russet and gold are woven in the green, making for a scenic drive to Véria.

GETTING THERE AND AROUND Trains on the Athens–Thessaloníki line branch off at Platý for Náoussa; the station is 7.5km east of the centre at Kopanós. For local taxis, call 23320 22636.

WHERE TO STAY

Esperides Spa Hotel [map, opposite] (17 rooms) 1.8m east of the centre, on the road to the station; 23320 20250; w esperideshotel.gr. A warm welcome awaits at the handsome hotel on a farm with lovely rustic-chic rooms, Coco-Mat beds, spa & excellent b/fast (inc). €€

Sfendamos Wood Village [map, opposite] (7 rooms) 3km from 3-5 Pigádia ski resort (see opposite); 23320 44844; w sfendamos.gr. On the mountain, Canadian-style log cabin chalets with fireplaces, sleeping 5, & 1 sleeping 10, plus an excellent restaurant (€€) by a roaring fire in winter. Experiences such as snowboarding, snowshoeing, & cross-country cycling are also available. B/fast inc. €€

Hayati Hotel (10 rooms) Ethn Anístasi 6, 100m from the main square; 23320 52120; w hayati-naoussa.gr. Traditional, homely rooms & a pleasant bar downstairs, plus a new sauna. Try to get a quiet room in the back. Delicious b/fast inc. €€–€

Archontikó Agonári [map, opposite] (4 rooms) 12km northwest of Náoussa & 4km from 3-5 Pigádia ski resort (see opposite); 23320 44588; m 69374 81603; w arxontiko-agonari.gr. Woodsy, folksy rooms with fireplace & colourful carpets in a stone-built mansion. B/fast served in-room. €

Guesthouse Militsa [map, opposite] (3 rooms) Milítsa, near Ag Nikólaos; 23320 22122; guesthouse.militsa. Charming guesthouse in an orchard, with a dbl, an apartment sleeping 4 & a maisonette for 6, all with kitchenette. Very simpatico owners live on site. €

Villa Vadola [map, opposite] (6 rooms) 9km south of Náoussa in Arkochóri; 23320 23068; w villavadola.gr. Charming B&B with stone walls & exposed beams & fireplaces; family rooms available & free bikes for exploring; plus a good traditional taverna (€) with pizzas. B/fast inc. €

 WHERE TO EAT AND DRINK

Archontikó Agonári [map, opposite]; 23320 44588; 09.00–21.00 daily. The excellent restaurant of the guesthouse (see above) attracts w/end diners from as far as Thessaloníki for its delicious bean soup, slow-cooked stews & glazed pork, served on the panoramic terrace. €€

Tésseris Epochés (4 Seasons) Ag Nikólaos; 23320 26571; noon–18.00 daily. Popular for its fresh grilled & smoked trout, baked aubergine dishes & starters; the pond & shady grove of Ag Nikólaos is a popular destination in itself. €€

Xarama [map, opposite] Arkochóri; 23320 21125; w estiatorio-xarama.gr; summer

NÁOUSSA

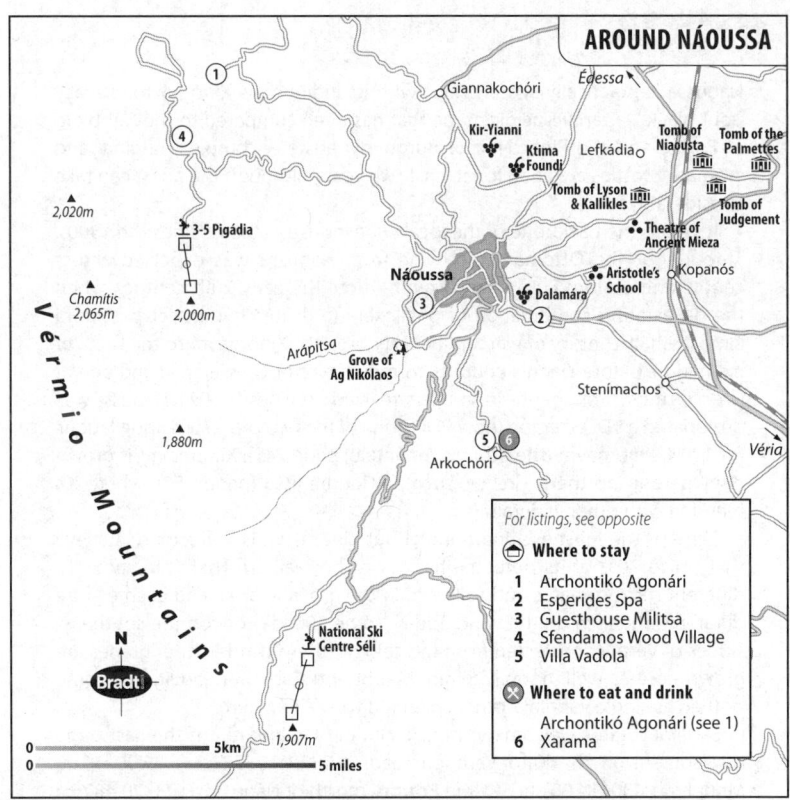

13.00–22.00 daily, winter to 20.00. Atmospheric rustic taverna, with superb views serving a wide range of game, succulent grilled steaks, wild mushrooms, stews & other dishes to go with homemade bread & a superb cellar of aged wines. Best to book. €€

Oinomagiremata Stéfanou Dragoúmi 1; 23320 23576; noon–22.20 Tue–Sat, noon–19.00 Sun. In the centre of Náoussa, a great place to try farm-fresh local cuisine, lovingly prepared, to go with a bottle of Náoussa wine. €€–€

Stou Thoma Vas Filíppou 1; 23320 24010; Στου Θωμά; 11.00–23.30 Tue–Sat, 11.00–19.00 Sun. Fresh seafood, friendly atmosphere & very reasonable prices. €

SPORTS AND ACTIVITIES Local company Trigiro (Stougiannáki 15; m 69744 08915) offers **hiking** or **cycling** excursions with **wine tasting** around Náoussa.

Ski resorts

3-5 Pigádia 16km west of Náoussa; 23321 02025; w 35pigadia.com. Small resort (2,005–1,430m) with 5 lifts & 10 runs but a very impressive 575m vertical descent & the only snow cannons in Greece. Plus 25km of cross-country trails, a hotel, football field, gym, indoor pool & sauna. Day ski pass €20, ages 6–18 €15.

National Ski Centre Séli 20km southwest of Náoussa; 23310 49226; w seli-ski.gr. 1,900m up Mount Vérmio, Greece's first (& for a long time only) ski resort was begun in 1934, when it hosted the first Panhellenic Ski competition. It has 14km of descents, cross-country tracks & snowboard slope. The E4 international trail goes through here. Day pass €22, under 12s €11.

5 | CENTRAL MACEDONIA (ΚΕΝΤΡΙΚΗ ΜΑΚΕΔΟΝΙΑ)

THE 'SOUR BLACK' GOLD OF NÁOUSSA

Náoussa is practically synonymous with its indigenous Xinómavro (literally 'sour black'), a tannic, acidic grape that has been compared to the Nebbiolo of Barolo and the Pinot Noir of Burgundy: austere, complex, original and aromatic. Bottles are aged for at least two years, although the finest can take considerably more.

It's been the backbone of the local wine industry at least since the 1500s. Throughout the Ottoman rule, wine from Náoussa was exported across central and eastern Europe and Egypt – until the early 20th century, when the devastating combination of phylloxera (a destructive insect pest) and almost a half-century of war and poverty brought Xinómavro to the brink of extinction, before Yiannis Boutáris, former mayor of Thessaloníki and one of Greece's most prominent wine makers, revived the vines. In 1971, Náoussa was designated a VDQS region (now PDO), one of the two protected appellations for 100% Xinómavro (the other is Amýntaio; page 245). Xinómavro is grown elsewhere in northern Greece, such as Gouménissa (page 157), where it's blended with other varietals.

Perhaps the most exciting thing about Xinómavro is that experts believe that up to 70% of its potential has yet to be realised. There are some 13 different microclimates and soils within the growing area, and each exert a different influence on the wine. Today, some 500ha grow on the southeast slopes of Vérmio, protected from the cold northern winds. Other grapes are grown here as well, notably Syrah, Merlot and Cabernet Sauvignon, some bottled as single varietals, others blended with Xinómavro.

Several estates welcome visitors, including **Dalamára** (on the east edge of Náoussa, on the Káto–Vermíou road; \ 23320 28321; ⏰ 09.00–16.00 Mon–Fri, 11.30–14.00 Sat); **Ktima Foundi** (north of Náoussa; \ 23320 48255; w ktimafoundi.gr; ⏰ 09.00–14.00 & 17.00–20.00 Mon–Fri); and highest of all, **Kir-Yianni** (north of Náoussa at Giannakochóri; \ 23320 51100; w kiryianni.gr; ⏰ 11.00–18.00 Tue–Sun, kitchen to 16.30; reservations strongly suggested), a beautiful winery with views, founded in 1968 by the late Yiánnis Boutáris. See map, page 147, for locations.

WHAT TO SEE AND DO
Ancient Mieza (\ 23310 29737; ⏰ summer 08.00–20.00 Wed–Mon, noon–20.00 Tue, winter 09.00–17.00 Wed–Mon; free) The exact location of Mieza, once the main city here, is a mystery, but bits of it keep cropping up in the orchards in a triangle between Lefkádia (Λευκάδια), Kopanós (Κοπανός) and Náoussa, most prominently a little Hellenistic **theatre** (signposted) and four remarkable **Macedonian tombs** (page 144).

Signs point to the **Tomb of Judgement**, where the guardian is based. Protected from the elements by a concrete hangar, this is one of the largest Macedonian tombs (8.5m high) and it reeks of new wealth, probably acquired by the occupant's campaigning with Alexander. The façade was given the works: four Doric half columns decorate the lower zone, with figures of the dead man, Hermes Psychopompos, and the judges of the dead, Aeacus and Rhadamanthys. Above, metopes show the centaurs and lapiths; the next register has a frescoed frieze in stucco relief of Macedonians fighting the Persians, above that an Ionic colonnade, with fake doors between the columns.

From here the guardian will hop in your car or walk with you to the **Tomb of the Palmettes**, some 200m away. This was discovered in 1971 by grave robbers, although it had already been broken into in antiquity, through the roof. It has four Ionic columns, painted to resemble marble, under a pretty frieze of palmettes and lotus flowers highlighted in blue and red. Three windblown palmettes in deep relief stand proud on the pediment, which is frescoed with a reclining mature couple; the key in the man's hand suggests that he held an important office. The great marble doors and their lock mechanism were discovered in situ, having fallen in. The ceiling in the antechamber is painted with a charming pattern of stylised palmettes and water lilies on a sky-blue background, perhaps a reference to Lake Acheron in the Underworld.

The smaller **Tomb of Niaousta** (or Kinch, named after the Danish archaeologist who discovered it) also has two chambers. It had an extraordinary lively painting (now sadly lost, although a copy of Kinch's drawing survives by the entrance) of a Macedonian horseman spearing a terrified Persian.

The fourth tomb, the 2nd-century BC **Tomb of Lyson and Kallikles**, is a few minutes' drive away. In order to preserve its colours, it has been left in its mound, so entrance is through a hatch in the roof and an iron ladder. The tomb was used by several generations of the descendants of Lyson and Kallikles, whose ashes were laid in 22 niches, husbands on top, wives on the bottom. The painted decoration almost seems new: a garland of pomegranates and ribbons links painted columns on the four walls, and trompe l'oeil weapons look as if they were hanging on nails or sitting on a shelf. The tiny antechamber is painted with a snake by an altar. It's a funny old place and can get claustrophobic after a few minutes. In more than one case, Macedonian tombs have been found with skeletons intact – of grave robbers who couldn't escape.

Aristotle's School (On Kopanós–Náoussa road; cultural centre ✆ 23320 43437; ⊕ 09.00–14.00 Mon–Fri; site ⊕ daylight hours; free) In late 343BC, Philip II invited the philosopher Aristotle to tutor his 13-year-old son Alexander (see below) and his contemporaries far from the court intrigue of the palace. The site of the school, Mieza's Sanctuary of the Nymphs (identified by descriptions left by Plutarch), is an idyllic place, set on a ledge above a gurgling stream. The three natural caves may have served as dormitories; the square-cut walls were the back of a stoa. The little cultural centre across the road (w sxoliaristotelous.gr) has a bookshop and shows

EDUCATING ALEXANDER THE GREAT

For nearly three years Aristotle taught natural sciences, maths, philosophy and poetry on his school's 'shaded walks' and made it his task to mould Alexander into a new Achilles, giving his pupil an annotated copy of the *Iliad* which the future 'Great' one would always keep by his side. The philosopher's spirit of enquiry may also have rubbed off, in the keen interest Alexander took in the geography and customs of his conquests. Yet many have speculated why Aristotle never mentioned Alexander in his writings; it may have been personal (Alexander had Aristotle's nephew put to death on suspicion of treason), but it may also have been Alexander's disregard for some of Aristotle's dearest precepts, most notably that non-Greek 'barbarians' should be treated as slaves – to the extent that Alexander compelled his officers to marry Persians, just as he married Roxane.

videos about the life of the philosopher and about the archaeological sites of the school and the theatre of Mieza.

ANCIENT PELLA

Although the area was inhabited from Neolithic times (16 *toumba* or mounds marking settlements were found in the area going back to 4600BC), Ancient Pella (Paliá Pélla, Παλαιά Πέλλα) was founded on a grand scale by King Archelaos, who moved his capital here from Aigai at the end of the 5th century BC; Philip II and Alexander the Great were born here, and Euripides wrote his uncanny play the *Bacchae* here for the theatre not long before he died (page 167). The largest city in Ancient Macedon, covering 4km^2, Pella boomed when Alexander's companions returned from Asia with gold burning holes in their tunic pockets. But Pella gradually lost its importance to Thessaloníki, and sometime in the 1st century BC it was hit by an earthquake. In c30BC a Roman colony (modern Néa Pélla, Νέα Πέλλα) was founded on the plateau to the north, and the ruins vanished in the alluvial mud of the Loudías, Aliákmonas and Axiós rivers.

Rediscovered by chance in 1914, excavations began in 1957 and have only revealed a fraction of the city and palace. The latter, set on the hill to the north as a giant belvedere overlooking the Thermaic Gulf, was famous, a 60,000m^2 complex with a swimming pool that wouldn't have looked out of place in Hollywood. 'Nobody would go to Macedonia to see the king, but many would come far to see his palace,' commented Socrates, who was invited to take refuge there – but still preferred to drink hemlock.

GETTING THERE AND AWAY From Thessaloníki, frequent **bus** departures to all the destinations served by KTEL Pellas (\ 23105 95435; w ktelpellas.gr (Greek only) or w ktelbus.gr/pel/ticketweb) – Édessa, Giannitsá, Skýdra, Aridaía – make a stop in Archaía (ancient) Pella (€4.10 each way), though you may have to ask the driver. **Driving** from Thessaloníki, head northwest (following signs to Édessa) and continue on the E02 – the ancient Via Egnatía. This, as in ancient times, goes through the centre of Pella.

 WHERE TO STAY AND EAT Giannitsá (see opposite) is the closest town to Ancient Pella for places to stay, while the surrounding region has a couple of notable restaurants that locals from nearby towns consider worth making a special trip.

Hotel Pella (32 rooms) Mitropoléos 3, Giannitsá; \ 23820 81433; w hotelpella.gr. Modern with large, quiet rooms, many with balconies. Free parking outdoors (garage parking €10), a small playground & a big choice at b/fast. €€

Alexandros (30 rooms) Kougioumtzídi 5, Giannitsá; \ 23820 24700; w hotelalexandros.eu. Functional hotel in the centre; big rooms with bathtubs, but parking can be tricky. €

Pelórios Néa Pélla; \ 23820 32930; ⊕ 11.00–midnight Tue–Sun. This classic taverna with a modern dining room & outdoor seating seems to do everything just right, meats from the spit especially. Very popular with locals & crowded on w/ends – call to book a table. €

Vasilikós Kallipoli; \ 23815 03707 (it's a good idea to call to confirm hours & to reserve); f mezedopoleionVasilikos; ⊕ 13.00–22.00 Wed–Sat, 13.00–17.00 Sun. More tractors than cars pass this casual place in the fertile heartland, a destination restaurant for local winemakers & farmers, where everything is made from scratch from seasonal local products, most of it cooked over a woodfire. Small & superb wine list, serious cooking. €

ANCIENT PELLA

ARCHAEOLOGICAL SITE (\ 23820 32963; w palaceofpella.gr; ⊕ Nov–Mar 08.30–15.30 Wed–Mon, Apr–Oct 08.00–20.00 Wed–Mon, noon–20.00 Tue, gradually earlier closings through Sep & Oct; €10, concessions €5, Nov–Mar €5 for everyone & free 1st Sun of month) Although it's hard to imagine now, King Archelaos chose the site for its natural defences. Pella was built on reclaimed marshland, surrounded by a wall and moat, with access to the sea via a shallow lagoon. A small island in the swamp, linked by a wooden drawbridge, doubled as a prison and treasury. As in Dion (page 133), Archelaos chose the fashionable Hippodameian grid for his plan, but with wider streets, bigger blocks and an excellent water and drainage system, built around a massive square **agora**. The scale allowed for palatial villas like the **House of Dionysos**, extending over 100m, with courtyards and *andrones* (men's entertaining rooms) decorated with superb pebble mosaics; a vivid *Stag Hunt* is still in place, the violence of the scene in marked contrast to the exceptionally lovely floral border. Many houses had upper floors and shady peristyle central courtyards.

The new **Archaeology Museum** (\ 23820 31160; w palaceofpella.gr/archaeological-museum-of-pella; ⊕ hours and fees as for archaeological site) at the foot of the hill where the palace once stood, recalls the atrium style of a Pella villa. A bust of Alexander greets you at the entrance, while inside, the floor mosaics steal the show, especially the *Lion Hunt*, showing Alexander and his companion Kraterus in Susa, when Kraterus saved Alexander's life; note how use of various sized pebbles and lead strips lend the work its dynamic volume. Others show a rare *Female Centaur*, *The Abduction of Helen by Theseus*, with a powerful quadriga of rearing horses, and a girlish *Dionysos Riding a Panther*. The famous painter Zeuxis is documented in Pella, and he may have been behind the trompe l'oeil architectural frescoes, embellished with multi-coloured coats of plaster that imitate marble – a style known as Early Pompeian, but really should be renamed Pellaean.

Elsewhere here are gold-trimmed helmets, weapons, golden funerary wreaths, jewellery and death masks, a reconstruction of a funerary bed, other grave goods, including a good 5th-century BC Attic vase showing the contest between Athena and Poseidon (page 375), and examples of local talent: marble sculpture (there's an especially fine dog that once sat on a tomb), coins, graceful clay figures and black glazed ceramics decorated with vine leaves, and an unusual penis-shaped rhyton, which must have been a hit at the symposia.

GIANNITSÁ (Γιαννιτσά; 10km west of Pélla) The capital of the prefecture and a big market town, Giannitsá is one of those intense bits of urbanity that dot an otherwise very rural landscape; at night, when everyone is out and about, you may as well be in Manhattan. Originally known as Yenice-i Vardar, it was founded by legendary Ottoman general Gazi Evrenos (who conquered most of Western Thrace and lived to be 129, at least according to his biography). His elegant mausoleum of 1417 stands near the centre, along with a pair of mosques, hammams and a rather peculiar but sturdy 17th-century clock tower. The 'Black Statue' in the centre commemorates the First Balkan War's Battle of Giannitsá (19–29 October 1912), which took place around a swamp formed by the Loudías River (south) and opened the way for the Greek army to reach Thessaloníki before the Bulgarians (page 61). In the late 1920s the swamp was drained, leaving the town with a rich agricultural plain. During the German Occupation, an Austrian soldier defected from the Nazis to the ELAS resistance forces on nearby Mount Páiko (1,657m), and in reprisal the SS and their Greek collaborators massacred 120 people in the primary school.

5 | CENTRAL MACEDONIA (ΚΕΝΤΡΙΚΗ ΜΑΚΕΔΟΝΙΑ)

ÉDESSA

Hanging off the slopes of Mount Vérmio, Édessa (Εδεσσα) is the only town in Greece sitting atop a 70m waterfall, formed when a 14th-century earthquake destroyed the town and diverted the Káranos River, sending it through the centre and over the edge of the cliff – 'the step on which God stands to ascend into heaven' according to poet Melélaos Lountémis – plummeting down through the trees and maidenhair ferns before a gargantuan pipe carries it all away. The Byzantines called Édessa 'the god-defended castle of Vodena' (its Slavic name, meaning 'waters') and built a mighty but now long-gone castle that guarded the Via Egnatía as it approached the Pindus Mountains. Its later history saw it ping-pong back and forth between Serbia, Bulgaria and the Byzantines, before becoming part of the Ottoman Empire, when the rail line was built and the town harnessed its water power to run a series of mills, now part of a unique open-air museum. Édessa is also famous for cherries, used to make jams and spoon sweets, and celebrated in a festival in late June.

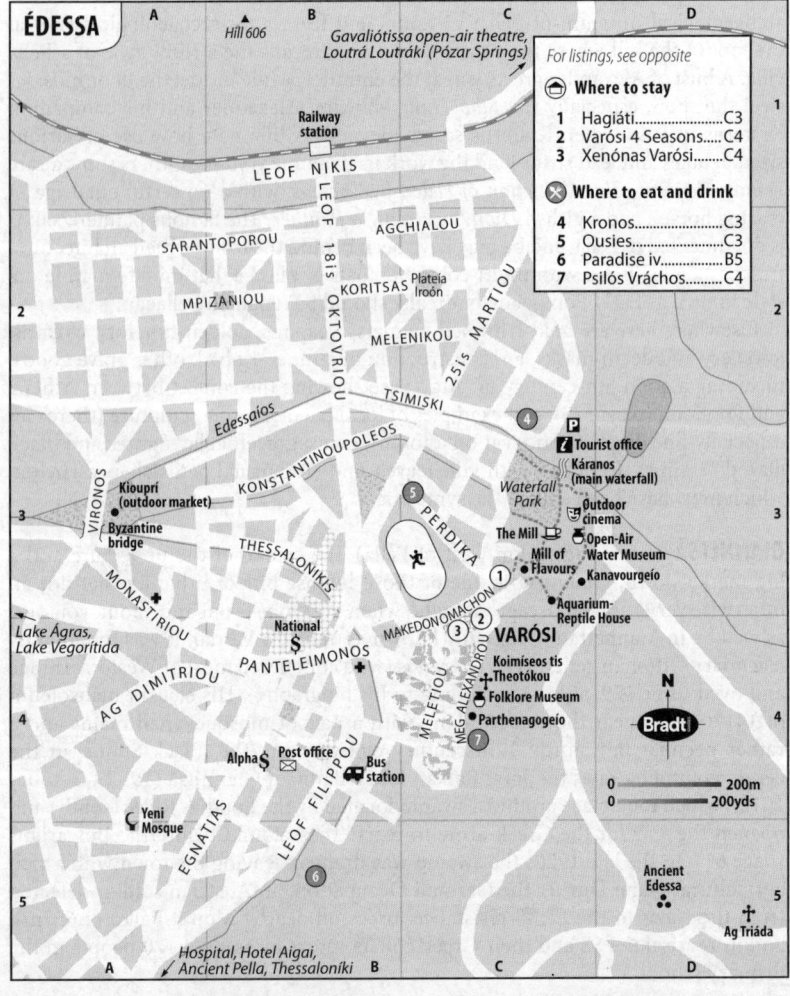

ÉDESSA

For listings, see opposite

Where to stay
1 Hagiáti.....................C3
2 Varósi 4 Seasons.....C4
3 Xenónas Varósi........C4

Where to eat and drink
4 Kronos.....................C3
5 Ousies......................C3
6 Paradise iv...............B5
7 Psilós Vráchos..........C4

ÉDESSA

GETTING THERE AND AROUND Édessa is 92km from Thessaloníki. **Trains** on the Athens–Thessaloníki line branch off at Platý for Édessa en route to Flórina. Édessa's station [152 B1] (28 Oktovríou; ⁂ 23810 23510) is in walking distance of the Waterfall Park. **Buses** run nearly hourly from Thessaloníki (2hrs 20mins; €9.70) to Édessa by way of Pella. Édessa's bus station [152 B4] (Pávlou Melá; ⁂ 23810 23511; w ktelpellas.gr) is in the centre and has regular connections to Véria and Aridaía, where you can pick up a connecting bus to Loutráki Aridaías/Pozar Springs (⁂ 23840 21249; Mon–Fri once a day, returning immediately with the same bus, Sat 3 times a day both ways, Sun twice a day both ways). There's a free **car park** [152 C3] by the Waterfall Park. For taxis in Édessa, call ⁂ 23810 23392.

TOURIST INFORMATION Pick up an Édessa city card (€5; which allows admission to all the watermills) at the tourist information office located at the Waterfall Park [152 C3] (⁂ 23810 20300; w edessacity.gr; ⊕ 10.00–16.00 daily). The office is also a great source of information on rafting, riding, trekking, boating and other excursions in the vicinity. There are free tours available for larger groups – call in advance for information.

WHERE TO STAY

Varósi 4 Seasons [152 C4] (10 rooms) Meletíou 48; ⁂ 23810 51440; w varosi4seasons.gr. Atmospheric rustic-chic inn within thick stone walls, with a terrace overlooking Ancient Loggos far below; most rooms have a balcony with a similar view. A roaring fire crackles in the handsome coffee bar on chilly nights. B/fast inc. €€€–€€
Hotel Aigai [map, page 128] (32 rooms) Filippoú 35, 4km southeast of Édessa; ⁂ 23810 29888; w aigai-hotel.com. Comfortable 4-star with a spa & indoor pool in a garden setting, with modern rooms & tasty b/fast (inc). €€

Hagiáti [152 C3] (7 rooms) Makedonomáchon 40; ⁂ 23810 51501; w hagiati.gr. Comfortable, well-equipped rooms in a historic stone building, 50m from the waterfall, with an atmospheric, antiques-filled coffee shop & courtyard. €€–€
Xenónas Varósi [152 C4] (8 rooms) Meletíou 45–47; ⁂ 23810 21865; w varosi.gr. In the quiet Varósi quarter, atmospheric pastel rooms with iron beds in a house of character built in 1818, with a pretty balcony & terrace; b/fast (inc) features local ingredients. €€–€

✕ WHERE TO EAT AND DRINK Édessa is famous not only for cherries, but also for *tsobléki*, a stew with meat, usually beef, slow cooked in a clay pot with aubergines and peppers. Pastry shops specialise in custard-and-almond-filled *flogéres*, 'flutes', in crispy filo.

Límni [map, page 128] Vryttá, 10km west of Édessa; ⁂ 23810 92195; ▇ estiatoriolimni; ⊕ 13.00–23.00 Wed–Mon, winter w/ends only. Signposted off the main road, lovely tranquil place overlooking the lake to have a delicious lunch or dinner with a magical sunset. Don't miss out on their excellent *mezédes*. €€
To Choriatikó Stéki [map, page 128] Platáni, 6km south of Édessa; ⁂ 23810 99495; ⊕ 13.00–23.00 Wed–Sun. Specialist in an array of vegetarian & vegan dishes, but meat choices too for any accompanying carnivores. €€
Ousies [152 C3] 25is Martíou 4; ⁂ 23815 02414; ▇ OusiesEdessa; ⊕ noon–midnight daily. Much-

loved *ouzerí* has a warm atmosphere, old photos & instruments on the walls, & delicious little plates of mushrooms, seafood, etc; elegant little desserts top it off. €
Kronos [152 C3] Dominikou Theotokopoulou 10; ⁂ 23810 22730; ⊕ 08.15–22.15 daily. Pastry shop in business since 1926; the place to try Édessa's famous custard-&-ground-almond-filled *flogéres*, wrapped in crispy filo.
Paradise iv [152 B5] Xenía Párko Parádeisas; m 69737 75683; ▇ Paradise Iv; ⊕ Jun–Aug noon–late daily. Summer cocktail bar around an outdoor pool, with occasional live music.

5 | CENTRAL MACEDONIA (ΚΕΝΤΡΙΚΗ ΜΑΚΕΔΟΝΙΑ)

Psilós Vráchos [152 C4] Meg Alexándrou 2; \23810 26118; ⊕ 09.00–01.00 daily. The 'High Rock' café at Édessa's highest point has magnificent views.

OTHER PRACTICALITIES
Alpha Bank [152 B4] Egnatías 23
National Bank [152 B4] Dimokratías 1
Hospital [152 A5] Térma Egnatías (Proástio); \23813 50100

Pharmacy Lousioti [152 B4] Panteleímonos 20
Pharmacy Trypsiani [152 A3] Makedonomáchou Stógiou 2
Post office [152 B4] P Méla 10–12

WHAT TO SEE AND DO

Waterfall Park [152 C3] (Párko Kataraktón; ⊕ always) Everyone gravitates here to this lovely park filled with channels of racing water, shaded by massive plane trees, and cafés and terraces with views over the falls – the main one, **Káranos** [152 C3], and 11 smaller ones. Steps lead down to the **Open-Air Water Museum** [152 C3] (\ 23810 20300; ⊕ 10.00–16.00 Tue–Sun; €2 per mill, or €5 for all with the Édessa city card; page 153) dedicated to water power, the 'White Coal' that powered Édessa into a mini Manchester of the Balkans, until the rights to the thundering waters, which were once voluminous enough to run textile, wheat and sesame mills, were bought by the electric company in 1954; by 1962 the mills were out of business. Original machinery dots the maze of pathways. The **Mill of Flavours** [152 C3], in a former sesame mill, has a little film on the making of tahini, once a speciality, and a chance to taste local products; another has an exhibition of local aromatic plants. The Giannákis watermill now holds the **Aquarium-Reptile House** [152 C3] with freshwater fish, snakes, crabs, turtles and eels. The biggest mill building at the bottom of the cliff (reached by a glass lift), the **Kanavourgeío** [152 C3], with all of its original machinery intact, was once Greece's largest rope and twine factory, where a workforce of more than 100 worked from 1913 to 1966; it was restored as a conference centre but is usually closed. The path eventually twists around to go under falls by a small cave. There's a snack bar in the midst of the **water museum** called The Mill [152 C3] (⊕ 10.00–23.00 Mon–Sat, 10.00–21.00 Sun) and a summer outdoor cinema.

Varósi [152 C4] Édessa's old Christian quarter is just south of the Waterfall Park, around the highest edge of the bluff. Before Édessa became an industrial centre, the whole town all looked like this; Edward Lear wrote the city was 'difficult to match in beauty'. A nest of resistance in World War II, half of the town was torched by the Germans after the Resistance fighters shot at a soldier. One of the biggest buildings to survive, the girls' school of 1877, the **Parthenagogeío** [152 C4], is now used for art exhibitions. Here too is the city's oldest surviving church, **Koimíseos tis Theotókou** [152 C4] (Meg Alexándrou 8), built in the late 14th century after the earthquake re-using columns and capitals (including a striking one with rams and eagles) from the acropolis of Ancient Edessa; inside are 14th-century frescoes.

Folklore Museum [152 C4] (Meg Alexándrou 10, Varósi; \ 23810 20300; ⊕ 10.00–16.00 Mon–Sat; €1.50) There are some handsome costumes here, including many locally made from the silk that was produced into the 1960s, along with an enormous loom and spinning wheel, photos, tools and other items used in daily life and work.

Kiouprí [152 A3] This little park has a handsome single-span **Byzantine bridge**, where an outdoor market takes place on Thursday mornings. To the south, the pretty but derelict **Yeni Mosque** [152 A5] (Plateía Mouseíou, visible from the outside) is the only one still standing in town.

Hill 606 [152 B1] North of the railway station, this 606m hill is Édessa's playground, with an open-air theatre and forest of Gavaliótissa, and paths through the trees up to the pavilion on top for 360° views.

Ancient Edessa [152 D5] (Lóngos; off the Thessaloníki road, or take a quite steep hike down through the Waterfall Park – the tourist information office can provide the route) Ancient Edessa reached its peak in Hellenistic and Roman times, and has walls standing 6m high in places and an impressive south gate and a colonnaded main street. Part of the temple of a local goddess called Mas (a version of the Great Mother) has survived with inscriptions on the columns related to the freeing of slaves, which seems to have been her speciality. Look for the whimsical late Roman-era funerary relief of the young Pig Pasifilos ('friend to all'), who was following his owner in a cart pulled by a quadriga of donkeys along the Via Egnatía when he was accidently run over and killed. In the 7th century AD the site was abandoned for the safety of the acropolis; many of the old stones went into the construction of the nearby 19th-century monastery of **Ag Triáda** [152 D5].

AROUND ÉDESSA

Lake Ágras (Vryttá Nisí Ágras (Βρυτά- Νησί- Άγρας) Wetlands, 6km west of Édessa) The water that supplies the waterfalls and irrigates the cherry orchards comes from this Natura 2000 site nicknamed Swan Lake, though it attracts nearly 200 species of bird, including ferruginous ducks, moorhens and little bitterns, along with 40 kinds of fish, otters, frogs and other creatures. The road after Ágras passes through the cherry groves – lovely in April when in bloom.

Aridaía (Αριδαία; 21km north of Édessa) Just past the railway station in Édessa, a narrow road winds up to a plateau with a special microclimate for peppers and tobacco, and increasingly vineyards. Aridaía, the main town, was renowned for its much prized Aridaía peppers, once considered the equal to Hungary's paprika until they went extinct decades ago after farmers planted other varieties in the vicinity and they cross-pollinated; others are still grown in the village just to the west, named **Piperiá** (Πιπεριά) in their honour. But pepper lovers can still find joy in Amýntaio (page 246).

Loutráki Aridaías (Λουτράκι Αριδαίας; 13km west of Aridéa; w loutrapozar. com.gr/en) Mount Vóras is known as Central Macedonia's 'little Switzerland', a popular weekend destination from Thessaloníki. Under its slopes, the Ag Nikoláou River (or Thermapótamos, 'burning ember' water), runs into the **Pózar Springs**. Also known as **Loutrá Loutráki**, its focus is around the waterfalls – the highest is 70m – in a lovely glen shaded by plane trees and willow groves. Most people aim for the two steaming-hot 37°C public pools (admission €3), one under a waterfall, popular with older generations in summer – and with the young in winter, who like to hit the springs after a ski trip (the outdoor pools are open until 21.00 or 22.00, and the indoor private pools – by reservation – until much later). There are some splendid walks; a 33km path with wooden bridges leads up the **Loutráki Gorge** and its 16 caves.

Órma (Όρμα), just south, is the base for walks in the dense **Mávros Dássos** (Black Forest) with its towering pine trees. According to the locals, they inspired

Philip II to invent the *sarissa*, a 6m spear or pike that greatly improved the strength of the Macedonian phalanx in close formation (page 136).

Where to stay
Hotel Eliton & Spa (20 rooms) \23840 91318; w elitonhotelspa.gr. 2.5km from the springs, rooms all come with Coco-Mat mattresses, balcony & gold, copper & silver décor; the superior rooms & suites have a fireplace. There's also a spa, indoor pool, sauna, hammam, solarium, excellent massages, & fitness equipment. B/fast buffet in the garden. €€€–€€
Nymfes Hotel & Spa (19 rooms) \23840 91570; w hotel-nymfes.gr. Stylish hotel in a peaceful wooded setting with relaxing, contemporary-style rooms, all with balcony overlooking the mountains & comfy beds; pricier rooms have fireplace or private hydro-bath. Indoor & outdoor pools, jacuzzi, hammam & sauna, & bar. B/fast inc. €€€–€€
Astéras (20 studios) 500m from the springs; \23840 91458; w hotel-asteras.com. Charming family-run place, with a flower garden; Mrs Katerína, the helpful owner, makes a lovely b/fast (inc). €€
Pózar Pallas Salt Cave & Spa (21 rooms) \23840 91357; w pozarpallas.gr. Modern hotel with classic rooms & suites, with colourful rooms (some with fireplace), built over northern Greece's only salt cave. The spa (w spatherapy.gr; ⊕ 10.30–23.00 daily), with a whole menu of treatments, is open also to non-guests. €€

Where to eat and drink
Hydrolithos \23840 91600; ⊕ 13.00–23.00 daily. Elegant, contemporary setting & creative cuisine making good use of local ingredients such as roasted Flórina peppers & aubergine purée with locally raised veal, prepared in a wood oven. Excellent wines by the glass. €€€
Diónysos Main square, Órma; \23840 94410; w dionisos.gr; ⊕ noon–midnight daily, closed Tue in winter. Airy & contemporary, with a gourmet touch & unusual twists on traditional starters, wines by the bottle or carafe. Book online. €€
Kókkino Pipéri [map, page 128] On the Loutráki–Órma road; \23840 91100; f KokkinoPiperiOrma; ⊕ noon–midnight daily. Out in the country, & crowded at w/ends; very tender meats & lots of vegetarian choices. €€

Vóras Kaïmáktsalan Ski Centre (36km northwest of Édessa; \23810 32000; w kaimaktsalan.gr; ⊕ Dec–early May) At 2,480m, this is the highest ski resort in Greece, situated on the northeast slope of **Mount Vóras/Kajmakčalan** (2,524m), straddling the border with North Macedonia, and with views that stretch as far as Mount Olympus and the Thermaic Gulf. It has ten red, blue and beginners' slopes, seven lifts, a snowboard park, 18km of cross-country trails and a smart chalet hotel (€€).

Palaió Ag Athanásios (Παλαίο Αγ Αθανάσιος) This handsome mountain village was abandoned in the 1980s, but with the opening of the ski centre 17km away, it found a new lease of life, as the descendants of the owners returned and converted the old houses into charming inns. Another traditional village, **Panagítsa** (Παναγίτσα), is, thanks to its up-draughts, a popular hang-gliding centre. Below stretches the great blue mirror of **Lake Vegorítida** (Λίμνη Βεγορίτιδα), originally called Lake Ostrovo (giving its name to the Ostrovo Unit, a Scottish women's World War I field hospital); today locals call it Mermaid Lake. Covering 54km², it's one of the deepest lakes in Greece (up to 70m) and filled with trout, carp and pike, and part of the Natura 2000 network (also see page 245).

Where to stay
Leventis Art Suites (9 Suites) Panagítsa; \23810 34141; w leventisartsuites.gr; ⊕ Oct–Mar. The term 'Art Hotel' is, for once, completely correct – absolutely extraordinary

antique-furnished suites with an avant-garde touch, & beautiful public areas that are like an art installation. B/fast inc. €€€–€€
Roúga Chalet-Suites & Spa (15 chalets) Palaío Ag Athanásios; 23810 31115; w rouga.gr. Near the village centre, cosy & romantic studios (including some for families) in stone chalets, with a good restaurant (€€), spa & playroom for kids. B/fast inc. €€€–€€

Montecristo Chalet (9 rooms) Palaío Ag Athanásios; 23810 31777. An attractive, traditionally styled guesthouse all in wood & stone, with lovely hosts & delicious b/fast (inc). €€
Metohi Inn (7 rooms) Palaío Ag Athanásios; 23810 39808. Resolutely traditional stone inn built around a beautiful courtyard. B/fast inc. €

 Where to eat and drink

Asága Palaío Ag Athanásios; 23810 39995; AsagaAgiosAthanasios; Oct & Nov 13.00–23.00 Fri–Sun, 30 Nov–summer same hours daily; summer closed. Warm & welcoming, succulent meats & salads plus a charming décor & hosts. €€
Pétrino Panagítsa; 23810 34033; 18.00–23.00 Mon–Fri, 13.00–23.00 Sat & Sun. Something different: the cuisine of Asia Minor,

with dishes such as suckling pig, wild boar with quince, kebabs served with homemade bread, rich desserts & local wines. €
Ouzerí Chóvoli (Χόβολη) Palaío Ag Athanásios; m 69843 71446; KafeOuzeriXoboli; 09.00–23.00 Mon–Tue & Thu, 09.00– midnight Fri–Sun. A whole range of tasty *mezédes* to go with your favourite tipple; also classic Greek coffee.

GOUMÉNISSA AND MOUNT PÁIKO

Gouménissa (Γουμένισσα) is famous for three things: its popular brass bands, its pretty main square with old plane trees and a French fountain (1918), and its wine, once the favourite tipple of Philip II. Today this is grown in Greece's smallest PDO wine region, its beautiful vineyards planted extensively (but not solely) with Xinómavro and Negóska grapes – the latter, nearly exclusive to Gouménissa, notably softens the wine and gives red Gouménissa its distinction. Several **wineries** in the area make worthwhile destinations: the beautifully situated Mikró Ktíma Títos (23430 43074; w mikroktimatitos.com), the organic and biodynamic Ktíma Tátsis (23430 43060; w ktimatatsis.gr/en), the organic Ktíma Chatzivarítis (m 69722 00102; w chatzivaritis.gr/en), and Ktíma Aidaríni (23430 41293; w aidarini.gr). Check websites of each for hours or, better yet, call to make an appointment. (In case you were wondering, 'Ktíma' means 'domaine'.)

The surrounding region is famed for its natural beauty – and its trees. **Gorgópi** (Γοργόπη) to the east has a truly monstrously large plane tree, and there's another just north, said to have been planted in the time of Alexander the Great at **Axioúpolis** (Αξιούπολη), a simple village on the Aliákmonas River with a remarkable huge frilly confection of a church called Áxion Estí (*Worthy It Is* – a famous work by the Nobel Laureate Odysséas Elýtis carries the same name).

Northwest of Gouménissa rises beautiful **Mount Páiko** (1,657m), its flanks covered by the largest chestnut forest in Greece; most of the 500–600 tonnes of chestnuts harvested here annually are exported to Italy. The small villages of **Gríva** (Γρίβα) and **Kastanerí** (Καστανερή) are immersed in green; further up on the 1,250m plateau is the potato-growing village of **Livádia** (Λιβάδια), once a major Vlach settlement with 4,000 people, famous for its warlike spirit in the Balkan Wars and a major resistance centre during World War II until the Germans burned the village to the ground. Today 400 people live there.

From Axioúpolis a good road ascends to tiny **Skra** (Σκρα) on Páiko's northeast slope, only 4km away from North Macedonia. It has a locally run **Museum of World**

5 | CENTRAL MACEDONIA (ΚΕΝΤΡΙΚΗ ΜΑΚΕΔΟΝΙΑ)

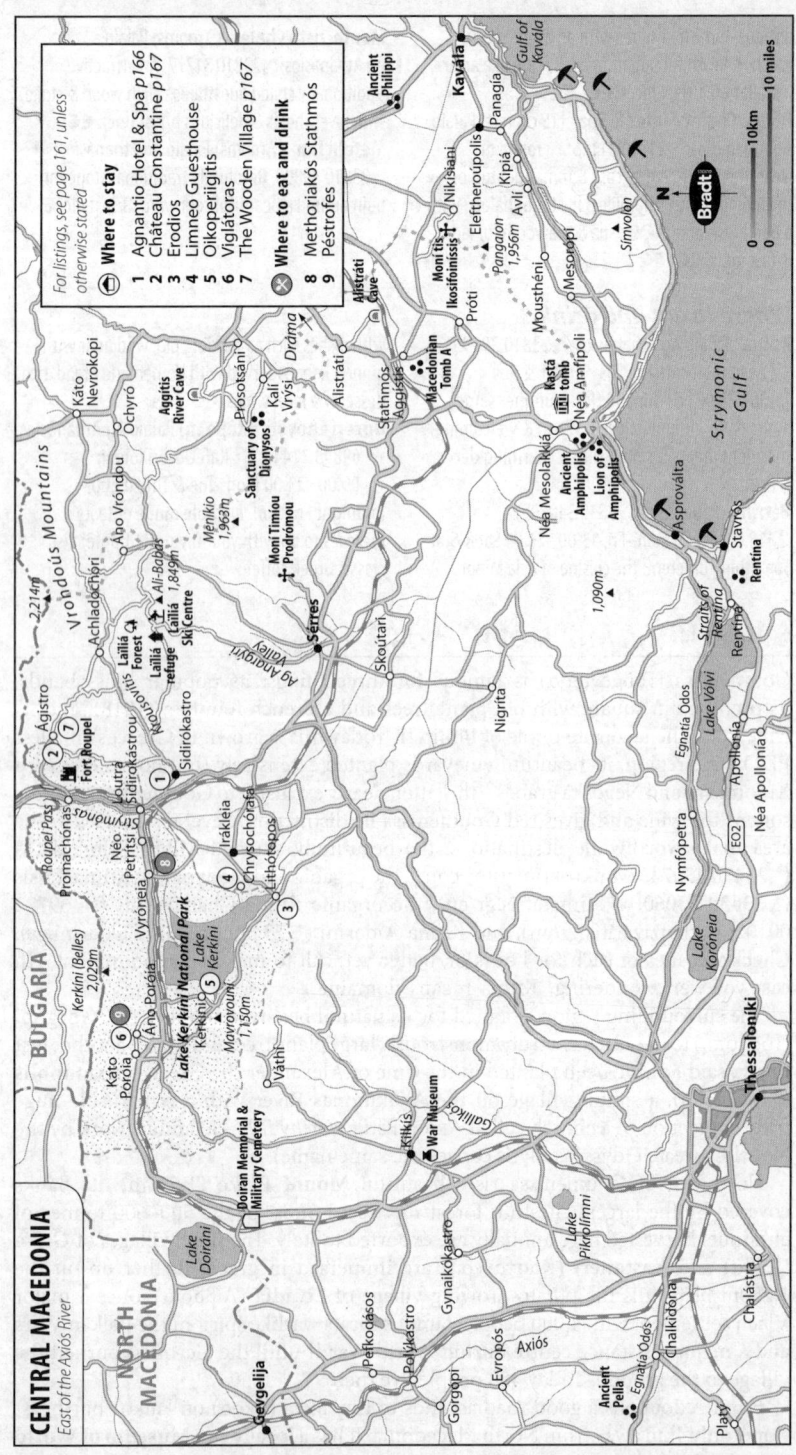

War I (ask for the key in the square) dedicated to the two-day Battle of Skra-di-Legen (29–30 May 1918), the first major battle fought by the Greek army in World War I, when they joined the French to defeat the heavily fortified Bulgarians. What most people make the long trek for, however, is the idyllic **Skra waterfalls** and its emerald lake, 5km south. It's a 20-minute walk through the woods and down about 100 steps – but the reward is one of those truly magical places where you half expect to see frolicking nymphs. The colour is derived from the white fossilised microorganisms that form its bed. It's very refreshing (and cold!) on a hot summer's day, but you won't have it to yourself. Bring a picnic.

WHERE TO STAY AND EAT

Dimosthénis Guesthouse (6 rooms) Kountourióti 17, Gouménissa; ☎ 23430 41302; w dimosthenis.gr. Friendly & comfortable traditional guesthouse. In winter guests gather around the fireplace in the comfy lounge, with a wine bar. B/fast inc. €€

Fanós Mezedopoleío Fanós (a small village 11km east of Skra); ☎ 23430 91500; ⊕ 13.00–19.00 Tue–Thu, 11.00–23.00 Fri–Sun. In an area settled by Greek refugees of Asia Minor, this is a beautiful & cosy spot to try some refined specialities, like *hünkar beğendi* (tender stewed beef served over smoky eggplant puree with a rich béchamel sauce). €

KILKÍS

Kilkís (Κιλκίς), a garrison town but not unpleasant provincial capital, played an important role in the 20th-century wars fought in the area. It was a major silk producer in the 1950s, but now it makes wine and produces aluminium. Kilkís first entered history in Roman times as Callicum (or Gallicum), named after the leather sieve used to collect gold. By the mid 19th century, it was the main market town in the area and populated largely by Bulgarians, and it was given to Bulgaria after the First Balkan War. During the Second Balkan War in 1913, as the Bulgarian army began its march to capture Thessaloníki, the Greeks, under their new king, Constantine, pushed them back in the gruelling Battle of Kilkís-Lachanás (15 June). The Greeks triumphed but suffered their worst casualties ever in modern times – 8,828 killed or wounded, while the Bulgarians lost 6,971. Kilkís itself was nearly completely destroyed. The pre-war population of some 13,000 Bulgarians were expelled to Bulgaria, while the Greeks living in Struma, Bulgaria, were relocated to Kilkís. In the 1923 population exchange, they were joined by Pontic Greeks.

But history hadn't finished with Kilkís. In November 1944, as Axis forces retreated, thousands of security battalion collaborators and members of the right-wing EDES (Greek Democratic National Army) resistance force gathered in Kilkís, defying orders by the Greek government in exile, in an agreement brokered by the British, to surrender to the Communist ELAS resistance. ELAS defeated them in a vicious street fight known as the Battle of Kilkís, the bloodiest confrontation before the Greek Civil War, with reprisals that have left a legacy of bitterness.

WHERE TO STAY

Evridiki (44 rooms) Sólonos 15; ☎ 23410 22512; w evridikihotel.gr. Contemporary, minimalist design in this recently renovated hotel in the heart of Kilkís. Rooms have deluxe Coco-Mat beds & fibre-optic Wi-Fi. Free parking & American buffet b/fast inc. €€

Habitat Hotel (36 rooms) Cnr Spártis & Ag Georgíou; ☎ 23410 24708; w habitathotel.gr. Shiny new business/boutique hotel, with everything from luxury suites to economy rooms, all with balcony. It has a charming restaurant (€€), a 2-storey

5 | CENTRAL MACEDONIA (ΚΕΝΤΡΙΚΗ ΜΑΚΕΔΟΝΙΑ)

underground car park & a branch of the city's best pastry shop. Greek/American b/fast buffet available. €€

Victoria (33 rooms) Dytikí Perifereiáki (west bypass); 23410 29700; w hotelkilkisvictoria.gr. Pleasant enough motel-style rooms, good for a night or 2, with a café serving b/fast (inc). €

✕ WHERE TO EAT AND DRINK Keep an eye peeled for Pontic dishes here – one company, Ragián, in Váthi (15km northeast of Kilkís; 23410 84267; w ragian.gr) produces Pontian cheeses such as cow's milk *tsiortan*, smoked *parcharotyr* and buffalo-milk *gais* (similar to mozzarella), along with pies and other products.

Me to N kai me to S 25 Martiou 6; m 69780 57506; ⊕ noon–23.00 Tue–Sat, noon–18.00 Sun. This relatively new spot in the city centre is a local favorite for tasty meze.

Mpalsamiko Politechníou 10; 23410 27707; f; ⊕ 16.00–23.00 Wed–Fri, noon–23.00 Sat & Mon, noon–19.00 Sun. Excellent *mezedopoleío* with especially good salads & meat dishes. €

Tratamento 25is Martíou 22; 23410 24651; f tratamentokilkis; ⊕ lunchtime until midnight Thu–Tue. A big step up from the usual taverna food, with lots of variety prepared with a lot of love. Don't miss their superb mushroom dishes in season. €

WHAT TO SEE AND DO

Archaeology Museum (Ouskoúni 12; 23410 22477; ⊕ 08.30–15.30 Wed–Mon) This little two-room museum houses finds from around the region, including Iron Age artefacts, jewellery and a collection of statues starring the late 6th-century BC kouros of Europos (the only kouros ever found in northern Greece) with rather willowy features that show an Ionian influence.

Cave of Ag Geórgios (Ag Geórgios hill, just northwest of the centre; 23410 20054; ⊕ 09.00–14.00 Wed–Sun, last entry 13.00; €5) Some 30,000 years ago, this cave (formed by thermal water trapped in aquifers) was a hyena den, and it yielded hundreds of Late Pleistocene bones – aurochs, deer, wild horses and asses and the only known Greek bone of a 'robust polecat'. Along with the usual stalactites, the cave has eccentric formations covered with what looks like petrified popcorn. The naturally moist air has special properties that help children suffering from respiratory diseases, according to Czech, Bulgarian and Ukrainian 'cave therapists', who began a programme of cures in 2002. A museum near the cave (temporarily closed for restoration at the time of writing) houses some of the fossils – because the hyenas chewed the bones, the skulls and teeth were the best preserved.

War Museum (2.5km southwest; 23410 76911; ⊕ 08.00–14.00 & 17.00–20.00 Tue–Sun; free) This little museum by the memorial on the Iroön, or 'Hill of Heroes' – the site of the Battle of Kilkís-Lachanás – displays uniforms, weapons, personal items, an audiovisual account of the battle and a relief map that puts it all into context.

AROUND KILKÍS Spring-fed, iodine-rich **Lake Doiráni** (37km north of Kilkís) is shared by Greece and North Macedonia, and after nearly being drained for irrigation a few years back has recovered completely (the fish caught here are exceptionally tasty; there's a pretty path along the shore at the village of Doiráni).

It's best known, however, as the site of three gruelling World War I Battles of Doiran, pitting the troops from six different nations – British, French, Greeks, Italians, Russians and Serbians – against the Bulgarians' heavily fortified position, commanded by General Vladimir Vazov, only to be repulsed three times. After the Third Battle (18–19 September 1918) the Allies suffered so many casualties they didn't renew the attack. Yet a few days later, they realised the Bulgarians had abandoned their position – their army's defeat by the French and Serbians at the Battle of Dobro Pole had forced Vazov to retreat to avoid being cut off from the rear – and on 30 September Bulgaria surrendered. The battles are remembered by the striking **Doiran Memorial** overlooking the lake and the **Doiran Military Cemetery** (3km northwest of Drossáto) on the southeast shore. The memorial, on its hill with two lions designed by Sir Robert Lorimer, commemorates all the 10,700 British and Commonwealth officers and servicemen who died in Macedonia.

The wounded were brought to the makeshift operating theatre in the church of the Taxiárchon in **Pefkodásos** (Πευκοδάσος), formerly the Bulgarian Smol, and subject of Stanley Spencer's *Travoys Arriving with Wounded at a Dressing-Station at Smol, Macedonia, September 1916* (1919), now in the UK's Imperial War Museum collection (w iwm.org.uk/collections/item/object/25132). Spencer personally witnessed the scene while serving here with the 68th Field Ambulance.

Gynaikókastro (Γυναικόκαστρο), 15km southwest of Kilkís between the Axiós and Gallikós rivers, is named after its still-impressive 'Castle of Women' built by Emperor Andonicus III in 1341, who made the walls so strong that women alone could hold them. Little **Lake Pikrolímni** (Πικρολίμνη; 'bitter lake'), just to south in the flat farm country, has three times the salinity of the Dead Sea and dries up in summer; the black muddy clay on its bed full of sulphates is good for everything from making you more beautiful to easing rheumatism and attracts people who come to wallow in the mud baths of its southeast shore.

LAKE KERKÍNI NATIONAL PARK

A legend among birdwatchers, Lake Kerkíni (Λίμνης Κερκίνης) lies south of the 2,029m Kerkíni (or Belles) range on the Greek–Bulgarian border and north of Mount Mavrovouní. Surprisingly, it's mostly artificial, formed by the damming of the Strymónas in 1932, to prevent flooding and create irrigated farmland on the Sérres plain for the influx of Asia Minor refugees. Although there were initial concerns over the environmental impact, the lake is a rare case where human intervention has dramatically improved the local biodiversity to the extent that it is now one of Europe's most important Ramsar wetlands. Redevelopment in 1980 has only made it better.

TOURIST INFORMATION Enquire at the **Lake Kerkíni Information Centre** (Káto Poróia; \ 23270 28004; w kerkini.gr; ⊕ 10.00–14.00 daily) and at **Oikoperigitis** (see below) for activities, including lake tours on traditional wooden boats with canopies, and excursions by 4x4, by bike or on horseback and canoe hire.

WHERE TO STAY *Map, page 158*

Oikoperiigitis (20 rooms) Kerkíni; \ 23270 41450; w oikoperiigitis.gr. A hotel dedicated to nature, in a peaceful setting on Lake Kerkíni's north shore. There are dbl rooms & suites (including 3 accessible ones), full of traditional character, which can sleep up to 6. There's a gym, & a good taverna (€€) downstairs. The hotel offers a long list of ways to explore the lake, including jeep, bike & canoe hire, & excursions with telescopes. B/fast inc. €€

Erodios (24 rooms) Lithótopos; \ 23250 28070; w hotel-erodios.gr. On the west bank near the dam, an attractive hotel shaped like an amphitheatre so all rooms have views over the lake; it also has a pool, pool bar & an excellent restaurant (€€). €€–€

Viglátoras (6 rooms) Áno Poróia; \ 23270 51231; w viglatorashotel.com. Delightful boutique hotel with great helpful owners in traditionally styled 1922 mansion, with a cosy sitting room around

the fireplace. Excellent homemade pies & cakes for b/fast (inc). €€–€
Limneo Guesthouse (8 rooms) Chrysochórafa; \ 23250 51581; w limneokerkini.gr. Friendly & well run, one of the few places to stay on the less-developed east shore of the lake. Fireplace in some rooms. €

✖ WHERE TO EAT AND DRINK Map, page 158

This is the place to try buffalo (*boubáli*) slow-cooked in a *gástra* (clay pot) or as *kavourmás*, sausages, burgers and meat balls, as well as fresh lake fish. Ottoman sweets include *tulumpa* (fried pastries in syrup) and *kazan-dibi* – similar to crème brulée, made with buffalo milk and caramelised on the bottom, flavoured with vanilla, rose water and mastic – and *mahleb* (the slightly bitter flavouring derived from seeds of the St Lucie cherry).

Péstrofes Áno Poróia (ask the locals for directions); \ 23270 51500; ⊕ summer 11.00–18.00 daily (Fri from noon), winter Fri–Sun only. Lovely woodland place under the trees, or around the fireplace in winter, serving delicious fresh & smoked trout (*péstrofes*) & local buffalo specialities. €€

Methoriakós Stathmós Vyróneia; m 69800 01484; f; ⊕ 10.00–18.00 Thu–Sun, but check before setting off. In the old railway station, atmospheric spot with old photos on the wall, & tasty buffalo dishes alongside vegetarian choices. €

WHAT TO SEE AND DO Bring your binoculars and telephoto lens. Located on the flyway from the Aegean and Black seas, the Balkans and Hungarian steppes, Lake Kerkíni attracts an impressive array of migratory birds (especially from September to late October, when an estimated 40,000 wildfowl arrive to overwinter or rest on the lake), as well as a host of permanent residents. Some 300 species have been spotted, including Dalmatian pelican, white pelican, greater flamingo, pygmy cormorant, ferruginous duck and pochards, and the endangered lesser white-fronted goose. The surrounding woodlands are home to the sombre tit; Alpine accentor wallcreeper; white-tailed, greater spotted and golden eagles; and grey-headed, Syrian and black woodpeckers.

There are dozens of amphibians and reptiles, and mammals – including wolves, jackals, boars, otters, wild cats and bats – although the animals you're most likely to see are the 3,500 or so shaggy black water buffalos raised along the lakeshore for milk and meat. More than 4,700 kinds of insect (some 50 of which were first discovered here) live by the lake; and over 1,300 species of flora, including water chestnuts, a 'meadow' of water lilies and 16 kinds of orchid grow here. The lake is also one of Greece's most successful freshwater fisheries.

You can drive up to the top of **Mount Mavrovouní** (1,150m), just west of the lake for the view, or if you're pressed for time, an easy way to see the lake is by way of the 17km drive along the southwest shore, starting at the dam at Lithótopos (Λιθότοπος), part of which was built with stones from the Lion monument and Kastá Tomb in Amphipolis (pages 170 and 171).

SÉRRES

On the edge of the broad Strymónas valley – hot in the summer, freezing in the winter – Sérres (Σέρρες) is Central Macedonia's second city. Settled by the 2nd millennium BC, 'Siris the Warlike' was first mentioned by Herodotus in the 5th century BC, but for much of its history it played second fiddle to Amphipolis (page 168). Today it is a well-run city brim-full of Balkan optimism in spite of a history that has seen it devastated on more than one occasion – most thoroughly during the Second Balkan War in 1913, when the retreating Bulgarians burned it out of spite. Some 70 workshops make jewellery; it's the home of Kri Kri, Greece's oldest ice cream maker; and there's increased use of local geothermal fields, especially for heating asparagus greenhouses and growing spirulina, the vitamin-rich green algae food supplement. It's a pleasant enough place once you get past its industrial outskirts, and a great base for the surrounding mountains and Lake Kerkíni.

GETTING THERE AND AWAY There's a twice-daily **train** service to Sérres from Thessaloníki (€4.70), Kilkís and Siderókastro, and once a day to Dráma. The station [163 A5] (w hellenictrain.gr/en) is 1km southwest of the centre, on the Periferiakí. The Kilkís–Sérres line stops at the little stations just north of Lake Kerkíni.

There are **bus** links every hour with Thessaloníki (1hr 15 mins; €9), two a day with Kavála (2hrs), and three on weekdays with Dráma (1hr 25mins). The bus station [163 B5] (\ 23210 22822; w ktelserron.gr) is just off Apameías, near the railway station.

For local **taxis**, try Radio Taxi (\ 23210 59100).

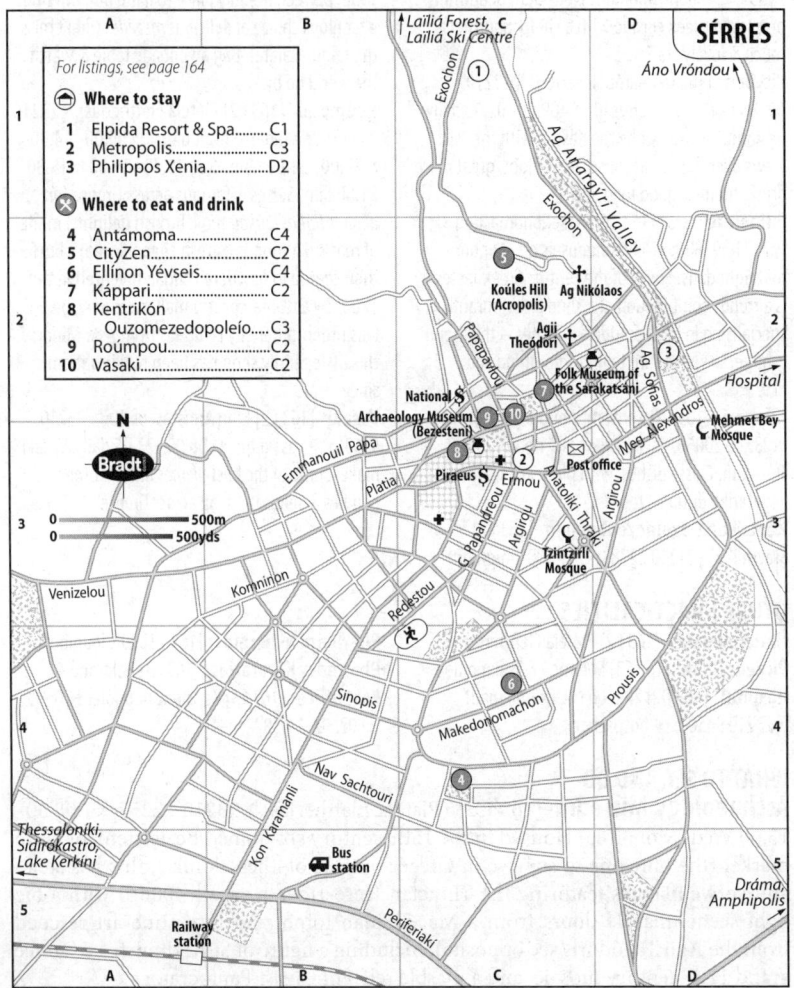

SÉRRES

For listings, see page 164

Where to stay
1 Elpida Resort & Spa..........C1
2 Metropolis......................C3
3 Philippos Xenia................D2

Where to eat and drink
4 Antámoma......................C4
5 CityZen..........................C2
6 Ellínon Yévseis.................C4
7 Káppari..........................C2
8 Kentrikón Ouzomezedopoleío.....C3
9 Roúmpou........................C2
10 Vasaki............................C2

WHERE TO STAY   For hotels outside of Sérres, see pages 166 and 167.

Elpida Resort & Spa   [163 C1] (111 rooms) Exochón St, just north of the centre in the Ag Anargýri valley; 23210 20000; w elpidahotel.eu. Modern with very comfy beds & a smart restaurant (€€€), & well equipped with tennis court, spa, great anti-stress massages, fitness & wellness centre, hammam, & indoor & outdoor pools. €€€–€€
Philippos Xenia   [163 D2] (57 rooms) Ag Sofías 1; 23210 99360; w philipposxeniahotel.com. Popular 4-star hotel next to the park but in easy walking distance of the centre, with a spa, fitness centre, indoor heated pool, sauna & hammam, & free parking, plus an elegant roof garden bar & restaurant (€€€) with views over the city, serving both Mediterranean & Japanese cuisine. €€€–€€
Metropolis   [163 C3] (30 rooms) Solomoú 49; 23210 54433; w hotelmetropolisserres.gr. Restored Neoclassical building near the bus station, with pleasant English-speaking owners. €

 WHERE TO EAT AND DRINK
Antámoma   [163 C4] Ag Georgíou 64; 23210 71533; ⊕ noon–midnight Wed–Sun. Beautifully presented Greek cuisine with a cheffy gourmet touch & lovely staff. €€
CityZen   [163 C2] Akrópoli Serrón; 23210 66118l; w cityzenserres.gr; ⊕ 09.00–02.00 daily. Restaurant/café/bar by the Kástro, with the best views over the city at sunset or at night, great drinks menu & good food. €€
Ellínon Yévseis   [163 C4] Makedonomáchon 37; 23210 98808; w ellinongeuseis.gr; ⊕ noon–midnight daily. South of the centre, 'Greek Tastes' is a trendy combination of a shop & restaurant, specialising in local products & dishes – the menu is huge, so you're sure to find something you like. €€
Káppari   [163 C2] Konstantinoupóleos 29; 23210 20066; Κάππαρη; ⊕ noon–23.30 Tue–Sun. Classy dishes, with plenty of seafood & vegetarian options, too. €€
Kentrikón Ouzomezedopoleío   [163 C3] Stavrídi 5; 23210 22783; ⊕ 11.00–midnight Tue–Sat, 11.00–evening Sun. Going strong since 1938, perfect, friendly place to hang out, offering a fabulous choice of delicious *mezédes* (don't miss the taramasalata). Bag an outside table & watch the world go by. €
Roúmpou   [163 C2] Plateía Eleftherías; 23210 23312; w akanesroumpou.gr; ⊕ 09.00–14.30 & 18.00–21.00 Mon–Sat, 10.30–14.00 & 18.00–21.00 Sun. Sérres is famous across Greece for *akanés laïliá*, *loukoúmia* ('Turkish delight') made of roasted almonds & fresh sheep & goat's butter then coated in powdered sugar. Invented in the 1700s by Ottoman pastry makers, the recipe was brought here by refugees from Asia Minor; this little family shop has been making them since 1927.
Vasaki   [163 C2] Ethn Antistáseos 10; 23210 55535; w vasaki.gr; ⊕ 08.00–23.45 daily. Vasaki makes some of the best *akanés* among other goodies & sends them all across Greece.

OTHER PRACTICALITIES
National Bank   [163 C2] Plateía Eleftherías
Piraeus Bank   [163 C2] Solomoú & Tsalapoúlou
Hospital   [163 D2] 2km on the Dráma road; 23210 94500; w hospser.gr
Pharmacy Avgerinos   [163 C3] 29is Iouníou 4
Pharmacy Karafotias   [163 C3] Solomoú 41
Post office   [163 C3] Konstantinoupóleos 10; ⊕ 07.30–14.30 Mon–Fri

WHAT TO SEE AND DO
Archaeology Museum   [163 C3] (Plateía Eleftherías; 23210 22257; ⊕ 08.30–15.00 Wed–Mon; free) Housed in the 15th-century six-domed Bezensteni, or cloth market (the only one to survive in Greece outside of Thessaloníki), this has steles and votive plaques featuring the Thracian Hero-rider, a vase (c400BC) with a big fight scene, marble doors from a Macedonian tomb, and Byzantine art rescued from the Agii Theódori (see opposite), including a figure of St Andrew from a once grand 11th-century mosaic, and a marble relief of Christ Pantocrator.

Folk Museum of the Sarakatsáni [163 D2] (Konstantinoupóleos 62; ⊕ call in advance for an appointment: m 69735 87186; ask if you may leave a donation) A fascinating museum devoted to Greece's ancient pastoral nomads, who donated all of the exhibits, including their striking costumes, life-size models of their thatched huts (*kalýves*; families generally required two, one for living and one for storing their clothes and loom), their cheese-making equipment, and more.

Agii Theódori [163 C2] (Íonos Dragoúmi 24; ⊕ usually closed) Built in the 11th century, the former cathedral was once a grand mosaic-filled basilica similar to the ones in Thessaloníki, but burned down twice, first in 1849 and then 1913, when the Bulgarians razed most of the town. It was rebuilt as it was, but lacks its splendid interior.

Koúles Hill (Acropolis) [163 C2] On the north edge of town, you can walk or drive up to the acropolis of Ancient Siris, now dominated by the ruins of the Byzantine castle, destroyed and rebuilt and destroyed several times in history; its fat ruined surviving tower (1350) was built under Serb ruler Stephan Dushan. Next to the walls and café stands a little Byzantine jewel of a church, **Ag Nikólaos**, from the same period.

Tzintzirlí Mosque [163 C3] (Anatolikís Thrakí 12; ✆23210 64454; ⊕ 10.00–14.00 Wed–Mon; free) Built in the 16th century, this is the best-preserved mosque in Sérres and is occasionally used for special exhibitions.

Mehmet Bey Mosque [163 D3] (Archélaou 14) The city's oldest and largest mosque was built in 1492 by the son-in-law of Sultan Bayezid II and is a picturesque ruin on the banks of the Ag Anargýri stream; originally it was surrounded by gardens. The park here, along the **Ag Anargýri valley**, has little waterfalls, restaurants and bars.

AROUND SÉRRES
Moní Timíou Prodrómou (10km northeast of Sérres; ✆ 23210 74544; ⊕ 09.00–13.30 & 16.30–sunset) Isolated on the slopes of Mount Meníkio (1,963m), this

THE SARAKATSÁNI

The Sarakatsáni have lived in the high mountains of the Balkans (in Greece in Epirus, Thessaly, Macedonia and Thrace) since the cows came home. There is even speculation, notably by Patrick Leigh Fermor in his book *Roumeli* (page 27), that they may be the last 'pure' ancient Greeks, a branch of the family who took to the hills sometime after the first Slavic speakers arrived around the 6th or 7th century AD, became shepherds and never built permanent homes, always remaining aloof in the high mountains; and it is true that their female costumes do look like designs from Geometric-era (9th century BC) vases. Extremely patriarchal and proud of being Greek, the Sarakatsáni were rivals of the region's other nomads, especially the Vlachs (page 260). Fermor quotes a popular Sarakatsán saying: 'If you hear a shepherd use the word *lapte* [the Vlach word for 'milk'] hit him over the head.'

The closing of the northern borders in 1923, however, undermined the Sarakatsáni's traditional way of life; some 15,000 found themselves on the Bulgarian side, where they still resolutely speak Greek. Since 1950 they have increasingly given up their *tselingáta* (temporary settlements) and settled down, many in this region.

picturesque monastery in a wooded ravine was founded in 1270 by Ioanníkio, a monk from Sérres who had been a hermit at Mount Athos; his nephew, Ioakím, added the pretty katholikón and built the walls, and managed to obtain an Ottoman *firman* in 1372 protecting the monastery's independence.

The monastery was a favourite of the Byzantine emperors. Gennádios Scholários, the first Patriarch of Constantinople under Ottoman rule, resided here as a monk in 1457–62 and 1465–72 and now lies in a special shrine. For 300 years the monastery's school offered Greeks a university-level education, but in 1917 its famous library was looted by the Bulgarian army.

After a long period of decline, the monastery has been restored and since 1986 it has housed nuns – currently numbering close to 30 – linked to Father Ephraim of Vólos, who did much to restore monastic life on Athos before moving to the USA as part of a campaign to restore Greek Orthodox spiritual life there. The katholikón, at the bottom of a sweeping cascade of cobbled steps, has a painted porch with a rather unusual vision of the *Assumption of the Virgin* and inside 13th-century frescoes by the Macedonian painter Manuel Panselínos. The small museum has relics of the mill, agricultural equipment, butter churns and old irons.

Laïliá Forest (Δάσος Λαϊλιάς) Part of the Natura 2000 network, the Laïliá Forest lies in the Vrondoús Mountains, named for the thunder that resounds in its peaks, said to be louder than anywhere else in the world. Near the 1,849m peak with an Arabian Nights name, Ali-Babas, grow the lofty beeches and pines where the local Beys once sent their harems in the summer, and the locals hit the **Laïliá Ski Centre** (26km from Sérres; 23210 58783; Dec–Mar Thu–Sun) in winter. Some 3km from the centre, there's a year-round **refuge** (1,500m; 23210 62400; w katafigiolailias.gr; Fri–Sun; 1 dorm, 10 dbls & quads, meals available; €) run by the Sérres Alpine Club. The skies are so clear up here that there's a small observatory, the **Astropyli** (23210 85225; astropyli.serres; call to visit), run by astronomy lovers in Áno Vróndou.

Sidirókastro (Σιδηρόκαστρο) Now a peaceful small town in the Strymónas valley, this was named for its 'Iron Castle' on the hill, built by Byzantine Emperor Basil II 'the Bulgar Slayer' in the early 11th century (his decisive defeat of the Bulgarians in the Battle of Kleidion in 1014 happened just over the Rupel Pass, when he reputedly blinded 14,000 captive Bulgarian soldiers and earned his cruel nickname); now only a few walls remain. Some 7km northwest, the recently renovated baths of **Loutrá Sidirokástrou** (Λουτρά Σιδηροκάστρου; 23230 22422; w spa.gr; year round 08.00–14.00 daily) exploit the high alkaline hot springs, good for your bones. One of the tributaries of the Strymónas, the pretty Krousovítis River, splashes down through a beautiful wooded region of plane trees known as 'the **Tempi of Sérres**', with five stone bridges along the way; get a lift up to **Achladochóri** (Αχλαδοχώρι) and make the 3-hour walk down.

Where to stay *Map, page 158*

Agnantio Hotel & Spa (21 rooms) 1km from Sidirókastro, on the national road; 23230 28200; w agnantiohotel.gr. Very pleasant family-run hotel with staff who try hard to please; all rooms have a balcony & there's an outdoor pool & wellness spa. Traditional Greek b/fast inc. €€

Fort Roupel (Ρούπελ; Promachónas (Προμαχώνας); 23210 95100; w roupel.gr; 09.00–13.00 daily; it's essential to ring ahead in order to arrange an English-speaking guide; free) The E79 carries on to the Bulgarian border, passing through the stern **Roupel Pass**, a narrow gorge formed by the Strymónas and guarded by arguably Greece's most famous fortification, which stopped the advance of German and Bulgarian armies in 1914. In 1916, the Greek army was ordered to surrender the fort to the advancing Bulgarian and German troops, allowing them to occupy Eastern Macedonia and Thrace, setting off the 'National Schism' between Venizélos and the king's party. In World War II, a handful of defenders defied all odds to hold out against the German and Bulgarian attack for three days (6–9 April 1941) – earning it the nickname the 'Thermopylae of Macedonia' – until they were forced to abandon their post after the Greek army surrendered in Thessaloníki. Still in use today, the fort has a memorial and guns from the war, and a small museum with photos, models, personal belongings and dioramas of the troops of 1941.

Ágistro (Άγκιστρο; 9km east of Promachónas) Ágistro is home to one of the most famous **hot springs** in Macedonia. The water, which comes out at 40.5°C, has been known for its healing and relaxation powers since AD950. Today, built around the old Byzantine baths, the new **Ágistro Hammam** (\ 23230 41420; w hamamagistro. gr; ⊕ 07.00–midnight w/days, 07.00–02.00 w/ends; €7/30mins, €10.50/1hr) offers private pools in little houses, big enough for a family or group of friends, which can be hired by the half-hour or hour.

 Where to stay and eat Map, page 158

Château Constantine (or Archontikó tou Kostí) (10 rooms) \ 23230 41180; w toarchontikotoukosti.gr. Atmospheric rooms in this 'Eco-Antique-Boutique Hotel', as it calls itself, with fancy PerDomire Italian beds, feather duvets, wood-burning stoves & pretty Mexican sinks. B/fast (in bed if you like) inc. €€–€

The Wooden Village (18 rooms) Ágistro; \ 23230 41008; w toxilino.gr. Get away from it all in these charming new wood-&-stone 2-storey cabins in the mountains, 3km from the spa. The cosy rooms have fireplaces, & there's a café, outdoor pool, & good traditional taverna (€€; open to non-guests). B/fast inc. €

SOUTH OF SÉRRES

In the shadow of Mount Chortiátis, the Egnatía toll road runs north of two shallow lakes, **Koróneia** (Κορώνεια) and **Vólvi** (Βόλβη), both part of a national park; the latter hosts some 200 species of bird, an endemic shad (*Alosa macedonica*) and, increasingly, flitting windsurfers. Along the old road parallel to the highway, the village of **Nymfópetra** ('Bridal stones') is named after a bizarre clutch of natural standing stones – the story goes they are a petrified bridal procession.

The old national road (the route of the ancient Via Egnatía) runs south of the lakes. **Apollonía** at Lake Vólvi was an Ottoman way station (there are remains on the edge of the village) and has a little spa by the lake in Néa Apollonía. East of here it enters the wooded **Straits of Rentína**, the 'Macedonian Tempe', formed by the Richíos River as it drains Lake Koróneia.

There was an important ancient road through the straits long before Roman times. The western entrance is guarded by two towns. **Ancient Arethusa** (signposted, but there's nothing to see) was chosen by elderly playwright Euripides for his retirement, but in 406BC, while his patron King Archelaos was hunting here, he was torn apart by the royal hounds (animals had it in for Greek playwrights; Aeschylus died when an eagle dropped a tortoise on his bald head). Although the Athenians requested his remains, Archelaos buried him at Pella: the site of his demise was often noted by passing ancient travellers.

On a hilltop just south of the road, was **Rentína** (signposted blue, just after Arethusa), a 20-minute hike up. Excavated since 1976 by the University of

5 | CENTRAL MACEDONIA (ΚΕΝΤΡΙΚΗ ΜΑΚΕΔΟΝΙΑ)

Thessaloníki, the site with its splendid views was inhabited from Neolithic to Byzantine times and forgotten by the 14th century. Impressive walls and towers still stand around the striking ruins of a 10th-century church. At the end of the strait, a right turn leads down Chalkidikí's east coast (page 114). Sandy beaches line the Strymonic Gulf around the north beach resort of **Asproválta**.

GETTING THERE AND AROUND KTEL Thessaloníki **buses** (w ktelmacedonia.gr) run on the old national road to Asproválta; for Néa Amfípoli, there are three buses a day from Thessaloníki on KTEL Serrón (\ 23210 22822; w ktelserron.gr) en route to Pangaíon. A **car** comes in handy: the archaeological site is sprawling.

ANCIENT AMPHIPOLIS In 2011, during the dark days of Greece's austerity crisis, the announcement by archaeologist Dr Kateрína Peristéri that one of the largest ancient tombs ever discovered in Greece had been found in Amphipolis came as a welcome distraction. The stunning finds have made it a household name, although it will be a while before visitors can see the great tomb for themselves. In the meantime, excavations continue apace and a network of paths between the sites is underway.

History Located in the fertile Strymónas valley, near the sea and Mount Pangaíon, antiquity's El Dorado (page 183), Amphipolis played an outsized role in ancient history. In the 7th century BC the Eretrians founded the colony of Eion at the mouth of the Strymónas (and minted a curious coin, showing a goose and a geometer's right angle). Athenian tyrant Pisistratos, sent into exile on Pangaíon, raised a fortune from its gold mines for his comeback from exile, and Athens, always remembering and always short of cash, tried to capture Eion in 497BC during the revolt of their Ionian allies against Persia. Instead, the Persians captured Thrace and built a fortress at Eion, which they stocked with supplies for Xerxes' army for his invasion of Greece.

Much to the annoyance of the Athenians, the Persians remained, until the great Athenian general Kimon besieged it in 475BC; when Kimon offered the Persian commander a chance to withdraw, he instead killed his family, destroyed the treasure and committed suicide. Kimon then diverted the Strymónas to wash against Eion's mud brick walls, causing them to collapse. Then he enslaved the population. Ten years later the Athenians founded a colony further inland called Ennea Odoi ('Nine Roads') that was soon wiped out in turn by the Thracians. In 437BC, Athens sent their General Agnon to try again. He named the new colony Amphipolis, 'City on both sides', because it was surrounded by the curving river.

The paint was still wet in 422BC when, during the Peloponnesian War, Spartan general Brasidas seized Amphipolis. Athens' general, Thucydides, rushed to the rescue with seven triremes, but managed only to save the port, a failure for which he was ostracised for 20 years (he settled on his estate at nearby Skaptesyle – as yet unidentified – and spent the rest of his life writing his famous history of the war and living off his gold mines). The Amphipolitans, for their part, were glad to be rid of Athens; Brasidas was an honest, just, noble and mild ruler, and when he died fighting off an Athenian attempt to recapture the city led by Kleon (who also died in the battle), he was given a hero's tomb and honoured with annual games.

Amphipolis resisted later Athenian assaults, but Philip II took it and the territory around Pangaíon by a sneak attack in 357BC, after the Delphic oracle told him 'Fight with silver spears and you shall win all'. He gave the city a measure of autonomy and set up his mint, producing Macedon's famous gold *staters*. Alexander then spent two years mustering his army here and building a fleet from the forests of Pangaíon

SOUTH OF SÉRRES

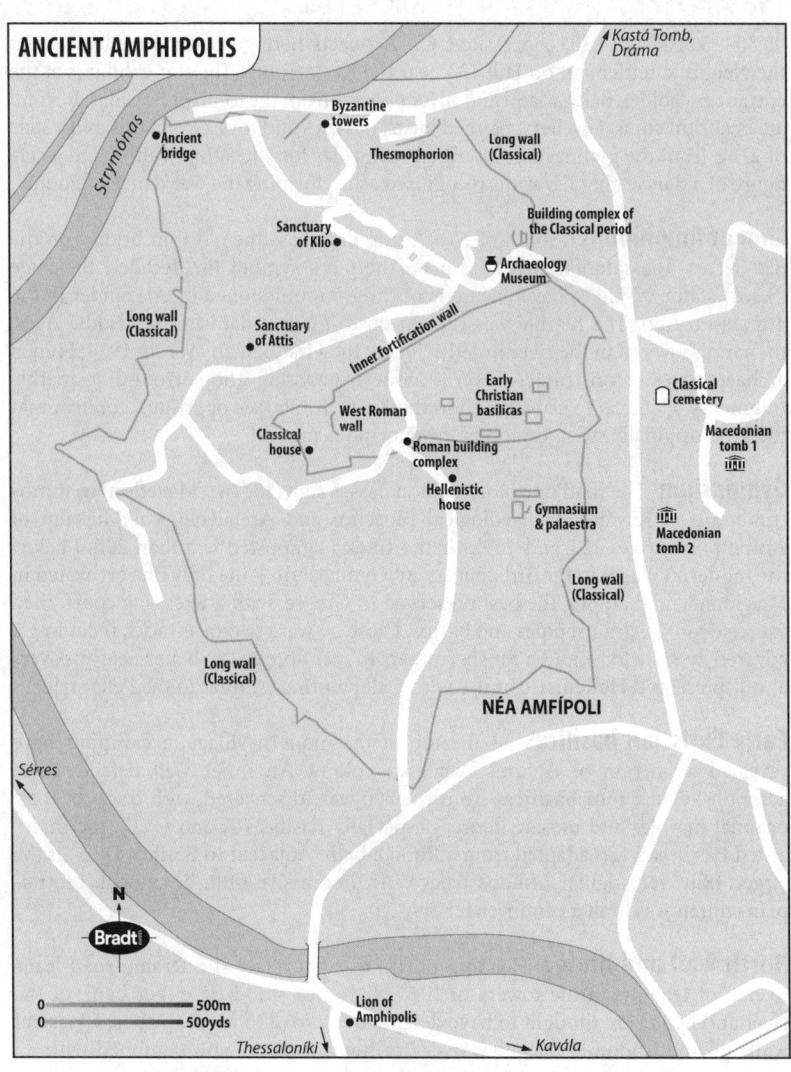

before invading Asia. After his death, his wife Roxane and son Alexander IV lived in Amphipolis until Cassander had them murdered in 308BC.

Under the Romans, the city became one of four administrative centres of Macedonia and a main station along the Egnatía, defended by massive walls, some as high as 7m. In AD500, it became an important bishopric until plague and the Slavs wiped it off the map in the AD700s. In the 13th century, Amphipolis was briefly resettled and fortified, then forgotten until it was replaced in the 20th century by Néa Amfípoli (Νέα Αμφίπολη). Proper excavations were only begun after World War II by Dimítrios Lazarídis. The city walls once stretched 7km, so the excavations cover a large area; to better understand the site, start at the archaeology museum.

Amphipolis Archaeology Museum 23220 32474; w odysseus.culture. gr; ⏱ May–Aug 08.00–20.00 daily, Sep–Oct gradually earlier closing, Nov–Apr

08.30–15.30 daily; €10, concessions €5) Artefacts here go back to c6000BC from the Neolithic settlement on Hill 133 near the Kastá Tomb. The star exhibit is at the entrance: a golden oak garland and silver ossuary from the tomb of Brasidas. Beyond are beautiful coins, jewellery, painted busts, mosaics and toys; two herms and a stele of 21BC from the gymnasium inscribed with rules for educating youths; and a clay figure of a dancer that Lazarídis recognised as performing the war dance of Pontus.

Lion of Amphipolis (South of Néa Amfípoli, across the old iron bridge, on the old Sérres–Thessaloníki road) It's been the city's symbol for decades: the huge (5.3m) statue is said to have been one of three commissioned by Alexander in the 4th century BC. The marble was broken up to make a dam in the Middle Ages, then rediscovered in the river in 1912 during the First Balkan War; in 1934, French archaeologists reconstructed it on a modern pedestal. The surrounding marble fragments, identical to slabs found in the Kasta Tomb (see opposite), confirm that the Lion originally stood on top of the enormous mound.

Gymnasium The road north of the Lion passes signs for **two Macedonian tombs** (finds are in Kavála's Archaeological Museum and Archaeological Museum of Amphipolis; pages 181 and 169), then a track (signposted less than 200m below the modern village) to the 3rd-century BC Gymnasium – the only one excavated in Macedonia, and among the best preserved in Greece, with a wrestling court, tiled exercise rooms, drains, pipes and basins. Close by were two racetracks, including a covered *xystus* wide enough for six runners to race abreast. A shelter nearby covers a well-preserved **Hellenistic house** with wall paintings similar to the Pella style.

Early Christian basilicas At the top of the modern village, excavations have revealed a portion of Agnon's Athenian colony. An inner wall defended the acropolis, where **four basilicas** from cAD500 were discovered, with traces of their original marbles and mosaic floors – especially Basilicas A and C (Γ); the three-aisled Basilica A was adapted from a Roman bath. Adjacent to Basilica D (Δ) is the large (48m) rectangular bishop's palace. An impressive fifth, hexagonal, central-plan church was built a century later.

North wall and bridge Heading north, a left turn off the Dráma road leads to one of two Byzantine towers of 1367 that once stood on either bank of the river and which are thought to have defended the road to Mount Athos. **Classical walls** of fine isodomic masonry, over 7m high in places and equipped with an impressive drainage system, confirm the accuracy of Thucydides' account of the battle between Kleon and Brasidas in 422BC, as do the three gates, one of which defended the river crossing. Signs point the way to a rare ancient find: the **ancient bridge** that once stretched 27m, linking Amphipolis to its long-gone port. Mentioned by Thucydides, it played a strategic role in the battle he lost. The hundred fossilised wooden piles are now protected under a roof; the oldest bits were carbon-dated to c600BC.

Three ancient temples were excavated in this area, although little remains above ground: near the Byzantine Towers, the **Thesmophorian**, a women-only sanctuary dedicated to Demeter and Persephone; south, towards the modern village, the **Sanctuary of Klio**, dedicated to Cleo, the muse of history (who doesn't get many of her own sanctuaries – one can't help but think Thucydides may have something to do with it); and, further south, the **Sanctuary of Attis**, a Hellenistic/Roman god imported from Anatolia.

Kastá Tomb (North of Néa Amfípoli, east of Néa Mesolakkiá; ☉ plans are to open it to the public in the near future) In 1956, when he was 12 years old, Alexándros Kohliarídis was out chopping wood with his father, and discovered what they first thought was a cave in a giant mound. They soon realised they had found something special. For 30 years Kohliarídis worked with head archaeologist Lazarídis excavating the mound, uncovering Iron Age and 5th-century BC tombs – and a 497m perimeter wall made of limestone covered in marble, standing 3m high, which was probably designed by Deinokratis, Alexander's chief architect. Lazarídis and Kohliarídis also came across a lot of broken marble, much of it imported from Thássos, now believed to be part of the mighty 10m pedestal that once supported the Amphipolis lion on top of the mound.

The present excavations inside the mound, led from 2010 to 2015 by Katerína Peristéri, revealed a Macedonian tomb unlike any yet found. At the bottom of 13 steps were three chambers from the late 4th century BC – around the time of the death of Alexander. Disappointingly, it was soon evident that the tomb had been robbed in antiquity. The entrance to the first chamber was guarded by two sphinxes (one of the heads was found in the first chamber); in the second were two beautiful caryatids. The floor outside the third chamber revealed a magnificent coloured pebble mosaic of Hermes Psychopompos (conductor of souls into the Underworld) and the abduction of Persephone by Hades in a chariot drawn by two white horses, similar to the scene in Vergína (page 143).

Behind the huge marble door, five skeletons were found: a baby, a 60-year-old woman, two men aged 35–40 and a burned man. In 2016, a frieze, believed to have been part of the lion monument, was discovered, showing a warrior resembling Alexander leading a funeral procession. The tomb is on such a vast scale that it may well have been commissioned by Alexander himself. Some believe it was for his dear friend and probable lover Hephaestion, and the woman – just perhaps – was Alexander's mother, Olympias, another victim of Cassander (page 60). The DNA may be recoverable, and there's been talk of possibly testing it against the relics of St Mark in Venice, on the theory that the Venetian merchants who stole the Evangelist's bones from Alexandria in the 8th century AD may actually have got Alexander the Great instead.

JOURNEY BOOKS
CONTRACT PUBLISHING FROM BRADT GUIDES

DO YOU HAVE A STORY TO TELL?

- Publish your book with a leading trade publisher
- Expert management of your book by our experienced editors
- Professional layout, cover design and printing
- **Unique** access to trade distribution for print books and ebooks
- Competitive pricing and a range of tailor-made packages
- Aimed at both first-timers and previously published authors

"Unfailingly pleasant"... "Undoubtedly one of the best publishers I have worked with"... "Excellent and incredibly prompt communication"... "Unfailingly courteous"... "Superb"...

For more information – and many more endorsements from our delighted authors – please visit: **bradtguides.com/journeybooks**.

Journey Books is the contract publishing imprint of award-winning travel publisher, Bradt Guides. All subjects are considered for Journey Books, not just travel. Our contract publishing is a complement to our traditional publishing, not a replacement, and we welcome traditional submissions from new and established travel writers. Please visit **bradtguides.com/write-for-us** to find out more.

6

Eastern Macedonia (Ανατολική Μακεδονία)

The eastern end of Macedonia encompasses its share of five-star attractions, starting with the handsome port town of Kavála with its sandy beaches, ancient Philippi and the pine-wooded beached-up island of Thássos. But there's plenty more: inland, Dráma makes a great base for exploring ancient forests, rare caves (including Greece's only river cave) and gorges, while the traditional border between Macedonia and Thrace, the spectacular twisting Néstos Gorge, offers superb opportunities for hiking and kayaking.

HISTORY

Administratively since 1987 Eastern Macedonia has included Western Thrace (page 202) and they share much the same history and landscapes dotted with *toumbas*, the mounds of early Bronze Age settlements, whose pottery resembled that of Troy. In the 13th century BC, these inhabitants were joined by the Thracians, an Indo-European people whose territory at its greatest extent stretched from Bulgaria to Gallipoli to the island of Évia. The Thracians spoke their own (mostly untranslated) language and never wrote anything down, so most of what we know about them is through the Greeks, who by the 8th century BC were busy colonising the coast. They usually gave the Thracians a bad press. They were both 'gods of war' (Ares, whose other name was 'Thrax', was their patron deity) and lazy drunkards who would sell their own children as slaves.

In art, Thracian women are depicted with tattoos, the men with long embroidered cloaks, boots and fox-skin caps, tails dangling à la Davy Crockett – which they still wore into the 19th century. These 'Butter-Eaters', as the Greeks called them, were tall, grey-eyed and fair- or red-haired, and famous for their music. Thanks to their gold mines, they had a remarkably rich material culture – in Bulgaria, excavations have revealed superb goldwork and frescoed tombs. The latter show how Hellenised the Thracian nobility became by the 4th century BC; several kings even claimed to be Greek through ancestral heroes.

Thrace, divided into 50 tribes, was the most populous land after India, according to Herodotus: 'If the Thracians could be united under a single ruler or combine their purpose, they would be the most powerful nation on earth and no-one could cope with them.' But instead of ruling the world, they were the first people in Europe conquered by the Persians under Darius I (512BC), and their soldiers were forced to join in the Persian invasions of Greece. After the Persian defeats at Salamis and Plataea, the Greek colonies in the region made a big comeback, until Philip II gobbled everyone up in 358BC.

6 | EASTERN MACEDONIA (ΑΝΑΤΟΛΙΚΗ ΜΑΚΕΔΟΝΙΑ)

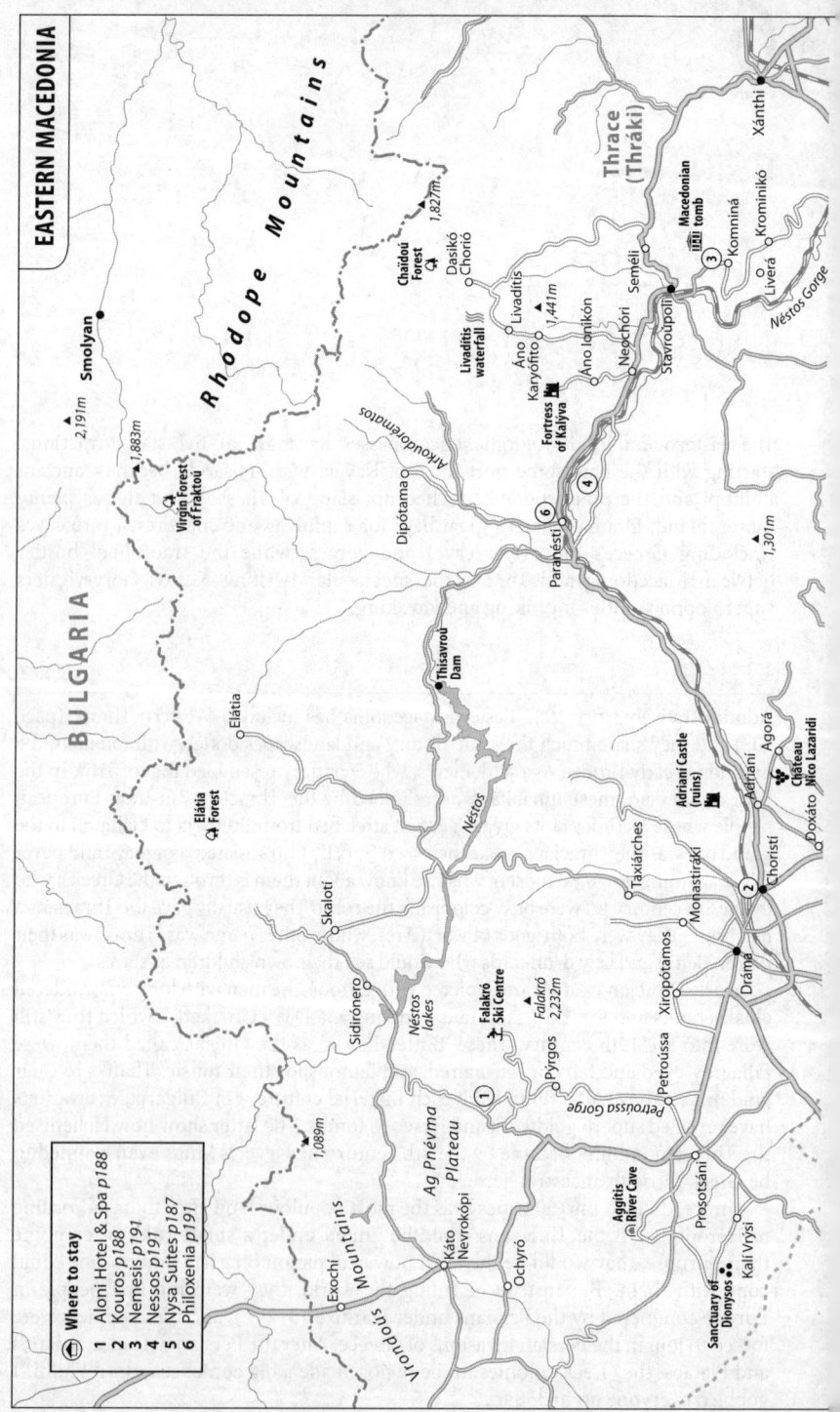

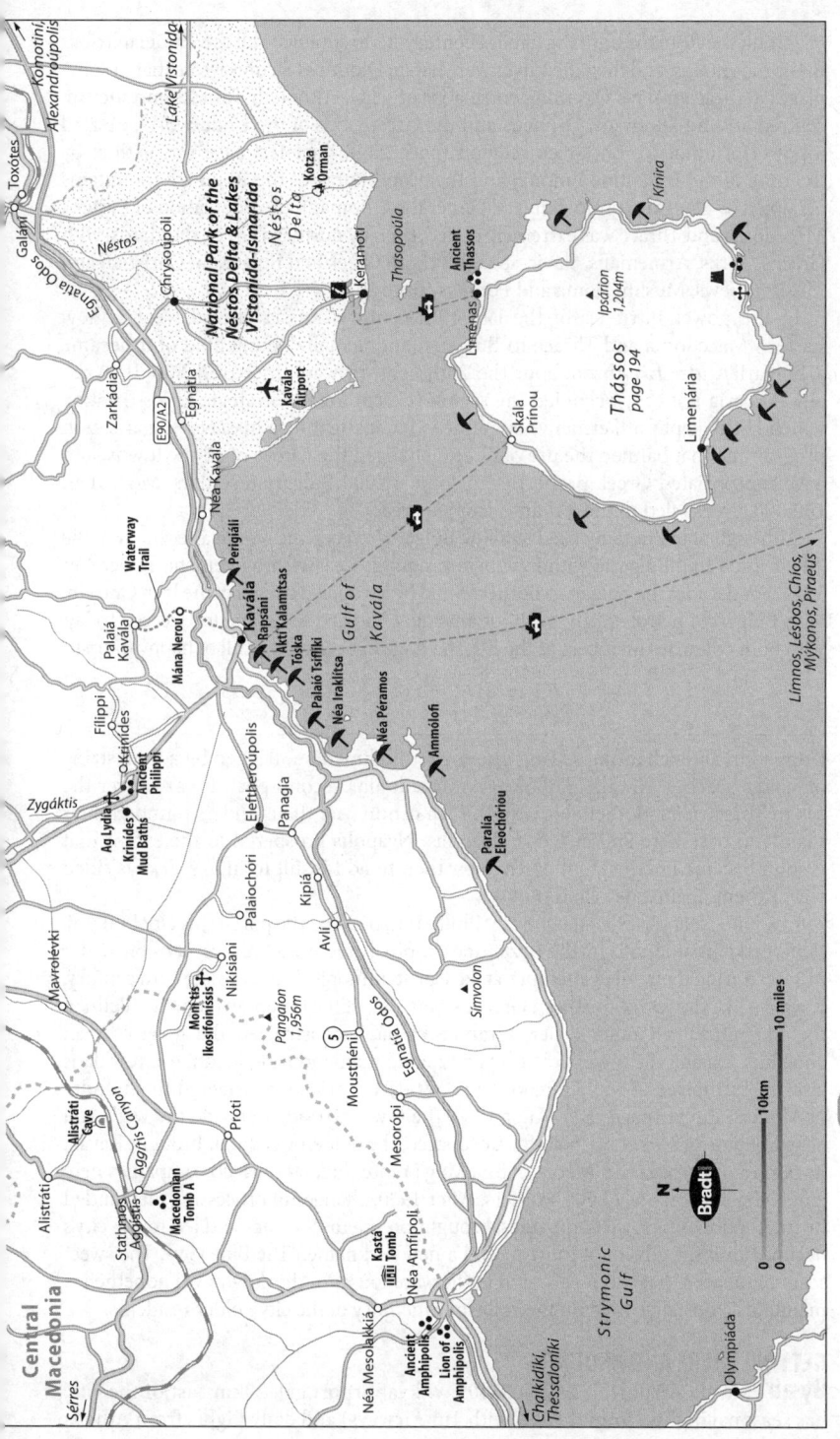

It took the Romans until the late 1st century BC to subjugate all the Thracian tribes in the mountains, and then their lives were harsh; Diodorus Siculus wrote that in some places a Thracian slave was only worth a jar of wine. Although Thracian mysticism, centred around Dionysos, Orpheus and the Great Gods of the Underworld, exerted a powerful influence on Greek religion (page 227), their language was extinct by the time of the Byzantine Empire, and their land north of the Rhodope mountains occupied by Slavs and proto-Bulgars. Under the Ottomans, the population of Eastern Macedonia and Thrace was extremely mixed, even by northern Greek standards, with Greeks, Turks, Armenians, Slavic-speakers (both Greek and Bulgarian, Christian and Muslim), Jews, Muslim Roma and Pomaks (page 202).

In the power intrigues of the late 19th century, Russia offered what is now Eastern Macedonia and Thrace to Bulgaria, and actually taking hold of it became a Bulgarian *idée fixe* throughout the 20th-century wars. In World War II, Axis-ally Bulgaria not only occupied the region (except for the strategic Évros frontier, which Hitler kept for Germany) but annexed it, instigating a massive Bulgarisation programme that banned the use of Greek, changed the names of all the towns, and gave expropriated Greek properties to some 45,000 Bulgarian settlers. More than 100,000 Greeks fled to the Italian-occupied areas.

Although Stalin initially tried to allow Bulgaria to keep the region after the war, the UK insisted that Bulgaria withdraw before signing a ceasefire agreement in October 1944. For decades the Bulgarian border would be a troubled stretch of the Iron Curtain, with Bulgarian patrols ready to shoot anyone who tried to escape to Greece. Today, with both countries members of the EU, the Aegean beaches are full of happy tourists.

KAVÁLA

Cupped in an enchanting setting under Mount Símvolon, fringed by a long string of sandy beaches, Kavála (Καβάλα) is Macedonia's second port. It gazes over the sea to Thássos, its mother ship – in the 7th century BC the islanders founded their mainland base here and called it Neapolis. Neapolis prospered to the extent that it soon became independent of Thássos, then to add insult to injury, always sided with Athens against its island mother.

In 350BC Neapolis was snatched by Philip II to become the port of his city Philippi. Renamed Christoúpolis by the Byzantines, it prospered until the Normans burned it in 1185 during their failed attempt to take Constantinople. From the late 14th century, Kavala – like the rest of northern Greece – was part of the Ottoman empire. Suleiman the Magnificent's Grand Vizier, Ibrahím Pashá, reconstructed the great Roman aqueduct, raising the town's fortunes and giving it an enduring landmark. Kavala is also the birthplace of Muhammad Ali (1769–1849), widely considered the founder of Modern Egypt (page 182). After 1864, the town expanded outside the walls and elegant mansions went up, paid for by tobacco, the golden weed that brought Kavála its period of glory as the 'Mecca of Smoking'; more than 60 tobacco companies here employed in excess of 12,500 workers. After 1930, changes in processing, demanded by international tobacco companies, brought on unemployment and led to the city's decline, until the advent of tourism and a new nickname: 'The Blue City'. The sweet scent of tobacco that was once cured in the warehouses of the downtown nonetheless maintains a nostalgic hold on the collective memory of the city's older residents.

GETTING THERE AND AROUND
By air Kavála Airport (📞 25910 53409; w kva-airport.gr), 29km east of the city, has seasonal flights (from the UK with Tui Airways) and daily flights from Athens

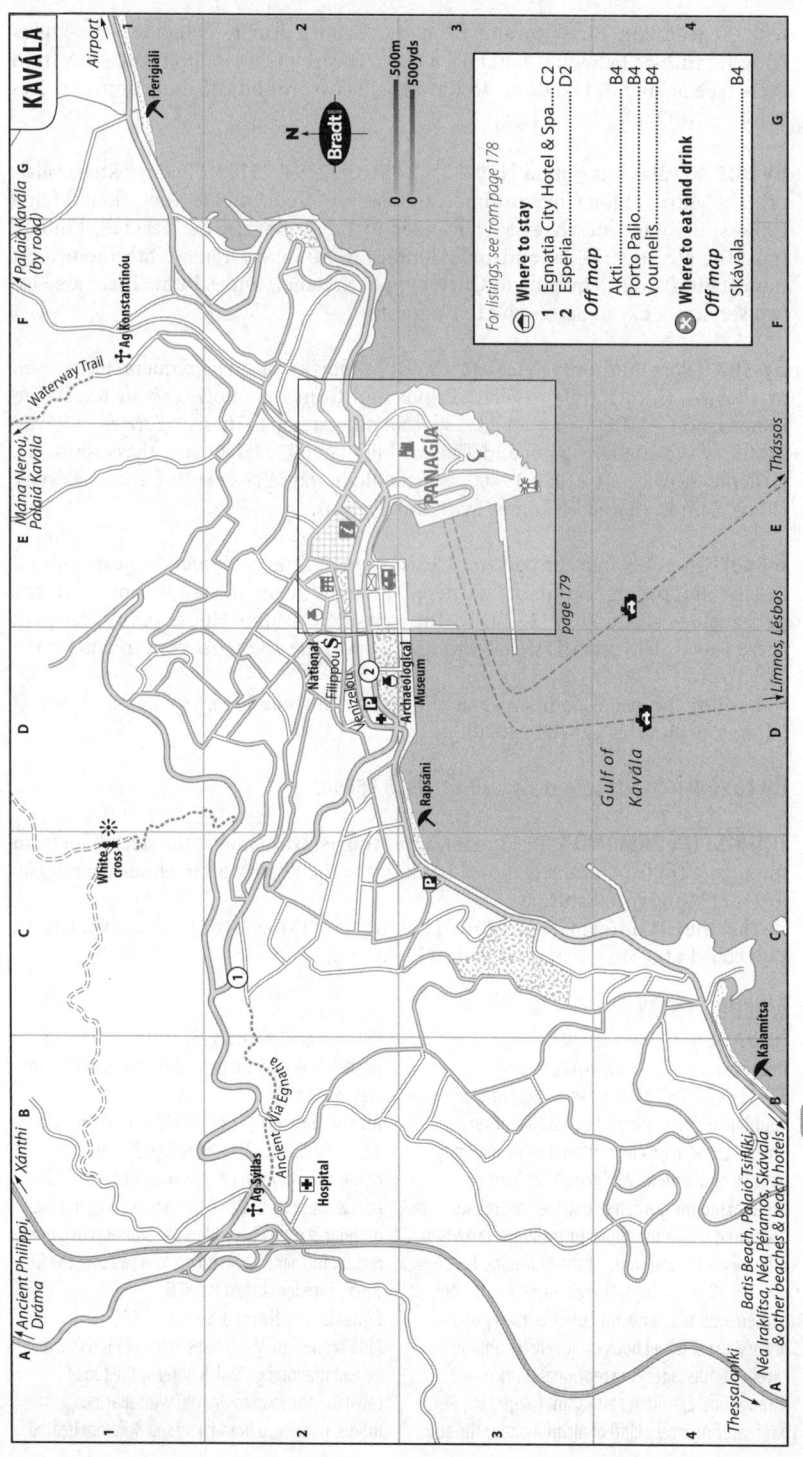

with Aegean Air. Buses to and from the airport usually coincide with flights (ring KTEL, see below); if not, take a taxi to nearby Chrysoúpoli and a bus from there (see below). A taxi direct to Kavála will cost around €45, but confirm prices before setting off.

By bus Kavála's bus station [179 A2] (↘ 25102 22294, 25102 23595; w ktelkavalas.gr) is at Mitropolítou Chrysostómou 4. Buses run frequently to Thessaloníki (2hrs express; €17) and nearly every half hour to Palaiá Kavála, the beaches, Philippi (take the bus to Krinídes and walk 30mins; €1.90) and Dráma (with the nearest train station) and frequently to Chrysoúpoli, Keramotí and Xánthi. There are also two services a day to Sérres and to Komotiní.

By sea (Port Authority ↘ 25102 23691; w portkavala.gr) Frequent ferries sail to Thássos, from Kavála to Skála Prínos and from Keramotí (east of Kavála) to Liménas, on ANEΘ (↘ 25930 22318; w anethferries.gr), Thassos Ferries (↘ 25930 24001; w thassos-ferries.gr) and Thassos Link (m 69734 04079; w thassoslink.gr). Hellenic Seaways (↘ 21089 19800; w hellenicseaways.gr) sails to Límnos, Lésvos, Chíos, Sámos, Ikaría, Mýkonos, Sýros and Piraeus.

By car There's a free car park on Chrisóstomou Smírnis Street 44 near Rapsáni Beach and paying car parks scattered around town, including one near the Archaeological Museum [177 D2]. The portside Customs House paying car park and Plateía Mehmet Ali (if you can find a spot) are the most convenient for the Old Town.

Besides the usual companies at the airport for **car hire**, try Evros [179 C2] (Kountouriótou 7; ↘ 25102 23020).

By taxi For local radio taxis, call m 69928 95694.

TOURIST INFORMATION In summer, a free **tourist train** makes the steep haul from the square (in front of the National Bank) up to the Kástro, on the hour from 09.00 to 13.00 Monday to Saturday.

The **tourist information office** [179 B1] (↘ 25102 31011; w visitkavala.gr; ⊕ 09.00–14.00 Mon–Fri) is on Plateía Eleftherías.

WHERE TO STAY
Town centre and around
Imaret [179 C3] (26 rooms) Poulídou 30–32; ↘ 25106 20151; w imaret.gr. This serene boutique hotel is one of the most beautiful in Greece. Located in a late Ottoman-era seminary built by Muhammad Ali (page 182), rooms, overlooking the garden or marble arcades, are decorated with sumptuous furnishings, carpets & fine linens (even some of the plumbing is original 19th century). There's an Islamic orange garden around a reflecting pool, a library of history, art & travel books, a lovely hammam, excellent massages & exceptional service throughout. Excellent restaurant (page 180) & bar featuring every kind of alcohol under the sun.

Over 12s only; b/fast (€25) features their own fresh-laid eggs & homemade goodies. Minimum stay. €€€€€
Airotel Galaxy [179 B1] (149 rooms) Venizélou 27; ↘ 25102 24812; w airotel.gr. Big, recently remodelled hotel in easy walking distance of the port & museums, with balconies overlooking the harbour & comfy beds. Plus panoramic roof garden restaurant/bar (€€) with great views over the Old Town. Excellent b/fast inc. €€
Egnatia City Hotel & Spa [177 C2] (105 rooms) 7is Merarchías 139; ↘ 25106 00250; w egnatiahotel.gr. Swish hotel at the top of town (on the road to Dráma) with spacious rooms, parking, a brand new spa & indoor heated

KAVÁLA

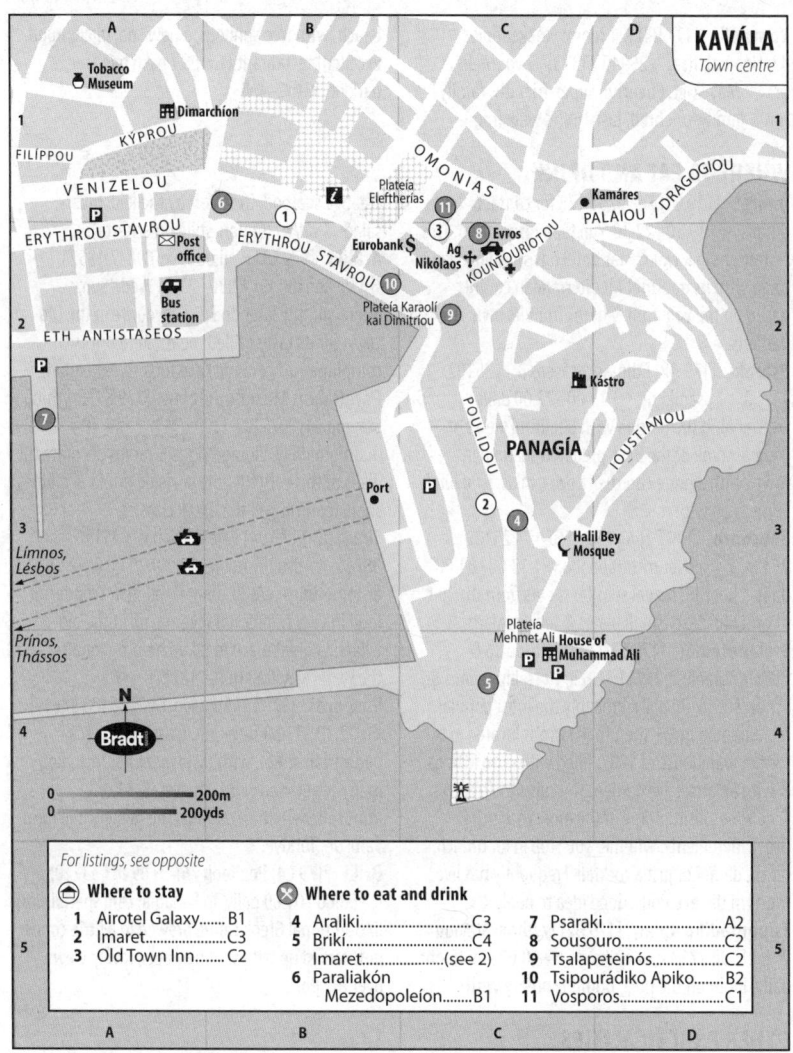

pool, & panoramic views from the roof garden & restaurant. €€

Esperia [177 D2] (21 rooms) Erythroú Stavroú 44; \25102 29621; w esperiakavala.gr. Central hotel with large rooms (some interconnecting) & balconies with sea views, in easy walking distance of the bus station & port. Limited but free parking in the underground garage (10 spaces, no reservations). Buffet b/fast inc. €€–€

Old Town Inn [179 C2] (10 rooms) Spetsón 14; \25102 11113; w oldtowninn.gr. Charming little hotel vintage 1929; bright rooms with balconies, AC & Wi-Fi located in the centre of the action between Panagía & Plateía Eleftherías. Owners speak good English & can help with parking. €

Kavála's beaches

Akti [177 B4] (16 rooms) Palaió Tsiflíki; \25104 41485; f Akti Hotel Kavala. Calm hotel with a beach bar on the sand, managed by a friendly couple. €€€

Porto Palio [177 B4] (33 rooms) M Merkoúri 33, Palaío Tsiflíki; \25104 41605; w portopaliohotel.gr. Relaxing hotel with a good taverna/bar on the child-friendly beach, with 3 family rooms, kind staff, anti-mozzie devices & parking. €€€–€€

6 | EASTERN MACEDONIA (ΑΝΑΤΟΛΙΚΗ ΜΑΚΕΔΟΝΙΑ)

Vournelis [177 B4] (21 rooms) Makedonías 43, Néa Iraklítsa; 25940 21353; w vournelis.gr; ⊕ May–Oct. Cheerful, super-friendly, family-run & family-oriented, just 1min's walk from a beach, with free sunbeds, a new spa, playground, excellent restaurant (€€) & beach bar. Free parking. €€€–€€

✴ WHERE TO EAT AND DRINK

Imaret [179 C3] See page 178 for contact details; ⊕ 19.30–22.30; call for a reservation. This restaurant in Kavála's star hotel has stunning views to go with its gourmet Mediterranean cuisine based on the veg, fruit & herbs from its own gardens. €€€€€

Psaraki [179 A2] Ethn Antistáseos 3; 25102 11750; w psaraki.gr; ⊕ 13.00–23.00 daily. Overlooking the marina with beautiful views of Kavála, some of the best-prepared seafood in town, with a huge choice of ouzos, rakís, tsípouro & wine to go with it. €€

Sousouro [179 C2] Ag Nikolaou 4; 25102 26111; ⨍ sousourostetoooooo; ⊕ 13.00–01.00 daily. Cheerful, casual spot for meats from the spit or grill plus tasty small plates & lovely salads. €€

Tsalapeteinós [179 C2] Cnr Dimitríou 36 & Plateía Karaolí; 25111 11073; w tsalapeteinos.gr; ⊕ 08.30–02.00 daily. Probably the most popular restaurant in town, the 'urban farm' is located in a former warehouse of 1907, filled with retro fittings & with an attractive garden. The cuisine is creative & delicious, using some of the more recherché Greek ingredients, whether you stop in for brunch, lunch, dinner or just a cocktail. Frequently has live music in the evenings. Good idea to book. €€

Tsipourádiko Apiko [179 B2] Erythroú Stavroú 2; 25102 27173; w apiko.gr; ⊕ 10.00–midnight daily. Right on the port, bright & breezy with creative seafood, fresh fish by the kilo, meats, salads & dákos (Cretan-style bruschetta). €€

Araliki [179 C3] Poulídou; m 69847 18521; ⨍ Το-Αραλίκ; ⊕ 12.30–23.00 Wed–Sun, opens slightly later on Fri. A favourite in the Old Town for its tasty grilled meats, kind prices & complimentary orange cake for a sweet ending. €

Paraliakón Mezedopoleíon [179 B1] Erythroú Stavroú 61; 25102 11005; ⨍; ⊕ 12.30–midnight daily. Vintage signs & radios decorate the walls of this very friendly portside drinks & nibbles shop, featuring all the Greek classics. €

Skávala [177 D4] Palaiá Kavála; 25130 08940; ⊕ usually noon–19.00/ 20.00 Fri–Sun, or sometimes w/ends only – call first. Wonderful food in very traditional taverna, up in the old village; a great place to fill up before – or after – the Waterway Trail (page 183). €

Vosporos [179 C1] Spetsón 17; 25108 34617; ⊕ 12.30–23.30 Tue–Sun. Classic décor & a pedestrian street, with tasty mezédes, including many vegetarian & fish choices, & a lively atmosphere in the evenings. The owners hail from Samsun, Türkiye. €

Brikí [179 C4] Poulídou 76; m 69443 33220; ⊕ 08.00–01.00 daily. In Panagía, café specialising in traditional Greek coffee brewed in a little copper pot, served up with spoon sweets; lovely views over the port.

OTHER PRACTICALITIES

Eurobank [179 C2] Venizélou & Ídras 10
National Bank [177 D2] Venizélou 36
Hospital [177 B2] Ag Sílas; 25135 01100; w kavalahospital.gr

Pharmacy Anastasiádi [177 D2] Erythroú Stávrou 68
Pharmacy Pistofidou [179 C2] Kountouriótou 20
Post office [179 A2] Mitropolítou Chrisostómou 8

WHAT TO SEE AND DO Venizélou Street, just in from Erythroú Stavroú, marks Kavála's original waterfront, where large tobacco warehouses (which are more stylish than they sound) are now being converted for new uses. The tobacco kings lived along Kýprou and Filíppou; one mansion, a white folly modelled on a Hungarian castle, now serves as Kavála's **Dimarchíon** [179 A1] (town hall).

One thing you will have already clocked is Kavála's landmark **Kamáres** [179 C1], the graceful three-tiered 280m aqueduct swooping 25m over the city. It was built (or more likely, it was built in Roman times and restored) in 1550 under Suleiman the Magnificent to supply the fortress and district of Panagía.

Archaeological Museum [177 D2] (Erythroú Stavroú 17; \ 25102 22335; ⊕ 08.30–15.30 Wed–Mon; €10, concessions €5) Come here for finds from Neolithic Dikili Tash (near Philippi) and Ancient Neapolis, including architectural elements from the 5th-century BC sanctuary of the virgin goddess Parthenos. From Amphipolis (page 168) there's lovely gold jewellery, a silver mirror, a strikingly modern painted bust of a woman and a reconstruction of a Macedonian tomb; from the other Greek colonies, a painted sarcophagus (c300BC) and a Cycladic amphora, with animal figures from 630BC. A column in the garden is crowned with an eagle and rams you wouldn't want to meet in a dark alley.

Tobacco Museum [179 A1] (K Palaiológou 4; \ 25102 23344; w tobaccomuseum.gr; ⊕ 08.00–16.00 Mon–Fri; €5) The place to learn all about small-leaf, sun-dried oriental tobacco, once grown throughout the Ottoman Empire and central to Kavala's fortunes: there's a rich collection of agricultural and industrial machinery, photos, documents, old tobacco art and ads, and lots of sweet-smelling tobacco – all enough to make you wish smoking were good for you.

Ag Nikólaos [179 C2] (Cnr Kontouriótou & Ag Nikoláou) This was once the city's main mosque built in 1530 by Ibrahim Pasha, brother-in-law of Suleiman, over the site of an early Christian church; a few stones remain beside the glittering gold-mosaicked **Bema of St Paul**, erected in 2000 to mark the spot where the Apostle landed and preached before heading to Philippi. The mosque was converted into a church in 1926. Many churches were converted to mosques during the Ottoman era, and then converted back into churches, but this is a rare example of one that started as a mosque (another, but reconstructed, is in Heraklion). The minaret has been used as a base for the bell tower. The surrounding lanes with their many bars are a favourite evening hangout.

Panagía Before it sprawled up the hills, Kavála was squeezed into the walls of its promontory. Now the peaceful district of Panagía, of leafy cobbled streets, stepped alleys and Neoclassical and Ottoman houses, it is the best place to get an idea of what Thessaloníki looked like before the Great Fire of 1917. The beautiful walk around the walls leads to the stubby white **lighthouse** at the tip, with views over town and sea; the steps lead to a great place to snorkel.

Imaret [179 C3] (Poulídou 30; \ 25106 20151; ⊕ 10.00–15.30 Tue–Sun for guided tours; €5) Just up from the port, this rambling yellow complex bubbles with metal-coated domes. In 1817, when Muhammad Ali (page 182) asked Kavála what favour he could grant it, the answer was this Islamic seminary, funded by

FESTIVALS IN KAVÁLA

Founded in 1957, the **Philippi-Thássos Festival** (w visitkavala.gr) takes place in July and August with performances of ancient drama, contemporary theatre, dance and classical concerts on Thássos and in the ancient theatre of Philippi. The Apostle Paul and the liberation of Kavála (26 June 1913) are celebrated with a host of cultural events – the **Eleftheria** ('freedom') – culminating on the feast day of Apostle Paul (29 June) with outdoor events and performances in the fortress, in Eleftherías Square, and elsewhere throughout the town.

the rents he received from Thássos. It later served as a charity, offering classes, a hammam, library, accommodation for 60 boarders and a soup kitchen, closing in 1923. Afterwards it was used as a restaurant, before falling into decay; in 2001 the Egyptian government ceded it to wealthy Egyptophile Anna Misirian, who beautifully restored the building as a monument and hotel (page 178).

House of Muhammad Ali [179 C4] (Poulídou 6; ☏ 25106 20515, 25106 20154; w moha.center; ⊕ 10.00–14.00 Thu–Mon; €3) This handsome house of 1720 still has its original chestnut floors, its panelling, fireplaces and men's and women's sections, offering an evocative glimpse of 18th-century life, although the only surviving piece of furniture is Ali's desk. In summer the gardens offer lovely views and are sometimes used for concerts. The house is the headquarters of the MOHA Research Centre, dedicated to highlighting the importance of the Islamic Golden Era (8th–12th centuries) to the arts and sciences. Dominating the square in front of the house is a flamboyant **Equestrian statue of Muhammad Ali** sheathing his scimitar, paid for by grateful Greeks, many of whom emigrated to Egypt during his rule.

Halil Bey (Old Music) Mosque [179 C3] (Anthemíou 2; ⊕ for exhibitions) This striking red mosque with its Frida Kahlo-like blue madrasa was built in 1530 over a Byzantine church, the ruins of which are visible through the glass floor. It was later used as a girls' school and between 1930 and 1940 served as the home of the local philharmonic band, hence its name. These days it houses temporary folklore exhibitions.

Kástro [179 C2] (Isidoroú 18; ☏ 25108 38602; w castle-kavala.gr; ⊕ May–Sep 08.00–21.00, Apr 08.00–20.00, Oct 08.00–17.00, Nov–Mar 08.00–16.00 daily; €4.50, concessions €2.50) On Neapolis's ancient acropolis high above Panagía, the well-preserved crenellated walls of the Ottoman castle (1425) replaced the Roman and Byzantine versions demolished in 1391, although here and there you can still pick out bits of older masonry. Purchased in 1964 from the Egyptian government

MUHAMMAD ALI: FOUNDER OF MODERN EGYPT

Son of a prosperous Albanian tobacco merchant and military commander, Muhammad Ali (1769–1849) was born in Kavála, in the same year as Napoleon and Wellington. Orphaned at an early age, and raised by his uncle, he spent much of his youth on Thássos before marrying a wealthy heiress from Dráma (his first of six wives) and mother of the first five of his reputed 95 children, many of whom were born to the 50 concubines in his harem.

Proud to have been born in the land of Alexander, and a great admirer of Napoleon, Muhammad followed in his father's footsteps. His work as a tobacco merchant put him in contact with the Enlightenment in the West, and his military career took off when his unit was sent to Egypt in 1801 after Napoleon's occupation. Sensing an opportunity, the charismatic Ali made himself a champion of the people, and went on to serve as viceroy of Egypt. He massacred the Mamluks who had controlled Egypt for the past 600 years, and then modernised the state, conquered the Sudan and, with French assistance, challenged the Sultan himself, founding the dynasty that ruled Egypt until King Farouk was forced to abdicate in 1952.

(which had inherited several of Muhammed Ali's properties in Kavála), it has grand views and a little café.

Ancient Via Egnatía [177 B2] (Intersection of Egnatía & Makedónia streets) You can stroll along an evocative kilometre of a branch of the ancient Roman road – still in use until the 20th century – that linked the city to Philippi. Near the top, at the church of **Ag Sýllas** (1936) marks the spot where SS Paul, Silas and Lazarus rested on their way to Philippi. Opposite the church, an unmarked paved road leads up to a car park; from here it's a 2.5km walk (or drive if you're very careful – it's best in a 4x4) to the big white **cross** high over Kavála, with its gorgeous views; there's no better place to watch the sunset.

Palaiá Kavála [177 E1] (Παλαιά Καβάλα; 14km from Kavála) Some say Thucydides (page 27) spent his exile in Palaiá Kavála, writing his famous history of the Peloponnesian War. Two well-signposted trails begin here: one, a bucolic 3km trail along a laughing stream through an ancient plane grove, past old watermills and a waterfall (great for a swim although it usually dries up by August). The second is the 10.5km **Waterway Trail** (O drómos tou neroú) [177 F1] over charming old bridges, forests of kermes oaks – host to the insects used to make crimson dye – and past superb views of Thássos, Mount Pangaíon and the plain of Philippi. After 5km you arrive at the **Mána Neroú** [177 E1], the 'mother of waters' cistern (5.5km), where the trail continues along the underground aqueduct that supplied the Kamáres. Signs along the way explain the construction of ancient aqueducts; at the end of the trail (or beginning if you want to walk up) is Kavála's church of **Ag Konstantinóu** [177 F1], located at the top of 13is Septemvríou Street.

KAVÁLA'S BEACHES Closest are the municipal beach **Rapsáni** (Ραψάνη) [177 D3], lined with bars and tavernas, and **Perigiáli** (Περιγιάλι) [177 G1], 2km east (buses 2 or 3), with sunbeds etc and views back to Kavála. **Kalamítsa** (Καλαμίτσα) [177 B4] to the south is another popular municipal beach (buses 4, 5 or 8).

The coast west of the city is scalloped with sandy beaches, hotels, villas, tavernas and campsites. **Bátis** (Μπάτη; 4km from Kavála; bus 8; w batis-sa.gr) is equipped with watersports, campsite, ballroom, bars, etc. Next is **Tóska** (Τόσκα) with a big hotel; then comes popular **Palaió Tsiflíki** (Παλαιό Τσιφλίκι; usually just 'Palaió') with its bars. **Néa Iraklítsa** (Νέα Ηρακλίτσα) still has a little fishing port tucked in its pine-wooded cape. The most beautiful, **Ammólofi** (Αμμόλοφοι), is 2km from **Néa Péramos** (Νέα Πέραμος; 18km from Kavála), where the sprawling ruins of a 12th-century Byzantine castle on the headland overlook a beautiful stretch of sand dunes, lapped by a crystalline sea; in summer there's a direct bus to the beach. Then there's **Paralía Eleochóriou** (Παραλία Ελαιοχώρέου; 27km from Kavála) with pine woods, clear water and Cuba Beach Bar, where the cool kids hang out.

ANCIENT PHILIPPI

In 360BC, the great powerhouse that was Thássos founded the colony of Krinídes ('fountains') on the edge of a 55km^2 peat bog (the largest in Greece). The city-state's aim was to control the Royal Macedonian road – the precursor of the Via Egnatía – between Amphipolis and Neapolis (Kavála), to exploit the gold, silver and timber of Mount Pangaíon; but four years later it was wrenched from them by Philip II, who, not one for false modesty, renamed it Philippi (Φίλιπποι). The new settlers partially drained the marshlands and laid out a town in the Hippodameian grid. Perennially in debt, Philip wanted to finance his ambitions in Asia, and it wasn't long before Pangaíon's mines were yielding 1,000 talents (33 tonnes) of gold a year, and Philippi replaced Amphipolis (page 168) as the kingdom's gold and silver centre.

In 41BC, the plain just west of the city walls witnessed the first of Philippi's two great turning points in history. In the aftermath of Caesar's death, the legions of Brutus and Cassius, occupying Rome's eastern provinces, met the nearly equal force of Mark Antony and Octavian, in the biggest confrontation ever between Romans. In the first round, Brutus defeated Octavian (who was ill but managed to escape to Antony's camp), and Antony defeated Cassius, who committed suicide. Twenty days later Brutus let himself be drawn into battle in the same place and was crushed by Antony, and committed suicide, bringing the last vestiges of the Roman Republic down with him. Antony settled his veterans in the town; in 30BC Octavian (now Augustus) granted others land in the city he renamed Colonia Augusta Iulia Philippensis, his 'Little Rome'.

With Augustus' patronage, Philippi soon grew into a large city. In AD49 or 50 it witnessed its second turning point, when St Paul came here to preach, and baptised his first convert, Lydia, who welcomed him into her home, and founded the first Christian church in Europe. Otherwise, he and his disciple Silas had a rough time of it: they were attacked and imprisoned after Paul exorcised a demon from a fortune teller. Paul returned six years later and seems, by his Epistle to the Philippians (cAD64), to have had a soft spot for the city.

The 5th century AD brought the first barbarian raids, followed in AD547 by the 'Justinian' plague, which decimated the population; then, in AD619, a powerful earthquake toppled it. After the Bulgarians took Philippi in AD838, the Byzantines rebuilt it and strengthened its walls, and it was still thriving when Arab geographer Idrisi visited it c1150. But by the time of the Ottoman conquest, the boggy plain had

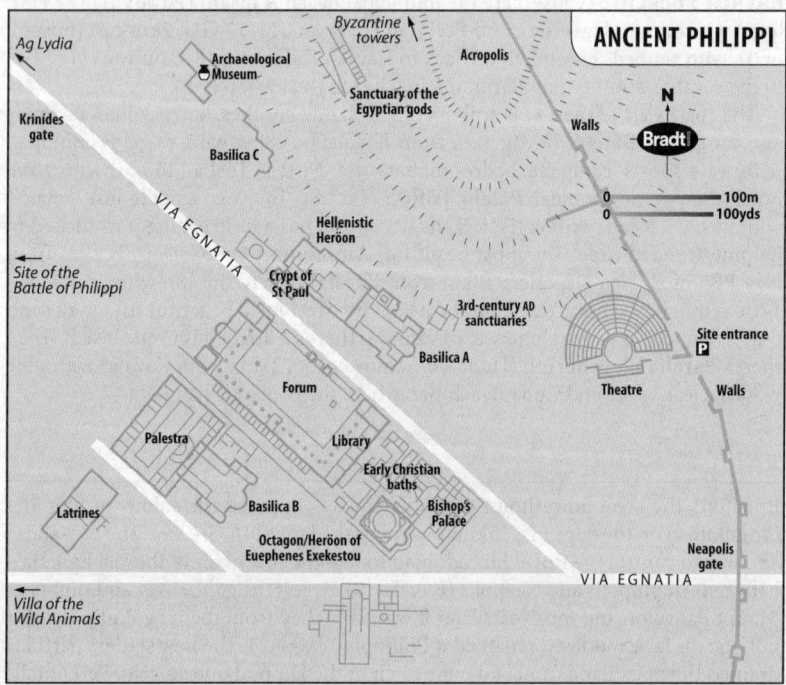

reverted to a marsh and its stones were used as a quarry. Excavations, begun by the French in 1914, continue apace, and in 2016, Philippi was inscribed on UNESCO's World Heritage List.

WHAT TO SEE AND DO
Philippi Archaeological Site and Museum (15km from Kavála; \25105 16251; w odysseus.culture.gr; ⊕ Nov–Mar 08.30–15.30, Apr–May & Oct 08.00–18.00, Jun–Aug 08.00–20.00, Sep 08.00–19.00 daily; you'll need a separate ticket for each: archaeological site €10, concessions €5; the museum €10, concessions €5) Most of Philippi's visible remains date from the Roman or Early Christian period. Just within the walls (4th century BC at the bottom, Byzantine on the top), however, is the large **theatre** built by Philip II in 356BC, at the base of the pyramid-shaped **acropolis**. The Romans remodelled the theatre in the 3rd century AD to give it an extra-large orchestra and protective 1.2m wall for blood spectacles; and it was partly restored in the 1950s for Philippi's summer festival (page 181). There's a graceful relief of a dancing figure from Philip's day, and others from the 3rd century AD, of Victory, Nemesis and Ares.

Around the hill, a large terrace was built for the 5th-century AD **Basilica A**; off to the right, carved into the rock, are reliefs, niches and walls that belonged to several small 3rd-century AD **sanctuaries**, dedicated to Sylvanus, Bendix (the Thracian Artemis), Heracles, Dionysos and Hermes. The paved atrium in front of the basilica incorporates parts of an older heröon; the **crypt** below, supported by props, is said to be the **prison of St Paul**, where Paul and Silas were liberated by a timely earthquake; their guards, impressed by their escape, at once converted to Christianity.

Further west are the remains of 6th-century AD **Basilica C** and the **Archaeological Museum**, with two floors of artefacts. The oldest are from Dikili Tash (w dikili-tash.fr) near Krinídes which goes back to 6500BC and has yielded some of the oldest gold ornaments ever found in the Balkans. From Philippi are mosaics, capitals, glass, coins and part of an inscription sent by Alexander for the town plan.

From the museum a path winds up to the shattered bits of the **Sanctuary of the Egyptian Gods**, then up to the top of the acropolis, with three stark **Byzantine towers** built over the ancient originals, offering a view over the site.

The rest of Philippi lies across the modern road, parallelling the ancient Via Egnatía – which doubled as the *decumanus*, or main north–south street – with its large paving slabs and sidewalks. Two side passages linked it to the vast **Forum**, with ruins of the **library** on the south end. Much of its stone (carefully scraped of all pagan reliefs) was re-used for the enormous **Basilica B**, erected in the reign of Justinian. Like Justinian's Hagia Sophia in Constantinople, it was an experiment on the evolution from Roman basilica to the cruciform Byzantine church. Only here, the dome collapsed (if it was ever built) and the discouraged architects abandoned the project, leaving just the massive piers standing picturesquely against the blueish backdrop of Mount Pangaíon. Several capitals, with their deeply incised acanthus leaves, are still in place, along with a mosaic inscription of AD343 left by Bishop Porphyrios. By the entrance arch lie scant remains of the **Palestra**, but with beautifully preserved **public latrines**, a veritable monument where some 50 Philippians could take their ease at the same time. Southwest is the large Roman **Villa of the Wild Animals**, named after the mosaic uncovered there.

East of the forum, the **Octagon**, unique in Greece, was Philippi's cathedral, built in the mid 5th century AD over an earlier chapel, believed to have been founded by St Paul himself, that burned down; traces remain of the mosaics, including an inscription left by Bishop Porphyrios in the AD340s. A cube on the outside, with a dome on top, the beautifully paved interior (including colourful mosaics) had an interior colonnade of 20 columns and a horseshoe apse projecting from one side; the original effect must have been similar to Ravenna's San Vitale. It was built over the vaulted Hellenistic funerary **heröon** belonging to a certain Euephenes Exekestou (whose name is also recorded as an initiate at Samothráki), who was somehow important enough to be buried in the city centre in the 2nd century BC. There are more baths just north of the Octagon (from the Christian era, and linked directly to its baptistry) and extensive remains of the **Bishop's Palace**.

Ag Lydía (⊕ As for archaeological site; free) Just west of Philippi, in a charming leafy setting on the little Zygáktis River, the church of Ag Lydía stands near the altar recording the first baptism in Europe – of a woman named Lydia, a well-to-do seller of purple dye and probably cloth from Thyatira in Lydia in modern Türkiye (Acts 16:14, 15). A modern church marks the site (where many Greeks bring their children to be baptised) with mosaics of St Paul's journeys and paintings that tell the story of Paul, Lydia and Philippi. Other remains of the ancient city, including a large cemetery, basilica and tombs, are scattered around the modern town of Krinídes.

Krinídes Mud Baths (3km west of Krinídes (Κρηνίδες); ☏ 25135 00300; w pilotherapia.gr; ⊕ Jul–Aug; from €6 for a 25min bath & thermal shower) Natural 'mature' clay combined with therapeutic hot spring water make for a perfect mud treatment, the ideal way to round off a day at the archaeological site. Men's and women's areas – enormous pools of mud you immerse yourself in – are separate, as you go in naked or nearly so; all you need is a towel. The showers of the natural therapeutic water wash it off well. A hammam and massages are available too, and there is a very nice on-site campground.

MOUNT PANGAÍON

A whiff of the uncanny lingers about the knobbly peaks of Mount Pangaíon (Παγγαίο; 1,956m), the Homeric 'Nysa' and myth magnet often topped with snow into April. It was the reputed birthplace of Dionysos. His oracle here was tended by the fiercest of Thracian tribes, the Satrai (who would be 'demonised' by the Greeks as Satyrs), where white horses were sacrificed and a priestess gave ambiguous oracles, similar to Apollo's Pythia at Delphi.

The mountain is also associated with Lycurgus, king of the Thracian Edonians, who scorned the young Dionysos as he crossed his land, axed his nursemaid Ambrosia, and forced the god to take refuge in the cave of sea goddess Thetis (page 347). The *Iliad* says Zeus punished Lycurgus' impiety with blindness and a short life, 'because he was hated by all immortals'. In another version of the myth, Lycurgus captures the Maenads, the followers of Dionysos, after the god escapes. They are miraculously freed, and Lycurgus, driven mad by the god, mistakes his son Dryas for a grapevine and cuts off his limbs with an axe. Lycurgus regains his sanity, but his country was barren until an oracle stated that Lycurgus had to die for the fields to become fertile again. So the Edonians took their king up Pangaíon and had him torn limb from limb by his own horses – subject of a trilogy of (lost) plays by Aeschylus.

In another myth, Orpheus – after rescuing his beloved wife Eurydice from Hades with the beauty of his music, only to disobey the injunction against looking back, losing her forever – foreswore women, took only male lovers and worshipped only Apollo. When he climbed Pangaíon to the oracle of Dionysos to watch the glory of the sun god, jealous Maenads tried to throw stones and branches at him; only these refused to touch him because of the enchantment of his music. So the Maenads tore him limb from limb. But they repented when their fury had passed, for according to great Classicist Jane Ellen Harrison, the Maenads were really the same as the Muses, and they buried his limbs by Mount Olympus. His head, still singing away, floated to Lésvos, where it prophesised in a popular oracle until Apollo, jealous, told him to shut up. Today monasteries dot Pangaíon's plane- and chestnut-wooded slopes along with tavernas popular on summer evenings.

 WHERE TO STAY AND EAT

Nysa Suites [map, page 174] (6 rooms) Mousthéni; 25920 93000; w nysasuites.gr. Elegant, luxuriously appointed modern suites with authentic architectural character in a historic stone mansion. B/fast inc. €€€€

Culinary Boutique Hotel Kladi Elias (4 rooms) Mesorópi; 25920 93293; m 69733 06955; w kladielias.gr. On the south slopes of Pangaíon, this is one of the best guesthouses in the area: chic boutique suites with mezzanines in an old stone house, with Coco-Mat bedding, including 1 with a wood stove. On the ground floor there's an excellent gourmet restaurant (€€€€) with a long list of local wines – try the pesto tomato couscous. B/fast inc. €€€

Neromylos Traditional Guesthouse (4 rooms) Nikísiani; 25920 62188; m 69429 40485; w neromyloshotel.gr. Soothing rooms in a former mill run by a lovely family, with family rooms, garden & good pizzas (baked in a proper wood oven) in the restaurant (€€). B/fast inc. €€

Botsani Mousthéni; 25920 93526; Μποστανι/Bostani; ⊕ 18.00–23.30 Tue, Wed & Fri, 14.00–23.30 Thu & Sat, 13.00–22.00 Sun. Superb traditional café/taverna spread under massive plane trees – a favourite retreat for beachgoers or anyone exploring Pangaíon & a place for lingering on a summer night – featuring home-cooked dishes & succulent grilled meats. They're famous for enormous, juicy pork chops & fine wines. €€

WHAT TO SEE AND DO The ancient road – the same one used by Xerxes' armies – runs through the rich valley and orchards between mounts Símvolon and Pangaíon. **Eleftheroúpolis** (Ελευθερούπολη), the local crossroads and market town, is dotted with old tobacco warehouses. From **Panagía** (Παναγία) you can drive up to the top of the Pangaíon (paved until the last stretch) for the views that seem to go on forever. Lush **Kipiá** (Κηπιά) has remains of a 5th-century AD basilica (fenced in, southeast of the village); a track east from here leads to another, built inside a ruined shrine of the Thracian Hero-rider. It also has, rather surprisingly, a **Wax Museum** (m 69378 03780; w kerinaomoiomata.gr; ⊕ Oct–May 10.00–18.00 daily, Jun–Sep 10.00–20.00 daily; €5, ages 13–17 €4, ages 6–12 €3, under 6s free), run by enthusiastic waxwork maker Theódoros Kokkinídis, where Greek politicians and celebrities keep company with the likes of Johnny Depp, Maria Callas and Princess Diana. **Avlí** (Αυλή) has a mountain path through beech trees and giant ferns. Pretty **Mousthéni** (Μουσθένη) just west, has a picturesque single-span stone bridge in the centre; **Mesorópi** (Μεσορόπη) is a charming village with a lush oasis of plane trees.

Palaiochóri (Παλαιοχώρι) on the north slopes, where most of the ancient mining took place, lies under the ruins of a castle known as the **Castle of Alexander**, or Vranókastro (a 40-minute walk from the end of the road), built by the ancient Macedonians to defend the mines, then re-used in the 12th century by the Byzantines. West in **Nikísiani** (Νικήσιανη) there are traces of the ancient mines, which were still a going concern in the 1st century AD. From here, a winding road through beech and chestnut groves leads to the most important of Pangaíon's many monasteries: **Moní tis Ikosifoiníssis**, a popular pilgrimage destination and said to be the oldest still-functioning religious house in Greece. Founded in the 4th century AD by the Blessed

Germanós, destroyed by the Turks in 1507, and wrecked by the Bulgarians in 1917 and 1943, it has since been rebuilt and is now inhabited by nuns, who safeguard an icon of the Virgin 'not made by human hands'. **Próti** (Πρώτη), on Pangaíon's west flank, is proud to have been the birthplace of late Greek prime minister and president Konstantínos Karamanlís, and his Neoclassical house stands in the centre.

DRÁMA

The Greeks may have invented theatre, but Dráma (Δράμα) has nothing to do with it; its name comes from *hydrama*, 'full of water'. Located under the south slopes of Mount Falakró ('Mount Baldy', though the locals prefer to call it 'the mountain of flowers'; 2,232m), this lively town was founded sometime around the 6th century AD. It built its fortunes first on rice and cotton, and then most profitably on smoke. A centre of the tobacco trade since the 18th century, it reached its golden age with the completion of the Thessaloníki–Istanbul railway line in 1895. Between 1914 and 1924, the surrounding plains supported 14,000 tobacco growers, who supplied 16 tobacco companies and filled 45 tobacco warehouses. Today it's the perfect base to visit the surrounding region, with its unspoiled natural beauty, unique caves, canyons and forests.

GETTING THERE AND AROUND Trains from Thessaloníki run to Dráma (once daily; 4hrs 15mins; €6.80), but note that the station is 10km out of town. **Buses** from Thessaloníki (2hrs; €15) and Kavála (50mins; €4) arrive at the more central bus station (Vitsi 1; 25210 32421; w kteldramas.gr). For a taxi, call m 69841 32954.

WHERE TO STAY
Town centre
Hydrama Grand Hotel (73 rooms) Ag Varváras 11; 25210 33322; w hydramagrandhotel.gr. This classy 5-star hotel occupies the palatial 19th-century Herman Spierer tobacco warehouse overlooking the Ag Varvára springs. Rooms are contemporary with chestnut-beamed ceiling, king-size bed, & – rare in Greece – loo with heated seat. There's a spa offering thermotherapy, Himalayan salt crystal cave, nano-bubble shower & gym, plus a wine bar with a state-of-the-art wine dispenser, a Scandinavian-inspired all-day coffee bar & an elegant à la carte restaurant (€€€). Charming staff. B/fast inc. €€€
Aya Hotel Agias Varváras 10–12; 25210 33090. Very chic modern décor with mid-century touches. Free parking; b/fast inc. €€€–€€

Kouros [map, page 174] (66 rooms) 3km south on the Kavála road; 25210 57200; w hotelkourosdrama.gr. Built in 2001, hotel with smart contemporary furnishings, a fine restaurant (€€€), enormous pool & free parking. American buffet b/fast inc. €€€–€€

Outside Dráma
Aloni Hotel & Spa [map, page 174] (18 rooms) 32km west in Vólvaka (Βώλακα); 25230 23714; w alonihotel.gr. Charming hotel 26km from the Falakró Ski Centre, with a small spa & excellent restaurant (€€), & a superb Greek b/fast using local products, inc. €€–€

WHERE TO EAT AND DRINK
Entrades Skra 84; 25210 22600; ; noon–17.30 Mon–Sat. Chic woodsy & brick décor; fresh, beautifully presented contemporary cuisine, including excellent seafood. €€€
Ellinikón Gefsipoleíon Ethnikís Amýnis 63; 25210 31389; Ελληνικον γευσιπωλειον; noon–23.00 Wed–Mon. Bright, contemporary

& good value for creative Greek dishes, including lovely salads, steaks, seafood, mushroom dishes & chocolate desserts. €€
Idonas D Gounari 32; 25210 32192; w idonas. gr; 11.00–midnight Wed–Sun. One of Dráma's favourites since 1986 & recently renovated with a garden courtyard. Famous for its succulent meat

dishes, but there are plenty of vegetarian choices, too. €€
Mpes Kai Piés Patriarchóu Dionisóu 3; \25210 34165; ⊕ noon–23.30 Tue–Sun. Lively young *tsipourádiko* with a merrily kitschy décor, serving seafood, skewers, salads, pies & other goodies to go with your glasses of *tsipouró* or local wine. €

SHOPPING Some of Greece's best Anatolian-style cured meats are made by the Sarímpogia family, originally from Cappadocia, and sold at their family-run shop, **Sary** (Kíprou 1; \25210 31533; w sary.gr; ⊕ 09.00–21.00 Mon–Sat). Look for beef, lamb and camel *pasturma*, *kavourmás*, pastrami, delicious cherrywood-smoked sausages with mountain herbs, and smoked turkey with pine nuts and chestnuts.

WHAT TO SEE AND DO Dráma boasts a lovely municipal garden, the **Párko Ag Varvára** (named after the St Barbara springs), with ancient plane trees shading its springs and waterfalls, streams, ponds, fountains and cafés. In the little lanes north of the park, you can find well-preserved **Byzantine walls**. The other main sight is the **Archaeology Museum** (Patriárkou Dionysíou 2; \25210 31365; w odysseus.culture.gr; ⊕ 08.30–15.00 Wed–Mon; €2), which houses prehistoric rhino bones and a giant mammoth tusk from the Aggítis River Cave (see below), and human finds dating back to the Palaeolithic era; there are iron swords from the precursors of the Thracians, and 7th-century BC finds from the Hellenisation of the area, notably from the Sanctuary of Dionysos (page 190), as well as tombstones, ceramics, hoards of coins and old photographs of Dráma.

AROUND DRÁMA
Aggítis River Cave (Σπήλαιο Πηγών Αγγίτη; 20km west of Dráma at Aggítis; \25220 60460; w caveaggitis.gr; ⊕ guided tours: winter 10.30–17.00 daily, spring & autumn to 18.00, summer to 19.00; spring/autumn ring ahead, as the water may be too high; €7) The Aggítis River rises in the depths of Mount Falakró, filled by the sinkholes in the Nevrokópi basin, then runs 25km underground – 12km of which have been explored since the cave's discovery in 1978. The tour, via an artificial entrance, takes you 500m along a causeway, where colourful stalactites, some

---

FESTIVALS AROUND DRÁMA

The villages of Kalí Vrýsi, Monastiráki, Nikísiani and Xiropótamos, near Dráma, are famous for the **Baboúgera** during Epiphany, when local 'goat men' don woolly capes of animal skins, giant horned masks and huge bells to re-enact ancient Dionysiac rites of death and rebirth, with plenty of alcohol, sexual innuendo, fake weddings, and drums and bagpipes to chase away any malingering bad spirits from the new year; they say Alexander the Great used the goat men to scare away the Persian elephant cavalry, and in Kalí Vrýsi they say they were useful in keeping Ottoman officials from taking their boys away as janissaries.

In **Mavrolévki**, the descendants of refugees from Eastern Thrace walk on coals (page 100) on 21 May – Feast Day of Saints Constantine and Eléni – each year.

The **Dráma International Short Film Festival** (w dramafilmfestival.gr), founded in 1978, celebrates new films of less than 35 minutes' running time and is considered one of the best of its kind. It takes place in September, alongside other events.

2m thick, nearly touch the water. The striking mill at the end once pumped out irrigation water for the surrounding tobacco fields.

Sanctuary of Dionysos (2.5km from Kalí Vrýsi (Καλή Βρύση) at Mikrí Toúmba; ⊕ always) Located on a hill, under a wooden shelter are the well-preserved Hellenistic-era walls of a rectangular sanctuary, which was destroyed by the retreating Gauls after their rout by Macedonian king Antigonus in the Battle of Lysimachae (277BC) – forcing them out of Greece and into Europe.

Alistráti (Αλιστράτη; 22km southwest of Dráma) Set on the slopes of Mount Meníkio (1,963m), Alistráti has a handful of traditional houses, deer, llamas and peacocks in its park, and sweeping views over the Dráma plain. But there are two other reasons for visiting: the **Alistráti Cave** (6km south; ✆ 23240 82045; w alistraticave.gr; ⊕ guided tours: Oct–Apr 09.00–17.00 daily, May–Jul & Sep 09.00–18.00 daily, Aug 09.00–19.00 daily; adults €8, students €4, ages 6–12 €3), one of the most beautiful in Greece, discovered in 1975 and a marvel of fantastical stalactite formations, including the finest gravity-defying eccentrics in Greece. The first kilometre of the tour is accessible for wheelchair users.

The second reason is the **Aggítis Canyon**, where it looks as if the very earth were wrenched in two. Its steep walls are decorated here and there with primitive rock etchings dated to the 5th century AD. The river itself is a favourite for rafting, with a 15km course; there's a good view and easy access at **Stathmós Aggístis** (Σταθμός Αγγιστης), with a secret beach and Roman bridge. Just south of the village is the 3rd-century BC **Macedonian Tomb A**, located in a burial mound.

Falakró Ski Centre (Φαλακρό; 46km north of Dráma; m 69733 70209, 69876 03409; ❋ FalakroOfficial; ⊕ Dec–Mar 09.00–16.00 Thu–Sun & hols) Greece's northernmost ski slopes (1,620–2,232m) have Greece's longest snow season and offer 20km of pistes for all abilities, with nine lifts.

Petroússa Gorge (13km northwest of Dráma) On the southwest slopes of Mount Falakró, this spectacularly sheer-sided gorge, stretching north of Petroússa to Pýrgos, resembles a 12km wooded corridor and is passable only in summer when the water levels are low.

Káto Nevrokópi (Κάτω Νευροκόπι; 44km northwest of Dráma) This friendly potato-growing village along the main road from Dráma to Bulgaria is famous as 'The Siberia of Greece', almost inevitably boasting the coldest winter readings (often down to −20°C) on the nightly weather report. There's a little museum, displaying arms, medals, personal belongings, etc in **Fort Lisse** (2km south at Ochyró; ✆ 25230 23822; w lisse.gr; ⊕ 09.00–14.00 Mon–Fri, 10.00–15.00 Sat & Sun, call for tour schedule) on the so-called Metaxas Line, a string of forts built along the Bulgarian border in the 1930s and where the Greek army bravely, if briefly, held back the Germans on 6–7 April 1941.

Elátia (or Karántere) Forest (Ελάτια) Around the highest peaks of the Central Rhodope, between the Bulgarian frontier and the artificial Néstos lakes (one dam, the 172m **Thisavroú**, is the highest in Greece), this 283,280ha forest is the largest spruce forest in Greece, dominated by towering Norwegian spruce and filled with streams and waterfalls. To the east along the Bulgarian border, the 1,972ha **Virgin Forest of Fraktoú** (Parthéno Dásos Fraktoú) is the second largest of Europe's last three primeval forests and has been protected since 1980 as a UNESCO World Heritage Site of Nature. It is home to brown bear and chamois, as well as 120 species of bird, and is a feast of colour in October. Here grow black and Scots pines, beech, European spruce and oaks, some 500 years old; some of the pines are nearly 60m tall.

Adrianí Castle (Αδριανή; 11km east of Dráma, then 4km north up a dirt road) There isn't a whole lot left of this ancient castle, built by Philip II, but the views are worth the drive. Some of the stone was used to build the nearby church of Ag Ioánnis.

Château Nico Lazaridi (◊ 25210 82049; w chateau-lazaridi.com; ⊕ 09.30–15.00 Mon–Fri; €5 tour; tastings, inc tour, priced according to package) Just southeast of Adrianí, the Château Nico Lazaridi is one of the best-known wineries in the area; visits include the estate's Magic Mountain contemporary art gallery.

Párko Arpaktikón – Raptor Park (Agorá (Αγορά); 5km east of Adrianí; m 69346 86917; w arpaktika.gr; ⊕ during the school year 10.00–14.00 Sat & Sun, demonstration at noon; in summer, due to the heat, hours are from 18.00, with a demonstration around 19.30; €5) Falconer Kóstas Eleftheriádis runs this educational park dedicated to raptors of several species.

THE NÉSTOS RIVER AND GORGE

Some of northern Greece's finest scenery lies along the Néstos (Νέστος) River, winding from Bulgaria into Greece for its last 140km and marking the traditional border between Macedonia and Thrace. Once past its artificial lakes, it weaves between Mount Falakró and the Western and Central Rhodope. Much of it belongs to the National Park of East Macedonia-Thrace, and it's one of the top spots in northern Greece for beautiful walks, river sports and birdwatching.

GETTING THERE AND AWAY Frequent buses from Kavála go to Chrysoúpoli and Keramotí en route to Xánthi (w ktelkavalas.gr); from Xánthi (◊ 25410 27200; w ktelxanthis.gr), there are two services daily to Toxótes and to Stavroúpoli.

TOURIST INFORMATION The **Néstos Delta Information Centre** (◊ 25910 51831; w en.fd-nestosvistonis.gr; ⊕ 09.30–15.30 Mon–Fri) is behind the Gymnasium (Middle School) in Keramotí.

WHERE TO STAY AND EAT *Map, page 174*

Kokkymelon Traditional Guesthouse [not mapped] (5 rooms) Toxótes; ◊ 25410 93551; w kokkymelon.gr. Elegant rooms with iron beds in the house of a former tobacco magnate, with shared kitchen & cosy sitting room. B/fast inc. €€

Nemesis (30 rooms) Komniná, south of Stavroúpoli; ◊ 25420 21005; w hotelnemesis. gr. Another unusual hotel with an unforgettable name, this one offers handsome rooms with beds made of stone (more comfortable than they sound), distributed in 8 mini stone castles, as well as a playground & peacocks, ostriches & deer to feed. B/fast inc. €€–€

Nessos (12 rooms) Paranésti; ◊ 25240 21021; w hotelnessos.gr. Not many hotels are named after the centaur with a poisoned shirt that killed Hercules. This one has red boudoir rooms named after Greek deities & has wonderful views over the river valley. B/fast inc. €€–€

Philoxenia (19 rooms) 300m from the centre of Paranésti; ◊ 25240 22001; w philoxeniadrama. gr. Comfortable rooms with mountain views & friendly owners, 3km from the river. B/fast inc. €

6 | EASTERN MACEDONIA (ΑΝΑΤΟΛΙΚΗ ΜΑΚΕΔΟΝΙΑ)

Ta Témpi tou Nestou [not mapped] Galáni, just east of Toxótes; ☎ 25410 93071; ⓕ Tempitounestou; ⏱ 13.00–01.00 Tue–Fri, noon–01.00 Sat & Sun. Good grilled meats & fresh salads, under the trees by the river. €

SPORTS AND ACTIVITIES The Néstos River, its gorge and surrounding woodlands are a wonderland for outdoor activities. Little **Paranésti** (Παρανέστι) is a base for activities on the upper river – for trail runners, it's synonymous with the 162km **Paranésti Virgin Trail** (ⓕ eparanestivft.eparanestivft), one of the most challenging in Greece.

Forestis Paranésti; m 69878 85626; w forestis. gr. Rafting down the Néstos & Arkoudorématos, paragliding, hiking, jeep excursions & more.
Leivaditis m 69870 93730, 69483 63078; w leivaditis.gr. Ioánna Porfilídou & Vasílis Georgiádis offer guided walks here, in the Thracian Meteora (page 215) & to Bulgarian 'ghost villages' & old Soviet-era installations in the Rhodope Mountains. In Jun they do a special week-long trek starting at the Néstos. A bespoke guided walk for a couple starts at €50.

Nestos Plus Zarkádia, Chrysoúpolis; ☎ 25910 24736; m 69781 07717; w nestosplus.gr. Horseriding along the Néstos, rafting & kayaking, mountain biking & hiking.
Riverland Outdoor Activities Bases at Toxótes & Keramotí; ☎ 25410 62488; m 69734 17189; w riverland.gr. Kayaking & rafting down the Néstos, off-road tours, birdwatching & mountain biking, as well as sea kayaking in the delta.
Vistonis Outdoor Activities Toxótes; m 69482 06351; w gonestos.gr. Canoeing, rafting & kayaking down the Néstos.

WHAT TO SEE AND DO Paranésti's **Natural History Museum of Rhodope** (☎ 25243 50100; ⏱ generally open w/ends – call to check; €3) offers a good introduction to the region, with dioramas of the Rhodope's habitat, fossils, stuffed bears, boars and wolves, and exhibits on geology and flora. North of Paranésti, near **Dipótama**, there are several pretty waterfalls along the **Arkoudorématos River** basin, one of the tributaries of the Néstos.

At Paranésti, the Néstos meets the Dráma–Xánthi railway line, laid out here in the 19th century by Ottoman engineers whose main concern was to protect it from coastal bombardments. Defensive considerations are nothing new here: half an hour's drive southeast, from the little village of **Áno Ionikón** (Άνω Ιωνικό), an easy 3.8km path ascends to the marble hilltop **Fortress of Kalýva** (627m) built by Philip II in 340BC to control the Néstos valley. It has a remarkable deep beehive cistern, and a well-preserved (and well-endowed) relief of Priapas to fend off evil on the gate.

The largest Néstos village, **Stavroúpoli** (Σταυρούπολη), has a tiny **Folklore Museum** (☎ 25423 50100; ⏱ by appt) of items collected by local café owner Stávros Karabatzákis (d1995) housed in the old tobacco tax office. It also has a beautifully preserved **Macedonian tomb** (3km southeast, off the Komniná road; ☎ 25410 51003/51783; ⏱ to visit, ring ahead; free) of c200BC, complete with marble couches and traces of its original paint. To the north, via Áno Karyófito (Άνω Καρυόφυτο), you can visit the beautiful 40m **Livadítis waterfall**. Start from the mountain village of **Livadítis** (Λειβαδίτης; 1,250m, population 5) and follow the signs – it's 5.7km, but the last 2.2km is a rough logging road. At the end is a shelter, and a well-signposted good 2km path to the waterfall through the beech woods. The water is cold, but refreshing on a hot day. In winter, it freezes to the delight of death-defying ice climbers.

South of Stavroúpoli begins the ravishing **Néstos Gorge**, the 'Thracian Tempi' where the river coils like a clock spring through the wooded limestone hills. Rare flowers dot the banks; Levant sparrowhawks and lesser spotted eagles hover overhead, while nightingales and Orphean warblers serenade from the trees; wild horses roam the meadows. A raft or kayak makes a fine way to enjoy the gorge, or follow a section of your choice along the E6 Nestos–Rhodope Trail (w topoguide. gr, choose the region Thrace, or download the app), passing the hard-to-find cave of the dryads, or wood nymphs, at **Liverá** (Λιβερά) and end at **Galáni** (Γαλάνι) near **Toxótes** (Τοξότες), where there's a beach – though the water is icy cold, even in August. Or take the riverside path from Galáni to Toxótes, past Liverá's abandoned railway station. If you're driving, the winding road up from Galáni to **Krominikó** (Κρωμνικό) offers some of the most breathtaking views of all.

Downstream, the **Néstos Delta** is a mix of wetlands and rich alluvial plain, where maize, cereals, asparagus, kiwis and rice are grown around the market town of **Chrysoúpoli** (Χρυσούπολη). **Keramotí** (Κεραμωτή) on a sandy peninsula is a low-key resort with excellent beaches, specialising in mussels and ferries to Thássos. Lagoons stretch for 50km east and west of the delta, while along the Néstos itself is the **Kotza Orman** (Turkish for 'Legendary Forest'), the last luxuriant remnant of a vast coastal woodland. From the Nestos Delta Visitors' Information Centre at the eastern edge of Keramotí there is a path into the Kotza Orman. The marshes of the delta are home or way station to some 300 kinds of birds, with flamingos a perennial favourite. This large national park continues into Thrace (page 211).

THÁSSOS

An island crowned with forests and lying in the sea like the backbone of an ass.

Archilochos, 7th century BC

Ringed with soft beaches and mantled with pinewoods, plane trees, walnuts and chestnuts, Thássos (Θάσος) is Greece's northernmost island. Unlike the other Aegean islands, it is rarely afflicted by the wind, but has a moist climate, much subject to lingering mists; on hot days the intense scent of pines by the sea casts a spell of dreamy languor. It's a very touristy place, favoured by British, German and Eastern European visitors, but it's also an island with a history and character, with fascinating relics of the past to explore. Wherever you sleep, come armed: the mosquitoes are vivacious, vicious and voracious. Sea urchins can be a problem too, but they're a sign that the sea here is very, very clean.

HISTORY In mythology, Zeus passed this way after abducting Europa from Crete. Europa wasn't a Cretan, but a Phoenician, daughter of King Agenor of Tyre. Agenor's son, Thasos, came searching for her, and left his name behind on the island. All this is mythology's way of telling us that there was an early Phoenician presence on Thássos, and recent discoveries suggest it was true. The western slopes are dotted with the mines they began, grubbing out the mineral that made Thássos a wealthy and busy place all through antiquity – gold.

Co-existing with the Phoenicians were the native Thracians. These were invaded and colonised c650BC by settlers from Páros. Connoisseurs of superb marble, they also established quarries here. The likeable Parian poet Archilochos was among the invaders, but found himself (or at least the persona he adopted) outmanoeuvred in battle: 'Some Thracian now is pleased with my shield/ which I unwilling left on a bush in perfect condition on our side of the field/ but I escaped death. To hell with the shield!/ I shall get another, no worse.'

The Parians went to great lengths to justify their presence on Thássos, with a legend about their Phoenician allies who had summoned Páros for aid. Then of course there was a command from the Delphic Oracle to found a city 'on the island

6 | EASTERN MACEDONIA (ΑΝΑΤΟΛΙΚΗ ΜΑΚΕΔΟΝΙΑ)

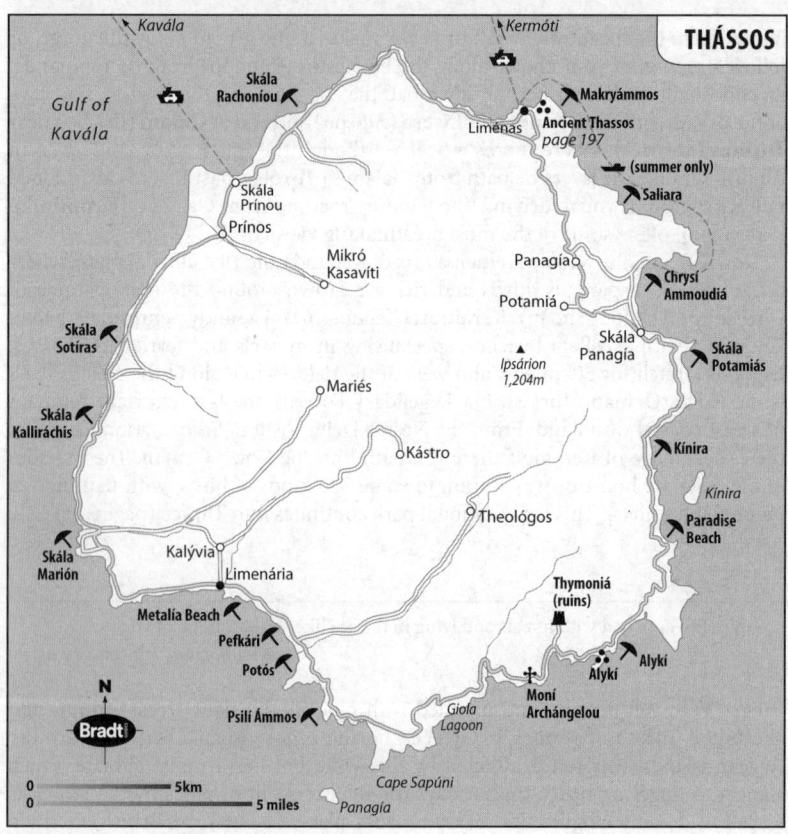

of mists'. It was certainly worth the fuss: every year they extracted 90 talents of gold and silver from the mines on the island and mainland coast, while founding colonies stretching from the Strymónos to the Néstos river deltas; their marble, timber, ships, oil and wine were in demand across the Aegean. Densely populated, the town was dubbed the 'Athens of the north'.

In 490BC, the Persians attacked the island and razed the city walls. When they reappeared a decade later under Xerxes, the defenceless Thassians prevented another attack by inviting them to a fabulous banquet, and with many slaps on the back sent them off to defeat at Salamis. Thássos revolted against the Delian League, when an increasingly imperialist Athens demanded huge chunks of its profits. In 463BC Athens sent Kimon to teach it a lesson, and after a three-year siege Thássos fell; the island would pass from Athenian rule to Spartan, and back again, twice in the course of the Peloponnesian War. In that troubled era the island produced another poet, Hegemon, who invented parody by twisting the words of well-known pieces in his plays. Audiences loved it, though Aristotle later complained that, while Homer made men appear better than they are, Hegemon made them seem worse.

In 340BC Philip II seized the island while gobbling up the rest of the mainland. In 197BC the Romans defeated the Macedonians and Thássos gladly became part of Rome, enjoying special privileges and a new period of prosperity. Thássos remained a Byzantine possession well into the Middle Ages. Among the uninvited guests in later years, the Genoese ruled briefly from 1307 and again from 1434, until the Turks chased them out in 1456. Russia occupied the island from 1770 to 1774. In 1813 the Sultan gave the island to Muhammad Ali (page 182), who had been brought up in the village of Theológos and loved Thássos; he lowered taxes and gave the island virtual autonomy. Egyptian rule lasted until 1902, when the Turks returned briefly before union with Greece during the Balkan Wars, in 1912. A last, bizarre occupation came in 1941, when the Bulgarians closed all the Greek schools, but hadn't the strength to keep Thássos from becoming a major resistance centre. Communist guerrillas kept up the fight after the war and were not put down until 1950.

GETTING THERE AND AROUND Frequent ferries operate between Kavála and Skála Prínou (75mins) and between Keramotí and Liménas (35mins; page 193). The island has a good **bus** network (25930 22162; w go-thassos.gr); from Liménas quay there are at least ten daily to Prínos, Skála Potamiás and Limenária, and six to Theológos, plus connections all round the island.

LIMÉNAS (Λιμενας) The bustling, unabashedly tourist-orientated island capital is officially Thássos Town, but it is better known as Liménas. It may not be pretty – especially the new port area – but it's lively; plane trees shade the squares, shops will sell you walnut sweets and honey, and the town beach, once relatively poor on this island of sandy beaches, has been improved with tonnes of new sand. Still, the town's inhabitants (many of whom came over from Türkiye in 1923) can hardly begin to fill the shoes of the once-great and wealthy city of Ancient Thassos, which was abandoned from the Middle Ages till the mid 19th century. Bits of it crop up everywhere.

Where to stay
Makryámmos Bungalows (206 rooms) On the beach of the same name; 25930 22101; w makryammos-hotel.gr; ☼ May–Oct. Recently renovated 4-star bungalows & 8 luxurious seafront suites on a beautiful beach, with several bars, watersports, tennis, a pool, a small deer park & a good restaurant. Good choice for families. Excellent buffet b/fast & dinner inc. €€€€€

A for Art (39 rooms) 18is Oktovríou; 25930 58405; w aforarthotel.gr. Fun, arty, quirky design hotel 70m from the port in a tobacco warehouse of 1907, with a very professional staff, pleasant outdoor pool & garden; plus an excellent range of cocktails in the bar with an antique piano & charming à la carte Lost Sheep restaurant (€€€) featuring stylish Mediterranean cuisine under a giant pine. B/fast inc. €€€–€€

Tarsanas (15 rooms) 1km west of the centre; 25930 23933; w tarsanas.gr. Studios & bungalows for 2–4, directly on the beach. Contemporary design with a pretty garden, beach bar & seafood taverna (€€). Popular with young couples. €€€–€€

Akti Vournelis (19 rooms) On the beach on the Prínos road; 25930 22901; m 69469 05995; w hotel-vournelis.gr. Basic but comfortable rooms, some with kitchenette & balcony. There's a nice pool, & the bar nearby has live Greek music in the evenings. €€

Laios (33 rooms) 18is Oktovríou 63, between the new port & town; 25930 22309; w laioshotel.gr. Unpretentious, spic-&-span rooms with AC & a pool; quiet, but in walking distance of the action. Has a small beach across the road. €€

Pegasus (33 rooms) Dimitriádou 12; 25930 22061; w thassos-pegasus.com. Within walking distance of everything, pleasant family-run hotel that works hard to please, with bright, colourful rooms, a restaurant, garden & pool with bar, & a fitness room. They have a minibus to take you to nearby beaches. Good b/fast extra. No children under 12. €€

Where to eat and drink
Mouses 18is Oktovríou, out towards the new port; 25930 23697; ☼ noon–midnight daily. Reliably good food – tasty mussels, *saganáki* & other seafood; beef & lamb casserole dishes. Live music some nights. €€

Simi Pétrou Axióti St, on the port; 25930 22517; ⊕ 13.00–23.00 daily. For over 60 years a good spot for seafood & seafood pasta, *souvlaki* & grilled chops. Vegetarian choices too, with their home-grown vegetables. €€

Tavernaki Polígnoto Vagí 7, in the centre; 25930 23181; ⊕ noon– 23.30 daily. Typical tavern food, though the cooking is a bit finer than most of the others. Nice outside tables on a pedestrian street. €€–€

What to see and do

Archaeological Museum (Megálou Alexándrou; 25930 22180; ⊕ Nov–Mar 08.30–15.30 Wed–Mon, Apr–May to 18.00, Jun–Oct to 20.00; €4, concessions €2) The museum stands on the site of Ancient Thassos's marketplace. Finds here hint at the wealth of the ancient city-state: there's a 7th-century BC plate showing Bellerophon on Pegasus slaying the Chimera; a 6th-century BC Kriophoros (a kouros, or young man, bearing a ram ready for sacrifice) over 11ft high, but left unfinished when the sculptor discovered a flaw in the marble by the ear; an Archaic relief (550BC) of a hunting scene and a beautiful ivory lion's head from the same period; a lovely, effeminate head of Dionysos from the 4th century BC; an elegant Hellenistic Aphrodite riding a dolphin; and Roman busts, including a fine one of Hadrian and another of Alexander the Great.

Ancient Thassos The ancient Parians built their most important buildings on the heights above the port. Exploring what remains makes a good half-day's hike, most of it in open countryside. The ruins are scanty on the whole, but it's still a fascinating walk amid some lovely landscapes and views. Across from the Archaeological Museum, the **Agora**, rebuilt as a colonnaded square under the Romans, is the most prominent survivor, with foundations and columns of porticoes and stoas, sanctuaries and a massive altar. A **heröon** in the centre of the Agora honoured the astonishing mid-5th-century BC athlete Theogenes, who won 1,400 victories in his career.

The mysterious paved '**Passage of Theoria**' (hard to make out), pre-dating the rest of the Agora by 500 years, leads back across Iraklíou Street to the sparse remains of the **Artemision**, the Temple of Artemis, where some of the most precious votive offerings in the museum were found. On the south side of the Agora are a Roman street, an exedra and a few tiers of the **Odeion** – a picturesque ruin, mostly still hidden under the lane. Further along are the foundations of a **Sanctuary of Heracles** and, towards the sea, the remains of an early Christian **basilica**, made of recycled ancient stones.

North of the Agora Beyond the Artemision, towards the ancient naval port, another group of ruins includes the **Sanctuary of Dionysos**, with its 3rd-century BC choreographic monument, erected by the winner of a drama prize. Beyond that is the **Sanctuary of Poseidon**, with two altars on its terrace; next to it, another altar remains in good enough condition to accept sacrifices to its divinity, Hera Epilimenia, guardian of ports. Remains of the naval gates with bas-reliefs survive in the open space towards the port: the scant remains of the **Chariot Gate** (with Artemis in a chariot) and the **Gate of Semel-Thyone** (with Hermes and the Graces, or Charities), facing Pétrou Axióti Street. This continues north, overlooking a small church set in the ruins of the ancient Thesmorphorion, sacred to Demeter.

Acropolis From the Sanctuary of Dionysos, a path from the end of Iraklíou leads eastwards to the beginning of the city's **walls**, last rebuilt in 411BC but repaired by the Genoese. Just inside the walls is the charming, well-preserved 5th-century BC

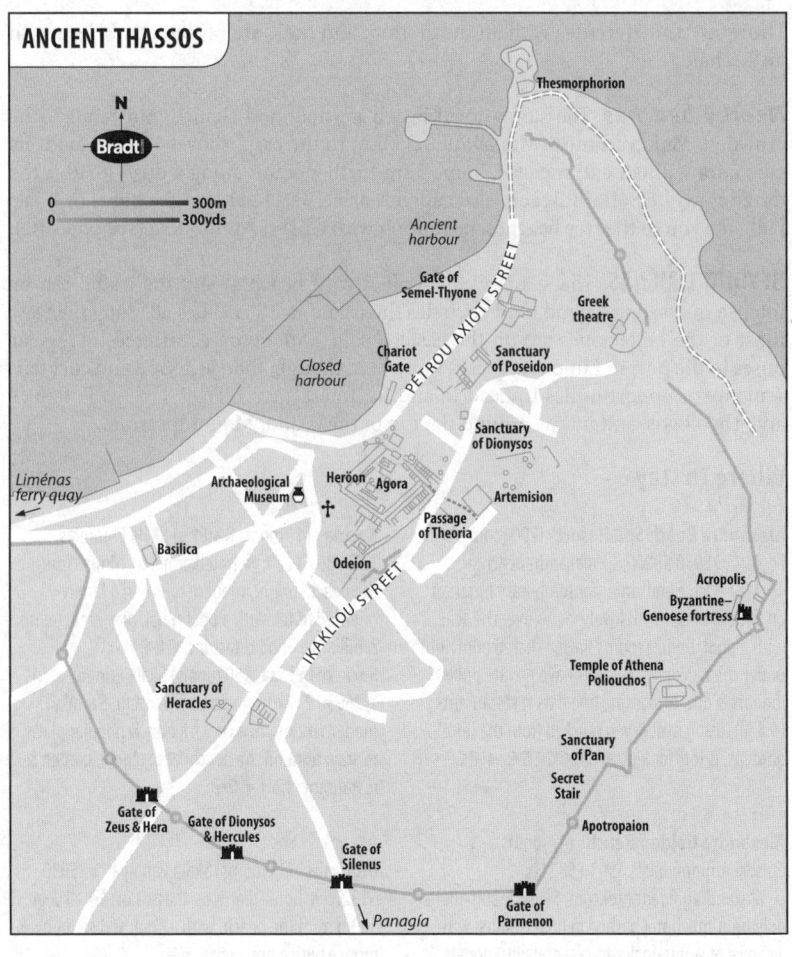

Greek theatre, affording a fine view over the pines and sea. Above, the acropolis is spread across three summits of a ridge, running north to south just inside the walls. On the first stands a Byzantine and Genoese **fortress** built out of the temple of Pythian Apollo, whose oracle had supposedly encouraged the Parians to colonise the island; note the relief of a funerary feast (4th century BC) by the guardroom. The second hill has the foundations of a 5th-century BC **Temple of Athena Poliouchos**, while the third and highest summit was a **Sanctuary of Pan**, with an eroded relief of Pan piping to his goats.

Around the back of the sanctuary, the vertiginous **Secret Stair**, carved in the 6th century BC, descends precipitously down to the remaining walls and gates (be careful if you attempt it: the stair-rail is rusted and there are big gaps between the steps). Here you'll find the watchful stone eyes of the Apotropaion (to protect the walls from the Evil Eye), the well-preserved **Gate of Parmenon**, still bearing its inscription 'Parmenon made me', and, best of all, the large **Gate of Silenus** (by the intersection of the road to Panagía), though a vigorous bas-relief of the phallic god (6th century BC) has lost its most prominent appendage to a 'moral cleansing' in the 20th century. Continuing back towards town are, respectively, the **Gate of**

Dionysos and Hercules with an inscription, and the **Gate of Zeus and Hera** with an Archaic relief.

Nearby beaches The sandy town beach is small and shaded, but tends to be crowded. **Makryámmos** (Μακρύαμμος), 3km to the east, is lovely, and defends its chic aura with an entrance fee. Some 5km further south along a dusty road is the dazzling white **Saliara Beach**, also called Marble Beach. Otherwise buses or boats will take you to the free beaches, beginning with Chrysí Ammoudiá (see opposite).

BEYOND LIMÉNAS Thássos is well supplied with beaches, and the traffic can be intense in season. A good road encircles the island, with beaches all along the way; most of the better ones are on the eastern side, and all are connected by regular buses to the port in Liménas. There's more to it, though, than just sand and cocktails – plenty of opportunities to head inland for interesting villages such as Potamiás and Theológos, and hiking around the top of the island, Mount Ipsárion.

 Where to stay

Luxury

Alexandra Beach Spa Resort (200 rooms) Potós; 25930 58000; w alexandrabeach.gr; ⊕ May–Oct. Handsome, contemporary hotel set on a rocky beach with lovely views over the sea, with a pool. Deluxe rooms have a shared pool right under the balconies, & suites have private pools indoors & out. Also a spa, fine bars & restaurants (€€€), using fruit & veg plucked from the hotel gardens, & lots for kids to do. €€€€€–€€€

Very expensive

Alexandra Golden Beach (47 rooms) Chryssí Ammoudiá; 25930 58212; w alexandragoldenhotel.com. Swish 5-star adults-only boutique hotel bathed in bold colours, with a choice of suites, including several with private pool; plus 2 swirly large pools & built-in jacuzzis, romantic loungers, spa & gourmet restaurant (€€€). Top-class service; transfers available from Kavála Airport or Liménas. €€€€€–€€€
Atrium (44 rooms) On the beach at the south end of Potós; 25930 53300; w atriumthassos.gr. Revamped & under new management. Elegant family rooms & suites for up to 6 people. Sauna & gym, restaurant (€€€), pool & garden. €€€€–€€€
Grand Beach (17 rooms) Limenária, on the beach west of the centre; m 69426 22914; w grand-beach-hotel.gr. Contemporary styled, rose-tinted rooms & studios, & apartments with balcony overlooking the beach; pool & restaurant (€€). Good for families, but books up early. €€€€–€€€

Expensive

Korina (41 rooms & suites) Skála Potamiás; 25930 61200; w hotelkorina.gr. 10mins from the beach; bright, modern rooms in a family-oriented hotel, with a pool & bar, play area, tennis & billiards. Good b/fast inc. €€€
Socrates Plaza (50 rooms) Skála Prínou; 25930 71770; w socrates-plaza.gr. Swanky modern rooms, in a very friendly & popular place to stay; right on the beach, with a pool, garden & restaurant (€€). €€€

Moderate

Dionysos (33 rooms) Skála Panagía; 25930 61822; w hotel-dionysos-thassos.gr; ⊕ all year. 100m from the beach, with a pool; stylish rooms & terrace with a great view. €€
Piatsa Michalis (18 rooms) Potós; 25930 52109; w piatsamichalis.gr. A variety of rooms & suites for up to 4 people, some with sea view, with one of the best restaurants on Thássos (see opposite); HB available. They also offer fishing trips & wine tastings. €€
Thássos (50 rooms) Pefkári; 25930 51596; w hotel-thassos.gr. 50m from the beach, basic but comfortable rooms & studios with balcony, sleeping up to 4. Pool, tennis court & watersports, & a restaurant (€) with traditional clay oven for pizzas. €€
Thalassies (25 rooms) Limenária Beach; 25930 52120; w thalassies-hotel.gr. Small, classy & welcoming beach hotel, recently renovated, fitness room, sauna & jacuzzi, billiards, pool, children's pool & games, plus a good restaurant. €€–€

Budget

Thássos Inn (15 rooms) Panagía; ☏ 25930 61612; w thassosinn.gr; ⊕ all year. Charming old family-run place to relax in the village centre. 3km from Golden Beach. Balconies with views. Café. €€–€

Hermes Hotel (16 rooms) Panagía; ☏ 25930 61220; w sotirelis.gr; ⊕ Apr–Oct. Basic rooms run by the Sotirelis family, who also make olive oil & run the last working watermill in Greece. Although they no longer make oil there, they will show you round. €

Lysistrata (12 bungalows) Potós; ☏ 25930 51678; w lysistrata.gr. Bungalows with kitchenette & patio in a delightful garden setting right on the beach, with bar. Room service available. €

✘ Where to eat and drink

Dionisos In the pedestrian zone of Limenária; ☏ 25930 51001; ⨍; ⊕ 11.00–midnight daily. One of the oldest tavernas on the island, famous for its *stifádo* & fish soup. Frequent live music. €€

Piatsa Michalis Potós; m 69455 43363; w piatsamichalis.gr; ⊕ 09.00–midnight daily in season. Great seafood platters, grills, stuffed calamari, risottos & salads, on a lovely vine-shaded terrace. Try their homemade *tsípouro*. Live music some nights. €€

Sta Kala Kathoymena Kínira; ☏ 25930 41289; ⊕ noon–23.00 daily. Lovely views, atmosphere & better-than-average taverna cuisine with tasty vegetable dishes, popular with the locals. €€

Fedra Chryssí Ammoudiá; ☏ 25930 61900; w fedra-restaurant.gr; ⊕ 09.00–23.00 daily in season. Lovely fresh fish, pasta dishes & light lunches. Open for b/fast. €

Krambousa Skála Potamiás; ☏ 25930 62190; w krambousa-taverna.gr; ⊕ 11.00–midnight daily in season. On a seaside terrace, excellent seafood & pasta, & mixed grills. One of the better places on the island. €

Stelios Theológos; ☏ 25930 31451; ⊕ noon–23.00 daily in season. With a cool, shady terrace, famous for spit-roasted lamb & kid raised on the family farm. €

Panagía (Παναγία) Directly south of Liménas, the road ascends 300m to charming Panagía, which is always a few degrees cooler than the coast. Its old whitewashed Macedonian houses, decorated with carved wood and slate roofs, overlook the sea, with their high-walled gardens watered by a network of mountain streams, some flowing directly under their ground floors; the church of Panagía has an underground spring. Down by the sea, 5 minutes by car, is the lovely, long town beach, **Chryssí Ammoudiá** (Χρυσή Αμμουδιά), or '**Golden Beach**' as it is commonly known.

Potamiá (Ποταμιά) South of Panagía, this is another large, well-watered mountain village with two museums. The **Polýgnotos Vagís Museum** (☏ 25930 61400; ⊕ in season 10.00–13.00 & 18.00–20.00 Tue–Sat, 10.00–13.00 Sun), dedicated to the locally born sculptor (d1965), who made it big in New York and is known for expressive portrait busts and paintings on traditional Greek themes. Down on the coast at **Skála Potamiás** (Σκάλα Ποταμιάς) – a friendly, laid-back resort lined with tavernas and rooms and a beach that some consider the best on the island – the small but interesting **Folklore Museum** (⊕ May–Sep 19.00–23.00 daily; free) is housed in an old stone building where boats used to be stored in winter; there are old photos and paintings of the locals, folk art and crafts, including an old working handloom and some of the island's stylish textiles, and a few more works of Polýgnotos Vagís. The museum holds dance classes and occasionally puts on concerts and folk dance shows.

Mount Ipsárion (Υψάριο) The highest point on Thássos, Mount Ipsárion (1,204m) is a solid block of white and greenish marble which provided the raw material for the ancient city. Today it is a popular excursion for the great views. There are two ways to reach the summit: for hikers, a marked, somewhat difficult path of a little over 10km from Potamiá, taking about 7–9 hours there and back. If you have a vehicle with good clearance, the other way is from the village of Mariés (see opposite), where a rough, 11km road leads to a viewpoint within 2km of the top.

East and south coasts Underneath Mount Ipsárion is **Skála Potamiás**. To the south, quiet **Kínira** (Κοίνυρα) has a small shingly beach closed off by an islet of the same name; only a kilometre further south are the white sands and shallow waters and taverna of **Paradise Beach**, folded in the pine-clad hills. As with most of the beaches on this coast, the water is shallow and safe for children. The northern edge is dedicated to naturists.

Continuing around the island, the little slate-roofed hamlet of **Alykí** (Αλυκή) is beautifully set on a tiny headland overlooking very popular twin beaches. Alykí was an ancient town that thrived on marble exports, and ruins are strewn around the northern beach and above it, including remains of an Archaic Doric double sanctuary dedicated to Apollo (the kouros statue discovered here is in the archaeology museum in Istanbul), and a pair of early Christian basilicas at the top of the headland, with the ancient marble quarries, partially submerged and beautiful, beneath. As an archaeological area it has been spared development beyond a few tavernas; there's a car park at the top. The remains of an ancient tower in cut stone stand nearby at **Thymonia** (Θυμωνιά; follow the signs).

Further along, **Moní Archángelou**, with its slate roof, is perched high over the sea on arid chromatic cliffs. Its nuns are in charge of a bit of nail from the Crucifixion, and the pretty courtyard and church are open to visitors (proper attire, even long sleeves, required – paradoxically, the pebble beach nestling in the cliffs below is frequented by naturists). West of the monastery and reached partly by dirt road is one of the most photographed spots of the island, the dramatic **Gióla Lagoon**, a natural pool of sea water surrounded by a high shelf of smooth rock.

Continuing clockwise, much of Thássos's resort hotel development has happened above the excellent sandy beaches of **Psilí Ámmos** (Ψιλή Άμμος), **Potós** (Ποτός) and **Pefkári** (Πευκάρι), with plenty of olive groves in between. Potós is a noisy, crowded place, but a good base for exploring inland; a handful of buses each day make the 10km trip up to the traditional slate-roofed village of **Theológos** (Θεολόγος), one of Thássos's greenest spots and the capital of the island until the 19th century, defended by a ruined Genoese castle, the **Kourókastro**. The church of Ag Dimítrios has 12th-century icons, and there's a **Folklore Museum** (\ 25930 31307; ⊕ summer 10.00–22.00 daily; €2) in a handsome old mansion with furnishings and items from the days when owning a mule was the status equivalent of owning a Mercedes. On the eastern outskirts of the village are the **Kefalógourna Waterfalls**, fed by a mountain spring – a fine spot for a cold dip in the shade. Use great caution, especially with children; there are no stairs, and the pools are quite steep-sided and deep.

Limenária (Λιμενάρια) With a population of about 3,000, Limenária is the island's second town, and draws a fair crowd of holiday-makers. It has a bit more village atmosphere than Liménas, surrounded by trees and a huge stretch of shady beach. In 1903 the German Speidel Company mined the ores in the vicinity – ruins of its plant are just south of the town, while the company's office, locally called the Palatáki, 'Little Palace', abandoned since 1963, stands alone and forlorn in a garden on the headland. Just east of town, near the old smelting works, is lovely sheltered **Metalía** (Μεταλλεία) **Beach** with fine sands, a taverna and an arty labyrinth in stone. From Limenária, excursion boats circle the coast of Mount Athos (page 119) – or you can hire a boat for a swim off Panagía islet. **Kalývia** (Καλύβια) just inland has reliefs embedded in the wall of its church, while 15km further up the road there's **Kástro** (Κάστρο), high on a sheer precipice, the refuge of the Limenarians in the days of piracy. Although abandoned in the 19th century, most of its old houses have been restored in the last decade as holiday homes, and there are a couple of summer tavernas.

West coast The flatter west coast of Thássos is farm country, lined with beaches that are generally less crowded – although they look good from a distance, they tend to be stonier. The somewhat ramshackle little port of **Skála Marión** (Σκάλα Μαριών) serves **Mariés** (Μαριές) proper, 10km inland, perhaps the least changed of the island's traditional villages. Just along the road, a sign points the way to the remains of an Archaic-era pottery workshop. **Skála Kallirráchis** (Σκάλα Καλλιράχης) and **Skála Sotíras** (Σκάλα Σωτήρος) have rocky beaches, while **Skála Prínou** (Σκάλα Πρίνου), the ferry port to Kavála with its workaday shipyards, nevertheless has some beaches in its environs, with fancy new hotels.

Inland from here is **Prínos** (Πρίνος), beyond which lies the small village of **Mikró Kasavíti** (Μικρό Καζαβήτι), in a lovely setting with beehives and charming old houses, many of which have been renovated. The last beach, at 11.55 if Thássos were a clock, is **Skála Rachoníou** (Σκάλα Ραχωνίνου), a peaceful low-key resort. An islet off the north coast, **Thassopoúla**, is pretty and wooded but, according to the locals, full of snakes.

7

Thrace (Θράκη)

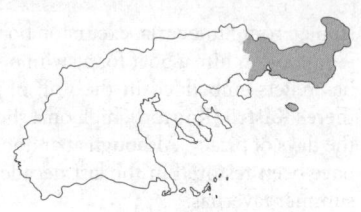

The soul of mystical Thrace is the frontier, the two-fold border of life and place, what you must safeguard but also overcome to meet the other and walk together without getting lost.

    Á Giannakídou, Founder and President of the Ethnological Museum of Thrace

Greece's least-known region, Thrace, or Thráki (Θράκη), is also one of its most fascinating. Anyone who has dabbled in the Classics will recognise Samothráki (Samothrace) and Abdera, birthplace of Democritus. Inveterate starers at maps may also recognise Xánthi, Komotiní and Alexandroúpolis. Naturalists know it for its wetlands, rivers and forests; they say as many different species of flora and fauna have been spotted between its borders – the Néstos and Évros rivers, the Rhodope mountain range and the Aegean Sea – as between Sweden and Italy. Depopulation after the brutal 20th-century wars has seen large swathes return to nature.

Greek Thrace encompasses only 12% of the historical land that stretched from the Bosporus into much of southeast Bulgaria. Now part of the region of Eastern Macedonia and Thrace (for much of its history, see page 13), it was exempted from the population exchange in the 1923 Treaty of Lausanne, on the understanding that Muslims could remain in Western Thrace while Greek Christians could remain in Istanbul. Ever since then, Thrace has been on the front lines of the on-and-off relationship between Athens and Ankara, which was good after World War II until the mid 1950s when the quarrel over Cyprus divided the two, leading to the pogrom against Greeks in Istanbul in 1955 and Athens retaliating by ruling that any non-ethnic Greek who left Greece forfeited their right to citizenship.

Muslim communities felt ghettoised and neglected – something later Greek governments have regretted. Another complicating factor is Thrace's mix of Muslim ethnicities: besides ethnic Turks, there are Slavic Pomaks and Roma. In accordance with the Treaty of Lausanne, Athens refers to them all as 'Greek Muslims' or the 'Muslim minority', the only officially recognised one in Greece. Although once-fraught Cold War relations with Bulgaria have vastly improved, especially since Bulgaria joined the EU, there have been issues with the current government in Ankara which has been actively promoting ethnic solidarity with 'Turkish Muslims', as the Erdogan government calls them, providing economic assistance through the Turkish consulate. The botched coup attempt against Erdogan in 2016 didn't improve relations, nor did the issue of Turkish servicemen (considered 'coup-plotters' by Erdogan) who were granted political asylum in Greece.

Today Muslims are the majority in Rodópi prefecture (55% of the population), with 42% in Xánthi, but just over 6% in Évros (Alexandroúpolis), where many of the Greek refugees ended up after 1923. There have been disputes over the appointment of muftis (Islamic jurists), the upkeep of mosques, and Sharia law;

THRACE (ΘΡΑΚΗ)

THRACE'S MYSTIC THREAD

Whereas the ancient Greeks anthropomorphised their gods, the Thracians wanted to become them. Warriors identified with the 'Hero-rider', lord of the Sun and the Underworld, who appears on funerary steles across northern Greece. The Thracian Great Gods, the Cabeiri, 'Earth and Sky', offered a mystic communion with divinity on Samothráki (page 227) which attracted initiates from across the Greek world. Most Greeks, however, drew the line at the most fundamental of all Thracian beliefs: that they were immortal and after death would go to paradise with their god-prophet Zalmoxis.

Yet the idea of achieving divinity in this life, for a moment if not for eternity, came to Greece in that most revolutionary of all Thracian religious imports, Dionysos, the god of wine, and secondly by following the teachings of another Thracian, Orpheus. During his orgiastic rites, Dionysos' followers, most famously the Maenads, were intoxicated with an enthusiasm that made them one with the god, capable of inhuman tenderness or inhuman cruelty, nursing wild fawns at their breasts or sinking their teeth into their raw flesh. Their rite of Omophagia, the eating of raw flesh, was a primitive version of communion with the godhead. Several myths attest to the arrival of Dionysos' cult in Greece, warning, too, of the terrifying consequences of denying his power. The 'rational' Greeks did their best to tame him. The idea of impersonating the god led to the impersonations of the stage and invention of theatre, the god as 'art'.

On the religious side, poet/prophet/shaman/religious reformer Orpheus invented the 'Mysteries of Dionysos', in which spiritual ecstasy was achieved, not through drunkenness, but by Apolline purification, symbolised by his music; in early Greek art, he plays his lyre not to tame wild beasts but to enchant uncouth Thracian tribesmen. But like Huckleberry Finn, something in the nature of Dionysos refused to be 'civilised', and Orpheus was a martyr to his own reforms; Maenads on Mount Pangaíon (or others say the women of Piería) tore him to pieces after he shunned their advances (page 186). He became the patron of the Orphics, who in their 'secret *logoi*' codified rules of living with the goal of attaining divine rapture in this life as well as the next. By Classical times, Orphism existed alongside Dionysian revels, sometimes in competition, sometimes intertwined, both subtly undermining the resolutely non-mystic pile that was Olympus.

References to the lost 'secret *logoi*' survive in Euripides and Plato (who were steeped in Orphism) and in the golden Orphic inscriptions discovered in southern Italy, and in the recently translated Dervéni papyrus (page 94). The early Church identified Christ with Orpheus, and since then Orphism has led to some surprising destinations, not least Renaissance Florence when Orphic 'natural magic' was revived by Marsilio Ficino, who translated Plato for the Medici and inspired the allegorical paintings of Sandro Botticelli. But such magic is a fragile thing, as Jane Ellen Harrison wrote in her 1908 classic, *Prolegomena*:

> The religion of Orpheus is religious in the sense that it is the worship of the real mysteries of life, of potencies rather than personal gods; it is the worship of life itself in its supreme mysteries of ecstasy and love. It is these real gods, this life itself, that the Greeks, like most men, were inwardly afraid to recognise and face, afraid even to worship. Now and again a philosopher or a poet, in the very spirit of Orpheus, proclaims these true gods, and asks in wonder why to their shrines is brought no sacrifice.

7 | THRACE (ΘΡΑΚΗ)

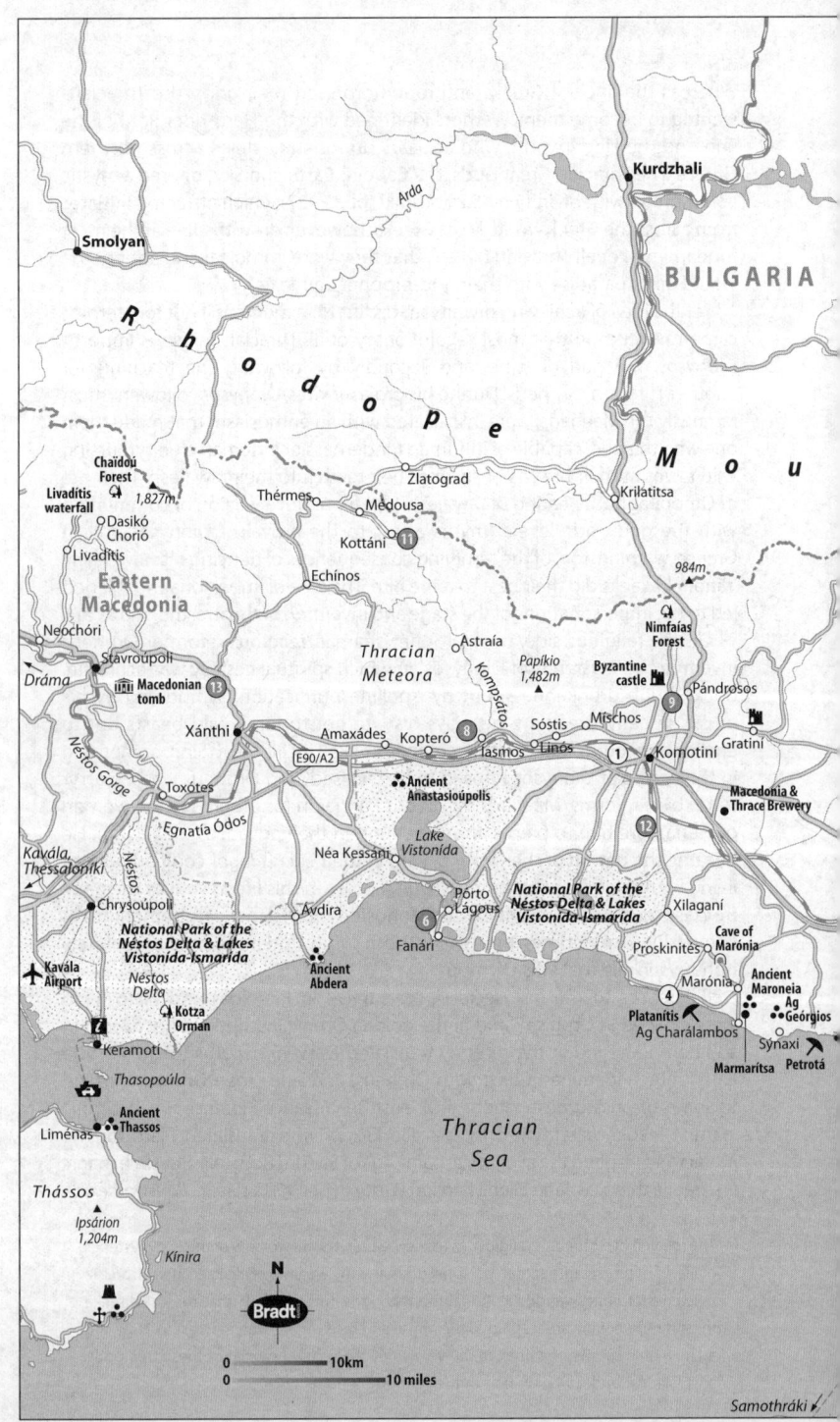

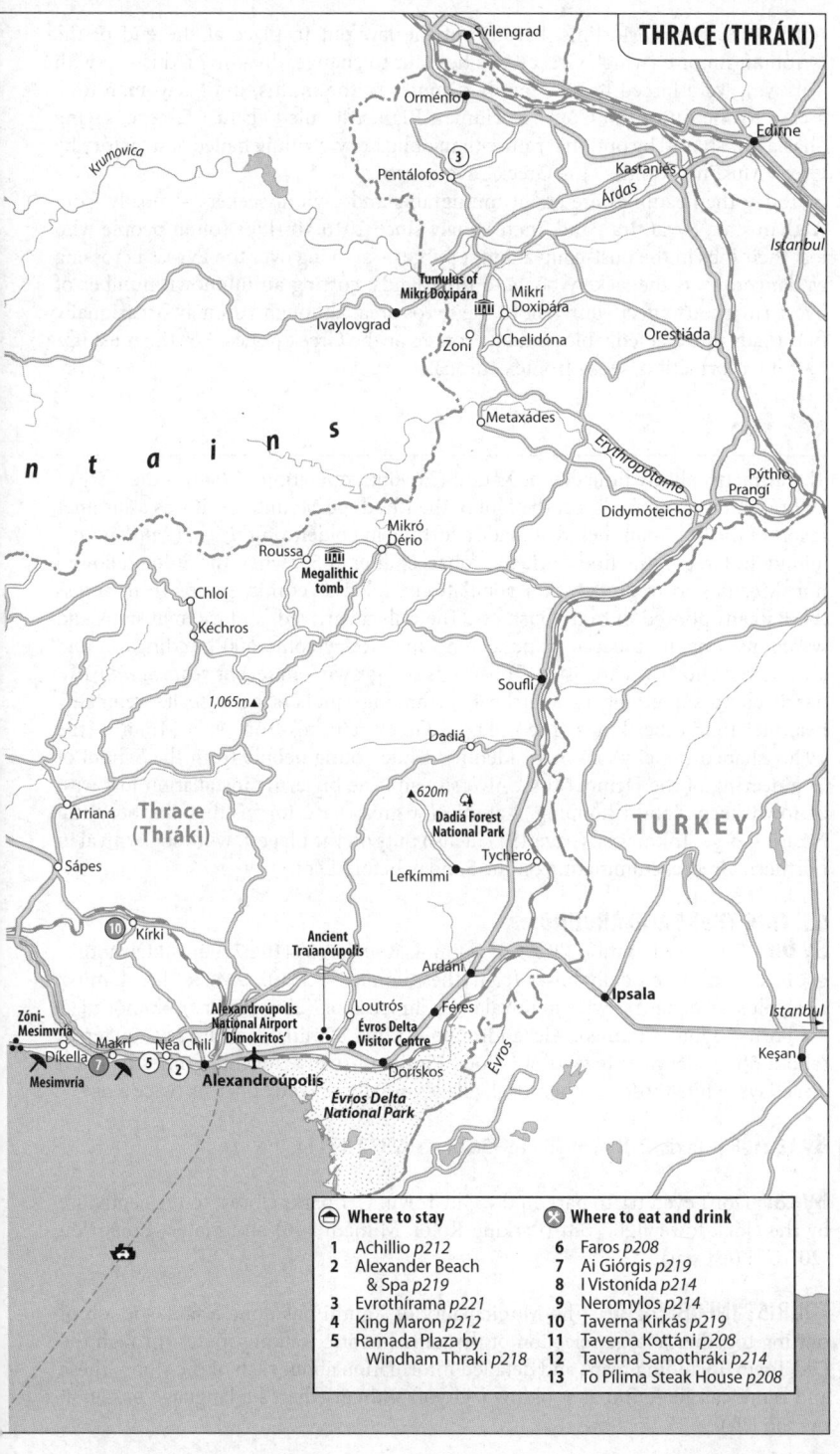

until 2018, Greek Muslims, because of the law put in place at the end of the Ottoman Empire (which Greece was hesitant to change, dreading a dust-up with Türkiye), were forced to take family disputes to the muftis, until a woman took a case to the European Court of Human Rights. It ruled against Greece, saying Sharia law should be optional rather than obligatory, a ruling hailed as a victory by Greek Muslims – and by the Greek government.

Today the headlines are about immigrants and asylum-seekers – mostly from Afghanistan, Syria, Iraq and, increasingly since 2016, Türkiye (often people who lost their jobs in the post-coup attempt purge) – arriving over the Évros, a crossing as dangerous as the rickety boats to the islands, costing an unknown number of lives. This won't affect your visit to the Évros area, although you may occasionally find roads unexpectedly blocked by Frontex or the Greek police. For the most up-to-date information, see w frontex.europa.eu.

XÁNTHI

The attractive, lively little city of Xánthi (Ξάνθη; population 65,000) – the 'City of a Thousand Colours' – lies at the foot of the Rhodope Mountains. It was a summer resort of the Ottomans before it made a fortune in golden *xanthíyaka* (*xanthós* as in 'blond' in Greek), the finest oriental tobacco; after 1859, when the Sultan allowed non-Muslims to trade, Xánthi's population tripled as ethnic groups from across the Balkans poured in to do business. The railway arrived, and the mansions and warehouses of the tobacco princes went up – today some 600 buildings in and around the Old Town are listed. Tobacco is still grown – in recent years *xanthíyaka* has become something of a niche item among smokers because it's reputedly healthier than other kinds. The influx of Greek refugees from Asia Minor in the 1920s shaped the city's culinary identity, while young people from the School of Engineering of the Democritus University and the big army installation just west of town keep Xánthi hopping. Xánthi is a great base for visiting the beautiful Néstos Gorge, 13km west (page 191). It also puts on the biggest, wildest Carnival in northern Greece, culminating on the Sunday before Lent.

GETTING THERE AND AROUND
By bus The KTEL station [207 C4] (Dimokrítou 6; \ 25410 27200; w ktelxanthis. gr) has six or seven daily buses from Thessaloníki (\ 23105 95423; 2hrs 45mins; €21), plus a frequent service to Kavála via Chrysoúpoli (2hrs 10mins), Komotiní (1 via Pórto Lágous; 70mins), Alexandroúpolis (2hrs 30mins), and Fridays to Sérres (about 3hrs). Services to Ávdira (about 45mins) usually run three times daily on weekdays, while those to other local villages are usually only once or twice a day.

By taxi For taxis, call m 69559 69936 or m 69872 89444.

By car Don't even try to park in the Old Town! Car parks closest to the centre are by the clock tower [207 B3] (Parking Roloi, Miltiádi 4–6) and Plateía Emporíou [207 C2] (exc Sat).

TOURIST INFORMATION The Municipality of Xánthi has done a fantastic job of putting together a large selection of thematic historic walking routes through the Old Town, including maps and detailed information about each of the stops. These and more can be found at w oldtown.cityofxanthi.gr (there's a language button at the top left).

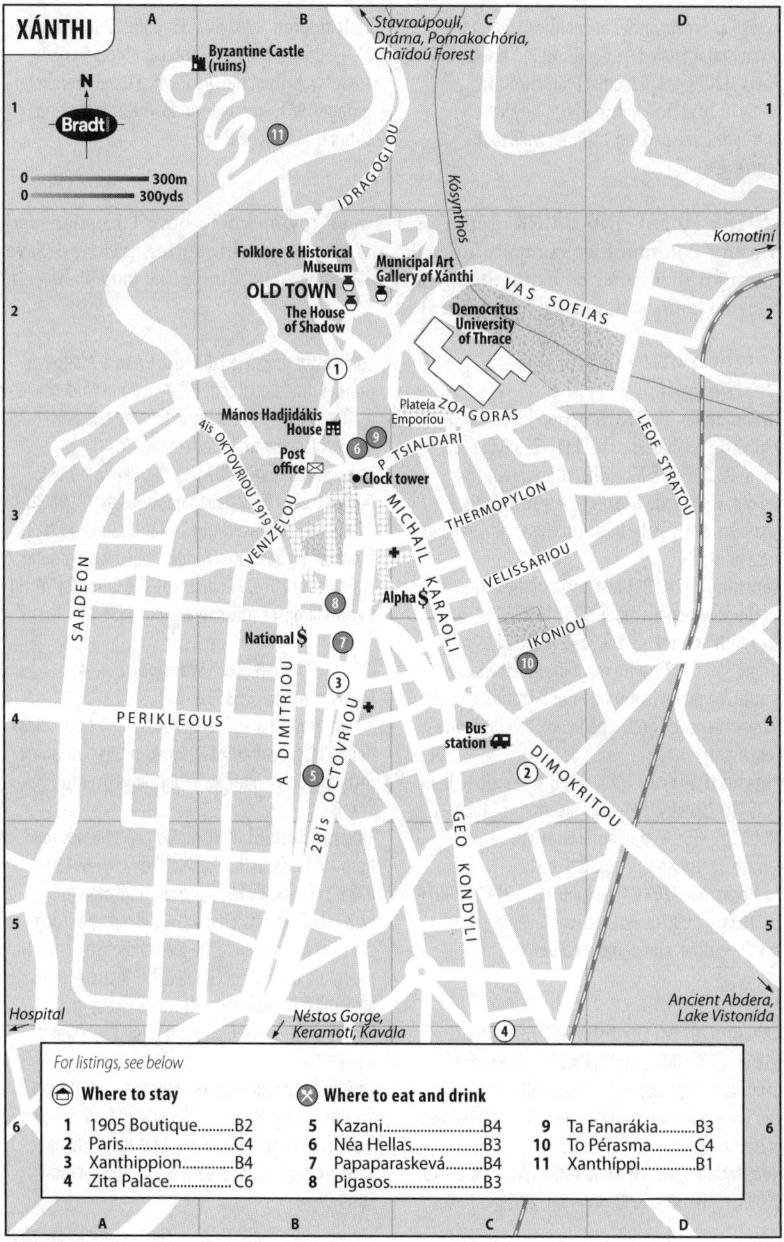

XÁNTHI

	Where to stay		Where to eat and drink		
1	1905 Boutique..........B2	5	Kazani..........................B4	9	Ta Fanarákia..........B3
2	Paris........................C4	6	Néa Hellas..................B3	10	To Pérasma..........C4
3	Xanthippion..............B4	7	Papaparaskevá..........B4	11	Xanthíppi..............B1
4	Zita Palace................C6	8	Pigasos........................B3		

WHERE TO STAY

1905 Boutique Hotel [207 B2] (6 rooms) Chasirtzóglou 5; 25410 77362; w 1905.gr. Located in the Old Town, 6 suites in a beautifully restored Neoclassical mansion built by the last pasha of Xánthi, & furnished with Coco-Mat beds & antiques. Delicious homemade b/fast inc. €€€

Zita Palace [207 C6] (97 rooms) G Kondýli; 25410 64414; w zpalace.gr. South of the centre, the only town hotel with a pool; good French,

as well as Greek, dishes are on the menu of the restaurant, L'Étoile (€€€). B/fast inc. €€€–€€
Paris [207 C4] (16 rooms) Dimokrítou 12; 25410 20531; w hotelparis.gr. Tidy little hotel with free parking, a 10min walk to the centre. €€–€

Xanthippion [207 B4] (53 rooms) 28is Oktovríou 212; 25410 77061; w hotelxanthippion.gr. 7mins' walk from the Old Town, a family-run hotel vintage 1981, with big windows & free parking. Buffet b/fast inc. €€–€

✖ WHERE TO EAT AND DRINK Xánthi is a 'sweet' town, where both Christian and Muslim communities compete to make the most mouthwatering pastries. Save room for them after enjoying the savoury dishes of Asia Minor, like *hunkár begendí* (stewed lamb with puréed aubergines).

Xánthi centre
Restaurants
Ta Fanarákia [207 B3] G Stavroú 18; 25410 73606; tafanarakia; ⏱ 11.00–23.00 Tue–Sat, noon–23.00 Sun & Mon. The 'little lanterns' is a delight, with modern takes on northern Greek & Anatolian classics; the fresh-cut chips with oregano are a must. €€

Xanthíppi [207 B1] Just north of the centre on the Stavroúpolis road; 25410 23627; xanthipphrest; ⏱ 09.00–23.00 daily. Going strong since 1974, with magnificent views over Xánthi & a menu featuring local & Ottoman dishes (*hunkár begendí*, grilled halloumi, a wide choice of kebabs, etc). €€

Pigasos (Pegasus) [207 B3] B Kostantínou Béni; 25410 29680; Pigasos Taverna; ⏱ noon–18.00 Thu–Tue. Popular grill with a pleasant terrace, featuring spit-roasted chicken. €

To Pérasma [207 C4] Ikoníou 16; 25410 78014; ⏱ 10.00–23.30 daily. Excellent taverna-*ouzerí* with beautifully prepared *mezédes*. €

Pastry shops
Kazani [207 B4] Chatzistavrou 278; 25410 65866; ⏱ 09.00–21.00 daily. Superb eastern delights: try the *kazán dibí* ('the bottom of the pan') made in a copper pot – the Ottoman version of crème brulée.

Néa Hellas [207 B3] Vas Konstantidoú 8; 25410 21095; ⏱ 08.30–22.00 Mon–Sat, 09.00–21.30

Sun. Pastry shop specialising in Greek & Anatolian pastries, traditional coffee & *dondurma* (Turkish 'battered' ice cream, made with salep & mastic) & *kaymak* (similar to clotted cream).

Papaparaskevá [207 B4] 28is Oktovríou 186; 25410 22677; w papaparaskevas.gr; ⏱ 08.30–21.30 daily. An institution in Xánthi since 1926, famous for chocolatey *karióka*, filled with ground walnuts (in 2016, Xánthi made the Guinness World Record largest *karióka*, weighing 383kg!).

Around Xánthi *Map, page 204*
Faros Fanári; 25350 31311; EstiatorioThalassinonoPharos; ⏱ 13.00–23.00 daily. Classy seafood of all kinds in this handsome restaurant on a bluff, with big views over the sea. €€€

Taverna Kottáni Kottáni, 5km up a bumpy road from Médousa, in the Pomakochória; m 69450 09855; ⏱ usually Fri–Sun, only until dusk (on account of the difficult road) – call before setting off. The 'taverna where the road ends', in a gorgeous mountain setting, chock-full of heirlooms & crafts. Mr Jemil & his wife serve delicious locally grown food & meats roasted on a spit turned by a water wheel. €

To Pílima Steak House Pílima; 25410 24242; PsestariaToPilema; ⏱ 13.00–22.00 Wed–Sun. One of the closest Pomak villages to Xánthi has a superb taverna for meat lovers, run by a local family. €

OTHER PRACTICALITIES
Alpha Bank [207 C3] Smýrnis 16; 25410 67808
National Bank [207 B4] Konistís 13; 25410 69162
Hospital [207 A5] Southwest of the centre, off Elthelontí Aimodíti; 25413 51100

Pharmacy Kerestétzis [207 C3] Dagklí 20; 25410 27072
Pharmacy Vasilíki [207 B4] 28is Oktovríou 201; 25410 78349
Post office [207 B3] Miltiádi 18; ⏱ 07.30–14.30 Mon–Fri

XÁNTHI

WHAT TO SEE AND DO Along with a railway station, the Ottomans gave Xánthi its landmark **clock tower** (1859) [207 B3], which once belonged to a market building that burned down along with much of the city centre in 1941. It marks the entrance to the charming **Old Town**, where granite cobbled streets and little squares twist around traditional houses and colourful tavernas. The shattered remains of the **Byzantine castle** [207 B1] that once guarded it stand on the wooded hill. Come on Saturday when shoppers from surrounding villages and Bulgaria come to haggle in several languages at northern Greece's biggest outdoor **bazaar** in Plateía Emporíou [207 C2].

Folklore and Historical Museum [207 B2] (Adíka 7; ✆ 25410 25421; w fex.org.gr; ⏰ 09.30–14.30 Tue–Sun; €2) This excellent museum is located in the Neoclassical Kougiomtzóglou Mansion, its 'twin' double-fronted façade built by the sons of a tobacco merchant. Exhibits cover Xánthi's glory days (1860–1940), work and entrepreneurs, but there are also toys, costumes, weavings, jewellery, school memorabilia, stamps and, in the garden, hammams for men and women.

Municipal Art Gallery of Xánthi [207 B2] (Cnr Orféos & Pindárou; ✆ 25410 76363; w pinakothiki.cityofxanthi.gr; ⏰ 10.00–14.00 Mon–Sat; free) This traditional house once belonged to artist Chrístos Pavlídis and features a number of his paintings, as well as temporary exhibitions of art and photography.

The House of Shadow [207 B2] (Orféos 33; ✆ 25411 08309; w vaitsis.com; ⏰ 11.00–19.00 Mon–Wed & Fri, 10.00–20.30 Thu & Sat, 10.00–14.30 & 16.30–20.30 Sun; free) Artist Triantáfyllos Vaïtsis specialises in creating unlikely looking sculptures that become something else entirely when a light is shone on them. Some of his pieces in the gallery make more than one shadow; others, outdoors, are visible only at certain times of day.

Mános Hadjidákis House [207 B3] (El Venizélou 17; ⏰ 08.30–14.45 & 17.00–21.00 Mon–Fri, 10.00–21.00 Sat & Sun; free) Composer Mános Hadjidákis (1925–94) was born in this handsome Neoclassical house with beautiful painted ceilings and spent his early years here before moving to Athens in 1932. He met his friend Míkis Theodorákis while participating in the youth wing of the Greek resistance, then went on to fame and fortune. Besides composing numerous orchestral works, Hatzidákis was a key figure in promoting the Greek blues, *rebétiko*, as a serious musical form, and wrote the scores for two classic films starring Melína Mércouri: Michael Cacoyannis's *Stella* (1955) and Jules Dassin's *Never on Sunday* (1960), for which he won an Oscar – you'll likely know the song 'Ta Paidiá tou Pireá'. His birthplace has been beautifully restored as a cultural centre and has a display of photos and memorabilia.

AROUND XÁNTHI
The Pomakochória (Πομακοχώρια) North of Xánthi you can slip off the beaten track to visit the villages of the Pomaks – the Turko-Slavic-Pomak-speaking Muslim minority – of the Central Rhodope. Their origins have produced all manner of theories (even the word 'Pomak' first appeared only in 1839); one, supported by Ottoman tax records, has it that the Pomaks were originally Christian and in the 17th century, when their mountains became a favoured hunting grounds of the Sultan, a large number of servants (who by law had to be Muslim) were required, so the locals were converted, willingly or not – part of the evidence is that many of their villages have Christian names. Pomak, a Slavic language related to Bulgarian,

is still spoken, but has never been written down. During the Bulgarian occupation in World War II, the locals were compelled to take Bulgarian names and speak Bulgarian, and until 1996 residents were not allowed to leave or have visitors without special permission, out of fears of collusion with the Bulgarian government. Many Pomaks have emigrated to Germany to find work, with some 2,000 having left one of the largest villages, **Echínos** (Εχίνος), 26km from Xánthi, with its three mosques.

Another 15km through the oak forest to the north is the little spa village of **Thérmes** (Θέρμες) with hot baths and where a large rock, near the ruins of an ancient Roman fort, is carved with a vivid relief from the 2nd century AD showing the Persian sun god Mithras – who was a favourite of the Roman legions – sacrificing a bull (to see it, ring the Ephorate of Antiquities in Xánthi: ℡ 25410 51003). Just beyond, a tiny road winds up to the smallest border crossing into Bulgaria – watch out for dogs sleeping in the middle of the road (if you want to make a brief foray into Bulgaria, try Zlatograd to Krilatitsa then back to Greece at Nymphaía north of Komotiní).

Médousa (Μέδουσα) on the Greek side has an old stone bridge, and beyond, where the pavement ends, there's the abandoned 300-year-old village of **Kottáni** (Κοττάνη), with its little mosque and famous taverna (page 208). It's a challenging road (4x4 may be best), but a charming destination and it is also the start of the hike to the ghost villages run by Vasílis Georgiádis (page 192).

Chaïdoú Forest (Δάσος Χαϊντούς; 49km north of Xánthi) Skirting the Bulgarian border, most easily accessible from **Dasikó Chorió** (Δασικό Χωριό), this forest was declared a Natural Monument for its endemic plants and massive beech trees. Some of the trees are over a century old and stand 30m high, amid meadows of yellow lilies and bare mountain slopes, home to bears, wolves, wild boar and more.

Ancient Abdera (26km south of Xánthi, on the Ávdira–Néa Késsani road; ℡ 25410 51003; ⊕ 08.30–15.30 Wed–Mon; €5, concessions €3) For his Eighth Labour, Heracles had to capture the four man-eating horses of Diomedes, the king of the war-like Thracian tribe of the Bistonians. The horses were tethered with iron chains to bronze mangers in their stables by Lake Vistonída; Heracles killed their guards, and was leading the horses to his ship when Diomedes attacked. Heracles crushed him with his club, but when he returned to the shore, he found that the horses had devoured his friend Abderus. To honour Abderus' memory, Heracles founded the city of Abdera and a games – though, out of respect, horseracing was banned.

Historically, the site was founded not once, but twice, in 656BC by Ionian colonists from Clazomenae and then in 545BC by new arrivals from Teos, including Anacreon, lyric poet of wine and women (and subject of 19th-century London drinking song 'To Anacreon in Heaven', which gave its melody to 'The Star-Spangled Banner'). Conquered by the Persians in 513BC and again in 496BC, Abdera hosted Xerxes' army in 480BC and nearly went broke as a result. This may be why its inhabitants had a reputation for stupidity – in spite of the fact that it was the birthplace of Democritus, the father of atomic theory (c460–370BC), and Protagoras (c490–420BC), the first and wisest of the Sophists, who gave his name to one of Plato's Dialogues and caused so much controversy with his statement 'Man is the measure of all things', interpreted by Plato to mean that all truth is relative.

The major port into Thrace, Abdera grew to become the third-richest city in Athens' Delian League, only to be conquered and sacked by Philip II, initiating its long decline, exacerbated by being too far off the Via Egnatía for the Romans. The **archaeological site** covers a massive 485ha but the most prominent features are concentrated around an enclosed area by the sea: the acropolis, where the Byzantines built a fortress, Polýstylon ('many columns'), over the Classical walls; you can pick out gates, the theatre, houses and a workshop where votive offerings were made. The acropolis is always open but keep an eye out for snakes.

Abdera Archaeological Museum (Modern Ávdira (Άβδηρα); ☏ 25410 51003; ⊕ 08.30–15.30 Wed–Mon; €5, concessions €3) With good explanations in English, this excellent museum concentrates on the numerous weapons excavated at the site, and items from everyday life – a medical kit, perfume pots, coins, knucklebones (used as toys), beautiful jewellery and bronze 'key rings' from Roman times, a painted sarcophagus and reconstructions of the tombs, and vases going back to 650BC.

Lake Vistonída (Λίμνη Βιστωνίδα; 26km south of Xánthi) The Egnatía Ódos detours north of beautiful Lake Vistonída, the largest lake in Thrace and fourth-largest in Greece, the same that caused a stir when the abbot at the Vatopédi Monastery discovered, in an 11th-century document, that it belonged to them (page 126). It has a unique 'mid-Mediterranean' ecosystem: the north half, fed by rivers, is brackish fresh water, while the south, linked to the sea, is home to saltwater species; Aristotle specifically mentioned it ('most species of fishes are found in Lake Vistonída'). In October 2018, it made the news again, when its shore – fences, trees, bushes, chapels and rocks – was wrapped in an extraordinary 1,000m-long web woven by harmless mosquito-eating Tetragnatha spiders. At other times you're more likely to see vast flocks of herons, swans, ducks, silver pelicans, flamingos and spoonbills.

Pórto Lágos (Πόρτο Λάγος), the largest village on the lake, is the site of the **National Park of Eastern Macedonia and Thrace Lake Vistonída Information Centre** (☏ 25410 96646; w epamath.gr; ⊕ 09.30–15.30 daily). The village has a pretty landmark – the small monastery of **Ag Nikólaos**, a dependency of the aforementioned Vatopédi monastery, on an islet, reached by a wooden causeway, itself linked by causeway to the church of **Panagía Pantánassa**. A series of sandy beaches backed by lagoons begins east of Vistonía Bay at the fishing village of **Fanári** (Φανάρι).

Ancient Anastasioúpolis (Turn south on a dirt road off the Xánthi–Komotiní road, between Amaxádes (Αμαξάδες) and Kopteró (Κοπτερό)) Known in ancient

---

WOMEN'S DAY, THRACIAN STYLE

Néa Kessáni, just north of Pórto Lágos, and Xilaganí to the east are two of several villages in northern Greece that celebrate the **Babo**, or **Midwife Festival**, on 8 January – a festival believed to be a last memory of a pagan festival of the goddess Demeter that was preserved in eastern Thrace, and brought over in the 1923 population exchange. An older woman in the village is chosen to be Babo the midwife – the same name as Demeter's nurse, who famously made the goddess smile while grieving for her daughter Persephone by lifting up her skirts. Traditional roles are reversed for the day: men stay home and do the chores while the married women gather to drink, tell dirty jokes, brandish sex toys and sing obscene songs. Men who try to enter the women's zone are lewdly teased or get a bucket of water over the head. Exceptions are made for the mayor or male musicians – but only if they cross-dress.

7 | THRACE (ΘΡΑΚΗ)

times as Stabulo Diomedis (Diomedes' Stable), this town once stood on the banks of Lake Vistonída (now 2km away) and was an important staging post on the Via Egnatía. Rechristened by Emperor Anastasius (dAD518), and fortified by Justinian, the city was destroyed by the Bulgarian Tsar Kaloyan in 1206, then rebuilt and renamed Peritheorion until it was abandoned in the 17th century, as the lakefront silted up. Now much overgrown, its walls and towers can be picked out by the very keen, along with the imperial gateway to the harbour with a Palaeologos monogram.

KOMOTINÍ

Seat of Democritus University and the prefecture of Rodópi, Komotiní (Κομοτηνή; or Gümülcine in Turkish) is a lively multi-cultural city of 54,000 on the Thracian plain. As Greek cities go, it's a relative newcomer; originally a 'daughter' settlement of Maroneia (page 216), it was a big fort on the Via Egnatía by the 4th century AD, playing second fiddle to nearby Maximianopolis (Byzantine Mosynopolis) until the Bulgarian Tsar Karolyan flattened it in the 13th century. In 1363 Komotiní was taken for the Ottomans by a Greek convert to Islam, General Gazi Evrenos Bey, who built the first mosque and settled Turks in the rural countryside – where many still reside today.

When Komotiní was given to Bulgaria after the Second Balkan War, local Greeks and Turks united in resistance to form the short-lived Republic of Gumuljina, until the city became part of Greece in 1919.

GETTING THERE AND AWAY Buses from the station at Maméli 15 [213 C4] (\ 25310 22912; w ktelrodopis.gr) run frequently to Xánthi (70mins; €5.20), Alexandroúpolis (70mins; €6.80), Thessaloníki (3hrs 15mins; €28.00), and usually twice daily to Fanári (about 30mins; €4) and Marónia (about 45mins, but check the routes – the one that goes first to the beaches takes longer; €3.10), and less frequently elsewhere. There are three buses daily to Istanbul (about 6hrs plus border crossing; m 69428 19387; €25/€45 return).

WHERE TO STAY

King Maron [map, page 204] (48 rooms) Platanítis, 35km south of Komotiní; \ 25313 06900; w kingmaron.gr. Stylish, recently built 4-star beach hotel perched on the shore with a path down to the beach. Bright suites & family rooms, a pool, restaurant & bar, plus a spa, gym, salt room & hammam. B/fast incl. €€€
Anatolia [213 D2] (53 rooms) Agchiálou 53; \ 25310 36242; w anatoliabaggage.com/hotels/anatolia-hotel-komotini. Snazzy contemporary rooms in greys, blacks & whites in easy walking distance of the centre. The good restaurant (€€) uses recipes from Cappadocia, Thrace, Armenia, the Pontus, etc. B/fast incl. €€

Democritus [213 C6] (52 rooms) Plateía Vizinoú 8; \ 25310 22044; w hoteldemocritus.gr. Central, comfortable, 2-star rooms with balcony, fridge & AC on the town's prettiest square. €€
Achillio [map, page 204] (45 rooms) 4km on the Xánthi road; \ 25310 22323; w achillio.gr. Built in 2005 & renovated in 2018, with a very helpful staff, classic rooms (inc family rooms), sat TV, pool, sauna & easy parking. €€–€
Rodopi [213 A4] (18 rooms) Ethn Makaríou 3; \ 25310 35988; w rodopihotel.gr. Comfortable hotel with a garden & friendly English-speaking staff, 1km west of the centre. €€–€

✖ WHERE TO EAT AND DRINK Komotiní is famous for its *loukoum* (aka Turkish delight) – including the *soutzouk loukoum*, long ropes made by stringing walnuts on a thread and dipping them in thickened grape must (*loukoum*), which are then dried and dusted with powdered sugar to resemble a sausage (*sucuk* is Turkish for sausage).

KOMOTINÍ

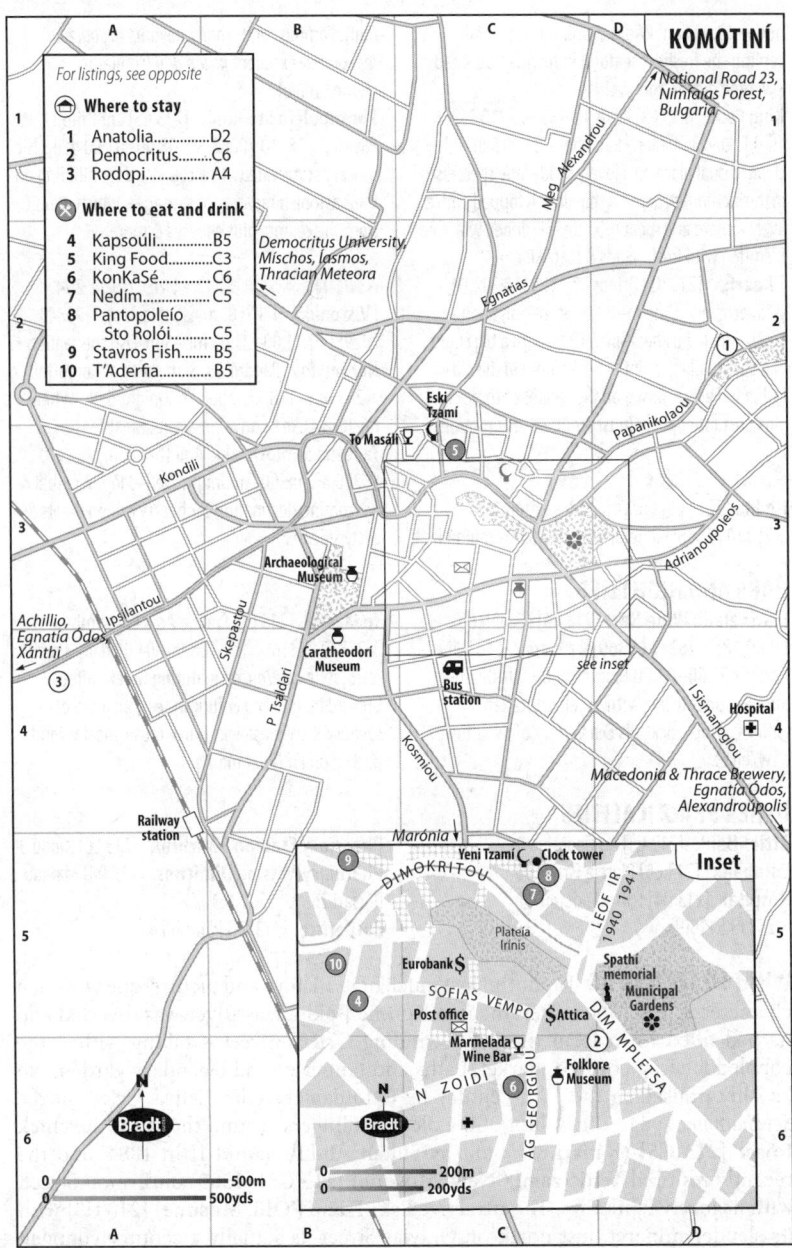

Komotiní centre
Restaurants

Kapsoúli [213 B5] Maronias 29; 25310 26767; w konkase.gr; ⊕ noon–midnight daily. A large menu of Greek seafood, meat, & vegetarian specialities. Very popular. €€

KonKaSé [213 C6] Nicholas Zoídi 29; 25310 32223; ⊕ noon–midnight daily. Contemporary, sophisticated interpretations of traditional dishes, based on prime local & seasonal ingredients. €€

Stavros Fish Restaurant [213 B5] Koúloglou 18; 25310 21669; ; ⊕ noon–23.30 Mon–Sat,

7 | THRACE (ΘΡΑΚΗ)

noon–18.00 Sun. Bright, luminous restaurant serving the freshest seafood in town; good salads & veggie dishes, too. €€

King Food [213 C3] Kilkís 12-13; ☏ 25310 31386; ⏲ 11.00–23.00 Mon–Sat, noon–23.00 Sun. This clean, casual place on a lovely shady lane specialises in terrific *lahmatzoún* – a thin dough topped with a lively tomato and meat mixture – & döner, wrapped & stuffed with fresh salads & tzatziki. €

T'Aderfia [213 B5] Orféos 33; ☏ 25310 20201; w aderfia.gr; ⏲ noon–23.00 Mon–Sat, noon–16.30 Sun. In business since 1935, with a big choice of dishes ready to point at & pick from in the old-fashioned way – based on the recipes of Thrace & old Constantinople. A must for lunch in Komotiní. €

Pastry shops and cafés

Nedím [213 C5] Cnr Orféos & S Kritón 15; ☏ 25310 22036; w nedim.gr; ⏲ 08.00–midnight daily. Famous for its many flavours of *soutzouk loukoum* & excellent *kazán dibí* (similar to crème brulée).

Pantopoleío Sto Rolói [213 C5] Cnr Kritón & Vas Pávlou; ☏ 25310 70068; ⏲ 08.00–01.00 daily. Hip grocery store/café with a courtyard for nibbling on their astonishing array of sausages, which dangle from the ceiling, plus cheeses & more.

Around Komotiní *Map, page 204*

I Vistonída (Ι/Ψ Η Βιστωνίδα) Íasmos; ☏ 25340 24298; ⏲ 11.00–23.00 Tue–Sun. Fish specialities. €

Neromylos Pándrosos, 8km north of Komotiní; ☏ 25310 32178; ⏲ noon–midnight daily. Where the locals like to drive for a rural meat feast. €

Taverna Samothráki Agii Theodori; ☏ 25310 55200; ⏲ 08.00–midnight Wed–Mon. A casual & welcoming destination for hearty grilled meats & zesty sides. €

BARS AND NIGHTLIFE

Marmelada Wine Bar [213 C6] N Zoídi (Plateía Eiríni) 18; ☏ 25311 00360; ☷ Μαρμελαδα Wine bar; ⏲ 08.00–03.00 Mon–Sat, 09.00–02.30 Sun. Rustic chic bar with excellent Italian coffees, wine, cocktails & a variety of live music at w/ends.

To Masáli [213 C3] Plateía Arch Chrisánthou 39; ☏ 25310 84416; ☷; ⏲ 08.00–04.00 daily. Popular retro-style café/*ouzerí* featuring Greek coffees brewed in hot sand & Turkish teas, an array of savoury & sweet snacks & live music most w/ends; packed on Fri & Sat nights.

OTHER PRACTICALITIES

Attica Bank [213 C5] Ag Georgíou 2
Eurobank [213 C5] Plateía Eirínis 40
Hospital [213 D4] I Sismánoglou 45; ☏ 25313 51100

Pharmacy Esagian S Michran [213 C6] Aínou 3
Pharmacy Mítsiou Dimítrios [213 D4] Markou Botsari 26
Post office [213 C5] Parasíou 4

WHAT TO SEE AND DO Komotiní lost much of its history and picturesque Ottoman character in the 1960s when the flood-prone Bokloutzás River was diverted and its bed filled in to form the wide, winding Orféos Street – taking with it the cobbled lanes, a covered market, baths and tanneries and legendary gardens, so lavishly praised in the 17th century by Ottoman traveller Evliya Çelebi in the *Seyahatnâme* (page 27). A hint of the old town lingers around the tall white **clock tower** [213 C5] (Kánari St), built by Sultan Abdul Hamid II in 1884, and the recently restored **Yeni Tzamí ('New' Mosque)** [213 C5] (1585) on Ermoú Street, with its lovely Iznik tiles. The attractive **Eski Tzamí ('Old' Mosque)** [213 C3] with its slender minaret, just north on Graviás Street, is actually a century younger, and has recently been restored; it gets quite a crowd on Fridays (if either are open, you can visit, dressed respectably and minus shoes).

Near the clock tower, colourful little lanes once renowned for their tin workshops, have recently been spruced up with pretty pergolas. The pedestrian-only **Plateía Irínis** [213 C5] is a favourite meeting place, by the shady **Municipal Gardens**, with a striking World War II memorial, the **Spathí** [213 D5] – a 15m high sword, where every Sunday morning there's a small military flag ceremony.

Folklore Museum [213 C6] (Ag Georgíou 13; \ 25310 25931; ☉ 09.00–13.30 Mon–Fri; free) A 19th-century mansion houses a collection of beautiful costumes, music boxes, icons and elaborately worked guns and yataghans.

Archaeological Museum [213 B3] (A Symeonídi 4; \ 25310 22411; w odysseus. culture.gr; ☉ 08.30–15.30 Wed–Mon; €5, concessions €3) Komotiní once had the best archaeological collection in Thrace, but many objects formerly housed here are now in the archaeological museums of Abdera and of Alexandroúpolis (pages 211 and 220). The now rather sparse exhibits range from prehistory to the Iron Age Greek colonies to Byzantine times, including a phallic altar dedicated 'to all the gods' and the star of the collection: a golden bust of Roman Emperor Septimius Severus found in Plotinopolis (Didymóteicho). The museum itself is a handsome building of 1976 by Aris Konstantinídis, one of Greece's most celebrated modernist architects.

Karatheodorí Museum [213 B4] (Stílponos Kyriakídis 93; \ 25310 85640; w caratheodorymuseum.gr; ☉ 09.00–14.00 Mon–Fri; €2) Considered the greatest Greek mathematician since ancient times, Konstantínos Karatheodorí (Constantin Carathéodory, 1873–1950) was born in Berlin of Greek parents from Néa Výssa (near Orestiáda), but spent most of his life in Germany and Belgium. He corresponded with Einstein and formulated the Carathéodory Theorum and the as-yet-unsolved Carathéodory conjecture. In 1919, Venizélos invited him to establish the Ionian University of Smyrna; instead he was one of the last people to escape the fire and slaughter there in 1922, with all his books, which are now in the library of Athens University. The museum houses an archive of his mathematical notes and dissertation.

Macedonia and Thrace Brewery [map, page 204] (12km southeast, off the Alexandroúpolis road in an industrial estate; visitor centre: \ 25310 38715; w verginabeer.com; ☉ 09.00–15.30 Mon–Fri, by appt only – contact via website; free) Heeding the words of Frank Zappa ('You can't be a real country unless you have a beer'), Dimítris Politópoulos founded this brewery in 1998 to produce Vergina, Greece's first Greek-made, widely distributed beer. It's made from local Thracian malt that they supply to other independent breweries in Greece and elsewhere in the Mediterranean.

AROUND KOMOTINÍ It's only 22km from Komotiní to the Bulgarian frontier, and the forests and mountains along the way are a refreshing retreat on a hot summer's day; there's a ruined Byzantine castle on the north end of the **Nimfaías Forest** (Δάσος Νυμφαίας), with magnificent views.

West of Komotiní, **Míschos** (Μίσχος) is a typical Pomak village with an elegant minaret and watermill in a gorge. Carry on west along the same road to **Íasmos** (Ιασμος), a mixed Christian–Muslim village where a triple-arched stone **bridge**, the longest in Thrace and last restored in the 18th century, carried the ancient Via Egnatía over the often tempestuous Kompsátos River. The foothills of **Mount Papíkio** (1,482m) to the north was the site of an early monastic state linked to Mosynopolis (the destroyed Byzantine administrative centre near Komotiní), although raids were so frequent that the monks all relocated to Mount Athos: ruins of their monasteries have been found outside of Míschos, and at **Linós** (Ληνός) and **Sóstis** (Σώστης).

Here too is one of the region's beauty spots, the '**Thracian Meteora**' (Thrakiká Metéora); head 15km north on a dirt road from Íasmos to **Astraía** (Αστραία), one of several abandoned Muslim villages in the area – then make a 90-minute walk on a well-marked trail. This beautiful empty region of beech forests and wild horses has three striking rows of surreal 80m sandstone monolithic rocks, a mini-version of Meteora, although minus any monasteries teetering on top. Instead, the rocks are perforated with perfect nesting places for vultures and rare birds of prey.

Marónia (Μαρώνεια; 29km southeast of Komotiní) This town with a scattering of old houses is near long sandy **Platanítis Beach**, and the picturesque little port of **Ag Charálambos** (Αγ Χαράλαμπος). It replaces the once vast ancient city of **Maroneia** (along the Marónia–Ag Charálambos road; w odysseus.culture.gr; ⊕ always; free; to visit the ancient theatre, contact the Ephorate of Antiquities of Rodopi at ✆ 25330 43016). Maron was a priest of Apollo who belonged to the Thracian tribe of Kikkones (Cicones), mentioned in the *Iliad* as allies of Troy.

In the *Odyssey*, Odysseus and his men brutally sack the Kikkones' capital Isamaros, sparing only Maron, who in gratitude gives Odysseus a dozen amphorae of strong wine. In the meantime, the Kikkones rallied and, after a battle, killed so many of Odysseus' men they were forced to flee. Maron's gift, however, soon comes in handy when the Greeks end up in the cave of Polyphemus the Cyclops, who intends to have them for lunch – until Odysseus intoxicates then blinds Polyphemus to make their getaway. The **Cave of Marónia**, where all this may have happened (although at least half a dozen other caves around the Mediterranean beg to differ, including a more convincing 'Cyclops cave' just east, near Makrí), is off the road to Proskinités (Προσκυνητές). Inhabited from Neolithic times, the cave today is home to ten species of bat, which flit among the stalactites.

The city that took Maron's name, founded by colonists from Chíos in the 7th century BC on the slopes of Mount Ismara, was captured by the Persians in 513BC, then prospered again under Athens in the Delian Confederacy and under the Romans. It was renowned across the ancient world for its wine, reputedly as fine as nectar, and produced a unique ancient celebrity, Hipparchia of Maroneia, who moved with her family to Athens. There she fell in love with the Cynic philosopher Crates of Thebes, a wealthy man who gave up all his possessions to find happiness in a life of virtue, free of desires for wealth and fame. To the dismay of her respectable family, Hipparchia married Crates, living with him as an equal in the streets of Athens, becoming a Cynic philosopher in her own right, the only woman out of the 82 philosophers listed in the 3rd-century AD *Lives and Opinions of Eminent Philosophers*, by Diogenes Laërtius.

Maroneia's sites are signposted: the west section of the 10km of Classical-era **walls** stands amid the olive groves, down a dirt road. Further along is a **Hellenistic villa**, with a fireplace, colourful mosaic floor, a room used for weaving and a bathroom. Near the seaside car park are overgrown remains of a monumental marble **double gate**, built for Emperor Hadrian's visit in AD124, and the foundation of an early Byzantine church. Another road to the coast passes the ruined 4th-century BC **Sanctuary of Dionysos**, and a sweet little Hellenistic **theatre**, with parapets added by the Romans to protect the audience from wild beasts in gladiator shows. Near the theatre are the ancient marble quarries, **Marmarítsa**, where the speciality was millstones; a dirt road leads down to a charming secluded pebble beach under the cliffs.

A trail climbs the slopes of **Ag Geórgios (or Ismaros)** to the remains of a 9th-century BC acropolis, tentatively identified as Homer's Ismara. Along the coast under the mountain the E6 path leads to **Sýnaxi**, with the ruins of a Byzantine monastery built over an ancient sanctuary, where pilgrims once set sail for

Gleaming white churches pepper Chóra (Skópelos Town) on the island of Skópelos PAGE 366 — above (GT/S)

The white-pebbled Ag Dimítrios beach on Alónissos is known for the clarity of its waters PAGE 372 — below (CI/S)

left (K/S) — Ancient Philippi, where St Paul made his first European convert PAGE 183

below (HK/S) — The Odeion at Ancient Nikopolis, the city founded by Augustus after defeating Antony and Cleopatra at Actium PAGE 292

bottom (AC/S) — Inspired by the excavations of an adjacent Neolithic settlement, Dispiló recreates a picture of lakeside Neolithic life PAGE 242

A replica of the Bronze Age Argo is sometimes moored in summer at Vólos, home port of Jason PAGE 337

above
(NN/S)

The dark mysteries at Samothráki's Sanctuary of the Great Gods of the Underworld attracted initiates from across the Mediterranean PAGE 229

below left
(GT/S)

The royal larnax that held the remains of Philip II and his burial wreath of golden oak, aglow in the semidarkness at the Royal Tombs of Aigai PAGE 143

below right
(AC/S)

above left (TP/S) — The Old Synagogue in Vería's Barboúta quarter was home to an important Jewish community before the Holocaust PAGE 141

above right (RG/S) — The Fetihie Mosque and tomb of Ali Pasha still stand within Ioánnina's medieval *kástro* PAGE 267

left (PK/S) — One of Greece's most unusual churches, Moní Ypséseos Timíou Stavró sits in isolation up in the Pindus Mountains PAGE 323

below (V/S) — The Russian monastery of Ag Pantelémonas rises above the shores of the Mount Athos peninsula PAGE 124

The extraordinary Moní Kipínas was built in 1212 in the cliffs of the Tzoumérka, Epirus PAGE 287 — above (G/S)

The Halil Bey (or Old Music) Mosque stands in the historic Panagía district of Kavála PAGE 182 — right (Sto/S)

The exquisitely decorated interior of Great Meteora dates back to the 16th century PAGE 322 — below (H/S)

top
(AC/S)

Among the wonders of Épirus is the dramatic Víkos Gorge, considered the world's deepest in relation to its width PAGE 278

above
(DM/S)

Mount Olympus is Greece's highest peak, and the legendary home of Zeus and his dysfunctional family PAGE 129

left
(VV/S)

A symphony in grey stone, Dílofo is one of the Zagorochória's many villages PAGE 278

Renowned among birdwatchers, Lake Kerkíni's wetlands also provide grazing for buffaloes PAGE 161   above (DM/S)

The little owl – *Athene noctua* – is a symbol of the goddess Athena and a frequent sight PAGE 5   below left (AD/S)

The lakes of Préspa and Kerkíni are both home to the majestic – and gigantic – Dalmatian pelican PAGE 5   below right (VM/S)

The pygmy cormorant is often spotted in the many rich wetlands of northern Greece PAGE 5   bottom left (DH/S)

Known for its sweet song and striking colouring, the golden oriole is at home on Mount Olympus and elsewhere PAGE 5   bottom right (JGG/S)

above
(SH/S)

The dramatic rock formations and dazzling blue seas at Lalária Beach on Skiáthos PAGE 361

MULTI-AWARD-WINNING
EXPERT-LED ARCHAEOLOGICAL & CULTURAL TOURS FOR SMALL GROUPS

WWW.PETERSOMMER.COM

Samothráki; the path carries on east to **Petrotá** (Πετρωτά) **Beach**, decorated with curious 3m volcanic formations called 'Poseidon's coastguards'.

Mesimvría (Μεσημβρίας) There's a fine, often quiet beach here, and the remains of a colony founded by Samothráki in the 7th century BC, as part of its *peraía* (literally 'land across' or mainland possession of an island state). It has since been identified as Zoni, another colony of Samothráki, hence the name of the small archaeological site, **Zóni-Mesimvría** (west of Mesimvría Beach; ↘ 25510 96214; ☉ summer 08.30–15.30 Fri–Sun, often closed out of season; €3, concessions €2). It was here that Apollonius of Rhodes wrote that Orpheus so enchanted the forest with his music that the trees began to follow him. There are well-preserved walls, blocks of houses, a Sanctuary of Demeter that yielded the votive offerings that are now in the Archaeological Museum of Alexandroúpolis, and a Sanctuary of Apollo. Unusual here are the numerous amphorae found buried upside down in several buildings, believed to have been used to protect the floor from rising damp. Some 2,000 ancient coins found here are now also in the Archaeological Museum of Alexandroúpolis.

The archaeological area around **Makrí** (Μακρή), discovered by accident during World War I, has been inhabited since Neolithic times (c4000BC), although the excavations you see are of early Byzantine churches. Makrí's beach, one of the best around Alexandroúpolis, is backed by an olive grove with trees up to 2,500 years old.

East of Komotiní On the Egnatía Ódos highway you can zoom across the cotton and tobacco fields to Alexandroúpolis in about an hour. Or there's an older, slower route starting in charming old **Gratiní** (Γρατινή) with a ruined Byzantine fortress of Gratianoupolis, which featured in several histories of the civil wars for the Byzantine throne. At **Arrianá** (Αρριανά) you can make a detour into the back of beyond and the isolated Pomak villages of **Kéchros** (Κέχρος) and **Chlói** (Χλόη). Further northeast, in **Roussa** (Ρούσσα), you can seek out a rare megalithic dolmen-style **tomb** (9th century BC) along the road east to **Mikró Dério** (Μικρό Δέρειο), from where a good road leads south to Alexandroúpolis.

ALEXANDROÚPOLIS

Alexander the Great founded a score of cities that he named after himself, but this Alexandroúpolis (Αλεξανδρούπολης; population 60,000) isn't one of them. Originally Ancient Sali, then Dedeağaç, a holy town of dervishes under the Ottomans, it was renamed in 1920 after King Alexander (who died of a monkey bite shortly thereafter). This young town with a multi-cultural heritage started out as a small fishing village in the mid 19th century, at the crossroads of Europe and Asia, then emerged as a key transport and trade hub with the opening of the railway and port. Alexandroúpolis today has excellent museums and very comfortable hotels, and makes a convenient base for exploring the surrounding region.

GETTING THERE AND AWAY
By air Alexandroúpolis National Airport 'Dimokritos' [map, page 204] (↘ 25510 89300; w alxd.gr) is 6km east of the centre, with several daily flights from Athens with Aegean.

By sea Fast Ferries (↘ 25510 82289; w fastferries.com.gr) sail for Samothráki (page 225); the ticket office is by the port [218 D5].

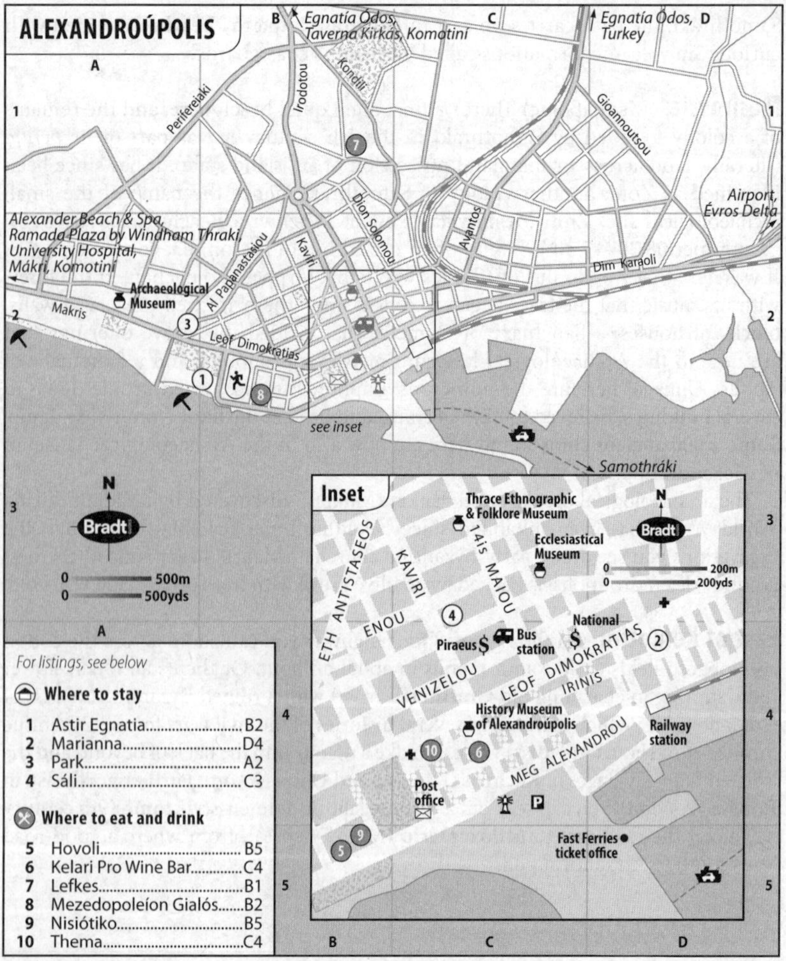

7 | THRACE (ΘΡΑΚΗ)

ALEXANDROÚPOLIS

For listings, see below

Where to stay
1. Astir Egnatia B2
2. Marianna D4
3. Park A2
4. Sáli C3

Where to eat and drink
5. Hovoli B5
6. Kelari Pro Wine Bar C4
7. Lefkes B1
8. Mezedopoleíon Gialós ... B2
9. Nisiótiko B5
10. Thema C4

By bus The bus station [218 C4] (Venizélou 33; ✆25510 26479; w ktelevrou.gr) has six buses daily to Thessaloníki (express 4hrs 30mins; €31.80), five to Xánthi (about 2hrs; €11.90), four to Kavála (2hrs 30mins–3hrs; €16.70), and ten to Orestiáda (2hrs; €9.80) via Féres, Souflí and Didymóteicho (all priced accordingly). There are also seven to Komotiní (see w ktelrodopis.gr).

By car There is an inexpensive and convenient public parking lot just below the lighthouse [218 C4].

WHERE TO STAY

Astir Egnatia [218 B2] (111 rooms) Egnatía Park; ✆25510 38000; w astiregnatia.com. A plush Grecotel experience, in a garden by the beach shared by sister hotel the Grand Hotel Egnatia, plus suites with private pools & 2 elegant restaurants (both €€€€) – the Bosphorus, serving creative Mediterranean cuisine, & Aesop's Myths, specialising in seafood & Mediterranean & Thracian cuisine with an international approach. €€€€€–€€€€
Ramada Plaza by Wyndham Thraki [map, page 204] (149 rooms) Km4 on the national road; ✆25520 89100; m 69725 52677;

ALEXANDROÚPOLIS

w ramadaplazathraki.com. Fall asleep to the sound of the waves at this recently renovated 5-star resort situated on its own little bay & wild beach. Thick rolling lawns, a pool with a view, a thalassotherapy wellness spa & gym, & an optional evening buffet & à la carte restaurant (€€) complete the experience. Great accessibility for the mobility impaired. B/fast inc. €€€€–€€€
Sáli [218 C3] (5 rooms) I Kavíri 16; ℡25510 25000; w sali.gr. Charming new boutique hotel in a former Neoclassical girls' school, full of character, with plush rooms, & cotton & silk sheets to sink into. B/fast €10. €€€€–€€€

Alexander Beach & Spa [map, page 204] (125 rooms) 2km west in Néa Chilí; ℡25510 39290; w alexbh.gr. Resort hotel with an indoor pool, spa, 2 outdoor pools & a little casino. Beach an awkward walk away; b/fast inc. €€€
Marianna [218 D4] (14 rooms) Cnr Dimokratías & Melgáron 11; ℡25510 81456; w mariannahotel. gr. Central, with small tidy rooms, fine for a night. B/fast inc. €€–€
Park [218 A2] (50 rooms) Dimokratías 458; ℡25510 28607; w parkalex.gr. Older budget hotel with a small pool in the courtyard. Greek b/fast inc. €€–€

✘ WHERE TO EAT AND DRINK

Ai Giórgis [map, page 204] Néa Makrí, 12km west; ℡25510 71777; w aigiorgis.com; ⊕ noon–midnight daily. Upmarket, elegant seafood restaurant, in a lovely setting overlooking the sea & sunset (try to book an outside table). Diners come from as far away as Türkiye to enjoy the superb prawns with orzo (kritharóto), beef cheeks with pickled cabbage, etc. Excellent wine list. €€€€–€€€
Nisiótiko [218 B5] Zarifi 1; ℡25510 20990; w nisiotiko.gr; ⊕ noon– 23.30 Tue–Sun. Some of the best seafood in town, including some more unusual dishes, in a luminous restaurant just off the waterfront. Great for Sun lunch. €€€
Hovoli [218 B5] Vas Alexándrou 50; ℡25510 37777; ꜰ hovolirestaurant; ⊕ noon–midnight daily. Run by an Armenian family, serving Armenian cuisine & renowned for their babaganoush & kebabs. €€
Lefkes [218 B1] Andronikoú 29; ℡25510 22418; ⊕ 19.30–23.30 Mon–Fri. Local favourite for meat dishes & Cretan rakí, often accompanied by live music. Reservations not accepted. €€
Mezedopoleíon Gialós [218 B2] Apolloniádos 26; ℡25510 83850; ⊕ noon–midnight daily. Waterfront taverna with superb little plates of seafood. €€
Taverna Kirkás [map, page 204] Kírki (Κίρκη), 25km northwest; ℡25510 22392; ⊕ sometimes w/ends only – call first. Lovely drive into the mountains for excellent Greek & Thracian dishes, including sarma (rice & lamb offal), stewed dishes in clay pots & grilled meats. €€
Kelari Pro Wine Bar [218 C4] Dikastirion 47 at Kanári; ℡25510 32086; ꜰ Kelari Pro; ⊕ 16.00–02.00 daily. Best wine cellar in Alex, with delicious dishes to go with your choice of bottle.
Thema [218 C4] Soulíou 8–10; ℡25510 25255; w themacafe.gr; ⊕ 09.00–04.00 daily. On the main pedestrian street, great atmosphere, great coffee, superb wines, cocktails, snacks & desserts, & cigars.

OTHER PRACTICALITIES
National Bank [218 C4] Dimokratías 240
Piraeus Bank [218 C4] El Venizélou 38
University Hospital [218 A2] Dragána; ℡25510 51000, 25513 52000
Pharmacy Georgíou Antonis [218 D3] Dimokratías 173
Pharmacy Kazakou Konstantina [218 C4] Dimokratías 355
Post office [218 C4] Meg Alexándrou 42

WHAT TO SEE AND DO
Lighthouse [218 C4] The city's 18m landmark was built by a French company in 1880 to guide ships through the Dardanelles. Today it's the main focus of the evening promenade along the waterfront, when traffic is banned.

Thrace Ethnographic and Folklore Museum [218 C3] (14is Maíou 63; ℡25510 36663; w emthrace.org; ⊕ 09.00–15.00 Tue–Sat, 10.00–14.00 Sun; €3, under 12s free; extremely interesting private guided tours available if you book) Housed in a beautifully restored Neoclassical mansion of 1899, this excellent self-funded museum is the life's work of an inspired woman. When Angéla Giannakídou began to amass this collection in the 1960s, these clothes and tools were still worn and used in the daily lives of many in the region – a way of life unchanged for countless generations. Perceiving the rapid changes in store, Ms Giannakídou sought to preserve these remarkable pieces and honour what they represent. Through the extraordinary traditional costumes (those of the Sarakatsáni in particular), ritual items, agricultural tools, musical instruments, copperware and ceramics, and objects related to the once-important silk-, wool-, flax- and cotton-weaving industries, visitors gain insight into the remarkably complex multi-cultural identity of Thrace – once part of the Roman Empire, then the Byzantine, then the Ottoman, and today divided among three nations for only a little over a century.

The museum runs an excellent shop (w riza.emthrace.org) whose aim is to provide an outlet for artisanal craftspeople to showcase their skill. Those wishing to experience something extraordinary can also contact the museum to arrange a unique culinary experience, centred around a historically accurate meal from a choice of eras and social strata, in a contextual setting. Ms Giannakídou's extraordinary contribution has been recognised by UNESCO.

History Museum of Alexandroúpolis [218 C4] (Dimokratías 335; ✆ 22510 28926; w ismo.gr; ⊕ 10.30–14.30 Tue–Sat; €3) This is one of the newest and sleekest history museums in Greece, financed by the Stávros Niárchos Foundation. Most of the photos, costumes, books, paintings and more were donated by the locals. It also has researcher Eléni Filippídi's important collection of items relating to the Sarakatsáni nomads (page 225). Explanations are in Greek but the staff loan out English translations.

Archaeological Museum [218 A2] (Leof Makris 44; ✆ 25510 22151; w amalexandroupolis.gr; ⊕ 08.30–15.30 Mon, Wed–Fri & Sun, 13.00–20.00 Sat; €10, concessions €5) This lovely new museum, opened in 2022, features objects from the maritime routes of Évros, Ancient Zone (Zóni), Mákri and the Peraia of Samothrace.

Ecclesiastical Museum [218 C3] (Enou 18; ✆25510 82282; w odysseus.culture.gr; ⊕ 09.00–13.00 Tue–Fri, 10.00–13.00 Sun) Housed in a grand Neoclassical building, the large collection of ecclesiastical items on display here includes portable icons of various eras and types, vestments, and manuscripts.

Cyclops Cave (Mákri, just west of Alexandroúpolis – ask locals, follow a couple of signs, & take a pleasant 500–700m walk from a parking spot) While there are other contenders, this beautifully situated cave just above Mákri is often considered the mythical dwelling of the Cyclops Polythemus encountered by Odysseus. It certainly looks the part.

THE ÉVROS

Thanks to decades of geopolitical turmoil, this northeasternmost corner of Greece has never been exploited the way it would have been had everyone been loveydovey. Although historically it's often been bad for humans, it has been great for nature, in particular for rare birds; according to the Ornithological Society of Greece (w ornithologiki.gr/en), the steppe eagle (*Aquila nipalensis*), the white-tailed lapwing (*Vanellus leucurus*), the little bustard (*Tetrax tetrax*), and the even more rare Arctic tern (*Sterna paradisae*), Egyptian goose (*Alopochen aegyptiacus*) and marbled teal (*Marmaronetta angustirostris*) are among the birds of the Évros (Εβρος; the classical Hebrus, Turkish Meriçi, Bulgarian Maritsa).

More recently, however, the Évros became widely known for the wildfires that raged through it in the summer of 2023 – some of the worst that Europe has experienced – and the forest is currently in a state of regeneration.

The second-longest river in the Balkans after the Danube, the Évros rises near Sofia and flows 530km into the sea, for 204km forming the border between Greece and Türkiye. It has also, after the EU–Turkish agreement to hold back asylum-seekers and immigrants trying to reach the Aegean Islands, become a major eastern Mediterranean route into Europe, although hardly a safer one; an estimated 2,000 people have drowned in the wide treacherous marshes, or died in the cold bleak emptiness of the border area or in the wildfires of 2023. Local Muslims give them a decent burial, while the local coroner, Dr Pavlos Pavlídis, who can rarely identify the deceased, saves all their belongings in the hope of someday returning them to their families.

WHERE TO STAY

Electra (50 rooms) Pantazídou 52, Orestiáda; 25520 21110; w hotelelectra.gr. Modern rooms with balcony, canopy beds & fireplace; plus a seriously large pool with slides, climbing floats & more. B/fast inc. €€

Evrothírama [map, page 204] (12 studios) 2km north of Pentálofos; 25560 61202; w eurothirama.wordpress.com. Stone-built guesthouse with traditionally furnished rooms, many with fireplace, on an isolated deer farm; the speciality in the restaurant (⏰ 11.00–20.00 Fri–Sat; €€) is slow-cooked venison. €€

Forest Inn Ecotourism Hotel (20 rooms) Dadiá; 25540 32263; m 69368 06068. In a quiet location near the national park information centre, a tidy & well-run inn, ideal for birdwatchers. Homemade pizza available Fri–Sun nights; excellent buffet b/fast inc. €€

Plotini (67 rooms) Ag Paraskeví 1, Didymóteicho; 25530 23400. Large, comfortable & modern hotel at the south end of town next to a park, with a pool in the garden. €€

Koukoúli (11 rooms) Souflí; 25540 22400; w koukoulihotel.gr. This silk house of 1850, where 30,000 cocoons were once housed, is now a pleasant hotel, with a snack bar. B/fast inc. €€–€

La Strada (10 rooms) Tycheró (Τυχερό), on the road to Souflí; 25540 42268; w hotellastrada.gr. Simple roadside inn with gnomes in the yard. €€–€

WHERE TO EAT AND DRINK

GlykáNisos (Anason) By the border crossing at Kastaniés; m 69824 84355; f anasonfishtavern; ⏰ 16.00–midnight Mon–Fri, noon–midnight Sat & Sun. Tasty, well-prepared seafood along with plenty of meats from the spit. It's so close to Türkiye the menu is in Turkish. €€

O Boufés kai to Masáli Prangí, 11km east of Didymóteicho; 25530 92263; f Ο Μπουφές Κ Το Μασάλι; ⏰ evenings Tue–Sat, plus lunch on w/ends. Wonderful place for great food & traditional Thracian music, where, if the mood is right, you may be inspired to join the customers dancing on the tables. €€

Mnímes Tycheró; 25540 41407; m 69451 54148; ⏰ 10.00–01.00 Wed–Sat, 11.00–midnight Sun–Tue. Translated, the full name means 'Memories of food & tradition' & it delivers the goods, often to live *rebétiko* at w/ends. €

O Simos Dadiá; 25540 32214; ⏰ eves Mon & Wed–Fri, lunch & dinner Sat & Sun. Reliable classic taverna. €

WHAT TO SEE AND DO

Évros Delta Visitor Centre (13km east of Alexandroúpolis at Loútra Traïanoupoli (Λουτρά Τραϊανούπολη); 25510 61000; w necca.gov.gr, search 'evros delta'; ⊕ 08.00–16.00 daily) The 9,500ha **Évros Delta National Park** is one of the richest natural habitats in Europe, where 304 of the 423 bird species recorded in Greece have been sighted. Although irrigation on both sides between 1950 and 1970 reduced the delta to a fifth of its original size – testified by the rather dreary landscapes here – it is now protected. This is a wonderful destination for birders, but requires serious planning: foreign citizens need a military zone entry permit from the Hellenic Police and Hellenic Army. The procedure is time-consuming; contact e mdpp.evros-dadia@necca.gov.gr for further instructions on the process. September and October are the best times to visit, but do drench yourself in mosquito repellent.

Across the road from the visitor centre are the visible remains of **Ancient Traïanoúpolis**, named after its founder, Emperor Trajan. For centuries this was an important administrative centre and station on the Via Egnatía before it was flattened by the Bulgarians and re-flattened by the Ottomans. Its landmark is an Ottoman inn, or *han*, built by Gazi Evrenos in 1375, which in its current state resembles a Nissen hut (remains of similar inns can be found in Türkiye, generally separated by some 30–40km – the distance one might travel with fully loaded pack animals in a day – along the old Persian Royal Road, the Silk Road, and other trade routes).

One attraction travellers looked forward to was a warm soak in the thermal **spa** – the modern one, now recently renovated, is in **Loutrós** (🕻 25510 61225).

Doriskos (Δορίσκος) The modern town on the Évros plain is next to the low hill of the unexcavated Persian fortress town founded by Darius the Great in 512BC, where proud Xerxes stopped to count his invading army by building a corral that could hold 10,000 men at a time. Herodotus also wrote that the Greeks were never able to capture it, even after their retreat, making it the last Persian stronghold in Europe, lasting into the mid 5th century BC.

Féres (Φέρες) An important defensive outpost of Constantinople, Féres has a ruined Byzantine aqueduct and, at the top of the town, the most important Byzantine church in Thrace, the **Panagía Kosmosotíra**, 'Our Lady, Saviour of the World' (🕻 25510 26103; w odysseus.culture.gr; free). Isaac Comnenus retired here from the Imperial family in 1152, and spent all his money creating a monastery with rooms for 100 monks and a majestic five-domed church. Converted into a mosque in the 1300s, and reconverted into a church in the 20th century, remnants of its frescoes and carved capitals hint of its once grand imperial decoration. **Ardáni** (Αρδάνι) has the turn-off for the border crossing to Istanbul, following the route of the ancient Via Egnatía; Ipsala on the Turkish side was once Kypsela, the largest city of the ancient Thracians.

Dadiá Forest National Park (Δαδιά; information centre 🕻 25540 32209; w dadia-np.gr; ⊕ 08.00–16.00 daily) Protected since 1980, this woodland is famous for its birds of prey – altogether 36 of the 38 species in Europe pass through in winter and spring, while some 80 birds live here year round; along with Extremadura in Spain, it's the last European refuge of the black vulture. Wolves, jackals, roe deer, bats, turtles and more than 40 kinds of reptile keep them company. However, the precious habitat has suffered serious damage from wildfires in recent years: first in July 2022 and then, in the summer of 2023, the Évros fires – the largest wildfires Europe had seen in decades – raged through the region, burning over 800km^2, including much of the Dadiá Forest. It was devastating.

The natural regeneration of the forest is in progress. At the information centre there are displays on the area's wildlife and maps of routes, including the petrified forest near **Lefkímmi**, south of Dadiá. Accessibility of the trails is based on conditions of the moment (check at the centre), especially from May to October, when the risk for wildfires is especially high. You can also get information from the centre about road accessibility – some places can only be reached by 4x4 or mountain bike.

Souflí (Σουφλί) On the edge of the protected area, Souflí has some fine old houses built during the late 19th and early 20th centuries, when the local silk industry, which employed thousands, was big business, along with wine and sesame oil. In 1922, the town lost most of its mulberry orchards (silkworms eat mulberry leaves) to the Turkish side of the border, and lost much of the rest of its business with the invention of rayon. Silk nonetheless remains the defining feature of the town, with several independently owned businesses producing fine silk, a few museums dedicated to the fabric and streets still lined with mulberry trees.

Silkline Mouhtaridis S A (Km1 Souflí–Alexandroúpolis national road, on your left as you enter Souflí; 25540 24113; w silkline.gr; 09.00–18.00 daily) A visit to this welcoming factory and showroom/shop serves as a fascinating introduction to both the enormously complex process of making silk and its connection to the culture of the region.

Silk Museum (Venizélou 73; 25540 23700; w piop.gr; Mar–mid-Oct 10.00–18.00 Wed–Mon, mid-Oct–Feb 10.00–17.00; €6, concessions €3) Located in the handsome Kourtídis Mansion (1883), this small museum covers the history of silk around the world, how it was made in pre-industrial times, and how Souflí became so successful at it, along with historical photos, some examples of traditional garments and an informative short film.

Art of Silk Museum (Vas Georgioú 199; 25540 22371; w silkmuseum.gr; Apr–Oct 09.00–21.00 daily, Nov–Mar 10.00–20.00 daily; free) Going on six decades now, the Tsiakíri family runs one of the few silkworm-egg-to-finished-silk businesses in Europe. There's a museum and an excellent guided tour in English; they also have a boutique full of lovely things.

Gnafala Folklore Museum (Venizélou 12; 25540 24168; w gnafala.gr; 09.00–21.00 daily, winter closes 20.00) 'Gnafala' is the first yarn made by a silkworm, and this family-run silk shop has a collection of costumes, jewellery, photos and everyday items.

Didymóteicho (Διδυμότειχο; 94km from Alexandroúpolis) This strategic town, piled theatrically on a steep hill where the Erithropótamos River flows into the Évros, has had its fair share of history. Founded by Roman emperor Trajan and named Plotinopoulis after his wife Plotina, it was captured by Frederick Barbarossa during the Third Crusade; in Byzantium's Civil War (1341–47), John Cantacuzenós, the Grand Domestic of Andronicus III, was proclaimed emperor here by the army. In 1361 the town fell to Sultan Murad I, who made it the Ottoman capital before moving to Adrianopolis (Edirne) in 1367. Greeks know it as a place where many have been posted during their mandatory military service, so much so that there's a famous song about it, the 'Didymóteicho Blues' by George Daláras and Lavréntis Machairítsas. There are picturesque back streets inside and around the Byzantine **castle** walls which were built over Plotinopoulis, with good views of the Évros.

Çelebi Sultan Mehmed Mosque (or Bayezid Mosque) (Plateía Dimarchíon) Begun by Sultan Bayezid I in the late 14th century and completed in 1420 by his son Mehmed I (recorded in the inscription over the door), this large square mosque is the oldest on European soil and the largest in Greece (outside of the new one built near Athens). The original interior decoration is well preserved, especially the *mihrab*, with a fresco depicting a heavenly city. It has, or rather had, a unique lead-covered wooden pyramid roof; restoration was begun in 2008 after the minaret partly collapsed in 1998, but in 2017 during the works the roof – like Notre Dame in Paris – accidently caught fire and was destroyed. Funds to fix it have been secured, and the Ministry of Culture, in conjunction with the scientific team of the National Technical University of Athens, will restore the mosque to its most recent historical phase, while highlighting previous stages of its structural history. At the time of writing, works were projected to finish in 2025.

Folklore Museum (Cnr Vatátzi & Kolokotróni; \ 25530 22316; w laografikodidym.wordpress.com; ⊕ 10.00–13.00 Mon–Fri) Didymóteicho's pride and joy, this excellent museum in the Neoclassical Chatzirvasáni Mansion boasts 2,500 items that cover the gamut of a vanishing way of life, including beautiful traditional costumes.

Municipal Art Gallery (\ 25530 23658; ⊕ 09.00–14.00 & 17.30–20.30 Tue–Wed, 09.00–14.00 Thu–Sat, 10.30–13.30 Sun; best to ring ahead; free) Housed in the stately Vafeiádis house inside the Kastro walls, with views over the two rivers, this gallery is filled with the works of locally born magical realism painter Dimitíos Nalbántis (b1957) who has also worked at the UN and designed stamps.

Military Museum (Vas Alexándrou; \ 25530 26518; ⊕ 09.00–14.00 Tue–Sat, 11.00–14.00 Sun; free) Located in a warehouse of 1907 made of Siberian wood, this museum has three floors of displays on the Greek army – uniforms, maps, guns – and audiovisual displays next to a courtyard decorated with weapons.

Byzantine Museum (Plotinoupóleos 9; \ 25530 23960; w odysseus.culture.gr; ⊕ 08.30–15.30 Wed–Fri & Sun, 13.00–20.00 Sat; €4) Built in 2009, the only Byzantine museum in Thrace has artefacts relating to the Via Egnatía, finds from Plotinopoulis and other archaeological sites, and items from local churches and convents.

Around Didymóteicho The easternmost village of mainland Greece, **Pýthio** (Πύθιο; 16km east) has a prominent Byzantine castle, once used as a retreat by Emperor John Cantacuzenós; it also has an evocative old wooden railway station (1896), little changed since the day that the Orient Express passed through on the way to Istanbul. One of Orthodoxy's most recently canonised saints, Cyril VI, former Patriarch of Constantinople, is buried in a new chapel here; hanged by the Ottomans in 1821 in Edirne during the Greek War of Independence, his body was thrown in the river and washed up here.

The last village in Greece up the Erythropótamo, **Metaxádes** (Μεταξάδες; 26km west of Didymóteicho) is one of the most beautiful villages in the area, with its well-preserved stone mansions from the days when its silk merchants travelled the Ottoman Empire.

North of Metaxádes, there's a surprise: the 2nd-century AD **Tumulus of Mikrí Doxipára** (between Mikrí Doxipára (Μικρί Δοξιπάρα), Zoní (Ζονί) and Chelidóna (Χελιδόνα), signposted: Ταφικός Τύμβος Μικρής Δοξιπάρας; ☏ 25520 96033; w odysseus.culture.gr, mikridoxipara-zoni.gr; ⊕ closed for works at the time of writing). Unique in Greece, it contained the incinerated remains of four people – probably members of the same family – buried here over the years, together with the five wagons that pulled their remains, complete with their metal axles, nails and decorative bits, along with the five horses that pulled them, a dog, boar tusks and countless other objects. Tumuli burials are common in this area, and this is one of the largest, and so far the only one with a horse and wagon burial – which were more common a thousand years earlier, in the Iron Age.

Orestiáda (Ορεστιάδα) This city of wide streets was founded in 1923 by Greek refugees from nearby Karagats (Orestiáda in Greek) and Adrianopolis (Edirne) in Eastern Thrace. Sugar beets grow in the flatlands around, and it has more than its share of bored young soldiers. Its multi-media **Historical and Folklife Museum** (Ag Theodóron 103; ☏ 25520 28080; w musorest.gr; ⊕ 10.00–13.00 Tue–Sun) tells the story of the city's foundation and a nostalgic evocation of the homes the refugees left behind in Türkiye, complete with a replica cart loaded with their possessions, their traditional music and instruments, professions, photographs and sports.

Kastaniés (Καστανιές) The Greece–Türkiye border was drawn west of the Évros River to encompass greater Edirne; the Árdas River just west is an important tributary of the Évros and also the scene of a very popular youth festival (w ardasfestival.gr) held in Kastaniés in July. Up until the 21st century, the village was a major producer of sorghum brooms, and you can still see a few about.

Orménio (Ορμένιο) Greece's northernmost town, 156km from Alexandroúpolis, is the last stop before Bulgaria and frontier town Svilengrad. This corner of Thrace is known as the Triethnés, the three nations, where Greece, Bulgaria and Türkiye meet. In 1371, Orménio witnessed the Battle of Maritsa, in which the Ottoman army defeated the Serbs, leaving the Évros running red with blood and opening up the way for the Ottoman conquest of Central Macedonia.

SAMOTHRÁKI

Samothráki (Σαμοθράκη), or Samothrace, is an island of lingering magic, of cliffs, nightingales, plane forests and waterfalls, sweeping around the Mountain of the Moon (Mount Fengári, 1,611m), the highest in the Aegean; Poseidon sat on its summit to watch the Trojan War. Often wind-whipped, and lacking a natural harbour, Samothráki was nevertheless one of the most-visited islands of antiquity, thanks to its sanctuary of the Cabeiri, the Great Gods of the Underworld. Today its natural beauty and 'mystical energy' attract a fair number of New Age types (not least because you can camp for free). Be aware that most hotels and restaurants close between October and Easter; and bring cash – the island's banks can run out, and not all places accept cards.

HISTORY Once densely populated, Samothráki owes its importance to its position near the Dardanelles – the strait named after the legendary

7 | THRACE (ΘΡΑΚΗ)

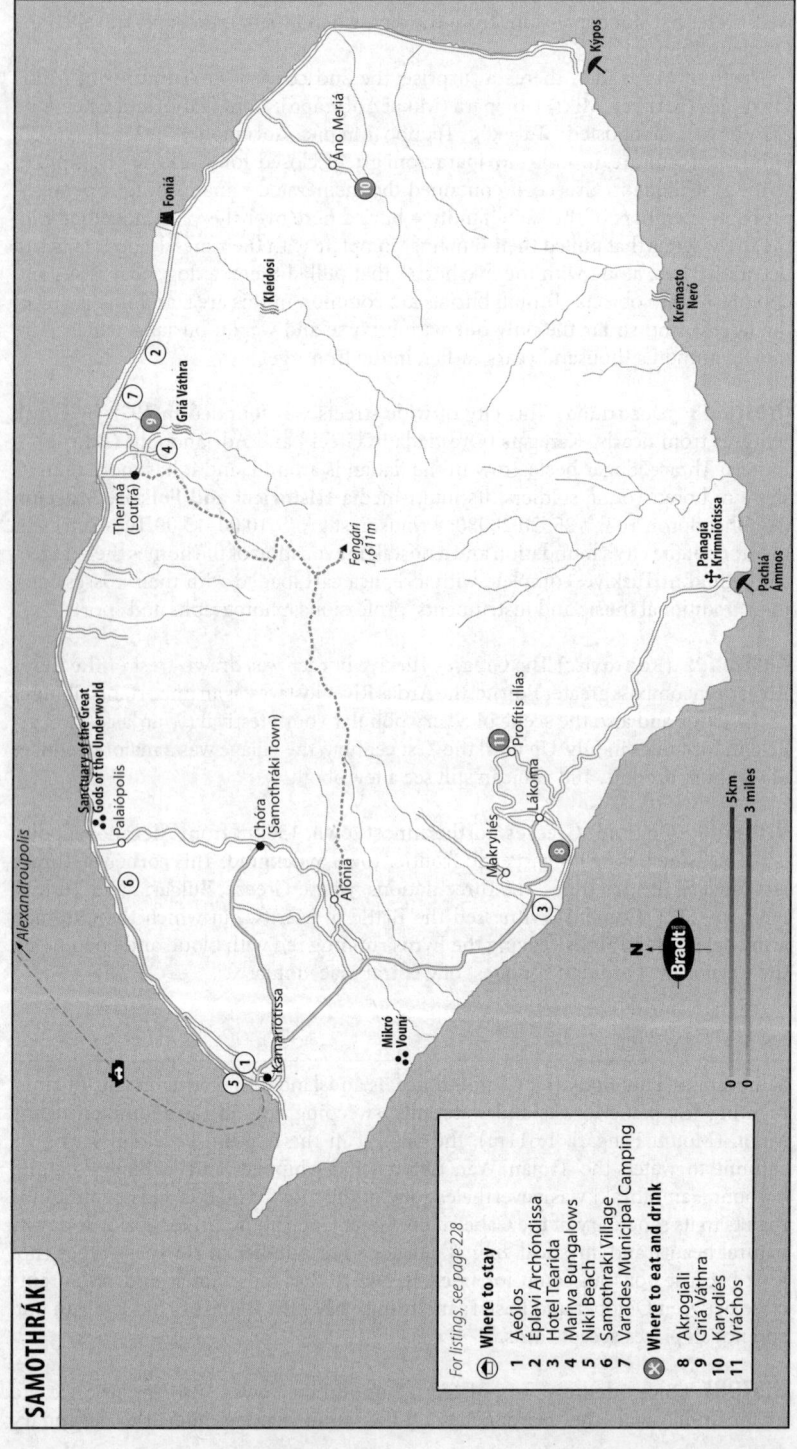

MYSTERIES OF THE UNDERWORLD

The Great Gods were chthonic or Underworld deities, older and more potent than the Olympian upstarts of the patriarchal state religion, at whom even first poet Homer could poke fun. But no-one dared to mess about with the Great Gods; no writer revealed the mysteries, although they (like the more famous Eleusis mysteries) may have offered promises for the afterlife. Although dedications found at the sanctuary were simply 'to the gods', their Thracian secret names were revealed by a Hellenistic writer: Mnaseas, Axieros, Axiokersos, Axiokersa and Kadmilos, whom the Greeks identified with Demeter, Hades, Persephone, Kore and Hermes.

The mysteries took place by torchlight. Anyone, male or female, free or slave, could undergo the two levels of initiation, the *myesis* and the more important *epopteia*. The *epopteia* began with a confession that may have been unique in the Greek world (the priest would ask the candidate 'which was the most lawless deed committed in his life'), followed by baptism, the winding of a purple sash below the abdomen, followed by the sacrifice of a ram. Initiation at Samothráki was thought to be sovereign against drowning; in myth, the Argonauts, at Orpheus' suggestion, were initiated before entering the Hellespont. Another peculiarity of the cult involved magnetised iron rings, perhaps symbols of attraction, given to initiates: several were found on site. King Lysander of Sparta and Herodotus were initiates, but it was in the Hellenistic era that the sanctuary knew its greatest fortune: Philip II of Macedonia fell in love with Olympias of Epirus, mother of Alexander the Great, during a ceremony. He was also keen to promote the only pan-Hellenic shrine in northern Greece to demonstrate his 'Greek-ness' to the bad-mouthing Athenians.

Samothracian Dardanos, founder of Troy; its oldest shrine (the rock altar beneath the Arsinoëion) goes back, according to Herodotus, to the pre-Indo-European Pelasgians – a period seemingly confirmed (Herodotus is usually right!) by recent excavations at Mikró Vouní on the island's southwest coast. In the 8th century BC Aeolians from Lésvos colonised Samothráki and mingled peaceably with the earlier settlers, worshipping the Cabeiri, the Underworld Gods of the Thracians, whose yet-undeciphered language survived in religious rituals into the 1st century BC (see above). By the mid 5th century BC, Samothráki's sanctuary was the religious centre of the North Aegean, attracting a steady stream of initiates, including Hellenistic and Roman rulers (notably the Ptolemys of Egypt) who also used Samothráki as a naval base, relying on its sacred soil for protection. St Paul stopped by in AD49, but failed to impress the locals, who kept their sanctuary running until the AD390s, when Emperor Theodosius ordered the closing of temples. But their fascination lingered: the Cabeiri make an appearance in Goethe's *Faust*, and excavations of the sanctuary were funded by the Bollingen Foundation, set up in honour of Carl Jung.

Without its sacred status, Samothráki itself was forgotten. Pirates forced the remaining inhabitants to the hills. In the mid 14th century, emperor John V Palaiologos gave the island to the Gattilusi family of Genoa in exchange for their assistance in helping him obtain the imperial throne of Byzantium. Afterwards it was ruled by the Turks, the Venetians, the Turks again (who razed much of it in 1821) and the Bulgarians, until it joined Greece in 1912.

7 | THRACE (ΘΡΑΚΗ)

GETTING THERE AND AROUND

By sea Fast Ferries (📞 25510 82289; w fastferries.com.gr) make the 2-hour journey from Alexandroúpolis nearly daily, sometimes twice a day. Book online, and well in advance, for July and August.

By bus Several buses a day run from Kamariótissa to Chóra, and three to Alónia, Palaiópolis, Thermá (Loutrá) and Pachía Ámmos, some run by KTEL (📞 25510 26479), others by the community (📞 25510 41218, 25513 50800; w samothraki.gr, insamothraki.com/samothrace-bus-schedules.html).

By taxi There are four taxi drivers on the island; contact them on m 69723 81762; m 69866 69272; m 69769 91270; and m 69728 83501.

By car There is only one petrol station (on the road to Chóra), and 20,000 goats, not one of whom has the least road sense.
In season, **hire cars** are in short supply: try, Rabbit (m 69764 35139), Kirkos (m 69953 81044) or Niki (m 69489 39192), all in Kamariótissa.

🏠 WHERE TO STAY *Map, page 226*

Hotel Tearida (12 rooms) Makryliés (6km south of Kamariótissa); 📞 25510 95111; ⊕ Easter–Sep. By the sea, new studios sleeping up to 4 with terrace & a pool. €€

Aeólos (56 rooms) 300m east of Kamariótissa; 📞 25510 41795; w hotelaeolos.com; ⊕ Apr–Oct. On a hill 50m from the sea, a quiet family-run hotel in a flowery garden; all rooms have balcony, some with sea view. €€–€

Niki Beach Hotel (37 rooms) Kamariótissa; 📞 25510 41545; w nikibeach.gr. 3-star hotel near a rocky beach with sunset views, a pool, garden & bar (but no restaurant), & a free shuttle from the port (500m) if you book. Greek b/fast €6. €€–€

Samothraki Village (27 rooms) Palaiópolis; 📞 25510 42300; w samothrakivillage.gr. Very pleasant contemporary choice with a pool & restaurant. B/fast inc. €€–€

Éplavi Archóndissa (6 rooms) East of Thermá; 📞 25510 98098; w archondissa.gr; ⊕ Apr–Oct. Charming studios & 2-room apartments (some sleeping 4), with private terrace or balcony, with traditional touches, kitchenettes & AC. 20m from the beach. B/fast available. €

Mariva Bungalows (50 rooms) Thermá; m 69324 37030; w mariva.gr; ⊕ May–Sep. Ivy-covered bungalows in the midst of a plane tree forest & hydrangeas; friendly & quiet, & now boasting a yoga salon. €

Varades Municipal Camping Thermá; 📞 25510 98424 ; f campingvarades. In a beautiful setting, basic facilities for caravans & tents in the woodlands by the sea. It's really cheap, & there is also a free campground. €

🍴 WHERE TO EAT AND DRINK *Map, page 226*

Akrogiali Lákkoma, 8km from Kamariótissa; 📞 25510 95123; w akrogialisamothraki.gr; ⊕ Jun–Sep 13.00–midnight daily. Excellent fish taverna with romantic sunsets. Also has 5 spotless rooms (€) for rent. €€

Karydiés Áno Meriá (signposted 3km from the coast beyond Thermá); 📞 25510 98366; ⊕ Jun–Sep noon–23.00 daily. Lovely lush setting & famous for semi-wild kid – the island's speciality – prepared 26 different ways, including cooked in parchment or stewed with quince. But lots of other dishes, too. €€

Griá Váthra Thermá; m 69720 75480; ⊕ May–Oct 13.30–midnight daily, may be closed Mon. Classic food, including kid, served in a shady grove. €

Vráchos Profítis Ilías; 📞 25510 95264; ⊕ 11.00–23.30 daily. The 'Rock' is legendary for its herby succulent wild kid on a spit, but they also do salads & greens. €

WHAT TO SEE AND DO Samothráki's workaday port, **Kamariótissa** (Καμαριώτισσα), is a simple place with an exposed rocky beach and an aeolian windmill park by

SAMOTHRÁKI

a small lagoon. A farm road leads in 2.5km to the fertile plain of Livádi and the archaeological site of **Mikró Vouní**, a proto-urban community of around 500 that survived until c1700BC, and was apparently a stop on the trade route of metals between the Minoans of Crete and the Black Sea; finds include a number of Minoan clay tablets in Linear A, dating to the 19th or 18th century BC – the first to have been found this far north. A building (⊕ May–Sep) covers some of the foundations.

Above Kamariótissa, **Chóra** (Χώρα), or Samothráki Town, where most of the island's inhabitants live, occupies a picturesque amphitheatre below the **castle** built in 1433 'by the glorious Palamedes Gattilusi' (as the proud marble inscription says, with its single- and double-headed eagles) who kept it for 20 years before it was captured by the Turks. Chóra has whitewashed houses with red-tiled roofs, a charming century-old bakery (famous for its bread kneaded five times), five mummified heads (of martyrs killed by the Turks for reconverting, up in the church) and an interesting little **Folklore Museum** (\ 25510 41227; ⊕ summer 08.00–14.00 & 17.30–23.45 daily – call first), with house furnishings, traditional costumes, textiles, embroideries, tools, photos and icons. At the entrance to Chóra stands a modern winged statue of Nike (Victory), not quite as grand as the one it lost to the Louvre but a dead ringer for Olympic gymnast Nadia Comăneci.

Pretty agricultural hamlets dot the slopes of southern Samothráki: **Alónia** (Αλώμια) has ruins of a Roman bath, while hilltop **Profítis Ilías** (Προφήτης Ηλίας) is famous for tavernas serving semi-wild kid, the island's speciality. From delightful **Lákoma** (Λάκκωμα) it's a windy 8km to the turn-off for the church of **Panagía Krimniótissa**, tottering on rocks and taking in huge views as far as the Turkish island of Imbros. Below lies the island's only sandy beach, **Pachiá Ámmos** (Παχιά Άμμος), with a taverna. A boat excursion is the only way to visit the spectacularly rugged southern coast east of Pachiá Ámmos, where you'll find **Krémasto Neró** ('hanging water'), a 180m waterfall, reputedly the highest in Greece and one of only a few in Europe outside of Greenland that spills directly into the sea.

Sanctuary of the Great Gods of the Underworld
(Palaiópolis (Παλαιόπολη), 7km from Kamariótissa; \ 25510 41474; w odysseus.culture.gr; ⊕ 08.30–15.30 daily; €6, concessions €3) The sanctuary, set in trees overlooking the sea, enjoys an idyllic setting, while goat bells tinkle on the mountain above. The first large structure you come across, the rectangular **Anaktoron** (House of the Lords), dates from the 6th century BC and was rebuilt twice, lastly by the Romans; first-level initiations were held here, but only the initiated, or *mystai*, were allowed in its inner holy of holies on the north side. A pile of carbon discovered in the Anaktoron suggests it had a wooden stage; a torch base is a relic of the night-time rites. Ancient writers referred to the Anaktoron's two bronze statues of Hermes in a state of excitement. Adjacent, by the Sacred Rock, is the **Arsinoëion**, at 20m in diameter the largest circular or *tholos* structure ever built by the ancient Greeks. It was dedicated in 280BC by Queen Arsinoë II, wife and sister of Ptolemy Philadelphos of Egypt. It had one door and no windows; no-one knows quite what went on there.

The rectangular foundation south of the Arsinoëion belonged to the **Temenos**, where ceremonies took place. Adjacent stand the five re-erected Doric columns of the **Hieron**, or 'New Temple', where the upper level of initiation or *epopteia* was held; it dates from 300BC and was last restored after an earthquake in the 3rd century AD. The Hieron's interior – 11m wide – was another ancient Greek record breaker, as the largest unsupported span. The apse to the south was the business end – the chthonic holy of holies. There are scant remains of a larger theatre and buildings where votive gifts were brought. To the north are the ruins of a building identified as the 4th-century BC **Hall of Choral Dancers**, source of the frieze in the museum (see below).

The hill above was the original entrance to the sanctuary, which included a tunnel leading up to the massive gateway donated by Ptolemy II: the **Propylae Ptolemaion**, once second only in grandeur to the great Propylaia on the Acropolis of Athens, made with the same Pentelic marble, imported here at huge expense, along with marble from Thássos (only the substructure survives). Initiates would then enter the **theatrical circle** for the beginning of the purification ceremonies. Next to it is a **Doric building**, also in Pentelic marble, dedicated by Alexander the Great's half-brother, Philip III Arrhidaios, and his posthumous son Alexander IV, who nominally reigned after Alexander's death.

The **museum** (same ticket) at the entrance to the site has a plaster replica of the *Victory of Samothrace*, a Hellenistic marble sculpture that, it is thought, stood on the prow of a marble ship above the theatre – though the original was discovered elsewhere, by Charles Champoiseau, the French consul at Adrianople (now Edirne, in Türkiye), in 1863 and taken to Paris that same year. The Louvre, of course, bagged the prize – and sent back a consolation copy. No-one is sure who dedicated the *Victory*, but a good guess would be Macedonian king Dimitrios Poliorketes (the 'Besieger') c300BC. The museum also has some good vases, especially an Attic *pelike* of 490BC with a dancing goat; the Archaic-style frieze of temple dancers donated by Philip II to decorate the Hall of the Choral Dancers; the entrance to the Temenos, or sacred area, with *steles* warning off the uninitiated; and, among the votive offerings found on the site, a perfect terracotta football.

Up the road, the unexcavated ancient city of **Palaiópolis** (⊕ 08.30–20.30 daily; free) served the sanctuary. The island's medieval Genoese bosses, the Gattilusi, used its stone to build their walls and watchtower and much of what remains is covered with plane trees. A path leads to the foundations of a church perhaps founded in honour of St Paul's visit. In 2008 a new building known as the '**Seat of St Paul**' and decorated with mosaics was erected to mark the spot where the first Christian in Europe set foot.

Thermá
(Θέρμα; or Loutrá; Λουτρά) The road continues east to Thermá, which, like much of this idyllic corner of Samothráki, is immersed in chestnut and plane trees. It has a small marina and a delightful little rustic spa where you can soak in therapeutic, sulphurous, mildly radioactive warm water. Follow the signs to the path to **Griá Váthra** (Γριά Βάθρα) – a short walk through a canopy of ancient trees takes you to a natural pool and little waterfalls that flow even in the scorching days of summer and where you almost expect to see a nymph in the dappled shade.

Mount Fengári
(Φεγγάρι) From Thermá, the end of the E6 trail, marked with red blobs, leads to the rocky ridge of the summit (1,611m). It's a walk of medium difficulty, but more exhausting than climbing Olympus because you'll be doing the 1,611m all at once and there are no shelters and only one very dribbling spring to replenish water bottles. Allow 11–12 hours there and back. And check the weather forecast: lightning strikes are common. If you make it to the top, you can enjoy the same view as Poseidon: a stunning panorama of the North Aegean from the T road in the east to Mount Athos in the west. Because of its altitude, Mount Fengári hosts a number of rare endemic plants: *Alyssum degenianum*, *Symphyandra samothracica*, *Herniaria degenii* and *Potentilla geoides*. The mountain's ancient name, Sáos, recalls the Saoi, 'the rescued ones', a secret society of men sworn into the mysteries of the Great Gods.

Foniá (Φονιά; 5km from Thermá) The medieval 'Killer' Tower, built by the Genoese, sits in the little delta of the Foniás River, which flows all year round. There's a beautiful 30-minute path up its ravine to an enchanting waterfall, where you can take a dip in the *vathrá* (pool). There are numerous other pools and falls further up, although as you climb higher it can get slippery; the highest waterfall, the 35m **Kleídosi**, is a 2-hour hike from Foniá. After this oasis, the road (and bus) continues to the long black pebble beach at **Kýpos** (Κύπος; 18km from Thermá), with crystal-clear water for snorkellers and a small café, and where clothes are optional at the far end.

8

Western Macedonia (Δυτική Μακεδονία)

Western (or, as it is known in many history books, 'Upper') Macedonia is a beautiful corner of Greece, but it's not one that often makes it on to magazine covers. It is a land of lakes and wetlands, reflecting the often starkly bare mountains that embrace them, where fishermen get around in their distinctive squared-off boats called *pláves*. Kastoriá, covering a hilly lake peninsula, is a Byzantine jewel, while the two Préspa Lakes, shared by Albania and North Macedonia, are pure poetry. Bears and wolves live in the wilderness; there are vineyards, fields of saffron and peppers, and the pristine Vália Cálda, one of the jewels of the Pindus National Park; and the famous River Party music festival in Nestório. And it won't be long before the remarkable archaeological finds around Amýntaio will bring a lot more interest to the region.

HISTORY

In ancient times there were several small Macedonian kingdoms here – Orestis, Tymphaia, Lyncestis, Elimeia, Eordaia and Pelagonia – not exactly household names, but by the 5th century BC Upper Macedonian kingdoms were allied to lowland Macedon; by 358BC they had one king and his name was Philip II.

Although Western Macedonia later saw the usual array of conquerors, including the medieval incursions of the Bulgarians and Normans, its very remoteness enabled its merchants in Siátista and Kastoriá to amass fortunes in central Europe without much interference from the Ottomans. Borders between countries were non-existent: Greeks, Vlachs, Jews, Albanians, Muslims and Slavs all lived together. Their old way of life began to change under Ali Pasha (page 268) and vanished in the turmoil of the 20th century. As the Ottoman Empire broke up, there was a rush for people, who had previously identified themselves only by religion, to decide on their 'national identity' so the competing countries could claim their lands within their borders. Even so, when the borders were set after the Balkan Wars, hundreds of thousands of Slavic speakers found their homes, where their ancestors had lived since the early Middle Ages, on the Greek side of the dotted line.

Because times were still very unsettled – especially after the Asia Minor Catastrophe (page 13) – there was increasing pressure to assimilate. As elsewhere in northern Greece, every non-Greek place name was renamed in the 1920s by a committee of scholars. In 1936, Prime Minister Metaxas, inspired by Mussolini, banned the use of minority languages, including Macedonian Slav (although it was the only language many knew). People were forced to change their names to Greek ones. Heavy fines, threats and beatings were the penalties for defying the rules; men were sent into exile on the Aegean islands, some for belonging to the Communist party, which from 1934 on was the only national Greek party to support the minority.

In World War II, some Macedonian Slavs welcomed the Bulgarians as liberators, but far more joined the resistance in the Communist National Liberation Front (Macedonia). As the Civil War heated up, the Greek Communist Party (the KKE) – egged on by Stalin and Tito – made the creation of a large independent 'Macedonia' their platform, which would include 'Aegean Macedonia', insisting that there had been an ethnic Slavic Macedonian people present since ancient times, complete with their own language and culture. Their provisional government in northwest Greece set up Slav-language schools and newspapers.

However, after the nightmare of the Occupation, when many Greeks naturally sympathised with the resistance, the Aegean Macedonia platform lost the KKE much of their national support. In 1947, Athens revoked the citizenship of anyone who fought against the Greek government and expropriated their property. There were atrocities on both sides – looting, torture and executions. In the spring of 1948, as the Greek government gained ground, the provisional government announced the evacuation of all children between the ages of 3 and 15 from the territory they controlled to Yugoslavia and Albania (the KKE claimed it was for their safety; the Greek government claims they were kidnapped to be brought up as little Communists). An estimated 30,000 would end up in various Eastern bloc countries.

Many were eventually joined by their families. Half of the 100,000 Communists who fled or were exiled over the borders at the end of the Civil War were Slav-speakers. Many ended up in Tashkent (Uzbekistan), others in Australia and North America; those who stayed in Greece were exiled to the islands and compelled to renounce their left-wing past. The lingering bitterness over the attempts to create an 'Aegean Macedonia' meant that in 1982, when Andréa Papandréou granted an amnesty to resistance fighters, only those of 'Greek ethnicity' were allowed to return and reclaim their property. The net result has been a vast depopulation, most hauntingly evident in the abandoned 'mud villages' of the Korésteia (page 248).

When Yugoslavia imploded in 1991 and the new state just north began calling itself the 'Republic of Macedonia', it brought forth a blast of Greek hysteria that few outsiders could understand. Papandréou blanketed Greece with 'Macedonia is Only Greek' signs, confusing foreigners who thought that Greece was claiming part of Yugoslavia. Nor did politicians in Skopje help matters with loose talk about open borders of a 'spiritual Macedonia' while erecting giant statues of Philip II and Alexander. The only winners in this debate were makers of nationalist keyrings, bumper stickers and lapel badges, with both sides using the Star of Vergína on their trinkets to prove their point.

At the height of the dispute Athens blocked the landlocked country's access to the sea, forcing a compromise that soothed Greek concerns: the new republic would be called the Former Yugoslav Republic of Macedonia, or FYROM. But at the same time, at least before the economic crisis, Greek business was investing heavily in the country, funding its banks, and running its telecommunications networks.

Although it's no longer illegal to speak Macedonian Slavic, the Greek government insists that those who do are a linguistic 'Slavophone Greek' minority rather than an ethnic one, because those 'whose national consciousness was not Greek moved to neighbouring states'. No-one knows how many there are (to avoid harassment, they call themselves the 'locals', or *dópio*, who speak the 'local language', or *dópia*). The Rainbow party, founded in Flórina in 1994, campaigns for minority recognition and to allow for the return of all refugees in North Macedonia, but never gets many votes.

8 | WESTERN MACEDONIA (ΔΥΤΙΚΗ ΜΑΚΕΔΟΝΙΑ)

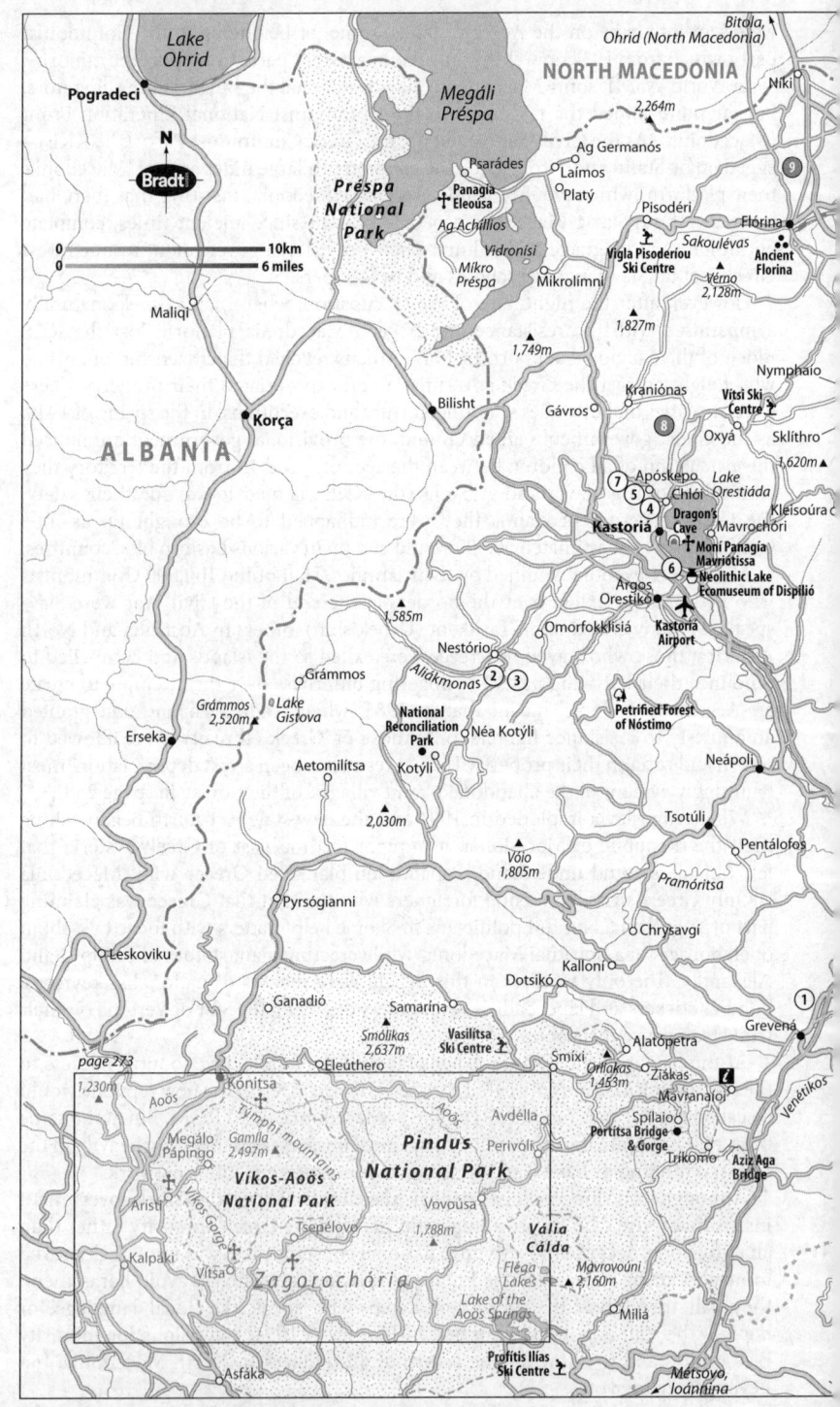

HISTORY

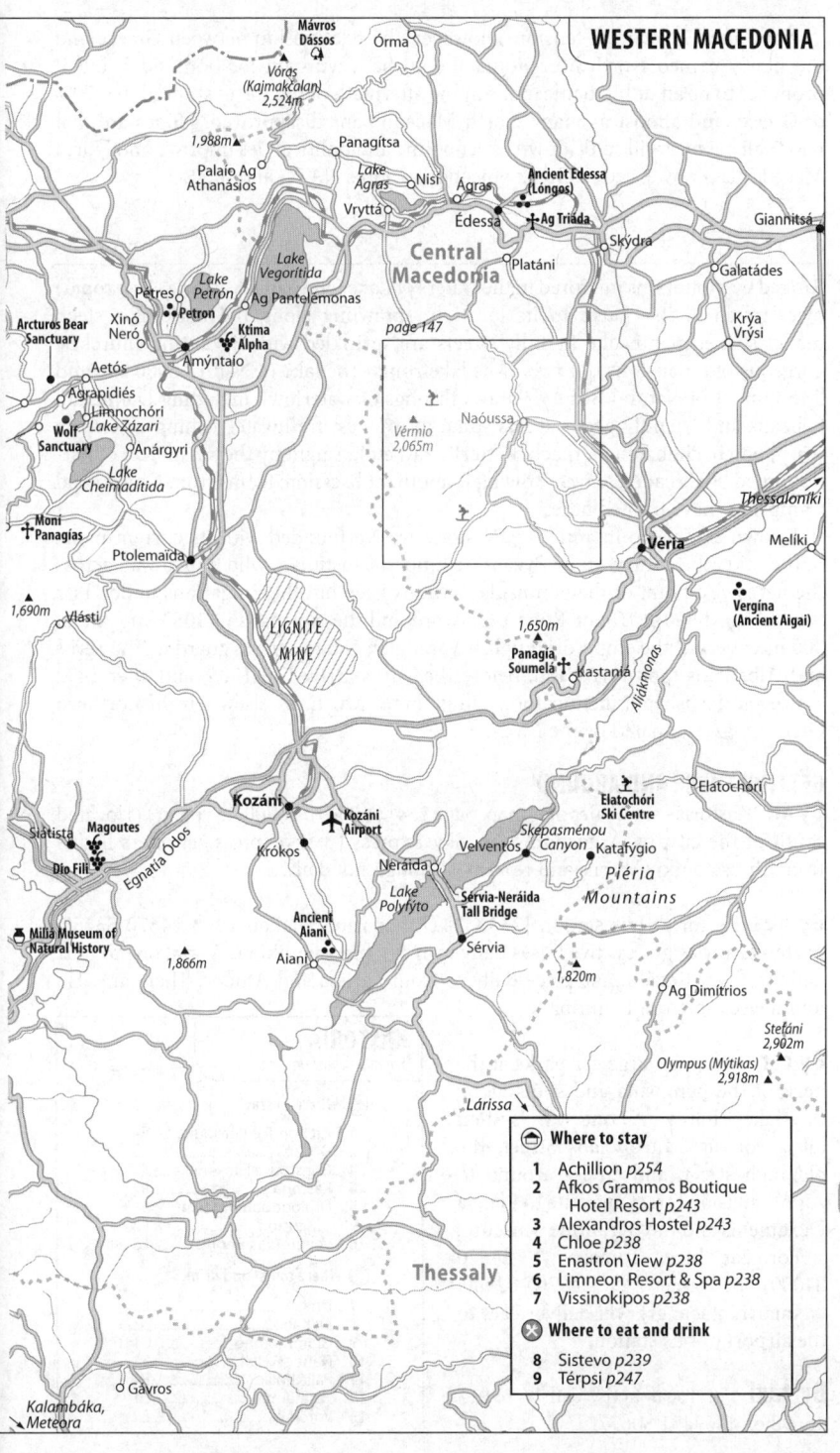

Now, after 30 years of tensions, however, the relationship between Greece and the newly named North Macedonia should be a win-win for both sides, but it promises to be an uphill battle: polls in the aftermath of the treaty showed that 70% of Greeks and almost as many North Macedonians disapproved. Hopes are that nationalist issues will settle down as economic and political ties improve and North Macedonia – now freed of Greek objections – joins NATO and the EU.

KASTORIÁ

Ringed by mountains mirrored in the waters of Lake Orestiáda, Kastoriá (Καστοριά) owes much of its charm to its location, sprawling along the neck of a steep mallet-shaped peninsula. Its hilly streets are sprinkled with Byzantine churches; gorgeous old mansions dot two of its lakefronts. The lake (a Natura 2000 site and 'Monument of Natural Beauty') draws throngs of waterfowl, including Dalmatian pelicans and friendly geese. It has some of the best freshwater fishing in Greece (carp, perch, chub, tench, roach, butterfly ray, etc), caught by the small fleet of flat-bottomed boats called *pláves*. Rowing is another obsession: teams from Oxford and Cambridge have trained here.

Known as Keletro in antiquity, Kastoriá was re-founded with its current name in the mid 6th century AD by Byzantine Emperor Justinian, who built a wall across the narrowest point of the peninsula. It didn't keep out the Bulgarians under Tsar Samuel in AD990–1018, or Robert Guiscard and the Normans in 1083, in spite of 300 members of the emperor's English Varangian Guard sent to guard it. The Serbs and Albanians took turns, too, before the Turks arrived in 1385; and after 1492 a sizeable Jewish population took refuge here, which, as elsewhere in northern Greece, was decimated by the Nazis.

GETTING THERE AND AROUND

By air Kastoriá's small airport [map, page 234] (24670 21700; w ypa.gr) is located south of the city, by Árgos Orestikó. Sky Express (w skyexpress.gr) offers flights from Thessaloníki, Athens and Kozáni, although not daily.

By bus Kastoriá's bus station [237 C2] (Athanasíou Diákou 14; 24670 83455; w ktel-kastorias.gr) has five buses daily to/from Thessaloníki via Véria, one to four daily to/from Kozáni, and once daily to/from Lárissa and Athens. There are also four a week to/from Ioánnina.

By car There are large car parks at the neck of the peninsula and spots along the lake shores. A one-way system takes you up Mitropóleos Street, the old high street, and circles around to Ag Athanasíou Street en route to Plateía Dexamenís and the Byzantine Museum.

For **car hire**, Tomaso (24670 84000) or Smart (24670 82900; w smartrentacar.gr) will deliver cars to the airport or bus station.

By taxi For local taxis, call m 69817 46698 or m 69471 80677.

KASTORIÁ
For listings, see from page 238

Where to stay
1. Archontikó Vérgoula........E4
2. Doltsó................................E3
3. Guestouse Filoxenía........F2
4. Kastoriá............................F2
5. Orologopoulos Luxury Mansion.........................E3
6. Venetoúla's Rooms............E3

Where to eat and drink
7. Doltsó................................E3
8. En Kairó............................D3
9. Grammofono....................C1
10. Nautical Hall.....................F1
11. Paliá Póli..........................E4
12. Pasatempos......................C1
13. Voroinó.............................E2

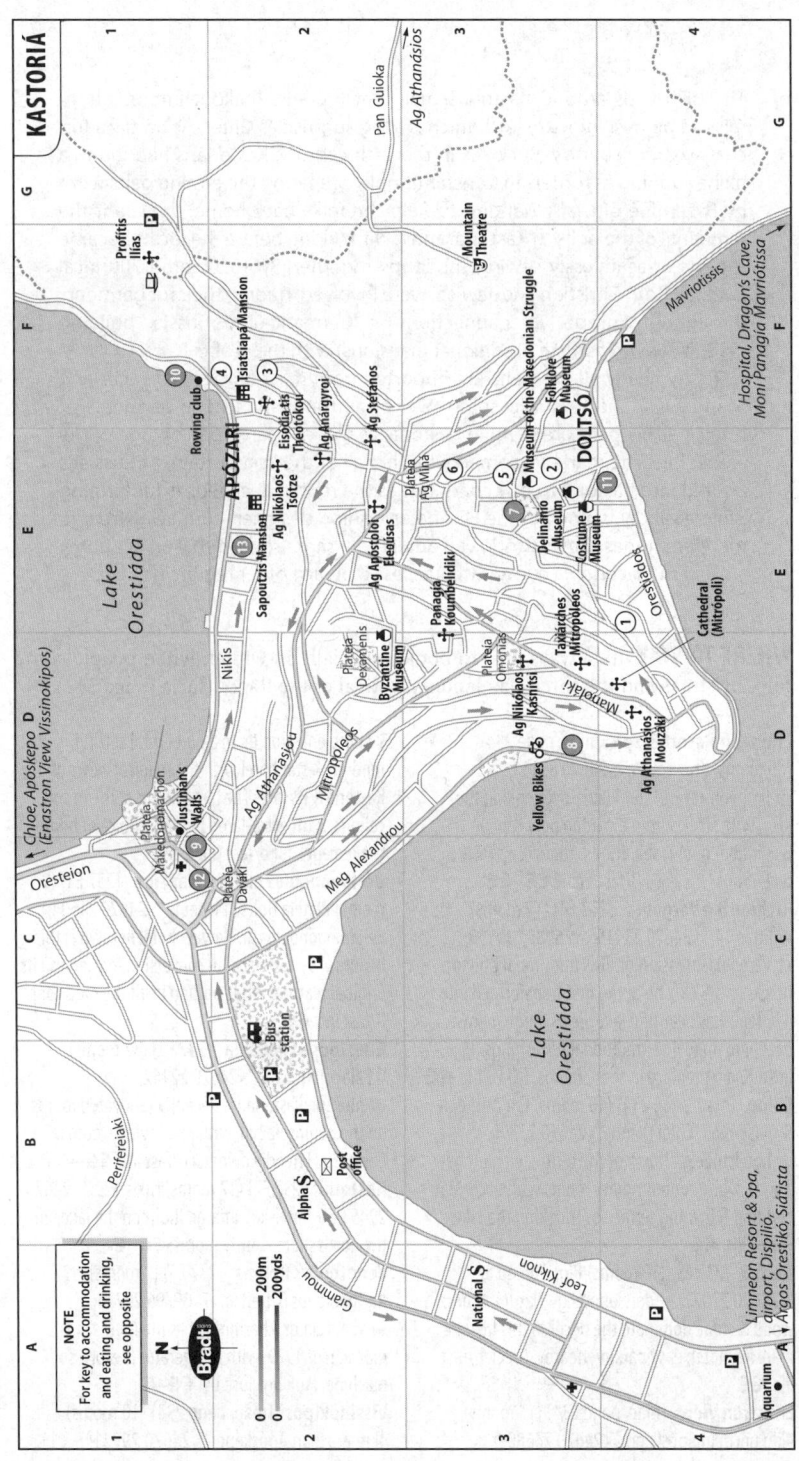

8 | WESTERN MACEDONIA (ΔΥΤΙΚΗ ΜΑΚΕΔΟΝΙΑ)

THE CITY OF MINK

The billboards around Kastoriá's main entry points make it impossible to miss its biggest industry: fur, which is a big surprise as Greece is hardly a fur-coat-wearing country. But back in the 14th century, Kastorians had found a niche working as furriers in Constantinople, preparing the ermine pelts worn by Byzantine officials. Wanting to help the folks back home, they sent the remnants of the pelts to Kastoriá, and it wasn't long before the locals became experts at seamlessly sewing the strips together. By 1520 some 700 local families, both Christian and Jewish, were involved, trading their fur garments throughout Europe via connections in Germany and Russia, building magnificent *archontiká* (traditional mansions) with the profits.

Today nearly all the pelts are imported from mink farms in the USA and Scandinavia and it is said some 90% of all the world's mink garments of small, narrow pelts are sewn in Kastoriá, as well as a large percentage of the whole furs. The market boomed with the fall of the Iron Curtain, as Russians poured into Kastoriá to buy coats, but as the rouble declined, as fur farming is increasingly banned in the EU and as fashion designers turn away from it, there are hopes that Kastoriá can adjust to a more tourism-based economy – Western Macedonia currently earns less than any other region in Greece.

 WHERE TO STAY It's always best to book, especially in winter, when people come for Christmas and the three-day January festival of the Ragoutsária (page 242).

Limneon Resort & Spa [map, page 234] (89 rooms) Km4 south; 24670 85111; w limneon.com. 5-star luxury overlooking the lake, with sleek suites, a garden pool & pool bar, indoor pool & spa, fitness room & a swish restaurant (€€€€). B/fast inc. €€€–€€

Archontikó Vérgoula [237 E4] (12 rooms) Aïdítras 14; 24670 23415; m 69857 39159; w vergoulasmansion.gr. This traditional Doltsó house of 1857 – one of the first transformed into a hotel – has beautiful lake views, large rooms (sleeping up to 4) & traditional furnishings, including a fireplace in some rooms. B/fast inc. €€

Chloe [map, page 234] (40 rooms) Cnr Anthéon & Giasemión, Chlói (Χλόι); 24670 21300; w hotelchloe.gr. North of the centre, elegant new, bright, white contemporary rooms with Coco-Mat bedding & inviting terrace overlooking the lake. B/fast inc. €€

Doltsó [237 E3] (10 rooms) Ríga Feréou 5; 24670 22022; w doltsohotel.gr. Natural tones, wood & stone dominate the décor in this historic mansion hotel; easy parking nearby. Greek b/fast inc. €€

Enastron View [map, page 234] (17 rooms) 4km north in Apóskepo; 24670 24680;

w hotelenastron.gr. In a quiet rural setting, modern 4-star hotel with the magical views of Kastoriá & its lake. The large rooms come in soft colours, with extra-large bed & a choice of home-cooked eggs for b/fast (inc). €€

Orologopoulos Luxury Mansion [237 E3] (9 rooms) Plateía Doltsó Picheón; 24670 21604; w orologopoulos.gr. Newest hotel in town is this beautiful 5-star mansion conversion, preserving its original features while adding in all the mod cons. B/fast inc. €€

Guestouse Filoxenía [237 F2] (37 rooms) G Palaeológou 23; 24670 22162; w filoxeniakastoria.gr. Recently renovated rooms on the peninsula hill, with lovely views from its balconies. Friendly owners; b/fast inc. €€–€

Kastoriá [237 F2] (37 rooms) Níkis 122; 24670 29453; w hotel-kastoria.gr. Right on the lake, on the north shore. Comfy rooms. €€–€

Venetoúla's Rooms [237 E3] (7 rooms) Ag Theológos 6, Doltsó; m 69796 26726; w venetula.gr. Charming en-suite rooms in a mansion of 1929, with refrigerator & espresso machine. Parking close by. €€–€

Vissinokipos [map, page 234] (10 rooms) 4km north in Apóskepo; 24670 29721;

KASTORIÁ

w hotelvissinokipos.gr. The 'Cherry Orchard' is an arty boutique guesthouse run by a lovely couple who can tell you all about the region (& the most beautiful motorcycle routes). Bar, board games & books galore; delicious b/fast inc. €€–€

WHERE TO EAT AND DRINK

Doltsó [237 E3] Tsakáli 2; ✆ 24670 23377; w ntoltso.gr; ⊕ to 22.30 Thu–Tue. Handsome traditional restaurant, specialising in bean dishes, meatballs, pork with plums, *sarmádes* (local meat-&-herb-filled cabbage rolls, topped with melted butter & red chilli flakes). Try the house red. €€

Nautical Hall [237 F1] Sougarídi 1; ✆ 24670 22330; f NauticalHallKastoria; ⊕ 18.00–midnight Thu, 18.00–04.00 Fri–Sun. Right on the water at the Rowing Club, with beautiful views & romantic lounge for a coffee & drink & an eclectic menu if you're peckish. €€

Paliá Póli [237 E4] Orestiádos 51; ✆ 24670 21401; ⊕ 12.30–midnight daily. In a mansion with a romantic lakefront courtyard, serving delicious baked lamb, *sarmádes*, local wines & beautiful Greek music. €€

En Kairó [237 D3] Meg Alexándrou 139; ✆ 24670 27247; f καφεποτείον έν καιρωι; ⊕ noon–midnight Wed–Mon. Excellent Greek coffee, well-prepared *mezédes* (don't miss the Flórina peppers) & *tsípouro*; often live traditional music on Sat eves. €

Grammofono [237 C1] Skapédeios Agorá 2; ✆ 24673 01336; f Γραμμόφωνο; ⊕ 18.00–01.00 Tue–Sun. Cheap & cheerful modern bistro/bar next to the town hall, with lovely food on a big menu & outdoor terrace. €

Pasatempos [237 C1] Ermoú 6; ✆ 24674 00113; f pasatemposkastoria; ⊕ 18.00–23.30 Tue–Sun. Mix of gourmet tapas & *mezédes* in a warm, welcoming spot. €

Sistevo [map, page 234] 11km north in Sidirochóri (Σιδηροχώρι); ✆ 24670 72193; ⊕ no specific hours – call to check. A simple, rustic place famous for its superb mushroom dishes in season, made with porcinis & the 'king of mushrooms', *Amanita caesarea*. €

Voroinó [237 E2] Níkis 80; ✆ 24670 22440; f Βοροινό; ⊕ 10.00–02.00 daily. Lake views in an attractive setting under exotic arches, with the owner's own *tsípouro* & a good wine list, & snacks. €

SPORTS AND ACTIVITIES Kastoria Outdoors (✆ 24675 03971; w kastoriaoutdoors.com) offers numerous activities from spring to autumn – canoeing on the lake, rafting, cycling, climbing and 4x4 tours of Mount Grámmos – while **Yellow Bikes** [237 D3] (Meg Alexándrou 119; m 69449 10255; w yellowbike.gr; ⊕ 10.30–20.30 daily; from €4 1st hr, then €1/hr, or €12/day) provides bike rental. **Vítsi Ski Centre** [map, page 234] (22km north in Oxyá; m 69830 37417; f Kastoria.Ski; ⊕ Dec–Mar) is a small three-slope ski and snowboarding station on Mount Vérno (2,128m).

OTHER PRACTICALITIES

Alpha Bank [237 B2] Athanasíou Diákou 42
National Bank [237 A3] Leoforos Kyknon 36
Hospital [237 F4] Mavriotíssis 33; ✆ 24673 50600

Pharmacy Samaras [237 C1] Ioustinianoú 7
Pharmacy Savvopoulos [237 A3] Grámmou 64
Post office [237 B2] Leof Kýknon 4

WHAT TO SEE AND DO

Byzantine Museum [237 D2] (Plateía Dexamenís, with free, easy parking; ✆ 24670 26781; w odysseus.culture.gr; ⊕ 08.30–15.30 Wed–Mon, to 17.00 summer, last entrance 20mins before close; €4, concessions €2) 'Dexamenís' means 'watertank' – the reservoir that lies under this square at the top of Kastoriá near the sadly dilapidated state Xenia Hotel. But the museum is better than ever, with a new layout and explanations in English. It houses works salvaged from local churches and fine examples of Kastoriá's 16th-century school of painting, including icons by masters Onoúfrio and Cretan Ioánnis Permeniótis (the latter went to Venice and trained with Giovanni Bellini). A film shows the step-by-step process of painting an icon (page 23). Near the museum, the Holocaust Memorial marks the spot where the city's thousand Jews were rounded up in March 1944; the 35 who survived never came back here to live.

Byzantine churches Enquire at the Byzantine Museum about visits to Kastoriá's often-locked Byzantine churches; there are 54 (originally 77), most quite tiny, with rustically ornate brick and stonework. The best include the city symbol, the 10th-century **Panagía Koumbelídiki** [237 D2], just south of the museum, off Karavangéli Street, named after its striking tall drum of a dome (*koumbes* in Turkish); it has 13th-century frescoes, including one on the exterior of *Elijah Being Fed by Ravens* and a stunning one inside of the *Dormition of the Virgin*. Just below, in Plateía Omonías, tiny **Ag Nikólaos Kasnítsi** [237 D3] with its striking brickwork has vigorous frescoes of 1180, including portraits of the donors, a magistrate and his wife.

Manoláki Street descends from here to the 10th-century **Taxiárches Mitropóleos** [237 D3], in Plateía Pávlos Mélas. Supported by modern brick buttresses, it has three aisles and unusual 13th-century portraits of the donors on either side of the giant figure of St Michael; within are fragments of even older frescoes and others of 1395. On the other side of the 19th-century cathedral, there's **Ag Athanásios Mouzáki** [237 D4], built by the Albanians during their brief tenure (1374–86), and decorated with saints in Byzantine finery.

There's another good clutch of churches to the east, starting with **Ag Apóstoloi Eleoúsas** [237 E2] at the top of Ag Anargýrou Street, with frescoes attributed to Onoúfrio (1545). Nearby are two of Kastoriá's oldest churches: lofty 10th-century **Ag Stéfanos** [237 E2] (on Eleoúsis St), with decorative brickwork, a women's gallery (the only one in Kastoriá) and sombre 10th-century frescoes; and the even taller **Ag Anárgyroi** [237 E2] (on Vitsíou), founded by Emperor Basil in 1018, after his army destroyed an earlier church. Dedicated to Cosmas and Damian, the doctor saints, it has rather severe 11th-century frescoes in the narthex and others, exceptionally lavish and courtly, from a century later, in the nave.

Apózari (Απόζαρι) In Ottoman times, when districts were divided by religion, this northeast corner by the lake was one of two Greek neighbourhoods. Its landmark is the recently restored **Tsiastsiapá Mansion** [237 F2] (\24670 28150; w odysseus. culture.gr; ⊕ 08.30–15.30 Wed–Mon; €3, concessions €2) of 1754, a rare *archontikó* with two wooden upper floors, decorated inside with charming friezes of flowers, baskets of fruit and imaginary cities; there's another good one nearby, the **Sapoutzís Mansion** [237 E2] on Christópoulou Street. And more churches: **Ag Nikólaos Tsótze** [237 E2], frescoed in the 1300s by a local, with some unusual iconography; and a bit further up, the little 17th-century Catholic **Eisódia tis Theotókou** [237 F2] (or the Tsiatsiapá), with rich paintings and an intricately carved iconostasis.

Plane trees and cafés rim the lakefront all the way to leafy **Plateía Makedonomáchon** [237 D1], with a well-preserved stretch of **Justinian's Walls**. Next to this is a little square with a bust that honours General James Van Fleet (General Patton's 'fighting fool'), who made Kastoriá his command centre when he was sent over in 1948, along with 250 advisors and US$400 million, to help end the Greek Civil War.

Doltsó (Ντολτσό) The southern Greek district of old Kastoriá has cobbled lanes lined with the grand *archontiká* of the fur barons. Some are now hotels and restaurants, and four have been converted into museums.

KASTORIÁ

Folklore Museum [237 F3] (Kapetán Lázou; ✆ 24670 28603; ⊕ 10.00–16.00 Tue–Sun; €3) The beautiful 17th-century Archontikó Nerantzí-Aivazi, home to the family of a wealthy furrier until 1960, has charming stained-glass windows and murals, and rooms laid out and furnished in the traditional style.

Delinánio Museum [237 E3] (Rígas Feríou 12; m 69801 79306; w delinanio. free.nf; ⊕ 11.00–14.00 Sat–Sun; €3) This mansion holds a colourful collection of women's garments from the 19th and 20th centuries, as well as embroideries and weavings, bridal gowns, linens for dowries and photos.

Costume Museum [237 E3] (Vizantíou; ✆ 24670 28603; m 69732 59113; w endmouskas.gr; ⊕ 11.00–13.00 Sun; €3) The Emmanuouil brothers were leaders in the fight against the Ottomans; today their handsome *archontikó* of 1750 has a collection of rare costumes and furs, jewellery and coins.

Museum of the Macedonian Struggle [237 E3] (Picheón 2; ✆ 24670 21144; ⊕ 09.30–13.30 Tue–Sun; €2) Set up in 2010 in another splendid *archontikó*, this museum is dedicated to the heroes of the early 20th-century Macedonian Struggle and the history of Macedonian Hellenism.

Around Kastoriá's peninsula From the crossroads of Plateía Ag Miná, you can drive up, following the signs, for the splendid views over the city from the café of **Profítis Ilías** [237 F1]. Other views are further along, from the **Mountain Theatre** [237 F3] or the summit (870m) marked by the church of **Ag Athanásios** [237 G3]. From here the road winds down to the hospital, and joins the 6km narrow road built in the 1950s around the peninsula, a favourite for Sunday walks, jogging and cycling (it's narrow and one-way after the Mavrotíssa to Apózari).

Just beyond the hospital at the peninsula's south tip is the **Dragon's Cave** (✆ 24673 05065; w spilaiodrakoukast.gr; ⊕ 09.00–17.00 Tue–Sun; €6, concessions €4, inc audio-guide in English). A rare cave located next to a lake, it was discovered by locals in the 1940s and opened to the public in 2009. It has thousands of stalactites – the ceiling resembles a real worm's-eye view of a carrot farm – reflected in seven little lakes.

A bit further on is the jewel of Kastoriá's Byzantine churches, the **Moní Panagía Mavriótissa** (✆ 24670 22714; ⊕ sunrise to sunset; bring a light to see the frescoes) founded by Emperor Alexis Comnenus in 1085, to mark the spot where he landed to boot out the Normans. The plane tree outside looks old enough to have been planted by the emperor himself – and maybe it was; it's more than 900 years old. There are two churches here, the katholikón and a 14th-century church dedicated to St John the Theologian. The exterior wall linking the two is vividly illustrated with a *Tree of Jesse*, two headless imperial portraits and, among other scenes, the rarely depicted Egyptian hermit *St Sisoës at the Tomb of Alexander the Great*. Under the figure of the Virgin in the apse of the katholikón is a small figure of Alexis; and there's a lively *Last Judgement* in the narthex, with a beard-pulling devil, and a wonderful *Last Supper*. It's interesting to compare them with the later frescoes in the church of St John, including the *Raising of Lazarus* in a fantastical setting and *Jesus Steering a Boat in a Storm*.

Aquarium [237 A4] (Zagólou 3; ✆ 24670 80229; w enydriokastorias.gr; ⊕ 09.00–17.00 Tue–Sun; €5, concessions €3, under 8s free) This is nothing less than the largest freshwater aquarium in the Balkans, with tanks holding 55 species of carp, catfish, eels and sturgeons, turtles and others from Greece's rivers and lakes, run with charm and enthusiasm.

8 | WESTERN MACEDONIA (ΔΥΤΙΚΗ ΜΑΚΕΔΟΝΙΑ)

WINTER DIONYSIA

One of the fascinating things about remote parts of Greece is how traditions that the church might have stomped out elsewhere have lingered. In Western Macedonia, the locals preserved some of their Dionysian rites by explaining to the priests that their masks were only 'beggars', *rogatores* (from the Latin *rogare* or 'to beg'), and had nothing to do with anything as pagan as chasing out the evil spirits at the beginning of a year. The Ragoutsária in Kastoriá on 6–8 January, the New Year's Argoutsária festival in Kleisoúra and the slightly later Fanoi ('Great Bonfires') Carnival in Kozáni all involve masks, costumes, parades, dancing in the street, music and gallons of wine and *tsípouro* – essential because it's usually freezing cold, if not snowing. And visitors are more than welcome to join in.

AROUND KASTORIÁ

Neolithic Lake Ecomuseum of Dispilió (Δισπηλιό, 7km south; 24670 21910; w limneosoikismos.gr; ⊕ 09.00–17.00 daily; €5, concessions €3) Discovered in 1932 when the lake was exceptionally low, and excavated in the 1990s, this settlement on stilts was once home to 3,000 people, from c5500BC to 3000BC. Among the finds are a boat, wooden walkways, jewellery, boat-shaped cooking pots and a bone flute – one of the oldest ever found. Thatched huts with replicas of tools and household items have been reconstructed around the settlement's centre fire. The site also yielded the wooden Dispilió tablet (dated 5260BC): the archaeologist, Giórgos Chourmouziádis, believes it shows symbols representing the earliest ever script by far; others say it was a cutting board. But recent finds may yet prove Chourmouziádis right (page 245).

Wax, Prehistory and Folklore Museum (Mavrochóri, on the east bank of the lake, 11km from Kastoriá; 24670 74870; KerinoMouseioKastoria; ⊕ 10.00– noon Sat, 10.00–16.00 Sun; €5, concessions €3) This charming museum created by a retired teacher combines antiques and waxwork figures performing traditional occupations and pastimes, including whooping it up at a wild wedding. There's a recreation of a colourful pre-World War II village square and, last but not least, local barber Níkos Pistikós's miniatures of the churches and mansions of Kastoriá.

Árgos Orestikó (Άργος Ορεστικό) Another 5km south of Dispilió, this town was the centre of the ancient Upper Macedonian kingdom of Orestis, founded or so they say, by Orestes, after being chased from Mycenae by the Furies for murdering his mother, Clytemnestra. Its small **Archaeology Museum** (Venizélou 9; 24670 44616; ⊕ 08.30–15.30 Wed–Mon; €3, concessions €2) has finds going back to 1100BC: bronze jewellery, spears, a shield from a phalanx and a delightful Archaic bronze figurine of a banqueter. Other artefacts are from nearby Dioklitianoupoli, a city founded by Diocletian cAD300, but abandoned under Justinian (probably because it was too hard to say) in favour of Kastoriá.

Petrified Forest of Nóstimo (Νόστιμο; 15km southwest of Árgos Orestikó; m 69778 33750; ⊕ Paleontological and Paleobotanical Museum: 10.00– 15.00 Wed–Mon officially, but call in advance to make sure; free) Accidently discovered in 1935 by a lignite miner, this petrified forest (*apolithoméno dásos*) has palm trunks going back 20 million years, along with rare maritime fossils and a giant tooth of a prehistoric herbivore.

Omorfokklisiá (Ομορφοκκλησιά, or Galishta; 23km southwest of Kastoriá) This tiny hamlet is named 'beautiful church' after the 11th-century **Ag Geórgios**, with a fresco of the saint killing the dragon over the door. This houses, along with some fine 13th-century frescoes, something very rare in an Orthodox church: a larger-than-life wooden statue in high relief of St George, brought here in the 1200s by two nuns from Ioánnina pulling a sled. Pilgrims press coins to the statue; if they stick, their prayers will be answered.

Nestório and around (Νεστόριο) The biggest village on the upper Aliákmonas River, 28km south of Kastoriá, Nestório is famous for its **River Party** (w riverparty. net), an alternative music festival that has been going strong since 1978, drawing thousands of Greeks and foreigners who free camp under the black pines. It's also the gateway for exploring the east slopes of **Mount Grámmos** (2,520m), Greece's fourth-highest mountain and the source of the Aliákmonas. There is some superb hiking and ski touring in the winter here; a favourite destination is jewel-like **Lake Gistova** on the Albanian border, the highest lake in Greece at 2,360m.

Aetomilítsa (Αετομηλίτσα), on the slopes of Grámmos, just south in Epirus, had long been the Communist headquarters during the Greek Civil War. Along with Mount Vítsi, Grámmos saw the very last battles in August 1949, when the Greek air force dropped bombs and US-supplied napalm on their positions, and the Communist party ordered a retreat through the last open pass into Albania. Today the **National Reconciliation Park** (Πάρκο Εθνικής Συμφιλίωσης; \ 24670 21853; w grammos-pes.gr; ⊕ Sun, but also ring ahead – it can close in bad weather) is up a dirt road east of Kotýli (Κοτύλη), set up by the Greek government in a lofty mountain meadow. It has a film, displays and photos of the Civil War, exhibits on the flora and fauna of Grámmos and a café/restaurant.

Where to stay and eat

Afkos Grammos Boutique Hotel Resort [map, page 234] (46 rooms) Ag Dimitríou 10, just south of Nestório; \ 24670 31534; w afkosgrammoshotel.gr. Delightful little eco-friendly 4-star resort, a great place to unwind with a summer infinity pool, spa & fabulous owners; most rooms have mountain views, & there's a superb restaurant (€€). €€€–€€

Hotel 1450 (12 rooms) Néa Kotýli; m 69465 07048. Named for its altitude & with stunning views to match. Cosy stone-built rooms, b/fast inc. €€

Alexandros Hostel [map, page 234] (10 rooms) On a hill south of the centre of Nestório, overlooking the river; \ 24670 31114; w hostel-alexandros.gr. Comfy rooms & 6 self-catering suites in a new building; b/fast inc. €€–€

To Spíti tou Gakoú (7 rooms) Néa Kotýli; \ 24670 31401; w tospititougakou.gr. Charming little guesthouse with a terrace, playground & friendly cat. B/fast inc. €€–€

EAST OF KASTORIÁ

The region east of Kastoriá and Flórina is already a popular destination thanks to the beautiful village of Nympháío, its bear sanctuary and four lakes. In the near future, the recent archaeological discoveries around the wine town of Amýntaio may well make it one of northern Greece's top sights.

KLEISOÚRA (Κλεισουρα) Among the beech forests of Mount Vítsi (2,128m), this was a flourishing Vlach village with a huge library before it suffered two 20th-century disasters, at the hands of the Turks in 1912 and the Germans in 1944. A sole survivor of the past is the fortified convent (1314) of **Moní Panagías** (2km east; \ 24630 94330) in a lovely green setting with a gorgeous gilt iconostasis and frescoes in the church, a popular pilgrimage destination for the relics of its holy ascetic, Sofia, a refugee from Pontus who died in 1974.

NYMPHAÍO AND AROUND (Νυμφαίο; 1,350m) A bit further east, the lofty Vlach settlement formerly known as Neveska is one of the most beautiful villages in Greece, with its grand stone houses and cobbled lanes. It was a silver- and gold-working centre with a population of 3,000 – until the 1929 stock-market crash. Abandoned after the Civil War, the village has been restored, in large part thanks to the Boutári wine family, and fills up at weekends. The big 19th-century stone-built Neveska House, now the **Museum of Goldsmithery** (⊕ by appointment m 69774 61695), has rare goldsmiths' tools, jewellery and household items, murals, portraits of local notables, letters, local furniture and costumes.

For Greeks, Nymphaío is practically synonymous with bears, thanks to the work of Arcturos (see below). The grand old Nikiis School building is now the **Arcturos Brown Bear Information Centre** (\ 23860 41500; w arcturos.gr; ⊕ 10.00–16.30 Wed, tours on the hour; €8, ages 5–17 €5, 4 & under free). Just to the northeast is the **Arcturos Bear Sanctuary** (w arcturos.gr; ⊕ 10.00-16.30 Thu–Tue, tours on the hour), where rescued bears unable to be reintegrated into nature live in a 20ha fenced ravine, amid a beech and oak forest, where they are unintrusively fed and cared for. In **Agrapidiés** (Αγραπιδιές), the same group of volunteers runs a **Wolf Sanctuary** (⊕ same hours as the Bear Information Centre), for rescued wolves, near pretty **Lake Zázari** (Λίμνη Ζάζαρη). Nearby, larger marshy reed **Lake Cheimadítida** (Λίμνη Χειμαδίτιδας) is a favourite wintering area for flocks of birds and sheep from the mountains.

 Where to stay and eat

Enterne (5 rooms) Nymphaío; \ 23860 31230; m 69772 66001. Antique-furnished rooms with mod cons in the heart of the village, with a bar & charming hostess. Good Wi-Fi, but no website – book by phone or via Booking.com. B/fast made to order (inc). **€€€–€€**

La Moára (8 rooms) Nymphaío; \ 23860 31377; w lamoara.gr. In 1990, Yiánnis Boutáris converted an old stone watermill (*moára* in Vlach) into a lovely little hotel with views over the garden & mountains, a pool table, library & board games. There are also 2 beautiful self-catering maisonettes sleeping 4. Ask about their truffle & mushroom hunting seminars. **€€€–€€**

Nymfes (5 rooms) Nymphaío; \ 23860 31114; w nymfeshotel.gr. In a classic stone house of 1923

ARCTUROS, GUARDIAN OF BEARS

Founded in 1992 by Yiánnis Boutáris, and named after the star that protects the constellations of Ursa Major and Minor, Arcturos is one of the best-known environmental NGOs in Greece. Originally a rescue centre for dancing and other bears and wolves held in captivity, with the goal of reintroducing them to the wild, Arcturos has successfully lobbied to ban dancing bears and bears in circuses, and works to reforest bear habitats, establish woodland paths, and make roads safer for wild animals. To keep track of them all, they run a National Bear Register, with bear DNA obtained from special fur traps. They also breed the endangered shaggy bear-like Greek Shepherd Dog, capable of defending flocks from bears and wolves, and donate them to shepherds; the waiting list is more than 1,000 long. They also work to protect other endangered animals in Greece: the chamois, red deer, roe deer, otter and jackal. Much of their funding comes from donations.

near the top of the village, a very cosy guesthouse with superb views, café, patio, small spa area & countless pictures of nymphs. Delicious Greek b/fast inc. €€€–€€
Agonari (7 rooms) Sklíthro; \ 23860 31080; w agonari.gr. Charming stone-built inn near Lake Zázari with an exceptional, elegant taverna, Thomas (€€); it's famous for rotisserie chicken (soúvlas), but the menu has much more, including a huge Greek cheese list & superb wines, too. B/fast inc. €€–€
La Galba (7 rooms) Nymphaío; \ 23860 31314. Small, cosy rooms, with a small garden. €€–€
Del Lago Limnochóri; \ 23860 41382; ⊕ noon–midnight daily. On the banks of Lake Zázari, a simple place specialising in the day's catch. €

Sports and activities Ártemis (Sklíthro; \ 23860 31028; w artemisoe.gr) organises horseriding, canoeing, hiking and mountain biking around Lake Zázari.

AMÝNTAIO AND AROUND (Αμυνταιο) This bustling agricultural town is the main settlement on the west shore of **Lake Vegorítida** (page 156). Its territory encompasses, to the west, **Xinó Neró** (Ξινό Νερό), named after its unusual carbonated 'sour water' spring, famous since ancient times and now available in bottles (in spite of its name, it's quite good). To the east is **Ag Pantelémonas** (Αγ Παντελεήμων), with a beach and long pier. To the north is Vegorítida's little sister **Lake Petrón**, with an important pygmy cormorant breeding colony; a 2km tunnel links it to Vegorítida, ending in a pretty waterfall near Ag Pantelémonas. The Hellenistic city of **Petron** (1.5km west of the modern village of Pétres; ⊕ always) was founded in the 3rd century BC as part of King Antigonos Gonatas' settlement policy in Upper Macedon; and prospered, especially when the Via Egnatía was built just south in 130BC – only to be abandoned a century later.

The 600–700m plateau south of the lakes is dotted with the Xinómavro vineyards of **PDO Amýntaio**. Prestigious wines were produced here from Hellenistic times until the outbreak of phylloxera, then vines were replanted in the 1960s and currently yield one of Greece's rare appellation of origin rosés, as well as PDO sparkling wines. **Ktima Alpha** (\ 23860 20111; w alpha-estate.com; ⊕ 10.00–16.00 daily) is open for visits by reservation. But there's more than water and wine up here: the plateau is also perfect for Flórina peppers (page 246). The Naoumidis family's 70ha of plantations and seed beds are kept carefully isolated from any pepper cross-pollination (w pipieriesflorinis.gr) to preserve the variety.

And there's more: back in 1898 when the Ottomans were building the Édessa–Flórina railway, they uncovered 376 Iron Age graves (1100–5th century BC, finds now in Istanbul). In 2001, a team led by archaeologist Paníkos Chrysostómou located many more graves between lakes Pétron and Cheimadítida – which has since proved to be the largest known Iron Age necropolis in the Balkans.

But they also found something even more intriguing: 13 settlements south of Amýntaio around **Anárgyri** (Ανάργυροι), belonging to a hitherto unknown culture dating back to c7500BC, which Chrysostómou calls the 'Civilisation of the Four Lakes'. People were living here during the Neolithic transition to agriculture and animal husbandry: the houses (similar to those at Dispilió; page 242), built on stilts, were linked to each other and the shore with wooden walkways – one measured at least 120m. Inside the settlements the archaeologists found a trove of stone, bone, horn and clay tools, huge storage jars for grains, the remains of wild and domestic animals and carbonised seeds from the ovens. Extremely rare finds of wood, preserved by the wet environment, include a four-legged stool, a pestle, dugout canoes, and floorboards carbon-dated back 7,500 years. Perhaps most intriguingly, they also found clay figurines of people and animals and pots marked with symbols and signs, which perhaps makes the Dispilió tablet not such an outlier.

If that wasn't enough, in 2017, while in Amýntaio, Chrysostómou's team discovered something else, just off the ancient Via Egnatía: the largest (4,856m²) and most lavish Roman villa ever uncovered in Greece, known by its own inscriptions as the **Villa of Alexandros and Memmia** (2nd–3rd century AD). These wealthy Philhellene Roman officials filled some 96 rooms with art and beautiful mosaics, notably in what the archaeologists have named the Europa Hall, the Nereids Hall, and the Beast-Warrior Hall. At the time of writing, they still have more to uncover and it's not yet open to the public.

✖ Where to eat and drink

Naoumidis Ag Pantelémonas; ☏ 23860 61238; Μεζεδοπωλειο-Ναουμιδης; ⏲ 13.00–23.30 daily. Restaurant with lovely views over Lake Vegorítida, run by the Flórina pepper dynasty, so expect the tasty red ones in many forms, but also generous portions of delicious trout, seafood & homemade bread. €€

FLÓRINA

Set in a wooded valley in Greece's far northwest, Flórina (Φλώρινα), 'the town where Greece begins', is a pleasant little city with numerous *archontiká*, or mansions – in this case of modest scale and in the local vernacular style, many now in a picturesque state of ruin. These are strung out along the duck-filled Sakoulévas River; much of the city had to be rebuilt after the Civil War. Flórina shares facilities of the University of Western Macedonia with Kozáni, so has a lively student population. The coldest city in Greece, it is known to many through the films of Théo Angelópoulos.

In ancient times Flórina was also near the border of Eordaia and Lyncestis, the latter the proudest of Macedon's highland kingdoms, whose rulers were descended from the Bacchiads, the royal family of Corinth. Philip II's mother was a Lyncestian, and her kinsman Leonnatus, Alexander's Companion, was so feisty that he took camel-loads of sand to Persia so he could challenge anyone, anytime, anywhere – to wrestle.

GETTING THERE AND AROUND Flórina's **train** station (Eyrydíkis St; ☏ 23850 22404), near the centre, is at the end of the line from Thessaloníki (3hrs 15mins; from €10), with two trains daily by way of Amýntaio, Xinó Neró, Ag Pantelémonas, Édessa, Naoússa, Véria and Platý. The **bus** station (Makedonómachon 10; ☏ 23850 22430; w ktel-florinas.gr), also central, has regular links to Athens, Thessaloníki, Kozáni, Édessa and Ioánnina. It's 36km to Bitola, North Macedonia's second city and site of Ancient Heraclea Lyncestis, and 102km to UNESCO World Heritage Site Ohrid. For **taxis**, call ☏ 23850 22700 or ☏ 23850 23100.

 WHERE TO STAY Both the Phaídon and Philippeon hotels are just north of the centre.

Hellinis (41 rooms) Pávlou Méla 31; ☏ 23850 22671; w hotel-hellinis.gr. Central & old-fashioned; the best bargain in town. €€–€
Phaídon Hotel (38 rooms) Víglas 1; ☏ 23850 44800; w phaidonhotel.gr. Recently built Neoclassical hotel, simple rooms, good value. B/fast inc. €€–€

Philippeon (33 rooms) Ag Paraskevís 38; ☏ 23850 23346; w hotelphilippion.gr. On a hill, adorned throughout with hand-painted murals, with balconies overlooking Flórina; good buffet b/fast €5. €€–€

✖ WHERE TO EAT AND DRINK
Flórina is famous across Greece for its long red peppers (usually sweet, although occasionally one has a bit of a bite), which are served

either roasted, stuffed with minced meat and rice or feta, or blended into a dip with tomatoes. The seeds are dried to make the region's famous chilli flakes (*boúkovo*), which are named after their place of origin – Bukovo in North Macedonia.

Térpsi [map, page 234] 5km north in Káto Kleinés; m 69321 98384; ⊕ 17.00–midnight Wed–Fri & Mon, noon–midnight Sat & Sun. In a pretty setting, Térpsi's menu features beautifully prepared stuffed mushrooms, linguini with porcini, chicken in orange sauce, devils on horseback – in short, not your typical Greek fare – accompanied by laid-back music. Book. €€

Aposperitis 25is Martíou 6–8; \ 23853 00794; f Αποσπερίτης; ⊕ 13.00–23.30 Tue–Sun. Bright & modern *mezedepoleíon* in the centre; the long menu includes vegan choices & fillet steaks to go with an excellent wine list. Great value for money. €

Florian Leóforos Eleftherías 7; \ 23850 26522; ⊕ 09.00–02.00 daily. 2 siblings grew up in a beautiful old family mansion on the riverbank, & then decided they wanted to share it with everyone, turning it into a beautiful contemporary café with all the authentic details intact. Fantastic homemade desserts. €

Gentéki Vas Georgíou 2 (beside the river); \ 23853 00599; ⊕ usually noon–midnight, to 15.00 Thu, to 18.00 Sun – call to confirm because sometimes they are gardening or tending their animals. Gíorgos & Iordána are dedicated to the culture of 'slow food', offering their own cheeses, pickled vegetables, preserves, home-grown organic produce, & even their own meats, with cooking done on a wood-burning stove. Meaningful & delicious. €

Kafeneíon Diethnés Meg Alexándrou 78; \ 23850 23585; ⊕ usually 08.30–19.00 Mon–Sat, but sometimes closed in the midday. Old Greece lives on at this coffee house from the 1920s, where Angelópoulos shot several scenes in his film *The Beekeeper*. Good *mezédes* including *kagianás* (scrambled eggs with tomatoes & feta), & fried cod with pickles & garlic. €

WHAT TO SEE AND DO The best thing to do in Flórina is wander around, especially along its riverbanks; if you've seen Angelópoulos's *The Beekeeper*, starring Marcello Mastroianni, or *Landscape in the Mist* and *Ulysses' Gaze*, much of the town may look familiar; it's especially evocative at twilight in the snow or mist.

Archaeology Museum (\ 23850 28206; ⊕ 08.30–15.30 Wed–Mon, summer to 19.30; €3, concessions €2) Flórina's well-arranged little museum by the railway station has finds from Armenochóri, home of a Neolithic acorn-eating people (5800BC). Funeral steles, with robust provincial carvings, stress the importance of the horseman in Macedonian hero cults; later steles identify the mortal dead with the gods (young women and concubines with Aphrodite, merchants with Hermes, etc). There are frescoes and items from Préspa's Byzantine churches, while the upper floor is devoted to finds from Hellenistic Flórina and Petron (page 248), cities built with the encouragement of the kings of Macedon to guard the frontier from hostile tribes. Finds include a clay drinking horn in the shape of a young man's foot, a blob of blackened resin (used for retsina-making?) and a little pot with a satyr's grinning face in the early Disney style.

Flórina Museum of Contemporary Art (Tag Fouledáki 8; \ 23850 29444; w mstf.gr; f mstflorina; ⊕ 17.00–20.00 Tue–Sat; free) Dedicated to 20th- and 21st-century Greek art, this museum was founded in 1977 in a handsome Neoclassical house by the river, but because of staffing problems doesn't always open.

Studio 83 (Next door to Kafeneíon Diethnís; m 69877 87661) Artist – and florist – Christina Papagrigoríou runs a fanciful garden shop and gallery, with three storefronts in a grand abandoned building filled with her own really lovely paintings on the walls, sacks of potting soil on the floor, and potted plants all around. Her plant and flower shop is across the street.

Ancient Flórina (South of the centre, signposted from the road to Kastoriá; ☉ usually; free) The foundations of the Hellenistic-era city (4th century BC–1st century AD) are on the wooded Ag Pantelémonas hill; a bit further up the road at the top of the hill (1,020m) is the **Cross of Florina**, with views to the surrounding mountains.

The Korésteia (South of Flórina towards Kastoriá) The Korésteia, its name derived from the ancient kingdom of Orestida, is dotted with some 22 eerie ghost villages of red mud-brick houses, once populated by Slavic speakers who fought in the Resistance and Civil War and are now all but abandoned, evocative and slowly returning to nature. Film-makers and photographers love the villages for their atmosphere; one of the largest is **Kraniónas** (Κρανιώνας).

PRÉSPA NATIONAL PARK

Préspa is a favourite with photographers. To cross the pass above Flórina is to descend into 'a giant and totally secluded cradle' of magical remoteness and stillness. Austere mountains surround two limpid sheets of water: Great or **Megáli Préspa**, the largest lake in the Balkans, the liquid frontier between Greece, Albania and North Macedonia; and **Míkro Préspa** lake, all Greek but for 2% in Albania. Although separated by a narrow spit of land, the lakes have diverse fish populations and the surrounding wetlands are a precious habitat for waterbirds. Míkro Préspa is home to what was until recently the world's largest colony of Dalmatian pelicans, the world's largest freshwater bird. Sadly the colony was struck by avian influenza in 2021, but the ongoing efforts of the Society for the Protection of Préspa (see opposite) have been meeting with some success.

Humans here have also faced challenges. At the end of the 9th century AD, Préspa belonged to the Western Bulgarian Empire. When it was dissolved in AD971, the son of the last emperor, Tsar Samuel, took refuge here, reorganised and made Préspa his base to seize much of Greece, until Emperor Basil II reconquered all the lost Byzantine territory (1018) and put an end to Préspa's day in the sun. During the Frankish and Turkish periods, the utter remoteness of the place attracted monks and hermits. Life was never easy for the rest of the population, and after the Civil War it lost nine out of ten inhabitants into Eastern bloc countries or to Australia, to the extent that the government offered free empty houses and land to Vlachs just to have warm bodies holding down the frontier.

Although the three governments on the borders weren't exactly chums, it came as a happy surprise when their leaders met in October 2000 to designate Préspa an international park (a Balkan first) to preserve its fragile environment – the result of a decade of hard work by Geórgios Kastadorákis and Myrsíni Malakoú, founders in 1990 of the award-winning Society for the Protection of Préspa (SPP; w spp.gr).

Today the SPP is aiming to strike a delicate balance between the needs of humans and nature: encouraging sustainable organic farming, sound fishing practices, modest tourism (converting traditional buildings into guesthouses) and a revival of cattle rearing – Préspa's unique breed of dwarf cows are needed to eat the reeds, to prevent them from taking over the lakes, while leaving sufficient cover for the pelicans to nest. So far it all seems to be working: bird numbers are on the increase, and new jobs promoting environmental tourism are bringing young people into the area.

In June 2018, Préspa made international news when prime ministers Aléxis Tsípras and Zoran Zaev signed the Préspa Agreement on North Macedonia's name. Part of the deal, much to the delight of many locals, will (someday) be the reopening of the border post north of Ag Germanós, closed more than 50 years ago by Greece's military dictatorship.

GETTING THERE AND AWAY There is only one road over the mountains to Préspa from the rest of Greece, and driving is by far the best way to get there as buses from Flórina are few and far between.

TOURIST INFORMATION The **Society for the Protection of Préspa** (SSP; Ag Germános; 23850 51211; w spp.gr) has created some useful apps, including Prespa Trails, covering a network of hiking and cycling trails (see the 'Resources' tab on the website). For birding, visit w prespawaterbirds.gr.

WHERE TO STAY Note that some of these take cash only.

Ag Germanós Traditional Hotel (10 rooms) Ag Germanós; 23850 51397; w prespa. com.gr. In a restored old stone house in the village centre; charming rooms with traditional furnishings; most have a little fireplace. B/fast inc. €€€–€€

Ariadni (17 rooms) Laímos, by Ag Germanós; 23850 51850; w ariadniguesthouse.gr. Fall asleep to the nightingales here; rooms, in traditional wood & stone, have lake views. Very kind, hospitable owners. B/fast inc. €€

Prespa Resort & Spa (15 rooms) Platý; 23850 51400; w presparesort.gr. Next to the highest stork's nest in Europe (on a special platform atop a telephone pole). Self-catering studios & apartments with a spa & wellness centre. €€

Philippos (4 rooms) Psarádes; m 69743 85619; w hotel-philippos.gr. Simple rooms in an old stone house of 1890 in the village square. €

Syntrofiá (5 rooms) Psarádes; 23850 46107; m 69425 03863; w syntrofia-prespes.gr. Simple guesthouse & taverna (€), right on the lake. Owner Germanós can arrange boating & fishing excursions. €

To Petrino (9 rooms) Ag Germanós; 23850 51344. Roomy old stone house, owned by the very hospitable Thómai Tsíkos. B/fast inc. €

Varnous (10 rooms) 10mins' walk from Ag Germanós; 23850 51880. Charming traditional hotel with a cosy sitting room, run by Chrístos, a mine of information about the area. Good b/fast €5. €

WHERE TO EAT AND DRINK The beans are especially good here (they say it's the water); the Fasolia Gigantes Elefantes Prespon Florinas have PGI (Protected Geographical Indication) status, and along with other dried beans are sold in shops all around the area. The lake fish is delicious – if it's on the menu, try *stifádo me griváadi*, a delicious carp and onion stew.

Stou Hássou Mikrolímni; 23850 46803; stouhassou; 10.00–21.00 daily. Lovely setting right on Míkro Préspa lake with tasty fish, mussels & pork with quince. €€

Taverna to Prespeion Ag Germanós; 23850 51442; noon–midnight daily. Great atmosphere in the village square, a favourite for its roasted peppers, homemade savoury pies, & grilled meats & good wines, with live music on holidays. €

SPORTS AND ACTIVITIES The **Prespa Experience** (in Peter's Grocery shop, Psarádes; m 69776 22652; w the-prespa-experience.com) has hiking information, and offers boat tours on Megáli Préspa. In winter locals flock to the **Vigla Pisoderíou Ski Centre** (on the Flórina road, 23850 45800; w vigla-ski.com; winter Sat–Sun) with five lifts and gorgeous views over the lakes.

WHAT TO SEE AND DO Préspa's dozen hamlets (total population c1,300, down from 13,000 a century ago) are an echo of the Greece of decades ago. All but one are located on Mikró Préspa, geologically the oldest lake in Europe, and the best for spotting pelicans. **Mikrolímni** (Μικρολίμνη), the first village you come to, looks across to uninhabited Vidronísi (Βιδρονήσι), 'Otter Island', where birds nest around a ruined chapel. The biggest village, **Ag Germanós** (Αγ Γερμανός), has a ravishing early 11th-century domed church (next to a modern church), covered top to bottom with frescoes. One of the SPP's recent projects was making the village's **watermill** operational again (for a tour, call ⎆ 23850 51211). There are more frescoes – good expressive ones from the 16th century – in the chapel of **Ag Nikólaos** in nearby **Platý** (Πλατύ; ask for the key in the village).

At the north end of the lake, **Ag Achíllios Island** (Αγ Αχίλλειος) was linked to the mainland in 2000 by a 650m pedestrian causeway, which hasn't spoiled its time warp; a modern legend has it that there can be only 11 houses here and if anyone builds a 12th, it will fall over. Yet back in the 10th century, this was the capital of Tsar Samuel. Like any medieval ruler he needed holy relics to get on the map, so he pinched the relics of St Achíllios in Lárissa and installed them in the elegant, now picturesquely ruined **basilica of Ag Achíllios**. Although sacked in 1072 by the Alemanni, the church remained in use until the mid 15th century; one of the graves here yielded a rare piece of Byzantine gold cloth, now in the museum in Thessaloníki. Folksy 15th-century frescoes decorate the church of **Ag Geórgios** (you'll need to seek out the key); other excellent ones are in the mid-16th-century **Panagía Porphyra** ('Our Lady All in Purple'), once attached to a monastery wrecked by the Germans in World War II.

The only Greek village on Megáli Préspa, atmospheric **Psarádes** (Ψαράδες), is another beautiful traditional settlement, under a rare cedar forest with dense wood that lasts forever. Local boatmen offer lake tours to the three 13th-century hermitages tucked in the steep cliffs; one hermitage, dedicated to **Panagía Eleoúsa**, is covered with pastel frescoes from 1410.

KOZÁNI

The capital of Western Macedonia and seat of its university, big bustling Kozáni (Κοζάνη) is worth a visit for its museum and a look around, but chances are it's not what you've come to northern Greece to see – though this so-called City of Books boasts the second-largest municipal library in the country. It lets its hair down every winter in a crazy Dionysian carnival called the Fanoi (page 242).

Once part of the Upper Macedonian kingdom of Elimeia, Kozáni was settled by families from Epirus, who in 1389 were the beneficiaries of a firman that put them under the protection of the Sultan's mother, so they paid no income tax, enjoyed complete freedom of religion and had no pesky Turkish officials in their midst. Thanks to these privileges, Kozáni became a major crafts centre, trading with Vienna, Budapest and Bucharest; one merchant, a certain Karayannis, was the great-grandfather of conductor Herbert von Karajan. Today it's probably best known as the battery of Greece with its lignite mine and power plant just north, which employs many of the locals.

GETTING THERE AND AROUND Kozáni's **airport** (⎆ 24610 36098), 4km southeast of town, is limited to small planes; there are several flights a week from Athens and from Thessaloníki on Sky Express (w skyexpress.gr), which also serves Kastoriá. The **bus station** (Giánnari 22; ⎆ 24610 34455; w ktelkozanis.gr) has hourly services to Thessaloníki (1hr 40mins; €12.70), three to Athens (6hrs 30mins; €47.50) and less frequently to the other cities of Western and Central Macedonia. Imperial Car Rental (\21119 85264; w imperial-car-rental.com) can arrange a **car** for you at the airport or bus station.

WHERE TO STAY AND EAT
Iberis (14 rooms) Siátista; \24650 47054. Stylish & family friendly with a pool & restaurant. B/fast inc. €€–€
Tria Pigadia Plateía Tria Piagádia, Chóra, Siátista; \24650 22991; ⊕ call for hours. Taverna with rustic charm & delicious lamb & vegetable dishes, plus local cheeses & wines. €
Vasilikós Mezedopoleío Drízi 5–7, Kozáni; \24610 33230; ⊕ noon–midnight daily. Cheerful contemporary space & small plates to match, lovely grilled seafoods & meats. €

WHAT TO SEE AND DO
Museum of History, Folk Life and Natural History (I Dragoúmi 9–11; \24610 33978; w mouseio-kozanis.gr; ⊕ 08.30–14.00 daily; €3, concessions €1.50) Allow a couple of hours for this wonderful museum, the life's work of local teacher Konstantínos Siabanópoulos: its six floors in a Macedonian-style building and a new wing include a fascinating array of petrified trees, elephant fossils, taxidermy of local wildlife and nature's hiccups – a five-legged lamb, a goat with one head and two bodies, and an impressive mess of rope found in the stomach of a cud-crazed cow. There's a collection of mini buildings, weapons, all kinds of silver, an archaeological collection, items from traditional professions, 19th-century photos, costumes, Neolithic art, memorabilia from the wars and, at the top, beautiful rooms reconstructed from old mansions – one, belonging to a doctor, with intricate floral decoration and figures from Euclid's geometry – plus a collection of postal franking stamps and antique radios.

AROUND KOZÁNI
Towards Ptolemaïda (Πτολεμαΐδα; 30km north of Kozáni) You've probably already clocked the billows rising from the chimneys of the power plant just north of Kozáni, where the coal-blackened landscape looks like a vision of Mordor. The biggest (1,618km²) lignite mine in the Balkans feeds the beast and supplies a huge percentage of Greece's electricity. Part of the EU bail-out deal was to privatise the mining company, but there's also environmental pressure to phase out coal, which would lead to massive job losses in a region with some of the highest unemployment in Greece.

Monastery of Panagía Soumelá (Kastaniá (Καστανιά); 39km northeast of Kozáni) The old national road (EO4) from Kozáni towards Véria takes in a vertiginous view over the Aliákmonas Valley and the Monastery of Panagía Soumelá, 'the paladin of Asia Minor Greeks'. As Pontic refugees fled Trabzon in 1922, they buried their most sacred treasures from the fantastical cliff monastery of Soumelá, including the icon of the Virgin attributed to St Luke. In 1931, the Turkish government agreed to let them retrieve it, and after spending 20 years in the Benaki Museum in Athens it was moved to this lofty spot in a specially built church – once a de rigueur stop along the road, with cafés and tavernas, but these days a bit neglected now that most traffic goes along the Egnatía Ódos.

Krókos (Κρόκος; 5km southeast of Kozáni) One of the most charming Minoan frescoes in Crete shows blue monkeys gathering saffron, but today in Greece it is only grown commercially here, appropriately, in a town called 'Crocus'. The local saffron co-operative (w safran.gr) produces DOP deep red Krókos Kozánís. The 'red gold' was also one of the rare success stories to come out of the economic crisis: before 2000 the co-operative produced only 30kg for the Greek market; after 2008, planting increased from 240ha to 546ha. Production reached close to 4 tonnes, but has been in decline – climate change is resulting in smaller flowers and threads, and therefore lighter yields. Around 70% is sold abroad.

Ancient Aiani (Aianí (Αιανή); 20km south of Kozáni) Aiani was the capital of ancient Elimeia, and it may well be the cradle of the kingdom of Macedon itself. It was inhabited from Neolithic times until the 1st century BC, and excavations have yielded some matt-painted pottery from the Middle Helladic period (1900–1600BC) and artefacts that suggest close contacts with the Mycenaeans, essential for those claims of descent from the kings of Argos (page 142). Nor were the Upper Macedonian kingdoms as uncouth as previously thought: the oldest buildings date back to the early 5th century BC – a century before Philip II united the kingdoms – and contained the oldest Greek inscriptions yet found in the area. Excavations (signposted at Megáli Ráchi, 1.5km northeast of modern Aianí) have uncovered several houses on the plateau, including the rather fancy ashlar house with staircases. The Royal Necropolis is 700m away; its Archaic and Classical tombs are in precincts that once had painted interiors, stone roofs and temple-like features that suggest early versions of later Macedonian tombs.

Aianí's **Archaeology Museum** (\ 24610 98800; w mouseioaianis.gr, odysseus. culture.gr; ⊕ 08.30–15.30 daily; €4) had to be enlarged to take in numerous finds from rescue digs. There are beautiful Archaic ivory plaques, *kouroi*, lions, horses and clay figurines with traces of paint, some beautiful black-figured vases and an uncanny terracotta head from the 6th century BC called the 'kore of Aianí', wearing heavy make-up and the blank, unsmiling stare of a fashion model.

Around Aianí Just east of Aianí, artificial **Lake Polyfýto** is swollen by the waters of the Aliákmonas; the dam was built in 1973, although, if there's a drought, it looks more like the Bonneville salt flats. The E65 swoops over the long and narrow lake on the gracefully curved 1.3km **Sérvia-Neráida Tall Bridge** to the Byzantine town of **Sérvia** (Σέρβια). Its name comes from the Latin '*servo*' or look-out, as it once defended an important pass between Macedon and Thessaly, used by Alexander the Great and St Paul. The romantically ruined castle built by Justinian (bombed by the Germans in the war, so only one tower survives) overlooks vaguely anthropomorphic rocks in the gorge that are said to be the defenders, petrified when the castle was captured by the Turks in 1393. The path up to the castle passes the impressive ruin of an 11th-century basilica.

North of Sérvia, in a lush valley of the Aliákmonas, **Velventós** (Βελβεντός) is famous for its peach orchards and has a pretty walk up the bucolic **Skepasménou Canyon** to a waterfall. A mountain road from here winds up in 23km to the scruffy little village of **Katafýgio** (Καταφύγιο) on the slopes of the Piéria Mountains; this was the native village of the most famous modern Greek of all – Geórgios Zórbas, the original for Kazantzákis' *Zorba the Greek* (who is remembered, appropriately enough, in the name of the local *ouzerí*).

Siátista (Σιάτιστα; 27km southwest of Kozáni) Remote, surrounded by grey, barren mountains, Siátista was founded after the fall of Constantinople in a region the Ottomans didn't care for, attracting immigrants from Thessaly and Epirus who wanted to live in relative independence. They became wealthy merchants, selling furs, leathers, wine and raki, setting up deals with Russia, the Austro-Hungarian Empire and Venice. Many locals would eventually leave for less remote parts, including Theódoros and Afráti Dimitrioú, who, in 1790, moved to Zagreb and became immersed in Croatian culture; their son, poet Dimitrija Demeter, wrote in Greek and Croatian and helped to found the Croatian National Theatre.

Others stayed and ploughed their profits into lavishly decorated *archontiká*, some 50 of which survive in the town's two distinct neighbourhoods, **Chóra** in the north and **Geránia** to the south, which meet in the middle in **Plateía Trís Pigádia**. The houses have heavily fortified ground floors – because of the town's isolation, brigands were always a problem. A few have preserved interiors from their long lost world, with colourful murals, wood-carved ceilings, stained glass and more. To arrange a visit of the **Archontikó Dólykira** contact the Cultural Association Markídes Poúliou (m 69454 98032, 69725 72465; w markides.gr); you can ask them about others open for visits too.

The former high school houses the **Paleontological Collection** (\ 24650 22805; ⊕ by appointment), with molars, tusks and bones of the mastadons, mammoths and prehistoric straight-tusked elephants (*Elephas antiquus*) whose bones were preserved in the clay deposits of an ancient lake.

The local wine business is enjoying a revival, making good use of Moshómavro, 'black muscat' grapes. Visit **Magoutes** (Mitropolítou Athinagorá 1; \ 24650 22654; w magoutes.com), makers of, among other wines, Siátista's naturally sweet *liastós* from raisins, which used to sell for ten times as much as a bottle of regular red wine; and **Dio Fili** (Ag Nikánoros 5; \ 24650 22224; w diofili.gr; ⊕ 09.00–17.00 Mon–Fri, 11.00–17.00 Sat–Sun) who make a delicious rosé Xinómavro.

North of Siátista, lush mountain village **Vlásti** (Βλάστη) is another pretty place that boomed in the 19th century. It once boasted 6,500 people and three schools, but now gets by with 100 souls in the winter. Many of its fine Neoclassical houses have been repaired, and it's become something of a summer resort. South, in **Miliá** (Μηλιά), just off the main road to Grevená, paleontologists from Aristotle University in Thessaloníki made headlines in 2007 when they uncovered the world's longest ever (4.39m and 5.02m) mastadon tusks in the deposits of the Aliákmonos, which now hold pride of place in the **Museum of Natural History** (\ 24620 61271; ⊕ 09.00–14.30 Mon–Fri, 09.00–17.00 Sat–Sun).

Mastorochória West of Siátista, on the slopes of Mount Vóio (1,805m), are a collection of settlements known as the 'Master-builder villages' who travelled in groups and spoke their own secret language, building stone bridges, mansions and *kalderimí* across the Ottoman Empire. Recently the old paths around Mount Vóio itself are being reopened, thanks to a project by the University of Western Macedonia (w monopatia-pindos.uowm.gr). Today only a few dozen people live in each of the *mastorochória*: among the prettiest are **Chrysavgí** (Χρυσαυγη), with its bridges and waterfall; **Pentálofos** (Πεντάλοφος, 1,050m), with its statues of a builder and a Pindus woman; **Dotsikó** (Δοτσικό); and **Kalloní** (Καλλονή).

PINDUS NATIONAL PARK

Greece's largest national park covers 2,000km^2, extending south to Epirus's Zagorochória – the bulk of it is there, where you'll find the main description (page 271). But some of its most beautiful bits are in the prefecture of **Grevená** (Γρεβενά), the 'Official Greek City of Mushrooms' – of the 7,000-plus kinds of fungus that grow in Greece, 2,600 varieties have been discovered in Grevená's surrounding forests. The town makes up for its lack of monuments with statues of giant mushrooms – near some of these, in Plateía Eleutherías, there is a mushroom shop called **Idígefston** (📞 24625 01260) if you want to take some dried mushrooms home. Along with mushrooming, this is also a popular area for rafting, notably on the Venétikos River, a tributary of the Aliákmonos. There is a healthy population of bears in these parts, as signs along the main roads warn. As one of the least-populated corners of Greece with next to no light pollution, at night the stars blaze like fire.

TOURIST INFORMATION The best source of information on activities in the park is the **Pindus National Park Information Centre** (Μαυρανaίοι (Μαυραναίοι); 📞 24620 87563; w pindosnationalpark.gr; ⊕ 08.30–15.30 Mon–Fri – call before visiting).

WHERE TO STAY

Valia Nostra (21 rooms) Smíxi; 📞 24620 80151; w valianostra.gr. Rustic, chic mountain lodge in wood & stone, with gorgeous views from the large glassed-in lounge & loft rooms (most have a fireplace). It has a heated indoor pool & works with local adventure companies. €€€€–€€€

Koukounari (5 rooms) Smíxi; 📞 24620 24821; w koukounari-flower.gr. Comfy contemporary-style inn, a great place to unwind around the fireplace. Greek b/fast inc. €€€–€€

La Noi Traditional Hostel (7 rooms) Samarína; 📞 24620 95660; w lanoi.gr. Charming family-run inn, with good advice on local walks to the lakes & waterfalls; delicious pies & other goodies for b/fast (inc). €€

Achillion [map, page 234] (34 rooms) 2km on the Kozáni road, Grevená; 📞 24620 85600; w hotelachillion.gr. Modern hotel with views over the surrounding mountains & an outdoor pool. Buffet b/fast inc. €€–€

Valia Calda (23 rooms) Perivóli; 📞 24620 82020; w valiacalda.com. Lovely mountain views at 1,350m. Modern & welcoming, & very friendly. B/fast inc. €€–€

Vasilitsa V1850 (5 dorm rooms, each sleeping 10) Smíxi; 📞 24621 00346; m 69779 93674. Big stone-built refuge up at the ski centre with a cosy bar overlooking the mountains. €

Villa Alexandra (11 rooms) Ziákas; 📞 24620 25659; w villaalexandra.gr. Simple rooms, a great base for walks in the Válía Cálda. B/fast inc. €

✗ WHERE TO EAT AND DRINK

Aulais Pavlou Melá 6, Grevená; 📞 24620 25402; w aulais.gr; ⊕ noon–midnight Wed–Mon. This famous restaurant in the centre of Grevená is your chance to try the local pride & joy – funghi. Over the course of the year dishes feature more than 100 kinds of fresh wild edible mushroom in nearly every course; at w/ends there's often live music, too. €€

Perdika Spílaio; 📞 24620 82234; ⊕ 13.30–22.00 Mon–Fri, 13.00–22.00 Sat, 12.30–19.00 Sun. Classic village taverna, woodsy & atmospheric, famous for its succulent meats, game & mushrooms. €€

Trapeza Gefseon Plateía Aimilanou 22, Grevená; 📞 24620 87111; w trapezageuseon.gr; ⊕ noon–midnight daily. Smart contemporary dining rooms, & interesting dishes with local cheeses & mushrooms, as well as grilled meats. €€

Barbamichalis Samarína; 📞 24620 95231; ⊕ 10.00–midnight daily. In the main square, lots of tasty meats on the spit, including game dishes in autumn. €

SPORTS AND ACTIVITIES Activities here include rafting, hiking and 4x4 tours.

Active-Nature m 69376 67799, 69871 11398; w active-nature.gr. Ioánnina-based firm offering rafting down the Venétikos.

Greek Adventure 📞 24620 87999; w greekadventure.gr. White-water rafting, canyoning, trekking & 4x4 tours in the Válía Cálda. Tailor-made experiences can also be arranged.

Pindus Hiking m 69489 49789; w pindushiking.gr/en. Specialists in hiking tours in the high mountains, including the Válía Cálda.

Vasilítsa Ski Centre Smíxi; \ 24623 53530;
w vasilitsa.com. 18 pistes topping at 2,000m on
'the little queen' peak of Smólikas. In summer, mountain bikers roam the slopes.

WHAT TO SEE AND DO The confines of the national park encompass five Vlach villages, including **Smíxi** (Σμίξη), site of the Vasilítsa Ski Centre, **Avdélla** (Αβδέλλα) – birthplace of Yiánnis and Miltiádis Manákis, 'the Fathers of Balkan cinema', who shot their first film, *The Weavers*, here in 1905, starring their 114-year-old grandmother Déspina – and **Perivóli** (Περιβόλι), closest to the pristine 6,780ha protected zone of **Vália Cálda** (Βάλια Κάλντα).

Vália Cálda, Vlach for 'Warm Valley' (a bit of joke as it's often colder and wetter than anywhere else), is cut off from the rest of the world by mountains, where human activity is limited to walks. It's a land of deep black and white pine and beech forests, cliffs and streams and rapids feeding into the idyllic **Arkoudórema** ('Bear Creek'), a tributary of the Aoös that crosses the entire valley, home to 80 different species of bird, brown bears (one of their most important habitats in Greece), wild goats, wolves, otters and tiny wildcats. In late spring, wildflowers and butterflies fill the meadows, and fireflies rule the night. The autumn colours rival New England. The one walk not to miss is the easy 2-hour hike up from the Arkoudórema to the **Fléga Lakes** (1,700m) for the magical views.

The largest village in the park, **Samarína** (Σαμαρίνα), is one of the highest in the Balkans at 1,600m, set on the majestic slopes of Smólikas, Greece's second-tallest mountain at 2,637m. Surrounded by pine forests, its nickname is 'Good Samarína' for its fresh air and healthy climate, where snow on the cliffs lingers into May. The inhabitants are traditionally shepherds and cattle herders, and are famous for their fluffy *flokáti* rugs (which they claim they've been making since the 5th century AD) and their appearance in the famous Greek song 'Children of Samarína' about their role in the Greek War of Independence. The massive old stone church of the **Megáli Panagía** is striking for a pine tree growing out of its apse. On 15–18 August, Vlachs from across Greece gather in Samarína for its traditional *panegíri* to join hands in the 'Great Dance', men in a centre ring, women outside, singing their ancient Vlach songs. You can also pick up the new Pindus trail here (page 274).

Also in the park, on the slopes of **Mount Órliakas** (1,453m; a favourite of mushroom hunters, and where there are current plans to build an educational observatory), the village of **Spílaio** (Σπήλαιο) has a path (or road) down to the most photogenic stretch of the Venétikos, as it flows under the 18th-century **Portítsa Bridge** before passing through the sheer 198m cliffs of the **Portítsa Gorge**, at places only 5.5m wide. Downriver, on the road above **Tríkomo** (Τρίκωμο), there's a turn-off for the stunning 71m single-span **Aziz Aga Bridge**, with the biggest stone arch in Macedonia, built when Ali Pasha improved the roads linking the Zagorochória to Thessaloníki. It is so big that a bell was hung over the arch to tinkle when the wind was up and warn that the crossing was dangerous; there's a nice place to swim nearby.

9

Epirus (Ήπειρος)

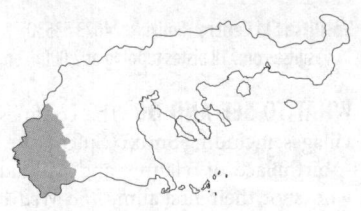

Bounded by Albania on the north and the Ambracian Gulf on the south, Epirus has historically played as hard-to-get as a fairy-tale princess: the starched, vertical pleats of the Pindus Mountains skirt its eastern side, an implacable barrier to admirers and assailants alike, while the breath from its malarial swamps along the Ionian Sea promised danger and death to those foolhardy enough to attempt its western defences. *'Noli me tangere'* (touch me not) could have been its motto, right up until the 20th century. Now modern roads have breached its mountain fastnesses, and determined agriculturalists have painstakingly tamed its swamps, its intricate, varied and extravagant beauty is accessible to all.

Although most visitors come for the beaches, the sheer glory of the lush Pindus Mountains and the sublime Víkos Gorge ensure a steady stream of hikers, kayakers and rock climbers, along with birdwatchers and botanists. The archaeological sites – Roman Nikopolis, beautiful Kassope, the very ancient oak tree oracle at Dodona and the oracle of the dead at the Necromanteíon – are choice. Yet even as Epirus yields to its suitors, it hasn't surrendered its soul: each corner has kept its personality, costumes, music and dialect, especially in the unique Zagorochória, one of the most enchanting regions of Greece.

HISTORY

Impassable mountains and swampy coasts always discouraged civilisation. The Mycenaeans were here, but not in force; in historical times, the Molossian tribe had royal dynasties and grandly claimed descent from Achilles, but Epirus's early history is pretty much a blank until the 7th century BC, when wealthy Corinth took an interest, founding Amvrakia (at present-day Árta) and other small cities. Except to visit Dodona and the Necromanteíon, Classical-era Greeks really didn't pay attention to Epirus, or ever write much about it.

In 400BC, Tharypas, the Molossian king, tried to form a federation of states and raise the cultural level of his pastoral countrymen. Olympias, wife of Philip of Macedon and mother of Alexander the Great, came from this dynasty, a connection that would henceforth give the Macedonians a tie to and claim upon Epirus. In 307BC, Pyrrhus, a second cousin to Alexander, became King of Epirus, with his capital at Amvrakia, where he instituted all the trappings of a respectable Hellenistic city-state.

Pyrrhus is one of Greek history's great might-have-beens. He was the only ruler to understand the existential threat the Greeks faced in the Roman Republic, and he was determined to do something about it. The strong state he built in Epirus enabled him to campaign all across southern Italy from 280BC. A brilliant general, with a big army trained in Macedonian warfare, he won several significant victories over the legions. Somehow nothing ever came of them. Pyrrhus never had the money or the men to follow up his triumphs, and his own indecisiveness often cost him dearly. He spent years distracted in fights with Rome's enemy Carthage, with whom he might more profitably have been allied.

In the end Pyrrhus withdrew from Italy in 275BC, and turned his armies in the other direction in a mad scheme to make himself ruler of the Peloponnese. He died in a street battle in Argos, when the aged mother of an Argive soldier fighting Pyrrhus in the street below hit him on the head with a well-aimed roof tile. Probably he never dreamed that 'Pyrrhic victories' would become a byword for battles won at too high a price.

Rome, busy putting an end to Carthage in the long Punic Wars, was in no hurry to press its advantage in Greece. Once Carthage was comfortably digested, though, the Republic turned its attention back eastwards. Squeezed by Rome on one side and Macedon on the other, the Epirótes threw in their lot with the latter. After they were trounced in 168BC, they suffered Roman reprisals; 70 towns were levelled, thousands killed and 150,000 sold into slavery. Epirus never recovered and its villages were decimated again in 38BC when Octavian needed citizens for Nikopolis, the grandiose city he founded after defeating Antony and Cleopatra at Actium.

The enforced *pax romana* didn't last long. After 90BC, one horde after another decimated Epirus – Thracians, then Germanic tribes, the Bulgars in AD502, then more Slavs, even Saracens (in AD877), then Bulgars again, then the Normans under Bohemund in 1082. The only infiltrators to stay, aside from Slavs, were the Vlachs (page 260). After the capture of Constantinople in 1204, many wealthy Greeks fled to Epirus, and in 1205 Michael Angelos founded a breakaway Greek state, the Despotate of Epirus, with Árta as its capital. This gave the region a little breathing space, and a lot of new churches.

In 1349, Serbian King Stefan Dushan had his Epiróte interlude. Then the local Albanians and Serbs entered the field, vying for the tattered football that was Epirus; both factions bolstered their sides with Turks, who took the ball themselves in 1431 and played it better than most. Ottoman Epirus was actually prosperous, although there were uprisings by the Greek Súliots in the mountain villages of the south; the Venetians kept the pot boiling, as did the Great Powers. Ioánnina's Ali Pasha brought a kind of peace and prosperity until his death in 1822, then factionalism and rebellion reigned as the Epirótes tried to join the new Greek state they had helped create. Although the Árta area joined in 1881, the rest had to wait until 1913. That should have been the happy ending, but there was one last drama to be played.

On 28 October 1940, Mussolini, without provocation, invaded Greece through Epirus. The bulk of the Italian army moved to Kalpáki north of Ioánnina, while the rest infiltrated the mountains. The Epirótes joined the Greek army in defending their homes, the women carrying ammunition when the packhorses died of cold. It was a heroic effort and the Italians were driven back, a victory celebrated in Greece every 28 October as Óchi Day, the day Greece said 'No'. The Germans came in 1941 and burned towns and villages in reprisal for their fierce resistance which just would not stop, leaving Epirus decimated, and depopulated, as all the Muslim Albanians (the Chams) who had collaborated with the Italians were exiled to Albania. The Civil War that followed completed the process.

Nowadays the invaders are tourists, and Epirus has managed to take them in its stride, even if the resort of Párga does look under siege in August. At least these hordes have brought prosperity, and in their own way have made it possible for the Epirótes to continue living in their villages, just as they always have.

9 | EPIRUS (ΗΠΕΙΡΟΣ)

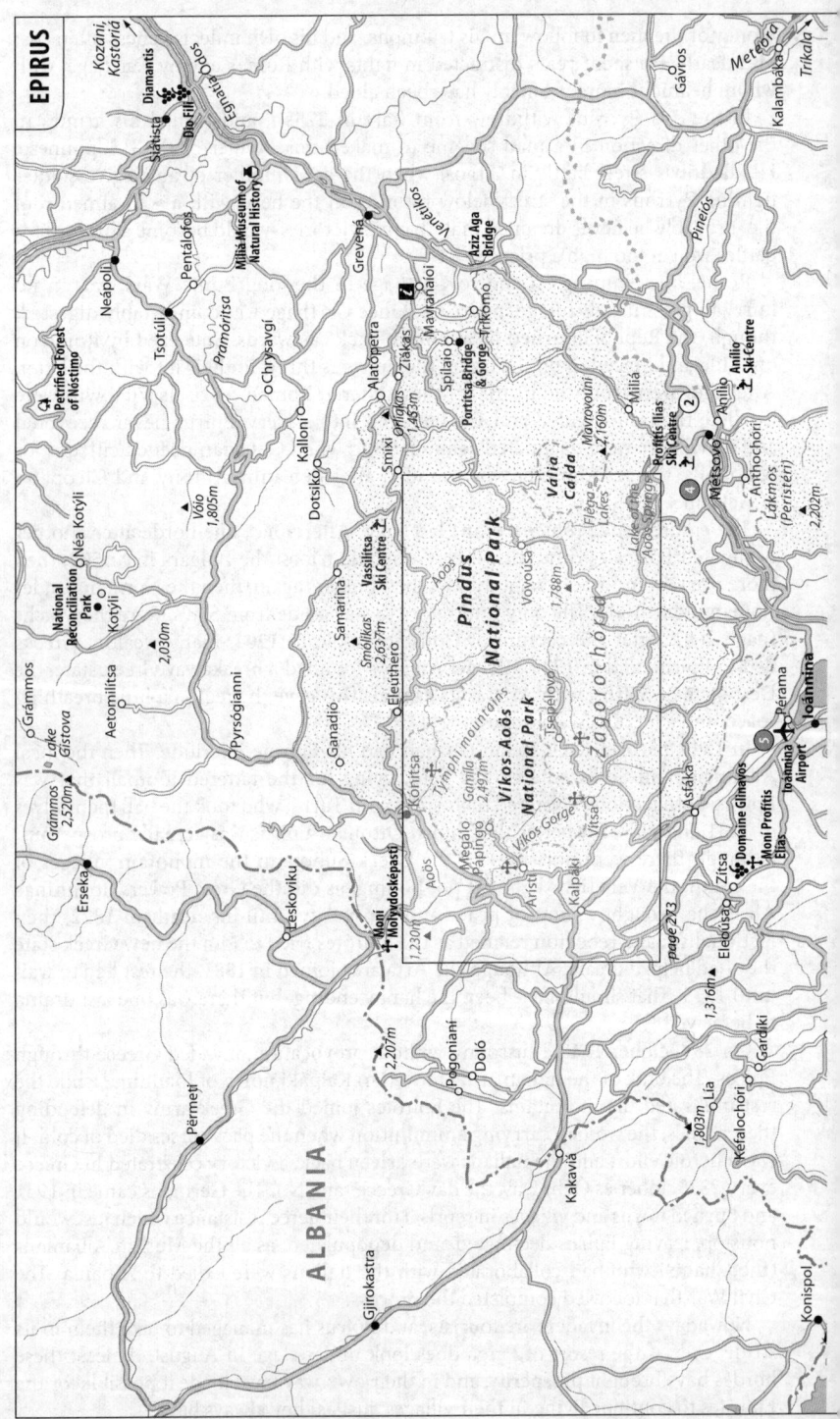

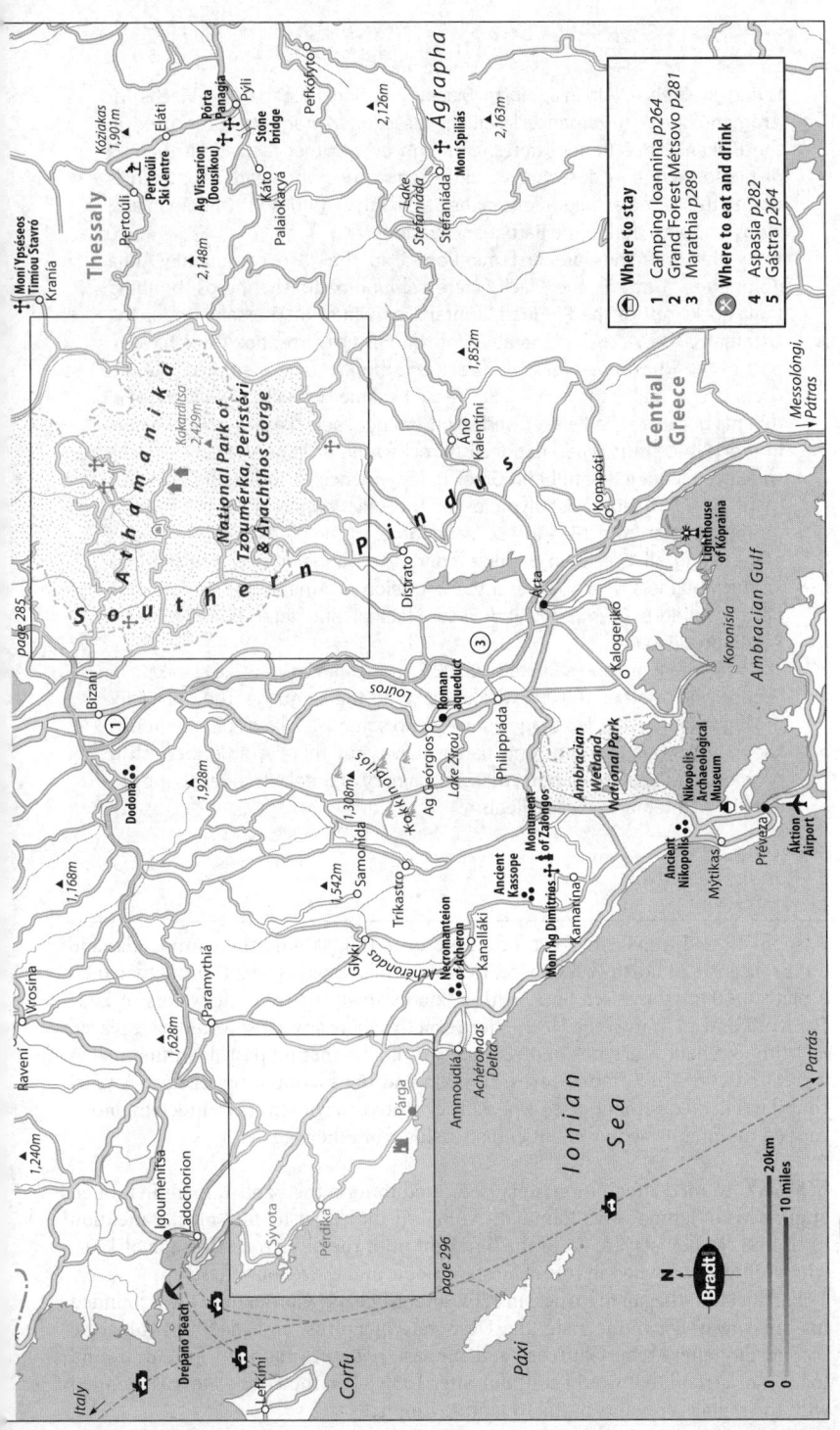

9 | EPIRUS (ΗΠΕΙΡΟΣ)

VLACHS: THE 'CHAMELEONS OF THE BALKANS'

Living in Greece, Albania, North Macedonia and Bulgaria, the Vlachs (or Aromani) speak a Romance language descended from the Latin used in the Balkans since Roman times, although every other fact about them is disputed. Were they descendants of the legionaries who headed for the hills during the Avar-Slav migrations in the 5th to 7th centuries AD? Or Romanians, who fled south during the Barbarian invasions?

By the time they are first mentioned, in the 11th century (in Anna Comnene's *Alexiad*), the Vlachs were semi-nomadic shepherds, bringing their flocks out of the Pindus Mountains to winter in Thessaly. Under the Ottomans, the Vlachs, as members of the Eastern Orthodox Church, were part of the *Rum millet* (aka the Greek community), and identified, like the Greeks, as Romaioi; those living in Greece became Hellenised, while those in Albania became Albanianised and so on – hence their 'chameleon' nickname. In the 19th century when nationalism rocked the Balkans, the Greek Vlachs were prominent in the fight for Greek independence, including Rígas Feraíos (page 11) and Giorgákis Olýmpios of Thessaly, Ioánnis Koléttis of Epirus (prime minister from 1844 to 1847, and father of the irredentist Megáli Idéa of reuniting all Greeks in a single country), Evángelos and Konstantínos Záppas (builders of schools and the Zappeion in Athens, and co-founders of the modern Olympics), and Field Marshal and later Prime Minister Aléxandros Papágos.

Today there are an estimated 300,000 Aromanian or Vlachiká speakers in Greece, and another 100,000 who understand the language. The University of Thessaloníki offers language courses, and some 200 Vlach cultural groups keep the language, songs and dances alive, but there is little interest in promoting a separate identity; the vast majority of Greek Vlachs are happy to remain 'an integral part of Hellenism'.

IOÁNNINA

A sophisticated university town of a little over 100,000 and the commercial and cultural centre of northwest Greece, Ioánnina (Ιωάννινα) is beautifully situated on a plateau 600m above sea level, with a citadel towering over the waters of Lake Pamvótis and an island off its leafy shore exactly where any artist would have placed it. With excellent museums and remnants of its fascinating past, Ioánnina makes a great base for the Pérama Caves, Dodona and the surrounding villages. A year-round weekend destination, it's especially evocative in winter, surrounded by snow-capped mountains, with romantic mists rising from the lake.

HISTORY Named after a monastery dedicated to John the Baptist, Ioánnina (often anglicised to 'Janina') was founded cAD527. It didn't get its first official mention until AD879, then stayed out of the limelight until the disastrous Crusade of 1204, when refugees crowded in from Constantinople and the Peloponnese.

Fortifications began in earnest in 1205, after Michael I Comnenus Ducas founded his breakaway Byzantine state, the Despotate of Epirus, and made Ioánnina the second city after Árta. Churches and monasteries were founded in and around Ioánnina, a trend that would continue after 1335 when the Despotate was reunited with the ragtag remnants of the Byzantine Empire.

IOÁNNINA

In 1430, having seen what had happened to Thessaloníki (page 61), Ioánnina surrendered to Sultan Murad II's army under Sinan Pasha, a defeat that ironically marked the beginning of its golden age. Sinan Pasha granted the city tax privileges, a promise to leave the churches alone and even placed the *kástro* off limits to Turks – a privilege that a Christian rebellion in 1618 put paid to, when they were kicked out in favour of Muslims and Jews. But despite that glitch, Ioánnina remained wealthy and relatively free. Silver guilds thrived; churches were decorated by the Epiróte school of artists. Educational institutions sprang up, and wealthy families sent their children abroad for schooling.

By the time Ali Pasha took over in 1788, Ioánnina was booming, with a population of 35,000, of which only 5,000 were Turks. He managed to get the fortress into splendiferous shape by 1809, in time to impress Byron. The burning of Ioánnina in 1820, some say by Ali, others by the Sultan's forces, marked the start of the decline. In 1878, the Congress of Berlin assigned Ioánnina and the rest of Epirus to Greece, but nobody took them up on it until 1913. This late start has left Ioánnina's lakeside *kástro* and its minarets intact, a rare exotic touch.

GETTING THERE AND AWAY

By air Ioánnina's airport [262 A1] (✆ 26510 83600; w ioanninaairport.eu) is 5km north on the Kónitsa road. Olympic, Aegean and Sky Express fly from Athens, and there are seasonal charter flights from Scandinavia. Get there in 10 minutes on city bus 2 (✆ 26510 22239). A taxi to Ioánnina centre should cost around €7.

Airport car hire
Avis ✆ 26510 46333
Europcar ✆ 26510 35723
Hertz ✆ 26510 27400 (airport), 26510 65002 (town)

By road Buses provide all the public transport in Epirus. The intercity bus station is at G Papandréou 45 [262 B2] (✆ 26510 25014; w ktelioannina.gr). By **car**, Ioánnina is a 3–4-hour drive from Athens on the A5 or from Thessaloníki on the Egnatía Ódos, and half an hour from Igoumenítsa.

GETTING AROUND

By car Parking in the historic centre is not easy, as large parts have been pedestrianised. There's a car park in Plateía Dimokratías [262 B7] and an underground garage beneath Plateía Pýrrou [262 B7] (w stathmosioanninon.gr); there's also a large free car park along the lake by the *kástro* [262 C6], and two others that charge €5/day and €10 overnight.

By taxi Cruising taxis abound; otherwise you can hang about the *kástro* entrance on Karamanlís Street [282 C5]. Radio taxis are available via m 69771 94800 or m 69430 73994.

By boat Boats leave from the quay [262 C5] under the *kástro* every 30 minutes in summer for the island (between 08.00 & midnight) and every hour in winter (08.00–22.00) for the 10-minute crossing (€2.50 one-way).

By bike A cycle path circles the lake; hire a bike at Ora gia Podílato (aka Ioannina Bike Rental) [262 B2] (Leof Georgiou Papandreou 84; ✆ 26510 32581; m 69082 76751; w oragiapodilato.gr; ⊕ 09.00–14.30 & 18.00–21.00 Mon & Wed, 09.00–14.30 & 17.30–21.00 Tue, Thu & Fri, 09.00–14.30 Sat; €10/day, helmet €2/day).

9 | EPIRUS (ΗΠΕΙΡΟΣ)

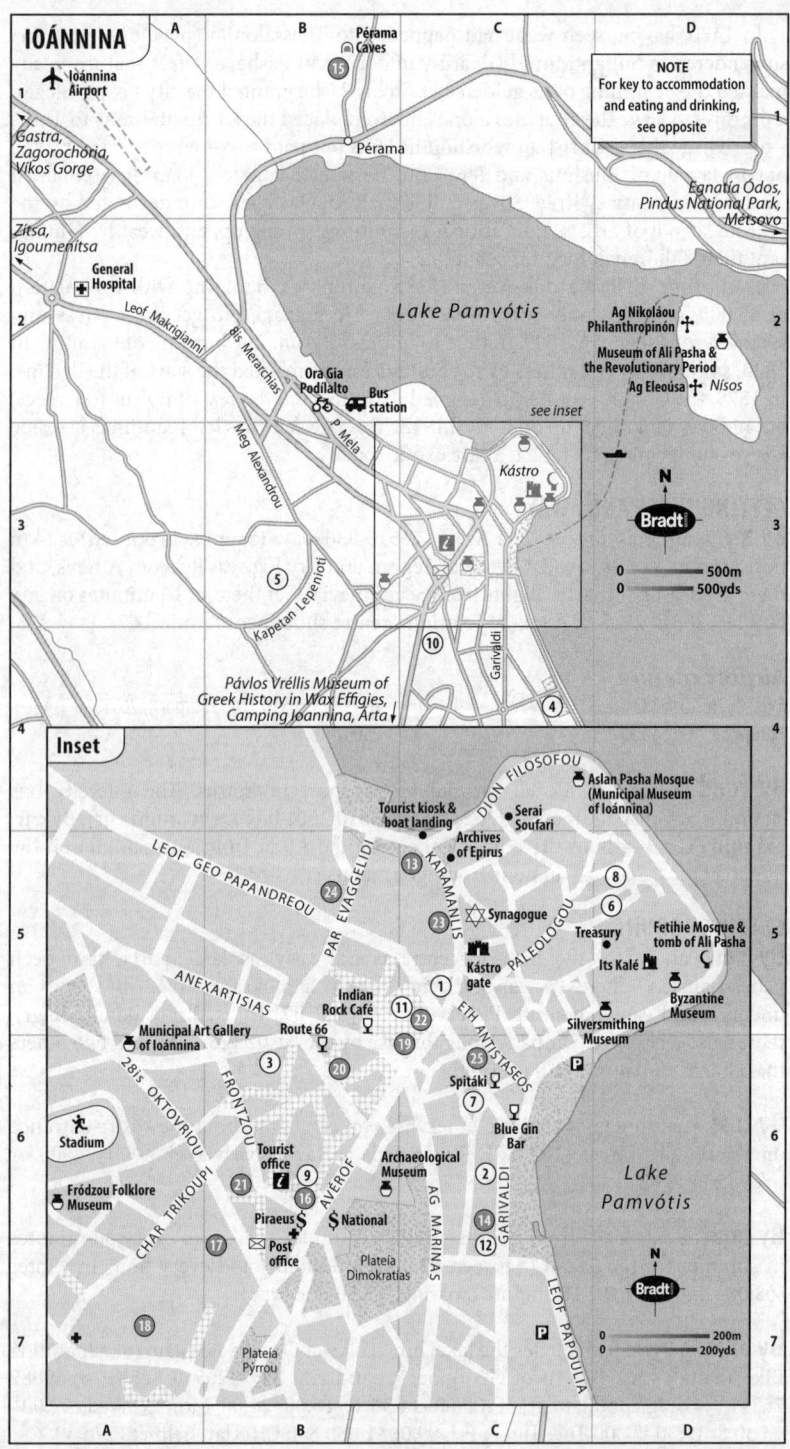

IOÁNNINA

TOURIST INFORMATION AND TOURS The **tourist office** is centrally located at Moulaïmídi 10 [262 B6] (📞 26510 37017; w travelioannina.com; ⏰ 08.00–15.00 Mon–Fri). In summer there's also a tourist kiosk by the boat landing [262 C5] (⏰ 10.00–20.00 or 21.00 daily).

This lovely and densely packed city narrates quite a tale; a half day (€120) or full day (€200/6hrs) with guide, museologist and historian **Nikos Zacharakis** (m 69328 06844; e nick-zacharakis@hotmail.com) is very well spent.

ORIENTATION Plateía Pýrrou [262 B7], high above the lake, is the modern centre. It spills into Avérof [262 B6], the city's high street. Towards the bottom, a rabbit warren of streets on the left is all that remains of the bazaar. As Avérof turns into Karamanlís Street, the gate leading into the *kástro* [262 C5] (the walled old town, built around the walled inner sanctum of the rulers) comes into view on the right. Karamanlís Street ends at the popular lakeside cafés where boats leave for the island with no name [262 C5].

 WHERE TO STAY Book well in advance for weekends. Cheaper places line the streets of Pérama, leading to the cave, from where there are frequent buses to the centre.

Expensive

Du Lac Congress & Spa [262 C4] (170 rooms) Cnr K Papoulia & Ikkou; 📞 26510 59100; w hoteldulac.gr. 5-star hotel by the lake, but a long walk from the *kástro*. Done up in a pleasant, pared-down Epiróte style, equipped with pool, children's pool, spa & wellness centre. The Du Sel restaurant (€€€) is one of the best in the area, with Epiróte dishes & non-Greek options if you need a change of pace. B/fast inc. €€€

Antique [262 C5] (12 rooms) Neoptólemou 8; 📞 26510 39999; w hotelantique.gr. Charming rooms in a 150-year-old Neoclassical building, that took 7 years to restore. Lavishly furnished throughout, with carpets & paintings. Nearest parking 180m away (but you can drop off your bags). Superb b/fast inc. €€€–€€

Fróntzu Politía [262 B3] (12 rooms) Ágia Triáda hill; 📞 26510 21011; w frontzupolitia.gr. In a protected monument complex, monastery-style suites appointed with handmade lamps & carpets & authentic details. The property also offers superb dining, a traditional-style café, & the best views in town. Bikes available for exploring. €€€–€€

Its Kalé [262 D5] (7 rooms) A Paleológou 64; 📞 26510 32777; w itskale-hotel.gr. Next to its namesake (Its Kalé; page 267) in the *kástro*, boutique hotel with immaculate rooms in whites & soft tones, a garden, & bikes to borrow; great b/fast (inc) served in a room with a glass floor over ancient plumbing. €€€–€€

Kamáres Boutique Hotel & Spa [262 C6] (9 rooms) Zalokósta 74; 📞 26510 74120; w hotelkamares.gr. Once an opulent 18th-century mansion, one of the few to survive a great fire, this beautifully atmospheric hotel has been awarded a Michelin key. Unique rooms rich in authentic,

IOÁNNINA
For listings, see above

Where to stay
1 Antique...................................C5
2 Archontariki...........................C6
3 Dioni..B6
4 Du Lac Congress & Spa......C4
5 Fróntzu Politía......................B3
6 Its Kalé....................................D5
7 Kamáres Boutique
    Hotel & Spa.........................C6
8 Kástro......................................D5
9 Kentrikón...............................B6
10 Lake Spirit..............................C4
11 Stoés Boutique....................C5
12 Z Hotel....................................C7

Where to eat and drink
13 Diethnés.................................C5
14 Dodóni Traditional..............C6
15 Filémata..................................B1
16 Fýsa Roúfa..............................B6
17 Maison.....................................B7
18 Meráki.....................................A7
19 Metsovitiki Folia...................C6
20 Montage Café Bar................B6
21 Motley.....................................B6
22 Nava Gastrobar....................C5
23 Presveia..................................C5
24 Seirios.....................................B5
25 To Magazáki Pou Légame...........C6

traditional detail & craftsmanship, plus a lovely spa. Private parking. B/fast €15. €€€–€€
Stoés Boutique Hotel [262 C3] (16 rooms) Efthimíou Chrístou 11; 26510 75700; w stoeshotel.reserve-online.net. Also awarded a Michelin key, this luxurious boutique hotel occupies a former historic commercial arcade (stoa) – a protected monument in the heart of the historic Jewish quarter. Dramatic spaces & a stylish ambiance rich in original architectural details & character. Private parking inc. B/fast €15. €€€–€€

Moderate
Archontariki [262 C6] (6 rooms) Zalokósta 50; 26510 78010. This charming little hotel in a mansion in the historic centre has equally charming owners, offering traditional rooms with pretty painted fireplaces & parking. B/fast €10. €€
Kástro [262 D5] (7 rooms) A Paleológou 57; 26510 22866; w hotelkastro.gr. A lovely renovated old house inside the *kástro*; quiet, well run & with easy parking. The rooms for 3 on the 2nd floor are terrific. Great hosts, too. Excellent b/fast €4. €€
Lake Spirit [262 C4] (10 rooms) Chatzí Pellerén 3A; 26510 25250; w lakespirit.gr. New hotel away from the historic centre (with easy parking), with luminous rooms in rich earthy tones, Coco-Mat beds, gym & sauna, & a bistro. Free parking & bikes to rent. B/fast inc. €€
Z Hotel [262 C7] (8 rooms) Garibáldi 39; 26510 25087; w zhotel.gr. Cool & contemporary near the boat landing; super-comfortable beds, & a popular bistro with lake views. Free parking; b/fast inc. €€

Budget
Camping Ioannina [map, page 258] Km13 Ioannina–Athens national road; 26510 45437; w camping-ioannina.gr. A camping/glamping option, with furnished tents & cabins & facilities for those with their own set-up, including WC & hot showers, washing machines, barbecue, minimarket, library, & cooking & washing up areas, plus a summer cinema, sports facilities & playground. €
Dioni [262 B6] (52 rooms) Tsirigóti 10; 26510 27864; w dionihotel.com. Older, central hotel, recently renovated; nearly all rooms have a balcony. Ask for a room on the top floor for the view. Free private parking. €
Kentrikón [262 B6] (9 rooms) Kolétti 5; 26510 71771; w hotel-kentrikon.gr. Right in the centre, with recently remodelled rooms & free parking in the hotel garage. B/fast €5. €

WHERE TO EAT AND DRINK
Cafés and bars line the lakefront, but also look at the pedestrian lanes of the old market area around Anexartisías Street. Be sure to try local craft beer Stala, brewed by Epirus Brewery, as well as their unusual Paguru cream ale and fruity, floral Naia.

Restaurants
Presveia [262 C5] Karamanlís 17; 25620 79366; Πρεσβεία; ⏰ 18.30–00.30 Tue & Wed,14.00–00.30 Thu, 13.30–00.30 Fri–Mon. You'll find some of Ioánnina's best creative cooking & generous portions in this house in the former Jewish quarter & in its secret courtyard. Good for salads & risotto dishes, beef fillet & desserts; good vegetarian dishes, too. €€€
Nava Gastrobar [262 C5] Efthimíou Chrístou 11; 26510 70717; nava_gastrobar; ⏰ 08.00–01.00 daily. Inventive use of local & seasonal ingredients, fresh & stylish presentations, select wine list. Beautiful spaces inside the historic Stoés boutique hotel (see above). €€€–€€
Seirios [262 B5] Evaggelídi 1; 26510 77070; w seirioskouzina.gr; ⏰ 13.00–01.00 daily. Pleasant garden terrace not far from the lake makes a lovely place to dawdle over well-prepared traditional dishes, with loads to choose from on the menu. It's 'the all-day restaurant', so pop in whenever you're hungry. €€€–€€
Gástra [map, page 258] Eleoúsa, km7 on the Kostáki road; 26510 61530; w estiatorio-gastra.gr; ⏰ 13.00–midnight Tue–Sun. Past the airport, on the Kónitsa road opposite the Dodóni ice cream factory. All Ioánnina comes to this large restaurant for *gástra*, tender lamb or kid titbits slow cooked in round casseroles under a lidful of burning coals in a special oven on the terrace. €€
Dodóni Traditional Restaurant [262 C6] Garivaldi 33; 26510 21970; ⏰ noon–03.00 Mon–Sat, noon–18.00 Sun. *Tsípouro* & more in a high-ceilinged old spot. Lots of delicious nibbles, including many veggie choices. €

IOÁNNINA

Filémata [262 B1] By the Pérama Caves; `26510 81192`; Φιλέματα – Filemata; ⏰ 18.30–02.00 daily. Smart bistro perfect for après cave. Order drinks, & delicious complimentary *mézes* follow, including mushrooms in season, chicken in pastry, smoked pork, & ice cream. €

Fýsa Roúfa [262 B6] Avérof 45; `26510 26262`; fysaroyfa; ⏰ always. One of the last old-school restaurants anywhere, with delicious 'ready dishes' lined up on the steam table to point at. Also tripe soup for hangovers, & often *magiritsa* – the traditional Easter soup made with lamb offal & dill. €

Metsovitiki Folia [262 C6] Avérof 101; `26510 22033`; ⏰ 12.30–22.30 Mon–Sat. Popular terrace without, traditional touches within, & above-average grilled meats, fries with oregano & salads. €

To Magazáki Pou Légame [262 C6] Eth Antistáseos 44; `26510 33106`; ⏰ 14.00–23.00 Tue–Sun. Small, stylish & run by a wonderful chef, with creative takes on Greek & Mediterranean classics. Great wine list. €

Cafés and pastry shops

Diethnés [262 C5] Plateía Mavíli; `26510 35513`; ⏰ 08.00–22.30 daily. Local pastry masters renowned for their baklava since 1950.

Maison [262 B7] Vlachleídi 3; `26510 27797`; Maisonloannina; ⏰ 08.00–01.00 daily. Big new design café serving gourmet coffees, brunch, cocktails & homemade ice cream.

Meráki [262 A7] Sakká 12; `26510 65144`; Παραδοσιακό καφενείο 'Μεράκι'; ⏰ 08.00–03.00 daily. Colourful, friendly café-bar adorned with folk art made by the owner.

Montage Café Bar [262 B6] Kániggos 10; `26510 33771`; ⏰ 08.00–04.00 Mon–Sat, 10.00–04.00 Sun. Charming garden courtyard in the middle of town, a favourite hangout with lovely music in the evening.

Motley [262 B6] Márkou Mpótsari 3; `26510 38310`; Motley coffeesweet; ⏰ 08.00–midnight daily. Great coffee, waffles & chocolate pastries.

BARS AND NIGHTLIFE

Blue Gin Bar [262 C6] Eth Antistáseos 40; m 69068 94946; TheBlueGin; ⏰ 21.00–05.00 daily. Superb cocktails, including many original ones made from local ingredients; plus soul, blues, rock & funk.

Indian Rock Café [262 B5] Anexartisías 14; `26510 73190`; Rock café Indian, Ιωάννινα. Still going strong since 1998.

Route 66 [262 B6] Stoá Liampéi 15; m 69370 23130; ⏰ 20.00–03.30 daily. Cool atmosphere & drinks under the stone vaults.

Spitáki [262 C6] Eth Antistáseos 42; `26510 33110`; SpitakiCocktailBarloannina; ⏰ 20.00–06.00. Great cocktails, funky kitschy décor & great atmosphere.

OTHER PRACTICALITIES

National Bank [262 B6] Avérof 4
Piraeus Bank [262 B6] Avérof 1
General Hospital [262 A2] Leof Makrigiánni 60; `26513 66111`

Pharmacy Kontochristos [262 A7] Plateía Párgi
Pharmacy Zacharis Loukas [262 B6] Avérof 2
Post office [262 B7] Plateía Markoú Bótsari; ⏰ 07.30–14.30 Mon–Fri

WHAT TO SEE AND DO

Municipal Art Gallery of Ioánnina [262 A6] (Koraï 1; `26510 75131`; ⏰ 08.00–14.30 Mon–Fri, 10.00–13.00 & 18.00–21.00 Sun; free) Housed in the Neoclassical mansion of art-loving mayor Vasilis Pyrsinella, this is the oldest municipal art gallery in Greece, with some 500 works, including charming 19th-century genre paintings.

Archaeological Museum [262 B6] (Plateía 25is Martíou 6; `26510 33357`; w efaioa.gr; ⏰ summer 08.00–20.00 Wed–Mon, winter 08.30–15.30 Wed–Mon; €10, concessions €5) This excellent museum, designed in the 1960s by modernist Aris Konstantinídis, houses 3,000 artefacts from the Palaeolithic to the Roman period, with good explanations in English. From Dodona come 150 lead sheets with questions for the oracle – relatable in their poignance and occasionally delightful in their pettiness ('Was it Pistsos that stole the wool from the bed mattress?') – and intricate nails and the round 'handle' of the *bouleuterion*'s door. This bronze disc has holes for string coming from the latch inside. Pulling it down released the latch; pulling it taut from the inside locked the door. Until recently, many mountain houses still used the same system.

The Necromanteíon (page 299) is also well represented with terracotta figurines of Persephone, votive hydrias and fragments of the so-called windlass mechanism for lowering supplicants into its inner sanctum. The finds from Vítsa are especially graceful; some from the 8th century BC are reminiscent of Mycenaean pottery. There are grave goods from a Molossian cemetery (13th–4th century BC) from Liatovoúni near Kónitsa, and a marble sarcophagus from Thesprotia. A triangular stone axe the size of a fist from 200,000BC, unearthed in Préveza in 1991, is the oldest tool ever found in Greece and its edges still look like they could do the trick. There's gold jewellery from Árta, coins, pretty clay jugs and a turtle's carapace used to make a lyre.

Fródzou Folklore Museum [262 A6] (M Angélou 42; 26510 20515; w ehm. gr; ⊕ 09.00–15.30 Mon–Fri, 09.00–14.30 Sat; €2, concessions €1) The wonderful costumes of Epirus are the stars here, ranging from elaborate waistcoats embroidered with silver and gold thread to the black-and-white geometrical costumes of the Sarakatsáni, from the austere skirts and headscarves of the ladies from Pogóni to the black flower-embroidered aprons of Métsovo.

The *kástro* [262 C5] This fortress on its rocky height, with walls that once dropped directly into the limpid waters of the lake, is still a vital precinct of the city, and easier to reach now that the moat has been filled in. Its quiet cobbled lanes are filled with houses, mostly built after 1900, but with architectural hints of their medieval predecessors.

Synagogue [262 C5] (Just left of the *kástro* gate; 26510 25195; ⊕ by appt) Jews have lived in Ioánnina ever since its foundation, and, isolated from other Jewish communities, developed their own customs and traditions (for instance writing in Greek, but using Hebrew letters). Never numbering more than 5,000, about half of Ioánnina's Jews emigrated to the USA in the early 1900s. Because Ioánnina was initially ruled by the Italians in World War II, Jewish lives continued much the same until 1943, when the Germans took control. On Greek Independence Day, 25 March 1944, the entire community was rounded up, forced into trucks and taken away to Auschwitz. Today some 50 Jews live in Ioánnina – one, in fact, Dr Moses Elisaf, was elected in 2019 as Greece's first Jewish mayor, serving until his death in 2023.

The pretty white 19th-century Ottoman synagogue is filled with light. It's one of the best preserved synagogues in Greece, partly thanks to Kehila Kedosha Janina in New York City, the only Romaniote (Greek Jewish) synagogue in the West, founded in 1906. But the most memorable sight in the synagogue is the marble tablets listing the names of the 1,832 men, women and children who never came back.

A 5-minute walk leads to the **Serai Soufari** [262 C4], built by Ali Pasha as a Cavalry School, and the **Archives of Epirus** [262 C5] (which occasionally hosts exhibitions), along with remains of the library, Byzantine baths and Ottoman hammam.

Aslan Pasha Mosque/Municipal Museum of Ioánnina [262 C4] (Noútsou 2; 26510 26356; ⊕ 08.30–16.30 Mon–Fri, 09.00–15.00 Sat & Sun; €2) Built in 1618, with a well-proportioned dome, this handsome mosque functioned until 1924, and

IOÁNNINA

still has recesses in the vestibule for the shoes of worshippers. Its collection of 15th–20th-century religious and everyday items, donated by local families, evokes the days when Ioánnina was home to large Christian, Jewish and Muslim communities living in harmony.

Its (Iç) Kale [262 D5] (⊕ 08.00–20.00 daily; free) Also known as the Acropolis, the *kástro*'s inner castle took its present shape when taken in hand by Ali Pasha early in the 19th century. Entered through an impressive gate, it resembles a park, with views that must have been appreciated by all of Ali Pasha's visitors. His palace and seraglio were here. To fit them in, he flattened the hill and incorporated a Norman round tower, the calling card of Bohemund who passed through in the 11th century but didn't have Ali's staying power. The late 18th-century **cookhouse** with its four distinctive chimneys, has been nicely transformed into a café.

Byzantine Museum [262 D5] (✆ 26510 25989; ⊕ summer 08.00–20.00 Wed–Mon, winter 08.00–15.30 Wed–Mon; €5, concessions €3 – inc admission to Fetihie Mosque & Treasury) The Byzantine Museum was built in 1960 as a royal pavilion in the style of an Epiróte mansion on the site of Ali's seraglio. Its collection includes not only Early Christian and Byzantine icons and sculptural bits and bobs, but also ceramics, silver and books, including a rare printed book from Venice from 1499.

Fetihie Mosque [262 D5] (See Byzantine Museum for hours & details) Otherwise known as the Victory Mosque, this mosque of 1611 (remodelled in 1795) has a prettily painted mihrab and dome, and excellent acoustics. Propped against the back wall, without a word of explanation, is a curious relief of a man and woman, halfway transformed into a merman and mermaid. In front of the mosque is the surprisingly modest **Tomb of Ali Pasha** (minus his head). There's no name or epitaph, but it is topped by an ornate black ironwork cage, replacing the one melted down in 1940. It is hard to decide if it's intended to commemorate Ali or to keep his restless spirit firmly underground.

Treasury [262 D5] (See Byzantine Museum for hours & details) Located near the ruins of the tower, this houses fine examples of Ioánnina's silverwork.

Silversmithing Museum [262 D5] (✆ 26510 64065; w piop.gr; ⊕ Mar–mid-Oct 10.00–18.00 Wed–Mon, mid-Oct–Feb 10.00–17.00 Wed–Mon; €8, concessions €4) This museum in the bastion walls covers the history of local silversmiths, who have been famous since Byzantine times for the silver chiselling that took their name, *gianiótiki*, and their intricate silver wire filigree based on Byzantine, Baroque and Arab designs. Niello work, where black enamel is used on a recessed background to highlight embossed designs, is especially dramatic, and goes back to the Mycenaeans. Into the mid 19th century, buyers came from as far afield as Russia, and master craftsmen grew wealthy supplying them. There are audiovisual displays, maps, tools, Christian and Jewish religious items, amulets, jewellery, silver pistols and the silverware of noble families – once an essential part of a dowry. There are also contemporary works by the 90 members of the Association of Silversmiths (w ioanninasilver.com).

Lake Pamvótis and the Island [262 C–D2] Fed by small rivers and drained through karstic sinkholes, Ioánnina's beautiful lake, the largest in Epirus, reflects the surrounding mountains. Its reed-fringed, car-free island (population 100), is the city's most popular destination. One of its claims to fame is an omission: it's the only inhabited lake island in the world without a name – it's just 'island', or **Nísos** in Greek. The whitewashed houses in the village, with their Epiróte white lace curtains, are the remains of a settlement of Maniátes from the south Peloponnese who sought refuge here in the 16th century, in the footsteps of the Byzantine aristocrats.

With its six monasteries, this is the third largest monastic state in Greece, after Mount Athos and Metéora. The monasteries house some extraordinary Byzantine frescoes, and walking to them amid the reeds and birdsong is reason enough to visit. You'll see small boats from time to time; their daily catch – eel and carp particularly – makes a nice lunch at one of the restaurants in the central square, where you'll also find *vatrachopódara* (frog's legs), a local speciality.

The **Lake Pamvóti Information Centre** (26510 21835; w lakepamvotis.gr; 10.00–16.00 Sat–Sun, summer also Wed–Fri; free) is on the island.

Museum of Ali Pasha and the Revolutionary Period [262 D2] (East of the village; 26510 81791; w museumalipasha.gr; 09.00–16.00 daily; €3,

EVERYONE'S FAVOURITE DESPOT: ALI PASHA

I talk not of mercy, I talk not of fear
He neither must know who would serve the Vizier:
Since the days of our prophet the Crescent ne'er saw
A chief ever glorious like Ali Pashaw
Byron, *Childe Harold's Pilgrimage*, 1812

Many historians present Ali Pasha (1744–1822) as simply another in the series of ruthless, cruel double-dealers fostered by the chaotic, despotic Ottoman Empire. But Ali, who defies neat definition, was much more. Born in Tepelini, Albania, he began as a well-connected bandit with a terrifying Greek mother, Khamco, who could have shown the Hell's Angels a thing or two and was the source, Ali said, of his early dreams of 'power, treasure, and palaces'. He helped the Sultan in the war of 1787 against Austria and got appointed pasha of Trίkala for his pains. But Ali wanted Ioánnina. He curried favour with the local Greeks (all of his court dealings were in Greek, and he even had a Greek inscription over the gate of Its Kale, claiming to be a descendant of Pyrrhus) and then forged a decree from the Sultan who, short-handed at the time, honoured it.

Ali ably administered Ioánnina, at the same time swallowing Préveza (1798) and having the poor Súliots for dessert (1803). Aided by his sons, Veli and Mukhtar, he instituted a rough and ready order in his expanding territories, which at one point included much of present-day Albania, Epirus, Macedonia, Thessaly and even the Peloponnese. By 1807, this charming, wily sociopath was more king than Sultan's representative, allying himself with the French when it suited him or the British, who gave him Párga in 1817.

Illiterate, but clever enough to employ the wealthy, literate Greeks he admired, Ali created a court that, when it suited him to thumb his nose at the Sultan, hosted Greek freedom fighters Karaiskákis, Bótsaris and Androútsos, and intellectuals such as Kollétis. He was called the 'Lion of Ioánnina' and he was indeed lionised by the many foreign Philhellenes who came his way. These included Byron (1809), who was especially susceptible to Ali's blend of magnetic charm and concessions €1) The small 16th-century Moní Ag Pandeleímonos, where you can see the holes in the floor made by the bullets that killed Ali Pasha, is now a museum dedicated to his life and times. There are stunning traditional costumes from around Epirus, Turkish ceramics, lavish belt buckles and other jewellery, and the magnificent weapons collected by Fótis Rapakoúsi: fabulous swords and daggers and an amazing array of firearms, including muskets with balls the size of hen's eggs, an efficient-looking 19th-century flick knife with a deer-foot handle and two *cheirovomvídes* (hand grenades) that look like festive candles. There are silver *baláskes* (shot holders), shaped like and worn somewhat like Scottish sporrans from the belt, and small, intricately decorated *medoulária* (tiny square containers holding grease, for cleaning the guns). Along with silver buckles, tobacco boxes and pen holders, they graphically show how war and everyday life were inextricably mixed. Weapons, made for death, were meant to be treasured for life. When fully kitted up, it can truly be said that Epiróte warriors were 'dressed to kill'. A highlight of Mr Rapakoúsi's collection has also recently gone on display: the revolutionary declaration of Alexandros Ypsilantis, written in his own hand.

amoral cruelty. Visiting Ali's sumptuous court, with its blend of oriental barbarism veneered with Hellenic sophistication, became something of a literary industry, and his hospitality was as effusive as his pockets were deep. Even today, when Greeks want to say that they have it made, they will invariably say that they are like the 'Pasha in Ioánnina'.

His cruelty was legendary even in his own time. He roasted an enemy of his mother's on a spit, to honour her dying wish. In 1801 he ordered the execution of Kyra Frosyni, a beautiful Greek aristocrat whose husband was often absent and rejected his advances (or had a love affair with his son, Muhtar Pasha), by throwing her and 16 companions accused of adultery into the lake. He had Katsandónis, a prominent Greek independence fighter, executed by breaking every bone in his body with a sledgehammer. Considering the atrocities Ali admitted to, along with some apocryphal ones, he has had amazingly good press. And when all is said and done, he was good for Ioánnina, and not as hated in his lifetime as some historians have made out. He did not consider himself, nor was he then considered, as much an outsider as the British or French or even some of the more sophisticated expatriate Greeks who visited Ioánnina.

The Sultan, not the Greeks, ended his amazing career. He began by placing Ioánnina under siege and burning it in 1822. Only the *kástro* held out, negotiations were opened and the 81-year-old Ali was promised a full pardon if he would retire to Ioánnina's island – only to be asked to present himself for beheading. He refused – 'My head…will not be surrendered like the head of a slave' – and fought until he was finally shot through a hole in the floor of the little Moní Ag Pandeleímonos, where he had taken refuge. The Sultan insisted on his head being sent to the Porte and displayed for three days, just to be sure he was gone for good.

Ali's resistance gave Greeks the opportunity to start planning for their own uprising. Perhaps that is why many Greeks look on him with a certain affection today. Most portraits displayed in Ioánnina depict him as a benevolent old codger, quietly smoking his famous *chiboúki*, the 63-inch decorated pipe with a rosewood bowl.

9 | EPIRUS (ΗΠΕΙΡΟΣ)

Ag Nikoláou Philanthropinón [262 D2] (West of the village; ☎ 26510 25949) The best known of the monasteries founded by the Philanthropinón family stands out for its exceptional frescoes, done when the local school of painting was at its height. In the additions of 1560, Solon, Aristotle, Thucydides and Plutarch were added to the usual Orthodox worthies – not the first time ancient Greeks have been lovingly placed in the company of saints. They look quite at home.

Ag Eleoúsa [262 D2] (400m past Ag Nikoláou Philanthropinón) Remote and hospitable (the monastery keeps longer hours than the others), this beautiful 13th-century monastery is rich in art and inspiration. The interior of the chapel is covered in its entirety, primarily the 16th-century work of the brothers Giórgos and Frángos Kontáris; the story of the loaves and fishes and of the denial of St Peter are among the recognisable scenes. Also notable is the unique icon of Christ with a globe beneath his feet.

After centuries of constant occupation, this monastery had been abandoned by the 1960s. It was revitalised less than a decade ago by a young monk, with the help of a couple of young people from the island.

AROUND IOÁNNINA The scenery around Ioánnina is lovely, and its many villages shared the city's prosperity. If you are using the city as a base, you might also consider a day trip to Dodona (page 283).

Pérama Caves [262 B1] (5km north in Pérama, Πέραμα; buses 4, 5, 8 & 16 from Ioánnina; ☎ 26510 81521; w spilaio-perama.gr; ⊕ tours every 15mins 09.00–17.00 daily; €7, concessions €3.50) This 1,100m-long complex, accidently discovered in 1940, is distinguished by the remarkable size of its chambers and 19 different kinds of stalagmite and stalactite. To exit, you must climb 163 stairs, but the temperature stays at a pleasant constant 17°C.

Pávlos Vréllis Museum of Greek History in Wax Effigies [262 B4] (12km south in Bizaní (Μπιζάνι); ☎ 26510 92128; w vrellis.gr; ⊕ 10.00–16.00 daily; €7, students €4, ages 8–17, over 65s & large families €3, under 8s free) There's no place like it in Greece: sculptor Pávlos Vréllis's extensive adaptation of Madame Tussauds to modern Greek history has been going strong since 1983, with 150 figures and no lack of gruesome displays or visitors.

Zítsa (Ζίτσα) The vineyards of high-altitude Zítsa produce a naturally sparkling white wine made from Debina grapes, which have to be kept fenced in to save them from the grape-loving wild boar. Visit the **Domaine Glinavos** (at Monastíri, up a steep hill east of the village; ☎ 26580 22212; w glinavos.gr; ⊕ 1hr tours 10.00–14.00 Mon–Fri, w/ends by appt; €3, €20 with tastings). From Domaine Glinavos you can wind south (there's no very direct route) to the 14th-century sturdy stone **Moní Profítis Elías**, which enjoys 'the most beautiful situation I ever beheld' according to Lord Byron, who visited in 1809 and gave it a mention in the Second Canto of *Childe Harold's Pilgrimage* (which is carved in the stone over the door). Its icon screen is elaborate even by Epiróte standards.

Kalpáki (Καλπάκι; formerly Elaía) A statue of a Greek warrior stands guard on the hill over this village, which saw the first major land victory for the Allies in World War II on 28 October 1940 (commemorated with a national holiday and parades), when the vastly outnumbered Greeks pushed back the Italians invading from Albania at the Kalamás River. The Battle of Elaía-Kalamás (2–8 November) is covered in the **War Museum of Kalpáki** ✆ 26530 42140; ⊕ May–Sep 10.00–14.00 & 17.30–20.00 daily, Oct–Apr 09.30–15.00 daily; free) with posters, photographs, clothing and more.

Kalpáki belongs to the **Pogóni** (Πωγώνι) region, which extends west towards the Albanian border. Sparsely populated even by local standards, the Pogóni is famous for its festivals and churches built in a squat, muscular basilica style with tall cupolas. It was the birthplace of legendary Kítsos Harisiádis, considered the greatest and most soulful *klaríno* player Epirus ever produced (which is saying something in this land of Balkan Benny Goodmans) – he never left Epirus, but made enough recordings in the late 1920s to be reworked in a new album (page 26). It's a great place to go if you're suffering from *mal de civilisation*: aim for picturesque **Doló** (Δολό), with lovely views over the Kouvarás Gorge, and **Pogonianí** (Πωγωνιανή), where marked trails have charming informative plaques in English reading 'Dear Tripper'. The main E853 road crosses into Albania at **Kakaviá** (Κακαβιά).

THE ZAGOROCHÓRIA

The Zagóri (Slavic for 'land behind the mountain'; known as Paroraia in ancient times) is surrounded by spectacular peaks and scored by ravines, including the fabulous Víkos Gorge. At its core the Víkos–Aoös National Park (one of Greece's four GeoParks), created in 1973, and the jagged Týmphi range (2,497m), aptly nicknamed the 'Greek Alps', form a backdrop to 46 settlements.

It was the Zagóri's isolation, and the difficulty in sending unwilling Turkish troops into the hills, that allowed its villages, the Zagorochória, to remain autonomous during the Ottoman occupation. After conquering Ioánnina, Sultan Murad II agreed to a treaty to let 14 villages in the core rule themselves in exchange for an annual tribute; no Turks were allowed to enter the Koinon ('Common') of the Zagorochória unless they were invited. In 1480, the Vlach villages to the east were allowed to join the Koinon; by 1670 there were 60 villages. They were governed by a council of elders, with a small military force. Education of both boys and girls was promoted and the area prospered as a result, attracting Philhellene benefactors and visitors from far and wide, as well as Greek scholars, and renegades.

Many of the highlanders used their relative freedom to become merchants, organising caravans of goods on the Silk Road, while sending funds home to their wives, to hire the finest builders to build their lordly mansions, or *archontiká*. The good times ended in 1820, when, after crushing Ali Pasha, 1,500 Ottoman troops arrived in the Zagóri and defeated the local troops raised by Filikí Etaireía ('Friendly Society') member Alexis Noutsos. Afterwards the Zagorochória were still allowed to appoint their own governor and keep their schools, but lost the rest of their autonomy and had to pay steep taxes until becoming part of Greece in 1913.

Now designated a national treasure, it is the totality of the Zagorochória that takes your breath away. Grey stone houses and grey stone churches are knitted together by lanes and *plateías* paved with the same ubiquitous stone. Local stonemasons, many hailing from the so-called Master-builder villages in the north (page 253) exported their talent to the Pelion and throughout the Balkans until well into the 20th century. At home, they built paved mule paths (*kalderímia*) and connected rocky chasms with poetic stone bridges that have become the region's trademark. They were the only roads linking the Zagorochória until the 1950s.

The Zagóri encompasses three mountain zones. Arbutus, holly oak, pine and cypress are found with cyclamens, anemones and camomile in the 'maquis' (490–800m). In the mountain zone (800–1,980m) the oak, black fir, beech, maple and

ZAGÓRI ARCHITECTURE

Houses in the Zagorochória are surrounded by stone walls, just high enough for looking over to be impossible. Doorways with triangular stone lintels lead into flower-decked flagged courtyards, which often have low stone benches outside the house entrance. Symmetrical windows, sheathed in thin black bars, have drab wooden shutters that often turn in rather than out, giving houses a blank expression.

But Zagóri houses, like geodes, are grey on the outside only. Raised wooden floors flank the fireplace to accommodate mattresses covered in fluffy *flokáti* rugs or brightly embroidered blankets and pillows – seating by day, beds at night. The typical fireplace is a plastered apron projecting into the room over an open stone hearth. In summer, an embroidered cloth, or *tzakópano*, is placed over the mantel, as important a piece in any dowry chest as embroidered linen or the white lacy half-curtains that grace every window.

Houses with separate living rooms have closed wooden benches lining the sides of the room, all topped with embroidered cushions. Ceilings are board and batten, but wealthier houses boast elaborate criss-crosses over tiny squares, and special mouldings for the chandelier. Cupboards are built in, with matching wainscotting so that some walls are all wood, painted bold dark blues, greens, even red, providing the background for folk art motifs that sometimes spill over to the white plastered walls. Deep windows are lined with wood; doorways can be low. Where space was at a premium, the animals lived downstairs and their owners up, and outside stone staircases often added an ornamental flair. Other mountain houses have similar features. But here, utility became an art and many of Greece's best designers have taken leaves out of the Zagorochória book.

Even looking down is interesting. Village lanes, the cobblestoned *kalderímia*, are stone-paved with precision, and without the benefit of cement. Many were constructed in a shallow 'v' so rainwater drained away from the walls. Steep paths have a stepped strip in the middle, so animals had a firm footing while the wheels of their carts ran smoothly on either side. On gentle inclines the entire *kalderímia* might be lined with steps shallow enough for cart wheels to roll over.

Churches in the Zagorochória are basilican and quite grand, frescoed by a local school of painters. Arches are popular here, especially in the colonnaded porch that inevitably runs down the one side and sometimes two, with benches perfect for inclement Sundays. The isolated bell towers were made to impress, but cupolas (*troúlis*) are rare and restricted to one per church, if at all. The style is so uniform that it is only the crumbling stonework that distinguishes a very old church from a new one.

chestnut trees share space with lilies, peonies and crocuses. The alpine zone, above 1,980m, is carpeted with rare blooms in spring. Monodéndri is the most visited village, the two Pápingos the most dramatic, but each and every Zagóri village has its own style and atmosphere. The hotels stay open all year, and often winter is priciest. You will eat simply but well: even tiny settlements have restaurants serving local meat and pittas, large flaky pastry pies loaded with cheese and spinach. The classic is crispy *alevrópita*, 'flour pie', named for its thin crispy crust, topped with golden baked feta.

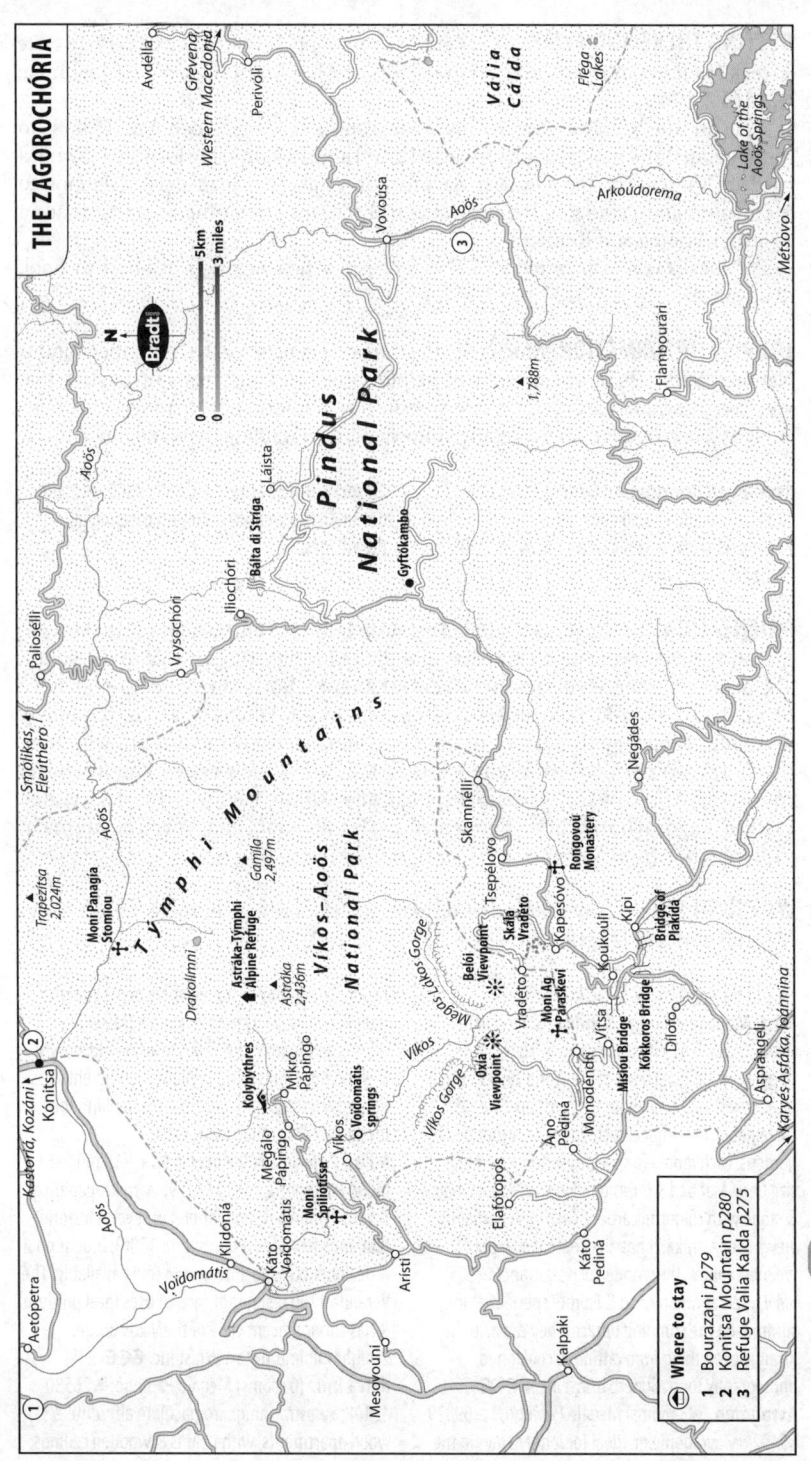

9 | EPIRUS (ΗΠΕΙΡΟΣ)

GETTING THERE AND AWAY Buses are in short supply. There may be service once a week from Ioánnina to either Monodéndri or Megálo Pápingo (KTEL Ioannina; ↘26510 25014).

By car, the Central Zagorochória are an hour from Ioánnina (53km to Monodéndri) and most easily approached by turning east from the Ioánnina–Kónitsa road in Karyés. For the Western Zagorochória, take the road north (signposted Mesovoúni and Pápingo). The nearest petrol stations are on the Ioánnina road in Asfáka, Klidoniá and Kónitsa.

For local **taxis**, call m 69555 73799 or visit w taxi-zagori.gr. It's best to book in advance.

TOURIST INFORMATION Much of this area is encompassed by the Pindus National Park. There are all sorts of helpful brochures and maps in English that you can download from the park website (w pindosnationalpark.gr). See also w vikosaoosgeopark.com for detailed information on walking trails and much more.

Asprángeli Information Centre ↘26530 22241; ⏱ 08.30–15.30 daily
Pápingo Information Centre ↘26530 25096; ⏱ 08.00–15.00 daily

Zagóri Municipality ↘26533 60300; w zagori.gov.gr. Useful website in English covering all the villages.

ORIENTATION The Zagóri is bounded by the Ioánnina–Kónitsa highway to the west, the Aoös River to the north and east and the Ódos Egnatía highway to the south. The densest cluster of villages in the **central Zagorochória** surround Monodéndri: Elafótopos, Áno and Káto Pediná, Vítsa, Aspránqeli, Dílofo, Vradéto, Kapésovo, Koukoúli, Kípi; slightly further out are Negádes, Tsepélovo and Skamnélli, then Iliochóri and Vrisichóri, with little Láista farthest east. The **western Zagorochória** consist of Arísti, Víkos, Megálo Pápingo and Mikro Pápingo. The less-visited **eastern Zagorochória**, best represented by Flambourári and Vovoúsa, are most easily reached from Métsovo.

WHERE TO STAY Many hotels and restaurants take only cash; there are ATMs in Monodéndri and Megálo Pápingo.

Western Zagorochória

Aristi Mountain Lodge & Villas (24 rooms) Arísti; ↘26530 41330; w aristi.eu. A 'National Geographic Unique Lodge of the World' built in the local grey stone, & run with the most up-to-date sustainable, low-impact techniques & surrounded by gardens. Each room is a spacious suite with a king-size Coco-Mat bed & is designed in traditional wood & stone with colourful carpets, each with gorgeous views over Astráka. It has an excellent spa, pool & wellness centre; the wonderful restaurant (€€€), Salvia, serves organic veg & Epiróte specialities in summer on the stunning terrace. They can also arrange everything from rafting to cooking to photography tours. Superb b/fast inc. €€€€
Avragónio (23 rooms) Megálo Pápingo; m 69829 85492; w avragonio.gr. Ideal for longer stays in the

Zagóri: beautifully designed apartments straight out of *Country Living* magazine, in a cluster of houses dating from the 1760s re-using old stones & wood from ruins with fireplaces in different sizes. Very cosy library/club room/bar overlooking the lovely pool & Gamílla peaks. €€€
Mikro Papigo 1700 Hotel & Spa (15 rooms) Mikró Pápingo; ↘26530 41179; w mikropapigo.gr. Award-winning designer hotel in several historic buildings (the oldest dates from 1700); indoor pool & designer eco-spa. Private 4x4 tours available. The Veranda 1700 restaurant (€€€) uses local produce & has a magnificent view of the Víkos Gorge. 2-night minimum stay. B/fast inc. €€€
Astra Inn (6 rooms) Megálo Pápingo; ↘26530 42108; w astra-inn.gr. Immaculate all-white & wood apartments, with beams & wooden ceilings,

in traditional stone buildings. The restaurant (€€) is one of the best, using local organic products – wild trout, mountain herbs, cheeses, & mushrooms & truffles in season. €€€–€€
Gamila Rocks Mountain Hotel (10 rooms) Arísti; 26530 41070; w gamilarocks.com. Little hotel, with a spa & outdoor hydro-pool to relax in after a stroll through the gorge (they offer transportation there). Comfortable rooms with views, comfy beds & Dunlopillo linens, herbal toiletries; plus billiards & a wine bar. The owners love motorcycles & can offer suggestions on the most exciting routes. B/fast inc. €€€–€€
Saxonis Houses (10 rooms) Megálo Pápingo; m 69371 51624; w saxonis-papigo.gr. Rooms in 3 stone houses separated by lush pergolas. Owner Nikos Saxonis abandoned a big advertising job in Athens years ago to create this haven of rural bliss (Coco-Mat beds, Laura Ashley linens, no TVs, although there's a library & occasional film showing). Week-long activity packages available. Hearty b/fast inc. €€€–€€
Papaevangelou (14 rooms) Megálo Pápingo; 26530 41135; w hotelpapaevangelou.gr. Run by a delightful couple, beamed woodsy rooms in old stone buildings around a courtyard; lots of fireplaces. Free parking, great b/fast (inc) with fresh baked bread. €€
Taxiarches (21 rooms) Arísti; 26530 41888; w taxiarches.gr. Large hotel with extensive grounds by Zagóri standards, with great views. It has its own minibuses & the on-site Rafting Athletic Centre offers every imaginable activity, including paragliding & mushroom hunting. Kind hosts; meals available by request. B/fast inc. €€
Zissis (20 rooms) Arísti; 26530 41088; w zissishotel.com. Traditional-style buildings complete with stone roofs & an attractive courtyard, run by a friendly local family. The colourful woodsy rooms sleep up to 4; there's also a good terrace restaurant (€€). 2-night minimum, sometimes b/fast inc. €€
Astráka (12 rooms) Megálo Pápingo; 26530 41693; w papigoastraka.gr. One of the first inns in the area, a traditional house of 1864 with mattresses framing the fireplace & a common living room; they also run a good restaurant (€€). The hosts know all the trails, & for a small fee can transport luggage etc. €€–€
Dias (12 rooms) Mikró Pápingo; 26530 41257; w diaspapigo.gr. A well-run, traditional inn, with colourful rooms & great views. The courtyard is cosy, the food terrific (good soups & spinach *pítes*), & the Tsoumánis family make visitors feel at home. €€–€

Central Zagorochória
Kipi Suites (8 rooms) Kípi; 26530 71995; w ariahotels.gr. New, ecologically sound suites at one of the highest points in the village, with a panoramic terrace. All with king-size bed, private entrance & fireplace. B/fast inc. €€€
Drakolimni (31 rooms) Tsepélovo; 26530 81318. Newer, traditional-styled hotel – with a car park & bar. €€
Villa Paroraia (6 rooms) Tsepélovo; 26530 81088; w villaparoraia.gr. Recent luxury conversion of an 18th-century mansion packed full of charm, with extra-long Coco-Mat beds on hardwood floors, & painted ceilings. Delicious homemade b/fast. €€
Víkos (7 rooms) Monodéndri; 26530 71370; w vikoshotel.com. Built in traditional style, with ornate ceilings & a terrace; all rooms have hydromassage shower. Summer cocktail bar, & restaurant that translates as 'Grandma's Secrets' (€€). Free parking nearby. €€–€
Zagori Philoxenia Hotel (18 rooms) Monodéndri; 26530 71040; w zagoriphiloxenia. gr. Cosy, traditional, woodsy & welcoming. B/fast inc. €€–€
Archontiko 1787 (6 rooms) Tsepélovo; 26530 81216; w archontiko1787.gr. Mary, the charming owner, runs a delightful cosy & colourful guesthouse in an 18th-century mansion. Great b/fast inc. €
Kadi (8 rooms) Tsepélovo; 26530 81029; w kadi.gr. Charming old stone inn, with lovely owners. B/fast inc. €

Eastern Zagorochória
Kerasies (10 rooms) Vovoúsa; 26560 23003; w kerasies.gr. 3 traditional buildings, with handsome contemporary rooms in 2 & a shared space in the 3rd, with a bar, library & games. B/fast inc. €€–€
Refuge Valia Kalda [map, page 273] (50 bunks in mixed dorms) 3km south of Vovoúsa; 26560 22200; m 69773 14779; w katafigiovaliacalda.eu. Recently built, with 50 bunk beds spread between 5 large rooms, with a restaurant (€) & a camping area, near a swimming hole with a waterfall. Towels, sheets & soap provided. €

✕ WHERE TO EAT AND DRINK

Western Zagorochória The best restaurants are attached to the hotels: the Astra Inn, the Astráka, Aristi Mountain Lodge, Mikro Papigo 1700 & Dias.

Adriano Pizza & Pasta Megálo Pápingo; ✆ 26530 25014; f adrianopizzapapigo; ⏲ 18.00–23.00 Wed–Sun. A surprise in the Zagorochória: one of the best Italian restaurants in Greece, with a chic dining room & delicious, authentic Italian *antipasti*, seafood, stews & desserts. €€

Pantheon Megálo Pápingo; ✆ 26530 42239; ⏲ winter noon–22.00 daily. At the hotel of the same name, with big views & generous portions of mouthwatering oregano pork, lamb chops, trout & moussaka. €€

Stérna Megálo Pápingo; ✆ 26530 25090; w sternashop.gr; ⏲ 08.30–21.00 daily. Handcrafted gifts, & café serving tasty homemade cakes & spoon sweets, as well as craft beers & homemade *tsípouro*.

Central Zagorochória

Kanela & Garyfallo Vítsa; ✆ 26530 71671; w kanela-garyfallo.gr; ⏲ hours & days may vary, call or check Google. A restaurant totally dedicated to mushrooms, in a stone building once used as a film set, with stunning views. €€

Sta Riza Vítsa; ✆ 26530 71550; f Στα ριζά/ sta riza; ⏲ 13.00–21.00 Fri–Tue. Great views from this modern stone-built restaurant, & big portions of succulent meats, mushroom & chicken pie, & good vegan choices, too. €€

Lithos Dílofo; ✆ 26530 22600; m 69442 34072; w lithos-dilofo.gr; ⏲ Nov–Jul noon–22.00 Thu–Mon, Aug–Oct noon–22.00 usually daily. Energetic Tákis runs this little restaurant using local ingredients & 'grandma's recipes', with great salads, homemade bread & spoon sweets. €

Oi Pites tis Fróssos Monodendri; ✆ 26530 71320; ⏲ 13.00–21.30 daily. Rustic savory pies, a specialty of Epirus, are the star – handmade, flaky & delicious. The *alevrópita* (flour pie) is a specialty, & there is also plenty of other hearty homestyle fare. €

Eastern Zagorochória

La Punti Vovoúsa; ✆ 26560 44905; ⏲ 09.00–23.00 daily. Next to the river & bridge, simple but filling food, & lots of potatoes. €

SPORTS AND ACTIVITIES

If you're striking out on your own, pick up the indispensable *Anavasi Pindus-Zagori 1:50,000 Topo/Hiking* map. Central Zagóri paths are marked with a 'Z', while those in the east and Métsovo are marked with a 'P'. The most beautiful is the Ioánnina to Kónitsa O3 trail (a branch of the E6) passing through the Víkos Gorge and seven of the Zagorochória. Or you can run: in late July the **Zagóri Mountain Run** (w zagorirace.gr) features three races – a hardcore 44km marathon plus ultra-race across Týmphi, a 21km half-marathon and a 10km entry race.

Alpine Zone ✆ 26510 23222; m 69746 59999; w alpinezone.gr. Day-long treks down the Víkos Gorge, into the Pindus National Park & to the Drakolímni; rafting on the Voïdomátis.

Fly & Fun m 69374 71156; w paragliding.gr. Tandem paragliding trips over the region.

Papigo Rafting Megálo Pápingo; m 69324 16011; w papigoadrenaline.com. White-water rafting, canyoning, & trekking to the Drakolímni.

Robinson Expeditions m 69443 13485; w robinson-trip.com. Based in Kípi, English-speaking Konstantinos Vasilíou & his team offer walking, mountain biking & river trekking/canyoning tours, as well as rock climbing.

Trekking Hellas Káto Voïdomátis (on the Ioánnina–Kónitsa road); m 69447 50009; w trekking.gr. Day hikes through the most spectacular part of the gorge; they also offer 3hr rafting trips down the Voïdomátis, & longer excursions in the Zagorochória.

White Pegasus Megálo Pápingo; m 69770 11275; w whitepegasus.simplybook.it. Horseriding for all ages & abilities.

WESTERN ZAGORÓCHIA

The road to the two Pápingos passes through lovely **Arísti** (Αρίστη), with its upmarket resorts, then descends to the Voïdomátis River, here serene and bubbling in a wide bed festooned with plane trees. The 16th-century **Moní Spiliótissa**, perched on the rock face, is beautiful, as are the views from its bell tower; don't miss the elaborate iconostasis inside.

The road then corkscrews up in 15 switchback turns, but the reward is two of the Zagorí's prettiest villages, starting with **Megálo Pápingo** (Μεγάλο Πάπιγκο), where the perfectly set stone paving begins. Visitors are invited to leave their cars here (you can drive, but reconnoitre first). Compact, neat and homogenous, Megálo Pápingo is so like a stage set you almost expect Dorothy and the Scarecrow to appear around a corner. Wide Astráka (2,436m), Týmphi's most imposing peak, aptly nicknamed 'the Tower', looms above, impossible to escape, softening only at sunset when it takes on a rosy glow. Some 2km closer to the Tower, **Mikró Pápingo** (Μικρό Πάπιγκο; no cars) is a village from another time. Between the two Pápingos, and handy to both, are the **Kolybýthres**, or Rogovo Ovires – swimming holes, where a picturesque stream has been dammed up. Paddling here amid the fractured flagstone is one of life's great experiences.

Trails leave from Mikró Pápingo to the Zagóri's famed beauty spots: the Víkos Gorge (page 278); and the **Drakolímni**, 11 small lakes formed by glaciers 10,000 years ago on Týmphi's slopes, starting at 1,500m. The largest and most spectacular, 2,050m up on **Gamíla**, takes about 5½ hours there and back. The 'dragons' in the name are rare newts, *Triturus alpestris*, which inhabit the lakes. The landscapes are truly extraordinary: if you want to linger, book a bunk at the **Astráka-Týmphi Alpine Refuge** (1,950m; m 69732 23100; w astrakarefuge.com; ⊕ May–Oct; €), which has a kitchen and restaurant.

CENTRAL ZAGOROCHÓRIA If you make the turn up into the mountains in the south via **Aspráŋgeli** (Ασπράγγελοι), one of the first things you'll see is the **Monument to the Women of the Zagorochória**, honouring the role they played in the resistance in World War II, building bridges and hauling ammunition and supplies to the fighters. Aspráŋgeli itself was burned to the ground in reprisal; today it's the administrative centre for the Zagorochória.

Next up is **Vítsa** (Βίτσα), with its pretty stone-roofed churches, and **Monodéndri** (Μονοδένδρι), the classic entrance into the Víkos Gorge with a fine collection of mansions, and an attractive shady *plateía* by the imposing 19th-century church of Ag Athanásios. In the late 18th century, orphaned brothers Mánthos and Geórgios Rizários left the village for Moscow to work in their uncle's trading company and made their fortune. They were big supporters of the Greek War of Independence and later spent their money supporting orphans and founding schools, including one in Monodéndri, giving many full scholarships; today the village still has the Zagorochória's boarding school. Their name lives on in the **Rizarios Handicrafts Centre** (part of a free school where local girls learn traditional crafts) with a shop, and the **Exhibition Centre** (\ 26530 71573; w rizarios.eu; ⊕ 09.00–16.00 daily; €3), featuring black-and-white photos.

Signs point the way to the gorge and the **Moní Ag Paraskeví**, built right at the edge of the precipice in 1412 by a wealthy couple who wanted to thank the saint for curing their daughter's eyesight but at the same time wanted to shelter the monks from invaders. The donors are depicted among the frescoes inside if you can drag yourself away from the vertiginous views. The monks' loo took advantage of the sheer drop to the bottom; just taking one of its round seats would have been an act of faith. A scary path leads to the Megáli Spiliá, a cave used as a hideout in tough times.

An 8km road ascends from Monodéndri through fantastical heaps of flysch, the naturally fissured flagstone that made the architecture of the Zagorochória possible, and on to the **Oxía** (Οξυά) **Viewpoint** with a heart-stopping view of the Víkos Gorge. Its great depth is emphasised by the closeness of the canyon walls. Víkos means 'echo'; you can easily test it out.

A trek in the Víkos Gorge Over eons and eons, the Voïdomátis ('Bulls-eye') River ground its way through Týmphi's limestone tablelands to produce the Víkos Gorge, a narrow, 12km-long phenomenon of nature with sheer walls towering 900m in places, and only 1,100m between its rims, which according to the Guinness Book of Records makes it the deepest in the world. It begins in earnest just north of **Kípi** (Κήποι) and ends near the village of **Víkos** (Βίκος).

June, September and October are the best months for a walk; summers can be hot. In winter and spring the Voïdomátis runs full in the gorge and walking can be dangerous. The most popular trek is from Monodéndri to either Víkos or the Pápingos: it takes 7 hours, and you will need a big water bottle, snacks, proper walking boots and walking sticks. The 45-minute walk down the stepped *kalderími* is enough to discourage duffers. The tricky bit is getting back to where you started – which is where an organised trek might come in useful. Ask at your hotel or book with a taxi.

The path along the river follows part of the marvellous O3 trail which begins in Ioánnina and ends on Mount Grámmos. After 4½–5 hours, the steep walls recede, the **Voïdomátis springs** come into view and an ascent can be made either to the village of Víkos (30mins) or to the Pápingos (1½hrs). Happily, Heraclitus was not thinking of mule paths when he said 'the path up and down is one and the same'; going up is actually a lot easier on the legs. The trail from Monodéndri south to Vítsa also goes to the bottom of the gorge, but is shorter (2hrs or so).

Of similar duration but less strenuous is the route from Monodéndri to Kípi, by way of the pretty Mísiou and Kókkoros bridges, before reaching the track to Vítsa up the 17th-century **Vítsa Stairs**.

A circle around Mount Týmphi This is an excellent day trip by car, taking in the other highlights of the Central Zagorochória, but could easily stretch to two or three days or more. Be sure to fill up before setting off. Many of the villages were destroyed by the Germans or during the Civil War and only have a handful of inhabitants who returned and rebuilt.

Start in **Dílofo** (Δίλοφο), with its impressive mansions built over two hills and a minuscule *kafeneíon* in the main square. The road descends to the **Kókkoros bridge**; to the right is charming, low-lying **Kípi** and its remarkable triple-span **Bridge of Plakída** (1814) humping over the river like a giant green caterpillar. Kípi's **Folklore Museum of Agápios Tólis** (✆ 26530 71826; m 69448 15482; ⊕ 10.00–16.00 Wed–Sun; free) has more than 40,000 items collected by Tólis throughout his life. The footpath linking Kípi to Tsepélovo (see opposite) is one of the most beautiful.

Backtrack to the bridge crossroads for **Koukoúli** (Κουκούλι) with its handsome church and the **Kóstas Lazarídis Natural History Museum** (✆ 26530 71775; ⊕ 09.00–noon Wed–Sun; free), founded by the botanically minded schoolteacher, who collected the 2,500 species of dried local plants from the Zagóri. Many are unique to the area and have been used for centuries by local healers, the Vikoiatroí; some of their cures go back to the writings of Hippocrates.

The next village is lofty **Kapesóvo** (Καπέσοβο), with the turn-off left for a thrilling detour up to the highest of the Zagorochória, **Vradéto** (Βραδέτο; 1,340m). The extraordinary and oft-photographed **Skála Vradéto**, coiling tightly down into the Mégas Lákos Gorge (a branch of the Víkos Gorge), was, until 1973, the sole access to the village, by way of Kapesóvo. An easy 2.2km (30mins) path at the end of a dirt

KÓNITSA AND AROUND

road in Vradéto leads up to the truly breathtaking **Belói Viewpoint** over the Víkos Gorge. In late spring, the area is a riot of butterflies and wildflowers – some 350 different plant species have been recorded just here.

Tsepélovo (Τσεπέλοβο), on the far east end of the Víkos Gorge, is a metropolis by Zagóri standards, with 200 people, a post office, a lovely main *plateía* and houses with doors and windows in bright greens, reds and blues. South, the lovely stone-roofed **Rongovoú Monastery** (1050) has good frescoes but is always locked.

Skamnéli (Σκαμνέλλι) is next, sitting pretty on an open hillside with vistas to the south, as well as to Týmphi's peaks (for a closer look, try the trail from here to Kónitsa). Some 13km after Skamnéli, there's the chance for a detour to tiny **Láista** (Λάιστα) by way of the **Gyftókambo** ('Gypsies' meadow'). A good number of nomadic Greek Sarakatsáni shepherds gather for an annual fair in the first week of August; amid the towering pines their traditional huts, set up as a permanent exhibition, resemble organic yurts.

Back on the main road, head north to **Iliochóri** (Ηλιοχώρι; 'sun village'), immersed in trees, with an easy 30-minute trail down to the gorgeous triple **Bálta di Stríga** (Μπάλτα Ντι Στρίγκα) waterfalls – the highest is 25m – with their crystalline pools, perfect for a dip. The next village, **Vrysochóri** (Βρυσοχώρι), which claims the ancestors of film-maker John Cassavetes (like many Epirótes, they moved to Thessaly – Cassavetes' father was born in Lárissa), also has a lot of water, and its own private gorge. The road winds down to the Aoös River and up again for **Paliosélli** (Παλαιοσέλλι), the base for making the 5½-hour hike up to the region's 'other' (but equally spectacular) newt-dwelling lake, the **Smólikas Drakólimni** on the slopes of **Smólikas** (2,637m), the second-highest mountain in Greece. After Paliosélli comes **Eleúthero** (Ελεύθερο); along the road the peaks of Týmphi are lined up, an amazingly long and jagged panorama; and beyond lies Kónitsa.

EASTERN ZAGOROCHÓRIA To continue east for the **Vália Cálda**, see page 255; from the south the gateway is **Vovoúsa** (Βοβούσα), with its **Pindus National Park Information Centre** (✆ 26560 22843; w pindosnationalpark.gr, ⊕ ring in advance). It's a pleasant mountain village, probably named after the sound of the Aoös rushing through its centre. The Germans destroyed it in 1943, but fortunately left its stone **bridge** of 1748.

KÓNITSA AND AROUND

It's not one of the Zagorochória, but Kónitsa (Κόνιτσα) can be a useful gateway into the area. The name in Slavic means 'horse bazaar' and it still has plenty grazing on its doorstep in the huge flat and green valley created by the confluence of the Aoös and Voïdomátis rivers, where trout fishing is popular. The emerald Aoös River gorge may not be as spectacular as the Víkos, but it's lush, beautiful and less visited.

GETTING THERE AND AWAY Three to five buses (✆ 26550 22214) go from Ioánnina on weekdays (fewer at weekends). The station is on the north edge of town.

WHERE TO STAY

Bourazani [map, page 273] (20 rooms) 14km west of Kónitsa, on the road to Moní Molyvdosképastou; ✆ 26550 61283; w mpourazani.eu. Woodsy family-run hotel/restaurant (€€) near the Aoös in a game park, where the deer & wild boar star on the menu. There's a pool, & a chance to take nature tours around the park. B/fast inc. €€

Gefyri (11 rooms) On the river by the old bridge; ℡ 26550 23780; w gefyri.gr. Attractive, warm & welcoming hotel, with contemporary rooms featuring extra-long Coco-Mat beds. It has a charming pool if you don't want to swim in the Aoös, & an excellent cocktail lounge & Thymeli Bistrot (€€). €€

Konitsa Mountain Hotel [map, page 273] (23 rooms) On the Distrátou road; ℡ 26550 29390; w konitsahotel.gr. Colourful hotel at the top of the town with mountain views & cosy rooms with wooden floors; also sauna & fitness centre. Good source of local info. B/fast inc. €€

WHAT TO SEE AND DO Kónitsa spills down the side of Mount Trapezítsa (2,024m) as far as the majestic Aoös as it weaves its way through the verdant gorge and under a delicate single-spanned **bridge**, the longest in the Zagóri at 40m, built in 1870 by master stonemason Kóstas Frontzos. Many walks begin here, although perhaps the most beautiful is one of the easiest: the riverside 1½-hour walk to **Moní Panagía Stomíou** (w monastiriakonitsis.wordpress.com), set on a small plateau of the Týmphi over the narrowest part of the Aoös Gorge. Burned down by the Nazis for its resistance during the war, the monastery has since been rebuilt with a bright red roof. Another beautiful monastery on the Aoös is 19km west, on the Albanian border: the striking **Moní Molyvdosképastou**, with a 15m narrow dome, founded in AD670 by Byzantine Emperor Konstantínos IV Pogonato, who left behind a miraculous icon of the Virgin, famous for granting fertility – which may be why it's a popular wedding venue. The curious name means 'of the lead roof', although the lead was melted down and turned into bullets by the Ottomans long ago.

At **Klidoniá** (Κλειδωνιά), 12km south of Kónitsa on the Ioánnina road, the Voïdomátis leaves the gorge to flow northward to join the Aoös, in an idyllic setting with another handsome 19th-century stone **bridge** as a landmark. Paths follow the river to a delightful picnic area under the plane trees.

North of Kónitsa lie the **Mastorochória** ('Master-builder villages'; page 253). The 'capital' in Epirus is **Pyrsógianni** (Πυρσόγιαννη; population 119); **Ganadió** (Γαναδιό) has a traditional *kafeníon*.

MÉTSOVO

Location, location, location. At the crossroads of Thessaly, Macedonia and Epirus between Mavrovoúni (2,160m) to the north and Lákmos, or Peristéri (2,202m), to the south, Métsovo (Μέτσοβο; population 3,000) is one of the most famous mountain resorts in Greece. Once an important stop on the Roman Via Egnatía (the name derives from the Latin *mansio*, or 'mansion'), it's still an important tour bus stop.

The largest Vlach town in Greece, Métsovo astutely managed to become the centre of a small independent state in Ottoman times, one that made its living from livestock, wool, hides and dairy products. Ali Pasha added it to his bailiwick in 1795; in 1854 it was nearly totally destroyed by Turkish troops. But Métsovo was not only rebuilt; it thrived (see opposite).

GETTING THERE AND AWAY The KTEL **bus station** is at the junction of the E90, a 5-minute taxi ride from town. Buses connecting Ioánnina with Thessaloníki pick up passengers there (consult KTEL Ioánnina; ℡ 26510 83071).

As in ancient times, Métsovo is a major stop on the Egnatía, although now, instead of making the vertiginous crossing over the pass, you have to watch while **driving** for the exit between the tunnels.

For **taxis**, call m 69476 94717 or m 69455 86256.

THE MIRACLE OF MÉTSOVO

It's a story that involves wine and cheese, and two great nephews of 'National Benefactors of Greece' who had made their fortunes in Alexandria. Michaíl Tosítsas (1787–1856), a good friend of Muhammad Ali (page 182), was the Greek consul to Alexandria and in charge of the remarkable building works undertaken by Ali, while becoming extremely wealthy in banking and commerce with connections as far as Livorno, in Tuscany, where he and his descendants were made Barons. His great nephew, and last surviving descendant, Baron Michaíl Tosítsas (or Tossizza; 1885–1950), was born in Livorno and would later run the family banking business in Switzerland and France, and by all accounts was a well-educated solitary eccentric.

The second great-uncle was George Avérof (1815–1899), who also moved to Alexandria, made a fortune in banking, property and shipping, then donated most of his wealth to good causes in Greece, including the restoration of the Marble Stadium in Athens for the first modern Olympics. His great-nephew Evángelos Avérof was an important political figure for 50 years in Greece, serving as Minister of Foreign Affairs and Defence.

In 1937, Avérof, who loved his native Métsovo but lacked the deep pockets of his great-uncle, began corresponding with Baron Michaíl, evoking the dire need in the land of his ancestors. By the time the two men finally met in Switzerland in 1947, Tosítsas (who never visited Greece) had decided to set up a foundation for the development of Métsovo, with Avérof in charge – on the condition that he added his name to his surname.

So Evángelos Avérof-Tosítsas went to work, and built a free hospital for the locals, the Folk Art Museum, the ski centre, a sawmill, and a model dairy, sending the offspring of local farmers to study cheese-making (especially provolone) in Italy, leading to the creation of the Tositsa Foundation's PDO *metsovone* smoked sheep's cheese. He also built 107 schools across Epirus and a residence in Athens where university students from Epirus could stay free of charge.

When he wasn't spending the baron's money on good causes, Evángelos Avérof-Tosítsas pursued his own projects. He planted the first Cabernet Sauvignon vines of Greece in Métsovo, and bottled the result at home in his *katógi* (basement). Since then, the winery has gone from strength to strength, also using native grapes Gudába, Vlachovóna and Piknoása at Yiniets ('vineyard' in Vlachiká). At 1,150m, Yiniets has the highest vines in Greece, where the grapes mature slowly and are harvested only in October, resulting in a distinctive wine; while his excellent collection of modern Greek art is a rarity in a small mountain village.

TOURIST INFORMATION The tourist information office is in the town hall (cnr N Cháli & Avérof; 24560 41207; w metsovotour.epcon.gr; ⊕ 07.30–14.00 Mon–Fri). The **Pindus National Park Information Centre** (26560 42720; w pindosnationalpark.gr; ⊕ 08.30–15.30 Thu–Sat) is at the village entrance.

WHERE TO STAY
Grand Forest Métsovo [map, page 258] (62 rooms) Anílio, exit 7a off the Egnatía; 26560 29001; w grand-forest.gr. Surrounded by black pine forests, this resort was declared Europe's Leading Landmark Hotel in 2019. Many of the beautiful suites have fireplaces, along with indoor & outdoor

pools, riding stable, spa, gourmet restaurant (Metsovo 1350m; €€€€) & a stunning glassed bar with a wooden cathedral ceiling. B/fast inc. €€€

Aroma Dryos Eco & Design Hotel (16 rooms) Avérof 1; 26560 29008; w aromadryos.gr. On a hillside, with enormous mountain views, welcoming family-run, ecologically sustained hotel with handsome rooms named after trees. Lots of lovely details; b/fast inc. €€

Kassaros (26 rooms) Tzoumáka 3; 26560 41800; w hotelkassaros.gr. Very stylish 2-star hotel, with flowery balconies & cosy, elegant rooms (many with spectacular views), Coco-Mat beds with carved wooden bedsteads, sauna & hydromassage. Inviting lobby with a bar & a fireplace. Free parking; b/fast inc. €€

Katogi Averoff Hotel & Winery (15 rooms) 5min walk from Métsovo's central square; 26560 42505; w katogiaveroffhotel.gr. Characterful rooms with wooden furniture, walk-in shower with Apivita toiletries & splendid views overlooking the vineyards & mountains. Wine bar; parking; Greek b/fast inc. €€

Victoria (27 rooms) 900m from the centre; 26560 41771; w victoriahotel.gr. Quiet & pretty, with a sauna & outdoor pool. The large reception-bar is in the Epiróte style, with a fireplace. €€–€

Adonis (15 rooms) Just off the central square; 26560 42300; w adonismetsovo.gr. There's a charming family atmosphere here & spacious rooms; most have a fireplace (some with hydromassage tubs), plus private underground parking & a cosy bar. €

Asteri (43 rooms) Th Tossítsa 58; 26560 42222; w asterimetsovo.com. Traditional-style hotel built in 1995, some rooms with mountain view, fireplace or spa bath. Weaving & cookery classes available; free parking. €

Galaxias (10 rooms) Central square; 26560 41202; w hotel-galaxias-metsovo.gr. Family run, & one of the older hotels, with colourful weavings in the cosy old-fashioned rooms. Next to a popular garden restaurant with the same name (see below). B/fast €8. €

✖ WHERE TO EAT AND DRINK Look for *kontosoúvli*, large chunks of marinated pork, lamb or chicken slow-roasted on a rotisserie, meatballs with leeks, all kinds of pies, *metsovone* PDO smoked cheese, and red Katógi wine.

Aspasia [map, page 258] Votonósi, 10km west of Métsovo; 26560 22882; ⊕ noon–20.00 daily. Going strong since 1955, this taverna may not look like much but serves superb succulent grilled lamb chops by the kilo, golden fried feta with honey & carrot sweets; good red wines, too. €€

Apókentro Tzoumaka 1; 26560 41801; ⊕ noon–midnight daily. Hearty homestyle fare in a cosy cabin with views. Good house wine. €

Galaxias Central square; 26560 41202; ⊕ 08.00–midnight daily. Next to the hotel of the same name (see above), this garden restaurant serves excellent traditional specialities – try the lamb in white sauce with roast potatoes – & wines of Métsovo. €

Tría Platánia Anílio; 26560 42333; ⊕ 11.00–20.00 Thu–Fri & Sun, 11.00–21.30 Sat. Excellent little family-run grillhouse with tasty lamb & friendly service. €

SPORTS AND ACTIVITIES Run by Olympian cross-country skiers Leftéris and Viola (who won a gold medal in Salt Lake City in 2002), **Go Active Métsovo** (m 69425 69618; w goactive-metsovo.gr) offers hiking, mountain biking, SUP and canoeing on Aoös Lake, canyoning and rafting.

Two **ski centres** are in easy striking distance: Profítis Ilías, with three lifts, and the newer Anílio Ski Centre (26512 00520; w aniliopark.gr) with five lifts and a snowboarding slope. One of Greece's **top cross-country ski routes** is the 30km Métsovo-to-Miliá trail.

WHAT TO SEE AND DO
Kentrikí Plateía Métsovo's cobblestoned main square is lined with bars, tavernas and shops filled with the most awful tat this side of Athens. In the middle of the square stands a bronze statue of a mother and baby bear, marking the beginning of

the beautiful 40km Ursa Trail. The church of **Ag Paraskeví** houses relics of the saint, a beautiful iconostasis, copies of the 5th-century mosaics from the tomb of Galla Placidia in Ravenna and ten Russian icons donated by wealthy locals; unusually it has a double pulpit.

Métsovo Folk Art Museum – Tossízza Mansion (26560 41084; w metsovomuseum.gr; guided tours every 30mins 10.00–16.00 Fri–Wed; €5, concessions €2/€3) Founded by Evángelos Avérof-Tosítsas in 1955, in the restored Tosítsa (Tossízza) mansion (1661), its collections are displayed as if the house were still lived in; there's a beautiful collection of icons, Byzantine coins, and prints. The third floor is dedicated to the founder.

Avéroff Museum (26560 41210; w averoffmuseum.gr; 10.00–16.00 Wed–Mon; €5, students €2.50) Opened in 1988, the Avérof-Tosítsas collection is dedicated to 19th- and 20th-century Greek art, representing everything from genre painting and portraiture through to the works of the Generation of the 30s and later 20th-century modernism (page 25). Also here are Cóstas Baláfas' compelling photos of Métsovo in the 1960s and 1970s.

Averófeios Garden (Up G Avérof St) The story goes that George Avérof prayed to St George in the chapel here, asking for success when he went to Alexandria. To thank the saint, he sent back a gardener to plant this large park around the chapel with a sample of every tree in the Pindus. There are gorgeous views over the Metsovítikos valley.

Moní Ag Nikoláou (On the road to Anílio; 26560 41390; 08.00–14.00 & 16.00–19.00 daily; free) This venerable monastery immersed in vineyards was renovated c1700, with icons and murals from the 17th and early 18th centuries, some by Epiróte painter Ephstáthios. On the outside, left of the door, is an unusual depiction of the Virgin breast-feeding the infant Jesus. The monks here, together with those of the Votsás monastery, tend some of Greece's highest-altitude vineyards and make delicious, award-winning wines under the label Imperator. You can sample them in an exceptionally lovely tasting room (m 69476 64890; w im-votsas.gr) with mountain views, directly beside the monastery.

Museum of Hydrokinesis (Southwest in Anthochóri) An open-air museum dedicated to water power, with its three restored mechanisms. Beside the river is also a unique restaurant and coffee shop in a lovely setting, To Mantáni (m 69486 70997; tomantani; €€–€).

Lake of the Aoös Springs (15km north of Métsovo) In 1987, the source of the Aoös was dammed to form Greece's highest (1,350m) and arguably most beautiful mountain lake, covering 11.5km^2 and sprinkled with romantic pine-clad islets, while cattle and horses graze on the banks.

DODONA

> Ancient Greece is defined as the land around Dodoni and the river Acheloos. It is inhabited by two tribes, the tribe of Selloi (Σελλοί) and the tribe with the ancient name Graekoi (Γραικοί), now called Hellenes (Έλληνες)…
>
> Aristotle, *Meteorologica*, chapter 14

According to Herodotus, Dodona's oracle was founded in 1900BC by a clan of prophets, the Selloi or Helloi, who never washed their feet and slept on the bare ground to stay in close contact with a sacred oak whose roots harboured the god, and whose leaves whispered prophecies, intelligible to their ears alone. Greece's second most important oracle after Delphi was not for the faint-hearted: Epiróte winters are bone-chillingly cold. Archaeological finds here go back to Mycenaean times, back when the oracle was dedicated to the Mother goddess Dione. Eventually she was joined by Zeus Naios 'of the spring' (dedications found on the site were addressed to both). Achilles himself invoked 'Zeus of wintry Dodona' in the *Iliad*; Odysseus visited the oracle, to ask whether he should return to Ithaca openly or disguised.

By historical times a steady stream of ordinary people came, seeking solutions to everyday problems. Questions, scratched on lead tablets, remained much the same: 'Am I her children's father?', 'Should I sail to Syracuse at a later date?' and 'To which god should sacrifice be offered as to govern the land the best way and have an abundance of good things?' The response to the last one would be worth having, but answers were not recorded.

In the Archaic period, the tree was surrounded by a ring of bronze cauldrons, the offerings of wealthy petitioners. By the 5th century BC, it 'got civilised' when a small temple was built beside it, followed by a circuit wall and a small city. By Plato's day, barefoot prophets were out; frenzied priestesses received the oak's message. By Hellenistic times, the tree was a wind chime, its message amplified by cauldrons suspended in its branches. During the reign of Pyrrhus (297–272BC), a gigantic 17,000-seat theatre was built, along with a stadium to accommodate the Naia, a festival featuring horse races, drama and athletic contests, all to enhance the king's prestige as well as to compliment Zeus.

Even later, a bronze statue of a boy held a baton; when the wind moved it, it struck a row of contiguous copper pots and that sound was interpreted. Or perhaps it was just a case of 'different strokes for different folks'. Cult practices may have been written in stone, but they altered over time to meet the needs of new generations. Pilgrims continued to come for a century – Julian the Apostate stopped by in AD362, before his Persian campaign, 30 years before his successor, Theodosius, had the sacred oak chopped down and banned pagan practices for good.

GETTING THERE AND AWAY Dodona is 21km southwest of Ioánnina; drive or take a taxi.

DODONA ARCHAEOLOGICAL SITE (26510 82287; ⊕ summer 08.00–20.00 daily, gradually earlier closings through Sep–Oct, winter 08.00–15.00 daily; €15, concessions €8) Visitors enter through the remnants of a **stadium**. Some of its seating remains up against the retaining wall of the enormous **theatre**, built into the acropolis hill. Destroyed by Aitolíans in 219BC, it was rebuilt by Philip V of Macedon soon after. The Romans damaged it, then patched it up as an arena during Augustus' reign, replacing the front rows with a protective wall to shield audiences from wild beasts. Note the rusticated isodomic ashlar masonry of the cavea's retaining walls, once buttressed by towers – an unusual touch for a Greek theatre. Double gateways with Ionic half columns lead to the *parados* and orchestra where the horseshoe drainage channel is still in good shape. A ceremonial entrance led to the topmost gallery from the once-grand acropolis: this is roughly quadrilateral with thick walls and towers and not much else.

Beside the theatre, the large 3rd-century BC **bouleuterion** or council house had a porch with Doric columns and an inner roof supported by Ionic columns. Like many buildings in this era, only its base was of stone, the upper walls being mud brick; wooden bleachers provided seating. The complicated ruins of the **prytaneion** to the south show that a hospitality suite was required as early as the 4th century BC.

Further east are a cluster of **small temples to Aphrodite, Themis, Dione and Heracles**, built from the mid 4th century on, and amid them a **Temple of Zeus**. Only the unusual relationship of its temple wall to later colonnades indicates that the oak must have been on the east side of the court. The archaeologists have planted a new one, so you can pose questions of your own.

THE TZOUMÉRKA

Southeast of Ioánnina towards Árta, the Tzoumérka (Ancient Athamania) is one of Epirus's lesser-known gems – a landscape of pristine, often breathtaking, nature, shepherds, gorges, waterfalls and 47 tiny villages. Since 2009, much of it belongs to the National Park of Tzoumérka, Peristéri and the Árachthos Gorge, bordered by the Árachthos River to the west and to the east by the Acheloós. Two ranges of the Southern Pindus, Lákmos (or Peristéri; 2,295m) and the Athamaniká Mountains, topping out at Kakardítsa (2,429m), form a mighty wall between the two rivers, sprinkled with rare forests of foetid juniper (*Juniperus foetidissima*) at 1,000–1,500m and black pine along with fir and more typical species. Although little known outside of Greece, the Tzoumérka has become something of a best-kept

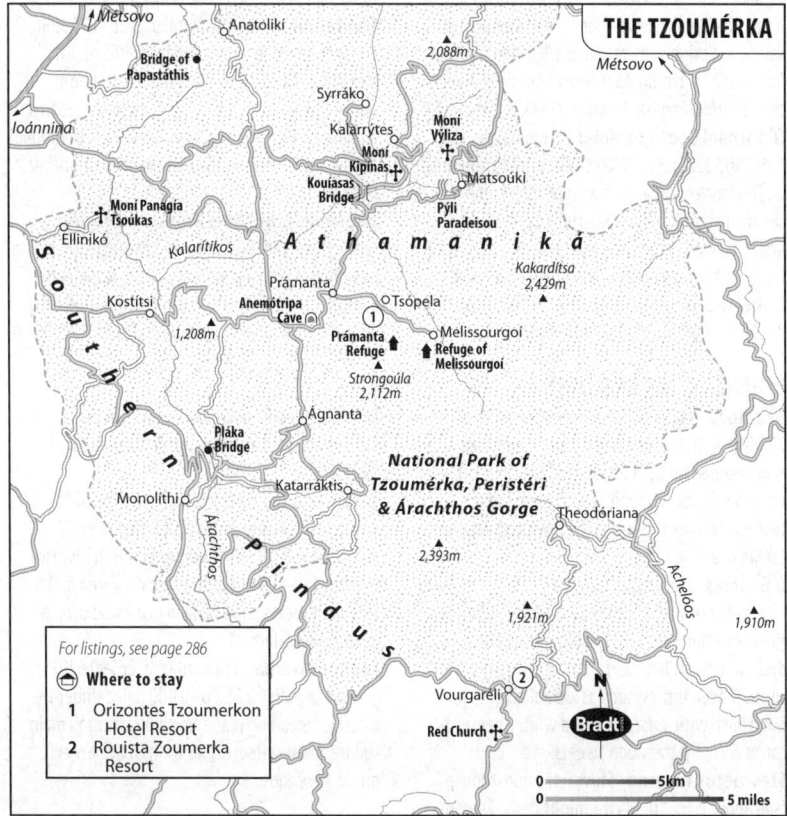

secret among the Greeks themselves, and some lovely mountain hotels have opened up, perfect for lingering in unspoiled nature.

GETTING THERE AND AROUND Bus 15 from Ioánnina goes to Ellinikó but you'll really need a car here. It's 62km from Ioánnina to Prámanta.

TOURIST INFORMATION For information on the National Park of Tzoumérka, Peristéri and the Árachthos Gorge, see w tzoumerka-park.gr. Try also w discovertzoumerka.com.

WHERE TO STAY

Orizontes Tzoumerkon Hotel Resort [map, page 285] (12 rooms) Pramánta; 26590 61002; w orizontestzoumerkon.gr. In a gorgeous mountain setting, this stylish wood-&-stone hotel has marble baths & cast-iron wood-burning stoves in each room to keep them snug in winter. The beautiful glassed-in restaurant overlooks pines & mountains. €€€–€€

Anavasi Mountain Resort (13 rooms) Tsópela, 1.5km from Pramánta; 26590 61141; w anavasihotel.gr. Comfy rooms with Coco-Mat beds & mountain views. There's an indoor pool & sauna, & a bright, airy restaurant/bar that serves teas made from mountain herbs. The lovely owners speak perfect English. Excellent Greek b/fast inc. €€

Old School Boutique Hotel (9 rooms) Syrráko; 26510 53286; m 69782 00002; w oldschoolhotel.gr. The former primary school now offers rooms sleeping up to 4, plus a colourful, cosy café bar. Cars aren't allowed in the village but they have a special buggy to transport your luggage. B/fast inc. €€

Princess Lanassa (16 rooms) Kostítsi; 26590 22600; w hotellanassa.gr. 10mins from the Árachthos rafting centre, a modern stone-built hotel with stupendous mountain views & 5 chalets; it has a restaurant, tennis, pool & a small spa. B/fast inc. €€

Rouista Zoumérka Resort [map, page 285] (19 rooms) Vourgaréli; 26850 22200; w rouista.com. Beautiful minimalist stone-&-wood inn, with comfy beds in handsome rooms, many with beamed ceiling. The lounge-café has a stunning central fireplace, & there's a terrace with superb mountain views. Excellent b/fast inc. €€

Stavraetos (8 rooms) Syrráko; 26510 53296; m 69464 24324; w syrrakostavraetos.gr. The Vaítsis family has converted the family home above the main square into a guesthouse: rooms all have beamed ceiling, wooden floor & traditional furnishings. Excellent taverna (see below); b/fast inc. €€

Napoléon Záglis Guesthouse (10 rooms) Kalarrýtes; 26590 61518. In the centre, charming guesthouse with a panoramic patio. Napoléon & Lampríni are kind hosts, & run taverna-cum-shop Ákathnos (see below) 20m away. B/fast inc. €€–€

WHERE TO EAT AND DRINK

Ákathnos Napoléon Záglis (see above); ⊕ 08.00–22.00 daily. In the same family for 5 generations & unchanged for decades, serving delicious kid casserole & jugged rabbit. If you've run out of toothpaste, note this is also the town's *pantopoleio* ('seller of all'). €€

O Boútzas Prámanta; 26590 61235; w mpoutzas.gr; ⊕ 13.00–22.00 daily. A family-run institution since 1937, a big restaurant, dedicated to grilled meats, but also very good for soups & oven dishes, such as kid baked in a clay pot. Finish with *galótyri* (a mild white cheese) & carrot & courgette spoon sweets. €€

Stavraetos Taverna Stavraetos guesthouse (see above); ⊕ 10.30–midnight daily. Famous for its handcrafted *tsípouro*, delicious pies, kid slow cooked in a clay pot & homemade sweets. €€

Taverna Ta Tzoumérka Ktistádes (outside Ágnanta); 26850 31163; Ταβέρνα Τα Τζουμέρκα; ⊕ 11.00–midnight daily. It's worth making a special trip to this rustic taverna for its succulent meats, bread baked in a wood oven & exceptional salads. €

Xagiáti Taverna Prámanta; 26590 62075; caféXagiati; ⊕ 08.00–01.00 daily. Under the massive spreading plane tree in Prámanta's main square, great coffee, drinks & often live Greek music at w/ends.

THE TZOUMÉRKA

SPORTS AND ACTIVITIES An enthusiastic young couple runs the **Tzoumerka Activities Centre** (Ágnanta; m 69452 47715, 69476 34197; w tac.com.gr), which offers a climbing wall, gymnastics, biking, rope games, punching bags, traditional dancing and archery. They are a great source of information on local trekking, climbing, mountain biking, skiing and paragliding.

There are several mountain refuges with simple restaurants for **hikers** with sleeping bags (€13 pp per night), including the **Prámanta Refuge** (10 rooms; 26593 00645; w tzoumerkarefuge.com; €) and the **Refuge of Melissourgoí** (6km east of Pramánta; m 69743 74172; f Katafigiomelissourgwn; €), whose owners are expert mushroom hunters.

Two of Greece's top **rafting** rivers are here: the Árachthos and its tributary, the Kalarítikos. Good local guides include: **Alpine Zone** (26510 23222; w alpinezone.gr), who also offer canyoning excursions from May to November; and **Trekking Hellas** (Frásta, Agnáta; 26820 46535; w trekking.gr).

WHAT TO SEE AND DO Ellinikó (Ελληνικό), 19km from Ioánnina at the west end of the park, was the birthplace in 1942 of modern sculptor Theódoros Papagiánnis. In his retirement, he set up the **Museum of Contemporary Art Theódoros Papagiánnis** (26510 89220; w theodoros-papagiannis.gr; ⊕ 09.30–15.00 daily; free) in and around the former elementary school, with his own works on the human condition (including some made of ruins from the Athens Polytechnic uprising in 1974 that led to the overthrow of the junta) and those of other sculptors who are invited to Ellinikó in summer. Another 5km east, the venerable **Moní Panagía Tsoúkas** (26510 89223; ⊕ 09.00–18.00 daily) was founded in 1190 by Isaac II Angelos, with a venerated icon of the Panagía and truly spectacular views over the mountains and narrow Árachthos Gorge.

Two of Tzoumérka's prettiest villages are further east: **Syrráko** (Συρράκο) and **Kalarrýtes** (Καλαριτες), both with cobbled streets studded with old stone mansions, fountains and beautiful main squares and churches that tell of past wealth. Syrráko's **Kósta Krystálli Folk Art Museum**, once home of the poet, is full of objects donated by residents; the **Ermeineía Fotiádou Traditional House** evokes life from 150 years ago (⊕ both open by request). It's a 90-minute walk from here up to the chapel **Ag Apostóli** (1,520m) for views that stretch all the way to Ioánnina.

Contemplating Syrráko across the Chroúsia ravine, Kalarrýtes, 'the eagle's nest of Epirus', hangs 1,200m up the slopes of Mount Peristéri. It was renowned for its gold and silver work (which helped finance the village's impressive triple domed church of Ag Nikóláos); one local, Sotíris Voúlgaris, left the village for Italy in 1877 and founded the famous Roman jewellery firm BVLGARI.

Kalarrýtes and Syrráko are close if you're a crow, but 24km by twisting mountain roads – or a beautiful 90-minute hike along the trail up and down the gorge, past a famous stone stair, waterfalls and watermills. In summer, check if a minibus is running between the villages to take you back to where you started. Or, hike from Kallarytes to the historic **Kouíasas Bridge**, by the waterfalls of the same name, stopping at the idyllic Cafe Mylos Kouiasas – about a 2-hour round trip. For all hikes, a storm can have affected access, so ask locals before setting off.

From **Matsoúki** (Ματσούκι), 8km east of Kalarrýtes, it's 2km up the steep cobblestone road and path to the 14th-century **Moní Výliza** (Μονή Βύλιζας; 1,050m). The reward is 360° views; its name derives from the Latin *viglio*, or 'vigil'. Inside are 18th-century frescoes, while the adjacent church has a magnificent iconostasis. But 'easy access' are not words in the Greek monk vocabulary. The most astonishing monastery in Epirus, **Moní Kipínas** (Μονή Κηπίνας; south of Kalarrýtes; ⊕ often open by day, but you can also call keyholder Father Lambrós: 26590 61790) was built in 1212 in a sheer vertical rock face high over the Kalarítikos, a tributary of the Árachthos. Half hewn out of living rock, the narrow interior, manned by a single monk, is evocative with its smoke-darkened 17th-century murals; a secret door leads down to the massive cave where resistance fighters and the local population took refuge in times of danger.

The Kalarítikos winds around to join the pale green **Árachthos** (the ancient Inachos), Epirus's longest river, which drains much of the eastern Zagorochória through a narrow gorge, only visible through the spray of a raft. Seventy stone bridges span it, including the striking if ruined four-arched **Bridge of Papastáthis**, at the beginning of the gorge in **Anatolikí**, and the recently rebuilt **Pláka bridge**, further south, at 40m the longest single-span stone bridge in the Balkans. Two early versions, in 1860 and 1863, failed – the 1863 version dramatically collapsed on the day of its official inauguration. The last one, built by local master Kóstas Bekas of Prámanta in 1866, stood over 17m high and marked the border between Greece and the Ottoman Empire between 1880 and 1912. It survived German bombs in World War II – only to have its centre collapse in torrential rain and a flash flood in 2015. In summer 2018, €4.75 million was set aside for its repair, using as much of the original stone as possible, and the bridge reopened in 2020.

In the centre of the national park, **Prámanta** (Πράμαντα) is a modern metropolis by Tzoumérka standards, complete with a bank and ATM machine, under the rounded, strikingly isolated 2,112m peak of Mount Strongoúla. Just up the road, in the resort hamlet of **Tsopéla** (Τσόπελα), you can visit the **workshop of Giórgos Polyzos**, a jeweller whose hobby is recreating ancient Greek instruments – the lyre, the *kithara*, the *varvitos*, *phorminx*, *pandourida*, and more.

Some 5km south of Prámanta, the stalactite **Anemótripa Cave** (m 69492 31710; 10.00–16.00 daily; tours €3) translates, rather indelicately, as 'wind hole'. First explored in the 1960s, it has three levels; you can visit the first 250m of the middle cave, over a rushing underground river. Further south, lush **Ágnanta** (Άγναντα) is another important village, with its terraces cut into the emerald slopes and watermills. **Katarráktis** (Καταρράκτης) means 'waterfalls' and there are a majestic pair (signposted) outside the village, reached by an easy 4km path from the road, although by high summer they revert to a trickle.

Southeast, between the Goúra and White Goúra (two tributaries of the Acheloós), **Theodóriana** (Θεοδώριανα) is filled with springs and watermills; and beautiful **twin waterfalls** plunge 25m side by side in a forest, up the road from the main square. In **Vourgaréli** (Βουργαρέλι), one of the larger Tzoumérka villages in the south, water gushes from sculpted fountains and gurgles under the tiny stone Neraidogéfiro ('Fairy Bridge'). There are several historic churches here, including ruggedly handsome **Ag Geórgios** (1690), where the locals gathered to join the 1821 Greek revolution, and 3km south, the Byzantine **Red Church** (named for the colour of its bricks). It has the only surviving 13th-century murals in the Tzoumérka; the portraits of its founders, Theódoros Tzimeiskis and his wife, María, in the narthex are among the oldest-surviving portraits in Greece. It also has a rare surviving original wooden door.

THE AMBRACIAN GULF

The Ambracian Gulf, almost closed off by the Préveza Peninsula (where an underwater tunnel makes heading south much easier), harbours fish, sea horses and jellyfish, including one bruiser that looks like a giant fried egg. Octavian (later Augustus) chose the Gulf's sheltered waters to build his new city, Nikopolis, now an extensive ruin brooding just north of Préveza. Historic Árta, at the northeast end, is separated from open water by silt, marshes and lagoons, favoured by migrating birds. And a perfect bird's-eye view of the Gulf waits from the heights of Ancient Kassope. In the restaurants, look for the large prawns (*gámbari*), which are a speciality of the Gulf (in season late spring through autumn), grilled sardines and *koutsomoúra*, a kind of red mullet, as well as *tsípouro Zambela* – a prized spirit made from the Zambela grape – and fruity Graviera cheese.

ÁRTA (Άρτα) Set on a height in a loop of the Árachthos River, Árta was the capital of the long-gone Despotate of Epirus and displays glittering gems of Byzantine architecture in a very plain setting. Its large 13th-century castle built on classical blocks would be impressive if the main Ioánnina–Préveza road didn't occupy the same space. The city does have the only university department of Folk and Traditional Music, though.

Known as Amvrakia in the 9th century BC, when it was founded as a colony of Corinth, the 4th century BC found it semi-independent under Macedonian control. In 294BC it became the capital of Pyrrhus I. Pyrrhus' meteoric career (page 256) saw him lead Epiróte armies all over southern Italy, often defeating the mighty Romans. Nothing came of all his efforts. The Epiróte Kingdom was eventually swallowed up by Rome, and Amvrakia withered as the Romans transferred its population to their new city, Nikopolis.

The city reappears in the early Middle Ages, as Árta, a busy trading centre between Venice and the east. After the sack of Constantinople in 1204, it became the capital of the Despotate under Michael I Komnenos Doukas. The following decades were a golden age for Árta, although it eventually fell victim to the constant wars of the surviving Byzantine princelings. In 1313 the Despotate came under the rule of the Italian Orsini family, initiating a long period of chaos and warfare. Árta was snatched back by the reviving Byzantines (twice), taken by the Serbs and the Albanians, and then by Italian counts of Cephalonia. Finally, in 1449, it fell to the Ottoman Empire, remaining principally in Ottoman hands with brief interludes of rule by the Republic of Venice and by France, before becoming a part of Greece in 1881.

Getting there and around Árta's bus station (⚲ 28610 27348; w ktelartas.gr) is on the highway at Plateía Krystálli and has a regular service from Athens (4 a day), Ioánnina (4 a day during the week, 2 a day w/ends) and one or two a day to Lárissa/Vólos, Préveza, and Thessaloníki. Motorists planning only a short stay should park off the highway near the castle; the adventurous can follow signs to the '*kentro*' and Plateía Kilkís for the few parking places there.

Where to stay and eat

Cronos (55 rooms) Plateía Kilkís; ⚲ 26810 22211; w hotelcronos.gr. Centrally located, large modern rooms, most with balcony. Parking extra. €€

Marathia [map, page 289] (10 rooms) 8km north at Chanópoulo (Χανόπουλο); ⚲ 26820 85397; w hotelmarathia.gr. A pet-friendly (call first) contemporary country retreat in a pretty setting with natural thermal spring waters (massages also available), a garden & traditional restaurant (€). €€

En Arti 1887 Café Ioánnis Apokolípti 9; ⚲ 26810 75059; f enarti1887; ⏲ 08.00–02.00 daily. Upmarket & in a great outdoor setting in Plateía Skoufá, with coffees by day & cocktails by night. In season they put on a schedule of jazz & blues nights.

What to see and do Central Árta is compact; the walk down Pýrrou Street from the castle clock to Plateía Kilkís takes all of 20 minutes. En route you'll pass

Ag Vasílios, a small 13th-century church famous for its brick-and-tile decoration. Just past that to the right (near no. 27) look for **Ag Theodóra**, built in the same era by Theodóra, wife of the Despot, with elaborate brick-and-tile work in its narthex. Recessed in its own little square, it was once surrounded by a monastery. Inside, Theodóra's tomb has capitals snitched from Nikopolis.

Just before Pýrrou Street flows into small Plateía Kilkís, the plain Byzantine church of **Ag Constantínou and Eléni** is signposted on the left (beyond 'Pizza Venezi'). It shares a tiny square with a 4th–3rd-century BC **theatre**. Bits of Ancient Ambracia appear whenever holes are dug; just beyond the theatre, practically in the square on Pýrrou Street, are the ruins of a 6th-century BC **Temple of Apollo**.

An equestrian statue of Pyrrus stands near Plateía Skoufá. Just to the east, on its own marble-tiled square, is Árta's jewel, the fabulous 13th-century church of **Panagía Parigorítissa** (✆ 26810 28692; ⏰ 08.30–15.00 Tue–Sun) dedicated to 'the comforting mother'. This unusual square church with imposing brickwork is topped by five cupolas (*trouli*), the central one sitting on three tiers of ancient columns, each tier resting on the butt ends of two columns. The Refectory houses a small archaeological collection with finds from local cemeteries. The clay ex-votos are lovely, including a terrific little cockerel. One case has the moulds from which many were made – votives were quite an industry in Árta. Even then, funerals were big business.

Bridge of Árta A multi-arched bridge for packhorses built in 1602 is easily visible from the modern bridge at the west end of town, and famous for its legend and popular song:

> Forty-five master builders and sixty apprentices
> Were laying the foundations for a bridge over the river of Arta
> They would toil at it all day, and at night it would collapse again.
> The master builders lament and the apprentices weep:
> 'Alas for our exertions, woe to our labours,
> For us to toil all day while at night it collapses!'
>
> A bird appeared and sat on the opposite side of the river.
> It did not sing like a bird, nor like a swallow,
> But it sang and spoke in a human voice:
> 'Unless you sacrifice a human, the bridge will never stand.
> And don't you sacrifice an orphan, or a stranger, or a passer-by,
> But only the chief mason's beautiful wife,
> Who comes late in the afternoon and brings his supper.'

The heartbroken master mason tells the bird to tell his wife to come very late that day, hoping the others would have gone, but the bird tells her to come earlier, and the masons trick her into going into the foundations to look for the master's wedding ring, when she is buried. Folklore, maybe, but even now in many villages chickens are slaughtered and their blood drained into the foundations of new structures. Maybe it's a good thing Árta has only one stone bridge. In modern Greek, 'the bridge of Árta' means anything that takes forever, going around in endless, pointless circles.

Archaeology Museum (Cnr Aráchthou & Manoliássis, just south of the bridge; ✆ 26810 21191; w efaart.gr; ⏰ 09.00–16.00 Wed–Mon; €4, concessions €2) This well-designed museum opened in 2009, and gives a good picture of Ancient Amvrakia, with objects of everyday life, funeral steles and ancient clay ex-votos – making an interesting contrast to the Christian ones in Panagía Parigorítissa.

Around Árta Pretty **Lake Ziroú** (Λίμνη Ζηρού; 22 km north of Árta), surrounded by woods, is popular with locals for swimming and canoeing. In early August, it's the site of the **Zero Festival** (f), which combines lake fun by the day and Greek rock and other concerts by night.

At **Ag Geórgios** (Αγ Γεώργιος) just north of Ziroú, are the impressive ruins of the **Roman aqueduct** (31BC) that once transported the water to Nikopolis (page 292) through a tunnel dug by thousands of enslaved people, and over a magnificent stone arcade that passes above the Loúros River. Just south of the arcade, signposted on the main road, is the beginning of the tunnel. Clamber to the top of it for the spectacular view over the remnants of **Kokkinopilós** (Κοκκινοπηλός), a red, dune-like expanse now partially covered in vegetation, left over after Africa and Greece went their separate ways. Although there's nothing to see, this may be the oldest archaeological site in Greece; stone tools found here go back as far as 250,000 years.

Down in the Ambracian Gulf, 27km south of Árta, the islet of **Koronisía** (Κορωνησία) is connected to the mainland by a causeway – a fantastic short drive. Here fishermen still use the age-old *ivaria* technique of cane traps that was passed on to them by their fathers and grandfathers. Along with fishermen in nearby **Kalogerikó** (Καλογερικό), they have set up a co-operative which has the exclusive fishing rights in the lagoon but also the responsibility to preserve the natural habitat. Koronisía has a beach and fish tavernas, and it was once a monastic centre; parts of the charming church of the Panagía go back to the 10th century.

The Gulf holds Greece's biggest wetlands, and the **Ambracian Wetland National Park** (w amvrakikos.eu) is one of the most important for rare birds and plant life, hosting more than 300 species, including an important colony of silver Dalmatian pelicans, attracted by the Gulf's rich sea life. Besides its famous prawns, it is home to oysters and mussels, and a big pod of dolphins; monk seals and loggerhead turtles are occasionally sighted. Along the coast to the east, the little **Lighthouse of Kópraina** (Κόπραινα) built in 1893 is now a museum of lighthouses (⊕ irregularly; ask at the seafood taverna). It's a lovely calm place, with wonderful swimming where little ponies mooch about along the shore.

PRÉVEZA (Πρέβεζα) The 20,000 citizens of Préveza live in a new city by Greek standards, just 700 years old, decorated with a Venetian castle and a newer one built by Ali Pasha. Once a dull provincial town with so-so beaches, linked by a rust bucket ferry with Áktion, it appealed only to duck-hunters. Now the ferries are gone, replaced by the first underwater tunnel in Greece. It's a pleasant, modern town, a good base for touring the Gulf and seeing the nearby ruins of Nikopolis.

The coast north of Préveza is lined with resort after resort on a lush and indented coast, many of which are filled with foreign-owned holiday flats, thanks to the proximity of the airport. But the beaches are stunning, and the villages, Párga in particular, attract thousands, many of whom never leave their sunbeds. But there are treats in store for those who do, from the mysterious Necromanteion to the lovely Achérondas Gorge.

Getting there and away
By air Préveza's Áktion Airport (✆ 26820 22089; w pvk-airport.gr) is just south of the 'channel tunnel' and has numerous flights from the UK, eastern Europe and

Scandinavia in summer. There is a regular bus from the airport to Préveza; a taxi will cost at most €30.

By bus Préveza's **bus station** (2km north of town on the Ioánnina road; 26820 22213; w ktelprevezas.gr) has buses to Athens, Ioánnina, Igoumenítsa and Árta.

Car hire
Avis Airport; m 69572 19700
Budget In town & airport; 26450 28846
Hertz Airport; 26824 40056

Where to stay

Dioni Boutique Hotel (34 rooms) Plateía Th Papageorgíou; 26820 27381; w dioniboutiquehotel.gr. Well-appointed, quietly elegant rooms & suites off the main street, Leof Írinis, 10mins south of the bus station. Free parking; b/fast (inc) served on the roof terrace. €€€€–€€€

Pension Alexandros (54 rooms) Ag Georgíou 27; 26820 23481. Dbls & trpls, many with kitchenette & balcony, & a lovely garden on the seafront. Rooms are basic but still a good bargain; this is the nicest of a row of similar places out by the castle south of town. All have lawns leading to the sea. €€–€

Where to eat and drink
It's a great town for seafood, featuring those big prawns from the Gulf, and *petáli*, a grey mullet split in half and grilled, often with vegetables. Tavernas and *ouzerís* are concentrated on the pedestrian streets around **Saitan Pazar**, an alley that got its name, 'Devil's Market', from the Turks – they say the local boys would smear its cobblestones with grease, and wait to see if they could get the stiff-booted Turkish soldiers to slip and fall on their bums.

Ambrósios Grigoríou E 9; 26820 27192; Αμβρόσιος; noon–01.00 Tue–Sun. In the pedestrian centre, an excellent seafood taverna with outside tables in a nice setting. €€

Trelí Garída Adrianópoleos 7; 26820 25691; noon–midnight daily. The 'Crazy Prawn' also has great grilled octopus & seafood pasta. €€

Tzitzikas In Psatháki, a 5min drive from downtown; 26820 25080; 13.00–16.00 & 19.00–23.00 daily. In a shady setting by the water, this is real Turkish cooking with a real Turk, Hassan, in the kitchen. Locally very popular, & famous for classics like *hünkar beggendí* (lamb stew with aubergine purée). €€

Psátha Dardchanéllou 4; 26820 23051; 12.30–23.30 daily. In the pedestrian centre, simple taverna fare – but every local swears by it, especially for its casserole dishes. €

What to see and do Préveza's pretty waterfront along Venizélou Street is closed to traffic, tavernas line its pedestrian streets, and the swimming is not bad near Ag Geórgios castle, south of town. The only big attraction here, however, is the ruins of Préveza's forebear, the lost Roman city of Nikopolis.

Ancient Nikopolis After Actium, Octavian promptly began planning his trophy 'Victory City', on the site of his camp, emptying most of Epirus and Aetoloakarnanía to the south to populate it. He inaugurated the quadrennial Actian Games to celebrate his victory, and along the way gave Rome a base ideally located for its interests in Greece.

Nikopolis became the biggest city in what is now Greece. St Paul visited in AD64 and may have written his Epistle to Titus there; by the 3rd century AD it had 300,000 inhabitants and the games were still going strong, especially after Julian the Apostate appeared and reinstituted paganism in the following century. An attack by

THE BATTLE OF ACTIUM

Long before Préveza was born, this corner of Greece had its one brush with big-league history. The strait that leads into the Ambracian Gulf suddenly became a strategic place in 31BC, during the wars that followed the assassination of Julius Caesar. On one side were lovers Mark Antony and Cleopatra (Roman political boss Marcus Antonius and Queen Cleopatra VII of Egypt, to be precise, or Richard Burton and Elizabeth Taylor for anyone who has seen Joseph L Mankiewicz's budget-busting *Cleopatra*, 1963). These two joined forces at Ephesus and proceeded across Greece on their way to Rome. On the other side is Octavian (the scheming Roddy McDowall in the film), who had seized control in Rome and led his armies down to meet them.

Antony and Cleopatra's fleet spent the winter of 32BC sheltered in the Ambracian Gulf while their armies marched across northern Greece from the east to catch up. Octavian, wasting no time, occupied Epirus, including the north shore of the Gulf. Antony frittered away much of the spring and summer in indecision, and when he finally took his fleet out, they were outnumbered by Octavian's navy 500 ships to 250.

The battle began on 2 September 31BC, as Antony's forces massed to break out of the Gulf. What followed was total confusion; historians today can't sort out what happened. By one account, Cleopatra took advantage of the initial clash to abandon Antony and take her fleet back to Egypt. Antony too escaped from the debacle, perhaps abandoning his own men to follow her. By another account, Antony's admiral defected to Octavian as soon as the battle was joined, and Antony and Cleopatra had no choice but to flee. Both would soon meet their ends in Egypt. After the naval disaster, Antony's armies on shore, numbering 20,000, quickly melted away for home. Octavian had won all the chips, and would soon be calling himself Caesar Augustus. Peace was restored, but it meant the end of the Republic, and the beginning of the Roman Empire.

the Goths in AD268 was the first of many; in the early 6th century AD, Justinian had to refortify a small corner as a stronghold of last resort. Subsequent Slav invasions convinced the Byzantines to relocate to the more defensible site of Náfpaktos on the Corinthian Gulf which became the new government seat. With no political function, more invasions (Arabs, Bulgars and others) and little trade, Nikopolis dwindled, and finally was abandoned in the 11th century, most of its inhabitants moving to the new city of Préveza.

Archaeological Museum (5km north of Préveza; 26820 89892; May–Oct 08.00–20.00 Wed–Mon, Nov–Apr 08.30–15.30 Wed–Mon; €8, concessions €4, inc archaeological site) Originally the finds from Nikopolis were kept in the old mosque in Préveza. The Italians looted it in 1941 (and the Greek government demolished it after the war). The new museum is well designed and chronologically arranged, with a timeline of the city, with good explanations in English, and finds from recent excavations: sculptures, coins, ceramics and objects of everyday life, along with some vivid reliefs of hunts.

Archaeological site (8km north of Préveza; 26820 41336; see museum for opening times & prices; tickets also available on the site) The ruins of Nikopolis are melancholy although the countryside is grand. Crumbling Roman brick is just

9 | EPIRUS (ΗΠΕΙΡΟΣ)

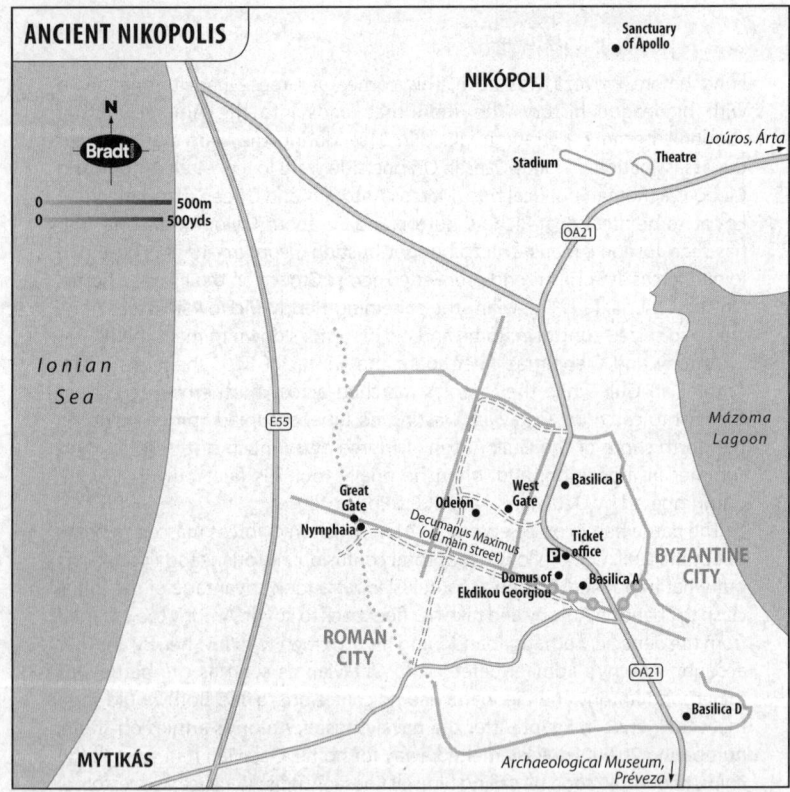

not as attractive as Greek marble, and weed-choked grass adds to the sense of lost glory; few great cities of antiquity disappeared so completely. It may take some time for its scale to sink in; the ruins are scanty, but they are spread over some 10km². You'll want a car or bike.

To make sense of it start from the north, by modern Nikópoli (Νικόπολη). Just off the Árta road is the huge **theatre**; its proscenium walls still stand as does some of its upper portico, where you can see holes for the canvas awnings that protected the audience from sun or rain. It took some hard knocks in World War II, when it was used as an air-raid shelter – the ancient city was a military camp, and bombed by the Italians in 1941 – and lately it has all been fenced off as they await funds to repair it. The long grassy depression that was the **stadium** for chariot races is just to the west. In its present state it resembles the Circus Maximus in Rome, both thoroughly cannibalised by later ages for building stone. Ali Pasha was especially rapacious; he carried away much of Nikopolis for his castles and took all the ancient sculpture still visible to give as diplomatic presents. Follow the signs up through the village 400m north of the theatre, to the few stones that remain of the **Sanctuary of Apollo**. Despite its name, this sanctuary was also dedicated to Poseidon and Ares, Augustus' tutelary gods, and built as a victory trophy. The site marks the spot where Augustus looked down on the naval battle of Actium.

This area was the big northern suburb of Augustus' city. Along the road to Préveza from the theatre, you'll pass some remnants of the city walls into the much-shrunken **Byzantine city**. Prominent on the low hill are the ruins of the **Domus of**

Ekdikou Georgiou, a luxurious Roman villa where visiting emperors (Germanicus, Hadrian and Nero) are known to have called, later owned by the Ekdikou, whose job was to defend the people from oppression. Near here is '**Basilica A**' (Basilica of Doumétios, 6th century AD), with some excellent mosaic floors, decorated with roundels of hunting scenes and an ocean teeming with fish. Other mosaics can be seen in '**Basilica B**' and '**Basilica D**'.

From here you can see Justinian's impressive L-shaped **wall** (6th century AD) which enclosed the Byzantine remnant, with alternating bands of brick and stone and arrays of towers. You can drive on the dirt road through the arched West Gate, and head left to the beautifully preserved **Odeion**, the concert hall built when Augustus was still alive. Concerts and plays are occasionally staged here in the summer.

Beyond it to the west are the ruins of the **Great Gate**, and just inside it are two elaborate fountain houses, the **Nymphaia**. Even now they stand 8.3m tall and would have impressed newcomers arriving in Komares (today's Mýtikas), the city's port. The Nymphaia were the terminals of the Nikopolis Aqueduct, which ran over the top of the city walls on both sides. A nympheum (*nimfaion* in Greek) was originally a sacred area considered as a home of the nymphs. Under the Romans the term referred to the monumental covered fountains: serving simultaneously as reservoirs, sacred places (marriages were celebrated in them) and places for travellers to freshen up as they came into town.

From the Great Gate, the main street, the **Decumanus Maximus**, runs straight towards the sea, surrounded on both sides by innumerable graves and funeral monuments, of which almost nothing above ground remains. North and south of the Odeion stretched the most important parts of Augustus' city. Here, too, little remains as far as the walls, still impressive in some places; the best view is from the side road to Mýtikas.

Ancient Kassope (23km north of Préveza, via Kamarína (Καμαρίνα); 26820 51010; summer 08.30–15.30 Wed–Mon; €2) Kassope wasn't a very important city, but it occupies a gorgeous site 600m up with views over the Préveza-Árta plain. It was founded in the 4th century BC by the tribe of the Cassopaei as their capital, but, although it flourished, it didn't last. The Romans sacked it in 167BC and after Actium they forced the inhabitants to resettle in Nikopolis. A lovely walk through a pine forest leads to the entrance.

The city was built on a Hippodamian grid plan that once boasted 500 buildings. The layout is still discernible around the **agora**, with Kassope's most substantial ruin, the perfectly preserved substructure and polygonal 'Cyclopean' wall (so called for the immense size of its stones) of a building identified as a **Katagogeion** (inn or hostel); Aphrodite was Kassope's chief goddess so may have had a lot of visitors. From its side you can look down the perfectly straight main street, connecting the eastern and western gates. Outside the western gate you can explore the remains of a **Macedonian tomb**, a rare one located this far from Macedon.

The remaining stoas, temples and so on pale in comparison with the view. The remnants of the small 2,000-seat **Odeion**, used for assemblies, provide a great spot for drinking it in. More Cyclopean walls, the city's fortifications, can be seen to the south and east. A small **theatre** graces the slope just above the city.

While at Kassope, look up to the east towards the 18th-century **Moní Ag Dimítrios**, the start of a steep path to the huge **Monument of Zalongos** (George Zongolopoulos, 1961) featuring a row of Souliote women apparently ready to dance off the mountain top. That is exactly what they did in 1806. The Souliotes were a confederation of some 60 villages in this rugged area, who had maintained a

9 | EPIRUS (ΗΠΕΙΡΟΣ)

relative independence from the Ottomans for centuries. In 1803 they were getting arms from Napoleon, which alarmed the Sultan enough to send Ali Pasha to put them down, which he did with his customary brutality. On this spot, 60 Souliote women and children, trapped by the Turks, chose this dance of death rather than be captured and killed. All Europe heard the grisly news; poets and painters captured the scene, contributing much to the agitation for Greek independence.

PÁRGA

Epirus's biggest beach resort is also a historic town, which grew up around its lofty medieval castle on a headland. Behind it, the brightly painted houses of Párga (Παργα) spill down to a quay packed with restaurants and bars as far as the beach of Kryonéri, which is separated by another mini headland from boulder-strewn Píso-Kryonéri Beach.

Párga is not so much a town as a holiday village. The French started it all in 1957 with a Club Med on Váltos Beach and donkey taxis to the village, and since then its pleasant, red-roofed houses have largely been hijacked by package tour companies. The medieval stepped lane to the *kástro* is a shop-lined pedestrian highway. Two or three streets above Plateía Andístassis still have a few Greek homes, but most of the locals running the Párga machine live in outlying villages. It sounds awful (and it is in August), but Párga is still beautiful. The 100m of water separating the beach from Panagía Island may not be pristine, but there are other beaches nearby and the island and castle (lit up at night), combined with the greenery and headlands, are hard to beat. If restaurants use foreign names like Rudi's, rest assured that their Greek owners are just doing what Párga has always done: dealing with foreigners as best they can.

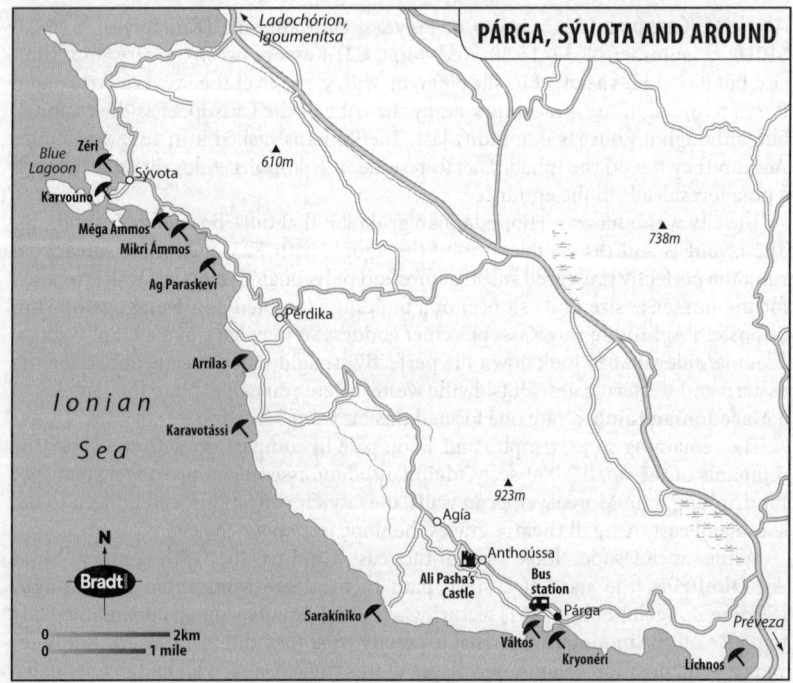

PÁRGA

GETTING THERE AND AROUND

By bus The bus station (Agíou Anthanaíou 53; m 69779 85905) is 1km east of the port on the Morfis–Anthousas road. There are three or four buses a day to Préveza (w ktelprevezas.gr), and two a day to Igoumenítsa, as well as two services daily in summer to Sývota via Pérdika (w ktel-thesprotias.gr).

By boat Water taxis connect Párga to Líchnos and Váltos beaches all day. Caiques to the Necromanteíon leave regularly from the town pier. You can also hire a small boat for a half or full day of exploring on your own from Parga Boat Rental (m 69463 05132; w pargaboatrental.gr; from €90/day low season, €140/day Aug).

By car Párga's waterfront is a pedestrian walk, which helps make both parking and driving around difficult. Leave your car in one of the impromptu unpaved car parks, a few streets in from the shore.

By taxi Call m 69444 44064 for local radio taxis.

TOURIST INFORMATION AND TOUR OPERATORS

Kanaris Travel Anexartisías 51; \26840 31490; w kanaris.gr. On the quay, with a handy service point listing local bus schedules & prices. They also rent bicycles.

Synthesis Travel Alex Bága 6; \26840 31700. They can book ferries, car rentals, & excursions to the Necromanteion, the Achérondas River, Albania, Corfu, Páxi & Antipáxi; plus itineraries for hikers, divers & mini-cruises.

WHERE TO STAY
Párga's hoteliers block-book many rooms with holiday firms but keep others for independent travellers. Expect big reductions in April and October, and book well ahead in high season.

Villa Rossa (34 rooms) Kryonéri Beach; \26840 31237; w villarossa.gr. Tucked under the cypress-clad promontory overlooking the beach, this big red house was built in 1903 for tobacco merchants Telemachos & Aphrodite Bozios (after he died she ran the house as a girls' school & became the first woman elected to public office in Greece). The Italians who made it their HQ during World War II gave it its name, & recently the former tobacco warehouse & stable have been converted into airy studios & apartments using original & recycled material. They have e-bikes & SUP boards; an organic farm supplies the wonderful Mediterranean restaurant (book at \26840 31532; €€€€), which has great views over Párga. Limited private parking available; b/fast inc. €€€€€–€€€€

Adams (51 rooms & suites) Edém; \26840 32160; w adamshotel.com; ⊕ Apr–Oct. Elegant, spacious rooms in a rather grand new building above a good-sized pool. Lots of olive trees; plus sauna & fitness room, parking & restaurant (€€€). Almost 1km from the beach on the road into town, though. €€€€

Rezi (50 rooms) Ríga Feréou 12; \26840 31417; w hotel-rezi.gr; ⊕ May–Oct. Left on the road to the sea as you enter town. Just back from the beach; nice rooms, pool & bar, & quieter than some. €€€

Villa Coralli (21 rooms) Ag Athanasíou 7; \26840 31069; w villacoralli.com. Friendly, new & well maintained, with parking, on the road backing Kryonéri Beach. The view of Panagía Island & the castle from the terrace is perfect. B/fast inc. €€€

Dolphin Apartments (16 apartments) Líchnos Beach; \26840 32439; ⊕ Apr–Nov. A gracious establishment in a peaceful spot just above the beach; good for families. Big rooms with kitchens have a fabulous view, & are far enough up from the beach that you may enjoy their pool (kiddies' pool attached). €€€–€€

Angela (30 rooms) Ag Athanasíou 12; \26840 31614; ⊕ Apr–Nov. Right on Píso-Kryonéri Beach & convenient for the centre; great views from the seaside rooms; garden & café terrace; some rooms with kitchenettes. €€

9 | EPIRUS (ΗΠΕΙΡΟΣ)

Torini (11 rooms) Mandilará 1; m 69758 51843. One of many around the main Spíros Livadá St above town, 600m from the beaches. Friendly & adequate; fine rooms for the price. €€

✖ WHERE TO EAT AND DRINK
Párga has a bit of everything, all open day and night from May through to September, but in winter take what you can get.

Bacchos Anexartisías 63; ☎ 26840 32700; ⏰ 10.00–midnight daily. One of the best choices on the promenade, with good lamb & seafood. €€

Golfo Beach Píso-Kryonéri Beach; ☎ 26840 32336; ⏰ 08.00–midnight daily. Tucked away from the hurly-burly in a pretty setting, where you can linger while keeping an eye on the kids playing on the pebble beach. Classic Greek cuisine & seafood (try the *stifádo*) prepared with TLC; live Greek music Mon, Wed & Fri. €€

Tango Club Váltos Beach; ☎ 26840 31252; f TangoBeachParga; ⏰ summer 10.00–01.00 daily. A restaurant-pool-café complex with good food; good for kids, too. €€

Sakis Patatoúkou Thémeli; ☎ 26840 32262; ⏰ 17.00–23.00 daily. A bit of a rarity in Párga – a proper friendly taverna under the pergola, serving the classics. €

MED Club Patatoúkou 25; ☎ 26840 32032; w medclubparga.gr; ⏰ 09.30–03.00 daily, kitchen to midnight. Hip lounge & cool cocktails with sublime views, looking straight across at the castle.

Pargas Distillery – Amicos Cocktail Bar Patatoúkou 26; ☎ 26840 31234; ⏰ noon–midnight daily. Relaxing setting & wonderful cocktails, including great mojitos, *ouzo*-based cocktails, & some fun ones with dry ice.

SPORTS AND ACTIVITIES Párga has a diving club, water-skiing and parasailing on its larger beaches, along with canoe rentals. In Glykí, the Pony Club (m 69866 17090; w ponyclub.gr) offers rafting, tours through the gorge and pony rides for children.

WHAT TO SEE AND DO Párga's romantically ruined **Venetian Castle** (10–15min walk up a steep alley & steps; wear sensible shoes; free) sits on its rock 600m above town and sea, still bearing a Lion of St Mark above the gate. Built in the 13th century, it remained Venetian with two brief interruptions (Barbarossa in 1537, Ottomans in 1571) until 1797, when the Turks took it again, only to lose it in 1801–07, when Párga had a brief fling at independence under Russian protection. Then the French had it, just long enough to build the crumbling little fort on the island opposite, followed by the British, who sold it to Ali Pasha. The Pargiótes were paid compensation, but being forced to move to Corfu did not sit well. When Párga joined Greece in 1913, its citizens returned, bringing their flag and icons. There are plenty of ruins to explore, wonderful views from Ali Pasha's harem building on top, and even a few rusting cannons, plus a café with lovely views, especially at sunset.

A footpath leads down to long, wide, sandy **Váltos Beach**, immediately west of Párga and linked by a footpath from the Venetian castle; in winter it offers some of the best surfing in Greece. **Líchnos Beach**, 4km east, is a spectacular, south-facing sandy bay with a fabulous view of Ammoudiá's dune-like headlands over the water. Water taxis are the best way to go; parking is almost impossible, and pricey.

AROUND PÁRGA
South of Párga The approach to the **Achérondas Delta** offers a vista of flat agricultural land, punctuated by the new resort of **Ammoudiá** (Αμμουδιά) by the lovely sandy beach where the river flows into the sea. Part of the delta, still willow- and cane-bordered marsh, is a Natura 2000 site, home to 150 species of bird, along with otters, turtles, foxes and badgers and 450 species of flora.

In ancient times this was a swampy lake, formed by three of the rivers of Hades – the Acheron, River of Woe; the Kokytos (aka Cocytus), the River of Lamentation (today the Mávros or Black River); and the Fire-flaming Pyriphlegethon (today the Voúvos). The lake's malarial waters were drained in the 1960s, turning the island that once supported the shrine to Hades and Persephone into a knobby hill. The shrine, better known as the **Necromanteion of Acheron** (℡26840 41206; ☉ summer 08.00–20.00 daily, gradually earlier closings Sep–Oct, winter 08.30–15.30 daily; €10, concessions €5), is signposted off the Igoumenísta–Préveza E55, but the nicest way to arrive is by boat up the Achérondas (book through Párga's travel agencies), now full of dragonflies, turtles and kingfishers, instead of woe.

But in ancient times visitors came in trepidation to communicate with departed loved ones through the Oracle of the Dead. In Homer, Odysseus came to its 'wild shore' to consult the seer Teiresias about how to get home. Supplicants underwent complicated rituals, including a special diet, animal sacrifices, all-night vigils and maybe hallucinogenic drugs before being led through a dark labyrinthine corridor and lowered by a winch – the flanged bronze rings and ratchet wheels belonging to this mechanism are in Ioánnina's archaeology museum. Exactly what transpired is unknown. Corinth's tyrant Periander sent envoys to contact his wife, Melissa. He had misplaced something she gave him in trust. So she was raised from the dead to answer the archetypal spousal question: 'Honey, what did you do with the...?' She told him, but only after he had guaranteed her a new wardrobe.

The ruins, topped by the small 18th-century church of Ag Ioánnis, were discovered in the 1950s by Sotíris Dakáris and date from the late 4th to early 3rd century BC. There are three rooms on the left of a corridor, which may have been where supplicants stayed; bones and ash found in the corridor at right angles to this suggest animal sacrifices. Another right-angled turn leads to the small labyrinth, and right again to the central square chamber, 21 x 21m with very thick 3.4m polygonal walls and adjacent storerooms, three on each side, where jars once held grains and grapes; below the square chamber is another the same size, with 15 arches supporting the roof that was inaccessible in antiquity.

Some have suggested that this is not the Necromanteion at all but the foundations of a Hellenistic tower fort, with a catapult (the bronze bits), an underground cistern and clay storage pots in case of siege. Well, archaeology is not able to answer all questions, but the matter could be settled easily if we could just contact Melissa.

Achérondas Gorge In spite of being the River of Woe, the pale turquoise Achérondas is one of the most beautiful and cleanest rivers in Greece. It runs through attractive country, especially when it squeezes through a narrow limestone gorge near **Tríkastro** (Τρίκαστρο), where you can pick up a 10km (4–4½ hours) trail that follows its rim.

At **Glykí** (Γλυκή), the 'sweet' village, the river widens and meanders placidly to the sea; summer restaurants place tables on its shady gravel bed. Rafting is popular in spring, and in summer many people wade the river narrows (swimming is required in places; you'll need swim shoes and waterproof protection for your camera and wallet – sold at the tourist stands in Glykí. From the stone Dalas Bridge, about an hour's wade, you can follow a land path back to Glykí. Or for a less strenuous wading experience from Glykí, it's 10 minutes to the **Dragon's Cave** (Spiliá tou Drákou), where the spring bubbles out icy cold. The dragon who lived here was fouling the water until St Donatus came along and slew it. When the Venetians in Párga heard the story, they stole the dragon's bones and saint's relics and installed them in the 12th-century church of San Donato on the island of Murano, where they reside to this day.

North of Glykí you can drive into the wild mountains to the Súliot villages – **Samonída** (Σαμονίδα) is one of the closest. In the 16th century, these 11 remote villages formed the Súliot Federation, 12,000 members strong, and all dedicated to freedom from the Turks. They were an ornery lot, and their consistent resistance has made them popular heroes today. A blood-and-thunder film called *The Súliots* is shown like clockwork every 25 March (Independence Day) on Greek television. Their independence lasted until 1803 when Ali Pasha dislodged them, only to ally himself with them 17 years later against the Sultan. The Sultan prevailed in 1822, and the Súliots abandoned their villages, strongholds and curiously shaped wells. Even today, only a few old-timers and romantics inhabit this once powerful stronghold.

North of Párga Beyond Párga's Váltos Beach, the coastal road winds through olive trees to **Anthoússa** (Ανθούσα) and its beach, under **Ali Pasha's Castle** (⊙ 08.00– sunset; free) on its hill. The tourist train from Párga (m 69457 93049; w pargatrains. com; €8, concessions €6) goes several times a day. Built by Italian engineers in 1814, the castle's dungeons and roof are accessible; the views on a clear day reach as far as Lefkáda. Below is a curl of fine sand, **Sarakíniko** (Σαρακίνικο).

The road to Sývota ascends through barren windswept **Agía** (Αγία) and down again through olive groves to **Pérdika** (Πέρδικα; 'Partridge town'). A tourist stopover perched high above the sea, Pérdika is at the junction of the roads to two gorgeous beaches, **Arrílas** (Αρίλλας) and **Karavotássi** (Καραβοστάσι). The corniche road past Pérdika offers bird's-eye views of the indented coast; the best beach along here is sand-and-pebble **Ag Paraskeví** (Αγ Παρασκευή), facing a small wooded islet.

SÝVOTA

Tucked in a small bay in an amoeba-shaped headland, among a cluster of mini pine-wooded fjords, islets and sandy beaches immersed in magical blue-green Ionian colours, Sývota (Σύβοτα) has been popular with the yachting set since the 1960s. It's smaller and more upmarket than Párga.

 WHERE TO STAY Sývota is chockful of holiday apartments; check online booking sites for options.

Domotel Agios Nikolaos (67 rooms) 600m from the centre; \26650 93017; w domotel.gr; ⊙ May–Oct. Recently renovated, contemporary 5-star hotel with idyllic views over the jagged coast, with a handsome pool, private beach & beach bar. B/fast inc. €€€€€

Sývota Seascape (6 residences) Ag Pareskeví; \26650 91105; m 69406 08830, 69446 54390; w sivota-seascape.gr. Large residences & villas – some of which have private pools – on a lush property overlooking the sea. Each has a chic, fully equipped kitchen & dining area, plus Coco-Mat mattresses, Korrés bath products & Nespresso machines. €€€€–€€

Méga Ámmos (40 rooms) Méga Ámmos Beach; \26650 93447; w hotel-megaammos.gr; ⊙ Apr– Oct. Peaceful hotel-bungalow complex immersed in gardens 2km south of Sývota's centre, within a 2min walk of the beach, with a restaurant, pool & playground. €€€

✱ WHERE TO EAT AND DRINK

Ionian Fish Restaurant Méga Ámmos; \26650 93506; ⊙ 13.00–22.00 daily. Delightful seafood taverna by the beach with good grilled veggies to go with the fish; also tasty starters. €€€–€€

Ammos Center Méga Ámmos; m 69571 12209; w ammoscenter.com; ⊙ 08.00–23.00 daily.

Excellent food & cocktails, great staff – a place to laze the day away by the beach. €€

Parasole By the marina; \26650 93188; w parasole.gr; ⊙ noon–midnight daily. Excellent hand-tossed pizzas & pasta, & good people-watching, too, with tables on the quay. €€

Stavedo Zéri Beach; **** 26650 93544; ⏱ 09.00–20.00 daily. Laid-back beach bar with good sandwiches, chips & salads; & sunbeds by the beach. €

SPORTS AND ACTIVITIES If you haven't brought the yacht, one of the best things to do is rent a small motorboat (for up to 5 people) to explore the surrounding islands, sea caves and beaches. Prices start at €70 a day, plus fuel. Try **Sivota Rent a Boat** (in the port; w sivotarentaboat.gr) or **Rent a Boat Sivota** (Zéri Beach; w rentaboatsivota.gr).

WHAT TO SEE AND DO Besides playing a game of chess on the giant outdoor chess board, and hanging out along the quay, the thing to do in Sývota is hit the beach. Within walking distance there are several, all with tavernas and sunbeds: head north for **Zéri** (Ζέρη) **Beach** on a lagoon, with the warmest water in the area, or south for **Karvoúno** (Καβούνο) in a sheltered bay, or **Méga Ámmos** (Μέγα Άμμος); further along is **Mikrí Ámmos** (Μικρή Άμμος), tucked in a wooded inlet, and totally occupied by the sunbeds of a pricey beach bar (it looks private, but it's not).

For the other beaches, you'll need a boat (see above). One of the best is on the islet of Mávro Óros: with exotic golden sands and clear turquoise waters of the **Blue Lagoon** (aka Pisína), along the channel to Ag Nikólaos island.

IGOUMENÍTSA

Igoumenítsa (Ηγουμενίτσα) calls itself the gateway to Europe, but most tourists think of it as the back door to Greece. Burned down by the retreating Germans and rebuilt without a lot of charm, it's Greece's third-largest passenger port after Piraeus and Pátras, and receives a growing number of cruise ships. Since the completion of the Egnatía Ódos, it has also become Greece's biggest cargo port. No-one ever says anything nice about it, but its 15,000 inhabitants like their home and the leafy waterfront north of the old port, with its cafés, isn't the worst place in the world. But there is no compelling reason to stay unless your ferry leaves or arrives at an awkward time.

GETTING THERE AND AROUND
By bus The bus station (Leof 49 Martíron; **** 26650 22309; w ktel-thesprotias.gr) is near the old port, with four daily buses to Ioánnina, three to Athens, and two each to Párga, Thessaloníki and Sývota.

By sea (Port Authority: Ladochórion, by the new port; **** 26653 61800) **International ferries** to Italy depart from the New Port with its own exit on the Egnatía Ódos. It's always best to get a ticket online in advance, but if you haven't, agents are in the New Passenger Terminal (**** 26650 99300). Note that even if you do have a ticket purchased online, you still need to present your passport and pick up a paper ticket in person at the passenger terminal. Arrive at least 2 hours before your departure time for the formalities, or even earlier if you'd like to find a comfortable place to sit on board.

Domestic ferries to Corfu (around once an hour) and Páxi (once a day in high season) depart from the old port to the north; for schedules see w kerkyralines.com.

Car hire
Avis Ag Apostólou 147; **** 26650 27999; w avis.gr   **Go Car** Ag Apostólou 39–41; **** 26653 06765

By taxi There are ranks by the port, or call m 69459 34196.

WHERE TO STAY AND EAT
Angelica Palace (38 rooms) Ag Apostólou 63; 26650 26100; w angelikapallas.gr. As good as it gets, bright & modern, with a pleasant atrium & restaurant (€€). €€
Aktion (26 rooms) Ag Apostólon 17; 26650 22707; w hotel-aktaion.gr. Pleasant, recently renovated hotel near the old port, run by the same family for generations. Reception stays open for late-night ferries. B/fast inc. €€–€

Lithos Eth Antístasis 74; 26650 00819; ⊕ noon–22.00 Mon & Wed–Sat, noon–18.00 Sun. Well-prepared Greek classics along the front. €€
Maistrali Drépano Beach; m 69494 73958; ⊕ coffee from 08.00, kitchen 13.00–23.30 daily. Lovely summer restaurant by the beach, with beautiful sunsets & seafood – one of the best in town. €€

WHAT TO SEE AND DO The **Archaeology Museum** (Oktovríou 2; 26650 28539; w igoumenitsamuseum.gr; ⊕ Apr–Aug 08.00–20.00 Wed–Mon, gradually earlier closings Sep–Oct, Nov–Mar 08.30–15.30 Wed–Mon; €10, concessions €5), just north of the centre, is filled with finds from Thesprotia, Epirus's extreme northwest, dating from 100,000BC to the 17th century AD. The Mycenaeans arrived here in the 14th century BC (reflecting the region's appearance in the *Odyssey*), followed in Archaic times by colonists from Corinth; among the most interesting finds is a breastplate with gold highlights. The other thing to do is hit **Drépano Beach**, 5km west of Igoumenítsa.

IGOUMENÍTSA TO IOÁNNINA The road to Ioánnina is a yawner by Greek standards, but there's an exit off the Ódos Egnatía for **Paramythiá** (Παραμυθιά), a charming old hill village off the beaten track – its name means 'fairy tales' and it holds a very lively Saturday morning market. Off the slower more scenic E92, you might want to stop at **Vrosína** (Βροσίνα), an old-fashioned village in a dip in the road that has a stone bridge and tavernas.

There is a tempting detour north of Vrosína to **Lía** (Λία), 24km north on the border with Albania, a picturesque drive via **Ravení** (Ραβενή) and **Gardíki** (Γαρδίκι). Lía was made famous by Nicholas Gage in his book *Eleni*, the story of his mother who was executed during the Civil War for arranging for her children to escape to the USA (page 27). Gage has returned frequently to Lía and, in August 2018, with the US ambassador to Greece in attendance, the **Yfantis Museum** opened in the old school house (ask locally for the key), with three newly discovered icons by Theóphilos (page 341), works donated by painter Sotiris Sorogas (who hails from the area), and exhibits on the village and famous visitors (including John Malkovich, who played Gage in the film *Eleni*).

10

Thessaly (Θεσσαλία)

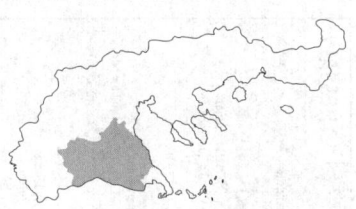

'In the entire world, the best land is the Thessalian land,' declared the oracle at Delphi, and although its mighty plain of wheat, cotton and corn – by far the largest in Greece – has delighted farmers since Neolithic times, the mountains on either side of the plain reserve some truly magical corners for the rest of us. Two of its five-star beauties, the Pelion and the Sporades Islands, are covered in the next two chapters, but this chapter has its fair share of wonders: otherworldly Meteora, where monasteries defy gravity on perpendicular rocks; Lake Plastíra, a mighty blue mirror in the high Pindus Mountains; and lush Mount Kíssavos (or Óssa) with a stunning line-up of beaches. Although its cities – Lárissa, Tríkala and Kardítsa – aren't on many itineraries, each has its special sights and charms. Even the plain can have a weird fascination, especially in late September, when freshly picked cotton lines the roads like snow; in August it's often the hottest place in Greece.

HISTORY

Thessaly has been compared to the Nile Delta. Densely inhabited since early Neolithic times, it nevertheless has little to show for itself thanks to a reliance on mud-brick instead of stone. Tradition and linguistics suggest that the very first Indo-European proto-Greek speakers, identified often as the Pelasgians, invading from the north with their horses c2500BC, got this far, saw that the plain was good, and stopped. Myth reflects this in the story of Hellene, the son of Deukalion (the Greek Noah). He lived in Thessaly and fathered the ancestors of the three major Greek tribes, the Aeolians (of Thessaly), the Dorians and the Ionians, before giving his name to the entire 'Hellenic' race.

The epic tradition was born here, too: critics even in antiquity believed that the heroes of the *Iliad* were 'dragged down to the Peloponnese from homes in Northern Greece'. Agamemnon started off as a Thessalian chieftain; 'horse-rearing Argos' was originally the plain of Thessaly. Achilles was one of the few who stayed put, in Phthia (or Achaea Phthiotis) – believed to be modern Fársala, land of the Myrmidons. Achilles' grandfather was king Aeacus of Aegina, whose population had been wiped out by a plague sent by Hera. Aeacus begged Zeus to repopulate Aegina with as many people as ants on a tree, and these were the Myrmidons or 'Ant People' – reflecting perhaps a historic colonisation from Thessaly.

Circa 1140BC, a fresh wave of Greek speakers, the Thessali, moved in and gave the region their name. With the best cavalry in Greece, they developed into a horsey set of oligarchic squires under a chieftain, or *tagos*, and reduced everyone else to serfs. They were big news in the 6th century BC, when they controlled the

10 | THESSALY (ΘΕΣΣΑΛΙΑ)

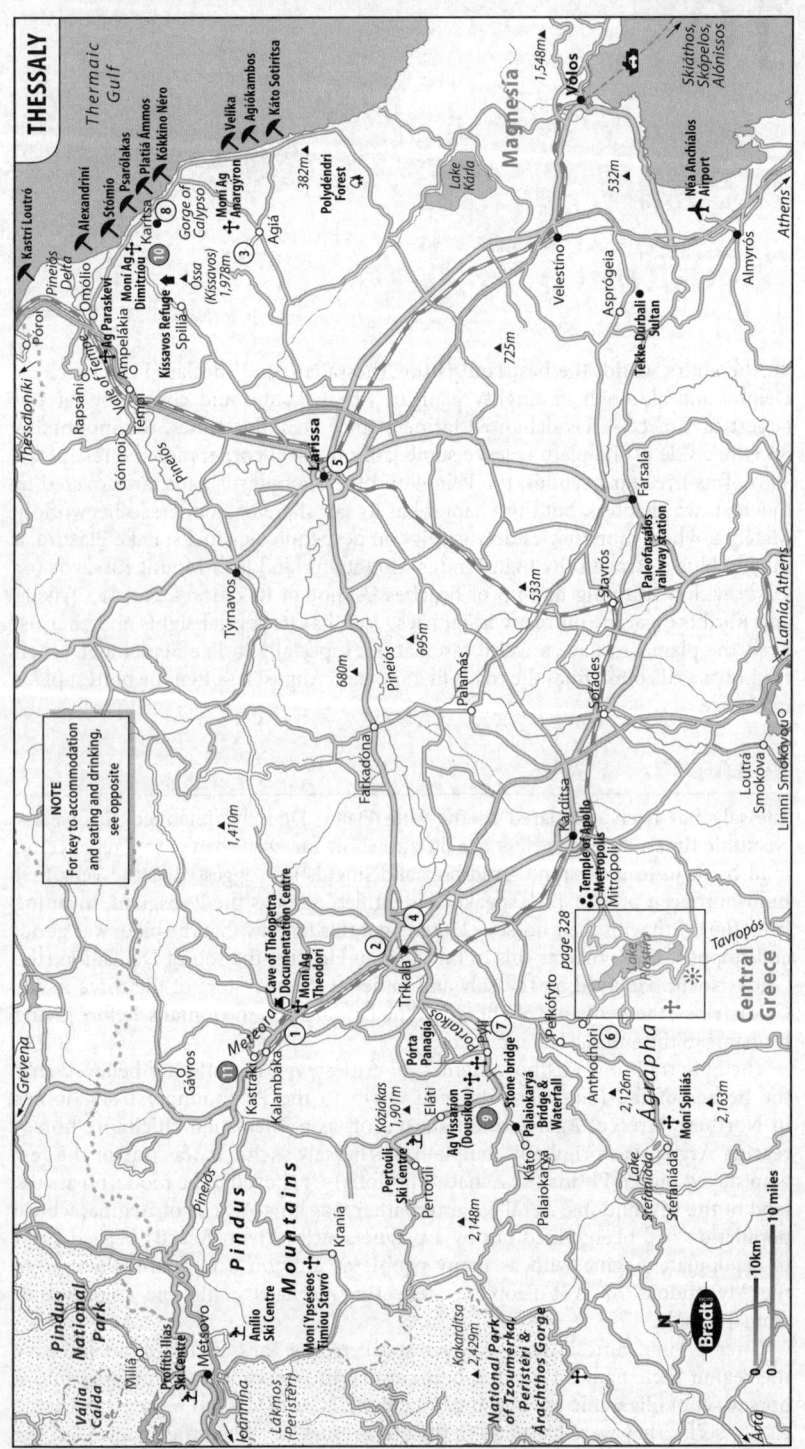

LÁRISSA

> **THESSALY**
>
> 🛏 **Where to stay**
> 1 Amalia *p319*
> 2 Ananti City Resort *p313*
> 3 Archontikó Soulioti *p309*
> 4 Gallery Art *p313*
> 5 Larissa Imperial *p307*
> 6 Montanema *p327*
> 7 Mouzaki Palace *p327*
> 8 Xenonas 1963 *p310*
>
> ✖ **Where to eat and drink**
> 9 Anavrusoúla *p325*
> 10 Arioprino *p310*
> 11 Mankláras *p320*

Amphictyony at Delphi, but on the whole they were considered backward by other Greeks (the poet Simonides wrote that the Thessalians were the only people who never cheated, because they were too stupid), and their alliance with Persia in 492BC lost them the last of their Panhellenic clout.

Gobbled up by Philip II of Macedon after foolishly asking for his assistance, Thessaly remained part of Macedon until T Quinctius Flamininus liberated them at the battle of Cynoscephalae (Kynos Kephalai) in 197BC, before making the region a Roman province in 168BC. Later overrun by Huns, Goths, Slavs and Bulgars, it hosted a complicated game of Risk after 1204, played by Frankish barons, Catalan mercenaries, Epiróte despots, Byzantine emperors and the Serbs, who so wore themselves out that when the Turks arrived in 1396 they encountered little resistance. The Turks remained until 1881, when they ceded Thessaly to the kingdom of Greece.

LÁRISSA

On the banks of the Pineiós River, which crosses the entire region from Meteora to the Aegean, Thessaly's capital, Lárissa (Λάρισα; population 178,000), is Greece's fourth city – an agricultural and industrial centre, university city and major transport hub. It has been inhabited since prehistoric times; its very name is a Pelasgian, pre-Greek word for 'citadel'. In the Classical age, Lárissa's Aleuadai dynasty ruled all Thessaly and were patrons of both the poet Pindar and the father of medicine, Hippocrates of Kos, who spent his last decade here, living into his 80s and maybe even reached 100 – sources vary.

Renamed Yeni-şehir i-Fenari (the 'New Citadel'), it became the main military base of the Ottomans for hundreds of years, with a majority Turkish population; today it's the site of the headquarters of NATO in Greece, and the Greek Air Force. Although little remains of its ancient glories, Lárissa does have several excellent museums and a lively pedestrian district at its core.

GETTING THERE AND AROUND
By air The closest airport is near Vólos (page 334), 71km southeast.

By train Lárissa's railway station [306 C4] (Ptolemaíou St; w hellenictrain.gr) is served by four high-speed trains from Athens (€32.50) and Thessaloníki (€14) daily, with nearby Vólos now serviced by bus, and Kalambáka, Tríkala and Kardítsa reached by train to Paleofársala then continuing by bus.

By bus The bus station [306 C2] (cnr Georgiádou & Olýmpou; ✆ 24105 67600; w ktellarisas.gr) has 9–13 buses to Thessaloníki (€15.30), 8–14 to Vólos (€7), and one to Ioánnina. For service to Tríkala and Kalambáka, see w ktel-trikala.gr.

By car Lárissa is 150km from Thessaloníki and 355km from Athens, with north and south exits off the National Road (E75). There's a convenient underground car park under Plateía Laoú [306 D6].

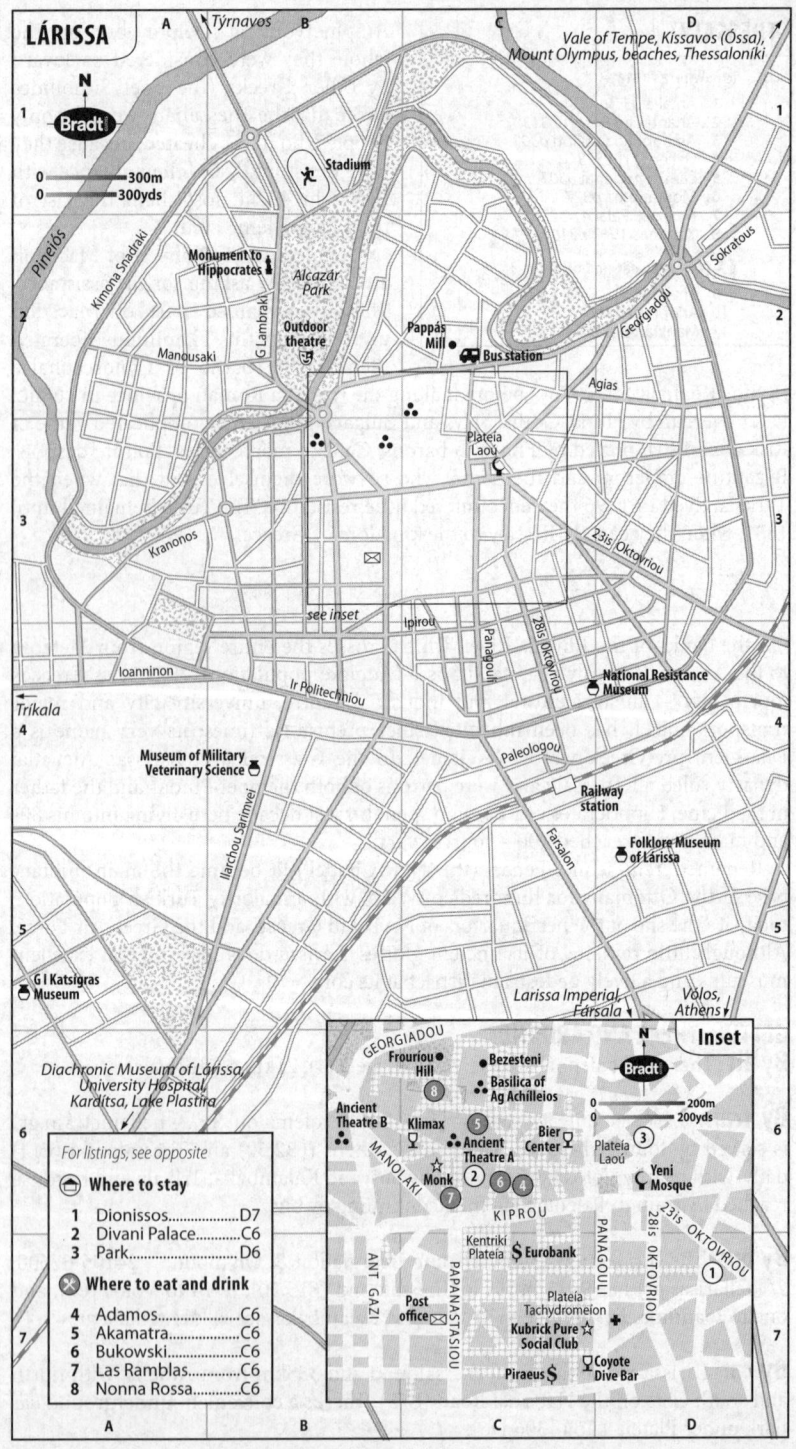

WHERE TO STAY

Divani Palace [306 C6] (74 rooms) Papanastassíou 19; \24102 52791; w divanilarissahotel.com. Opposite Ancient Theatre A, central 5-star hotel with a spa, indoor pool & gym. American buffet b/fast inc. €€€–€€
Larissa Imperial [map, page 304] (150 rooms) Farsálon 182; \24106 87600; w larissaimperial.com. Just off the 1st Lárissa exit coming from Athens (or 4th if coming from the north), this is the city's smartest hotel; bedrooms are in bungalows or the main building & have views over the pool or garden; there's also a spa, jacuzzi, gym, sauna, etc. B/fast inc. €€€–€€
Park Hotel [306 D6] (56 rooms) 31is Avgoústou 1; \24102 57071; w parkhotellarisa.gr. By Plateía Laoú, pleasant modern & comfy, with a sun terrace & nearby parking for €10/day; also bikes available for guests. Greek b/fast buffet €7. €€
Dionissos [306 D7] (84 rooms) Lámbrou Katsóni 24; \24102 30101; w dionissoshotel.gr. Classic city hotel with sat TV. Central but convenient for motorists with its numerous parking options, indoors & out. €

WHERE TO EAT AND DRINK
Lárissa's surprising contemporary and international restaurant scene clustered in the pedestrian area offers comfort if you can't face another Greek salad. It's also a wonderful place if you love coffee – the locals are very picky and drink more than anyone else in the country.

Akamatra [306 C6] Výronos 5; \24140 03803; f akamatralarissa; ⊕ 13.30–midnight Tue–Sun. Casual, colourful spot in the pedestrian zone, with tables in a garden. International & Greek cuisine. €€
Bukowski [306 C6] Panós 11; \24105 36729; ⊕ 13.00–01.00 daily. Popular gastropub with tasty cocktails & drinks, & creative gourmet dishes to go with them. €€
Nonna Rossa [306 C6] Skylosófou 9; \24104 12352; w nonnarossa.gr; ⊕ noon–midnight daily. Cool, contemporary Italian bar-restaurant-pizzeria by Theatre A, with great cocktails & music. Good choice of dishes from pasta & *bistecca fiorentina* to pizza & salads. €€
Adamos [306 C6] Panós 9; \24105 30566; f Ψητοπωλείο "Αδάμος"; ⊕ 07.00–23.00 Tue–Sun. Carnivore heaven in business for nearly a century, with succulent grilled meats sold by the kilo. €
Las Ramblas [306 C6] Apollónos 8; \24111 10390; w lasramblas.coffee; ⊕ 07.00–01.00 daily. Coffee specialists, who also do a decadent sweet or savoury b/fast & brunch.

BARS AND NIGHTLIFE

Bier Center [306 C6] Lapithon 12 ; \24102 59703; f BierCenterLarisa; ⊕ 19.30–23.00 daily. Huge choice of brews from around Europe & Greece.
Coyote Dive Bar [306 C7] Patróklou 9A; \24140 01671; f; ⊕ 20.00–03.00 Mon–Sat. Rock music bar popular with the young & young at heart.
Klimax [306 C6] Ifaístou 2; \24102 51108; f klimaxwine; ⊕ 08.00–midnight daily. Coffees, big choice of wines & cheese, & jazz.
Kubrick Pure Social Club [306 C7] Protopapadáki 12; m 69773 56011; w kubrickpsc.gr; ⊕ 08.30–00.30 daily. Cosy atmosphere with plenty of wood & stone, with superb coffees & cocktails, & lots of events, live music & exhibitions.
Monk [306 C6] Apóllonos 13; m 69875 23123; f Monkbarla; ⊕ 11.00–03.00 daily. Famous for creative cocktails & DJs.

OTHER PRACTICALITIES

Eurobank [306 C7] Meg Alexándrou
Piraeus Bank [306 C7] Nikifórou Mandilará 25
University Hospital [306 B5] Mezoúrlo Hill; \24135 01000
Pharmacy Gatoudis [306 D7] Panagoúli 21
Post office [306 C7] Papanastasíou 62; ⊕ 07.30–14.30 Mon–Fri

WHAT TO SEE AND DO Lárissa's bustling pedestrian heart opens up into two big squares, **Kentrikí Plateía** [306 C7] and **Plateía Tachydromeíon** [306 C7], both of which have fountains built in the 1990s by the city's award-winning landscape sculptor Nella Golanda. The **Potamós Fountains** in the latter celebrate the mighty Pineiós River and the city's past – the water splashes through marbles resembling the ruins of an Archaic temple.

Ancient Theatre A [306 C6] (Cnr Venizélou & Papanastasíou; ⊕ closed at the time of writing for restorations, but visible from the street) Lárissa's oldest surviving theatre was built in the 2nd century BC at the foot of the citadel-acropolis hill, after the Romans liberated the city from Philip V of Macedon. To celebrate, Lárissa founded the Eleutheria games, with theatrical and athletic events honouring Zeus the Liberator. The theatre has 11 well-preserved tiers of marble seats and in its heyday sat 10,000; part of the stage survives as well, although the Romans later converted it into an amphitheatre for the gory events they loved. Dramatic performances moved over to **Ancient Theatre B** [306 B6] (cnr Ergatikís Protomagiás & Tagmatárchou Velissaríou sts; ⊕ by appt with the Ephorate of Antiquities – call ☏ 24135 08200) just west, but its slope was unfortunately razed in the 1950s before the large orchestra and lower ring of seats were discovered in 1978. Originally it had 14 stairways and must have been massive; now, wedged between the street and apartment blocks, it's a bit sad.

Frouríou Hill [306 C6] The only hill in the area, Lárissa's acropolis has been inhabited since 6000BC. It once had a famous temple of Athena Polias, of which a few old marbles still survive in the outer walls. Other bits were re-used in the late 15th century by the Ottomans to build the **Bezesteni** [306 C6], a handsome cloth market with 21 shops; one of its ornate doorways still survives. Just south are the foundations of the large 6th-century AD **Basilica of Ag Achílleios** [306 C6], with a pretty mosaic floor in the narthex and two vaulted tombs decorated with painted crosses, one of which once held the city's first bishop and patron saint, Achílleios (dAD330); but in the early 11th century, Tsar Samuel of Bulgaria conquered Lárissa and carried off his relics to Préspa (page 248).

Alcazár Park [306 B2] This pretty wooded park along the banks of the Pineiós (described by Homer as *argyrodinis*, 'silver swirling river') offers respite on a hot day, complete with a pond, outdoor theatre, minigolf and café. Just to the west of the park, the **Monument to Hippocrates** [306 B2] marks the site of the famous physician's tomb, which was revealed in 1826 by a flood. There's a small museum below the statue (usually locked) which has a copy of his tombstone, and photos of ancient medical instruments.

Pappás Mill [306 C2] (Georgiádou; ☏ 24106 14449; doll museum ⊕ 10.00–14.00 Sat–Sun, but ring ahead) For more than a century this five-storey mill (1883) ground the flour and made Lárissa's pasta; today it houses a cultural centre, hosting Thessaly's regional theatre, music performances, a summer cinema, and the Tipitoúmba puppet theatre and little doll museum (closed temporarily at the time of writing) with some 300 dolls and puppets.

Yeni Mosque [306 D6] (Plateía Blána) One of the few vestiges of Lárissa's Ottoman rule, this rather homely little yellow mosque of 1900 with a minaret is slated to become a city history digital museum.

National Resistance Museum [306 C4] (Ioustaianoú 42; ☏ 24102 80220; ⊕ 09.00–13.00 & 18.00–20.00 Tue–Fri, 10.00–14.00 Sat; free) A small museum run by volunteers, with photos and busts of World War II resistance leaders.

AROUND LÁRISSA

Folklore Museum of Lárissa [306 D5] (G Gourgióti; \ 24102 39446; w larissa-dimos.gr/en/sights/folklore-museum; ⊕ 08.00–14.00 Mon–Tue, 08.00–20.00 Wed–Fri, 10.00–14.00 Sat; €3) Behind the train tracks (there's a subterranean passage from the station), this is an exceptional, well-arranged collection of over 20,000 items from the 15th to the mid 20th century, including traditional costumes, furniture, prints, embroideries, art, rural tools and trades and photos of pre-industrial Thessaly.

Museum of Military Veterinary Science [306 B4] (In the old military stables, Stratópedo N Plastíra; \ 24109 93552; w army.gr/en/news-announcements-en/museum-of-the-hellenic-army-veterinary-service; ⊕ 08.00–14.00 Mon–Fri; free) If there was going to be a museum dedicated to caring for military horses, it would have to be here in the land of the cavalry.

G I Katsígras Museum [306 A5] (Georgiou Papandréou 2; \ 24106 21205; w katsigrasmuseum.gr; ⊕ 10.00–14.00 & 18.00–21.00 Tue–Sun; free) Located southwest of the centre in a brand new building, this municipal gallery has an excellent collection of 19th- and 20th-century Greek paintings collected by art-loving surgeon Dr Katsígras; it also has the furniture once owned by archaeologist Heinrich Schliemann, discoverer of Troy and Mycenae.

Diachronic Museum of Lárissa [306 B5] (Mezoúrlo Hill, southwest of the ring road (take city bus 1); \ 24135 08242; w odysseus.culture.gr; ⊕ Apr–Oct 08.00–20.00 daily, Nov–Mar 08.30–15.30 Wed–Mon; €10, concessions €5) This new, well-laid-out archaeology museum is where Lárissa shows its true age, with rich displays of Palaeolithic and especially Neolithic (7th–4th millennium BC) artefacts and figurines, discovered on the surrounding plain. The bizarre Bronze Age two-sided menhir from Souflí Magoúla carved with a female figure laden with necklaces and triangular helmet is unlike anything else ever found in Greece. Other finds include a Mycenaean gold signet ring from the necropolises of Megálo Monastíri, on the road to Vólos. There are striking Archaic and Classic vases and steles, including one showing a breast-feeding mother, Roman reliefs and Early Christian mosaics, Byzantine jewellery and carvings, Christian, Jewish and Muslim tombs and charming murals from Ampelákia.

AROUND LÁRISSA

When the locals need to get in touch with nature, they don't have to go too far. The beaches and big mountain to the east – Óssa to ancient Greeks, but Kíssavos to most modern ones – don't get the same attention as its mountain neighbours Olympus and Pelion, but are all the better for it.

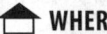
WHERE TO STAY

Panorama Suites & Spa (7 suites) Stómio; m 69349 99097; w panoramastomio.gr. Mykonos-style luxury & glamour, award-winning boutique suites, all with sea view & private pool, a spa & concierge service & gourmet restaurant (€€€€); 50m from the beach. **€€€€**
Archontikó Soulioti [map, page 304] (7 rooms) Metaxochóri, near Agiá; \ 24940 22040; m 69491 99657; w souliotismansion.com. Charming traditional mansion featuring antique-furnished rooms & an irresistible stone-paved terrace; they can offer good advice on local mountain walks & activities. **€€**
Ennéa Moúses (10 rooms) Ampelákia; \ 24950 93458. Traditional '9 Muses' hotel, by the square, but not always open. **€**

THESSALY (ΘΕΣΣΑΛΙΑ)

Xenonas 1963 [map, page 304] (7 rooms) 800m above Kókkino Néro Beach; 24950 92303. Handsome old stone guesthouse in a garden setting, with studios & self-catering apartment, a pool & hot spring bath, excellent restaurant (€€) & lovely owners, Julia & Markos. €

✖ WHERE TO EAT AND DRINK

Akrogiáli Stómio; 24950 91055; ⏰ 11.00–midnight daily. Classic seafood taverna right on the beach. €€

Bougázi Spiliá; 24950 71442; ⏰ 17.00–midnight Tue–Sun. Lovely food, including great roast potatoes & homemade desserts in the village centre. €€

Krasomana Rapsáni; 24950 61160; ⏰ 11.00–18.00 Tue–Fri, 09.00–midnight Sat, 09.00–20.00 Sun. Probably the nicest place to eat around the Vale of Tempe; typical taverna fare & great local wine in a lovely square with views. €€

Arioprino [map, page 304] 40km mark on the Karítsa–Spiliás road; m 69786 86734; f ArioprinoCafe; ⏰ spring–autumn 10.00–midnight Sun–Mon, 10.00–03.00 Fri–Sat. A very laid-back slice of old Greece in the oak forest. Limited menu, but good. €

O Platanos Ampelákia; 24950 93130; ⏰ 10.00–midnight daily. In the square, a place to dawdle in the dappled shade over the classics while quaffing the local wine. €

SPORTS AND ACTIVITIES Karítsa-based adventure company **Olympos Trek** (m 69325 45001; w olympostrek.gr) offers a wide range of activities: rafting on the Pineiós, rock climbing in the Vale of Tempe, canyoning in the Calypso Gorge, tours of the delta on mountain bikes, and more, for every level of fitness.

TÝRNAVOS (Τυρναβος; 17km northwest of Lárissa) Týrnavos is famous for its Tyranvou-Katsarou *tsípouro* distillery – the first company to produce ouzo, in 1856 – and its large Vlach community. It is known best of all, though, for Thessaly's biggest carnival, culminating on Sunday with a riotous parade of floats and masks, followed on Clean Monday by the Bouráni, a festival with not-so-distant echoes of ancient Greek fertility festivals (see below).

VALE OF TEMPE (Κοιλάδα των Τεμπών) Back in the Quaternary era, the great plain of Thessaly was a lake, until an earthquake opened a crack between mounts Óssa and Olympus. It wasn't long before the water thundered through, creating a 10km cleft – only 25m across at its narrowest point, with walls 500m high – that allowed the

> ### NOT SO CLEAN MONDAY
>
> Throughout Greece, Clean Monday is the day to fly kites and eat seafood. In Týrnavos, however, it's time to celebrate penises in every possible form – in phallus-shaped loaves of bread, lollipops, chocolates, candles and alcohol, sold in phallus-shaped bottles. The name comes from the spinach and vinegar soup *bouráni*, prepared by the men in a cauldron in the main square. All passers-by are dragged over, made to give it a stir and a taste with a shot of *tsípouro*, then made to kiss the giant phallus. There's a rocking penis throne to ride, with endless amounts of music, dancing, drinking, teasing and plenty of obscenities. You could be in a 5th-century BC Dionysia, although the custom was first recorded only in 1898. Until World War II, it was exclusively male, and included a lot of cross-dressing; it was considered too rude for daughters, wives and mothers to see. The military Junta banned it, but since then it's been more popular than ever – all good-natured fun for the entire family.

lake, now the Pineiós River, to drain into the sea. The ancients liked to imagine the mountains had been torn apart in the war of the gods and giants, when the giants tried to pile Pelion on Óssa to reach Olympus – hence the famous expression of futility. The lush glen entered myth again when Apollo was serving his eight years as the shepherd to Admetus (page 17) and spotted Daphne, daughter of the river god, bathing in the Pineiós, and fell in lust. As he pursued her, she begged the gods on nearby Olympus to save her, which they did, more permanently than she may have wished, by turning her into a laurel tree (*dafni*). Apollo plucked a branch and replanted it in Delphi, and used it to crown the victors of the Pythian Games; every nine years a messenger would come to Tempe to collect a new bunch.

The Vale of Tempe provided a convenient gate between southern and northern Greece, but it was a gate that could never be closed; attempts to block invaders (the Persians in 480BC, Alexander the Great in 336BC, the Romans in 168BC, Germans in 1941) never succeeded, because the invaders all too soon located the track inland to Gónnoi and turned the position.

The train tracks that once passed through the Vale are gone, but for decades the national road drowned out the nightingales in what was one of the most dangerous stretches of highway in Greece. In 2017, however, three tunnels, including the 6km T2 Tunnel – the longest in the Balkans – were completed with EU aid. There are several car parks along the now fairly quiet road, most of them near the suspension bridge crossing the Pineiós for the 13th-century chapel grotto of miracle-working **Ag Paraskeví**, patron saint of eyesight and of the Roma.

Near the south entrance to the glen, in the village of **Témpi** (Τέμπη), are the romantic ruins of **Hasa Baba Tekkés**, a Dervish monastery. From here a little mountain road winds up to **Rapsáni** (Ραψάνη), with its lovely views and PDO wine, renewed in the 1980s by the Tsántali family (page 49). A small **Wine Museum** (📞 24950 61259; ⏱ by appt) tells all.

To continue north to Mount Olympus, see page 129.

AMPELÁKIA (Αμπελάκια) Just before the Tempe toll booth, a narrow road on the right winds 5km up Óssa's west slope to pretty Ampelákia (population 480). The name means 'vineyards', but what has made the village a subject of international study was the founding, in 1780, of the world's first co-operative, the *koiné syntrophiá* ('common company'), by the producers of a glossy red cotton thread dyed with local madder roots which was in demand across Europe, especially in Germany and Austria. In its heyday, Ampelákia had 24 dyeing mills and a population of 6,000, most of whom were bilingual (one bylaw of the company provided that merchants should be sent abroad to learn languages). The co-operative even had an office in London.

Although it didn't last long – the Napoleonic Wars wreaked havoc on the trade and Ali Pasha's demands of 60,000 pilasters a year in tribute were too swingeing – you can get an idea of what it was like in its prime at the **Mansion of George Schwartz** (German for his name, Mávros; 📞 24950 93302; ⏱ 08.00–15.00 Wed–Mon; €5), built in 1787 by the president of the co-operative. Used as residence and the co-operative's headquarters, it's decorated with charming murals of real and imaginary landscapes, carved wood and stained glass from Vienna – a delightful mix of Balkan, Islamic and central European.

MOUNT ÓSSA (KISSAVOS) This 1,978m cone rising by the sea is a verdant botanical garden, much of it designated the Óssa Aesthetic Forest and special protection area by the Natura 2000 network. From **Spiliá** (Σπηλιά), a lush Greek village on the west slope, a good 11km road rises to the **Kíssavos Refuge** (1,604m; ⏱ open for groups on w/ends by pre-arrangement – call m 69799 88954; €), from where, without too much difficulty and in about 90 minutes, you can walk to the summit and its tiny chapel of Profítis Ilías for the sublime vision of Olympus in all its glory, the views stretching all the way to Mount Athos on a clear day.

Some 20 sand-and-pebble **beaches** dot the 50km coast under Kíssavos, starting to the north with busy **Kastrí Loutró** (Καστρί-Λουτρό) north of the evocative **Pineiós Delta** – where 200 species of bird have been counted – followed by little **Alexandriní** (Αλεξανδρινή) near the river itself. To continue south, you'll need to go by way of **Omólio** (Ομόλιο), with its bizarre top-heavy church, and aim for **Stómio** (Στόμιο), a small resort famous for its bottomless springs. Just up from Stómio is the once-isolated **Moní Ag Dimitríou** (\ 24950 91220; ⊕ call for hours; skirts below the knee for women, trousers for men, & shirts with sleeves for everyone), founded perhaps in the 6th century AD. An important hideout for fighters during the Greek War of Independence, it has recently been rebuilt, complete with crenellated walls and towers, around the katholikón with some fine old frescoes.

Two roads continue along the coast; along the lower one, a 10-minute walk through the trees, is the beautiful isolated beach of **Psarólakas** (Ψαρόλακας). The upper road goes by way of **Karítsa** (Καρίτσα), with a pretty main square and a gravel road, to the spectacular **Gorge of Calypso**, with a 70m waterfall and crystal pool, a favourite spot for canyoning.

Further south, the beach at **Platiá Ámmos** (Πλατιά Άμμος) is adorned with picturesque black boulders and plane trees that offer shade in the afternoon. Next south is much bigger **Kókkino Néro** (Κόκκινο Νερό; 'red water'), with big plane trees, a Byzantine bridge, and an outdoor spa gurgling reddish water full of iron hydroxides. And south of here is **Velíka** (Βελίκα), **Agiókambos** (Αγιόκαμπος) and **Káto Sotirítsa** (Κάτω Σωτηρίτσα), all part of what they claim is the longest (14km) beach in Greece.

Inland, the big farming town of **Agiá** (Αγιά) is 3km away from the 12th-century **Moní Ag Anargýron**. In a pretty woodland setting, the church has 17th-century frescoes, while above it steps climb the rock face to three older monasteries and hermitages, some with some sincere, if rather primitive, paintings (especially a Crucifixion scene) dating to the 12th century.

FÁRSALA (Φάρσαλα; 44km south of Lárissa) Fársala may well have been Homer's Phthia, the capital of Peleus and the Myrmidons and birthplace of Achilles. Although battered in an earthquake in 1954, there are some Mycenaean-era walls by the north gateway to the acropolis. A new park has a statue of Thetis baptising baby Achilles in the Apidános Springs; and there are the remains of a vaulted, possibly Mycenaean tomb on the west side of town, on Lamiás Street. The name may ring a bell: it was on the plain of Fársala, on 9 August 48BC that Julius Caesar, against the odds and outnumbered two to one, defeated Pompey and most of the Senators, and essentially ended the Roman Republic – although its final death knells, also decided in northern Greece, would be at Philippi (page 184) and Actium (page 293).

TEKKE DURBALI SULTAN (Asprógeia (Ασπρόγεια), 30km east of Fársala) There is something unexpected here, on a small mountain ridge overlooking the plain: the romantic ruins of a Dervish monastery founded in 1400 by mystic saint Durbali Sultan, on the site of an old church of St George. It grew to become an important centre of the Bektashi, an order of Sufi mystics founded in the 13th century, who 'picked the best flowers from each religion' including Christianity. In the late 19th century, 55 dervishes lived here, and it stood out as a peaceful example of religious tolerance and co-existence. When Atatürk banned the Sufis, the *tekke* was taken over by Albanian Bektashi until 1973, when the last abbot died. Still owned by the sect today, the little mosque and shrine with the tombs of the Sufi saints have been cared for by Albanians who arrived in Greece after the fall of Communism.

TRÍKALA

Due west of Lárissa on the edge of the Thessalian plain, Trίkala (Τρίκαλα; population 82,000) is a pleasant little, surprisingly leafy, city of bicycles, bustling squares, a pretty clock tower and a charming park along the Lithaíos, 'the river of forgetfulness', a tributary of the Pineiós, where swans swim. It has attractive old quarters, but Trίkala is also Greece's first tech-savvy 'smart city'. Young mayor Dimítris Papstergioú was elected in 2014 when Trίkala was €45 million in debt; four years later it was half that, thanks to his willingness to let tech providers trial new ideas here. One scheme was to use technology to grow ancient medicinal plants – in the spirit of Asclepius, the god of health, who was born in the nearby mountains and whose statue in the city centre keeps an eye on things. The current mayor is Nikolaos Sakkas, elected in 2023.

GETTING THERE AND AROUND Trίkala's **train** station is on the same line as Kardítsa and Kalambáka, which at the time of writing was being serviced by bus from the Paleofársala train station. The **bus station** (✆ 24310 71337; w ktel-trikala.gr) is 4km southeast on the ring road in Rizarío, with 8–12 buses running daily to Kalambáka (30mins; €2.90). Other links include frequent buses to Lárissa, Kardítsa, Athens and Thessaloníki, as well as three a day to Vólos, and one or two to Ioánnina. For local **taxis**, call ✆ 24310 22111 or ✆ 24310 22022.

 WHERE TO STAY *Map, page 314, unless otherwise stated*
Trίkala is 22km from Meteora and a good, less touristy, base.

Ananti City Resort [map, page 304] (18 rooms) Loggáki; ✆ 24310 63950; w anantiresort.gr. Sleek hotel isolated on a hill, 3.5km north of Trίkala, with great views from the balconies & deck of the infinity pool. There's also an indoor pool & spa; the rooftop cocktail bar & Oltre restaurant (€€€) look out over the glittering city lights. B/fast inc. €€€
Aeton Melathron (46 rooms) Neárchou 16; ✆ 24310 63130; w aetonmelathron.gr. Just off the ring road on the north side of the city, this splashy 4-star hotel has indoor & outdoor pools & sauna; free parking & good restaurant (€€). B/fast inc. €€€–€€
Gallery Art Hotel [map, page 304] (25 rooms) Lárissa–Kardítsa ring road; ✆ 24310 63990;

w galleryarthotel.gr. Smart, new 4-star hotel by the bus station with big art reproductions, bar & snack bar. B/fast inc. €€
Lithéon (57 rooms) Óthonos 16; ✆ 24310 20690; w litheonhotel.gr. Classic central hotel overlooking the river & giant plane trees, with bright renovated rooms & helpful staff. Near the central bus stop; free parking; b/fast inc. €€–€
Panellinion (22 rooms) Plateía Ríga Feréou; ✆ 24310 73545; w hotelpanellinion.com. Charming hotel with antique-furnished, high-ceilinged rooms (some on the small side) in a Neoclassical building of 1913, right in the heart of town. No elevator (as it's a listed building). €

 WHERE TO EAT AND DRINK *Map, page 314*
Trίkala's tavernas are concentrated in Manávika, the former market and red-light district.

Kókkini Svoúra GastroPUB Asklipioú 21; ✆ 24315 51077; Κόκκινη Σβούρα Gastro PUB; ⏰ 11.00–18.00 daily. The

place for lunch, with a short daily menu on the chalkboard, generous portions & all delicious. €€

10 | THESSALY (ΘΕΣΣΑΛΙΑ)

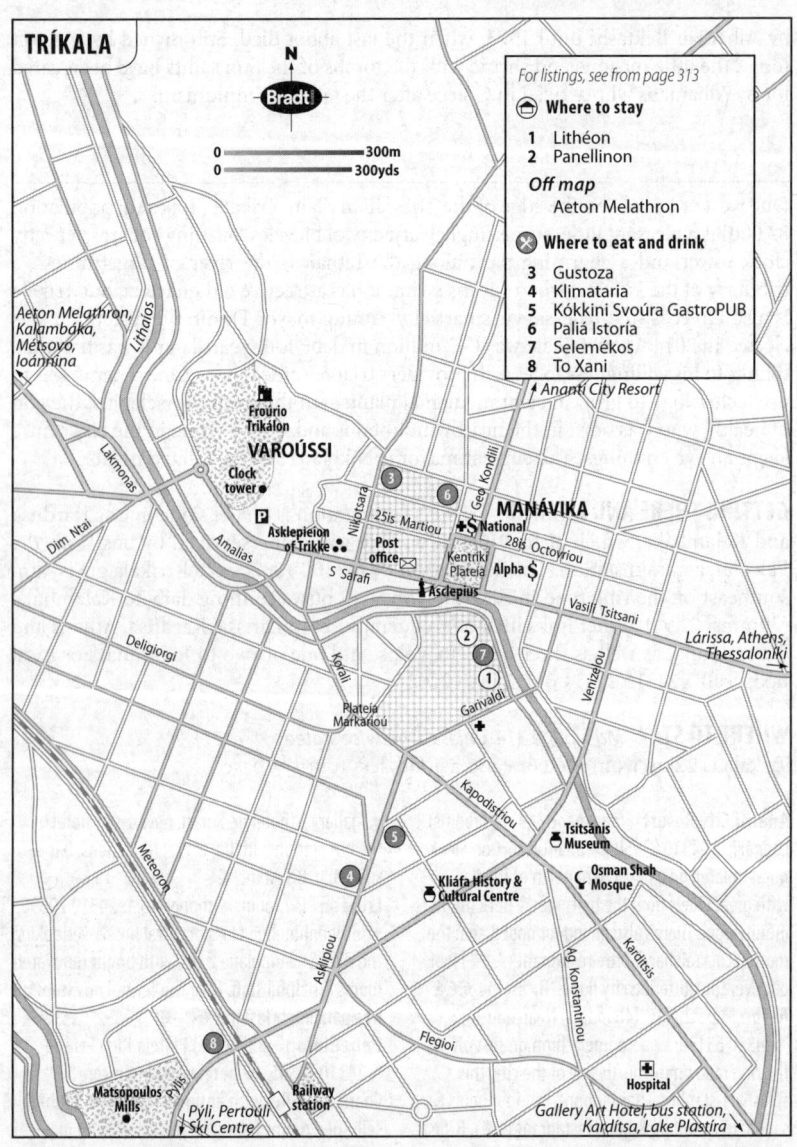

To Xani Pýlis 2; 24310 28502; w tavernatoxani.gr; ⏱ 13.00–23.00 daily. Old inn, near the railway station, for a lively night out, with a mix of traditional & less traditional dishes (baked stuffed potatoes, pork with cream & mushrooms), & superb meats, including treats for offal lovers. Good Greek wine list. €€

Gustoza Nikotsára 22; 24310 71606; w gustoza.blogspot.com; ⏱ 18.00–midnight Tue–Sun. Best pizzas in town, plus pasta dishes & salads. €

Klimataria Asklipioú 46; 24311 01576; ⏱ 11.30–04.00 daily. The place for *tsípouro* & nibbles & live *rebétika* music until late at night – just the thing after a visit to the Tsitsánis Museum (see opposite). €

Paliá Istoría Ipsilántou 3; 24310 77627; w palia-istoria.blogspot.com; ⏱ 12.30–23.30 Thu–Mon. Atmospheric traditional taverna, famous for its chicken pie. €

Selemékos Óthonos 10; `24310 22118;
⏲ 11.00–17.30 Mon–Fri, 11.00–16.30 Sat.
Choose from a daily selection of warm home-style

Greek comfort food classics from the glass case at this welcoming, casual spot. €

OTHER PRACTICALITIES
Alpha Bank Ir Alvanikoú Metópou 12
National Bank 28is Oktovriou 13
Hospital Kardítsis 56; `24313 50100
Pharmacy Dimitra Karaïskáki 46;
`24310 27277

Pharmacy Koulourídas Garïváldi 14;
`24310 20290
Post office S Safári 15

WHAT TO SEE AND DO
Froúrio Trikálon (S Saráfi 44; `24310 76647; ⏲ 08.30–15.30 daily; free) Justinian built this fortress in the 6th century AD over the ancient acropolis of Trikke, and it went through countless changes over the years. The Ottomans added the landmark **clock tower** that had to be rebuilt after World War II; inside are photos of old Tríkala, and steps up for the view over the city, at its most beautiful at sunset. **Varoússi**, the picturesque district just under the citadel with its mansions, was a posh residential quarter in Ottoman times.

Asclepeion of Trikke (Opposite the church of Ag Nikólaos on S Saráfi; `24310 76647; ⏲ closed for restoration at the time of writing, although some of it is visible from outside; due to reopen in 2028) Little remains of Ancient Trikke, outside of these Hellenistic foundations and part of a Roman bath in an overgrown field, all that survive of what Strabo described as the oldest Asclepeion in Greece.

Osman Shah Mosque (Daváki 6; `24310 76647; ⏲ during exhibitions) Also known as the Koursoum Mosque ('lead' mosque, for its dome) this is the only one in modern Greece built by the 16th-century master architect Mimar Sinan, who built many of the finest mosques in Istanbul. Osman Shah commissioned it in gratitude for a cure and was buried in the octagonal mausoleum next door. Inside (it has perfect acoustics) there are a few archaeological finds.

Tsitsánis Museum (Kardítsis 1; `24310 77977; w mouseiotsitsani.gr; ⏲ 09.00–15.30 daily; free) A must for any lover of Greek music: housed in a former Ottoman bath house and later prison, this museum and research centre honours Tríkala-born *rebétiko* composer and bouzouki maestro Vassílis Tsitsánis (1915–84), whose compositions changed the course of popular Greek music. There are interactive and audiovisual displays featuring Tsitsánis and his collaborators (including Theodorákis and Mános Hadjidákis) and some of his old 78s, too.

Kliáfa History and Cultural Centre (Cnr Ómirou & Themistokléous 12; `24310 23771; w kliafa.gr; ⏲ Oct–May 11.00–13.00 Mon–Fri, or by appt; free) Kliáfa, a soft drinks manufacturer and one of Tríkala's oldest companies, has moved into the suburbs, but the original factory built in 1926 now houses exhibits on the town's history and on the history of Kliáfa's fizzy pop, along with one of the world's biggest collections of bottle caps.

Matsópoulos Mills (Klinoú 10; ` 24310 20090; w mylosmatsopoulou.gr; ⏲ 09.00–16.00 Wed–Sun; free) Tríkala's flour mill (1884), located in the riverside park, was the first pasta factory in Greece and is now a cultural centre.

METEORA

The road from Trikala northwest to Kalambáka is mesmerisingly boring – until suddenly out of nowhere a forest of sandstone pillars appears, rising straight up from the valley floor. Eroded, iron grey and water scarred, their sometimes stubby, sometimes pointed pinnacles are visible for miles, and from a distance they look as two-dimensional as a cartoon backdrop. More than 800 smooth and windswept rocks, some over 360m high, cover 20km^2. Geologists drily call it debris left over from a primeval river delta that the earth pushed up to create a lofty, fault-filled plateau 60 million years ago, but it's really the mighty Pindus range's last and greatest conjuring trick, a spectacular geographical non sequitur, before it releases its spell on the landscape and subsides into the dull Thessalian plain.

Even if monks of old had not built in its improbable recesses and on its inaccessible peaks, the area would still be visited for the sheer grandeur of its scenery. Meteora (Μετέωρα) means 'things hovering in the air' – as in meteor – as apt a name for the rocks themselves as it is for the stupendous and unforgettable monasteries that crown them. Hiking among the rocks is magical, and, if you're very lucky, you might see a critically endangered Egyptian vulture – one of the last breeding pairs nests in the pinnacles.

Two villages provide the closest base for visiting: big bustling **Kalambáka** (Καλαμπάκα), formerly the Byzantine town of Stagoi, renamed 'strong castle', *kale mpak* in Turkish – but burned to the ground by the Germans in 1943 – and traditional, smaller **Kastráki** (Καστράκι) closer to the monasteries. It is marvellously photogenic, but what you won't see in most pictures are the dozens of tour buses parked under each monastery and the long snaking queues trundling up the steps. Try to go early in the day or out of season.

HISTORY The magical setting first attracted people 130,000 years ago; the cave of Theópetra (3km south of Kalambáka) is famous for its extraordinarily long period of human habitation. But what is bizarre, given the ancient Greek penchant for telling stories about every river, spring and mountain, is that, as far as anyone knows, Meteora was never mentioned in antiquity. Not once.

It was, however, a magnet for spiritual athletes: a ragtag group of misanthropic hermits came seeking salvation in Meteora's clefts and caves, perhaps as early as the 8th century AD, although no-one mentioned them until the 11th century. A small proto-monastic community developed at Doúpiani (present-day Kastráki), and built a small church to serve their few communal liturgical needs. Then, in 1336, Athanásios, a monk from Athos, founded the Great Meteora, the first monastery set at the very summit of the pinnacles themselves.

This and subsequent monasteries were coenobitic, which stressed hierarchical communal living – the kind of monasticism preferred by the Orthodox church to wild-eyed hermits in lonely caves who often ignored or, worse, challenged the church's authority and its more worldly approach to salvation. As these grander monuments to Orthodoxy sprang up, the hermits might have been forgiven for doubting whether the absence of solitude and conspicuous wealth made Holy Contemplation any easier.

The monasteries got an improbable boost in the Middle Ages during the short-lived Serbian interlude in Thessaly, thanks to the piety of their kings. Under the Ottomans, after serious initial setbacks, Meteora recovered and by the reign of Suleiman the Magnificent (1520–66) there were 13 substantial monasteries, replete with wooden galleries, corniced rooftops, and frescoed katholikóns, along with 20 smaller establishments. The second most important clutch of Orthodox monasteries after Athos

METEORA

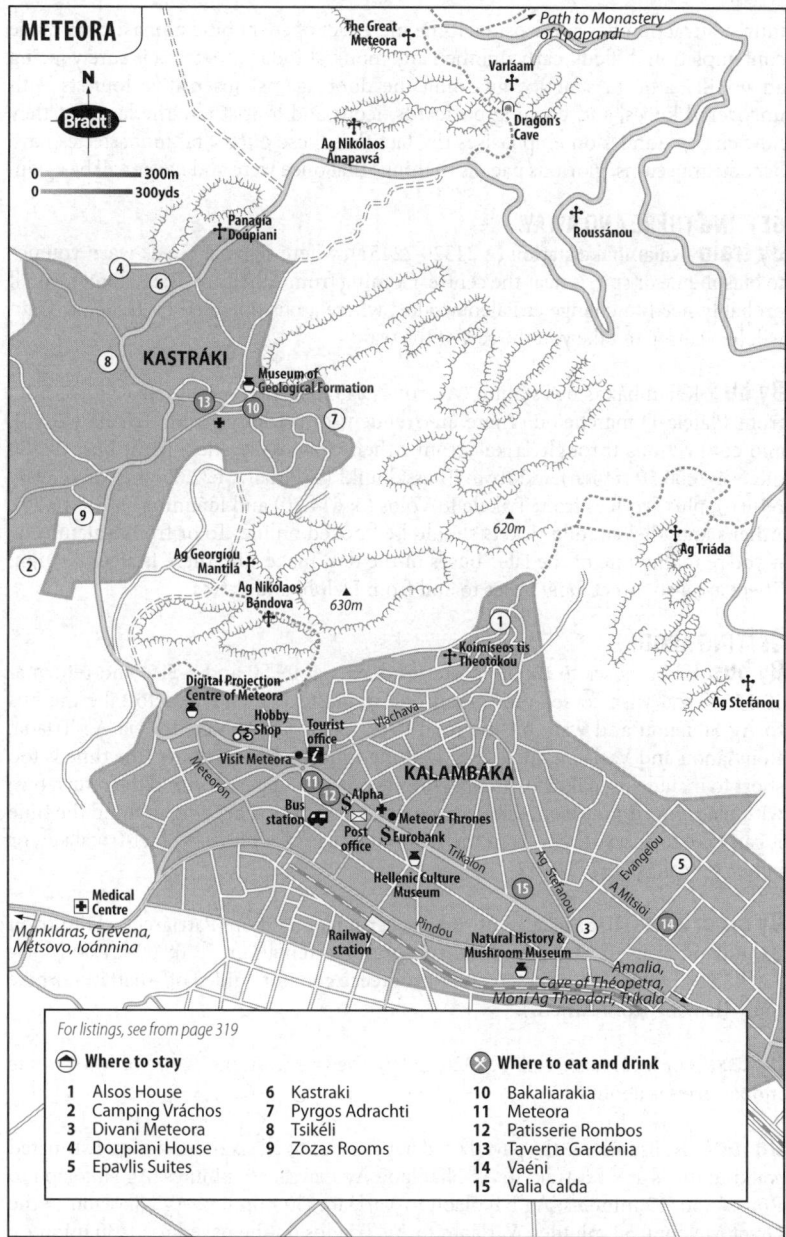

For listings, see from page 319

Where to stay
1 Alsos House
2 Camping Vráchos
3 Divani Meteora
4 Doupiani House
5 Epavlis Suites
6 Kastraki
7 Pyrgos Adrachti
8 Tsikéli
9 Zozas Rooms

Where to eat and drink
10 Bakaliarakia
11 Meteora
12 Patisserie Rombos
13 Taverna Gardénia
14 Vaéni
15 Valia Calda

itself, they were well endowed by princes hoping for salvation, owning lands as far away as Moldavia and Wallachia. Ironically, their decline began with Greek independence in 1830. The new state did not include Thessaly, leaving the monasteries suspended in the Ottoman Empire, as many monks abandoned them for the new Greek state.

The six survivors (two are now convents), the massif and the village of Kastráki are now a UNESCO World Heritage Site, but Meteora's renaissance as a mega

317

tourist attraction has a downside. If the mere fact of coenobitic monasticism made contemplation difficult early on, then any monk at today's Meteora is surely facing an uphill battle to sanctity, guarding the door against insensitive tourists with uncovered knees, and flogging postcards, icons and tourist tat. The fact that they now charge admission emphasises the fact that these once vital monasteries have become museums, glorious paeans to things that once were and never will be again.

GETTING THERE AND AWAY
By train Kalambáka station (\ 24320 22451), where signs in Greek warn you not to blaspheme or spit, is near the centre. Coming from Athens or Thessaloníki, you'll probably need to change at Paleofarsálos, where a bus operated by Hellenic Train will be waiting to take you the rest of the way.

By bus Kalambáka's bus station (Avérof; \ 24320 22432; w ktel-trikala.gr) is 50m from Plateía Dimarcheíou. There are frequent direct buses from Tríkala (€2.90), and connections through Tríkala from Athens (5–6 daily, inc a night bus; €32.50 one way/€56.50 return) and from Thessaloníki (4–6 daily; €22.60 one way/€39.00 return), plus services from Tríkala to Vólos (3; €14.70) and Ioánnina (1–3; €16.70). Athens and Thessaloníki tickets should be booked online. To or from Kalambáka, if you're taking one of the later buses of the day, make sure there is a connection. There are also direct daily buses to and from Delphi and Pátras.

GETTING AROUND
By bus KTEL buses to the monasteries depart at 09.00 and 12.15, and return at 13.15. If you wish to see more than one monastery, it's advised to take the bus to Ag Stefánou and walk on the road back to the Great Meteora via Ag Triáda, Roussánou and Varláam, for a total walking time of about 2 hours (the time is too short to include Ag Nikólaos Anapavsá). It's only about 4 hours until the return bus; with planning, it may be possible to see two monasteries, keeping in mind the time it can take to access them from the road. See bus schedules at w ktel-trikala.gr, or better yet call \ 24320 22432.

By car or bike Hire a bike, motorbike or car at Hobby Shop (Patriárchou Dimitríou 28, Kalambáka; \ 24320 25262; w meteora-bike-rentals.gr; ⊕ 08.00–21.00 Mon–Sat, 08.00–14.00 Sun). Also see w endurogreece.com for guided off-road motorbike tours (leaving from Athens).

By taxi For local taxis, call \ 24320 22310; the fare from the centre of town to the monasteries is about €12.

On foot Trails that use the paved road in places go to all six monasteries. Estimated walking times are: Kastráki to Ag Nikólaou Anapavsá, 30 minutes; Ag Nikólaou to Roussánou, 15 minutes; Ag Nikólaou to Varláam, 30 minutes; Ag Nikólaou to the Great Meteora, 50 minutes; Varláam to Ag Triádos on the paved road, 30 minutes; Ag Triádos to Ag Stefánou, 20 minutes. From the northeast corner of town, at the end of Kleisoúras Street, there is a spot to leave a couple of cars. From here, a well-defined trail ascends through the woods to Ag Triáda monastery. The walk to the monastery takes about 50 minutes at a relaxed pace, but it's quite steep in places. As the path is mainly stone, hiking shoes will be more comfortable than trainers. It's a beautiful hike, and a fitting way to reach a place that belongs to a distant past. The last portion of the climb from the main road is the most dramatic of all, with steps

METEORA

carved into the side of the mountain. If you continue from here, note that nearby Ag Stefánou closes at 13.00–15.00 in winter, and 13.30–15.30 in summer.

Accessibility Of all the monasteries, Ag Stefánou is the most accessible for people with limited mobility, with direct access almost to the door by car, but there are some stairs in the monastery itself.

TOURIST INFORMATION AND TOUR OPERATORS The **tourist office** (cnr Vlachává & Patriárchou Dimitríou; ✆ 24323 50245; w infotouristmeteora.gr; ⊕ May–Oct 08.00–21.00 Mon–Fri, 09.00–16.00 Sun) is in Kalambáka. Check the website for up-to-date opening hours.

The two tour operators on page 32 also offer packages from Athens and Thessaloníki.

Meteora Thrones Trikálon 28, Kalambáka; ✆ 24320 78455; w meteora.com. Tours, hikes, sunset & VIP private tours.

Visit Meteora Patriárchou Dimitríou 2, Kalambáka; ✆ 24320 23820; w visitmeteora. travel. Offers hiking, cave, & sunset tours.

 WHERE TO STAY *Map, page 317, unless otherwise stated*
Hotels are open all year, and bargains can be had outside of July and August.

Kalambáka

Divani Meteora (54 rooms) National road; ✆ 24320 23330; w divanimeteorahotel.com. At the east end of the village; queen-size beds, wooden floors & views of the rocks, plus outdoor & indoor pools & a spa. Buffet b/fast inc. €€€

Epavlis Suites Hotel (6 rooms) Koumariés; ✆ 24320 24830; w hotel-epavlis.gr. Quiet garden location amid the rocks, up a narrow road, with great views down over Kalambáka. Friendly, family-run mini-suites sleeping up to 5. Dinners available by request; b/fast inc. €€€–€€

Amalia [map, page 304] (172 rooms) 6km out of town on the Tríkala road; ✆ 24320 72216; w amaliahotels.com/meteora. As much personality as an airport, but set in a large garden with 4-star comforts, a big pool, lovely views of the rocks & restaurants. Popular with groups. B/fast inc. €€

Alsos House (10 rooms) Kanári 5; ✆ 24320 24097; w alsoshouse.gr. Recently renovated, simple rooms with balcony, & free private parking. B/fast inc. €€–€

Kastráki

Tsikéli (14 rooms) Metéoron 59; ✆ 24320 22438; w tsikelihotel.gr. Rooms, lawn & tables for the view & nice owners. B/fast inc. Adults only. €€€–€€

Doupiani House (9 rooms) Off the main road; ✆ 24320 75326; w doupianihouse.gr. A winner, in a quiet spot, with panoramic views & comfy traditional rooms. If you can't get a room here, go for a coffee on its terrace. B/fast inc. €€

Kastraki (27 rooms) On the main road; ✆ 24320 75336; w hotelkastraki.gr. Modern & comfortable. Try to get an upper room with the view. Buffet b/fast inc. €€

Pyrgos Adrachti (10 rooms) Off the main road; ✆ 24320 22275; w hotel-adrachti.gr. Near the highest spot in Kastráki, with very helpful owners & renovated, if smallish, rooms with gorgeous views of the rocks. B/fast inc. €€

Camping Vráchos On the main road; ✆ 24320 22293; w campingkastraki.com. On the outskirts of Kastráki with a pool, lots of shade & views. €

Zozas Rooms (15 rooms) On the main road; ✆ 24320 24408; w zozas.gr. Simple woodsy rooms 5mins from the centre, nice bar, parking. Excellent b/fast €5. €

✖ **WHERE TO EAT AND DRINK** *Map, page 317, unless otherwise stated*

Kalambáka

Meteora Trikálon 2; ✆ 24320 22316; w meteora-restaurant.gr; ⊕ noon–21.30 daily. Great collection of Greek & other knick-knacks to ponder while dining on well-prepared Greek classics. Locals love this place, too. €€

Vaéni A Mitsíoi; 24320 24915; ⏰ noon–midnight daily. Stands out for the giant wine barrel over the door & pleasant terrace; usually grilled meats, but don't miss the grilled mushrooms if they're on the menu. €€

Patisserie Rombos Trikálon 16; 24320 22269; ⏰ 08.00–22.00 daily. For 4 generations, this family has been making the finest rich, buttery *halvah sapouné* around, using all-local ingredients – goat butter, cornstarch, almonds, & even the sugar. €

Valia Calda Trikálon 91; m 69755 91006; w valia-calda.gr; ⏰ noon–23.00 daily. Good place for vegetarian & vegan dishes, along with meat choices, & mushrooms in season. €

Kastráki

Bakaliarakia Near Ag Pétrou church; 24320 23170; ⏰ noon–23.00 Mon–Sat. Grilled meats & potatoes but also excellent moussaka & house wine, & very nice owner. €€

Mankláras [map, page 304] On the Ioánnina road, just north of Kastráki; 24320 22677; ⏰ 13.00–21.00 Mon–Thu, 13.00–22.00 Fri, 13.00–23.00 Sat, 13.00–19.00 Sun. Going strong since 1958 – rustic setting, friendly folk & fresh good food, some of the best in the area. €€

Taverna Gardénia Agiou Athanasíou, near the Museum of Geological Formations; m 69727 00698; f; ⏰ midnight–23.00 daily. Grilled meats, salads, & homestyle specialities. A local favourite. €€

SPORTS AND ACTIVITIES Meteora is a big **rock-climbing** centre and, although it is technically illegal in some areas, you'll often see figures inching up the rocks' smooth surfaces or bouncing down their vertical walls on flimsy ropes. Visit Meteora (page 319) offers guided experiences, with all equipment provided. Meteora's unique rocks go as far north as Gávros, and there are wonderful **hiking trails** throughout the area. Both Meteora Thrones and Visit Meteora offer hiking tours. To strike out on your own, see the routes provided at w infotouristmeteora.gr (click on 'Activities'). Note that some routes will not be in shade – wear a hat, bring plenty of water, and take care not to venture out in the heat of the day, nor in dangerous winter conditions.

OTHER PRACTICALITIES

Alpha Bank Trikálon 26, Kalambáka
Eurobank Trikálon 42, Kalambáka
Medical Centre Southeast off the E92; 24323 50000. The nearest hospital is in Tríkala (page 315).
Meteora Pharmacy Trikalon 5, Kalambáka; 24320 22230

Pharmacy Tsarouha Eleftheria Ep Odo Kalambáka, Kastráki (near Taverna Gardénia); 24320 24266
Post office Trikálon 22, Kalambáka; ⏰ 07.30–14.30 Mon–Fri

WHAT TO SEE AND DO

Digital Projection Centre of Meteora (Cnr P Dimitríou & N Plastíra, Kalambáka; 24320 77997; ⏰ 35min shows every hr 09.00–16.00; €3, under 18s €2) The centre provides a popular introduction to the area: don 3D glasses to watch the virtual formation of Meteora and the history of its monasteries. Children are very welcome.

Koimíseos tis Theotókou (At the top of Mitropóleos St, Kalambáka; 24320 24962; ⏰ summer 09.00–13.00 & 15.00–20.00 daily, winter 09.00–noon & 14.00–18.00 daily) The Nazi destruction in 1943 spared this splendid 10th-century Byzantine church – one that most visitors miss in their rush to the monasteries. The interior is completely covered with murals from the 12th–16th centuries, including some by the sons of the great painter Theophánis of Crete, along with a beautiful iconostasis, parts of an early mosaic floor, and an unusual double-stair marble pulpit in the nave.

Hellenic Culture Museum (Cnr Chazpétrou & Meg Alexandroú, Kalambáka; 24323 75219; w bookmuseum.gr; ⏰ temporarily closed at the time of writing; call or check website for hours & entrance fees upon reopening) Greek education and literacy are the themes here, so expect a lot of books – including a copy of the first printed one exclusively in Greek. There's also a room of drawings and paintings of Meteora, and another dedicated to the fables of Aesop, a reconstructed classroom and more, much with English translations.

Natural History and Mushroom Museum (Píndou 20, Kalambáka; 24320 24959; w meteoramuseum.gr; 10.00–17.00 Mon–Fri, 10.00–18.00 Sat & Sun; €7, ages 4–18 & over 65s €5) This new museum has dramatic dioramas of local wildlife and, on the top floor, Greece's first mushroom museum with a weirdly fascinating collection of every local fungus, along with fun facts such as Ötzi the Ice Man used mushrooms to start fires and control parasites.

The museum also sponsors truffle-hunting expeditions. Specially trained truffle dogs lead the hunt, which is followed by a festive meal of mushroom and truffle pasta, cooked in the woods and covered with shavings of the day's discoveries. These excursions are organised from March to November; to check dates and to reserve, visit w meteoramuseum.gr/truffle-hunting. The price is around €60 per person, including lunch and local wines. Back at the museum, you can stock up on a variety of dried local mushrooms and truffle oil in their excellent shop.

Cave of Théopetra Documentation Centre (3km southwest of Kalambáka; 24320 72196; call for current hours) Local shepherds used to shelter their flocks in this cave near the Lithaíos River, never suspecting they were in a major archaeological site. Dr Nina Kyparíssi-Apostolíka, who excavated it between 1987 and 2007, found that it had been continuously inhabited from the Middle Palaeolithic (130,000BC) to the late Neolithic (3000BC) period – a record only matched by the Fránchthi Cave in the Peloponnese. A wall at the cave's entrance dates from c21,000BC, making it the oldest structure in Greece, and perhaps the world. Footprints of Neanderthal children were preserved when they walked in the ashes of a fire. Other finds include tools, pottery, bones and traces of seeds – offering clues on climate change. Recently they extracted DNA from a pair of Mesolithic tibias. The cave itself has been closed since 2016 due to a rock fall, but finds from inside are exhibited at the small documentation centre, accompanied by a short film, making for a brief yet worthwhile stop.

Museum of Geological Formation (Cnr Plateía Pétrou & Pávlou, Kastráki; 24320 22523; 08.00–15.00 Mon–Fri, 09.00–16.00 Sat & Sun; free) Kastráki's handsome old primary school reopened in 2018 as an interesting museum covering Meteora's past 30 million years, with videos and a series of well-presented displays, minerals and fossils.

THE MONASTERIES Monastery hours can fluctuate – check current hours with the tourist office (page 319) or with the individual monasteries you plan to visit.

Ag Nikólaos Anapavsá (24320 22375; Apr–Oct 09.00–17.00 Sat–Thu, Nov–Mar to 15.00; €5) This monastery was built by Dionysios, bishop of Lárissa, in the 16th century over the foundations of an older building. The katholikón (1527) in the centre of every monastery, symbolising the church as the centre of the human cosmos, traditionally faces east, but here it faces north; Meteora's topography required some rearrangements. Restored in 1960, its frescoes by Theophánis the Cretan are exquisite, and include one of the most charming scenes in Byzantine art,

VISITING THE MONASTERIES

Until the 1920s, many monasteries hauled visitors up in nets attached to winches; the 'flight' distance up Varláam was 373m, the flight time interminable. The classic reply to queries at how often the monasteries replaced the rope was 'When they break.' Handholds in the rocks, along with precarious rope or wooden articulated ladders were also employed. Supplies are still winched up, but roads, bridges and stairs chiselled into the rocks have made today's ascent a lot easier.

As per usual when visiting Greek monasteries, dress modestly. Both men and women should cover their knees and upper arms. For women, this means skirts or dresses (not trousers); shawls and skirts to be worn over clothing are handed out at the monasteries. Men should wear long trousers and shirts with sleeves.

Adam Naming the Animals. A footpath to Varláam just up the road leads to the base of Varláam's pinnacle for a look at the 90m-deep **Dragon's Cave**.

Roussánou (24320 22649; Apr–Oct 09.00–15.30 Tue–Thu, 09.00–15.00 Sun, Nov–Mar 09.30–14.00 Thu–Tue; €5) Dedicated to St Barbara, Roussánou looks as if it grew straight out of its rock pedestal; a frighteningly narrow bridge built in 1868 between two mini peaks replaced an earlier, even scarier approach. Founded in 1545 by Maximos and Joseph of Ioánnina, with art from 1560, it is now a convent with 13 nuns, whose new kitchen inside the entrance nicely highlights an ongoing dilemma for monasticism. How much of the modern world should this conservative institution embrace? Formica and spiffy new kitchen cupboards look wildly incongruous after the gruesome frescoes in the katholikón (the nuns' habits haven't changed much, though).

Varláam (24320 22277; Apr–Oct 09.00–16.00 Sat–Thu, Nov–Mar 09.00–15.00 Sat–Wed; €5) The second-largest monastery, now home to seven monks, Varláam is wonderful. Founded in 1517 by Theophánis and Nektários Apsarádas from Ioánnina, it was named after the hermit who originally built on the spot. Its 195 stairs were added in 1932, and its overhanging tower room contains a windlass and rope, next to a tiny lift. The katholikón (1544) has a carved and gilded iconostasis, frescoes by Frángos Katelános, and two charming cupolas, one in the main body of the church and one in the narthex. Varláam has a fascinating museum in the old refectory, with relics, ecclesiastical treasures and explanations of the monks' lives, featuring a great collection of old photos and a documentary filmed in Meteora in 1924 – including a scene of a monk with a mallet banging the *semantra*, the flat wooden beam all the monasteries have, said to replicate the 'bell' Noah used to summon the animals to the Ark.

The Great Meteora (24320 22278; w meteoromonastery.gr; Apr–Oct 09.30–15.00 Wed–Mon, Nov–Mar 09.30–14.00 Fri–Mon; €5) Sprawling over Platýs Líthos (flat rock), this is the big one, and well worth the trek up its 146 steps. It's the most popular among visitors, who keep its few monks busy. Founded by Ag Athanásos, who flew here on the back of an eagle, it's officially dedicated to the Transfiguration (Moní Metamórphoseos tou Kyríou). Its privileges were guaranteed in 1362 by Serbian emperor Symeon Uros, whose son, taking the name of Joásaph, became a monk here and built the first katholikón, at his own expense, in 1387–88; subsequent alterations never needed to be done on the cheap. Joásaph's original church is now the *ierón* behind the iconostasis of the 16th-century katholikón – the incorporation of older structures within newer ones, like so many Russian dolls, is common in Byzantine monasteries.

The cross-in-square katholikón under its lofty 12-sided dome was beautifully frescoed by Theophánis and his workshop, completed in 1552. The pictures are exquisite and well preserved: in the narthex, they depict all the gruesome details of the Roman persecution of the Christians, while the saints line up along the walls in the nave. On the pilasters, you can pick out the two founding fathers, Athanásos and Joásaph, each holding a model of the monastery.

On the north side of the katholikón, the vaulted refectory (c1557) is now a history and folk art museum. A seashell incense burner is one of its less serious exhibits; others cover the role of the Orthodox church in resisting the Nazis. The domed kitchen is interesting, as is the library, noted for its 640 fine manuscripts, codices – the oldest date back to AD861 – chrysobulls from various emperors and a rare printed volume of the Greek classics by Aldus of Venice. The cellar has a carpenter's workshop, with rare old wine barrels.

Before leaving, consider the 30-minute path to the restored 14th-century church of the long-gone **Monastery of Ypapandí**, tucked in a small cavern. A path leads up to the statue of the *klepht* Thýmios Vlachávas, who organised an uprising against the Ottomans in 1808 but was betrayed and captured by Ali Pasha; chances are you'll have the views all to yourself.

Ag Triáda (✆ 24320 22220; ⊕ 10.00–16.00 Fri–Wed; €5) Farther east, on an isolated 400m pillar with ravines on both sides, this 15th-century monastery will look familiar to James Bond fans, who will recognise the spectacular backdrop for some of the skulduggery in *For Your Eyes Only*, when it played the villain's lair. The 140-or-so-step approach is mostly through a tunnel, offering some relief for vertigo sufferers. A plinth on the outer wall of the church states it was built in the year 6984 since the creation of the world (1475); the small chapel of St John the Baptist (1682) has gorgeous paintings, as does the katholikón (the main chapel); take particular note of prophets in their dynamic, expressive poses – a departure from the impassive quality that characterises much Byzantine iconography – in the first dome. Four monks hold the fort.

Ag Stefánou (✆ 24320 22279; ⊕ Apr–Oct 09.00–13.20 & 15.30–17.30 Tue–Sun, Nov–Mar 09.30–13.00 & 15.00–17.00 Tue–Sun; €5) High on its pinnacle, the easternmost monastery (now a convent with 24 nuns) is separated by a deep gorge from the road; the two rocks are connected by a bridge, making this the easiest monastery to access. It was bombed during World War II by the Nazis, who suspected it was sheltering Resistance fighters, then abandoned and partially rebuilt, so it has a newer look. The fabulous view out over Kalambáka and the plain beyond is alone worth the journey. Its church of Ag Stefánou (c1350) has a timbered roof, some gold-leaf wood carvings, and wall paintings (c1545) by a local priest, Ioánnis of Stagoi. The katholikón, dedicated to Ag Charálambos (c1798), contains the said saint's skull, a gift of Vladislav of Wallachia. The templon (iconostasis) of 1814 is the work of master carvers from Metsovo, while the expressive interior was painted by the contemporary iconographer Vlasios Tsotsónis.

A distant dependency of Ag Stefánou, the 18th-century **Moní Ypséseos Timíou Stavró** (44km west at Doliáná, just north of Kranía (Κρανία); ⊕ Apr–Oct 10.00–18.00 Thu–Tue; free) is one of the most unusual churches in Greece. Nicknamed the 'Acropolis of Aspropotámos', it is built entirely of stone and punctuated by 13 tall domes. Although the rest of the monastery was burned down by the Germans, the church has been lovingly restored by the locals, and stands alone amid the pines, very much like an illustration in a fairy tale.

Around the main monasteries

Panagía Doúpiani (On the way to Ag Nikólaos Anapavsá) In the 12th century when the hermits felt the need to descend from their caves to worship together on holidays, they built this little stone chapel, decorated with 13th-century paintings.

Ag Georgíou Mantilá (South of Kastráki) 'St George of the Scarves' is located in a cleft in the sheer rock, instantly recognisable by what looks like a laundry line hanging at the entrance. The story goes that, in the 17th century, a Muslim man cut down a tree near the hermitage, but the tree fell on him, gravely wounding him. When his wife despaired, the locals told her that the trees were sacred to St George but that the saint might help if she offered something. All she had to give was her headscarf – and a few days later her husband was able to walk again. Ever since then, others have left brightly coloured scarves, and every St George's Day (23 April, unless that day falls during Lent, in which case it is celebrated on Easter Monday), locals gather as the youth of Kastráki use ropes to climb the cliff, carrying new scarves to replace the old ones, then sing and dance.

Ag Nikólaos Bándova Not all the monks lived on monoliths. The track in the gorge between Kastráki and Kalambáka leads to one of the original dependencies or *skete* of Ag Triáda, an impressive, recently restored monastery tucked in a ledge in a sheer cliff.

Moní Ag Theodori (4km southeast of Kalambáka; ✆ 24320 72716; ⊕ summer 08.00–13.00 & 16.00–19.00 daily, winter 08.00–noon & 16.00–18.00 daily) Anywhere else, this remarkable four-storey monastery teetering on a rock would be a major sight, but in Meteora it looks almost tame. Built in the 16th century, it was restored in 1999 and is now inhabited by nuns.

WEST OF TRÍKALA: PÝLI, ELÁTI AND PERTOÚLI

West of Trikala rise the jagged peaks of **Mount Kóziakas** (1,901m). Rather than head straight to Meteora, you can take a more picturesque, wiggly route on the EO30 via Pýli, a river town at the mouth of a narrow gorge under a vertiginous wall of the Central Pindus range. This is also the back gate to Lake Plastíra (page 327); the 20km drive through the mountains is a much nicer prelude to this pocket Eden than the highway from Kardítsa.

WHERE TO STAY AND EAT

Chatzigáki Manor (36 rooms) Pertoúli; ✆ 24340 91146; w chatzigaki.gr. This stone manor house has been transformed into a 5-star hotel with rustic-chic rooms, garden & terrace complete with mountain views. Beds are king-size, & there's an outdoor pool & fitness centre, excellent restaurant (€€) & staff, plus a playroom for the little ones. B/fast inc. €€€–€€

Giamandes (16 rooms) Eláti; ✆ 24340 71749; w giamandes.gr. Quiet hotel near the village entrance; large rooms come with sat TVs, wooden floors & mountain views; a hammam, sauna & jacuzzi await sore muscles. €€

Kroupi (14 rooms) Eláti; ✆ 24340 71312; w kroupi.gr. Simple lodgings just outside the centre, including apartments sleeping up to 5 with

WEST OF TRÍKALA: PÝLI, ELÁTI AND PERTOÚLI

magnificent views. The friendly owners are a font of local knowledge. €

Anavrusoúla [map, page 304] Km60 on the Pýli–Eláti road; ☏ 24340 71085; m 69727 04606; f anavrisoula; ⊕ noon–23.00 daily. Taverna with a trout farm, where they also make their own wine & *tsípouro*. Excellent pies & grilled meats, too. €€

Kanavia Eláti; ☏ 24340 71201; ⊕ 13.00–23.00 Thu–Tue. Better-than-average taverna fare brings customers back again & again. Don't miss the stewed dishes such as *kókkaras krasáto* (Greek coq au vin) if available; also mushrooms, including morels in season. €

SPORTS AND ACTIVITIES Pertoúli Ski Centre (Pertouliótika Livádia; ☏ 24340 91382; ⊕ Dec–Mar) has 2km of slopes (1,170–1,370m), three lifts, and three cross-country runs, and also offers snowboarding and night skiing. On the last weekend in June, it hosts the 'Gathering of the Sarakatsáni' (page 165) with traditional costumes, music, and dancing. **Pertoúli Extreme Sports** (m 69817 64200; w pertouliextremesports.gr) has horseriding, snowmobiles, and bikes for exploring the mountains, plus archery.

WHAT TO SEE AND DO Pýli (Πύλη; 16km southwest of Trikala) means 'gate'; its pretty **stone bridge** across the Portaíkos River, built in 1514 by Ag Vissaríon (St Bessarion II, bishop of Lárissa), may now be just a photo opportunity but was once part of a major highway in Byzantine times – the only route from the great plain of Thessaly to Árta and the South Pindus range. The village winery, **Kelári Pergantí** (m 69839 43028; ⊕ 09.00–14.00 & 17.00–20.00 Mon–Sat), makes some unusual wines, *tsípouro* and the Greek version of balsamic vinegar.

Across the modern bridge (or across the stone bridge and following the trail), **Pórta Panagía** (⊕ 11.00–17.00 Thu–Tue) is a small hodgepodge of a church founded on the site of an ancient temple in 1283 by Ioánnis Doukas, the Despot of Epirus, and once the katholikón of a long-gone monastery. The Despot liked the church well enough to be buried in it; a fresco over his tomb shows him in monkish gear being led to Paradise. Its mosaics, especially of the Virgin and Christ, are renowned, albeit the worse for wear after a fire in 1855. Mary stands on Christ's right, an unusual honour; both mosaics are offset by attractive marble frames. The domed narrow ceiling is still impressive.

Some 5km northwest, straight up a dirt road, **Ag Vissaríon (Dousíkou)** (☏ 24340 22420; ⊕ 08.00–noon & 15.30–19.00 daily; men only) has terrific views of the plain. A mere hour's drive from Meteora, Ag Vissaríon is worlds apart: this is the real McCoy, a fully functioning monastery. Founded in 1530, it's an austere square fortress, equipped with 366 cells, one for each day of the year. Only the maroon-and-white cupolas of its katholikón add a little whimsy; inside are excellent 16th-century frescoes and an 18th-century gilded iconostasis carved by artisans in Métsovo. By the outer wall, just beyond the old windlass gallery, a tiny trout fishery has been made out of an old water tank. The monks eat no meat, so the trout and their garden make them almost self-sufficient. Admission is forbidden to women, a rule written into the founder's will; the monks swear that every time the rule was violated, catastrophes occurred. A stone chapel has been built outside the gate for women to attend Mass; the saint is renowned locally for his cures.

Signposted just before Káto Palaiokaryá (Κάτω Παλαιοκαρυά), 10km west of Pýli on the Árta road, is **Palaiokaryá Bridge and Waterfall**. This is the bridge you see on the brochures: a great arching stone bridge with a sparkling waterfall behind, and another, smaller, one in front of it, in a bucolic setting perfect for a picnic or swim, although you won't linger – it's icy cold.

The mountain road winds up to **Eláti** (Ελάτη; 950m) and **Pertoúli** (Περτούλι; 1,150m). Both had to be rebuilt after 1943 but are now little mountain resorts; the lush meadows near the ski centre make a lovely spot for a picnic amid the grazing horses, cows and deer.

KARDÍTSA

The town with the sweetest name, Kardítsa (Καρδίτσα; the 'little heart') is the main gateway to Lake Plastíra. It's a smaller version of Tríkala, with a small university, lovely park, and friendly residents who get around on bikes. The old livestock fair in the centre is now the charming Paysílypo Park, where friendly squawking peacocks strut their stuff.

GETTING THERE AND AROUND Kardítsa's **train** station (✆ 24410 21402) on the south edge of the centre is on the same line as Tríkala and Kalambáka, which at the time of writing was being serviced by bus from the Paleofársala train station. The **bus** station (Dimokratías; ✆ 24410 21411; w ktel-karditsas.gr) has two buses daily (just one on Sundays) making a round of the villages around Lake Plastíra (Mesenikóla, Morfovoúni, Kalývia, Neochóri and others), as well as buses to other towns of interest in the region. There are also three to six buses daily to Tríkala and Lárissa, and three a day to Vólos, plus a few each day to Thessaloníki and Athens. For a **taxi**, call ✆ 24410 73001.

WHERE TO STAY AND EAT
Domotel Arni (31 rooms) Karaiskáki 4; ✆ 24410 22161; w domotel.gr. A surprise, just outside the pedestrian centre: a beautiful Neoclassical Rococo-style hotel that opened in 1921. Recently restored to its former glory, its public rooms are especially lovely, including the popular bistro (€€). Excellent staff; b/fast inc. €€
Kiérion (72 rooms) Mplatsoúka 22; ✆ 24410 71923; w hotelkierion.gr. By the central square, a comfortable, modern hotel. The roof garden with its small pool overlooks the city & surrounding mountains. B/fast inc. €€
Mikro Palati Plateía Plastíras; ✆ 24410 41258; ◷ 18.30–midnight Mon–Fri, 12.30–midnight Sat & Sun. The 'Little Palace' has a terrace on the square & tables upstairs, & a big menu – including slow-cooked lamb, kid with pilaf, or pork with prunes in a clay pot (*gástra*). €€

Gkekas Kolokotróni 3; ✆ 24410 23289; ◷ 10.00–17.00 & 20.00–midnight Mon–Sat. Classic *ouzerí*, with lots of seafood goodies & tables along the street. €
Steki tis Kyra Giotas Iezekiél 19; ✆ 24410 75071; ◷ 11.00–01.00 daily. Lovely atmosphere & music in the centre, serving tasty little plates to go with your tipple, with plenty of seafood choices. €
Avlí Rakomeládiko Irakleítou 4–6; m 69726 79216; f Αυλή Ρακομελάδικο; ◷ 23.00–03.00 daily. Sip hot *rakí* with honey & listen to live music.
Rebetiko Irakleítou 12; ✆ 24410 76013; ◷ 10.00–03.00 Mon–Sat, 11.00–03.00 Sun. Café with board games & live *rebétiko* music on Thu–Sat nights.

WHAT TO SEE AND DO
Archaeology Museum (Lachaná 1; ✆ 24410 25219; ◷ 08.30–15.30 Wed–Mon; €5) Located in the centre, this new museum covers the history of Western Thessaly from 250,000BC to Roman times, and goes out of its way to show how people lived here in the past. There's a reconstruction of a tell, one of the mounds that dot the Thessalian plain; a Neolithic house, complete with all its furnishings; Mycenaean-era artefacts, notably from the tholos tomb discovered in Ktimén (south of Kardítsa, near Loutrá Smokóva); elements of an Archaic temple of Apollo from

nearby ancient Metropolis (including a striking Art Deco-ish horse-head gargoyle and an unusual 6th-century BC bronze statue of Apollo as a warrior); and a replica tree with offerings from the Sacred Grove of Athena.

Fire Fighting Museum (Cnr N Plastíra & A Diákou; ⊕ 10.00–noon Mon–Fri, also 19.00–22.00 Tue & Thu; free) Inside Karditsa's now almost empty covered market from the 1920s, this charming little museum was set up by local firefighters in their former headquarters. Explanations of the equipment are only in Greek but it doesn't really matter.

LAKE PLASTÍRA

At 750m, Lake Plastíra (Λίμνη Πλαστήρα) looks like it's always been there, stretching 14km north to south, its indented sand-coloured shore emphasising its impossibly blue water. It bears the name of Karditsa-born Nikólaos Plastíras (1883–1952), nicknamed 'the Black Horseman', a general and three-time prime minister who tried (unsuccessfully) to reconcile left and right after the Greek Civil War. In 1925, he thought of damming the Tavropós River to provide electricity to the region, though the project wasn't completed until 1959. In the meantime, during World War II, the area now covered by the lake was a top-secret airfield, where the Allies dropped off supplies at night, guided by kerosene lamps. During the day the locals hid the airfield under brush and trees – the Germans knew it was somewhere and, although they never found it, burned down several villages anyway.

In places Lake Plastíra is 60m deep and holds up to 400 million cubic metres of water to irrigate Thessaly's dry plains, but it also doubles as a year-round resort, with smart hotels and guesthouses that draw weekending Athenians. The 70km drive around the lake is beautiful; the surrounding hills are all forest, perfect for walking, mountain biking, cycling and riding.

 WHERE TO STAY *Map, page 328, unless otherwise stated*

Pandion Luxury Boutique Hotel & Suites (18 rooms) Neochóri; 24410 93440; w pandion.gr. Charming, intimate stone-built hotel, where all rooms have lake views & fireplace; great staff, & delicious b/fast (inc). €€€€–€€€

Montanema [map, page 304] (33 rooms) Anthochóri; 24450 45220; w montanema.gr. 4.5km from the lake, this ecological 'handmade village' is deep in a pristine forest & wildlife preserve, offering lovingly built apartments & suites, all made with natural materials. The owners raise ewes to make feta, & free-range hens; guests are welcome to pick the ingredients for their salads. There's also a restaurant, bar & wine cellar (€€€). B/fast with bread baked in a wood-fired oven & homemade jams inc. €€€

Kazarma Lake Resort & Spa (50 rooms) Kalývia; 24410 92290; w kazarma.gr. Chic resort with a wide range of rooms & suites, along with an excellent restaurant (€€€) with a fireplace in the centre of the dining room, plus an outdoor pool & a playroom for kids. €€€–€€

Mouzaki Palace [map, page 304] (42 rooms) Mouzáki; 24450 43452; w mouzakipalace.com. Set on a wooded hillside, almost equidistant from Tríkala, Karditsa & Lake Plastíra, this new 4-star resort has an outdoor rooftop pool with wonderful views, plus indoor heated pool & spa. €€€–€€

Titagion (22 rooms) Lampéro; 24410 94660; w hoteltitagion.gr. Family-run stone-built hotel near the water, on one of the quieter shores of the lake, with a good restaurant; most rooms have a fireplace. Lovely owners; b/fast inc. €€

Nevros Resort & Spa (21 rooms) Neochóri; 24410 93201; w nevros.gr. Modern hotel where all rooms, some with fireplace, have lake views. There's also an outdoor pool, small spa, & a good restaurant (€€). B/fast inc. €€–€

10 | THESSALY (ΘΕΣΣΑΛΙΑ)

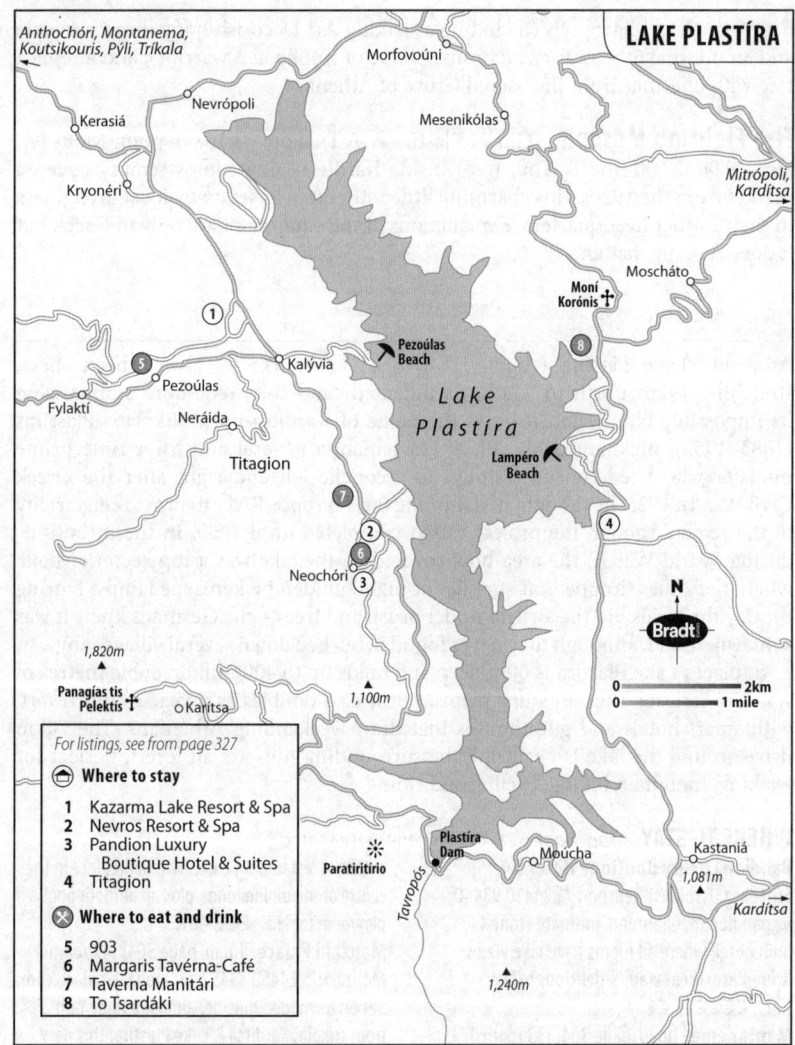

For listings, see from page 327

⌂ **Where to stay**
1. Kazarma Lake Resort & Spa
2. Nevros Resort & Spa
3. Pandion Luxury Boutique Hotel & Suites
4. Titagion

✕ **Where to eat and drink**
5. 903
6. Margaris Tavérna-Café
7. Taverna Manitári
8. To Tsardáki

✕ **WHERE TO EAT AND DRINK** *Map, above*

903 Pezoúlas; 24410 92000; 10.30–23.00 Sat–Thu, 13.00–23.00 Fri. Excellent taverna, famous for its succulent *kótsi* (slow-cooked pork shank with honey), mushrooms & salads. €€

Taverna Manitári Neochóri; 24410 93322; w manitari-limniplastira.gr; noon–19.30 Mon, Tue, Thu & Fri, noon–22.00 Sat & Sun. Come to the 'mushroom taverna' for grilled funghi with freshly made pittas, grilled chicken, colourful salads & gorgeous lake views. €€

Margaris Tavérna-Café Neochóri; 24410 93209; 07.00–midnight daily. Greek travellers rave about this small grocery/café/taverna with its simple décor of old maps & photographs, homemade feta & delicious sausage, & warm atmosphere. (Note that on Google it comes up as 'Margaris, tavern-brown'.) €

To Tsardáki Kardítsa-Kastaniás road, Tsardáki; 24410 20024; totsardaki; noon–19.00 daily. A taverna on the Karditsa–Kastanías road going strong since 1939 – long before there was even the lake. Traditional, lovely owners, & tasty dishes prepared in a wood-burning oven. €

LAKE PLASTÍRA

SPORTS AND ACTIVITIES On the north shore, **Saloon Fárma Zambétas** (Nevrópoli; ☏ 24410 92855; w lakeplastira.gr) offers horseriding for all ages, plus archery and boating. **Tavropós** (Kalývia; m 69777 40066; w tavropos.com) arranges all kinds of land- and lake-based activities from archery and cycling to kayaking and SUP; it also rents out mountain bikes, canoes and hydrocycles (water bikes).

WHAT TO SEE AND DO Along the road from Kardítsa and just past the modern village of Mitrópoli (Μητρόπολη), a sign on the right points the way to the 6th-century BC **Temple of Apollo Metropolis** (☏ 24410 61564; ⊕ 08.00–15.00 Tue–Sun; €5) – with its impressive foundations sheltered by a roof. Beyond, the northernmost of two roads winds up to the lake. Clockwise, the first village is **Morfovoúni** (Μορφοβούνι), home of the parents of Nikólaos Plastíras. It's also the site of a small **Plastíras Museum** (w plastiras-ota.gr/en/building/morfovouni-center-historical-studies), in a little stone house, with newspaper articles and memorabilia about his role in Greece's many 20th-century wars and complicated politics (if it's not open, ask around for the key). The lake road heads south to wine-growing **Mesenikólas** (Μεσενικόλας), with a charming main square and café, then to the fortified 16th-century **Moní Korónis** (☏ 24410 22250; w monikoronis.gr; ⊕ 10.00–14.00 Tue, Thu & Sat, 07.00–14.00 Sun), named 'the crown' for its majestic position. It has fine frescoes by the Cretan school and stupendous views across the plain of Thessaly to Olympus; the monks make wine, keep bees and have some impressive tools and barrels in the cellar. They also run a shop stocked with their own fine food products.

Beyond is the intersection of the south road from Kardítsa, and the road up to **Moscháto** (Μοσχάτο), while the lake road continues to rocky **Lamperó** (Λαμπερό) **Beach** where you can swim. Beyond **Kastaniá** (Καστανιά) and **Moúcha** (Μούχα) is the **Plastíra Dam** itself – and a row of souvenir shops. Just past the dam, still heading west, follow the signposted (3km, partly paved) road up to the **Paratiritírio** (Παρατηρητήριο; 1,350m), or observation tower, with a little kiosk to drink in the vision of the lake and all the mountains at your feet.

Heading up the west shore, **Neochóri** (Νεοχώρι) is the largest lake town, and a lot of it is new; the old village is under water. Near the shore, the **botanical garden** (m 69464 76683; w plastiras-ota.gr/en/building/botanical-garden; ⊕ Sep–Jun 10.00–15.00 Wed–Mon, Jul & Aug 10.00–13.00 (14.00 on w/ends) & 18.00–20.00 Wed–Mon; free) has flora from around the region. It's 9km southwest to **Karítsa**, an old mountain village immersed in trees; just northwest is the remarkable 15th-century monastery of **Panagías tis Pelektís** ('The Virgin Hewn in Rock'; call ☏ 24410 94747 for the caretaker; ⊕ often open 10.30–16.00 Sat & Sun) built on the instructions of the Virgin Mary herself on a cliff's edge, with two churches, both with fine Cretan frescoes and a striking painted iconostasis, and secret hideaway where the monks hid *klephts* and *armatoloí* during their fight against Ottomans. Abandoned in the 1920s, it has been restored; the views are otherworldly.

The monastery is in the **Ágrapha**, the mountainous region of the South Pindus range with six peaks over 2,000m, so little travelled in Byzantine and Turkish times that its name means 'unwritten' – the Greek equivalent of Terra Incognita. During Ottoman times, its impoverished, barren little villages here and to the south in central Greece were autonomous and fiercely independent. A fascinating wilderness, it is largely inaccessible in winter; in other seasons, you can dip into its capillaries by aiming for the handsome 11th-century grey stone **Moní Spiliás** (1,300m; ☏ 24450 31789; w monispilias.gr) overhanging a deep ravine, whose monks also played an important role in the fight for independence; many of its fine 17th-century paintings have survived. Just west is lovely turquoise **Lake Stefaniáda**,

10 | THESSALY (ΘΕΣΣΑΛΙΑ)

immersed in forests near the tiny village of **Stefaniáda** (Στεφανιάδα). Get there on the road via Pefkófyto.

Back on the big lake, north of Neochóri, **Kalývia** (Καλύβια) is the activity centre on the lake, with its popular **Pezoúlas** (Πεζούλας) **Beach**, a narrow spit of land with a café that juts into the lake. The lofty villages in the woodlands above – **Pezoúlas**, **Neráida** (Νεράιδα), **Fylaktí** (Φυλακτή) and, further north, **Kerasiá** (Κερασιά) – are especially charming. **Anthochóri** (Ανθοχώρι), further up, has an old stone bridge and an easy, well-signposted walk up through a ravine to a pair of waterfalls. **Nevrópoli** (Νευρόπολη) on the north shore is the last village before re-joining the road down to Kardítsa.

LOUTRÁ SMOKÓVA

Last but not least, in the far south you can soak in the warm waters of Loutrá Smokóva, extolled since the 17th century and once visited by Ali Pasha. Here, in the basic 1970s-style spa (35km from Kardítsa; ↘ 24430 61209/61210; ⊕ Jun–Oct 08.00–20.00 daily, Nov–May 10.00–18.00 w/ends, but ring first; €7–10), lightly sulphurous, therapeutic springs of 37–40.2°C fill a pool and private baths. There are also saunas and steam rooms.

✕ WHERE TO EAT AND DRINK
Drosostalia Límni Smokóvou; m 69825 22593; w drosostalia.gr; ⊕ noon–21.00 or later Thu–Tue. Views over the lake & superb food, not far from the hot springs. €€

11

Magnesía (Μαγνησία) and the Pelion Peninsula

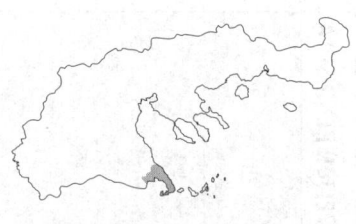

Thessaly's window on the Aegean, Magnesía (Μαγνησία) has been renowned for its exceptional, verdant beauty and climate since ancient times. The region around its lively capital Vólos (ancient Iolkos) attracted some of the very earliest inhabitants of Greece, and inspired some of the country's oldest myths, including Jason's search for the Golden Fleece – an adventure that mirrored early Greek explorations of the Black Sea. The bucolic Pelion Peninsula, home of the centaurs and summer holiday resort of the gods, is pure enchantment, covered with forests and waterfalls, ancient walking paths that meander down to some of the most dramatically beautiful beaches in all Greece, and traditional villages filled with attractive boutique hotels in historic mansions. But attraction is nothing new here: Magnesía's wealth of iron-attracting ores gave its name to 'magnet' and 'magnesium' after its legendary founder, an ancient Cretan shepherd named Magnes, who, while herding his flocks here some 4,000 years ago, found the nails in his boots got stuck on a large black lodestone.

VÓLOS

Modern Vólos (Βόλος; population 150,000) is just that – modern. In the Dark Ages people from Demetrias (page 339) moved here for greater protection, around the castle, of which only a few stones remain west of the station. In the 19th century the Sultan granted permission for the town to expand. Vólos, along with the rest of Thessaly, freed itself from Ottoman control and became part of Greece in 1881. The city has a strong working-class character and consciousness; this is the first place where *The Communist Manifesto* was translated into Greek, and the first place a labour union was established (both in 1908). A new harbour was built in 1912 and, with the population boost of Asia Minor refugees a decade later (who filled a whole new district, Néa Ionía), the city grew quickly, an industrial powerhouse processing and shipping cotton, fruit, cereals and tobacco. Shattered by earthquakes in 1955, it was rebuilt on a grid plan, and is a busy and likeable place, the sixth-largest city in Greece and home to the University of Thessaly. Italian artist Giorgio de Chirico (1888–1978) was born here, son of railway engineer Evaristo de Chirico; another famous son, Vangelis (1943–2022), composed the scores for *Chariots of Fire* and *Blade Runner*.

Vólos has exceptional archaeology and folk art museums, and others dedicated to bricks and butterflies. It's also a great place to watch the world go by over a glass of tsípouro before heading off to the Pelion or the Sporades.

11 | MAGNESÍA (ΜΑΓΝΗΣΙΑ) AND THE PELION PENINSULA

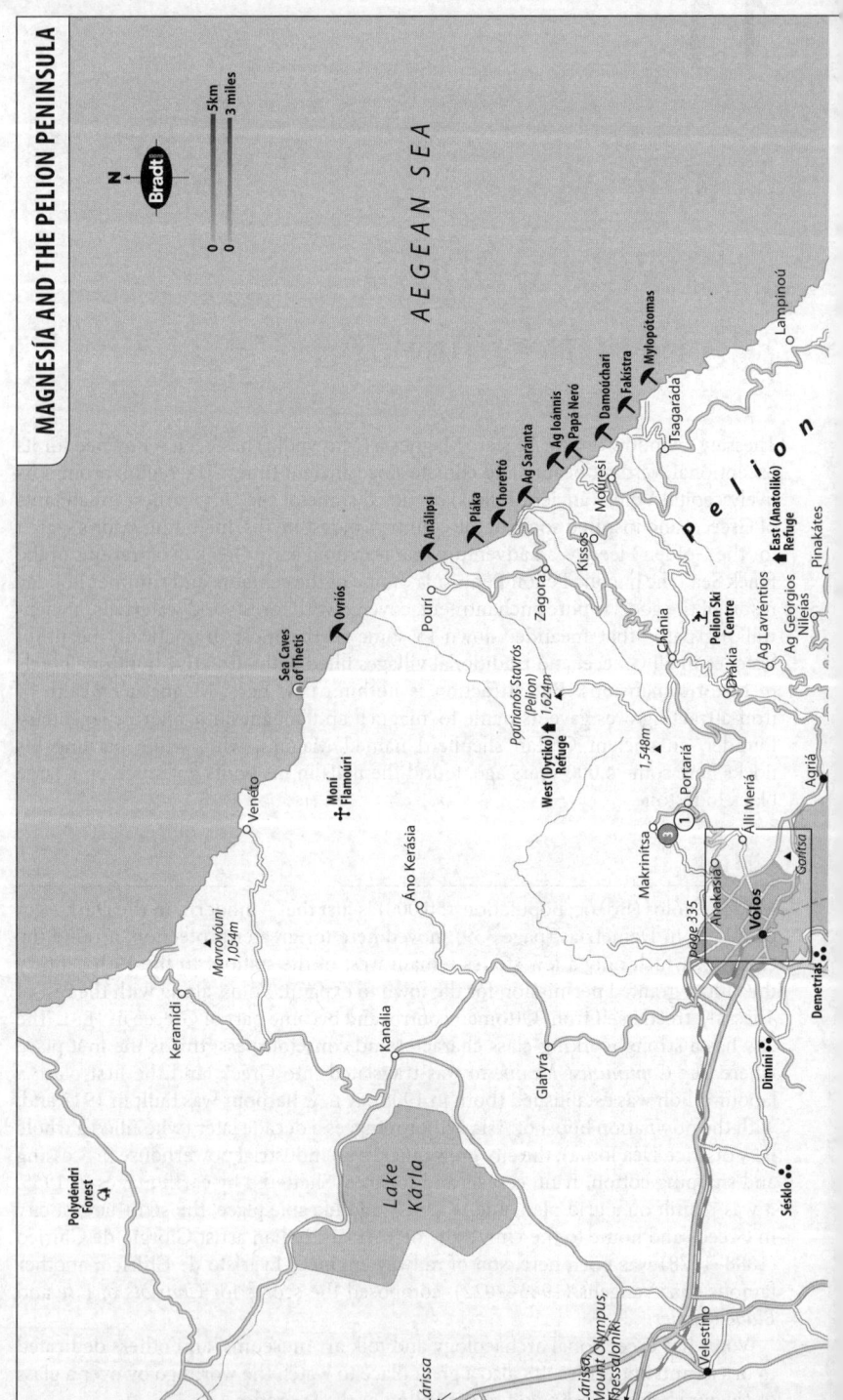

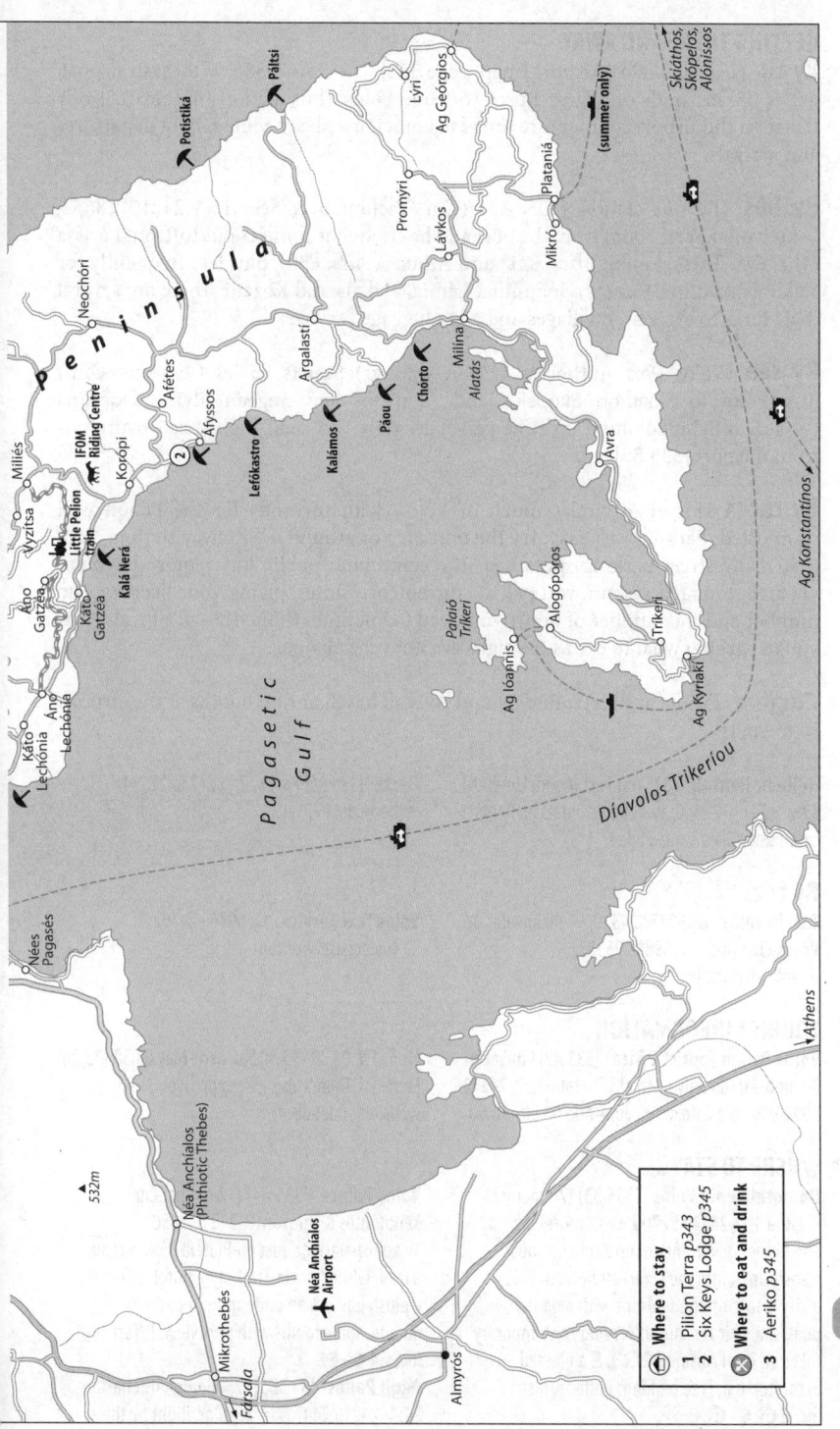

GETTING THERE AND AWAY

By air Néa Anchíalos Airport [map, page 332] (🖁 24280 76886; w thessalyairport.gr) is 38km south of Vólos. Buses to/from Vólos's bus station (45mins/€5; buy tickets at the airport counter) are timed to coincide with scheduled flight departures and arrivals.

By bus The bus station [335 A3] (Cnr Váchou 5 & Sékéri; 🖁 24210 28632; w ktelvolou.gr) is 300m from the port and has frequent connections to/from Lárissa (1hr; €7), Thessaloníki (3hrs; €21) and Athens (5hrs; €30), plus less frequently for Kalambáka (2hrs 15mins), Ioánnina, Lamía, Tríkala and Kozáni. There are several daily links to the Pelion villages and a left luggage service.

By sea (Vólos Port Authority: w port-volos.gr) **Seajets** ferries (w seajets.com) link Vólos to Skiáthos, Skópelos and Alónissos and **Aegean Flying Dophins** (w aegeanflyingdolphins.gr) runs passenger-only (no cars) high-speed hydrofoils from the port [335 B5].

By car A ring road circles much of Vólos, with turn-offs for the Pelion well signposted. Parking isn't easy; try the port area or around the railway station. Note that many street parking spots near the centre and public lots require payment via an automated system; you pay at convenience stores, giving your licence plate number and the number of hours you need (sometimes limited). Ask a local when you're parking what to do, as the signs are not very obvious.

Car hire Europcar, Hertz, Budget and Avis all have car hire booths at the airport. In town, try:

Hellenic Rentals [335 A5] Port (Agorá Liménos) K28; 🖁 24210 22880; w hellenicrentals.gr. Rents cars, motorbikes & quad bikes.

Hertz [335 A5] Port K27; 🖁 24210 22544; w hertz.gr

By taxi
Taxi in Vólos m 69473 24329; w taxiinvolos.gr
Vólos City Taxi m 69883 95383; w voloscitytaxi.gr

Vólos Taxi Service m 69369 24702; w volostaxiservice.com

TOURIST INFORMATION
Vólos-Pelion Tourist Office [335 A2] Cnr Sékeri & Lambráki (directly by the KTEL station); 🖁 24210 30930; w volosinfo.gr; ⊕ Jun–Aug 08.30–18.00 Mon–Fri, 08.30–15.30 Sat, Sep–May 08.30–15.30 Mon–Fri. There's also a free app (iVolos) – see website for details.

WHERE TO STAY
Domotel Xenia Volos [335 B3] (79 rooms) Plastíra 1; 🖁 24210 92700; w domotel.gr. The former government-run Xenia has been transformed into the smartest hotel in Vólos, a 'city resort' on the seafront with a garden, pool, spa, chic restaurant serving contemporary takes on local cuisine (€€€), & a glassed-in rooftop bar. Free parking; buffet b/fast inc. €€€€–€€€

Volos Palace [335 A4] (72 rooms) Cnr Xenofóntos & Thrákon; 🖁 24210 76501; w volospalace.gr. Just off Plateía Ríga Feréou, a cool, white Neoclassical-style hotel with a plush lobby & an underground parking garage; some rooms with port view. B/fast inc. €€€–€€

Aégli Pallas [335 B5] (75 rooms) Argonaftón 24; 🖁 24210 24471; w aegli.gr. Right by the

VÓLOS

Where to stay
1. Aégli Pallas B5
2. Ávra B5
3. Domotel Xenia Volos B3
4. Hotel Roussa B3
5. Volos Palace A4

Off map
Pyrassos A3

Where to eat and drink
6. Demíris A1
7. Kavouras B5
8. Kypsele A2
9. La Marimba B3
10. LoLa&LuNa B3
11. MeZen B5
12. Prosfygáki A1
13. Stáfylos A5

---

ferry port, in 2 recently renovated 19th-century buildings, smartly refurbished in 2016. B/fast inc. €€

Ávra [335 B5] (13 rooms) Sólonos 3; ☎ 24210 25370. Not too noisy, friendly, on a side street by the port & parking nearby. €

Hotel Roussa [335 B3] (15 rooms) Iatroú Tzánou 1; ☎ 24210 21732; m 69453 07147. A clean & modest place on the southeast end of the waterfront; AC rooms, all but the few on the ground floor with balconies & some with a view to the side or front. No b/fast, just a vending machine & shared lounge. Excellent value. Parking is also somewhat easier on this side of town. €

Pyrassos [335 A3] (20 rooms) Kasnéti 36, Néa Anchíalos; ☎ 24280 76256. Tidy little family-run hotel by the beach, 20mins from Vólos & 15mins from the airport. €

THE TSIPOURÁDIKA OF VÓLOS *Amber Charmei*

Vólos's working-class history and its unique, refined drinking and eating culture go hand in hand. In the 20th century, the city's docks and many factories provided plenty of employment, while an influx of refugees from Asia Minor provided plenty of hands, plus sophisticated palates. It became the custom for workers to stop off for a glass of *tsípouro* – a distilled spirit from grapes, which is sometimes flavoured with aromatics like anise – on their way home for lunch. A small bite would be served alongside. Then a different snack would be served with the second glass. In time, the agreeable custom grew to involve little individual bottles and a greater variety of snacks, becoming an event in itself. There are few more pleasant – nor more carefree – ways to dine. The only decision you need to make at a Vólos *tsipourádiko* is '*mè*' ('with', as in flavoured with aromatics) or '*horís*' (without). Each person will be brought a small glass or often a tiny bottle (25ml) of *tsípouro* and a *mezé* – a different dish for every person – selected by the house. Everyone shares. The choices are often seafood-forward, which goes well with the drink. Smoked or pickled fish, tangy slaws, fried shrimps, grilled octopus, zesty cheese dishes, fried peppers and so on are among the many selections. Another round of *tsípouro* and *mezédes*, and then another, continues in an orchestrated progression of tastes and textures. Empty bottles are left on the table, for patrons to keep track of how much they're drinking, and for waiters to compile the bill; they just count up the bottles, as each round is the same price (currently around €5), regardless of the *mezé* that accompanies it, plus a small extra charge for the first round to cover the bread and water.

This cultural ritual is reason alone to visit the city, and to venture from the centre, too. While one of the very best – Kavouras (see below) – is near the harbour, the destination neighbourhood for *tsipourádika* (the '-a' ending indicates the plural) is the working-class district of Néa Ionía, a short walk northwest of the port. This is mainly a lunchtime activity – most authentic *tsipourádika* open before noon, and start closing up around 17.00.

WHERE TO EAT AND DRINK

La Marimba [335 B3] Nikotsára 46; 24210 71167; f; ⊕ 20.00–01.00 Tue–Sun. For something different: scrummy Mexican cuisine, going strong since 1995. Great frozen margaritas, too. €€

LoLa&LuNa [335 B3] Filippou Ioan 2; 24210 57755; f trattorialolaluna; ⊕ 19.00–midnight Tue–Sun. Lovely Italian dishes, including fresh pasta, risotto, & seafood, on the east side of the waterfront. €€

Stáfylos [335 A5] Meloúnas 6; 24210 38548; f; ⊕ 19.00–01.00 Mon–Thu, noon–01.00 Fri–Sun. Generous & extremely delicious Cretan-style dishes plus vegan selections near the train station & good wine list; always packed so best to book ahead. €€

Demíris [335 A1] Efraimídou 23; 24210 65559; f Δεμιρης Παραδοσιακο Τσιπουραδικο; ⊕ 11.00–02.00 Tue–Sun. Classic *tsipourádiko* in Néa Ionía, with superb seafood *mezédes*: one of the best places to enjoy fresh bivalves on the half-shell. €

Kavouras [335 B5] Chatziargiri 3; 24210 28520; ⊕ 08.00–18.00 Mon–Sat. In a town famous for its unique *tsipourádika* (see above), this casual place in an alley behind the port is a local legend, with one outstanding little dish after another. €

Kypsele [335 A2] 2as Noemvriou 96; 24210 24677; ⊕ 08.30–22.00 Mon–Sat. Yogurt & various milk-based puddings are the thing to get at this petite, traditional (& very photogenic) dairy & pastry shop. €

MeZen [335 B5] Alonnísou 8; 24210 20844; w mezen.gr; ⊕ noon–midnight Tue–Sun. Inspired by the Barcelona tapas scene, this hip new *tsipourádiko* has a fab selection of bottles from all across Greece, with extremely good fusion *mezédes* to match the flavours. Shots around €2.50, with *mezé* around €5. €

Prosfygáki [335 A1] Dorileou 15, Néa Ionía; 24210 84587; ProsfigakiParadosiakoTsipouradiko; ⊕ 11.30–17.30 Mon–Sat. 'The Little Refugee' – a very popular neighbourhood spot with good seafood *mezédes* & pleasant outdoor seating. €

ENTERTAINMENT AND NIGHTLIFE Nightlife is concentrated around the church of Ag Nikólaos [335 C5] and the railway station, plus along the waterfront where cafés and bars are open late for those taking an evening promenade.

Coffee shops and bars

40 bar & coffee lab [335 C4] Koumoundoúrou 28–40; m 69871 06607; 40barvolos; ⊕ 10.00–03.00 daily. Popular simpatico hangout with great coffee, wines, cocktails & music.

Alter Ego Rock & Blues Bar [335 C4] Ag Nikoláou 38; 24211 09113; ⊕ 20.30–dawn daily. Since 1987, the place to go for old vinyl records on w/days, & live jazz & blues at w/ends.

Kyklos [335 A4] Mikrasiatón 85; 24210 20872; Τσιπουράδικο Ό Κυκλος'; ⊕ noon–midnight Mon–Sat, noon–19.00 Sun. A warm & welcoming traditional *tsipourádiko*, with wooden chairs & marble tables, plus live Greek music some Thu, Fri & Sat eves (check Facebook page).

Valentin Curious Bierkneipe [335 A4] Ferón 13; 24210 76663; ; ⊕ 19.30–03.00 daily.

One for beer lovers, with a German touch & outside tables.

Cinemas

Achílleion [335 B5] Cnr Koumoundoúrou & Iásonos; 24210 32818. Art Deco cinema of 1925 that survived the earthquake, used for cultural events (live streaming from the Metropolitan Opera etc).

Exoraistiki [335 B3] Dimitriádos 263; 24210 30303; w exoraistiki.victoria-cinema.gr. Outdoor summer cinema.

Theatre

Municipal Theatre [335 A4] Plateía Ríga Feréou; 24211 81063. Big summer theatre with 1,739 seats.

OTHER PRACTICALITIES

Alpha Bank [335 B4] El Venizélou 49
National Bank [335 B5] Iásonos 50
Hospital [335 C3] Polyméri 134; 24213 51804 (emergency room); w ghv.gr
Pharmacy Daliarkis [335 B5] K Kartáli 123

Pharmacy Tzortzákis [335 B3] Konstantá 144A
Post office [335 B5] Dimitriádos 209
Tourist Police [335 B2] Venizélou 158; 24210 39065

WHAT TO SEE AND DO Vólos's bustling waterfront and port lined with *tspourádika* has a bronze model of the *Argo* (1965) [335 B5], and sometimes in summer the working life-size reconstruction of Jason's famous ship is docked nearby (page 350).

City of Vólos Museum [335 A4] (Ferón 17; 24210 29878; w vmoc.gr; ⊕ 09.00–14.00 Tue–Fri, 10.30–13.30 Sat & Sun, also 18.00–21.00 Wed & Fri; free; free Wi-Fi & English translations via QR code) Housed in a former tobacco warehouse of 1920, this museum focuses on the city's history with an excellent selection of informative graphs, installations, photographs from the 19th and early 20th centuries, as well as old cigarette ads and many artefacts of interest.

Railway Museum of Thessaly [335 A4] (1st floor of the station, Papadiamánti St; 24210 23644; w ose.gr; ⊕ 07.30–14.30 by appt; free) The rail link to Lárissa was key to Vólos's success in the 19th century, and is documented here with photos,

11 | MAGNESÍA (ΜΑΓΝΗΣΙΑ) AND THE PELION PENINSULA

JASON AND THE ARGONAUTS

In the generation before the Trojan War, Pelias usurped the throne of Iolkos from the rightful king, his half-brother Aeson, and killed all his children – although Aeson's wife managed to save her newborn son, Jason, by getting her women to pretend he had been stillborn and drown out his cries with their own, and sending him to the Pelion to be raised by wise centaur Cheiron (who would later educate Achilles). In the meantime, an oracle warned Pelias to beware of a man wearing only one sandal. This, of course, was Jason, who lost a sandal in a river while helping an old woman cross – who was really the goddess Hera, who made his cause her own.

When single-sandalled Jason showed up in Iolkos and claimed his father's throne, Pelias agreed on the condition that he sail to Colchis (modern Georgia) and retrieve the Golden Fleece, guarded by an unsleeping dragon. The quest attracted 50 heroes, including Heracles, Peleus, Orpheus, Castor and Pollux, Meleager and Atalanta. Aboard their ship the *Argo*, built by Argus the shipwright, and following the constellations that Cheiron arranged in the sky to guide them, they set sail and had many adventures before Jason succeeded in his quest, thanks to a dragon-sleeping potion supplied by sorceress Medea, daughter of the king of Colchis, who had fallen in love with him.

After many adventures (see the 3rd-century BC epic *Argonautica* by Apollonius of Rhodes), the heroes returned to Iolkos. When Pelias still refused to surrender the throne, Medea showed Pelias' daughters how they could make him young again by killing an old ram and boiling it in a cauldron, only for it to emerge as a young lamb. The daughters then cut up Pelias and boiled him – so much for the wicked king; but as an accessory to the murder, Jason was still denied the throne, and he and Medea were exiled to Corinth. And the Golden Fleece? After Jason and Medea spent their wedding night on it and gave it to Pelias, it vanished from history. So, if the *Argonautica* was the prototype of the novel, as many have argued, the Fleece stands out as the first MacGuffin.

old clocks, ticket machines and Evaristo de Chirico's designs for the station and his Pelion rail line (page 350), which may be why his famous son often painted trains in his pictures, along with statues of Greek gods.

Roof Tile and Brickworks Museum N & S Tsalapátas [335 A2] (Nótia Pýli; \ 24210 29844; w piop.gr; ⊕ closed at the time of writing as the museum undergoes restoration following storm damage in 2023) Follow the roof-tile- and brick-making process every step of the way in this museum, set up in a factory founded in 1926 by the Tsalapátas brothers. It was the only Hoffmann kiln in Greece, which burned 24 hours a day until the mid 1970s, interrupted only by the Nazis and the 1955 earthquake.

Giorgio de Chirico Art Centre [335 B5] (Metamorfóseos 3; \ 24210 31701; ⊕ 11.00–14.00 Mon–Fri; free) No original de Chiricos here, but there are temporary exhibits and the permanent Alékos Dámtsas collection of contemporary Greek art and photographs of old Vólos.

Kítsos Makrís Folklore Centre [335 C3] (Kítsou Makrí 38; ℡ 24210 37119; w lib.uth.gr/LWS/en/ls/lkm.asp; ⊕ 09.00–14.00 Mon–Fri; free) This fascinating collection, now run by the University of Thessaly, occupies the house of folklorist Kítsos Makrís (d1988). It has an exceptional folk-art collection, including woodcarvings; paintings by Epiróte artist Ioánnis Pagónis, who decorated many Pelion churches, and other works by his son; paintings of ships and sea scenes by local artist Nikólaos Christopoúlos (1880–1967); and, the stars of the collection, 25 paintings by Theóphilos (page 341). It was Makrís who published *Theóphilos, the Painter*, the first book ever on the artist, in 1939.

Athanasákio Archaeological Museum [335 C3] (Athanasáki 1; ℡ 24210 25285; ⊕ 08.00–15.00 Tue–Sun; €4, concessions €2) Built in 1909, the Athanasákio is one of the oldest archaeological museums in Greece. Famous for its unique Hellenistic painted marble funerary steles from Ancient Demetrias (see below), it's also a place to reflect on Magnesía's true age, with its artefacts from Sésklo (page 340) dating back to 6500BC. Best of all is a large room devoted to the Neolithic that makes the era come alive like no other, with a delightful portrait gallery of little faces, seals, figurines (one looks decidedly contemporary), clay models of houses, reproductions of their tools, looms and buildings, and the wild wheat (*Triticum boeoticum*) they planted.

While in the vicinity, consider popping into the pretty hospital chapel of **Ag Triáda** [335 C3] to see the murals of saints (1951) by the 20th-century painter Geórgios Gounaropoúlos, rendered in his immediately recognisable, ethereal style.

Gorítsa [335 D3] (Just east of Vólos) A pretty tree-lined road leads up to the top of Gorítsa, the 'little mountain' (200m), crowned by the church of Zoodóchos Pigís. This stands on the acropolis of an as-yet unexcavated walled city (perhaps Orminio) built on a grid by Philip II. It has pretty sunset views over Vólos. Next east, along the road to the western Pelion, is the mighty Heracles Cement Plant, one of the largest in the world.

Entomological Museum [335 B1] (Záchou 98; ℡ 24210 48556; m 69452 96129; w entomologikomouseio.gr; ⊕ by appt) This is nothing less than the greatest private insect collection in the Balkans, founded by local scholar Dr Athanásios Koutroúmpas, whose collection features more than 100,000 insect species, including 40,000 species of butterfly and the largest moth in the world, *Thysania agrippina*, with a wingspan of 40cm.

Natural History Museum [335 A2] (Cnr Mikrasiatón & Záchou; ℡ 24210 36555; w volosmuseum.gr; ⊕ closed temporarily at the time of writing for works; free) Geology, biology, fossils (including mammoth tusks) and the evolution of man are covered here in this little museum.

AROUND VÓLOS As Thessaly's only outlet to the sea, this was an extremely busy area in the past, with a collage of archaeological sites from the early Neolithic to the early Christian era.

Demetrias (1.5km south of Vólos near Magoúla Pefkákia (Μαγούλα Πευκάκια); ℡ 22410 88091; w odysseus.culture.gr; ⊕ by appt, but check at the tourist office) This Hellenistic city founded in 294BC by the warlord-playboy King of Macedon,

11 | MAGNESÍA (ΜΑΓΝΗΣΙΑ) AND THE PELION PENINSULA

Demetrios Poliorketes, was his base when he wasn't out besieging Alexander's successors or holding orgies in the Parthenon. Later Macedonian kings followed suit and made it a favourite residence, and, although it dwindled under the Romans, it remained inhabited until the early AD600s. The **theatre** is the most prominent souvenir, along with foundations of a palace and walls reconstructed in the 1st century BC, using – and preserving for posterity – the unique painted funerary steles now in the archaeology museum.

Just west of the commercial port of Vólos are defensive walls of what is tentatively identified as **Ancient Pagasae**, the port of Iolkos, which gave its name to the Pagasetic Gulf.

Dimíni (Διμήνι; 6.5km west of Vólos; 24210 85960; 08.00–15.00 Tue–Sun; €2 inc admission to Sésklo, see below) The Neolithic farming settlement of Dimíni was inhabited in 4800–4500BC and had a central *megaron* (palace structure) and smaller houses enclosed by walls that hint of a troubled time. The site was resettled by the Mycenaeans; two impressive *tholos* tombs were discovered in the 19th century, and recently a palace was uncovered, believed to have belonged to Homer's 'spacious' Iolkos.

Sésklo (Σέσκλο; 18km west of Vólos, south of the Lárissa road; 08.00–15.00 Tue–Sun; €2 inc admission to Dimíni, see above) As old as Dimíni is, Neolithic Sésklo is much older, dating back to 6500BC, making it one of the oldest sites in the Balkans. Its 5,000 inhabitants fished, made sun-dried pottery (and later fired it, painting it the rich red colour synonymous with the 6th millennium BC Sésklo Culture) and imported obsidian from Mílos. They lived around a *megaron* – considered the oldest acropolis in Greece – in huts on stone foundations, made of branches and pebbles covered with clay. And they got by without an outer defensive wall, and enjoyed a lovely view.

Theóphilos (or Kontós House) Museum [335 D1] (Anakasiá, 6km northeast of Vólos; 24210 47340; 08.30–14.00 Mon–Fri, but ring first; free) The Kontós House is an extraordinary place to get to know the work of Theóphilos, a seminal folk artist. Yánnis Kontós, a mill owner, took in the roving artist, who decorated the entire upper floor with scenes and heroes of the Greek War of Independence, as well as Greek gods, village scenes, his benefactor Kontós on horseback, fanciful vegetation, crocodiles and a giraffe. Note that the drive there can be a bit of a challenge, although there is easy parking beside the museum; consult your GPS beforehand so as not to be led astray, or take a taxi (about €12) from town.

South, in **Álli Meriá** (Άλλη Μεριά) [335 D2], the Velentzas Bakery (1897) has nine murals by Theóphilos (undergoing restoration at the time of writing).

Néa Anchíalos (Νέα Αγχίαλος; 18km southwest of Vólos; 24280 76468; 08.30–15.00 Tue–Sun; €4, concessions €2) The modern seaside town of Néa Anchíalos is built over Homeric Pyrasos, which in the 4th century BC served as the port for the inland city of Phthiotic (Thessalian) Thebes, near the modern village of Mikrothebés. Under Demetrios Poliorketes, the city became the region's chief port. What has survived, however, is one of the most important Early Christian sites in Greece. No fewer than nine basilicas and a sumptuous baptistery from the 4th to the 6th centuries AD survive in the centre of the modern town, along with some with pretty mosaic floors and lovingly carved capitals on the columns, including a bizarre one with lions and strange blobby creatures.

GREECE'S GREATEST POPULAR ARTIST

Born on Lésvos, Theóphilos Hatzimichaíl (1866–1934) had piercing blue eyes and always dressed in a traditional white kilt (*foustanélla*) and clogs with tassels (*tsaroúchia*). After learning the basics of painting from his icon-painter grandfather, he left home at age 18, first serving as doorman at the Greek consulate in Izmir before ending up in Vólos and the Pelion in 1895. There he painted oils and murals, usually in exchange for his supper: fascinating scenes from daily life, or Greek history, folktales or mythology that were immediate, vivid, fresh and full of light and colour – often enough with helpful descriptions running along the painted frame or right in the middle of the action (reminiscent of ancient vases). He loved to lead local schoolchildren in costumed historical re-enactments during carnival and national holidays. Some people thought he was half mad, but entertaining, and the story goes that he returned to Lésvos in 1927 after someone played a cruel prank on him in a café, kicking away the ladder while he was painting. In other circles though, his star was rising. The artist Gíorgos Gounarópoulos saw Theophilos' works when he was in Vólos and was impressed; he brought him to the attention of Stratís Eletheriádis – also a native of Lésvos, but far better known internationally as Tériade, the noted art critic and publisher in Paris. Tériade ordered a number of works which were exhibited in Paris in 1936. He later financed and donated his own considerable collection of the artist's works to create the Theóphilos Museum on Lésvos, which is the other best place in Greece to see his art. Many of his paintings have been lost by their owners or their descendants, who must be kicking themselves: his works today are considered so essential to the cultural heritage of Greece that they cannot be exported, and can fetch up to hundreds of thousands of euros.

Almyrós Archaeological Museum (Athenéon 50, Almyrós (Αλμυρός); 24220 21326; 08.30–15.00 Tue–Sun; €2) In a handsome little Neoclassical building, this museum houses finds from Phthiotic Thebes and other local sites, including clay figures, ceramics, Neolithic tools, Hellenistic coins and statues.

Velestíno (Βελεστίνο; 17km west of Vólos) This was Ancient Pherae, which was mentioned in Homer as the kingdom of the hospitable Admetus. When Apollo was exiled from Olympus for killing the dragon Python, the guardian of the Delphic oracle, he worked as a shepherd for Admetus and became his lover, then helped him marry the princess Alcestis, daughter of Pelias. When Admetus forgot to make an important sacrifice to Artemis on his wedding night, she sent the Fates after him, but Apollo managed to get them drunk and made them promise not to take Admetus if anyone else would offer to take his place. Later, when Admetus' time came and even his elderly parents refused to die for him, Alcestis volunteered – only to be rescued from Hades by Heracles. She become a popular archetype of love and devotion, beginning with the play *Alcestis* by Euripides. Their son Eumelus, a suitor of Helen, would lead the army of Pherae and Iolkos to Troy.

Historically, Jason (d370BC) was the strongest ruler of Pherae, putting all of Thessaly under his rule; his nasty successor Alexander was murdered by his wife in 358BC, leading the ruling Aleuadae family in Lárissa to beg for help from Philip II of Macedon, who came and, as per usual, annexed the country while he was at it.

Today Ancient Pherae is mostly covered by the Vlach apple-growing town of Velestíno, birthplace of poet Rígas Feraíos ('of Pherae', 1757–98), who, fired by the American and French revolutions, proposed that Greeks and Turks alike should fight for liberty and the rule of law against the Sultan – 'better an hour of freedom than 40 years as a slave' – before he was captured in Trieste and murdered in Belgrade on orders from Istanbul. Little of this turbulent history survives, although the spring of Kefalóvryso in the town gardens may well be the fountain of Hypereia, 'the water loved by the gods' according to Sophocles. Excavations on the edge of town have also revealed the 4th-century BC foundation of the temple of Thaulios Zeus and walls of the acropolis.

Lake Kárla (Κάρλα; 12km northeast of Velestíno) Known as Boibeis in ancient times, Lake Kárla covered 180km² until it was completely drained for farmland in 1962. But much of the soil proved too saline to be useful and, in an ambitious €100 million project, 50km² of the lake has been gradually re-flooded – a pioneering wetlands restoration project and hopefully a model for the Balkan region; the local conservation project for the delicate lesser kestrel has won an award. The protected area includes the Mavrovóuni range that girdles the shore with steep cliffs, and the **Polydéndri Forest**, once owned by the Greek royal family.

Here too on the north slopes of Mount Pelion are some charming Pelion villages (most easily reached from the lake or via Glafyrá (Γλαφυρά) north of Vólos), which most visitors neglect: lofty **Áno Kerásia** (Άνω Κεράσια), car-free **Keramídi** (Κεραμίδι) and **Venéto** (Βενέτο), the latter two set above quiet beaches. There's a beautiful circular walk (for details, see w walking-pelion.blogspot.com) through wooded glades from Áno Kerásia, past the isolated 16th-century **Moní Flamoúri**, where four monks live without electricity and follow Athonite rules (women can't enter, but men can visit and stay the night).

THE PELION

Just behind Vólos rises Mount Pelion (Πήλιο; 1,624m), the 'healing mountain' named after Peleus (the father of Achilles) and a botanist's paradise covered with

CENTAURS

Half man, half horse, centaurs ('those who round up bulls') may have been the ancestral memories of horsey Thessaly's first cowboys. Myth has it, however, that Centauros was the product of the union between Ixion, the king of the Lapiths, and a cloud shaped like Hera, created by Zeus to confound Ixion's lusty designs. For his presumption, Ixion ended up tied to a fiery wheel in Hades, while Centauros mated with local mares to create the centaurs. Their wise and immortal king Cheiron tutored the healing god Asklepios, Jason and Achilles. Accidentally shot in the foot by Heracles, Cheiron was in such pain that he asked Zeus to give his immortality to Prometheus. Zeus complied, but immortalised the centaur anyway as Sagittarius, the constellation with the arrow pointing the way to the Golden Fleece. Pelion weddings had a habit of going wrong; one hosted by Peirithoös the Lapith, the king of Magnesía, led to the drunken misbehaviour of the centaurs that the ancient artists so liked to depict, contrasting civilisation (Greece and its gods) with the Other (not only centaurs, but Titans, Amazons, monsters and Persians).

medicinal herbs, olives, vineyards, chestnut groves and orchards, standing at the head of a peninsula that resembles a sock with a ball stuck in the toe. In summer its gorgeous beaches are a delight; and in the winter, Pelion, which gets more rain than any place on the Greek mainland, goes all misty and romantic, with a mantle of snow on the higher points – enough to support a small ski resort. And the peninsula's delightful hotels tend to stay open all year round.

The Pelion's traditional *archontikó* houses are topped with slate slabs that sparkle like silver in the sun. Thick walls of grey stone support overhanging Ottoman-style wooden floors, painted white. The second floor, with its fireplace, is designed to be snug in winter; the third, lined with windows and wooden shutters, is designed to be fresh and airy in summer. A frustrated longing for stained glass led to the custom of painting colourful geometric motifs over the real windows; lintels around the front doors are often of carved stone or marble. Flowerpots crowd every inch of space outside. Fountains splash, brooks gurgle, *kalderími* (cobbled paths) link the villages and enormous plane trees shade the squares. The old churches of the Pelion are different, too: rectangular with small apses, sometimes covered with sculpted marble plaques and topped with wide overhanging roofs, their artworks are often full of rustic charm.

HISTORY Although the peninsula was inhabited in antiquity, piracy forced its abandonment in the Middle Ages, except for a string of monasteries high on the mountain ridge. When Ottomans arrived in 1423, they preferred the fertile lower and easier-to-cultivate land along the Pagasetic Gulf around Lechónia and Argalastí, leaving the uplands to the Christians. Thanks to their benign neglect, villages sprouted up under the old monasteries that grew rich on silk and woollens, timber, fruit and olive oil, reaching their heyday of wealth in the 18th and 19th centuries, when stone workers from Epirus came and built bridges and *kalderími* for mules to transport their products down to the peninsula's tiny ports.

The merchants of Pelion travelled to Europe and came in contact with the Enlightenment, then returned home to found schools and libraries, notably in Zagorá and Miliés. Beautiful mansions went up, often financed by merchants who had moved to Alexandria in Egypt, and returned. The diaspora increased after 1881, when Thessaly became part of Greece (travelling had become much easier), although it came to an abrupt halt in the early 1960s with the election of Nasser, who nationalised Greek assets. In the meantime, new links opened up the Pelion, including a rail line to Vólos and roads, but after the ravages of World War II and the Greek Civil War, the whole area went into decline until the first visitors began to trickle in in the 1970s.

GETTING THERE AND AROUND Frequent buses (w ktelvolou.gr) from Vólos run to Portariá, Makrinítsa and Káto Lechónia, and five or so a day link up the other villages, but to really see the peninsula you need a car or a good pair of hiking boots. The Pelion is splendid walking country, criss-crossed by a hundred old cobblestone mule paths (*kalderími*), and little stone bridges. Download maps at w friendsofthekalderimi.org.

WHERE TO STAY *Archontikó* means mansion, and many in the Pelion have been converted into small inns. Most stay open all year – expect high-season prices on winter weekends and in summer. Always check ahead to see if they take credit cards.

North Pelion Portariá, which has a handy ATM by the car park under the main square, & a rare petrol station, is packed with options.

Pilion Terra [map, page 332] (24 rooms) 300m from Portariá on the Makrinítsa road; 24280 99799; w pilionterra.gr. Handsome stone-built hotel (& one of the few in the area with rooms for guests with disabilities) with extraordinary views. €€€–€€

Portariá Hotel & Spa (80 rooms) Portariá; ✆ 24280 90000; w portariahotel.gr. Contemporary hotel in the Pelion style, with indoor & outdoor pools, sauna, jacuzzi & gym, open to non-guests. B/fast inc. €€€–€€

Archontikó Karamarlis (9 rooms) Makrinítsa; ✆ 22480 99570; w archontikakaramarlis.gr. Each room in this 250-year-old mansion is decorated in a different period style, with a garden bar & lovely Neoclassical tea room. €

Archontikó Xanthá (7 rooms) Makrinítsa; ✆ 24283 00377; f archontikoxantha. At the highest point in town, extraordinary views, charming rooms (most with fireplace), & charming hosts. B/fast inc. €

East Pelion

Kalderimi Country House (7 rooms) Ag Tríada, Moúresi; ✆ 24260 49453; w kalderimihotel.gr. Warm, welcoming rooms in a traditional mansion of 1796. Handmade olive oil toiletries, plus yoga sessions, Thai massages & 'bio-dancing' on offer; organic Greek b/fast, inc. €€€

Lions 9 (8 rooms) Moúresi; ✆ 24260 49500; w lionsnine.com. Anna & Nikos run these handsome suites with terraces high over the sea, a few mins' drive from the beaches. B/fast inc. €€€

Aeolos (29 rooms) 20m from Choreftó Beach; ✆ 24260 22910; w aeolos.com.gr; ⊕ Apr–Oct. Lovely studios & apartments with balconies & Coco-Mat beds, around a small pool, in a quiet walled garden of olives & lemons. Minimum stay 2 nights. Buffet b/fast available. €€€–€€

Amanita Guesthouse (8 rooms) Tsagaráda; ✆ 24260 49707; w amanita.gr; ⊕ Apr–Oct & Christmas. One of the best: a traditional stone-walled mansion run by the delightful Filarete & Marianna, overlooking a 1.5ha organic garden, 5mins' drive from the beach; the owners offer a superb organic b/fast (inc). Filarete is passionate & knowledgeable about the local flora, & offers foraging excursions for mushrooms or culinary or medicinal herbs & greens. €€€–€€

Olga (6 rooms) Moúresi; ✆ 24260 49651; w hotelolga.gr. Rustic-chic rooms & suites with colourful contemporary art, Coco-Mat beds & stupendous views from the terrace. Delightful owners Dimitri & Lena cook up a superb b/fast (inc); don't miss their organic wine. €€€–€€

Paliá Damouchari (17 rooms) Damoúchari; ✆ 24260 49175; w pelion-damouchari.com. Comfortable open-plan studios with plenty of wood & stone, sleeping up to 4 in traditional buildings surrounded by olives. All have balcony & fireplace. €€€–€€

Lost Unicorn (8 rooms) Ag Paraskeví, Tsagaráda; ✆ 24260 49930; w lostunicornhotel.gr; ⊕ Apr–Oct & winter holiday w/ends. British Clare & Greek Christos run this delightful, ultra-cosy, book-filled inn with an excellent, candlelit restaurant (⊕ May–Sep Fri–Sun, & Aug eves; €€€) with a garden terrace, featuring the finest seasonal produce & Greek wines. Cooked-to-order full b/fast inc. €€

Oriades (5 rooms) Moúresi; ✆ 24260 48898; m 69739 93898; w oriades.com. Stone villa built in 1870 plus a handsome garden villa sleeping 4 with a fireplace; pretty garden & fruit orchard with hammocks, mountain views & free bikes for guests to borrow. B/fast inc. €€

Zagora (15 rooms) Ag Geórgios, Zagorá; ✆ 24260 22062; w zagorahotel.gr. Spacious apartments with great views over the sea, built in the traditional Pelion style, with gardens & a pool, plus bar & free parking. Buffet b/fast available; Wi-Fi in the lobby. €€

Marabou (18 rooms) 250m above Choreftó Beach; ✆ 24260 23710; w marabouhotel.gr. Friendly family-run hotel with a massive terrace, lovely views & an excellent restaurant (temporarily closed at the time of writing) serving great seafood with organic wines & their own homemade *tsípouro*. It's also the base for Pelion Scout (page 347). €€–€

Victoria's Guesthouse (2 apartments, 1 room) Damoúchari; ✆ 24260 49872; w gopelion.com; ⊕ Apr–Oct. Charming old hotel on the seafront, with a huge wooden terrace shaded by an enormous vine. The studios are simple, furnished with old wooden pieces & traditional weavings. €€–€

Faros (12 rooms) Mylopótamos; ✆ 24260 49994; f. Secluded hotel at the end of a rocky road immersed in olive groves. Lovely sea views, plus a garden, library & home-cooked meals; steps descend to the secluded beach below. Excellent b/fast €8. No credit cards. €

Rousis (10 rooms) Zagorá; ✆ 24260 23407. Family run, just off the central square with private parking. All rooms have a fireplace & most have sea view. The owner belongs to the local alpine club & is a great source of info on hikes. €

West Pelion
Sakali Mansion (9 rooms) Pinakátes; \24230 86560; w sakalihotel.gr. Beautiful restoration of a 19th-century mansion on a steep hillside, with a fireplace in every room & views down to the sea, with an outdoor pool, & a winter spa, jacuzzi & hammam. Lovely owners, too. Minimum stay 2 nights; b/fast inc. €€€€–€€€
Glorious Peleus Luxury Castle (11 rooms) Vyzítsa; \24230 86671; w gloriouspeleys.com. Built in 1791, this luxurious mansion-tower house-museum is full of antiques & attention to detail, with a library, charming sitting rooms, sauna, jacuzzi & a chance to experience 'sound therapy'. €€€
Archontiko Stathopoulou (6 rooms) Ag Geórgios Nileías; \24280 94071; w archontikostathopoulou.gr. Neoclassical complex built in 1888 by a merchant returning from Egypt, beautifully restored with mythological ceiling paintings. The pool terrace has lovely sunset views over the gulf; 4 independent villas available as well. €€€–€€
Santikos Mansion (8 rooms) Vyzítsa; \24230 86765; w santikoshotels.com. Built in 1860 this chic Greek country mansion has traditional furnishings, a charming lounge & a hot tub, plus views down to the sea. Good for families, but it's a 100m walk up from the car park. B/fast inc. €€€–€€
Karagiannopoulou Mansion (6 rooms) Vyzítsa; \24230 86717; w karagiannopoulou.com. A wonderful listed mansion of 1791, filled with traditional features & heirlooms; plus a shady garden. Delicious b/fast inc. €€
Palios Stathmos (8 rooms) Miliés; \24230 86425; w paliosstathmos.com. Next to the train station, traditional stone hotel immersed in greenery, with an excellent restaurant (€€). Often a minimum stay of 3 nights. €€–€

South Pelion
Six Keys Lodge [map, page 332] (6 rooms) Kaliftéri Beach, Áfyssos; \24230 33720; w sixkeys.gr. Stay within earshot of the waves on a semi-private beach in luxurious boutique rooms & with an award-winning restaurant (€€€€). B/fast inc. €€€€€–€€€€
Nikoleri Studios & Apartments (5 rooms) Lefókastro; m 69734 87427; w nikoleri-studios.gr. Peaceful unfussy spot with vine-covered terraces right on the sea, plus a shared garden with a barbecue. €€€–€€
Agia Kyriakí Guesthouse (5 rooms) Ag Kyriakí; \24230 91112; w agiakyriaki.gr. Pleasant & peaceful, in its own little garden. B/fast inc. €€–€
Des Roses (14 rooms) Plataniá; \24230 71268; w peliondesroses.gr. One of the first hotels here, run by a family who returned from Egypt in the 1960s & brought back their natural soap-making skills. B/fast made to order inc. €€–€
Trikeri Villas (6 rooms) Palaío Tríkeri; \24230 55056; w trikeri-villas.gr. On this small, car-free, island (a 5min ride by water taxi from Algopóros), you'll find seaside cottages in an olive grove by the sea with a playground, a 10min walk from the beach & tavernas. €€–€

✖ WHERE TO EAT AND DRINK
North Pelion
Kárdamo Oinomageireíon Makrinítsa; \24280 90131; ⊕ 13.00–23.00 daily. Breathtaking views from their terrace & tasty daily specials; try the kid in egg & lemon sauce if it's on the menu. €€
Kritsa Gastronomy Hotel Portariá; \24280 99121; w hotel-kritsa.gr; ⊕ 09.00–23.30 daily. On the main square filled with ancient plane trees, one of the very best restaurants in the area, with a constantly changing seasonal menu of Pelion dishes, & cookery classes (see w peliongastronomy.gr). Also 8 charming rooms (€€). €€
Aeriko [map, page 332] Between Portariá & Makrinítsa; \24280 99710; w aeriko-pelion.gr; ⊕ 10.00–01.00 daily. Romantic café-bar with some of the Pelion's very best views; at night all of Vólos sparkles below in a sea of lights. €
Alchemist Portariá; \24280 99744; ⊕ call for hours. Magical art-filled garden café to relax over a coffee & luscious desserts. €

East Pelion
El Resto Bar Ag Ioánnis; \24260 31005; w pelion-agapitos.com; ⊕ May–Sep 16.00–23.30 daily. Contemporary bar-restaurant

overlooking the sea in a swish hotel complex, where the award-winning chef prepares creative dishes, especially using locally sourced succulent meats, with a good wine & beer list. €€€

Agnáti Plateía Ag Taxiárchon, Tsagaráda; ☏ 24260 49210; ⊕ 12.30–22.30 Tue–Sun. Taverna under an enormous plane tree, serving stuffed courgette blossoms, grilled mushrooms, & meats cooked on charcoal or the spit. €€

Dipnosofistis Mylopótamos; ☏ 24260 49825; w dipnosofistis.com; ⊕ 11.00–01.00 daily. Atmospheric wine bar/restaurant under the plane trees on the road down to Mylopótamos Beach, featuring garden-fresh ingredients, exceptional wine list & cool music; very romantic by candlelight. €€

Galeos Ag Ioánnis; ☏ 24260 31116; ⊕ 17.00–23.00 Mon–Thu, noon–17.00 & 19.00–23.00 Fri–Sun. Excellent seafood taverna overlooking the beach, with good house wine. €€

Meintani (Niki's) Zagorá; ☏ 24260 22626; w meintani.gr; ⊕ 13.00–01.00 daily. Old-fashioned classic, with a flowery balcony; best for traditional slow-cooked dishes like *kleftikó* & stewed vegetables; in winter sit by the wood stove. €€

Paralos Ag Ioánnis; ☏ 24260 32052; f Paralosthebarexperience; ⊕ May–Sep 09.00–after midnight. The great staff make this a lovely place to relax on a sunbed under the eucalyptus trees, whiling away a day on the beach to good music, drinks & food. €€

Plimari Análipsi Beach; m 69777 06151; f plimari.tavern.pelio; ⊕ 13.00–22.00 daily. The perfect Greek seaside taverna, right on the water & serving organic veg from the garden with the owner's day's catch. €€

Tavernáki Vóntzos Moúresi; ☏ 24260 49416; w tavernaki-vontzos.gr; ⊕ 10.00–23.30 daily. For more than 50 years, reliable eats, with good stewed dishes such as lamb in lemon sauce & all the classic Greek sweets. €€

5F O Makis Kissós; ☏ 24260 31266; w ta5fomakis.gr; ⊕ 13.30–23.00 daily. Just off the square & still one of the Pelion's best tavernas, in business since 1939. Great home-baked bread & pies & daily specials slow cooked in the oven, along with fresh grilled meats. €

Synántisi Kissós main square; ☏ 24260 31620; w kissossynantisi.gr; ⊕ winter 13.30–22.30 Sat–Sun, summer 13.30–22.30 daily. Sit on the shady terrace, or by the fireplace in winter, at this family-run restaurant with some unusual local dishes, as well as mouthwatering *kontosoúvli* pork (slow roasted on a spit) & desserts. Book in Aug. €

Women's Agritourism Co-operative Zagorá; ☏ 24260 23566; w sweetstories.click; ⊕ 08.30–23.00 daily. Founded in 1993, the women run a café & shop selling Zagorá's famous *firíki* apple sweets, jams & other goodies. €

SPECIALITIES OF THE PELION

People from all across Greece (Epirótes, Vlachs, Slavs, islanders and others) found refuge in the relatively safe mountain villages of the Pelion and combined their own culinary traditions with the local produce; few had any money so most of the dishes they came up with were vegetarian. Don't miss the wild mushrooms in the spring and autumn, or deep red Zagorá apples and small, aromatic *firíki* apples (Centaurs' apples). The latter grow on trees that take 15 years to bear fruit, and then do so every two years, turning red only on the side kissed by the sun; they are often made into spoon sweets. Pelion jams and preserves (quince, fig, chestnut, cherries, bitter orange, walnut) are famous across Greece. Among the more unusual dishes you may find on menus are citrusy *krítama* (rock samphire) from the coast, preserved in salt and vinegar, and *tsitsíravla* (or *pistákia*), the tender shoots of the wild pistachio or terebinth, eaten fresh in salads in April and pickled with salt and vinegar to nibble with *tsípouro*. Other dishes you may see include *spetzofái* (fried green peppers, aubergine, goat or lamb sausage and tomatoes), stewed wild boar and *strapatsáda* (green peppers, feta, tomatoes and eggs).

West Pelion

To Salkimi Miliés; 24230 86010; noon–23.00 daily. Near the railway station, serving classic Greek & Anatolian dishes such as *hunkár begendí* (smoked aubergine puréed with bechamel, topped with sautéed lamb). €€

Drossia Taverna Pinakátes; 24230 86772; noon–late daily. *Drossiá* means shade, & this place on the edge of the village with its terrace under the trees is a classic, famous for succulent meats. €

Liostási Miliés; 24230 86082; Λιοστάσι / Liostasi; 13.00–midnight daily. Old-fashioned, laid-back taverna amid the olive groves, with extra tasty starters & often live music. Best to book; w/ends only out of season. €

To Panorama Miliés; 24230 86128; 10.00–23.30 daily. Classic taverna with a flower-covered terrace & views down to the sea. €

South Pelion

Manolas Ag Kyriakí; 24230 91311; Mar–Oct 11.00–midnight daily. Classic harbour-side seafood taverna, specialising in fish soup, crayfish & octopus. €€

Taverna Da Angelo (Psarotaverna 'O Aggelos') Kótes, Tríkeri; m 69797 50866; noon–23.00 daily. This seaside spot (a short walk from where you leave your car) is popular for fresh fish & seafood – mussels are a standout – delicious salads & sides, plus good house wine & very warm service. €€

O Achilleas Tríkeri; m 69740 72215; soyvlatzidiko.axilleas; 10.00–15.30 & 18.30–midnight Mon–Sat, 18.30–midnight Sun. The scent of meat in the grill greets you at this friendly spot on the central square of this inland village. €

SPORTS AND ACTIVITIES

IFOM Riding Centre Miliés; m 69811 76203. Riding for all ages & abilities from 1 to 3hrs; especially good for children & novices.

Mountain Escapes Tsagaráda; m 69324 18001; w mountainescapes.gr. Canyoning specialists.

Pelion Scout Choreftó; m 69949 55146; w pelionscout.com. Top provider of outdoor activities from their base in Choreftó, including hiking, boat trips (including the Sea Caves of Thetis), riding & cooking classes.

Pelion Ski Centre 12km from Portariá, on a 3km bypass road; 24213 13721; w pelionski.gr. Dec–Mar. 5 lifts, 3km of mostly intermediate slopes (1,471–1,170m), with a restaurant/bar & ski hire.

Zoumbosub Diving Centre Kaliftéri, Áfyssos; 24210 29574; w zoumbosub.gr. The pristine fish-filled waters here are made for diving; sites include numerous wrecks around the big peninsula.

WHAT TO SEE AND DO

North Pelion The northernmost, closest villages to Vólos are beautiful and have spectacular views, but are also the busiest, especially at weekends.

Portariá (Πορταριά; 650m), 12km from Vólos, was once famous for its trade in silk thread and is full of impressive mansions, nearly all of which are now guesthouses or hotels. The air is already noticeably cooler here and *kalderími* offer beautiful walks: the favourite is the panoramic, bucolic 5km **Path of the Centaurs**, signposted by the church of Ag Marína or 200m up the road to Makrinítsa, following a stream through the woodlands, criss-crossed by little wooden bridges. Also not to be missed is the **Portariá History Museum** (24280 99920; 10.00–14.00 Fri–Sun; free) in the Zoúlia mansion, which offers a look at local life in eras past. The apse of the 19th-century church of **Ag Nikoláos** is also of note, covered in elegant marble plaques carved with bas-reliefs.

'The balcony of Pelion', **Makrinítsa** (Μακρινίτσα), is 3km up the road, a favourite of coach parties (and often subject to a parking scrum at the entrance, as no cars are allowed). Makrinítsa's mansions are piled on such a steep slope that some have front doors on the third floor. Everyone congregates in the deeply shaded square, where a huge hollow plane tree dwarfs the church of **Ag Ioánnis** (1806), with a bijou apse covered with marble plaques, echoed in the decoration of the nearby **Lion fountain** of 1809 – the largest of some 50 in the village. Just above the square is the 13th-century church of **Panagía Theotókou**, used as a secret Greek school during the Turkish occupation, decorated with more marble plaques and stones bearing ancient and Byzantine inscriptions; and the newly remodelled **Byzantine Museum** (\ 24280 90016; w makrinitsamuseum.gr; ⊕ Apr–Sep 10.00–18.00 daily, Oct–Mar 10.00–16.00 Mon–Fri, 10.00–18.00 Sat & Sun) with an extremely rare Orthodox statue of the Virgin, wood carvings, and beautiful icons, including three by Theóphilos.

Although the 1,624m **Pourianós Stavrós** peak of Mount Pelion is a Greek Air Force installation and off-limits, you can get close by taking the path from Makrinítsa to Pourí (6hrs) via the West (Dytikó) Refuge. It was the giant twins Otus and Ephialtes who futilely piled Pelion on top of Ossa in their vain attempt to take over Olympus in the battle of gods versus giants or the Gigantomachia, the most popular of all Greeks vs 'Barbarians' themes in art. On a clear day the path takes in all of the villages along the Aegean coast of the peninsula and even the ghostly peak of Mount Athos, which was also involved in the mighty fray.

Above Portariá, lofty – at 1,200m – **Chánia** (Χάνια) is named after the old inns that welcomed travellers, a few of which survive. A road winds down here to Agriá via **Drákia** (Δράκεια), with a delightful main square, cobblestone streets and houses built by workers from Epirus. But more than any other Pelion village it has known tragedy: a monument remembers the 115 men killed by the Nazis in December 1943 as a reprisal for an attack.

East Pelion On the steep Aegean coast, microclimates collide: here chestnuts grow and rushing springs water plum, cherry and the peninsula's famous apple orchards just minutes up from classic Mediterranean shores. This is the Pelion at its most irresistibly bucolic, with the most gorgeous beaches tucked under the cliffs.

The Pelion's largest village, **Zagorá** (Ζαγορά), is spread out in four hamlets, each with its own square – Ag Paraskeví, Ag Kyriakí, Ag Geórgios and Metamorphósis. In Ottoman times it took advantage of its isolation to prosper, producing 32 tonnes of silk a year; in 1712 its merchants opened a secret school (where revolutionary poet Rígas Feraíos studied; page 11) and a library (w library-zagora.gr/#), now housing more than 10,000 books. The church of Ag Geórgios has a huge gilt iconostasis with lacy carvings, and the beaches below are lovely. **Choreftó** (Χορευτό), its old silk port, is long and sandy; or head 2km south for the more peaceful **Ag Saránta** (Αγ Σαράντα) with its tiny pebbles and iconic sea rock nicknamed the 'Monk' (arrive early as parking is limited and the sun goes behind the cliffs in late afternoon). To the north lie the pretty coves of **Análipsi** (Ανάληψης). The most peaceful beach of them all is 8km further on by way of little **Pourí** (Πουρί): **Ovriós** (Οβριός), at the end of a rough road best done in a 4x4. Further north, accessible only by sea, are the **Sea Caves of Thetis**, legendary home of shape-shifting sea goddess Thetis. After an oracle warned the lusty Zeus that the son of Thetis would be stronger than his father, Zeus arranged for her to marry the mortal Peleus and, keen to make the wedding a success, invited all the gods except for Eris ('strife'). In spite, Eris sent a golden apple inscribed 'to the fairest' to the wedding and set the Trojan War in motion, where Achilles, son of Thetis and Peleus, would meet his destiny.

Back towards the south, **Kissós** (Κισσός) up above is built in an amphitheatre around another leafy flagged square; its 17th-century church of **Ag Marína** has a lavish, intricate gilded iconostasis (1802) by Ioánnis Pagónis, nicknamed 'the jewel of the Pelion'. There's another wonderful iconostasis in the church at **Moúresi** (Μούρεσι), the next village over a gorge, where every house has a minimum of a hundred pots of gardenias, roses and camellias on its terrace.

Below, the beach of **Ag Ioánnis** (Αγ Ιωάννης), with its long coarse white sand, is the busiest organised beach on the east coast, with plenty of families, and is your best bet for nightlife in the area. Further south is quieter **Papá Neró** (Παπά Νερό) and **Damoúchari** (Νταμούχαρη), a charming hamlet with a ruined Venetian castle and a safe, minuscule port – once the most important one on the Pelion – so picturesque that it was used as the location for a scene in *Mamma Mia!* where Meryl Streep waltzes down to the harbour and joins the locals in a dance on a pier built for the film.

Huge boulders, deep forests and streams cutting into ravines surround **Tsagaráda** (Τσαγκαράδα), another village spread out in four hamlets, each with its own square. One, Ag Paraskeví, has the best centrepiece: a church of 1746, a pretty fountain and a truly magnificent **thousand-year-old plane tree**, just over 15m in circumference; a second one nearly as big shades the square of another hamlet, Ag Taxiárches. One of the loveliest and easiest walks on the whole Pelion descends to Damoúchari in about another hour.

There are more beaches below: sandy, pebbly **Mylopótomas** (Μυλοποτάμας) is divided in two by a mighty rock pierced by a natural tunnel. While there, make the 2km coastal walk from Damoúchari to dramatic, boulder-strewn **Fakístra** (Φακίστρα) **Beach**, one of the most beautiful in Greece, hemmed in by cliffs, passing by a 'secret school' built into the cliff, where Greek children learned to read during the Ottoman occupation.

West Pelion

The busier, drier and far more built-up west side of the peninsula along the Pagasetic Gulf is only a short hop from Vólos, with its easy-to-reach beaches that have a more classic Greek holiday feel. Beaches are more sheltered if less spectacular, but do get brilliant sunsets. The villages hanging high above the coast – Vyzítsa, Ag Geórgios Nileías, Pinakátes and Miliés – make the nicest places to stay. A spectacular corniche road links them to the north coast.

Heading down the coast from **Agriá** (Αγριά), the main seaside playground of Vólos, **Áno Lechónia** (Άνω Λεχώνια) is a busy market town with the train to Miliés. The string of lovely villages in the hills were the centre of Pelion's wine and *tsípouro* industry before it was devastated by phylloxera in the 19th century. **Ag Lavréntios** is named after its picturesque monastery, founded by a monk of the same name from Athos in the 12th century. It went through many subsequent changes, and has Byzantine murals and an icon of the *Birth of Christ* by Pagónis. It is also where international musicians gather in August and September, to participate in programmes, workshops and concerts organised by the Music Village; to take part in the sessions, or to see the programme of concerts, check w music-village.gr. Lofty **Ag Geórgios Nileías** (Αγ Γεωργίος Νηλείας) has spectacular views, but there are even better ones from the East Refuge (Ανατολικό καταφύγιο), an hour's walk further up the slopes of Pelion's long ridge (signposted 2km east, near Taverna Paliovígla).

To the south are two other stunning villages, **Pinakátes** (Πινακάτες), high atop its ravine, and **Vyzítsa** (Βυζίτσα), with its many springs and the largest collection of mansions and tower houses, built by wealthy merchants returned from Egypt. There are beautiful murals in the church of Ag Ioánnis Pródromos (1791); and below is the busy, organised sandy beach at **Kalá Nerá** (Καλά Νερά).

In West Pelion's most important village, **Miliés** (Μηλιές), the wise centaur Cheiron had his cave (right under the steel rail bridge). It was for centuries the major cultural centre on this side of the Pelion and boasts one of the peninsula's most beautiful churches, right near the station: **Ag Taxiárches** has a superb gilded iconostasis and pulpit, and frescoes of the Zodiac, Hell and other stories from

THE LITTLE PELION TRAIN

This 60cm-gauge train – one of the narrowest ever made – is nicknamed Moutzóuri ('Smudgy') from the old days of steam. Begun in 1894, six years after Thessaly became part of Greece, the railway was the project of Sicilian engineer Evaristo de Chirico (page 338), who designed its 11 stone viaducts and bridges over the ravines to reach its terminus in the hill village of Miliés. It made its first journey from Vólos in 1903, and its last in 1971, but has since been revived as a heritage train (w hellenictrain.gr/en/mythical-route; ⊕ at the time of writing departures from Ano Lechonia for Miliés left at 10.00 on Sat & Sun, returning at 15.00; €10 each way). The train travels 16km in 90 minutes with a stop in Áno Gatzéa, and gives you enough time to enjoy pretty Miliés before the return journey. It takes in lovely views over the mountains and the Pagasetic Gulf. Book in advance via w newtickets.hellenictrain.gr/Channels. HellenicTrainWeb (select the language in the upper right, where it says 'Γλώσσα') as it can sell out.

the Bible. The School of Miliés was founded in 1814 by three local scholars and writers, leaders of the Greek Enlightenment and members of the revolutionary 'Friendly Society', along with the **Public Library** nicknamed the 'Cure of the Soul' (\ 24230 86260; w vivl-mileon.mag.sch.gr; ⊕ 08.00–14.00 Mon–Fri, 10.00–14.00 Sat; free). One of the scholars, Ánthimos Gazís, proclaimed Thessaly's allegiance to Greek independence in May 1821 in Ag Taxiárches. It proved to be premature, and afterwards the school and library's fortunes went up and down, finally reopening for good after Thessaly joined Greece in 1881. The Germans destroyed the original library building during World War II, but some 4,000 rare volumes (including 15th-century books printed by Aldus Manutius in Venice) that survived out of 10,000 or so are here. Also nearby, in the town hall, is the **Museum of Miliés** (\ 24230 86602; ⊕ 10.00–14.00 Wed–Sun; free), with old photographs of the village and train, a replica of Gazís's Revolutionary flag and a folklore collection.

Back on the coast, **Káto Gatzéa** (Κάτω Γατζέα) is where the Reppos Shipyards built a 28.5m replica 50-oar (*penteconter*) *Argo* in 2004–06, using only five kinds of wood from trees growing in the Pelion, Bronze Age tools, rope and canvas, with only Mycenaean art and Homeric descriptions as their guide (Tim Severin's *Argo*, built in 1984 and used in the expeditions described in *The Jason Voyage* and *The Ulysses Voyage*, was a 16.5m scale model with 20 oars). The ship was successfully rowed by a team of 50 volunteers to Georgia, and in the summer it often reappears in Vólos harbour [335 B5]; to visit, contact Míkos Dókos (m 69465 01031; w argonautes2008.gr).

South Pelion The southern Pelion, with its olives, pines and cypresses, is more typical of the Greek coast, with sandy beaches. South of the big resort of Áfyssos, it grows increasingly empty.

It does have several small ports, with **water-taxis** linking the little port of Plataniá with Skiáthos. Get to Palaío Tríkeri by water-taxi from Alogóporos Beach just opposite the island, or from Ag Kyriakí in the far south (a signboard lists their mobile numbers).

Áfyssos (Άφυσσος) could play the role of a classic Greek village in a film. Its amphitheatre of traditional tile-roofed houses rises above the orchards and a coast scalloped with beaches; here the Argonauts stopped to take on water before sailing into the unknown. There are several peaceful coves to the north, tucked under olive trees and pines. Across the Pagasetic Gulf the mountains shimmer like a mirage.

The biggest village in the south is **Argalastí** (Αργαλαστή; population almost 2,000), a status it has held since Ottoman times. On Saturday mornings it holds the Pelion's only market. Its landmark, near its pretty square, is the tall marble bell tower of 1913 with a pair of Russian bells. A network of roads leads to beaches on either coast: to the east **Potistiká** (Ποτιστικά), a sandy beach with giant wrinkly monoliths in the middle, and more sheltered **Páltsi** (Πάλτση) to the south of Potistiká; to the west, choose between **Lefókastro** (Λεφόκαστρο), **Páou** (Πάου), **Chórto** (Χόρτο) and the longest, **Kalámos** (Κάλαμος).

Continue south to the turquoise coves dotting the gulf shore to **Milína** (Μηλίνα), a quiet resort with banana plants and beautiful sunset views facing the deserted islet of **Alatás**. Southeast of Milína, through a forest of olives, **Plataniá** (Πλατανιάς) is a little port looking across to the island of Évia. It has a long, sheltered crescent of sand, and an even nicer one reached by an 800m path at **Mikró** (Μικρό).

Further south the landscapes grow emptier and emptier. On the toe of the peninsula, **Tríkeri** (Τρίκερι) overlooks the narrow strait, the Diávolos Trikeríou, where the Greek triremes first tried to squeeze the invading Persian navy in 480BC, before succeeding at the Battle of Salamis. Tríkeri was settled by islanders of Palaió ('Old') Tríkeri after one too many pirate attacks. It is dotted with impressive mansions and for centuries was accessible only by boat; here the men spend so much time at sea, that women run things and even pass property down the female line. In the church of Ag Triáda there's a beautiful carved iconostasis and Napoleon's throne, of all things, brought here by a local sea captain from Barcelona, where Bonaparte was meant to sit – if he ever made it to Catalunya. Its whitewashed port of **Ag Kyriakí** (Αγ Κυριακη) with its bobbing fishing boats is 4km south.

The serene, wonderfully car-free islet of **Palaió Tríkeri** (Παλαιό Τρίκερι) is the only inhabited island in the Pagasetic Gulf, with 80 permanent residents, several quiet beaches (free camping – officially not permitted – may be possible on the westerly ones), two fish tavernas and 75,000 olive trees. In the centre of the island, a 15-minute walk from the port village of Ag Ioánnis, the pretty **Moní Panagía Evangelístria** was founded in 1837 after the discovery of a miraculous icon in the roots of an olive tree, and has beautiful pebble mosaics. Between 1948 and 1953 during the dark years of the Greek Civil War, 5,000 female political prisoners lived in the cells and tents around the monastery, 1,500 of whom were condemned to death. Yet their story is one of resilience; in spite of the extremely harsh conditions, they set up schools, an infirmary, a 60-voice choir and theatre.

12 | THE SPORÁDES (ΣΠΟΡΑΔΕΣ) ISLANDS

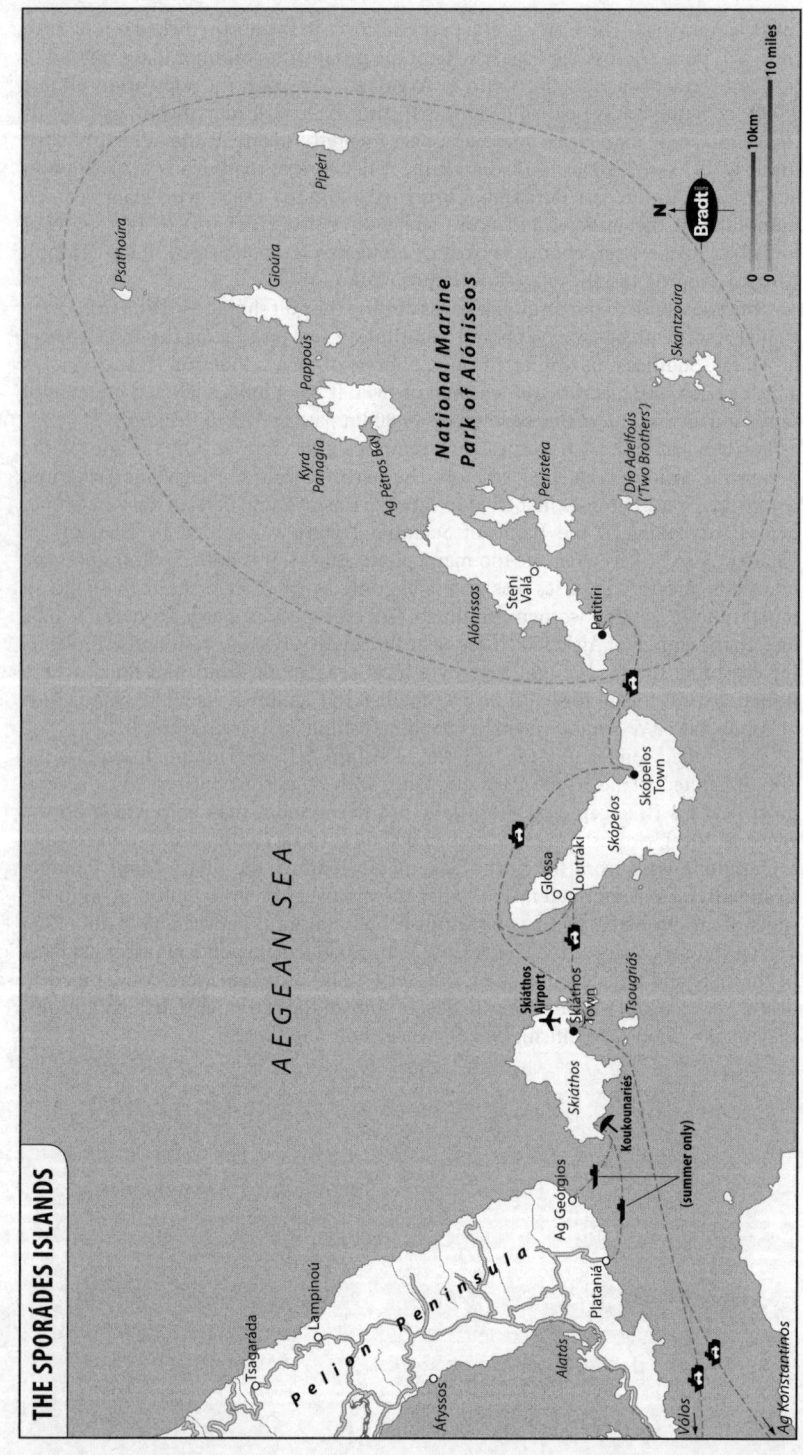

12

The Sporádes (Σποράδες) Islands

The Sporádes, the 'scattered' islands off the Pelion's Aegean shore, are as lovely as the peninsula itself, but because they are poor in antiquities or names that anyone remembers from school history, they were among the last Greek islands to be 'discovered'. Then an airport was built on Skiáthos: word spread, holiday photos were passed around showing beaches and villages that fit many people's image of a holiday paradise, and the rest is history. Three islands float temptingly a short hop off the coast: Babylonian Skiáthos, closest to the Pelion, with the most beautiful beaches; dignified Skópelos, which has kept much of its Greek character; and Alónissos, gateway to Greece's first national marine park.

HISTORY

The first settlers on the Sporádes were from Thrace. In the 16th century BC, Minoan colonists introduced the cultivation of olives and grapes. After their fall, Dolopians from Thessaly (first cousins of the Achaeans) took their place, using the Sporádes as bases for daring naval expeditions. In the 8th century BC, settlers from Chalkí (Évia) captured the Sporádes during the same colonisation drive that led them to Chalkidikí, and continued the bold sea traditions of the Dolopians. This increasingly brought them into conflict with Athens, until 476BC, when Kimon and the Athenians destroyed the Sporádes' fleets. The Athenians managed to present themselves as liberators rather than conquerors; the Sporádes adopted the model of Athenian democracy, and Athena became the prominent goddess in local pantheons.

When the Spartans defeated Athens in the Peloponnesian War, they briefly took the Sporádes. A greater threat came in the person of Philip II of Macedon, who claimed the islands in a dispute that attracted the attention of the entire Greek world. Philip's success in 322BC was a prelude to nabbing Athens itself.

In Roman times, the Sporádes retained their traditional links with Athens. The Byzantines, however, made them a place of exile for unruly nobles, who set themselves up as the local aristocracy until 1207, when the Gizzi of Venice picked up the Sporádes as their share in the spoils of the Fourth Crusade. Filippo Gizzi usurped control from a senior relative and ruled as a pirate king until Likários, admiral of Emperor Michael Paleológos, took him in chains to Constantinople. Afterwards, possession of the Sporádes see-sawed between Greeks and Franks, until Mohammed the Conqueror took Constantinople in 1453. The islanders invited Venice back as the lesser evil, although the Venetians were forced out when all their crafty agreements with the Ottomans crumbled before the attacks of the admiral Hayreddin Barbarossa in the 1500s.

Once they had the Sporádes, the Turks neglected them; the islands were so exposed to pirates that a permanent Turkish population never settled there. In the

1821 revolution, insurgents from Thessaly found refuge on the islands, and in 1830 the Treaty of London included them in the original kingdom of Greece.

SKIÁTHOS

One of the most popular destinations in the country, racy, cosmopolitan Skiáthos (Σκιάθος) is not for the shy teetotaller or anyone looking for a slice of 'authentic' Greece. An isolated peasant community in the early 1970s, Skiáthos catapulted faster than any other island into big-money tourism, so fast that corruption and violence were long a factor in local life. Away from the main road, it is as stunning as ever, rimmed with 62 gorgeous beaches. Add to this a host of lively bars and restaurants and you have the ingredients for a heady cocktail that attracts a fun-seeking crowd.

HISTORY When Xerxes sailed to conquer Athens in 480BC, his fleet met a fierce storm off Skiáthos. So many ships were damaged that Xerxes put in for repairs and, during his stay, invented the world's first-known navigational aid on a reef called Myrmes (now Lephtéris and still a menace to ships). 'Thither the barbarians brought and set up a pillar of stone that the shoal might be clearly visible,' Herodotus wrote. Thanks to its guidance, Xerxes slipped past the Athenian patrols towards his first sea battle at Artemissíon (a draw) and eventual defeat at Salamis. Part of the pillar can still be seen today, in the courtyard of the Naval Cadet School in Piraeus. The rest of Skiáthos's history follows that of the other Sporádes. The Gizzi ruled the island in the name of Venice and built the fort on Boúrtzi islet by the present-day town. The Skiathot navy assisted the Russians against the Ottomans at Cêsme, and the islanders revolted against the Turks in 1805, then sent so many ships to fight for independence that Skiáthos itself was left unprotected and prey to marauders.

GETTING THERE AND AWAY
By air Regular flights arrive year-round at Skiáthos's Alexándros Papadiamántis Airport (code JSI; w jsi-airport.gr) from Athens on Olympic, Aegean and Sky Express, plus a few from Thessaloníki on Olympic and endless charter flights in summer from all over Europe which bring nearly half a million passengers a year. Airport **taxis** are abundant and cost from about €10 to the centre. Backpackers can **walk** there in about half an hour.

Skiáthos Airport is a favourite with British plane-spotters, who gather at the beach and road right at the end of runway 2, where the planes come in just 10–20m overhead. Every year a few spotters get blown away by jet blasts – if they're lucky they land on the sand, if not they land in the tabloids.

By sea (Port Authority \ 24270 22017) Ferries and frequent hydrofoils connect daily with Vólos (page 334), with some ferries stopping at the islands in succession, making island hopping quite easy. There are also less frequent ferries from Ag Konstantínos in central Greece (buses from Athens) with seasonal service to Skiáthos and Skópelos.

GETTING AROUND
By sea Seasonal excursion boats go to Plataniá and Ag Geórgios on the Pelion, as well as Skópelos and Alónissos and nearby islets. Water-taxis (w skiathoswatertaxi.gr) in the Old Harbour go to the beaches. Some offer round-island trips, but the north side is fairly uninteresting and the sea can be rough.

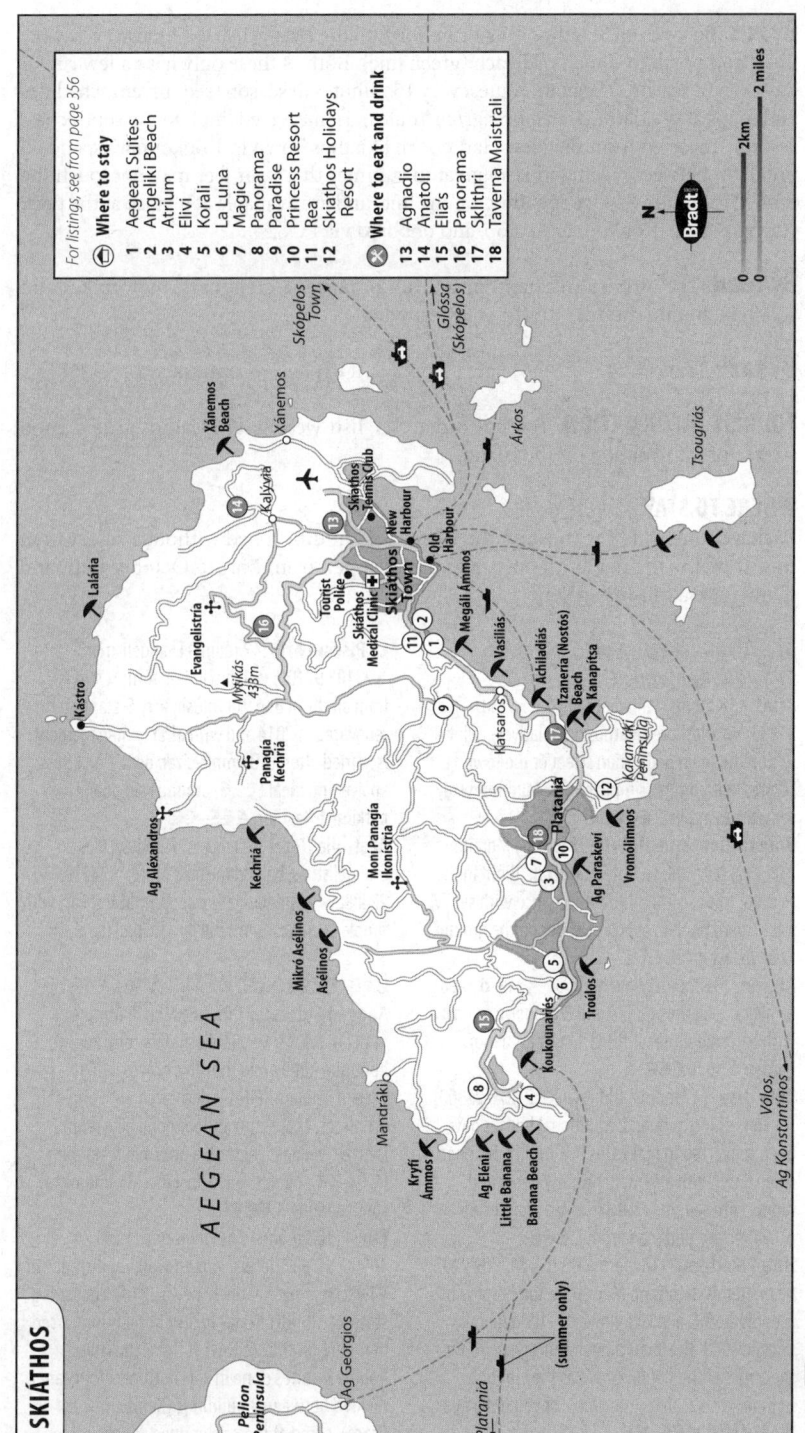

By bus Buses from Skiáthos Town run north to the Evangelistría Monastery (yellow line), and north to Xánemos Beach (green line). Both of these only have a few runs a day even in season. The main route, every 15 minutes in season (see current schedules and maps at w skiathostransports.gr/en/routes), is line 2 (red line), to the south coast resorts. These go from the New Harbour in Skiáthos Town to Koukounariés, and all points in between. Demand is so great in summer that your feet may not touch the floor. Tickets are €2–3, depending on the line, and are available at a kiosk at the port, Akrópoli stop, Koukounáries stop, and onboard via POS.

By road The airport and harbour are full of places to rent cars, motorbikes and scooters, but be careful – traffic is fast-moving.

By taxi Taxis (\24270 24461) are a popular, if expensive, option.

TOURIST INFORMATION The up-to-date English website w skiathos.gr is a good source of information on the island.

 WHERE TO STAY *Map, page 355*
Package tours rule the roost on the island, and finding a bed without a reservation in summer is the devil. All but a handful are open from May to October only, and many have a minimum stay.

Skiáthos Town *Not individually mapped*
Atlas (18 rooms) Papadiamántis; m 69801 31333; w atlashotelskiathos.gr. Relatively quiet (it's on the main pedestrian street of the town centre), with bright, simple rooms. Minimum stay sometimes applies. €€€€€
Bourtzi Boutique Hotel (38 rooms) Moraïtou 8; \24270 21304; w hotelbourtzi.gr. Right in the heart of town, contemporary elegance with sat TV, a courtyard pool & cool cocktail bar on the ground floor. B/fast inc. €€€€
Alkyon (36 rooms) New harbour; \24270 22981; w alkyon-skiathos.gr. Tasteful & modern; rooms with balcony, some with sea view, plus a roof garden & pool. €€€
Villa Orsa (17 rooms) Old town; \24270 22300. For something quieter, 2 traditional houses have been converted to make this beautifully designed small hotel with a garden; brightly decorated rooms with sea-view balconies & a wonderful b/fast terrace under an arbour. €€€
Hotel Meltémi (18 rooms) Port; \24270 22493; w meltemiskiathos.gr. Modest design hotel with friendly staff & a loyal following – it's generally booked solid. The bar is a good vantage point for the antics of the flotilla crowd as they moor & unmoor with zealous gung-ho. Conveniently near the bus stop. €€€–€€

La Piscine Art (42 rooms) Evangelistrías; \23105 92100; w lapiscine.gr. A short stroll from all the action, this plush, arty 5-star hotel, renovated in 2014 and with affable management, is named after its Olympic-sized pool. Don't miss an evening meal (€€€) around said pool. Free parking; b/fast inc. €€€–€€
Australia Hotel (23 rooms) Parodos, Odos Evangelístrias, behind the post office; \24270 22488; w australiaskiathos.gr. Central & cheap, with simple en-suite rooms; run by a helpful family. €

Beaches south of Skiáthos Town
Aegean Suites (21 rooms) Megáli Ámmos; \24218 88043; w santikoshotels.com. Swish boutique hotel amid the olive groves, where each of its glam suites is decorated with original art pieces. There's an outdoor pool, bike rental, jacuzzi, wellness centre & a gourmet restaurant (€€€€€), open to all. B/fast inc. Minimum stay some periods. €€€€€
Elivi (108 rooms) Koukounariés; \24274 40900; w elivihotels.com. In walking distance of 4 beaches, this relatively new (2018), cocooning, state-of-the-art 5-star luxury hotel is immersed in nature on the southwest tip of the island. Rooms & suites done in soft natural colours are divided between 3 buildings (Xenia, Nest & Grace), some of the pricier ones are complete

with private pool & garden; there are also a pair of pools purified by electrolysis, plus an Elemis spa, beach bars, several restaurants & bars, watersports, kids clubs, etc. B/fast inc. Minimum stay some periods. €€€€€
Princess Resort (130 rooms) Ag Paraskeví; \24270 49731; w santikoscollection.com/ princess. Bright & airy with very stylish & well-appointed rooms, enjoying one of the best positions on one of the best beaches. It has a buffet restaurant, watersports, a spa, & lots of diversions for children. Good b/fast (inc). Minimum stay some periods. €€€€€
Atrium (75 rooms) Ag Paraskeví; \24270 49345; w atriumhotel.gr. Elegant, spacious rooms on a hill above the beach, all with balcony & nearly all have a sea view. Excellent b/fast (inc) & a buffet restaurant for guests, plus pool. Good for children. €€€€€–€€€€
Angeliki Beach Hotel (17 rooms) Megáli Ámmos; \24270 22354; w angelikihotel. gr. 10 steps from the sea, in a peaceful setting with a shady garden, beach bar & plenty of loungers, & super staff. Minimum stay some periods. €€€€€–€€€
La Luna (34 rooms) On the hill overlooking Troúlos Bay; \24270 49262; w skiathoslaluna. gr. Well-equipped studios & maisonettes with AC, a lovely pool & great views, 10mins' walk from the sea. No restaurant, but weekly barbecue nights at the pool bar. Minimum stay some periods. €€€€€–€€€
Korali (41 rooms) Troúlos; \24270 49212; w skiathoskorali.gr. Studio suites & apartments, with fully equipped kitchens & balconies with sea views, & pool. Minimum stay some periods. €€€€–€€€
Magic (35 rooms) Ag Paraskeví; \24270 49453; w magic-hotel.com. 250m from beaches, nice hotel with nice owners & rooms with balcony, kidney-shaped pool with jacuzzi, plus restaurant (€€€) & bar. B/fast inc. Minimum stay some periods. €€€€–€€€
Skiathos Holidays Resort (17 suites & villas) Vromólimnos; \24270 21596; w skiathos-holidays.gr. In a single complex close to the beach, a wide choice of accommodation, from junior suites to 3-bedroom villas. Modern & minimalist, set in beautifully landscaped grounds. Minimum stay some periods. Wide range of prices. Generally €€€€–€€€
Rea (14 rooms) 5mins from Megáli Ámmos; \24270 23065; w reaskiathos.gr. Inland, in between bus stops 4 & 5, with well-equipped rooms, studios & an apartment sleeping up to 5 run by a wonderful, hospitable brother-&-sister team, complete with pleasant terrace & pool. €€€€–€€
Paradise (46 rooms) Katsarós; m 69811 98781; w paradiseholidays.gr. In a quiet position on the pine-wooded hillside a 10min walk from Vasiliás Beach. Very hospitable owners, bright rooms, large pool & restaurant. Free minibus to Skiáthos Town. €€€–€€
Panorama (36 rooms) Koukounariés; \24270 49382; w hotel-panorama.net. Opposite bus stop 24, by the lake, & 9mins' walk from the beach; pleasant, relaxed hotel with a pool. Minimum stay some periods. €€

✖ **WHERE TO EAT AND DRINK** *Map, page 355*
Skiáthos Town *Not individually mapped*
The Final Step Plateía Ag Nikólaos; \24270 21877; w finalsteprestaurant.com; ⏲ 19.00–late daily. Pam's creative Mediterranean cuisine, served on the white terrace high over the port, is a favourite for a special evening out in town. Lots of vegetarian & seafood choices, some with an Asian touch. €€€€
Windmill In a restored mill near the port; \24270 24550; w skiathoswindmill.gr; ⏲ May–Sep 18.45–23.00 daily. Food with an international flavour & a lovely view (book the 'honeymoon balcony'); very popular. €€€
Alexandros Near Trión Ierarchón church; \24270 22431; f Taverna Alexandros; ⏲ 06.00–midnight daily. Traditional taverna on a pedestrian street with tables under a big mulberry tree. Good lamb & salads; live music most nights in season. €€€–€€
Mesogia Taverna Grigoríou; \24270 21440; f mesogia taverna; ⏲ 18.30–midnight daily. Tucked away in the back streets, the island's oldest taverna (since 1925) has an excellent repertoire of Greek delicacies including outstanding courgette fritters (*kolokithakéftedes*) & grilled lamb. €€
Folia Dimitriádi (follow the road behind the National Bank); m 69945 58239; ⏲ 11.00–01.00 daily. Traditional, excellent & inexpensive; known for their moussaka. €

North of Skiáthos Town

Agnadio On the Evangelistría Monastery road; 24270 22016; 18.30–midnight daily. Very popular with its chic blue-&-white interior, its terrace with beautiful views & tasty Greek fare – great moussaka. Don't head up without booking. €€

Anatoli Kalývia; 24270 21907; AnatoliSkiathos; 18.30–23.00 daily. Family-run, with fresh seafood & a gorgeous view from the terrace, accompanied by Greta the cat. In the same area as Agnadio, past the turn-off to the monastery. €€

Panorama Ag Anágyri; m 69441 92066; w skiathospanorama.gr; 13.00–midnight Wed–Mon. As the name promises, fabulous views over Skiáthos Town & over the sea to Skópelos. The menu is mostly Italian: good bruschetta, pizza & pasta. (A bit hard to find: see the detailed map on its website.) €€

Beaches south of Skiáthos Town

Elia's Mandraki Village, Koukounariés; 24270 49301; w mandraki-skiathos.gr; 09.00–19.00 daily. Recently renovated garden restaurant serving beautiful modern Mediterranean cuisine, served with a smile. €€€

Sklithri Sklíthri, near Tzanería Beach; m 69469 32869; sklithritavernaskiathos; 13.00–22.30 daily. On the beach, serving delicious fresh fish & good pasta dishes. €€€

Taverna Maistrali Plataniá; 24270 49511; 13.00–01.00 daily. Old wooden favourite, with delicious takes on the Greek classics & a play area for the kids. €€

ENTERTAINMENT AND NIGHTLIFE Having eaten, you'll be spoilt for choice when it comes to bars. On a warm summer evening, the picturesque bars on the waterfront of Skiáthos Town and along the airport road come into their own; some stay open until dawn. In season, impromptu bars appear on many of the distant beaches, but the following are all in town.

Admiral Benbow Inn Polytechníou; m 69438 73124; 19.30–02.00 daily. Popular & friendly, with lots of music memorabilia, providing a little corner of old England playing golden oldies hits.

Andersson's Papadiamántis; m 69459 61789; w anderssonsbar.com; 18.00–02.00 daily. Forget the big Swedish flag out front. A comfortable & classy retreat; great cocktails & a nice terrace. Music quiz Tue & Fri nights.

Bourtzi On the Boúrtzi promontory; 24270 23900; w bourtzi-skiathos.gr; 10.00–23.00 daily, Jul–Aug until 02.00. A swanky bar with a lovely, candlelit sea-view setting. Cocktails, tapas, pizza & salads (€€€).

De Facto Grigoríou St; m 69863 86266 ; De Facto Bar Skiathos; 09.00–03.00 daily. Quiet & pleasant, the LGBTQIA+ meeting place on Skiathos for 20 years.

Kentavros Mitropolítou Ananíou; 24270 22980; Kentavros Bar; 21.30–04.00 daily. Funky jazz & blues atmosphere; great cocktail menu.

SPORTS AND ACTIVITIES

Achladies Watersports & Rental Boats Achiladiás Beach; m 69810 34270, 69895 01615; w skiathos-rent-boat.com. Hire boats with or without licence, or with a captain; plus parasailing & beach transfers.

Alpha Rentals New Harbour; m 69748 30745; w alpha-rentals.gr. Hybrid bikes & bicycles for exploring the island.

Dolphin Diving Centre Tzaneria (Nostós) Beach; m 69806 63065; w dolphindivingskiathos.com; May–late Oct. Diving courses, equipment rental & guided tours including cave dives, wrecks & coral.

Skiáthos Fishing Trips Old Harbour; m 69877 28444; . Snorkelling & fishing trips.

Skiathos Tennis Club Off the airport road (turn right at the Asterias supermarket); 24270 24054; w tennisclubskiathos.com; all year. Tennis courts floodlit on summer nights, restaurant & a swimming pool.

OTHER PRACTICALITIES There are plenty of banks and pharmacies in the narrow streets of Skiáthos Town; the post office is there too at Papadiamánti 3.

> ### ALEXÁNDROS PAPADIAMÁNTIS, THE MASTER OF NEO-HELLENIC PROSE
>
> It's safe to say that Alexándros Papadiamántis wouldn't recognise his hometown or island today. The Skiáthos that he immortalised in his short stories, with stark realism and serene, dispassionate prose, was a poor, tragic place, where most of the men were forced to emigrate or spend years at sea and the women lived hard lives of servitude to accumulate a *príka*, or dowry, for each daughter; this was such a burden that, when a little girl died, other women would comfort the mother by saying, 'Happy woman, all you need to marry this one off is a sheet.'
>
> Papadiamántis' strongest story, *The Murderess* (1903), concerns an old woman who, reflecting on the conditions of her own life, sees the monstrous injustice of the system and quietly smothers her sickly newborn granddaughter, to spare her daughter the need to slave away for her dowry. Always the island's herbal doctor (the one herb she could never find was one for contraception), the old woman believes that her destiny is to alleviate the suffering of others, and she kills four other daughters of poor families before being pursued to her own death. As she drowns, the last thing she sees is the wretched vegetable garden that was her own dowry. Twelve of Papadiamántis' stories have been beautifully translated by Elizabeth Constantinides as *Tales from a Greek Island*, complete with a map (it's usually available at the house) – a perfect read on Skiáthos, more than a century on.

Skiáthos Medical Clinic Periphery road; 24270 22111; w medskiathos.com

Tourist Police Periphery road; 24270 23172

SKIÁTHOS TOWN The capital and only real town on the island, Skiáthos is a gentle spread of traditional whitewashed houses and cobbled streets, overhung with bougainvillaea over a razzmatazz of in-your-face commercialism. It has two harbours, separated by the pretty **Boúrtzi** promontory, with the remains of a Venetian fortress, a café, summer theatre and cultural centre; you can dive off the rock here and pretend you're in a Martini ad. A couple of streets in from the harbour, you can climb the highest building in town – the **clock tower** by the church of Ag Nikólaos – for views over the coast and rooftops.

If hedonism palls, get a shot of culture at the **Papadiamántis House Museum** (Papadiamántis 12; 24270 23843; ⊕ summer 09.30–13.30 & 17.00–19.00 daily, call for winter hours; €1.50), dedicated to one of modern Greece's first and finest novelists, Alexándros Papadiamántis (1851–1911; see above), who grew up here; there's memorabilia, portraits, and traditional textiles and furniture.

Taxi-boats in the old harbour wait to whisk you off to **Árkos** (around €8 return), a gorgeous little islet with a fine sandy beach and a good taverna or, in half an hour, to **Tsougriás islet**. In the 1960s the Beatles wanted to buy it. It's uninhabited, an ideal place to escape the crowds, with its fine sand and excellent swimming. There's a taverna offering expensive sandwiches by the beach, and an old church that once served a community of a few fishermen and shepherds. Tsougriás has two other beaches, accessible by foot, for Robinson Crusoe fantasies. Skiathos Cruises (w skiathoscruises.gr) has three departures to Tsougriás each morning in season (€15), and also offers several other excursions.

BEACHES AROUND SKIÁTHOS Beaches, beaches, beaches are the key to Skiáthos's success, and they fringe the emerald green isle like lace. Mobile sardine tins called buses follow the south coast (w skiathostransports.gr/en). The stops are all numbered and located within walking distance of the best strands, all of which are equipped with tavernas and watersports hire. The most convenient beach from Skiáthos Town is **Megáli Ámmos** (Μεγάλη Άμμος) although it's generally packed. Moving westward, **Achladiás** (Αχλαδιάς; easiest reached by taxi-boat) is also chock-a-block in summer.

Beyond that, 5km from town, the Kalamáki Peninsula juts out with a coating of holiday villas. Beaches here include **Kanapítsa** (Καναπίτσα), a popular cove, and nearby **Vromólimnos** (Βρωμόλιμνος; 'dirty lake'), hard to pronounce and hard to find, but one of the finest places to swim on the island, with powder-puff sand; the restaurant-bar at the right-hand end of the strand is worth a stop for a tipple or two. **Plataniá** (Πλατανιάς) overlooks **Ag Paraskeví** (Αγ Παρασκευή), a lovely long stretch of beach with plenty of parasols and sunbeds.

Troúlos (Τρούλος) has a couple of tavernas and more good swimming. The last bus stop, 12km from Skiáthos Town, is the legendary **Koukounariés** (Κουκουναριές), a superb sweeping crescent bay of soft sand that escaped from the South Pacific, fringed with pines, although in August it seems that not only can you 'see a world in a grain of sand', as Blake wrote, but that each grain of sand has a world sitting on it. Tavernas, hotels and a campsite are hidden away from the sea behind trees and wetlands of Lake Strofiliás. Hyper-trendy Krássa, nowadays called **Banana Beach**, is up the hill with the sea on your left when you get off the bus at Koukounariés. **Little Banana** (or Spartacus), next door, is the gay/nudie beach where you can peel off everything and lie cheek-to-cheek in a bunch. Next is the lovely **Ag Eléni** (Αγ Ελένη), the last beach accessible by road, a quieter spot with a view across to the Pelion Peninsula and a welcome breeze; or take the dirt road just before the beach, which leads after 1km or so down to **Kryfí Ámmos** (Κρύφή Άμμος Άμμος) Beach, with a cool taverna.

INLAND AND THE NORTH COAST Skiáthos has a good network of paths, most of them now signposted. A donkey path (just before the turning to the airport road) will take you 4km through the most beautiful empty scenery on Skiáthos to the last working monastery, **Evangelistría** (✆ 24270 22012; w monievaggelistrias.gr; ☉ in season sunrise–sunset; monastery free, museum €2) – but you can also go by road on the minibus from the KTEL station in Skiáthos Town (departing 5 times a day – the last departure from town currently at 13.30 – with two extra trips very early Sun; schedule on the website; €4 return). Evangelistría was founded in 1797 by monks forced to flee Mount Athos for their support of the traditionalist Kollivádes movement. A lovely, peaceful place with a triple-domed church and garden courtyard, it became a refuge for both monks and scholars, as well as for the *armatoloí*, irregular Christian militia from Mount Olympus, who, with the support of the Russians, had raised a small fleet to harass the Turks. When Russia made peace with Türkiye in 1807, the *armatoloí* were abandoned, and many took refuge on Skiáthos; under Giánnis Stathás, they united in an irregular army, and over the monastery hoisted the blue-and-white Greek flag that they had just invented. The Ottoman fleet soon put an end to their pretensions, but a statement had been made that would inspire the War of Independence 14 years later. Only a rusting cannon and a few pieces (among other items) in the museum, cared for by four monks, recall the monastery's belligerent past.

Continue on from Evangelistría: the car park at the end of the road takes you within 600m of **Kástro** (Κάστρο), founded on a windswept niche in the 14th century when pirates were on the warpath. Kástro was the island's main town until 1829, when everyone moved down to Skiáthos Town. Eight of the original 30 Byzantine churches more or less still stand (one, Christós, has good frescoes and a chandelier) among the houses and a hammam. The view from the top is lovely and there's a quiet beach below, where the locals smuggled out trapped Allied troops during World War II. In *The Poor Saint*, Papadiamántis describes Kástro's churches:

> some of them stood on rocks or on reefs by the shore, in the sea, gilded in summer by the dazzling light, washed in the winter by the waves. The raging north wind whipped and shook them, resolutely ploughing that sea, sowing wreckage and debris on the shore, grinding the granite into sand, kneading the sand into rocks and stalactites, winnowing the foam into spokes of spray.

If the *meltémi* wind is blowing, you can see that he wasn't exaggerating.

A detour on the path leads to the pretty 15th-century Monastery of **Panagía Kechriá**, containing some fine frescoes painted after 1745; here too, at the end of the bumpy road (signposted), is the pure white contemporary and very photogenic church of **Ag Aléxandros**, its façade decorated with painted plates, in a truly spectacular setting high over the sea that has made it a favourite for weddings. The nearest beach to Kástro (a 4x4 comes in handy here) is lovely, isolated **Kechriá** (Κεχριά; 'Little Paradise') Beach, complete with a delightful taverna, olive trees shading a grassy meadow and the island's best sunsets.

In general, beaches on the north coast are windy. East of Kástro, the magical beach at **Laláría** (Λαλάρια, accessible only by sea from Skiathos Town) is a marvel of silvery pebbles, shimmering like a crescent moon beneath the cliff, with a natural arch closing off one end and nearby sea grottoes: Skotiní, 'the dark' (bring a torch); Galázia, 'the blue'; and Chálkini, 'the copper'.

West of Kastró, **Asélinos** (Ασέληνος) is a sandy beach in a bucolic setting with a taverna and reed sun shelters; but beware of the undertow. Inland, just off the road that leads to **Mikró Asélinos Beach**, is the exquisitely painted, candlelit chapel of the 17th-century **Moní Panagía Ikonístria** (◐ in season 08.00–20.00 daily; donation), overlooking the north coast, where an icon of the Virgin was found dangling in a tree and, like so many stubborn icons, refused to be moved. **Mandráki** (Μανδράκη) further west, is reached most easily by a lovely footpath from the lagoon behind Koukounariés, and has two stretches of sand and a snack bar.

SKÓPELOS

Where rambunctious Skiáthos has given its all to tourism, Skópelos (Σκόπελος), with its more modest pebbly beaches, remained aloof during the 1960s and 70s, the decades of slapdash cash-in-quick building. So not only has the island kept its integrity and serenity – the lure for a new wave of upmarket tourists, along with its star turn in the 2008 film *Mamma Mia!* – but it's also exceptionally beautiful, with dramatic scenery, dense pine forests, plum orchards and two truly pretty towns, Skópelos and Glóssa. It is a lovely island for long walks, especially outside of the heatstroke months of July and August.

HISTORY Known in antiquity as Peparethos, Skópelos was colonised by Prince Staphylos of Crete (who, according to some, was the son of Theseus and Ariadne). This tradition was given dramatic substance in 1927 when Staphylos' Minoan tomb containing a sword (now in the Archaeology Museum in Athens) was discovered by the cove that has always borne his name. Staphylos means 'grape': the local wine, described as an aphrodisiac by Aristophanes, was long an important export. The Minoans also founded the island's three settlements: Peparethos (Skópelos

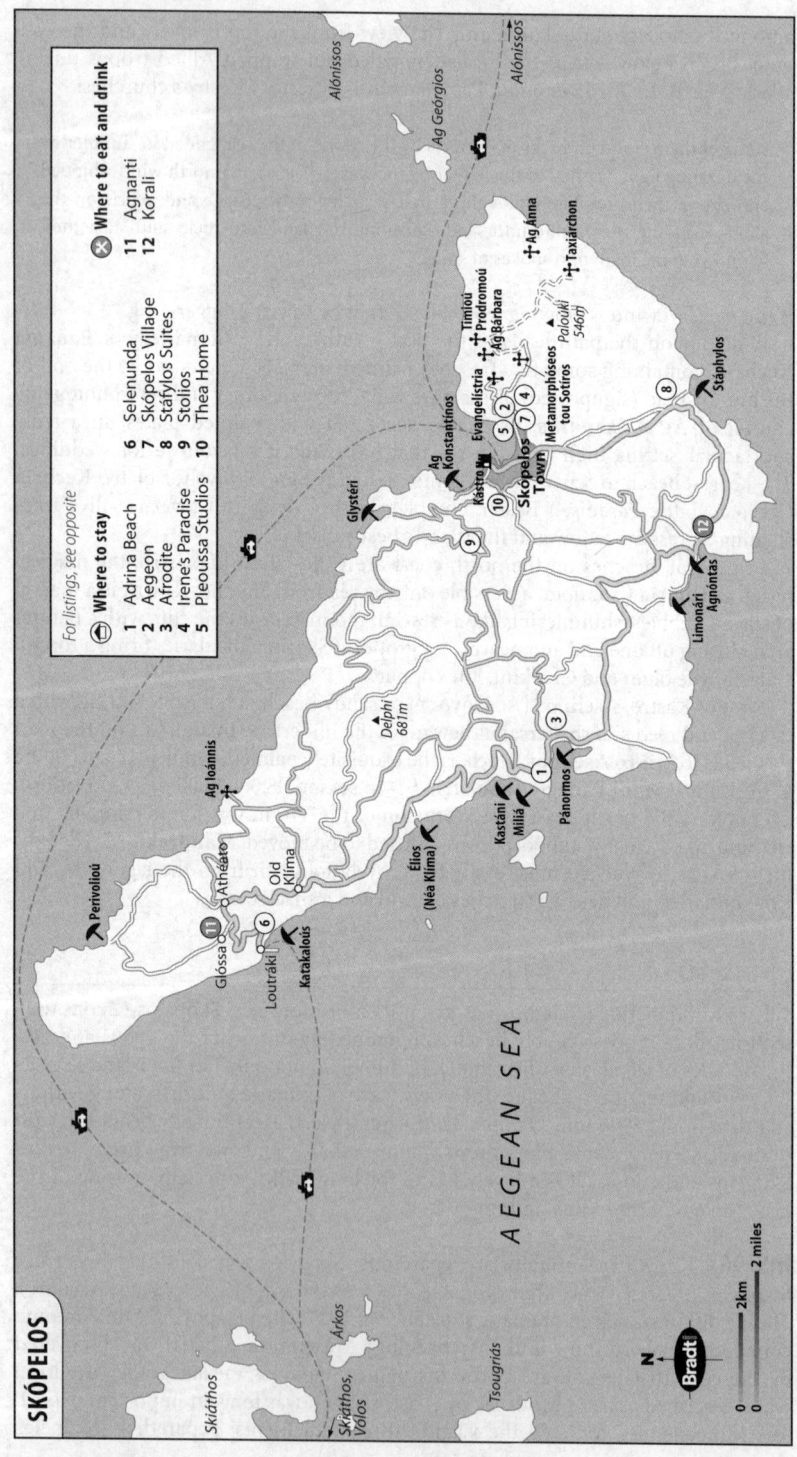

Town), Staphylos (Pánormos) and Knossa (Glóssa). Subsequent tradition recounts that King Pelias, usurper of the Iolkan kingdom in Magnesía (page 331), settled Skópelos in the 13th century BC.

Venetian renegade Filippo Gizzi used Skópelos as his headquarters, and his capture by the resurgent Byzantines meant a decline in local excitement until Barbarossa decimated the island in 1538. In later years Skópelos was a popular refuge from the Turks, who called the Sporádes the 'demon islands' for their ornery pirates. The Skopelitians joined in the revolt of the irregular militia in 1805 (page 354), and throughout the War of Independence the island's population soared, augmented by refugees from the mainland; in the 1820s, 70,000 people lived there, so many that there was fighting over food (the current population is less than 6,000 year-round, and 20,000 in August).

Skópelos was a prosperous place in the 19th century, known for shipbuilding and for its merchant fleet; many families made a living off their own small trading vessels. They declined with the advent of steamships, and the island's once-flourishing agriculture suffered when phylloxera decimated the famous vines in the 1940s. They've only recently been replanted, and once again you can try the island's born-again red Peparithios wine (at least while you're on Skópelos, as they don't make very much – yet).

GETTING THERE AND AWAY Ferries and **hydrofoils** link Skópelos daily with Vólos, Skiáthos and Alónissos. They often call at both Skópelos Town and Glóssa, but always check ahead (Port Authority ⟩24240 22180; in Glóssa ⟩24240 33033).

GETTING AROUND The main **bus** line (w skopelostransports.gr/en) runs several times a day from Skópelos Town to Glóssa (50mins), stopping by all the beach paths. Another line goes to Agnóntas and Stáphylos on the south coast, with some services continuing on as far as Kastáni. Buy tickets on board. In season there are also some private minibus services to the beaches. **Taxis** (w skopelosweb.gr; see under Travel/Transportation for the independent drivers and their numbers) are plentiful by the port of Skópelos Town, with a few based in Glóssa. A trip between the two costs about €35. There's also a **water-taxi** in season from Skópelos Town to **Glystéri Beach**. Sporades Water Taxi (w sporades-watertaxi.gr) serves various destinations, connecting also with the mainland. Sea Cab (w seacab.gr) connects Skópelos with Skiáthos.

Car hire
The Local Route Paralía Skópelos (Town port); ⟩24240 23682; w thelocalroute.gr
Magic Potóki St, just up from the port; m 69847 59509; w magiccars.gr. They also have motorbikes & 4x4s – for serious exploring you may want the latter.

TOURIST INFORMATION The websites w skopelosweb.gr, w skopelos.net and w skopelos.com are helpful and have listings of studios and apartments, etc. And you can find a little bit of everything else on a lovely blog called Skopelos News (w skopelosnews.wordpress.com).

Heather Parsons (m 69452 49328; w skopelos-walks.com), author of *Skópelos Trails*, offers intimate, in-depth **walking tours** around the island.

WHERE TO STAY *Map, opposite*
Unless otherwise mentioned, hotels here are open from April to October.

CARNIVAL ON SKÓPELOS

The three Sundays of Carnival (Apokriés) can be fun, if a little confusing. There is a calendar of events (w skopelos.net), but you can expect a general chaos of music and dancing, traditional costumes, dirty jokes, mocking children and lots of food. The main event comes on the first Sunday, when little boats called 'trátas' are made of cane and decorated with rubbish, sometimes with a chimney spewing fumes from burning wet garbage. The foul vessels are borne through the streets, while their bearers, bodies painted, drink and sing lewd songs until they finally make it to the harbour, where the boats are hurled into the sea and the merrymakers jump in after them.

Skópelos Town and around

Skópelos Village (48 rooms) Across the bay, 600m from town; 24240 22517; w skopelosvillagehotel.com. Attractive seafront bungalow complex with all the frills (2 pools, tennis & good facilities for kids). Greek b/fast inc. Minimum stay some periods. €€€€–€€€

Diónyssos [not mapped] (52 rooms) Venizélou; 24240 23210; w dionyssoshotel.gr. On the hill to the west of the port, upbeat hotel with an international flavour, with large pool & gardens, adjacent taverna & comfortable rooms. B/fast inc. €€€€–€€

Pleoussa Studios (11 rooms) Near the beach, a 10min walk from centre; 24240 23141; w pleoussa-skopelos.gr. Studios with wrought-iron bed & veranda; some with kitchenette. €€€

Stolios (6 rooms) 4km from town, high up at Ráches Skopélou; m 69729 09700; w skopelosweb.gr/studios/stolios. Very peaceful retreat, welcoming & well appointed; handsome new traditionally styled apartments with splendid views. €€€

Aegeon (15 rooms) 1km east of the port; 24240 22619. Stylish small hotel, set on a hill 300m above the beach, with pool, garden & panoramic views over Skópelos Town & its port. Family rooms available. €€

Thea Home Hotel (7 rooms) Ring road; 24240 22859; w theahomehotel.com. Great views & private balconies, & even a little kidney-shaped pool. Free transfer from the port, & free bicycles for guests. Lovely hosts. Don't miss their famous cheese pies. B/fast inc. Minimum 2 nights in peak season. €€

Akti [not mapped] (12 rooms) By the harbour & beach; 24240 22132; w aktiskopelos.

com. Big central rooms above a supermarket, recently freshened up. A good bet if you come unbooked. €€–€

Irene's Paradise (5 rooms) 1km from the beach; m 69455 08619; Jun–Sep. Small family pension with simple, nicely decorated studios & a garden in a secluded spot with pretty views & charming hosts. €€–€

Kir Sotos [not mapped] (12 rooms) On the port; 24240 22549; w skopelostravel.net/sotos. A popular place in a traditional island house. Each room has its own character & views of either the harbour or a flower-draped courtyard. €€–€

Between Skópelos and Glóssa

Adrina Beach (58 rooms) Pánormos; 24240 23373; w adrinabeach.com; May–Sep. Above the beach, a child-friendly complex in traditional style, all rooms with balcony, with a pool & restaurant (€€) & taverna open to non-residents. Minimum stay some periods. €€€€–€€

Stáfylos Suites (17 suites & studios) 7min walk from Stáphylos Beach; 24240 22220; w stafylos-suites.gr. Attractive, recently renovated complex with a lovely pool & sea views. Suites accommodate up to 4, all with balcony & kitchenette; b/fast €9. Minimum stay some periods. €€€–€€

Selenunda (21 rooms) Loutráki; 24240 34073; w hotelselenunda.com. In a quiet setting above the port, simple studios or apartments with balcony, kitchenette & glorious views. Minimum stay some periods. €€€–€

Afrodite (38 rooms, 8 apartments) Pánormos; 24240 23150; w afroditehotel.gr. Rural retreat; pleasant rooms with balcony; gym & bikes to rent. B/fast inc. €€–€

🍴 WHERE TO EAT AND DRINK *Map, page 362*

Skópelos has a distinctive cuisine, and is famous across Greece for its pies, filled with spinach or cheese, formed into a long roll, then twisted into a spiral and fried. The island has always had a lot of plum orchards, and another favourite dish is meats roasted with prunes or other fruits; you'll find these in most of the restaurants.

Skópelos Town *Not individually mapped*

Ouzerie Anatoli In the walls of the Kástro; ☏ 24240 22851; 📷 anatoliofficialpage; ⏱ 19.30–02.30 daily. Fantastic setting, with tables on a lovely terrace for this bastion of Skópelos tradition. Simple taverna fare. But the owner is Giórgos Xindáris, who plays *rebétiko* with his talented sons when he's in the mood, after 22.00. €€

Alexandros Chimou, Skópelos (inland from the ferry port); ☏ 24240 22324; ⏱ 18.30–23.00 daily. In a shady garden, reliable; good grilled meats & seafood with a couple of stews or baked dishes on offer, too. €

Finikas Behind the port by the huge palm tree; ☏ 24240 22008; ⏱ 18.30–midnight daily. Friendly little gem in situ since 1989, with local dishes served by lantern-light; try the roast pork stuffed with prunes. €

Between Skópelos and Glóssa

Korali Agnóntas; ☏ 24240 22407; w koralirestaurant.gr; ⏱ 13.00–23.00 daily. On the beach & for over 25 years serving seafood platters, seafood pasta (including lobster when available), grilled fish & other dishes, not all fishy. €€€

Glóssa

Agnanti Glóssa; ☏ 24240 33606; w agnanti.com.gr; ⏱ 13.00–23.00 daily. Founded in 1953 & now in the hands of the 2nd generation, Agnanti has evolved from a simple taverna into one of the best restaurants in the region, using excellent organic ingredients in both Skopeliot dishes & innovative ones, matched by lovely views from the roof terrace. €€

ENTERTAINMENT AND NIGHTLIFE The island of Skópelos has long been known as a centre of traditional music, especially *rebétiko*, which came here with Anatolian refugees in the 1920s. Some famous singers and musicians got their starts here. The best places to hear *rebétiko* are restaurants, especially the Ouzerie Anatoli (see above). The **Rembétiko Festival**, with the best local musicians, takes place in July (w skopelos.com/listings/rebetiko-festival). In the last week of August the **Folklore Dance Festival** (f dancefestivalgreece) hosts groups from around Greece. For other types of music, the bars along the port can give you an earful.

Mercurius Cocktail Bar On the port; ☏ 24240 24593; w mercurius.gr; ⏱ until 03.00 daily. The home of LED-illuminated fancy cocktails & vodka-soaked watermelons. Pop playlists & occasional live music.

Oionos ('Blue Bar') On the port; m 69424 06136; ⏱ 20.30–03.00 daily. Cocktails & snacks, outside tables on the alley & a convivial atmosphere. Blues, jazz & pop; live music some nights.

SPORTS AND ACTIVITIES

Dolphin of Skópelos Néa Paralía, Skópelos Town; ☏ 24240 29191; w dolphinofskopelos.com. Excursions by bus or boat, including a *Mamma Mia!*-themed tour & a barbecue sailing trip.

Kayaking Greece Miliá Beach; m 69742 99055; w kayakinggreece.com. Day trips, sunset tours & longer expeditions in the region.

Skopelos Cycling Doulidou St, Skópelos Town; m 69470 23145; w skopelos-cycling.gr. Rents mountain bikes & all the accessories & offers guided bike tours, including sunrise & sunset tours.

Thalpos Travel Upstairs on the waterfront in Skópelos Town; ☏ 24240 29036; w holidayislands.com. Can arrange night fishing trips, boat hire, culinary tours, round-island sails in a schooner, & diving trips.

OTHER PRACTICALITIES Everything you need is in Skópelos Town, including banks, pharmacy, the post office and the island's health centre (\ 24240 22222).

SKÓPELOS TOWN AND ITS HARBOUR Skópelos Town (usually just called 'Chóra'; Χώρα) is artfully arranged in an amphitheatre around the port, a handsome collage under old blue slate and post-earthquake red-tile roofs. The newer houses incorporate traditional features, while the national obsession for planting a seed wherever it has half a chance has resulted in a lush growth of flowers. The town claims 123 churches, many with charming iconostases; two to look out for are **Zoödóchos Pigí** and **Christó** (above the Commercial Bank) with a triangular, Armenian-style apse.

At the top rise the walls of the Venetian **Kástro**, so formidable that Skópelos was left alone during the War of Independence. A row of chapels along the edge offers saintly defence against the storms that crash into the island, and the 9th-century AD church **Ag Athanásios** has been restored after grave damage in the 1965 earthquake.

Beyond Plateía Plátanos and its enormous plane tree (*plátanos*) and fountain, **Panagía Eleftherótria** is a picturesque 18th-century stone church. At the end of town, fortified monastery **Episkopí**, built by the Venetians, shelters a 17th-century basilica. Further on, **Ag Regínos** has the sarcophagus of Ag Regínos, the first bishop and patron saint of Skópelos, who was martyred in AD362. Along the waterfront, cafés scent the evening with warm honeyed *loukoumádes*.

North of town, **Ag Konstantínos** has a pleasant shingle beach and the ruins of a Hellenistic water tower. If it's too crowded, try **Glystéri** further north; there's a pleasant taverna and a campsite amid the olive groves. Caiques offer excursions to the islet of **Ag Geórgios**, with a 17th-century monastery and wild goats.

MOUNT PALOÚKI (Παλουκι) The massif that looms over the southeast of Chóra was an important monastic colony for centuries. Hunters have been banned: birds twitter and butterflies dance over the lovely track (T1, with a continuation on the T2 trail – ask locally if they are open for mountain bikes as well), with spectacular views over the coast, beginning just beyond the strip of beach hotels. It's best to get an early start. Most of the monasteries have similar hours (⊕ usually 09.00 or 10.00–13.00 & 17.00–20.00), but some close on different days.

A dependency of Mount Athos monastery Xiropotámou (page 124), the first one here, **Evangelístria** (1712; 4km from town) enjoys magnificent views over the town, and is now occupied by two nuns who offer their weavings for sale. On the other side of the valley, up the hill, the 16th-century **Metamorphóseos tou Sotíros** (or just Sotíris; 7km from town) is a dependency of Moní Xenofóntos monastery on Athos (page 124) and is a very peaceful place, occupied by one slightly eccentric monk with friendly cats. Further afield, fortress-like **Ag Bárbara** (1648) has frescoes from the 15th century, but saw its last monk in 1980 (the key-holder, Mrs Magda, is usually there). Over the ridge is **Timioú Prodromoú**, with a beautiful iconostasis and a jam-making monk.

The path (now the T2) descends steeply to the abandoned **Taxiárchon**, with a welcome spring; during the war the local Resistance hid Greek and Allied soldiers here before they were smuggled to Türkiye. Further along, at the end of the path, is the little whitewashed and equally deserted **Ag Ánna**, the most peaceful of all, with splendid views over nearby Alónissos.

ACROSS SKÓPELOS TO GLÓSSA Buses from Skópelos Town to Glóssa can pass within 500m of some of the island's best beaches. **Stáphylos** (Στάφυλος), where the Minoan tombs were found, is now a popular family area, with several beaches. **Agnóntas** (Αγνώντας), the next stop, is a boaty little bay with good tavernas and a pebbly beach. Greeks have long memories: Agnóntas was named after a local victor in the 569BC Olympics, who disembarked here to wild acclaim. Nearby sand-and-pebble **Limonári** (Λιμνονάρι) has usually calm turquoise waters and a pair of tavernas. From Agnóntas a road cuts through the pines to pebbly **Pánormos** (Πάνορμος), set in a magnificent bay, followed by pretty pebbly **Miliá** (Μηλιά) and charming **Kastáni** (Καστάνη) – one of several film locations around the island. Further along, **Élios** (Ελιος) is a small resort that got its name from a dragon who demanded an annual tribute of human flesh, until St Reginos took the place of one of the victims and asked God for mercy (*éleos*); the dragon then let Reginos lead it over a cliff. Today it's better known as Néa Klíma. Beyond is the larger village of Old Klíma, and then just before Glóssa is tiny **Athéato** (Αθέατο), the 'invisible' and the oldest village on the island.

GLÓSSA (Γλώσσα) The north end of Skópelos is the quieter, more traditional part of the island. Glóssa, its main village, spills prettily down a wooded hill over hundreds of steps, guarded by a trio of ruined 4th-century BC towers. A scenic road descends to cliff-hugged **Perivolioú** (Περιβολιού) beach with a taverna and sunbeds, 5km from Glóssa; the colours are especially fetching in the afternoon light. A track leads in an hour to the outrageously pretty church of **Ag Ioánnis**, an eagle's nest with real eagles often soaring overhead; the last leg of the walk is up 100 steps carved in the rock, leading to the church hanging dramatically above the sea – now world-famous after its role in the wedding scene in *Mamma Mia!* in 2008, and still receiving a lot of cinema pilgrims. There's a small beach below.

A steep 3km below Glóssa, there's an untidy beach and tavernas at **Loutráki** (Λουτράκι; Ancient Selenunda), the peaceful port of Glóssa, with its cobblestone lanes, where the ferries call. South along the shore is peaceful white **Katakaloús Beach**, near the scant eroded remains of Selenunda's Roman-era baths.

ALÓNISSOS

Long, skinny Alónissos (Αλόννισος) is queen of its own little archipelago, but its a late bloomer when it comes to tourism. Few islands have suffered so many setbacks: in 1953 disease killed its old grapefruit orchards and vineyards; in 1965, a devastating earthquake hit its only town, Chóra, and politicians tried to force everyone to move to the port, Patitíri.

Despite the troubles Alónissos rebuilt itself, and it remains a slice of friendly, laid-back 'Old Greece' that is increasingly popular with nature tourists. In 1992, after the urging of environmental groups across Europe, Greece's first **National Marine Park** was set up in and around Alónissos and its archipelago to protect the endangered Mediterranean monk seal; at the website of the Hellenic Society for the Study and Protection of the Monk Seal (w mom.gr), you can learn more about the little grey *Monacus monacus* and how to help their efforts.

The seas of the marine park are now some of the cleanest in the Aegean, home to some 300 species of fish and coral; dolphins and whales are often spotted. The park, the largest marine park in Europe, covering some 2,260km^2, is accessible except for the exclusion zone around Pipéri island, but no camping or fires are allowed.

About 90% of Alónissos is accessible only on foot, crossed by trails offering stunning views and glimpses of the rare Eleonora's falcon and Audouin's gull. Holiday-makers and yacht flotillas have arrived, but not overwhelmingly so.

12 | THE SPORÁDES (ΣΠΟΡΑΔΕΣ) ISLANDS

Right now the island is very popular with Italians; others come for courses and seminars at the island's International Academy of Classical Homeopathy (w vithoulkas.com).

HISTORY The history of Alónissos is complicated by the fact that the modern island is not Ancient Halonnesos, but actually bore the name Ikos – the result of an overeager restoration of ancient Greek place names after independence, but in Alónissos' case the mistake was an improvement. As for the real Ancient Halonnesos, some scholars say it must have been tiny Psathoúra, northernmost of Alónissos' islets, where the extensive ruins of an ancient city lie submerged offshore; others place it as far away as Ag Efstratíos, an island near Límnos.

Inhabited from Neolithic times, Ikos/Alónissos was part of the Minoan colony of Prince Staphylos, who planted the first of the vines that were to make it famous. Peleus, the father of Achilles, was among the later settlers from Thessaly. The Athenians annexed the island in the 5th century BC and established a naval base to take care of the Dolopian pirates who plagued the surrounding seas. There followed a period of great prosperity, as the Ikians exported their wines across the Mediterranean. The Romans seized the island in 190BC, although they later allowed it to return to nominal Athenian rule. During the Middle Ages, Ikos went under the name of Achilliodromia, Liadromia or simply Dromos (road). The Franks took it in 1204, followed by the Venetians (1453) and the Ottomans (1538).

As for Ancient Halonnesos (wherever it may have been), it was governed throughout antiquity by Athens, which lost control of it in the 4th century BC to a pirate named Sostratos. In 341BC, in the lead-up to Athens' troubles with Macedon, Philip II captured the island, and when Athens complained he offered to return it. Skópelos then rushed in and grabbed it; Philip, however, crushed the opportunists and the island was returned to Athens. But afterwards it lost all importance, its port sank, and even its location faded from memory.

GETTING THERE AND AWAY ANES ferries (w anes.gr), Sea Jets (w seajets.com) and Aegean Flying Dolphins hydrofoils (w aegeanflyingdolphins.gr) connect Alónissos at least once a day year-round with Vólos, Skópelos and Skiáthos. A central booking site such as Ferry Hopper (w ferryhopper.com) makes short work of checking daily options. Excursion boats from Patitíri go up the coast, and to the islets of Peristéra, Kyrá Panagía and Gioúra.

GETTING AROUND There are public **buses** from the port at Patitíri to Chóra, frequently in season, and three or so a day from Patitíri to Stení Valá. In addition, Alónissos Transport runs summer services to the beaches up the east coast, as far as Ag Dimítrios. Hire a **car** at Turismo in Patitíri (m 69725 00362; w turismo.gr) or at Alónnisos Travel (\ 24240 66000; w alonnisostravel.gr).

TOURIST INFORMATION Alónnisos Travel (see above), by the port in Patitíri, is a good source of information and runs trips to the islets, as well as other activities. Also see the municipal website (w alonissos.gr). For more on the Marine Park, see w necca.gov.gr/mu-sporades.

WHERE TO STAY Most hotels on the island are open from May to October; prices can fluctuate a lot throughout the season.

Patitíri and around

Atrium of Alónissos [map, opposite] (29 rooms) Vótsi; \ 24240 65750; w atriumalonnissos.gr. Complex above Roussoúm Yialós Beach, with comfortable, well-kept rooms overlooking the sea & central pool with bar. €€€€–€€€

Ikion Eco Boutique Hotel (13 rooms) Patitíri; \ 24240 66360; w ikion.com. Intimate & stylish, some rooms with sea view & balcony. They pride themselves on their elaborate b/fasts (inc); special diets catered for. €€€€–€€€

Marpunta Resort [map, opposite] (105 rooms) Marpoúnta; \ 24240 65212; w santikoscollection.com/marpunta. Bright, all-inclusive resort with all the bells & whistles, with 3 private beaches & plenty of sports, etc. Minimum stays apply. €€€€–€€€

Paradise (31 rooms) Patitíri; \ 24240 65160; w paradise-hotel.gr. On the cliff promontory, facing east over pine trees to the open sea. Simple, smallish rooms, with beautifully tiered terraces below the pool, a perfect spot for evening drinks. €€€–€€

Alkyon (34 rooms) Patitíri; \ 24240 65602; w thealkyonhotel.gr. Right on the harbour, modern white hotel with well-appointed balcony rooms & studios. €€

Arhodico (10 studios) Patitíri; \ 24240 65270. Comfortable apartments in a modern building near the beach, some with full kitchen, all with balcony & parking. €€

Dimitris (8 rooms) Vótsi; \ 24240 65035; w dimitrispension.gr. With its own bar, pizzeria (€) & terrace; all rooms have balcony over the little harbour; 2 with kitchenette. €€

Haravgi (19 rooms) Patitíri; \ 24240 65090; w haravgi.gr. Well-scrubbed & wholesome rooms & studios above the port, with a pretty terrace. €€

Liadromia (20 rooms) Patitíri; \ 24240 65521; w liadromia.gr; ⊕ year round. Up on the cliffs, this place is full of character, with attractive rooms, all with a balcony. It has a rooftop bar & b/fast terrace; 6 rooms have a kitchenette. €€

12 | THE SPORÁDES (ΣΠΟΡΑΔΕΣ) ISLANDS

Vótsi (15 rooms) Vótsi; 24240 65510; w pension-votsi.gr. Very nice, welcoming pension 2mins' walk up from the waterfront, with good-sized, spotless rooms & studios, communal kitchen & sea-view terrace. Minimum stays apply. €€–€

Chóra
Konstantina Studios (9 studios & suites) 24240 66165; w konstantinastudios.gr. A variety of suites & studios with sea views & a pretty garden. Excellent b/fast €5; good for families. €€€€–€€€
Chiliadromia Studios (10 rooms) 24240 65814; w chiliadromia.gr. Bright, pleasant rooms, some with sea view. €€

North of Patitíri
The Infinity 180 Luxury Suites & Spa [map, page 368] (3 suites) 6km from Patitíri; m 69824 89619; w theinfinity180.com. Laze in luxury far, far from the madding crowd amid the pines & olives, with infinity pool & hypnotic views over the sea. Gorgeous suites with private terraces, superb Amani 180 spa (bookable by the day for non-guests) & bar; meals available & amazing staff. B/fast inc. €€€€€

Alónissos Beach [map, page 368] (7 suites & 86 bungalows) Chrysí Miliá Beach; 24240 65281; w alonissosbeach.com. An elegant complex with stylish rooms set 700m above the beach, with pool, bar, restaurant (€€) & plenty of activities: spa & fitness centre, beauty salon, tennis, billiards. €€€€–€€€
4 Epochés (22 rooms) Stení Valá; 24240 66101; w 4epochesalonnisos.com. The '4 Seasons' is a peaceful complex near the entrance to the village, built around an oval pool. Very family friendly. B/fast inc. €€€–€€
Milia Bay [map, page 368] (21 apartments) 3km north of Patitíri; m 69764 38898; w miliabay.com. On the cliffs high above the sea, a complex of studios & apartments for 2–6 people, all with sea view, with a pool & a snack bar that has a telescope for starry nights. €€€–€€
Ikion (10 rooms) Stení Valá; 24240 65158; w ikiongroup.gr. Begun in 1965, before there were even roads on the island. Simple rooms & studios with Coco-Mat bedding, plus a bistro (€) & scuba-diving facility. Minimum stays some periods. €€–€

✕ WHERE TO EAT AND DRINK
If you're in the mood for seafood, Alónissos is the place; the Aegean, for some reason, is quite salty here and that makes the fish especially tasty. Some 80 island fishermen still make a living, hauling in Mediterranean lobster (*astakós*) and tuna, exporting it as far away as Japan.

Patitíri
Ostria 24240 65243; 10.00–23.30 daily. On a flower-decked terrace on the harbour, an eclectic menu, with plenty of seafood (stuffed sea bream, octopus, swordfish), as well as lamb grilled with honey or *kleftikó*; also some surprises, such as barbecued chicken wings. €€
To Kamáki 24240 65245; tokamakialonissos; noon–midnight daily. On the main street, an *ouzerí* serving some of the best fish in town – stuffed squid a speciality – & really tasty seafood starters; also caters for fish-haters & vegetarians. Good value, & live music some nights. €

Chóra
Astrofegia 24240 65182; 19.00–23.30 daily. The name means 'starlight,' & they've been shining since 1980. Innovative Greek & Mediterranean dishes, using local ingredients, & the best choice of wines on the island. Owner Yánnis Toúndas used to play football for Panathenaïkos. €€
Panselinos 24240 66371; w panselinos.gr; 09.00–midnight daily. Just outside the centre, a mix of Greek & international cooking. Salads, pasta, delicious chicken breast flambéed in ouzo & *giovétsi* lamb. €

North of Patitíri
Eleonas Leftós Gialós; 24240 66066; 09.00–23.00 daily. Beach bar & restaurant offering elegant outdoor dining under the olive trees. Seafood, taverna fare, & interesting desserts, with an emphasis on local produce & wines. €€
To Fanari Stení Valá; 24240 66013; 08.00–23.00 daily. Deservedly popular, family-run fish taverna, on a pretty terrace, serving tasty seafood linguine dishes & vegetarian choices. €

ALÓNISSOS

SPORTS AND ACTIVITIES The crystal seas here make for superb diving and snorkelling. For excursions, including to Alónissos' underwater museum (page 372) with the famous 5th-century BC Peristerá shipwreck, and for diving lessons, see **Triton Dive Center** (\ 24240 65804; w bestdivingingreece.com), **Ikion Diving Alónissos** (m 69404 48004, 69841 81598 (WhatsApp); w sporadesdiving.gr), and **Alónissos Seacolours Dive Center** (\ 24240 65912; w alonissos-seacolours.gr).

OTHER PRACTICALITIES All services are concentrated in Patitíri, including the health centre (\ 24240 65208).

PATITÍRI (Πατητήρι) In 1965, when an earthquake shattered Chóra, the junta then in power forced the homeless into prefab relief housing at the port, Patitíri, and prevented their return to Chóra by cutting off the water and electricity. Patitíri has since spread its wings to merge with the fishing hamlet of **Vótsi** (Βότση). The big stone building by the port is the **Alónissos Museum** (\ 24240 66250; w alonissosmuseum.com; ⊕ May & Sep 11.00–18.00 daily, Jun–Aug 11.00–20.00 daily; €4, concessions €2/€3). Founded by Kostas and Angela Mavríkis, it's an impressive undertaking for such a small island. The best part is the floor dedicated to pirates: cutlasses, cannonballs, battle axes, irons and chains, from the centuries when pirates were the scourge of the Aegean. Other rooms commemorate the Greek War of Independence, traditional crafts and economy. There are frequent exhibitions, and a collection of sculptures by artists who have made Alónissos their home.

There's a small beach at Patitíri, and a prettier one at Vótsi, just north. To the south, **Marpoúnta** (Μαρπούντα) has the submerged remains of a Temple of Asklepios; beyond are the nicer beaches at **Výthisma** (Βύθισμα) and **Megálos Moúrtias** (Μεγάλος Μουρτιάς).

CHÓRA (Χώρα) Set high up above the sea, Chóra has outstanding views, especially of the frequent cinemascope sunsets. After the 1965 earthquake, Germans and Brits bought the houses for a song and restored them, agreeing to do without water and electricity (although now they've been hooked up, as the resentment of the former residents has diminished). It's a busy place in season, with plenty of tavernas and bars.

AROUND ALÓNISSOS Caiques run out to the island's best beaches, most of which have at least a snack bar. Heading north from Patitíri, the first really good one (especially for children) is **Chrysí Miliá** (Χρυσή Μηλιά), in a small cove enveloped with pines and with a pair of tavernas. The 5th-century BC capital of Ancient Ikos was found by the shingly rose-tinted beach **Kokkinó Kástro** (30mins by caique from Patitíri); if you know where to look, you can make out some of its walls in the sea. This was also a stomping ground in the Middle Palaeolithic era (100,000–33,000BC) – the simple stone tools, now in the City of Vólos Museum (page 337), are among the oldest ever found in the Aegean.

Further north, 10km from Patatíri, sheltered **Stení Valá** (Στενή Βάλα) is a pretty but simple place with a handful of tavernas and is a favourite of yachties. It also has the rescue centre of the Hellenic Society for the Study and Protection of the Monk Seal (MOm; page 367), a private charity dedicated to the survival of one of the world's rarest animals, the grey monk seal (*Monacus monacus*), extinct in France since 1920, and only rarely spotted in Spain and Italy – decimated by pollution, loss of habitat and fishermen, who, looking on them as rivals, used to kill them on sight.

The largest remaining population in the world, with an estimated 300 of the last 500 seals, lives in Greece, and the 30 or so seals on the islet of Pipéri are the largest single community.

For years, the Greek government's funding and management of the National Marine Park was spotty at best, and scandalous at worst – in 1995–96, the Defence Ministry even used two of the protected islets for live target practice. Through private initiatives such as MOm, things have improved. Their patrol boat in the park and seal hospital here have worked hard to revive Alónissos' colony.

Beaches just north of Stení Valá are well sheltered in the embrace of nearby **Peristéra** islet, and offer the best fishing and watersports on the island. **Kalamákia** (Καλαμάκια) has small pensions and tavernas. The island's biggest and most beautiful beach, **Ag Dimítrios** (Αγ Δημήτριος), 6km north of Stení Valá, dramatically covers a headland and has a bar, sunbeds and the ruins of a Byzantine fountain and an ancient settlement in the sea.

Isolated beaches are plentiful off the remote northern coast. Here at the old shepherd's village of **Gérakas** (Γέρακας) a biology station funded by the EU was opened with fanfare, then hardly ever used.

ALÓNISSOS ARCHIPELAGO The islands scattered around Alónissos' shores make for exceptional sailing. Olive-covered **Peristéra** (Περιστερά; 'dove') islet off the east coast was Alónissos' Siamese twin until separated by a natural upheaval. Peristéra has good sandy beaches, popular for evening barbecue excursions. In 1992, divers found the largest Classical-era shipwreck yet discovered off its shores, a 5th-century BC Athenian vessel, nicknamed 'Parthenon of the Shipwrecks', that carried 4,000 amphorae of wine from Skópelos, Alónissos and Macedonia. This submerged archaeological site is now Greece's first undersea museum, opened in August 2020, with both the mayor of Alónissos and the regional governor of Théssaly participating in the inaugural 30m dive. Now anyone can visit the site by participating in organised dives with experienced divers – see w museum.alonissos.gov.gr/en for details. Those wishing to stay on dry land can still have an interactive experience of the shipwreck at the information centre (\24240 66502; w museum.alonissos.gov.gr/en/the-museum-2), with 3D representations of archaeological findings and marine flora and fauna, as well as a virtual dive through the wreck.

Lovely, wooded **Kyrá Panagía** (Κυρά Παναγία) or Pelagós, the largest island, is 2 hours or so from Patitíri and still belongs to the Great Lávra monastery (page 127) on Mount Athos, which hires out the land to goatherds. Kyrá Panagía's own 12th-century monastery has been abandoned for decades but was recently restored and waiting for any new monks who might fancy a dose of isolation. In the bay of Ag Pétros lie the sunken remains of a 12th-century Byzantine ship that yielded a cargo of ceramics. Kyrá Panagía has sandy beaches, a pretty stalactite cave (a reputed home of the Cyclops), and plenty of opportunities for bushwalking.

Another abandoned monastery linked to Athos stands on verdant **Skantzoúra** (Σκάντζουρα), which offers excellent fishing in its many coves and caves. **Pappoús** (Παππούς), home to hares, has the remnants of a 7th-century AD church, while a rare breed of goat skips about steep, forbidding grey **Gioúra** (Γιούρα; Ancient Geronta), nibbling on its maquis. It has a few Classical and Roman remains and up a steep path yet another, wonderfully dramatic 'Cyclops' cave with stalactites, although it's currently closed to visitors.

Further out, volcanic **Psathoúra** (Ψαθούρα) is the island base of one of the most powerful lighthouses in Greece. The submerged city by the lighthouse is probably

Ancient Halonnesos, but the reason most people stop is a gorgeous 'tropical' sandy beach.

Pipéri (Πιπέρι) at the east end of the Marine Park, is the home to the monk seal colony and Eleonora's falcons; no-one is allowed within three nautical miles of it without special permission.

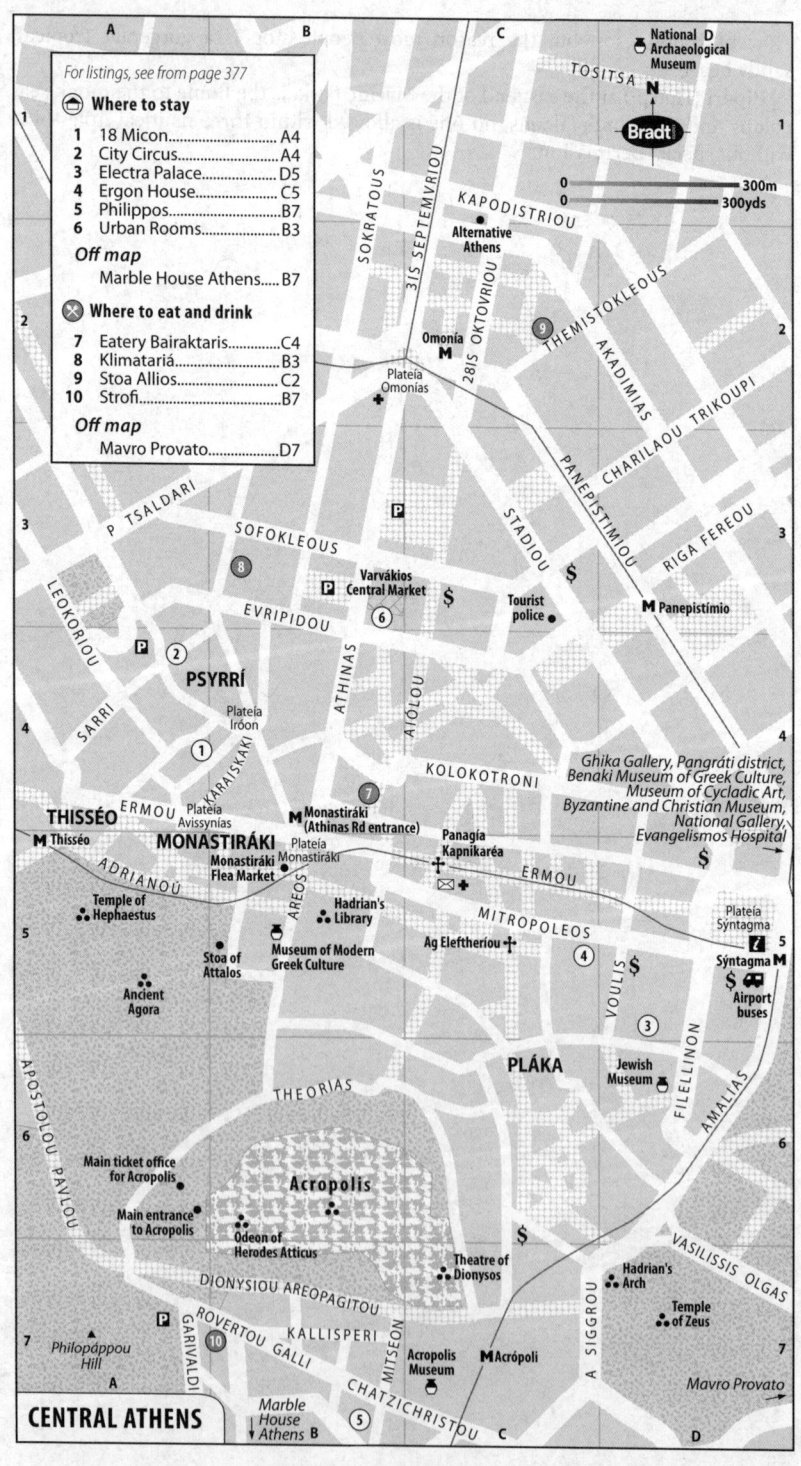

13

Athens (Αθήνα)

With Andrew Bostock and Amber Charmei

If you are flying in or out of Athens, it's a fine opportunity to stop in on the city itself. Lysippus nailed it in the 4th century BC: 'Who doesn't desire to see Athens is stupid; who sees it without liking it is even more stupid, but the height of stupidity is to see it, like it, and then leave it.' While modern Athens has in the past been characterised as a haphazard expanse of concrete, its reputation is on the rise, with its architectural variety spanning Neoclassicism to Art Deco and Modernism. A mix of contemporary urban energy, a sociable Mediterranean lifestyle, a surprising wealth of green spaces like Mount Lycabettus, and an easy intimacy with its ancient past make Athens a prime destination for a cultural city break.

HISTORY AND MYTHOLOGY

The history of the city often called the 'cradle of Western civilisation', where Socrates and Plato, Pericles and Sophocles once hobnobbed, is well known, and widely covered elsewhere. After the rise of Alexander the Great, but especially after the fall of Rome and through the centuries of Ottoman occupation, it was reduced to a backwater. A village of just 7,000 when it became the capital of modern Greece in 1834, it quickly acquired its grand Neoclassical character under the reign of its first king, Otto (originally of Bavaria). Growth continued apace, with a large influx of Greek refugees from Asia Minor in the early 1920s. Refugees of more recent decades and many young and creative residents from all over the world have given the city an increasingly cosmopolitan character, while its enviable Athenian lifestyle remains intact.

The myth behind the naming of Athens involves its first king Cecrops, an odd character who had the torso and head of a man, but the tail of a snake. According to the myth, when deciding which god – Poseidon or Athena – should be the city's patron deity, Cecrops asked each to present the city with a gift. Poseidon struck the ground with his trident and produced a flowing spring out of the Acropolis. For her turn, Athena struck the ground with her spear, and planted the first olive tree. Athena duly won and the city was dedicated to her.

GETTING THERE AND AWAY

BY AIR For information on flights to Athens, see page 33.

GETTING TO AND FROM ATHENS AIRPORT
By bus Bus X95 goes directly from the airport to central Plateía Sýntagma [374 D5] in 45–65 minutes (traffic depending) for €6 per person (ages 6–18, students & over 65s €3, under 6s free). Purchase tickets in the kiosk by the bus stop directly outside the arrival area. The airport bus runs round the clock (w oasa.gr/en/visit-athens/airport-express-bus-lines or w aia.gr/en).

By metro The metro from the airport (€9, or €16 return, ages 6–18, students & over 65s €4.50, under 6s free) takes about 40 minutes to downtown Athens, but take care: this line in particular is rife with gangs of pickpockets (usually well-dressed men who work in pairs) who prey on new arrivals and escape with wallets and bags just as the doors shut. The last train from the airport leaves before midnight (schedules at w stasy.gr/en/timetables/line-3).

BY CAR The ring road means that you can get to central Athens quicker than you might think, using a map app on your smartphone, but can be stressful if you're not used to driving abroad. Once in Athens, park – if you're lucky you might find a spot on the street, otherwise in a private car park (around €15/day) – then use public transport or walk to explore. If staying in a hotel, book in advance and ask where to park. Also note that for nearly the whole of the year on weekdays, the city centre enforces an odd/even number plate system in order to limit congestion. With few exceptions (certain low-emission or electric vehicles), only vehicles with plates ending in even numbers may circulate on even-numbered dates and those ending in odd number may circulate on odd-numbered dates.

GETTING AROUND

Walking is the best way to drink in the sights and sounds of Athens. Just be aware that pavements sometimes disappear on smaller streets, or will be full of parked cars. Traffic can be hairy when crossing roads, and even pedestrian streets often have mopeds whizzing up them – keep your wits about you.

Taxis are relatively inexpensive, and most trips in the centre will cost only a few euros (there's a minimum charge of €4). If you hail one, be sure the meter is running. To avoid confusion about the fare, only enter an empty taxi, and feel free to say no if the driver asks about picking up other fares en route (once a common practice, but less so now). Licensed yellow taxis can also easily be ordered through the Uber app. The public transportation system, consisting of three metro lines plus trams, buses and trolleys, is excellent and also inexpensive (€1.20 for a 90min journey). Multi-day tickets include a three-day tourist ticket with travel to and from the airport for €20, and a five-day ticket (no airport transfer) for €8.20. There are ticket machines at metro stations and there are also some other points of sale, such as Plateia Kannigós and other squares where many buses stop. If you have an ATH.ENA ticket, you can load up electronically, and for single rides you can now tap your contactless card or digital debit card (making sure you do not incur extra charges from your bank at home for using your card abroad). The correct fare is automatically calculated. You can find full details about everything transit related, in English, at w oasa.gr/en.

TOURIST INFORMATION AND CITY TOURS

There are **Athens Info Points** at the airport on the arrivals level [374 D5] (⏱ 08.00–20.00 Mon–Fri, 09.00–17.00 Sat & Sun) and at Syntagma Square (⏱ 09.00–20.00 Mon–Fri, 09.00–17.00 Sat & Sun).

Alternative Athens [374 C1] Chalkokondíli 24; ✆ 21101 26544; w alternativeathens.com; ⏱ 09.00–18.00 Mon–Fri. Offers some of the best walking tours of Athens.

Athens Free Tour w athens-free-tour.com. Book online for their 2½–3hr introduction to Athens, meeting up near Hadrian's Arch. Tipping is welcome & customary (perhaps €10–20 pp).

OTHER PRACTICALITIES

WHERE TO STAY

Electra Palace [374 D5] (185 rooms) Nav Nikodímou 18–20; ☎ 21033 70000; w electrahotels.gr. Luxury in the Pláka, with heated indoor pool & gym, & roof-garden restaurant & pool with fabulous Acropolis views. B/fast inc. €€€€€

Ergon House [374 C5] (38 rooms) Mitropoleos St 23; ☎ 21001 09090; w houses.ergonfoods.com/ergon-house-athens. Natural materials & collaborations with local artists & designers bring warmth to these appealingly minimalist rooms, serene yet in the very heart of things. Superb artisanal b/fast inc. €€€€€–€€€€

18 Micon [374 A4] (15 rooms) Aesópou & Mykónou; ☎ 21032 35307; w 18miconstr.com. A converted 1950s warehouse in the heart of Psyrrí, with a minimalist décor that reflects the building's industrial roots. It's quiet at night, despite the plethora of eateries & bars within easy walking distance. Stellar buffet b/fast inc. €€€€

Philippos [374 B7] (52 rooms) Mitsaíon 3; ☎ 21092 23611; w philipposhotel.gr. Warm contemporary style just steps away from the Acropolis metro & the Acropolis museum. B/fast inc. €€€€

City Circus [374 A4] (15 rooms) Sarrí 16, in Psyrrí; ☎ 21302 37244; w citycircus.gr. Although it calls itself a hostel & has a youthful air, it is sophisticated enough that many older guests will be perfectly happy here. The communal areas are relaxed & informal, & the included b/fast (if you book directly through their site) is a sociable event. Dorms €, private rooms €€

Marble House Athens [374 B7] (16 rooms & 1 apartment) Anastasiou Zinni 35, Koukaki; ☎ 21092 34058; w marblehouse.gr. This budget-friendly favourite in an excellent location near the Metro station Sygrou-Fix has a variety of room configurations – dbls, family, trpls – some with en suite & some with shared baths. Optional AC €5/day, b/fast €5. €€

Urban Rooms [374 B3] (8 rooms) Evripídou 30; m 69463 36795; w urban-rooms.hotelsathens.org. Backpacker-oriented hotel set on the 3rd floor of an apartment block on Athens' 'spice street': clean dbl rooms with writing desk & spotless shared bathrooms. The owner is a good source of local info. €

 ## WHERE TO EAT AND DRINK

Strofi [374 B7] Rovértou Gálli 25; ☎ 21092 14130; w strofi.gr; ⊕ noon–midnight Tue–Sun. Greek & Mediterranean classics & stunning Acropolis views, especially at night when the Parthenon is bathed in golden light. Book a table online. €€€€

Mavro Provato [374 D7] Arrianoú 31; ☎ 21072 23466; w tomauroprovato.gr; ⊕ 13.00–midnight Mon–Sat, 13.00–19.00 Sun. Hop in a taxi to Pangráti, a lively neighbourhood away from tourist Athens, for a superb array of little dishes on the chalkboard & fine wines. Best to book. €€€

Klimatariá [374 B3] Plateía Theátrou 2; ☎ 21032 16629; w klimataria.gr; ⊕ noon–02.00 daily. Classic taverna, full of atmosphere & live music most nights & Sun lunch. Not to be missed. €€

Stoa Allios [374 C2] Gamvétta 14; ☎ 21038 25961; w noon–23.30 Mon–Sat. A classic, casual seafood taverna experience & a great favourite with locals in the know. €€

Eatery Bairaktaris [374 C4] Aiolou 29; ☎ 21032 20203; w linktr.ee/eateryathens; w 09.00–midnight daily. On one of the loveliest & liveliest pedestrian streets, well priced street food, gyros, souvlaki & plenty of vegetarian choices. €

OTHER PRACTICALITIES

ATMs and banks are plentiful in Athens. In addition to the pharmacies listed below, check w xo.gr/pharmacies-on-duty/athens to locate an open pharmacy near you, even after hours or on weekends and holidays.

Evangelismos Hospital [374 D5] Ipsilántou 45–47; ☎ 21320 41000

Pharmacy Lolas [374 C5] Mitropoléos 54

13 | ATHENS (ΑΘΗΝΑ)

Pharmacy Omonías [374 B2] Platía Omonía 19A
Post office [374 C5] Mitropoléos 60; ⏰ 07.30–20.00 Mon–Fri

Tourist Police [374 C3] Dragatsaníou 4; ☏ 21032 22230

WHAT TO SEE AND DO

EXPLORING ATHENS ON FOOT The area around the **Acropolis** (see oposite) and the fascinating if touristy **Pláka** and **Monastiráki** districts just below it are the oldest part of Athens, sprinkled with ruins and Byzantine churches; its little windy streets are all that was left of Athens when it became the capital of Greece in the early 19th century. Ancient Athens will soon be before you; walk from Monastiraki Square along Areos Street, passing **Hadrian's Library** [374 B5] on your left then continuing to Thisséo along the pedestrian street Andrianoú, which runs right beside the **Ancient Agora** [374 A5] with its **Stoa of Attalos** [374 B5] and the splendid **Temple of Hephaestus** [374 A5]. One of the metro lines shares the route; the colourful, graffiti-covered metro cars add much to the scene as they pass. From Thisséo, follow the broad and lively pedestrian thoroughfare Apostolou Pavlou – the best place in the city from which to get a full view of the Acropolis as it emerges on your left. Where the road merges with Dionysiou Aeropagitou – named for Athens' patron saint – a network of shaded paths leads to the Acropolis and to **Philopáppou Hill** [374 A7]. It seems as though these trails have always been here, but in fact they were the work of architect Dimítris Pikiónis and a team of traditional artisans in the 1950s, making use of elements of demolished Neoclassical buildings; the work at this juncture is especially decorative. Sweeping views of the city's Classical monuments are framed by native Attic vegetation along the stroll. At the highest point of the walk, go higher still up Philopáppou Hill for a magical view of the Acropolis and the city below, especially at sunset when the Parthenon glows rosy pink.

Continuing along Dionysiou Aeropagitou with the Acropolis rising on your left brings you to Syggrou Avenue – one of the busiest thoroughfares of downtown – and two other major landmarks: **Hadrian's Arch** [374 D7] and the **Temple of Zeus** [374 D7]. Head left here for a walk along busy Amalias Avenue. Bordering the National Gardens, this brings you to the Parliament, with the Evzones in their ceremonial dress standing guard at the Monument of the Unknown Soldier. This is the heart of downtown; from here, the Benaki Museum of Greek Culture, the Ghika Gallery and the Museum of Cycladic Art are a brief stroll away.

In the morning, **Athinás Street** is the place to be. For a bold taste of Athenian life, head to the **Varvákios Central Market** [374 B3], a wonderful 19th-century building, with ironwork reminiscent of a Victorian railway station, great piles of fresh fish and seafood on ice, and rather slick floors. Meats on vivid display – not for the squeamish – are off to either side. The shops on and around Athinás still cluster in the old-fashioned manner, with lines of candle and icon shops, baskets and birdcages, hardware, and herb and spice shops.

To see these things and more through local eyes, book a personalised, small group walking tour (page 376).

MUSEUMS In addition to the Acropolis and National Archaeological museums (see opposite), excellent museums include the **Benaki Museum of Greek Culture** [374 D5] (w benaki.org; ⏰ 10.00–18.00 Mon & Wed–Sat, Thu until midnight permanent collection free, 10.00–16.00 Sun; €12, concessions €9, Thu from 18.00 until midnight free), which has an extraordinarily broad collection dedicated to

WHAT TO SEE AND DO

Greek culture across the millennia, and the **Museum of Cycladic Art** [374 D5] (w cycladic.gr; ⊕ 10.00–17.00 Mon & Wed–Sat, until 20.00 Thu, 11.00–17.00 Sun; see website for current admission prices), which is the best place to see the elemental white figurines that inspired modern artists from Brancusi to Picasso. For a thorough introduction to modern and avant-garde 20th-century Greek culture, visit the **Ghika Gallery** [374 D4] (w benaki.org; ⊕ noon–20.00 Thu, 10.00–18.00 Fri–Sun, closed in Aug; €9, concessions €7). At the **National Gallery/Alexandros Soutsos Museum** [374 D5] (w nationalgallery.gr; ⊕ noon–20.00 Wed, Thu–Mon 10.00–18.00, last entrance 1hr before close; €10, concessions €5), centuries of Greek painting are on display; the collection of 20th-century art is particularly strong. The **Byzantine and Christian Museum** [374 D4] (w byzantinemuseum.gr/en; ⊕ 08.30–15.30 Wed–Mon; €8, concessions €4) offers an excellent overview of the Byzantine Empire spanning antiquity to the influence of Byzantium on modern art, and has some marvellous pieces on view. The small museums in Pláka – the **Jewish Museum** [374 D6] (w jewishmuseum.gr/en) and the **Museum of Modern Greek Culture** [374 B5] (w mnep.gr/en), which has exhibitions at three different spaces close to one another by the Ancient Agora – are also well worth a visit if time allows.

Acropolis Museum [374 C7] ♆ 21090 00900; w theacropolismuseum.gr; ⊕ summer 09.00–17.00 Mon, 09.00–20.00 Tue–Thu & Sat–Sun, 09.00–22.00 Fri, winter 09.00–17.00 Mon–Thu, 09.00–22.00 Fri, 09.00–20.00 Sat–Sun; €20, concessions €10) This is a fabulous museum, notably filled with an army of Archaic kouros and kore statues and reliefs that survived from the original Acropolis temples destroyed by the Persians in 480BC. The Karyatids are also magnificent. The top floor, with its views straight on to the Parthenon, displays panels of the frieze remaining in Greece with white plaster casts of the sections in the British Museum, representing the dreams of someday reuniting them. The museum's videos and displays are a great introduction to the Acropolis site itself.

National Archaeological Museum [374 D1] ♆ 21321 44800; w namuseum.gr; ⊕ summer 13.00–20.00 Tue, 08.00–20.00 Wed–Mon, winter 13.00–20.00 Tue, 08.30–15.30 Wed–Mon; summer €12, winter €6) Greece's treasure chest holds the gold mask of Agamemnon, the fabulous bronze Poseidon, the Minoan frescoes from Santoríni, the incredible Antikýthira Mechanism and much more.

THE ACROPOLIS [374 B6] ♆ 21032 14172; w odysseus.culture.gr; ⊕ Apr–Aug 08.00–20.00 daily, gradually earlier closings through Sep–Oct, Nov–Mar 08.00–17.00 daily; Apr–Oct €30 inc Theatre of Dionysos, concessions €15, Nov–Mar €15 for all; timed-entry tickets available at w hhticket.gr; the Acropolis is now accessible to people with limited mobility, with an elevator and paved pathways, though it's a good idea to call the chief guard's office at the number above in advance) Pericles' 5th-century BC Athens was a marvel. Architects Iktinos and Kallikrates set the bar high, using complex calculations to make the Parthenon appear perfect from every angle, while the sculptor Pheidias directed the building programme and oversaw the extraordinary sculptural decoration. Ancient and modern architects consider the entrance gate, the Propylaea, its equal in beauty. It can be very hot and very busy here, though; try to arrive when it just opens or late in the day to avoid the crowds.

Embedded in the Acropolis hill, the **Theatre of Dionysos** [374 C7] (⊕ as for Acropolis) is the world's oldest: founded in the 6th century BC, it witnessed the first performances of nearly every surviving ancient Greek tragedy and comedy. For decades, attending a performance at the **Odeon of Herodes Atticus** has been one of the most memorable ways to enjoy a summer night. This 2nd-century AD theatre – the 'Heródeon' to Athenians – is one of the venues of the annual Athens-Epidaurus festival (w aefestival.gr). At the time of writing, the Heródeon was planning to close for at least three years of renovations at the end of the 2025 season. In the meantime, the festival's full programme, spanning ancient drama to contemporary and avant-garde music, theatre and dance, will continue in the meantime at the other stages, including Epidaurus, a 2-hour drive south of Athens.

Appendix 1

LANGUAGE With Andrew Bostock

The first battle when dealing with Greek is the alphabet. While never an easy one, this is somewhat helped by the fact that letters, with a few exceptions, are always pronounced the same. This means that once you learn the alphabet, with due notice to proper word stress, you are fully able to read Greek. You may not understand any of it, of course, but it can come in useful when transliterating signs and menus.

Greek grammar can also be a bit of a nightmare, with all nouns being masculine, feminine or neuter. Adjectives and articles then have to agree with them. For instance 'a beer' is '*mía bírra*', while 'a coffee' is '*éna kafé*' (Greek does not distinguish between 'a' and 'one'). Verbs are even more complicated but don't be disheartened, the Greeks themselves cheerfully admit that they make mistakes all the time. They will love you for making an attempt at the language, and will excuse even major mangling.

Transliteration – using the Latin alphabet to write words originally written using the Greek alphabet – is an adventure of its own. Greek spelling often references the ancient Greek roots of many words. A long 'E', for instance, could be written ι, η, υ, οι or ει. It's often a pleasure for etymologists, and quite fun for everyone else too, once you get into the spirit of it. This is why on one sign a place might be 'Dáphne' and another 'Dáphni', or why one salt cod restaurant might be called 'Bakaliarákia' and the one next door called 'Mpakaliarákia' – the version starting with 'Mp' is the direct transliteration of the Latin 'B' sound.

THE GREEK ALPHABET

Greek letter	Sound	Name
Αα	a normal 'a' sound	alpha
Ββ	'v'	vita
Γγ	a mixture between 'g' and 'y'	gamma
Δδ	somewhere between 'd' and 'th' (as in 'that')	delta
Εε	'e'	epsilon
Ζζ	'z'	zita
Ηη	'i'	ita
Θθ	'th'	thita
Ιι	'i'	yiota
Κκ	'k'	kappa
Λλ	'l'	lamda
Μμ	'm'	mi
Νν	'n'	ni
Ξξ	'x'	xi
Οο	'o'	omicron
Ππ	'p'	pi

Ρρ	'r'	ro
Σσ (ς at the end of a word)	's'	sigma
Ττ	't'	taph
Υυ	'i'	ipsilon
Φφ	'f'	fi
Χχ	'h' or 'ch' as in loch	chi
Ψψ	'ps'	psi
Ωω	'o'	omega

DIPHTHONGS AND CONSONANT DOUBLES

Greek letters	Sound
Αι αι AI ai	short 'e' as in bet
Ει ει/OI οι EI ei / OI oi	'i' as in machine
Ου/ου OU ou	'oo' as in too
Αυ/αυ AU au	'av' or 'af'
Ευ/ευ EU eu	'ev' or 'ef'
Ηυ/ην HU hu	'iv' or 'if'
Γγ/γγ GG gg	'ng' as in 'angry'
Γκ/γκ GK gk	hard 'g'; but 'ng' within a word
Ντ/ντ NT nt	'd'; but 'nd' within a word
Μπ/ μπ /MP mp	'b'; but 'mp' within a word

WORDS AND PHRASES
Essentials

Do you speak English?	*Miláte angliká?*
Good morning	*Kalí méra*
Good evening	*Kalí spéra*
Good night	*Kalí níkta*
Hello	*Yássas* (formal or plural)
	Yássou (informal singular)
Goodbye	*Yássas* or *yássou* as above
My name is…	*Me léne…*
What is your name?	*Póse léne?*
Pleased to meet you	*Haíro polí*
I am from…	*Eímai apó tin…*
…England/Britain	*…angliá*
…America	*…amerikí*
How are you?	*Ti kánete?* (formal or plural)
	Ti kánis? (informal singular)
Fine, and you?	*Kalá, ke esis?*
Please	*Parakaló*
Thank you	*Efcharistó*
You're welcome	*Parakaló*
Excuse me/pardon me/sorry	*Signómi*
I want...	*Thélo...*
Do you have...?	*Échetai...?* (formal or plural)
	Écheis...? (informal or singular)
OK	*Endáxi*
Yes	*Ne*
No	*Óchi*
Certainly	*Málista*

LANGUAGE

I understand		*Katalavéno*	
I don't understand		*Then katalavéno*	
Do you understand?		*Katalavénetai?* (formal or plural)	
		Katalavéneis? (informal or singular)	
Have a good trip!		*Kaló taxídi!*	

Questions

How?	*Pos?*	When?	*Poté?*
What?	*Ti?*	Who?	*Pios?*
Where?	*Poo?*	How much?	*Póso?*
Which?	*Píos?*	Why?	*Yiatí?*

Numbers

1	*éna* or *miá*	20	*íkosi*
2	*thío*	21	*íkosi éna*
3	*tría*	30	*triánda*
4	*téssera*	40	*saránda*
5	*pénde*	50	*peнínda*
6	*éxi*	60	*exínda*
7	*eftá*	70	*evdomínda*
8	*októ*	80	*ogdónda*
9	*enéa*	90	*eneнínda*
10	*thékka*	100	*ekató*
11	*énthekka*	200	*diakósa*
12	*thóthekka*	300	*trakósa*
13	*thekatría*	400	*tetrakósa*
14	*thekatéssera*	500	*pendakósa*
15	*thekapénte*	600	*eksakósa*
16	*thekaéxi*	700	*eftakósa*
17	*thekaeftá*	800	*oktakósa*
18	*thekaoktó*	900	*eneakósa*
19	*thekaenniá*	1,000	*chília*

Time

What time is it?	*Ti óra ine?*	tomorrow	*ávrio*
It's...o'clock	*Íne...*	yesterday	*kthés*
today	*símera*		

Days

Monday	*Theftéra*	Friday	*Paraskeví*
Tuesday	*Triti*	Saturday	*Sávatto*
Wednesday	*Tetárti*	Sunday	*Kiriakí*
Thursday	*Pémpti*		

Months

January	*Ianuários (Yenáris)*	July	*Ioólios*
February	*Fevrooários*	August	*Ávgoostos*
March	*Mártios*	September	*Septémvrios*
April	*Aprílios*	October	*Októvrios*
May	*Máios*	November	*Noémvrios*
June	*Ioónios*	December	*Dekémvrios*

Getting around

I'm going to…	*Páo sto…*	train	*tréno*
How far is it?	*Póso makriá ine?*	plane	*aeropláno*
How long will it take?	*Póses óres?* (how many hours?)	ship	*plío*
ticket	*isitírio*	taxi	*taxí*
		car	*aftokínito*
bus station	*stathmós leoforíon*	scooter	*papáki*
railway station	*stathmós too tréno*	petrol	*venzíni*
airport	*aerodrómo*	bicycle	*podílato*
port	*limáni*	on foot	*me ta pódia*
bus	*leoforío*		

Directions

Where is…?	*Poo íne…?*	south	*nótia*
left	*aristerá*	east	*anatoliká*
right	*thexiá*	west	*ditiká*
north	*vória*		

Signs

Entrance	ΕΙΣΟΔΟΣ	Closed	ΚΛΕΙΣΤΟΣ
Exit	ΕΞΟΔΟΣ	Caution	ΠΡΟΣΟΧΗ
Open	ΑΝΟΙΚΤΟ		

Accommodation

hotel	*xenodochío*	shower	*dous*
campsite	*cámping*	air conditioning	*klimatismós*
I'd like a room…	*Thélo éna domátio…*	toilet	*tooaléta*
…for one night	*…yia mía vradís*	breakfast	*proinó*
bed	*kreváti*		

Food and drink

I'm vegetarian	*Íme chortofágos*	water	*neró*
bread	*psomí*	milk	*gála*
eggs	*avgá*	coffee	*kafé*
fish	*psári*	tea	*tsái*
cheese	*tyrí*	beer	*bírra*
yogurt	*yiaoúrti*	wine (white, rose, red)	*krasí* (*áspro* or *lefká*, *rosè*, *kókkino*)
honey	*méli*		
the bill	*to logariasmó*	cheers!	*yámas!*

Shops

bank	*trápeza*	pharmacy	*farmakío*
post office	*tachithromió*	bakery	*foúrno*

Emergencies and health

Help!	*Voíthya!*	doctor	*yatró*
police	*astinomía*	hospital	*nosokomío*

Other

boy/girl	*agóri/korítsi*	hot/cold	*zestí/krío*
big/small	*megálo/mikró*	good/bad	*kaló/kakós*

GREEK GESTURES AND EXCLAMATIONS Sign language is an essential part of Greek life. 'Greekspeak' for 'no' is usually a click of the tongue, accompanied by raised eyebrows and a tilt of the head backwards. 'Yes' is usually indicated by a forward nod, head tilted to the side. If someone can't hear you, they will shake their head from side to side and say '*Oríste?*'

A circular movement of the right hand usually implies something very good or in great quantities. Unless you mean ill, never hold out the flat of your palm in someone's general direction.

Greek people also use exclamations which mean a lot, like *po, po, po!*, an expression of disapproval and derision; *brávo* comes in handy for praise, while *ópa!* is useful for 'Whoóps!', 'Lookout!' or 'Watch it!', or if someone's dancing, 'Go for it!'; *sigá sigá* means 'Slowly, slowly!'; *éla!*, 'Come!' or 'Get on with you!'; and *kíta!*, 'Look!'

Appendix 2

GLOSSARY

acropolis	fortified height, usually the site of a city's chief temples
agíos, agía, agíi	saint/saints, abbreviated to 'Ag'
agora	market and main civic area
aktí	coast
ámmos	sand
amphora	tall jar for wine or oil, designed to be shipped (the conical end would be embedded in sand)
áno/apáno	upper
archaía	ancient ruins
archontikó (pl. *archontiká*)	mansion
bouleuterion	council chamber
caique	small wooden boat
cavea	the concave seating area of an ancient theatre
cella	innermost room of a temple
chóra	'place'; often what islanders call their 'capital' town
chorió	village
chthonic	pertaining to the Underworld
Cyclopean	used to describe walls of stones so huge that only a Cyclops could carry them
dimarchíon	town hall
Dodekaorton	the 'Twelve Feasts' of the Orthodox church
EAM	National Liberation Front (Ethnikó Apeleftherotikó Métopo); the communist party resistance during World War II and the Greek Civil War
EDES	Greek Democratic National Army (Ellínikos Dímokratikos Ethnikós Strátos); right-wing resistance army during World War II
ELAS	Greek People's Liberation Army (Ellinikós Laïkós Apeleftherotikós Stratós); military branch of EAM
entablature	all parts of an architectural order above the columns
eparchía	eparchy, an Orthodox diocese, now used to refer to an area outside a big city
exonarthex	outer porch of a church
heröon	a shrine to a hero or demigod, often built over a tomb
hoplite	foot soldier with a large circular shield, often interlocked with other hoplites to form a unit called a phalanx
iconostasis	in an Orthodox church, the decorated screen between the nave and altar

GLOSSARY

kalderími	stone-paved pathway
kástro	castle or fort
katholikón	monastery church
káto	lower
KKE	Communist Party of Greece (Kommounistikó Kómma Elládas)
klephts	brigands or outlaws who took to the mountains under Ottoman rule, carrying on a constant guerilla war against the Turkish authorities. The *armatolí* (page 129) were hired to control them, but they often changed sides.
kore	Archaic statue of a maiden
kouros	Archaic statue of a naked youth
krater	large bowl for mixing wine and water
ktima	estate
limáni	port
limenarchíon	port authority
loutrá	hot spring, spa
megaron	central hall of a Mycenaean palace; also used for grand official buildings ('Mégaro Maxímou' houses the offices of the prime minister, 'Mégaro Mousikís' the concert hall)
meltémi	north wind that cools and sometimes plagues the Aegean in summer
metóchi	income-generating property owned by a monastery (often far from the monastery itself), usually land rented out to farmers or herders
metopes	sculpted panel on a frieze
moní	monastery or convent
monopáti	path
náos	temple
narthex	entrance porch of a church
ND	New Democracy (Néa Demokratía); centre-right party
néa	new
nisí/nisiá	island/islands
nómos	law
nomós	province
odeion	concert hall, originally roofed
ósios	blessed
palaestra	area of a gymnasium set aside for wrestling
palaia/palaió	old
Panagía	the 'all holy': the Virgin Mary
panegýri	saint's feast day
Pantocrator	the Almighty: a figure of the risen Christ in Byzantine churches
paralía	beach or waterfront
PASOK	Panhellenic Socialist Movement (Panellínio Sosialistikó Kínima)
pendentive	triangular architectural construction that supports a round dome on a square room
pithos	large storage jar
plateía	square
polis	city-state
pótamos	river
propylon	entrance gate; a propylaea has more than one door

prytaneion	meeting chamber of the officials of an ancient city
pýli	gate
pýrgos	tower
rhyton	drinking horn
skála	technically 'stair' – indicates a seaside location
spílio	cave or grotto
spíti	house
squinch	triangular inset in a square chamber to support a round dome; the alternative solution to a pendentive
stási	stop, like a bus stop
stathmós	station, for buses, trains or petrol
stoa	a portico not attached to a large building; in an agora, often lined with shops; also a covered commercial arcade
SYRIZA	Coalition of the Radical Left (Synaspismós Rizospastikís Aristerás)
temenos	sacred precinct
tholos	circular building; often a Mycenaean beehive tomb
xenónas	guesthouse

Appendix 3

FURTHER INFORMATION

In addition to the following, don't ignore the many works by Greek publishers in English, available in Greek bookshops, notably the series of modern Greek fiction translated into English by Kedros Press and the regional architectural guides by Melissa.

BOOKS
History, art and culture

Beaton, Roderick *Greece: Biography of a Modern Nation* Penguin, 2019. New up-to-date account that explains why modern Greece is the country it is today.

Campbell, John *Honour, Family and Patronage: A Study of Institutions and Moral Values in a Greek Mountain Community* Oxford University Press, 1964. Classic anthropological work on northern Greece's Sarakatsáni nomads.

Clark, Bruce *Twice a Stranger* Harvard University Press, 2006. A vivid account through interviews and new research of the traumatic Exchange of Populations that changed the face of northern Greece.

Clogg, Richard *A Concise History of Modern Greece* Cambridge University Press, 2002. Readable account of a messy subject.

Gage, Nicholas *Eleni* Ballantine Books, 1983. This Greek-American journalist's history of his mother's execution during the Civil War (page 27) for saving her children is still one of the best and most poignant accounts of a period many Greeks still find hard to discuss.

Gkotzaridis, Evi *A Pacifist's Life and Death: Grigorios Lambrakis and Greece in the Long Shadow of Civil War* Cambridge Scholars Publishing, 2016. Excellent analysis of Greece during the Cold War, and the assassination of MP Grigoris Lambrákis (page 93).

Graves, Robert *The Greek Myths* Penguin, 1955 (but often reprinted). The classic, down to the often off-the-wall footnotes.

Green, Peter *Alexander to Actium: The Historical Evolution of the Hellenistic Age* University of California Press, 1993. Massive, scholarly and highly readable account of unbridled ruthlessness, decadence, murder and incest.

Hammond, N G L *Alexander the Great* Bristol Press, 1980. General biography by one of the finest Alexander scholars, who first suggested that Vergína was Ancient Aigai, with a detailed section on Ancient Macedon.

Kalyvas, Stathis *Modern Greece: What Everyone Needs to Know* Oxford University Press, 2015. A detailed history of modern Greece, from its conception through its eventful centuries. The Gladstone Professor of Government at Oxford University, Kalyvas is also one of the most engaging voices in contemporary Greek culture.

King, Christopher *Lament from Epirus: An Odyssey into Europe's Oldest Surviving Folk Music* W W Norton & Co, 2018. Musicologist King fell in love with pre-Homeric sounds of Epiróte music and went to seek it on its home ground; he also produced a new album with

historic recordings by Kítsos Harisiádis called *Lament in a Deep Style 1929–1931* (Third Man Records).
Lane Fox, Robin *Alexander the Great* Penguin, 1986. Sweeping, sympathetic and fluent epic account of the 'last Homeric hero'.
Mazower, Mark *The Balkans* Phoenix, 2002. A concise background to the Macedonian issue.
Mazower, Mark *Inside Hitler's Greece* Yale University Press, 1995. Vivid account of life during the Occupation.
Mazower, Mark *Salonica, City of Ghosts: Christians, Muslims and Jews* HarperCollins-Publishers, 2004. Essential reading; a riveting biography of Thessaloníki and its unique multi-cultural history.
Pettifer, James with Tom Buchanan *War in the Balkans: Conflict and Diplomacy before World War I* I B Tauris, 2015. An excellent account of events that still affect northern Greece.
Rice, David Talbot *Art of the Byzantine Era* Thames & Hudson, 1985. A classic.
Runciman, Steven *The Great Church in Captivity* Cambridge University Press, 1968. Not for the faint-hearted, but Runciman is one of the few who can explain the Greek church to Westerners; in this case, he examines its tricky role under the Turkish Occupation.
Speake, Graham *Mount Athos: Renewal in Paradise* Denise Harvey, 2014. A beautifully illustrated history of the Holy Mountain.
Walbank, F W *The Hellenistic World* Fontana/Harvard University Press, 1993. The lively period from Alexander to the Romans.
Ware, Timothy *The Orthodox Church* (2nd edition) Penguin, 1993. The classic, with all you've ever wanted to know about the national religion of Greece, told clearly and concisely by a bishop and theologian.

Literature and travel Anything by Alexándros Papadiamántis is worth reading. Read *Tales from a Greek Island* (John Hopkins, 1994) if you can get your hands on it – but recently new translations have appeared that might be easier to find: *The Murderess* (NYRB Classics, 2010); *Fey Folk* (Aiora, 2013) and *The Merchants of Nations* (Sunstep, 2016).

Byron, Robert *The Station* Phoenix, 2000. By far the zestiest traveller's account of Mount Athos, originally written in 1928.
Fermor, Patrick Leigh *Roumeli: Travels in Northern Greece* Penguin, 1983. Beautiful, evocative book written in the 1960s, when Sarakatsáni shepherds still roamed and Meteora was all but abandoned. Fermor wears his wisdom and excellent scholarship lightly.
Hoffman, Julian *The Small Heart of Things* University of Georgia Press, 2013. Evocation of the Préspa Lakes.
Kassabova, Kapka *Border* Granta, 2017. Evocative, magical, personal account of the border between Greece, Bulgaria and Türkiye.

Nature and outdoors
Catsadorakis, Giorgos *Prespa: A Story for Man and Nature* The Society for the Protection of Prespa, 1999. Account by a renowned Greek biologist.
Mayer, Christian *Ski Touring with Sea View* Anavasi, 2016. Winter skiing in northern Greece.
Mills, Steve *Birdwatching in Northern Greece* Birdwing, 2011. An extensive guide to the best sites, also available at w nhbs.com.
Salmon, Tim *The Mountains of Greece, Trekking in the Pindos Mountains* Anavasi, 2006.
Salmon, Tim, with Michael Cullen *Trekking in Greece* Cicerone, 2018. With details on the E4.

WEBSITES
w ekathimerini.com Up-to-date Greek news in English.
w emy.gr Hellenic weather service.

FURTHER INFORMATION

- **w greece-is.com** Articles on culture, cuisine and destinations.
- **w greekreporter** Daily news from Greece.
- **w gtp.gr** Greek Travel Pages, for all the latest news on Greek tourism, plus ferry schedules and accommodation listings for every village in Greece.
- **w topostext.org** Former diplomat and ancient historian Brady Kiesling's library of ancient texts attached to a detailed gazetteer, available as a free app.
- **w travel.gr** Travel recommendations across Greece.

Index

Page numbers in **bold** refer to main entries and those in *italics* refer to maps.

Abdera, Ancient 202, **210–11**
Abdul Hamid II (Abdul the Damned), Sultan 61
accidents, road 43
accommodation 43–5
 prices 44
 see also places by name
Achérondas Delta 298
Achérondas Gorge 299–300
Achinás, Alexándros 92
Acropolis (Athens) 378, **379–80**
Actium, Battle of 10, **293**, 312
administrative regions 3
Aeschylus 186
Aetomilítsa 243
Áfyssos 350–1
Áfytos 110
Ag Achíllios Island 250
Ag Charálambos 216
Ag Dimítrios 133
Ag Geórgios 291
Ag Geórgios Nileías 349
Ag Germanós 250
Ag Ioánnis (Pelion) 349
Ag Ioánnis (Sithonía) 112
Ag Kyriakí 351
Ag Lavréntios 349
Ag Pantelémonas 245
Ag Paraskevi beach (near Párga) 300
Ag Saránta 348
Aggítis Canyon 190
Aggítis River Cave (near Dráma) 189–90
Agía (Epirus) 300
Agiá (Thessaly) 312
Agiókambos 312
Ágistro 167
Ágnanta 288
Agnóntas (Skópelos) 367
Ágrapha 329
Agriá 349
agriculture 19
Aianí, Ancient 6, **252**
Aigai, Ancient 142–5
air travel
 domestic 41
 international 33–4
 Thessaloníki 63–6
Akté Peninsula 102, **116–19**
Alatás 351
Albania, border 35, 243
Alexander I of Greece 12, 217
Alexander III the Great of Macedon 8–9, 22, 60, 119–21, 129, 134, 143, 149, 168–9, 170, 171, 217, 311
Alexander IV of Macedon 145, 169
Alexandriní Omólio 312
Alexandroúpolis 202, **217–20**, *218*
Ali Pasha 232, 257, 261, **268–9**, 271, 300
Aliákmonas, River 3
Alistráti 190

Alistráti Cave 190
Alónia (Samothráki) 229
Alónissos 3, **367–73**, *368*
 getting there and around 369
 history 368–9
 sports and activities 371
 where to eat and drink 370
 where to stay 369–70
Alónissos Archipelago 372–3
Alónissos National Marine Park 4, 367, 372
Alykés 118
Alykí (Thássos) 200
Ambracian Gulf 288–96
Ammoudiá 298
Ammoulianí island 118
Ampelákia 311
Amphipolis, Ancient 168–71, *169*
Amphipolis, Battle of 111
Amýntaio 232, **245–6**
Análipsi 348
Anárgyri 245
Anastasioúpolis, Ancient 211–12
Anatolikí 288
ancient/archaeological sites 54–5
 Acropolis (Athens) 378, **379–80**
 Aigai 142–5
 Anchíalos 340
 Ancient Abdera 210–11
 Ancient Agora (Athens) 378
 Ancient Aianí 252
 Ancient Amphipolis 168–71, *169*
 Ancient Anastasioúpolis 211–12
 Ancient Arethusa 167
 Ancient Dion 133–6, *134*
 Ancient Édessa 155
 Ancient Flórina 248
 Ancient Kassope 256, **295–6**
 Ancient Mieza 148–9
 Ancient Nikopolis 288–9, **292–5**, *294*
 Ancient Olynthos 107
 Ancient Pella 150–1
 Ancient Pherae 341–2
 Ancient Philippi 173, **183–6**, *184*
 Ancient Pydna 136–7
 Ancient Siris 175
 Ancient Stageira 115–16
 Ancient Thássos 196–8, *197*
 Ancient Theatre A (Lárissa) 308
 Ancient Torone 114
 Ancient Traïanoúpolis 222
 Arch of Galerius (Thessaloníki) 85–6
 Asclepeion of Trikke (Tríkala) 315
 Civilisation of the Four Lakes People (near Anárgyri) 245
 decumanus maximus (Thessaloníki) 87
 Demetrias 339–40
 Dimíni 340
 Dodona 283–5

Gymnasium (Amphipolis) 170
Hadrian's Arch (Athens) 378
Kamáres (Kavála) 180
Kastá Tomb (Amphipolis) 171
Leivithra 132
Macedonian tomb (near Stavroúpoli) 192
Makrí 217
Maroneia 216
Necromanteion of Acheron (near Párga) 299
Odeon of Herodes Atticus (Athens) 380
Palace (Aigai) 145
Palace of Galerius (Thessaloníki) 85
Persephone Tomb (Vergína) 143–4
Prince's Tomb (Vergína) 145
Rentína 167–8
Rhomaois Tomb (Vergína) 145
Roman Agora (Thessaloníki) 79
Roman aqueduct (Ag Geórgios) 291
Royal Tombs of Aigai (Vergína) 143–5
Sanctuary of Dionysus (near Dráma) 190
Sanctuary of the Great Gods of the Underworld (Samothráki) 229–30
Sésklo 340
Stoa of Attalus (Athens) 378
Temple of Apollo Metropolis (Mitrópoli) 329
Temple of Hephaestus (Athens) 378
Temple of Zeus (Athens) 378
Theatre of Dionysos (Athens) 379
Tomb of Eurydice (Vergína) 145
Tomb of Philip II (Vergína) 144
Tumulus of Mikrí Doxipára 225
Villa of Alexandros and Memmia (near Amýntaio) 246
Zoní-Mesimvría 217
Anemótripa Cave 288
Angeloúdis, Stélios 62–3
animal husbandry 19
Áno Ionikón 192
Áno Kerásia 342
Áno Pólis (Thessaloníki) 88
Anthochóri 330
Anthoússa 300
antiparochí 24
Antony, Mark 10, 184, 293
Aoös, River 3, 274, 279, 280, 283
apartments 44
Aphrodite 17
Apollo 17
Apollonía 167
Apózari (Kastoriá) 240
Aquarium (Kastoriá) 241
Árachthos River/Gorge 288

392

INDEX

archaeological sites *see* ancient/ archaeological sites
Archaic Age 7-8, 21
architecture
　Mastorochória 253, 280
　Zagóri 272
Arcturos Bear Sanctuary (Nymphaío) 244
area 2
Ares 17, 173
Argalastí 351
Argead dynasty 142
Árgos Orestikó 242
Aridaía 155
Arísti 276
Aristotle 27, 102, 116, 283
Aristotle University of Thessaloníki 95
Aristotle's School (Náoussa) 149-50
Árkos islet (Skiáthos) 359
Arkoudórema 255
Armenistís 114
Arnaía 108
Arrianá 217
Arrílas 300
art, modern Greek 25
Árta 257, 260, **289-91**
Artemis 17
Arvanites 20
Asélinos (Skiáthos) 361
Asia Minor Catastrophe 13, 25, 232
Asprángeli 277
Astraiá 215
asylum seekers 4, 17, 202, 206, 221
Atatürk (Mustafa Kemal) 12, 13, 90
Athéato (Skópelos) 367
Athena 17, 375
Athens 374, 375-80
　airport 33
　getting there and around 375-6
　history and mythology 8, 13, 375
　what to see and do 378-80
　where to eat and drink 377
　where to stay 377
Athinás Street (Athens) 378
Athos 119
ATMs 40-1
Avars 60
Avérof, George 281, 283
Avérof-Tosítsas, Evángelos 281, 283
Avlí 187
Axiós Delta National Park **99-100**, 137
Axiós, River 3
Aziz Aga Bridge 255

Balkan Wars 12, 61, 151, 159, 163, 195
Bálta di Stríga waterfalls 279
barbarian invasions 10, 184, 257, 305
Barbarossa, Frederick 223, 298
Barbarossa, Haryreddin 353
bars 48
　see also places by name
Basil II, Emperor 10
bats 38
Bavarians 11
Bayazid I, Sultan 60
Bayazid II, Sultan 11, 60, 62
beaches
　Alónissos 371-2
　Blue Flag 4
　Kavála 183
　Pelion Peninsula 348-51
　Skiáthos 359-61
　Skópelos 366-7
　Thássos 196, 200-1

Thessaloníki 99
Thessaly 312
bears 4, 232, 244
Belle Epoque 97
Bema of St Paul (Kavála) 181
Bema of St Paul (Véria) 141
Benjamin of Tudela 62
Bey Hamam (Thessaloníki) 79-80
Bezestén (Thessaloníki) 82-3
birdlife 4-6, **53**, **162**, 220-1
Bit Bazár (Thessaloníki) 82
bites and stings 36-8
Blue Lagoon (Sývota) 301
boat trips
　Chalkidikí 103
　Mount Athos 116-17
borders 2, 3
　crossing 35
Bouráni (Týrnavos) 310
Boutáris, Yiánnis 62
Brasidas, General 168
breakfast 45
Bridge of Árta 290
Bronze Age 4-5, 173
Brutus 10, 184
Bucephalus 134
budgeting 41
Bulgaria
　border 35, 166, 176
　Eastern Macedonia and Thrace 176, 209-10
Bulgars 10, 257
bus travel 41-2
　Thessaloníki 66, 67
Byzantine baths (Thessaloníki) 90
Byzantine Civil War 223
Byzantine Empire 10, 11
　culture 22-4
Byzantium 10

Cabeiri 86, 203, 225, 227
Caesar, Julius 184, 293, 312
cafés 47-8
camping 44-5
canoeing 53
car hire, Thessaloníki 63-6, 67
car travel
　driving in Greece 42-3
　getting to Greece 34
carnival 29, 146, 206, 242, 250
　Skópelos 364
Carrás, Yiánnis 113
Cassander of Macedon 9, 59, 60, 111, 134, 136, 171
Cassius 184
castles and fortifications
　Adrianí Castle 191
　Ali Pasha's Castle (Anthoússa) 300
　Byzantine castle (Xánthi) 209
　Byzantine walls (Dráma) 189
　Castle of Alexander (Palaiochóri) 187
　Castle of Platamónas 133
　Classical walls and ancient bridge (Amphipolis) 170
　Eptapýrgio (Thessaloníki) 89
　Fort Roupel 166-7
　Fortress of Kalýva (Nestos valley) 192
　Froúrio Trikálon (Tríkala) 315
　Gratianoupolis Byzantine fortress 217
　Its (Iç) Kale (Ioánnina) 267
　Justinian's Walls (Kastoriá) 240
　Kástro (Ioánnina) 266
　Kástro (Kavála) 182-3
　Kástro (Limenária) 201
　Kourókastro (Theológos) 200

Kroúna Tower (Ierissós) 118
Prosphóriou Tower (Akté Peninsula) 119
Stavronikíta Tower (Kassándra Peninsula) 110
Theodosian Walls (Thessaloníki) 89
Venetian castle (Párga) 298
Venetian fortress (Skiáthos) 359
White Tower (Thessaloníki) 91-2
Cave of Ag Geórgio (Kilkís) 160
Cave of Marónia 216
Cave of Théoptera Documentation Centre (near Kalambáka) 321
Cecrops, King of Athens 375
censorship 14
centaurs 342
centipedes 37
Central Macedonia 128, **129-71**, 158
Cergína 30
Chaïdou Forest 210
Chairóneia, Battle of 8
Chalkidikí 3, 4, 29, **102-27**, **104-5**
　east coast 114-16
　getting there and away 103
　history 102-3
　sports and activities 103-6
　where to eat and drink 106
　where to stay 106
Chalkís 102
Chánia 348
Chantiótis 110
Charles, Prince 126
Château Nico Lazaridi (Adrianí) 191
children, travelling with 39
Chlói 217
Chóra (Alónissos) 371
Chóra (Samothráki) 229
Choreftó 348
Choriátis 98
Christianity 9, 10, 20-1, 59, 60
Chroúsou 110
Chrysavgí 253
Chrýssa (Vardéa-Mavrimicháli) 25
churches and cathedrals
　Ag Apostóli (Thessaloníki) 91
　Ag Ekateríni (Thessaloníki) 91
　Ag Geórgios (Omorfokklisiá) 243
　Ag Gregórios Palamás (Thessaloníki) 88
　Ag Ioánnis (Glóssa) 367
　Ag Konstantinóu (Kevála) 183
　Ag Kýrikos and Ioulítta (Véria) 141
　Ag Lydía (Philippi) 186
　Ag Minás (Thessaloníki) 83-4
　Ag Nikólaos (Kavála) 181
　Ag Nikólaos Orphanós (Thessaloníki) 90
　Ag Panteleímonos (Thessaloníki) 86
　Ag Sofía (Thessaloníki) 87-8
　Ag Sýllas (Kavála) 183
　Ag Vlásio (Véria) 141
　Agii Theódori (Sérres) 165
　Anastásis Sotíros Christoú (Véria) 140-1
　Basilica of Ag Athanásios (Toróni) 114
　Basilica of Ag Dimítrios (Thessaloníki) 80-1
　Basilica of Bishop Sofronios (Ag Geórgios) 112
　Byzantine churches (Kastoriá) 240
　early Christian basilicas (Amphipolis) 170
　Holy Catholic Cathedral of the Immaculate Conception (Thessaloníki) 84

393

INDEX

Koimíseos tis Theotókou (Kalambáka) 320
Metamórfosis tou Sotíros (Thessaloníki) 86
Ósios David (Thessaloníki) 89–90
Palaiá Mitrópoli (Véria) 141
Panagía Acheiropoiétos (Thessaloníki) 88
Panagía Chalkeón (Thessaloníki) 79
Panagía Doúpiani (Meteora) 324
Panagía Parigorítissa (Árta) 290
Pórta Panagía (Pýli) 325
Profítis Ilías (Thessaloníki) 90–1
Protáton (Karyés) 123
Red Church (Vourgaréli) 288
Rotonda (Thessaloníki) 86
Taxiarchón (Thessaloníki) 90
Churchill, Winston 13
Cicero 59
cinema 27–8
  Thessaloníki 76
city-states (*polis*) 7–8
Civilisation of the Four Lakes People 245
Classical Greece 8–9, 21–2
Clean Monday 310
Cleopatra VII of Egypt 10, 293
climate 2, 3
clock tower (Komotiní) 214
clock tower (Xánthi) 209
clothing 39–40
coffee 47–8
Colonels, The 14
colonies 7
Communist party (KKE) 13, 14, 233, 243
concessions 54–5
Congress of Berlin 261
conservation 4
Constantine I, Emperor 10
Constantine I of Greece 12, 14, 92
Constantine II of Greece 14
Constantinople 10
corruption 18
COVID-19 pandemic 18
Crete, Battle of 13
crops 19
Crusades 10, 60, 223, 260, 353
cuisine
  classic Greek 45–6
  specialities of Northern Greece 47
cultural etiquette 56
culture 21–8
currency 2, 40
cycling 43
  Thessaloníki 66
Cyclops Cave (Alexandroúpolis) 220
Cynoscephalae, Battle of 9, 305
Cyprus 14–15, 202
Cyril and Methodius, Sts 27, 60

Dadiá Forest National Park 4, 222–3
Damoúchari 349
Darius I of Persia 173
de Chirico, Evaristo 26, 331, 338, 350
de Chirico, Giorgio 25–6, 331, 338
debit/credit cards 40
debt, national 16, 17
December Events (Dekemvrianá) 13–14
Deinokrates 119, 121, 171
Delian League 8, 111, 194, 210
Demeter 17
Demetrias 339–40
Demetrius I Poliorketes (the Besieger) of Macedon 9
Democritus 27, 202

Demotic 19, 20
Dervishes 311, 312
Despotate of Epirus 257, 260
Déstos Delta 193
dialling codes 2
Diáporos 114
Didynóteicho 223–4
Dílofo 278
Dimarchíon (Kavála) 180
Dimíni 340
dinner 45
Diodorus Siculus 176
Dion, Ancient 133–6
Dionysos 17, 176, 186, 203
disabled travellers 39
Dodona 256, 283–5
dogs 38
Doiran, Battles of 160–1
Doiran Memorial 161
Doiran Military Cemetery 161
Doló 271
Doltsó (Kastoriá) 240–1
Dorískos 222
Dotsikó 253
Dragon's Cave (Glyki) 299
Dragon's Cave (Kastoriá) 241
Drákia 348
Drakolímni 277
Dráma 173, 188–91
Drénia Islands 118
Drépano Beach (Igoumenítsa) 302
dress code 40, 56
  monasteries 322
driving
  in Greece 42–3
  to Greece 34
Dushan of Serbia 257

earthquakes 10, 62
Easter 29
Eastern Macedonia 173–201, *174*–5
  history 173–6
Eastern Orthodox Church 20
Echínos 210
economy 16, 17–18, 18–19
Édessa 29, 129, *152*, 152–7
education 21
Egypt, Muhammad Ali and 182
Eláti 324, 326
Elátia (Karántere) Forest 190–1
Elatochóri 133
electricity supply 2, 40
Eleftheroúpolis 187
Eleúthero 279
Eliá Beach (Sithonía) 112
Élios (Skópelos) 367
Ellinikó 287
embassies 33
emigration 16
Enchanted Ones (Las Incantadas) (Thessaloníki) 80, 92
English language 20
Enipéas Gorge 132
Epaminondas, General 8
Ephraim, Abbot 126
Epirus 256–302, *358*–9
  history 256–7
Erdoğan, Recep 17, 202
Eretria, Ancient 102, 110, 168
Euripides 27, 203
Europa 193
European Central Bank 16
European Commission 16
European Union 15, 18, 176
Évros area 220–5
Évros Delta 4, 221–2
Évros Delta Visitor Centre (Loutra Traïanoupoli) 221–2

Évros, River 3, 17, 202, 206, 221
exchange rate 2

Falakró Ski Centre 190
Fanári 211
Fársala 312
Feraíos, Rígas 11, 27
Féres 222
ferries, international 34–5
festivals 29, 50–3
  Bouráni (Týrnavos) 310
  Dráma area 189
  Kavála 181
  Thessaloníki 82–3
  Thrace 211
  Western Macedonia 242
fire-walkers (Anasternárides) 100
Fléga Lakes 255
flora 4
Flórina 246–8
Foniá (Samothráki) 231
food and drink 45–9
  Pelion 346
footwear 40
forests 3
Franks 10, 353, 368
Frederíka, Queen 14
free/discounted admissions 54–5
Frouríou Hill (Lárissa) 308
Fylaktí 330

Gage, Nicholas 302
Galáni 193
Galátista 107
Gamíla 277
Ganadió 280
Gardíki 302
GDP 2
Genoese 194, 200, 227
geography 3
George I of Greece 11–12, 61, 92
George II of Greece 13
gestures 56, 385
Giannitsá 151
Gióla Lagoon (Thássos) 200
Gioúra island (Alónissos) 372
Glóssa (Skópelos) 367
Glykí 299
Golden Dawn 16
Golden Fleece 331, 338, 342
Gorge of Calypso 312
Gorítsa (near Vólos) 339
Goths 10
Gouménissa 157–9
government 18
Gratiní 217
Great Depression 13
Great Famine 13
Great Fire (Thessaloníki, 1917) 61, 63, 181
Great Idea (Mégali Idéa) 11–12
Greek Civil War 13–14, 92, 233, 243, 327, 351
Greek Dark Age 7
Greek Democratic National Army (EDES) 159
Greek diaspora 14
Greek National Schism 12
Greek People's Liberation Army (ELAS) 13, 14, 159
Greek War of Independence 11, 61, 103, 146
Grevená 4, 253
Griva 157
Grove of Ag Nikólaos (Náoussa) 146
guerrilla campaigns 14
guesthouses 44

INDEX

Gyftókambo 279
Gynaikókastro 161

Hades 17
Hadjidakis, Mános 26, 209
Hatzimichaíl, Theóphilos 25, 26, 302, 340, **341**, 348
health 35–8
heatstroke 36
Hébrard, Ernest 62
Hegemon 194
Helios 17
Hellene 303
Hellenistic Age 9, 22
Hephaestos 17
Hera 16–17
Heracles 17
Hermes 17
Herodotus 173, 227, 284
Hestia 17
Hesychasm (Quietness) movement 60
highlights 29–30
hiking 54
  Mount Olympus 131–2
  safety 38
  Víkos Gorge 278
Hipparchia of Maroneia 27
Hippocrates 308
Hippodomus of Miletus 21
history 6–18
Hitler, Adolf 176
Homer 7, 10, 27, 186, 194, 216, 299, 303, 341
hot springs 54, 166, 167
hotels 43–4
  see also places by name
House of Muhammad Ali (Kavála) 182
human rights 14

Ibrahím Pashá 176
Iconoclasm 10, 20, 23
icons 23
Ierissós **118**, 125
Igoumenítsa 301–2
Iliochóri 279
Imaret (Kavála) 181–2
IMF 16, 17
immigration 206
independence movement 11–13
internet 55
Ioannídes, Dimítrios 14
Ioánnina 29, **260–71**, *262*, 302
  getting there and away 261
  history 260, 271
  nightlife 265
  what to see and do 265–71
  where to eat and drink 264–5
  where to stay 263–4
Italians, World War II 13, 176, 257
itineraries, suggested 30–1

janissaries 60, 61, 92
Jason and the Argonauts 7, 331, **338**
jellyfish 37
Jewish community 19
  Eastern Macedonia 176
  Sabbetaians 98
  Thessaloníki 11, 12, 13, 62–3
John IV Cantacuzenós, Emperor 20, 223, 224
John V Palaiologos, Emperor 227
Justinian I, Emperor 60

Kabeiri 86, 203, 225, 227
Kalá Nerá 349
Kalambáka 316, 318–19

Kalamítsi 114
Kalámos 351
Kalarrýtes 287
Kallithéa 110
Kalloní 253
Kalogerikó 291
Kalpáki 270–1
Kalývia 201, 330
Kamariótissa (Samothráki) 228
Kapesóvo 278
Karagátsia 118
Karamanlís, Constantínos 14, 15
Karamanlís, Kóstas 15, 126
Karanos of Macedon 142
Karavotássi 300
Kardítsa 303, **326–7**
Karítsa (Lake Plastíra) 329
Karítsa (Mount Óssa) 312
Karoúlia 127
Karvoúno (Sývota) 301
Karýdi 114
Karyés 123
Kassándra Peninsula 102, 103, **108–11**
Kassope, Ancient 256, **295–6**
Kastanerí 157
Kastaniá 329
Kastaniés 225
Kastoriá 232, **236–41**, *237*
  around Kastoriá 242–3
  east of Kastoriá 243–6
  getting there and around 236
  sports and activities 239
  what to see and do 239–41
  where to eat and drink 239
  where to stay 238–9
Kastoriá Peninsula 241
Kastráki 316, 317, 318–19
Kástri 112
Kastrí Loutró 312
Kástro (Skiáthos) 360–1
Katafýgio 252
Katarráktis 288
Kateríni 136
Káto Gatzéa 350
Káto Nevrokópi 190
Káto Sotirítsa 312
Kavála 29, 173, **176–83**, *177*, *179*
  beaches 183
  festivals 181
  getting there and around 176–8
  what to see and do 180–3
  where to eat and drink 180
  where to stay 178–80
Kavourótrypes 114
kayaking 53
Kechriá (Skiáthos) 361
Kéchros 217
Kefalógourna Waterfalls (Theológos) 200
Kentirikí Plateía (Métsovo) 282–3
Keramídi 342
Keramotí 193
Kerasiá 330
Kilkís 129, **159–61**
Kimon, General 168, 194, 353
Kípi 278
Kipiá 187
Kissós 348
Kleídosi (Samothráki) 231
Kleisoúra 243–4
Klidoniá 280
Klybýthres 277
Kókkino Néro 312
Kokkinopilós 291
Komotiní 202, **212–15**, *213*
  around Komotiní 215–17

Konak (Ministry of Macedonia and Thrace) (Thessaloníki) 81–2
Kónitsa 279–80
Korésteia 233, **248**
Koronisía 291
Kottáni 210
Kotza Orman 193
Koukoúli 278
Koúles Hill (Acropolis) (Sérres) 165
Kouvarás Gorge 271
Kozáni 250–1
  around Kozáni 251–3
Kraniónas 248
Krémasto Neró waterfall (Samothráki) 229
Krinídes Mud Baths 186
Krókos 251–2
Kýpos (Samothráki) 231
Kyrá Panagía island (Alónissos) 372

Ladádika (Thessaloníki) 85
Lagadás **99**, 100
Laïliá Forest 166
Láista 279
Lake Ágras 155
Lake Cheimadítida 244
Lake Doiráni 160
Lake Kárla 342
Lake Kerkíni National Park 4, 5, 129, **161–2**
Lake Koróneia 167
Lake of the Aoös Springs 283
Lake Pamvótis and the Island (Ioánnina) 267–8
Lake Petrón 245
Lake Pikrolímni 161
Lake Plastíra 303, 324, **327–30**, *328*
Lake Polyfýto 252
Lake Stefaniáda 329–30
Lake Vegorítida 245
Lake Vistonída 4, 126, 211
Lake Vólvi 167
Lake Ziroú 291
Lákoma (Samothráki) 229
Lalária (Skiáthos) 361
Lambrákis, Grigóris 93
Lampero Beach (Lake Plastíra) 329
language 2, **19–20**, 381–4
Lárissa 303, **305–9**, *306*
  around Lárissa 309–13
Lausanne, Treaty of 12, 18, 202
Lazarus 183
Lefkádia 129
Lefókastro 351
Leivithra 132
Leo III, Emperor 20
Leptokariá 132
LGBTQIA+
  rights 62
  Thessaloníki 77
  travellers 39
Lía 302
Líchnos Beach (Párga) 298
life expectancy 2
Lighthouse (Alexandroúpolis) 219
Lighthouse of Kópraina 291
Limenária (Thássos) 200–1
Liménas (Thássos) 195–8
Linós 215
Lion of Amphipolis 170
literature 27
Litóchoro 132
Livadítis 192
Livadítis waterfall (Néstos valley) 192
Liverá 193
London, Treaty of 354
Loudía, River 3
Loutrá Smokóva 330

395

INDEX

Loutráki Aridaías 155–6
Luke, St 9
lunch 45
Lycurgus, king of Thracian Edonians 186
Lysander of Sparta 227

Macedonia and Thrace Brewery (Komotiní) 215
Macedonia, Former Yugoslav Republic of 15, 18, 233
Macedonian Empire 8–10
Macedonian Front 12
Macedonian Wars 136
Maenads 186, 187, 203
Magnesía and the Pelion Peninsula 331–51, *332-3*
Makários, Bishop 14
Makrinítsa 347–8
Makrýgialos 136
Malakopí Arcade (Stoá Malakopí) (Thessaloníki) 84
Mána Neroú 183
Mandráki (Skíathos) 361
Mános Hadjidakis House (Xánthi) 209
Mansion of George Schwartz (Ampelákia) 311
Manuel II Paleológos, Emperor 60
maps, road 43
Mariés (Thássos) 201
Marónia 216–17
Mastorochória 253, 280
Matsópoulos Mills (Tríkala) 313
Matsoúki 287
Mavróbara 110
Mávros Dássos 155
media 55
medical expenses 36
medicines, prescription 35, 40
Médousa 210
Medrese Tzamí (Véria) 141
Méga Ámmos (Sývota) 301
Megali Ámmos 118
Megálo Pápingo 277
Mehmed IV, Sultan 98
meltémi wind 3
Méndi 110–11
Mesenikólas 329
Mesimvría 217
Mesorópi 187
Metaxádes 223–4
Metaxás, General Ioánnis 13, 232
Meteora 29, 303, **316–24**, *317*
  history 316–18
  sports and activities 320
  what to see and do 320–4
  where to eat and drink 319–20
  where to stay 319
Methóni 137
Metro (Thessaloníki) 67
Métsovo 280–3
Michael I Comnenus Ducas (Michael Angelos) 257, 260, 289
Midas, King 137
Mieza, Ancient 148–9
Mikrí Ámmos (Sývota) 301
Mikró 351
Mikró Dério 217
Mikró Kasavíti (Thássos) 201
Mikró Pápingo 277
Mikró Vouní (Samothráki) 229
Mikrolímni 250
Miliá 253
Miliés 349–50
Milína 351
military dictatorship 13, 14
Miller, Emmanuel 80

Minoan culture 5, 353, 361, 368
Míschos 215
Mitsotákis, Konstantínos 15
Mitsotákis, Kyriákos 18
mobile phones 55
Modiano Market (Thessaloníki) 83
monarchy, abolition of 13
monasteries and convents
  Ag Bárbara (Skópelos) 366
  Ag Dionýsios (Mount Olympus) 132
  Ag Dionysíou (Mount Athos) 125
  Ag Eleoúsa (Ioánnina) 270
  Ag Georgíou Mantilá (Meteora) 324
  Ag Nikólaos Anapavsá (Meteora) 321–2
  Ag Nikólaos Bándova (Meteora) 324
  Ag Nikólaos Monastery (Lake Vistonída) 126, 211
  Ag Nikoláou Philanthropinón (Ioánnina) 270
  Ag Panteleímonos (Mount Athos) 124
  Ag Pávlos (Mount Athos) 125
  Ag Stefánou (Meteora) 323–4
  Ag Triáda (Meteora) 323
  Ag Vissaríon (Dousíkou) 325
  cave hermitage Ag Dionýsios (Mount Olympus) 132
  Chilandaríou (Mount Athos) 125
  Docheirariíou (Mount Athos) 124
  Esfigménou (Mount Athos) 125
  Evangelismós tis Theotókou (Ormýlia) 107–8
  Evangelistría (Skíathos) 360
  Evangelístria (Skópelos) 366
  Great Lávra (Mount Athos) 127
  Great Meteora 322–3
  Hasa Baba Tekkés (Témpi) 311
  Iviíron (Mount Athos) 126–7
  Karakállou (Mount Athos) 127
  Konstamonítou (Mount Athos) 124
  Koutloumousíou (Mount Athos) 124
  Lake Pamvóti monastic state 268
  Metamorphóseos tou Sotíros (Skópelos) 366
  Meteora 316–18, **321–4**
  Monastery of Panagía Soumelá (Kastaniá) 251
  Monastery of Ypapandí (Meteora) 323
  Moní Ag Anargýron (near Agiá) 312
  Moní Ag Dimitríou (Stómio) 312
  Moní Ag Nikoláou (Métsovo) 283
  Moní Ag Paraskevi 277
  Moní Ag Theodori (Meteora) 324
  Moní Archángelou (Thássos) 200
  Moní Flamoúri (near Áno Kerásia) 342
  Moní Kipínas (near Kalarrýtes) 287–8
  Moní Korónis (Mesenikólas) 329
  Moní Molyvdosképastou (near Kónitsa) 280
  Moní Panagía Evangelístria (Palaió Tríkeri) 351
  Moní Panagiá Ikonístria (Skíathos) 361
  Moní Panagía Mavriótissa (Kastoriá) 241
  Moní Panagia Stomíou (near Kóntisa) 280

Moní Panagía Tsoúkas (near Ellinikó) 287
Moní Spiliás 329
Moní Spiliótissa 277
Moní Timíou Prodrómou 165–6
Moní tis Ikosifoiníssis (Mount Pangaíon) 187–8
Moní Vlatádon (Thessaloníki) 89
Moní Výliza (near Matsoúki 287
Moní Ypséseos Timíou Stavró (Dolianá) 323
Moní Zygoú 119
Osíou Grigoríou (Mount Athos) 125
Panagía Kechriá (Skíathos) 361
Panagías tis Pelektís (Lake Plastíra) 329
Pantokrátor (Mount Athos) 126
Philothéou (Mount Athos) 127
Roussánou (Meteora) 322
Símonos Pétra (Mount Athos) 124–5
Skíti Timíou Pródromou 127
Stavronikíta (Mount Athos) 126
Tekke Durbali Sultan (Asprógeia) 312–13
Timioú Prodromoú (Skópelos) 366
Varláam (Meteora) 322
Vatopédi (Mount Athos) **125**, 126, 211
Xenofóntos (Mount Athos) **124**, 366
Xiropotámou (Mount Athos) **124**, 366
Zográfou (Mount Athos) 124
Monastic State of Mount Athos 18
Monastiráki (Athens) 378
money 40–1
monk seals 371–2, 373
Monodéndri 277
Monument to the Women of Zagorochória (Asprángeli) 277
Morfovoúni 329
Morosini, Francesco 11
Moscháto 329
mosques
  Alatzá Imaret (Thessaloníki) 81
  Aslan Pasha Mosque (Ioánnina) 266–7
  Çelebi Sultan Mehmed Mosque (Didymóteicho) 224
  Eski Tzamí (Komotiní) 214
  Fetihie Mosque (Ioánnina) 267
  Halil Bey (Old Music) Mosque (Kavála) 182
  Hamzá Bey Mosque (Thessaloníki) 82
  Mehmet Bey Mosque (Sérres) 165
  Osman Shah Mosque (Tríkala) 315
  Tzintzirlí Mosque (Sérres) 165
  Yeni Mosque (Lárissa) 308
  Yeni Tsamí(Thessaloníki) 96
  Yeni Tzamí (Komotiní) 214
mosquitoes 36–7
motorcycles
  getting around 42–3
  getting to Greece 34
Moúcha 329
Mount Athos 10, 18, 20, 27, 102, **119–27**, *120*
  getting there 116–17, 201
  history 119–22
  monasteries 123–7
  staying at the monasteries 122–3
  visiting 122–3
Mount Fengári (Samothráki) 230
Mount Grámmos 243
Mount Ipsárion (Thássos) 199–200

INDEX

Mount Ítamos 113
Mount Kíssavos 303
Mount Kóziakas 324
Mount Mavrovouní 162
Mount Olympus 3, 4, 30, 129–30, 311
Mount Olympus National Park 129–37
  getting there and around 130
  sports and activities 131–2
  what to see and do 132–7
  where to eat and drink 131
  where to stay 130–1
Mount Órliakas 255
Mount Óssa (Kissavos) 311–13
Mount Páiko 157–9
Mount Paloúki (Skópelos) 366
Mount Pangaíon 183, **186–8**, 203
Mount Papíkio 215
Mount Pelion 342, 348
Mount Símvolon 176, 187
Mount Smólikas 3
Mount Týmphi 278–9
Mount Vérmio 137, 145, 152
Mount Vóras 155
mountains 3
Moúresi 348
Mousthéni 187
Moutzóuri (train) 350
mud villages (Korésteia) 233, 248
Muhammad Ali 176, 181, **182**, 281
Murad I, Sultan 223
Murad II, Sultan 61, 261, 271
museums and galleries 54–5
  Abdera Archaeological Museum 211
  Acropolis Museum (Athens) 379
  Almyrós Archaeological Museum 341
  Alónissos Museum (Patitíri) 371
  Amphipolis Archaeology Museum 169–70
  Archaeological Museum (Alexandroúpolis) 220
  Archaeological Museum (Ancient Pella) 151
  Archaeological Museum (Ancient Philippi) 185
  Archaeological Museum (Díon) 136
  Archaeological Museum (Ioánnina) 265–6
  Archaeological Museum (Komotiní) 215
  Archaeological Museum (Liménas) 196
  Archaeological Museum (Nikopolis) 293
  Archaeology Museum (Aianí) 252
  Archaeology Museum (Árta) 290–1
  Archaeology Museum (Dráma) 189
  Archaeology Museum (Flórina) 247
  Archaeology Museum (Igoumenítsa) 302
  Archaeology Museum (Karditsa) 326–7
  Archaeology Museum (Kavála) 181
  Archaeology Museum (Kilkís) 160
  Archaeology Museum (Sérres) 164
  Archaeology Museum (Thessaloníki) 92–4
  Art of Silk Museum (Souflí) 223
  Atatürk Museum (Thessaloníki) 90
  Athanasákio Archaeological Museum (Vólos) 339
Avéroff Museum (Métsovo) 283
Benaki Museum of Greek Culture (Athens) 378
Byzantine Museum (Didymóteicho) 224
Byzantine Museum (Ioánnina) 267
Byzantine Museum (Kastoriá) 239–40
Byzantine Museum (Makrinítsa) 348
Byzantine Museum (Véria) 141
City of Vólos Museum 337
Costume Museum (Katoriá) 241
Cultural Centre of Ierissós 118
Delinánio Museum (Katoriá) 241
Diachronic Museum of Lárissa 309
Digital Projection Centre of Meteora (Kalambáka) 320
Ecclesiastical Museum (Alexandroúpolis) 220
Entomological Museum (Vólos) 339
Ermeineía Fotiádou Traditional House (Syrrákos) 287
Fire Fighting Museum (Karditsa) 327
Flórina Museum of Contemporary Art 247
Folk Museum of the Sarakatsáni (Sérres) 165
Folklore and Ethnological Museum of Macedonia-Thrace (Thessaloníki) 96
Folklore and Historical Museum (Xánthi) 209
Folklore Museum (Chóra) 229
Folklore Museum (Didymóteicho) 224
Folklore Museum (Édessa) 154
Folklore Museum (Katoriá) 241
Folklore Museum (Komotiní) 215
Folklore Museum of Agápios Tólis (Kípi) 278
Folklore Museum of Lárissa 309
Folklore Museum (Stavroúpoli) 192
Folklore Museum (Theológos) 200
Fródzou Folklore Museum (Ioánnina) 266
G I Katsígras Museum (Lárissa) 309
Geology-Paleontology Museum (Thessaloníki) 95
Gerovassilíou Wine Museum 99
Ghika Gallery (Athens) 379
Giorgio de Chirco Art Centre (Vólos) 338
Gnafala Folklore Museum (Souflí) 223
Hellenic Culture Museum (Kalambáka) 320–1
Historical and Folklife Museum (Orestiáda) 225
History Museum of Alexandroúpolis 220
House of Shadow (Xánthi) 209
Jewish Museum (Athens) 379
Jewish Museum (Thessaloníki) 63, 83
Karatheodorí Museum (Komotiní) 215
Kítsos Makrís Folklore Centre (Vólos) 339
Kliáfa History and Cultural Centre (Tríkala) 315
Kósta Krystálli Folk Art Museum (Syrráko) 287
Kóstas Lazarídis Natural History Museum (Koukoúli) 278
Métsovo Folk Art Museum – Tossízza Mansion 283
Military Museum (Didymóteicho) 224
MOMus Experimental Center for the Arts (Thessaloníki) 85
MOMus Museum of Modern Art (Thessaloníki) 91
MOMus Museum of Photography (Thessaloníki) 84
Municipal Art Gallery (Didymóteicho) 224
Municipal Art Gallery of Ioánnina 265
Municipal Art Gallery (Thessaloníki) 97
Municipal Art Gallery (Xánthi) 209
Municipal Museum of Ioánnina 266–7
Museum District (Thessaloníki) 91
Museum of Ali Pasha and the Revolutionary Period (Ioánnina) 268–9
Museum of Byzantine Culture (Thessaloníki) 94
Museum of Casts and Antiquities (Thessaloníki) 95–6
Museum of Cinema (Thessaloníki) 84
Museum of Contemporary Art Theódoros Papagiánnis (Ellinikó) 287
Museum of Cycladic Art (Athens) 378–9
Museum of Geological Formation (Kastráki) 321
Museum of History, Folk Life and Natural History (Kozáni) 251
Museum of Hydrokinesis (Anthochóri) 283
Museum of Litóchoro 132
Museum of Miliés 350
Museum of Military Veterinary Science (Lárissa) 309
Museum of Modern Greek Culture (Athens) 379
Museum of Natural History (Miliá) 253
Museum of the Macedonian Struggle (Katoriá) 241
Museum of the Macedonian Struggle (Thessaloníki) 88
Museum of World War I (Skra) 157–9
National Archaeological Museum (Athens) 379
National Gallery/Alexandros Soutsos Museum (Athens) 379
National Resistance Museum (Lárissa) 308
Natural History and Mushroom Museum (Kalambáka) 321
Natural History Museum (Vólos) 339
Natural History Museum of Rhodope (Paranésti) 192
Neolithic Lake Ecomuseum of Dispilió (near Kastoriá) 242
Olympics Museum of Thessaloníki 96
Paleontological Collection (Siátista) 253
Papadiamántis House Museum (Skiáthos Town) 359
Pávlos Vréllis Museum of Greek History in Wax Effigies (Bizani) 270

397

INDEX

Plastíras Museum (Morfovoúni) 329
Polycentric Museum of Aigai (Vérgina) 143
Portariá History Museum 347
Railway Museum of Thessaly (Vólos) 337–8
Roof Tiles and Brickworks Museum N & S Tsalapátas (Vólos) 338
Silk Museum (Souflí) 223
Silversmithing Museum (Ioánnina) 267
Studio 83 (Flórina) 247–8
Telloglio Fine Arts Foundation (Thessaloníki) 96
Theóphilos (Kontós House) Museum (Anakasiá) 340
Thessaloníki History Centre 87
Thessaloníki Science Centre and Technology Museum (NOESIS) 98
Thrace Ethnographic and Folklore Museum (Alexandroúpolis) 219–20
Tobacco Museum (Kavála) 181
Tsitsánis Museum (Tríkala) 315
War Museum (Kilkís) 160
War Museum of Kalpáki 271
War Museum of Thessaloníki 95
Wax Museum (Kipiá) 187
Wax, Prehistory and Folklore Museum (Mavrochóri) 242
Yfantis Museum (Lía) 302
mushrooms 253–4
music 26
  Thessaloníki 76, 77
Muslim community 13, 18, 19, 176
  Thrace 202–6
Mussolini, Benito 13, 232, 257
Myceneans 4, 7
Mylopótamos 349
mythology, Greek 16–17
  centaurs 342
  Jason and the Argonauts 338
  mysteries of the Underworld 227
  Thessaly 303, 311
  Thrace's mystic thread 203
Mýtikas 132

Náoussa 145–50, *147*
National Liberation Front (EAM) 13
national parks 4
  Ambracian Wetland 291
  Axiós Delta **99–100**, 137
  Dadiá Forest 4, **222–3**
  Évros Delta 222
  Lake Kerkíni 161–2
  Mount Olympus 129–37
  National Park of Eastern Macedonia and Thrace 191, 211
  National Reconciliation Park 243
  Pindus 232, **253–5**, 279
  Préspa 248–50
  Tzoumérka, Peristéri and the Árachthos Gorge 285, 286, 288
  Víkos–Aoös 4, 271
NATO 14
natural history 3–6
nature reserves 4
Navarino, Battle of 11
Nazi regime 13, 62, 63, 257
Néa Anchíalos 340
Néa Fókea 110
Néa Róda 118
Néa Skióni 110
Necromanteíon 256
Neochóri 329

Neolithic period 6
Néos Marmarás 112
Neráida 330
Nestório 232, **243**
Néstos River/Gorge 3, 173, **191–3**, 202, 206
Nevrópoli 330
New Democracy (ND) party 15, 18, 62
newspapers 55
Nicaea, Second Council of 23
Nikephóros Phokás, Emperor 10
Nikísiani 187
Nikíti 112
Nikopolis, Ancient 256, 288–9, **292–5**, *294*
Nimfaías Forest 215
Normans 176, 232, 257
North Macedonia 18, 236
  border 35
nudism 56
Nymfópetra 167
Nymphaío 244–5

Ochi Day 13, 50, 257
Octavian (later Augustus) 10, 184, 288, 293
Old railway station (Thessaloníki) 85
Olympiáda 115
Olympus Riviera 133
Olynthian (Chalcidian) League 102
Olynthos, Ancient 21, 107
Omorfokklisiá 243
opening hours 55
  cultural attractions 54
Oresiáda 225
Orliás Waterfalls 433
Orlov, Alexei 11
Órma 155
Orménio 225
Órmos Panagiás 114
Ormýlia 107–8
Orpheus 186–7, 203, 227
Orphism 203
Otto of Greece 11, 375
Ottoman Empire 11, 12, 21, 227, 232, 257, 261, 271, 275, 353
  cultural legacy 24
  Thessaloníki 60–1
Ouranoúpoli **118–19**, 124
ouzo 48
Ovriós 348
Oxiá 278

Pachiá Ámmos (Samothráki) 229
packing 39–40
Palaiá Kavála 183
Palaiá Leptokariá 132–3
Palaió Ag Athanásios 156–7
Palaió Tríkeri 351
Palaiochóri 187
Palaiokaryá Bridge/Waterfall 325
Palaíos Panteleímonas 133
Palamás, Gregory 60
Paliosélli 279
Páltsi 351
Pan 17
Panagía (Kavála) 181
Panagía (Mount Pangaíon) 187
Panagía (Thássos) 197
Pángalos, General 13
Panórama (Thessaloníki) 98
Páou 351
Papá Neró 349
Papadiamántis, Aléxandros 27
Papadópoulos, Colonel George 14, 20
Papandréou, Andréas 14, 15, 233

Papandréou, George 14, 16
Pappás Mill (Lárissa) 308
Pappoú island (Alónissos) 372
Paradise Beach (Thássos) 200
Paramythiá 302
Paranésti 192
Paratiritírio 329
Párga 257, *296*, **296–300**
Paris Peace Conference 12
parks and gardens
  Alcazár Park (Lárissa) 308
  Aristotle Park (Stágira) 116
  Averófeios Garden (Métsovo) 283
  botanical garden (Neochóri) 329
  Hill 606 (Édessa) 155
  Kioupré (Édessa) 154–5
  Municipal Gardens (Komotiní) 214
  Parko Ag Varvára (Dráma) 189
  Parko Arpaktikón – Raptor Park (near Adrianí) 191
  Sheikh-sou Forests (Thessaloníki) 97
  Waterfall Park (Édessa) 154
Páros 193
Parthenónas 112–13
PASOK (Panhellenic Socialist Movement) 15, 63
passports 32–3
Path of the Centaurs (Pelion) 347
Patitíri (Alónissos) 371
patron saint's days 50
Paul I of Greece 14
Paul, St **9**, 62, 129, 137, 141, 181, 183, 184, 185, 292
Pefkári (Thássos) 200
Pefkochóri 110
Pefkodásos 161
Pelion Peninsula 4, 30, 303, **331, 342–51**
  getting there and around 343
  history 343
  sports and activities 347
  what to see and do 347–51
  where to eat and drink 354–7
  where to stay 343–5
Pella, Ancient 150–1
Peloponnesian War 102, 168, 194, 353
Pentálofos 253
people 19
Pérama Caves 270
Pérdika 300
Pericles 8
Peristéra islet (Alónissos) 372
Perivóli 255
Perseus of Macedon 136–7
Persian Empire 8, 173, 194
Pertoúli 324, **326**
Petrálona Cave 107
Petrified Forest of Nóstimo 242
Petroússa Gorge 190
Pezoúlas 330
Pezoúlas Beach (Lake Plastíra) 330
pharmacists 35–6
Philip II of Macedon 8, 22, 60, 103, 129, 133–4, 137, 142–5, 168, 173, 176, 183–4, 192, 194, 210, 227, 232, 305, 339, 341, 353, 369
Philippi, Ancient 173, **183–6**, *184*
Philippi, Battle of 10, 59, 184, 312
Philopáppou Hill (Athens) 378
Phoenicians 193
Pinakátes 349
Pindus Mountains 3, 256, 303
Pindus National Park 232, **253–5**, 279
Pindus Trail 54, 255

398

INDEX

Pineiós Delta 312
Pineiós, River 3
Pipéri island (Alónissos) 373
plague 10, 184
Pláka (Athens) 378
plants, harmful 38
Plastíra Dam 327, 329
Plastíras, Colonel Nikólas 12
Plataea, Battle of 8, 173
Plataniá 351
Plateía Aristotélous (Thessaloníki) 79
Plateía Elftherías (Thessaloníki) 84
Plateía Irínis (Komotiní) 214
Platiá Ámmos 312
Plato 144, 203
Platý 250
Pogóni 271
Pogonianí 271
politics 18
Polk, George 92–3
Polýchrono 110
Polydéndri Forest 342
Polýgyros 106
Pomakochória 209–10
Pomaks 19, 20, 176, 209–10, 215, 217
Pontic Greeks 19, 159
population 2
population exchange (1923) 13, 19, 62, 103, 202, 331
Póroi 133
Portariá 347
Porto Carras 113
Pórto Koufó 114
Poseídi 111
Poseidon 17, 119, 225, 375
postal services 55
Potamiá (Thássos) 199
Potistiká 351
Potós (Thássos) 200
Pourianós Stavrós peak (Mount Pelion) 348
Prámanta 288
prehistory 6–7
Préspa Lakes 30, 232
Préspa National Park 248–50
Préveza 291–6
prices
    accommodation 44
    restaurants 46
    typical 40
Prínos (Thássos) 201
Profítis Ilías (Samothráki) 229
Protagoras of Abdera 27
Protítsa Gorge 255
Psarádes 250
Psarólakas 312
Psathoúra island (Alónissos) 372–3
Psilí Ámmos (Thássos) 200
Ptolemaïda 251
public holidays 2, **49–50**
Punic Wars 9, 257
Pydna, Ancient 136–7
Pýli 324, **325**
Pýli Paradeisou 287
Pyrrhus, King 142, 256–7
Pyrsógianni 280
Pýthio 224

rabies 38
Rainbow Party 233
rainfall 3, 29
rakí 48
Rapsáni 311
Ravení 302
red tape 32–3
refugees
    Asian/Middle Eastern 19, 206
    European refugee crisis 16, 17, 221

from Asia Minor 13, 19, 62, 103, 202, 331
Regime of the Fourth of August 13
religion and beliefs 2, **20–1**
republic, Greek 15
restaurants 47
    prices 46
    see also places by name
Rhodope Mountains 3, 129, 202, 206
Roma 19, 20, 176
Romans 9–10, 176, 256–7, 311, 312
    cultural legacy 22
    see also archaeological/ancient sites
Rongovoú Monastery 279
Roupel Pass 166
rules of the road 42, 43

Sabbetaians 63, **98**
safety 38
saffron 252
sailing 372
Salamis, Battle of 8, 173, 351, 354
Salonica *see* Thessaloníki
Samarína 255
Samonída 299
Samothráki 3, 30, 202, 203, **225–31**, *226*
    getting there and around 228
    history 225–7
    what to see and do 228–31
    where to eat and drink 228
    where to stay 228
Sapoutzís Mansion (Kastoriá) 240
Saracens 10, 257
Sarakatsáni **165**, 220
Sarakíniko 300
Sárti 114
scorpions 37
Sea Caves of Thetis 348
sea travel 34–5
sea urchins 37
seasons 3, 29
Sérres 129, **162–7**, *163*
    south of 167–71
Sérvia 252
Sésklo 340
shopping **53**, 55
    Thessaloníki 77–8
Siátista 252–3
Sideritis scardica 133
Sidirókastro 166
Silas 9, 137, 183
Silkline Mouhtaridis S A (Souflí) 223
SIM cards 55
Simítis, Kósta 15
Sinan Pasha 261
Sithonia Peninsula 111–14
Skála Kalliráchis (Thássos) 201
Skála Marión (Thássos) 201
Skála Potaiás (Thássos) 200
Skála Prínou (Thássos) 201
Skála Rachoníou (Thássos) 201
Skála Sotíras (Thássos) 201
Skála Sykiás 114
Skála Vradéto 278
Skamnéli 279
Skantzoúra island (Alónissos) 372
Skepasménou Canyon 252
Skiáthos 3, **354–61**, *355*
    entertainment and nightlife 358
    getting there and around 354–6
    history 354
    sports and activities 358
    where to eat and drink 357–8
    where to stay 356–7
Skiáthos Town 359

skiing 54, 132, 147, 156, 190, 249, 255, 282
Skópelos 3, **361–7**, *362*
    entertainment and nightlife 365
    getting there and around 363
    history 361–3
    sports and activities 365
    where to eat and drink 365
    where to stay 363–4
Skópelos Town 366
Skotína 133
Skra 157–9
Slavic-speaking community 19
Slavs 10, 60, 176, 232, 233, 257
Smíxi 255
Smólikas 279
Smólikas Drakólimni 279
Smyrna (Izmir) 12
snakes 37
snowfall 3
Sóstis 215
Souflí 223
Souli 11, 295–6
Sparta 8, 168, 353
spas 54
Spathí (Komotiní) 214
Spathiés (Sithonía) 112
Spiliá 311
spirits 48
Sporádes 3, 30, 303, *352*, **353–73**
    Alónissos 367–73, *368*
    history 353–4
    Skiáthos 354–61, *355*
    Skópelos 361–7, *362*
    sports and activities 53–4
Stageira, Ancient 115–16
Stágira 116
Staktópoulos, Grigóris 92–3
Stalin, Joseph 13, 14, 176, 233
Stáphylos (Skópelos) 366–7
State Conservatory of Thessaloníki 84
Stathmos Aggístis 190
Stavrós 115
Stavroúpoli 192
Stefaniáda 330
Stení Valá (Alónissos) 371
Stómio 312
Straits of Rentína 167
Strymónas, River/Valley 3, 162, 166, 168
studios 44
Súliot Federation 300
sunburn 36
supermarkets 53, 55
surfing 298
synagogues
    Old Synagogue (Véria) 141
    Synagogue (Ioánnina) 266
    Thessaloníki 62, 63, 83
SYRIZA 16, 18
Syrráko 287
Sývota 300–1

tap water 56
tavernas 47
Taxiárchon (Skópelos) 366
taxis 43
    Thessaloníki 67
telephones 55
temperatures 3, 29
Témpi 311
Thassopoúla (Thássos) 201
Thássos 3, 173, 176, **193–201**, *194*
    Ancient Thássos 196–8, *197*
    beaches 196, 200–1
    getting there and around 195
    history 193–5

399

INDEX

what to see and do 196–201
where to eat and drink 195–6, 199
where to stay 195, 198–9
theatre, Thessaloníki 77
theme parks
  Magic Park (Thessaloníki) 99
  Waterland (Thessaloníki) 99
Theodorákis, Míkis 26
Theodóriana 288
Theodosius I, Emperor 59
Theológos (Thássos) 200
Thermá (Samothráki) 230
Thermaic Gulf 3, 59
Thermal Baths of Ag Paraskevi (Kassándra Peninsula) 110
Thermopylae, Battle of 8
Thessalonike 60
Thessaloníki 3, 30, *58*, **59–100**, *64–5*, *68–9*
  airport 34, 63–6
  around Thessaloníki 97–100
  entertainment and nightlife 75–7
  festivals and events 82–3
  getting around 66–7
  getting there and away 63–6
  history 9, 10, 11, 12, 13, 58–63
  Old Imperial City and around 85–96
  orientation 70
  other practicalities 78–9
  shopping 77–8
  southeastern suburbs 96–7
  sports and activities 78
  tourist information/tour operators 67–70
  what to see and do 79–100
  where to eat and drink 72–5
  where to stay 70–2
Thessaloníki, Edict of 59
Thessaloníki International Fair 95
Thessaly 303–30, *304*
  history 303–5
Thrace 202–31, *204–5*
Thracian Meteora 215–16
Thracians 173
Thucydides 27, 168, 183
Thumonia (Thássos) 200
ticks 37–8
time zone 2
Timothy 9
tipping 56
Tito, Marshal 14, 233
tobacco 176, 181, 206
toilets 38
Toróni 113–14
Tosítsas, Michaíl 281
tour operators 31–2
  Thessaloníki 70
Tourbe of Musa Baba (Thessaloníki) 90
tourism 17, 18, 25, 56
tourist information 31
  see also places by name
Toxótes 193
Traïanoúpolis, Ancient 222
train travel
  internal 41
  international 34
  Thessaloníki 66

travel
  getting around 41–3
  getting there and away 33–5
  travelling positively 56
travel clinics 36
Treasury (Ioánnina) 267
Tríkala 303, **313–15**, *314*
  west of 324–6
Tríkeri 351
Tríkomo 255
Trikoúpis, Harilaos 12
Trípiti 118
troika 16
Truman Doctrine 14
Tsagaráda 349
Tsepélovo 279
Tsiastsiapá Mansion (Kastoriá) 240
Tsiódras, Sotíris 18
tsípouro 310, **336**
Tsípras, Aléxis 16, 18
Tsopéla 288
Tsougriás islet (Skíathos) 359
Türkiye 13, 17, 202, 206, 221
  border 35, 225
  Greek relations with 12
Turkokratía 11
Týmphi range 271, 277, 278–9
Týrnavos 310
Tzoumérka *285*, 285–8

unemployment 17

vaccinations 35
Vafiádis, Márko 13, 92
Vale of Tempe 133, **310–11**
Vália Cálda 232, 255, 279
Váltos Beach (Párga) 298
Vangelis 26, 331
Varósi (Édessa) 154
Varvákios Central Market (Athens) 378
Varvára 116
vegetarian/vegan food 46
Velestíno 341–2
Velíka 312
Velventós 252
Venetians 10, 11, 61, 227, 257, 298, 353, 354, 363, 368
Venéto 342
Venizélos, Elefthérios 12, 13, 61
Vergína 129, **142–5**
Véria 129, **137–42**, *139*
  getting there and around 138
  nightlife 140
  what to see and do 140–2
  where to eat and drink 139–40
  where to stay 138–9
Via Egnatía 10, 59, **183**, 280
Víkos 278
Víkos Gorge 30, 256, 271, 277, **278**
Víkos–Aoös National Park 4, 271
Villa Ahmet Kapandjí (Thessaloníki) 97
Villa Allatini (Thessaloníki) 97
Villa Galini (Porto Carras) 113
Villa Mehmet Kapandjí (Thessaloníki) 97
Villa Modiano (Thessaloníki) 97
Villa Mordoch (Thessaloníki) 97
villages, depopulated 25
villas (accommodation) 44

visas 32
Vitruvius 22
Vítsa 277, 278
Vlach Folklore Association (Véria) 141–2
Vlachs 20, 165, 232, 255, 257, **260**, 271, 280
Vlásti 253
Voïdomátis, River/springs 3, 278
Vólos 331–42, *335*
  around Vólos 339–42
  entertainment and nightlife 337
  getting there and away 334
  what to see and do 337–9
  where to eat and drink 336–7
  where to stay 334–5
Vóras Kaïmáktsalan Ski Centre 156
Vourgaréli 288
Vovoúsa 279
Vradétο 278
Vrosína 302
Vrysochóri 279
Vyzítsa 349

watersports 54
Waterway Trail (Kavála) 183
Western Macedonia 232–55, *234–5*
  history 232–6
Western Thrace 173
wetlands 4, 5
white-water rafting 53, 287
wildfires 4, 38, 221
wildlife 3–6
wine **48–9**, 148, 191, 245, 253, 311, 325, 370
Wisliceny, Dieter 63
wolves 4, 232
women travellers 38
Women's Day (Thrace) 211
World War I 12, 61, 157–9, 160–1
World War II 13, 62, 176, 233, 270–1, 277, 308, 311, 327, 348

Xánthi 202, **206–9**, *207*
  around Xánthi 209–12
Xerxes I of Persia 8, 102, 118, 168, 194, 210, 354
Xiná 110
Xinó Neró 245

Yalta Conference 13
Years of Stone 14
Young Turk movement 12, 61
Yugoslavia, collapse of 15, 233

Zagorá 348
Zagorochória 30, 256, **271–9**, *273*
  central 277–9
  eastern 279
  getting there and away 274
  sports and activities 276
  western 276–7
  where to eat and drink 276
  where to stay 274–5
Zalmoxis 203
Zéri Beach (Sývota) 301
Zérvas, Konstantinos 62
Zeus 16–17, 119, 129, 133, 186, 193
Zevi, Sabbetai 98
Zítsa 270

INDEX OF ADVERTISERS

Peter Sommer second colour section
Wanderlust 388